Employment Distribution by Major Industrial Sector, 1900–2000
(Data displayed graphically in Figure 2.3 on text page 31.)

 W9-AWS-388

Year	Agriculture	Goods-producing industries*	Nongovernment Services	Government Services
1900	38.1%	37.8%	20.0%	4.1%
1910	32.1	40.9	22.3	4.7
1920	27.6	44.8	21.6	6.0
1930	22.7	42.1	28.1	7.1
1940	18.5	41.6	31.1	8.8
1950	12.1	41.3	36.4	10.2
1960	6.6	41.4	38.8	13.2
1970	3.8	39.8	40.5	15.9
1980	3.5	35.9	43.9	16.7
1990	2.7	32.0	49.8	15.5
2000	2.5	24.2	57.9	15.2

*Includes transportation and public utilities.

Sources: U.S. President, Economic Report of the President (Washington, D.C.: U.S. Government Printing Office, 1991), Table B–43; and U.S. Bureau of Labor Statistics, Employment and Earnings, 38, no. 1 (January 1991), Tables 1, 25; U.S. Bureau of Labor Statistics, Monthly Labor Review 124, no. 6 (June, 2001), Tables 18, 19.

TABLE 2.4 Unemployment and Long-Term Unemployment, Selected European and North American Countries, 2000

	Unemployment: Overall Rate	Percent of Unemployed Out of Work > One Year	Unemployment: Long-Term Rate
Belgium	7.0%	56.3%	3.9%
Canada	6.8	11.2	0.8
Denmark	4.7	20.0	0.9
France	9.5	42.5	4.0
Germany	8.1	51.5	4.2
Netherlands	2.8	32.7	0.9
Norway	3.5	5.0	0.2
Sweden	5.9	26.4	1.6
United Kingdom	5.5	28.0	1.5
United States	4.0	6.0	0.2

Source: OECD, Employment Outlook (Paris: OECD, 2001), Tables A and G.

MODERN LABOR ECONOMICS

THE ADDISON-WESLEY SERIES IN ECONOMICS

MODERN LABOR ECONOMICS
Theory and Public Policy
Eighth Edition

RONALD G. EHRENBERG
School of Industrial and Labor Relations

Cornell University

ROBERT S. SMITH
School of Industrial and Labor Relations

Cornell University

Addison
Wesley

Boston San Francisco New York
London Toronto Sydney Tokyo Singapore Madrid
Mexico City Munich Paris Cape Town Hong Kong Montreal

Editor in Chief: Denise Clinton
Acquisitions Editor: Victoria Warneck
Associate Editor: Roxanne Hoch
Production Supervisor: Meredith Gertz
Supplements Editor: Andrea Basso
Marketing Manager: Adrienne D'Ambrosio
Design Manager: Regina Hagen Kolenda
Senior Media Producer: Melissa Honig
Composition, Illustration, and Packaging Services: Electronic Publishing Services Inc.,
    N.Y.C.
Cover Designer: Leslie Haimes
Senior Print Buyer: Hugh Crawford
Cover Image: ©Lisa Berkshire/Illustration Works

Library of Congress Cataloging-in-Publication Data

Ehrenberg, Ronald G.
        Modern labor economics : theory and public policy / Ronald G. Ehrenberg, Robert S.
    Smith.—8th ed.
            p.cm.—(The Addison-Wesley series in economics)
        Includes index.
        ISBN 0-201-78577-3
        1. Labor economics. 2. Labor policy. 3. Personnel management. I. Smith, Robert
    Stewart. II. Title. III. Series.
    HD4901 .E34 2002
      331—dc21
      2002019350

Brief Contents

Detailed Contents

CHAPTER 5 QUASI-FIXED LABOR COSTS AND THEIR EFFECTS ON DEMAND   131

CHAPTER 6 SUPPLY OF LABOR TO THE ECONOMY: THE DECISION TO WORK 163

CHAPTER 10 WORKER MOBILITY: MIGRATION, IMMIGRATION, AND TURNOVER 310

CHAPTER 11 PAY AND PRODUCTIVITY: WAGE DETERMINATION WITHIN THE FIRM 344

CHAPTER 12   GENDER, RACE, AND ETHNICITY IN THE LABOR MARKET   377

CHAPTER 15   UNEMPLOYMENT   503

Preface

Modern Labor Economics: Theory and Public Policy has grown out of our experiences over the last three decades in teaching labor market economics and conducting research aimed at influencing public policy. Our text develops the modern theory of labor market behavior, summarizes empirical evidence that supports or contradicts each hypothesis, and illustrates in detail the usefulness of the theory for public policy analysis. We believe that showing students the social implications of concepts enhances the motivation to learn them and that using the concepts of each chapter in an analytic setting allows students to see the concepts in action. The extensive use of detailed policy applications constitutes a major contribution of this text.

OVERVIEW OF THE TEXT

Modern Labor Economics is designed for one-semester or one-quarter courses in labor economics at the undergraduate or graduate level for students who may not have extensive backgrounds in economics. Since 1974 we have taught such courses at the School of Industrial and Labor Relations at Cornell University. The undergraduate course requires only principles of economics as a prerequisite, and the graduate course (for students in a professional program akin to an MBA program) has no prerequisites. We have found that it is not necessary to be highly technical in one's presentation in order to convey important concepts and that students with limited backgrounds in economics can comprehend a great deal of material in a single course. However, for students who have had intermediate microeconomics, we have included nine chapter appendixes that discuss more advanced material or develop technical concepts in much greater detail than the text discussion permits.

After an introduction to basic economic concepts in chapter 1, chapter 2 presents a quick overview of demand and supply in labor markets so that students will see from the outset the interrelationship of the major forces at work shaping labor market behavior. This chapter can be skipped or skimmed by students with strong backgrounds in economics or by students in one-quarter courses. Chapters 3 to 5 are concerned primarily with the demand for labor, while chapters 6 to 10 focus on labor supply issues.

Beginning with chapter 11, the concepts of economics are used to analyze several topics of special interest to students of labor markets. The relationship between pay and productivity is analyzed in chapter 11, and the earnings of women and minorities—encompassing issues of discrimination—are the subjects of chapter 12. Chapter 13 uses economic concepts to analyze collective bargaining in the private and public sectors. Chapter 14 offers an analysis of the growth of earnings inequality over the past two decades, and it serves the dual role of both investigating an important current phenomenon and reviewing many key concepts presented in earlier chapters. Chapter 15 treats the macroeconomic issue of unemployment.

In addition to the use of public policy examples and the inclusion of technical appendixes, the text has a number of important pedagogical features. First, each chapter contains boxed examples that illustrate an application of that chapter's theory in a nontraditional, historical, business, or cross-cultural setting. Second, each chapter contains a number of discussion or review questions that allow students to apply what they have learned to specific policy issues. To enhance student mastery, we provide answers to the odd-numbered questions at the back of the book. Third, updated lists of selected readings at the ends of chapters refer students to more advanced sources of study.

This eighth edition provides updated references to the professional literature, updated coverage, new boxed examples, and end-of-chapter problems; solutions to the odd-numbered problems appear at the end of the book.

ACCOMPANYING SUPPLEMENTS

Supplements enrich the eighth edition of *Modern Labor Economics* for both students and instructors.

The **Study Guide** is available in paperback (ISBN 0-201-88269-8). For each chapter in the text, the Study Guide offers: (a) a brief summary of the major concepts, with numerical examples when appropriate; (b) a review section with multiple-choice questions; (c) a problems section with short-answer essay questions; (d) an applications section with problems and questions related to policies or labor market issues; (e) answers to all questions and problems; and (f) one or more newspaper articles that illustrate concepts central to the chapter.

In addition to the Study Guide, students receive a cohesive set of **Online Study Tools** that are available on the Companion Web site, www.aw.com/ehrenberg_smith. For each chapter, students will find a multiple-choice quiz, additional examples and applications, web links to labor data sources, and PowerPoint lecture presentations.

For Instructors, an extensive set of course materials exists in one central location online, at www.aw.com/ehrenberg_smith. All resources are password-protected for instructor use only. An **Online Test Bank** by Lawrence A. Wohl consists of 500 multiple-choice questions that can be downloaded easily by instructors via the Web site, and edited for use in problem sets and exams.

Also available via the Web is the **Online Instructor's Manual**, written by co-author Robert Smith. The Online Instructor's Manual presents answers to the even-numbered review questions in the text, outlines the major concepts in each chapter, and contains two new suggested essay questions per chapter (with answers).

Finally, an **Online PowerPoint lecture presentation** is available for each chapter. The slides, consisting of figures from the text with accompanying lecture notes, can be downloaded easily from the book's Web site. The PowerPoint lecture presentations can then be used electronically in the classroom, or they can be printed for use as **Overhead Transparency Masters**.

ACKNOWLEDGMENTS

Enormous debts are owed to four groups of people. First are those instrumental in teaching us the concepts and social relevance of labor economics when we were students: Frank Brechling, George Delehanty, Dale Mortensen, John Pencavel, Orme Phelps, and Mel Reder. Second are the generations of undergraduate and graduate students who sat through the lectures that preceded the publication of each new edition of *Modern Labor Economics* and, by their questions and responses, forced us to make ourselves clear. Third, a special debt is owed Robert Whaples, who contributed several boxed examples and problems to this eighth edition.

Fourth, several colleagues have contributed, both formally and informally, to the recent editions. We appreciate the suggestions of the following people:

John Abowd
Cornell University

Francine Blau
Cornell University

George Boyer
Cornell University

Donald Bruce
University of Tennessee

Ted Chiles
Auburn University

Gary Fields
Cornell University

Darren Grant
Georgia Southern University

Paul Grimes
Mississippi State University

Richard Hannah
Middle Tennessee State University

Joseph W. Hunt Jr.
Shippensburg University

Robert Hutchens
Cornell University

George Jakubson
Cornell University

Lawrence Kahn
Cornell University

Douglas Kruse
Rutgers University

Daniel Millimet
Southern Methodist University

Robert L. Moore
Occidental College

Kevin Murphy
Oakland University

Kevin M. O'Brien
Bradley University

Catherine O'Connor
Bucknell University

Walter Oi
University of Rochester

Peter Orazem
Iowa State University

Steve Raphael
University of California, San Diego

Tim Schmidle
Workers' Compensation Board, New York State

Jeremy Schrauf
State University of New York, Albany

Eric Solberg
California State University, Fullerton

Peter Soule
Park College

Kristen Stein
Colorado University

Wendy Stock
Montana State University

Leonie Stone
State University of New York, Geneseo

Lawrence A. Wohl
Gustavus Adolphus College

Ronald G. Ehrenberg
Robert S. Smith

1

INTRODUCTION

Economic theory provides powerful, and surprising, insights into individual and social behavior. These insights are interesting because they help us understand important aspects of our lives. Beyond this, however, government, industry, labor, and other groups have increasingly come to understand the usefulness of the concepts and thought processes of economists in formulating social policy.

This book presents an application of economic analysis to the behavior of, and relationship between, employers and employees. The aggregate compensation received by U.S. employees from their employers was $5.6 trillion in the year 2000, while all *other* forms of personal income that year—from investments, self-employment, pensions, and various government welfare programs—amounted to $2.4 trillion. The *employment* relationship, then, is one of the most fundamental relationships in our lives, and as such it attracts a good deal of legislative attention. Knowing the fundamentals of labor economics is thus essential to an understanding of a huge array of social problems and programs, both in the United States and elsewhere.

As economists who have been actively involved in the analysis and evaluation of public policies, we obviously believe labor economics is useful in

1

understanding the effects of these programs. Perhaps more important, we also believe policy analysis can be useful in teaching the fundamentals of labor economics. We have therefore incorporated such analyses into each chapter with two purposes in mind. First, we believe that seeing the relevance and social implications of concepts studied enhances the student's motivation to learn. Second, using the concepts of each chapter in an analytical setting serves to reinforce understanding by permitting the student to see them "in action."

THE LABOR MARKET

There is a rumor that a former U.S. Secretary of Labor attempted to abolish the term *labor market* from departmental publications. He believed it demeaned workers to regard labor as being bought and sold like so much grain, oil, or steel. True, labor is unique in several ways. Labor services can only be rented; workers themselves cannot be bought and sold. Further, because labor services cannot be separated from workers, the conditions under which such services are rented are often as important as the price. Put differently, *nonpecuniary factors*—such as work environment, risk of injury, personalities of managers, perceptions of fair treatment, and flexibility of work hours—loom larger in employment transactions than they do in markets for commodities. Finally, a host of institutions and pieces of legislation that influence the employment relationship do not exist in other markets.

Nevertheless, the circumstances under which employers and employees rent labor services clearly constitute a market, for several reasons. First, institutions such as want ads and employment agencies have been developed to facilitate contact between buyers and sellers of labor services. Second, once contact is arranged, information about price and quality is exchanged in employment applications and interviews. Third, when agreement is reached, some kind of *contract*, whether formal or informal, is executed covering compensation, conditions of work, job security, and even duration of the job. These contracts typically call for employers to compensate employees for their *time* and not for what they produce. This form of compensation requires that employers give careful attention to worker motivation and dependability in the selection and employment process.

The end result of employer-employee transactions in the labor market is, of course, the placement of people in jobs at certain rates of pay. This allocation of labor serves not only the personal needs of individuals but the needs of the larger society as well. Through the labor market, our most important national resource— labor—is allocated to firms, industries, occupations, and regions.

LABOR ECONOMICS: SOME BASIC CONCEPTS

Labor economics is the study of the workings and outcomes of the market for labor. More specifically, labor economics is primarily concerned with the behavior of employers and employees in response to the general incentives of wages, prices, profits, and nonpecuniary aspects of the employment relationship, such as working conditions. These incentives serve both to motivate and to limit individual choice. The focus in economics is on inducements for behavior that are impersonal and apply to wide groups of people.

In this book we shall examine, for example, the relationship between wages and employment opportunities, the interaction among wages, income, and the decision to work, the way general market incentives affect occupational choice, the relationship between wages and undesirable job characteristics, the incentives for and effects of educational and training investments, and the effects of unions on wages, productivity, and turnover. In the process, we shall analyze the employment and wage effects of such social policies as the minimum wage, overtime legislation, safety and health regulations, welfare reform, payroll taxes, unemployment insurance, immigration policies, and antidiscrimination laws.

Our study of labor economics will be conducted on two levels. Most of the time we shall use economic theory to analyze "what is"; that is, we shall explain people's behavior using a mode of analysis called *positive economics*. Less commonly, we shall use *normative* economic analysis to judge "what should be."

Positive Economics

Positive economics is a theory of behavior in which people are typically assumed to respond favorably to benefits and negatively to costs. In this regard, positive economics closely resembles Skinnerian psychology, which views behavior as shaped by rewards and punishments. The rewards in economic theory are pecuniary and nonpecuniary gains (benefits), while the punishments are forgone opportunities (costs). For example, a person motivated to become a surgeon because of the earnings and status surgeons command must give up the opportunity to become a lawyer and must be available for emergency work around the clock. Both the benefits and the costs must be considered in making this career choice.

Scarcity   The pervasive assumption underlying economic theory is that of resource *scarcity*. According to this assumption, individuals and society alike do not have the resources to meet all their wants. Hence, any resource devoted to satisfying one set of desires could have been used to satisfy another set, which means that there is a cost to any decision or action. The real cost of using labor hired by a government contractor to build a road, for example, is the production lost by not devoting this labor to production of some other good or service. Thus, in popular terms, "There is no such thing as a free lunch," and we must always make choices and live with the rewards and costs these choices bring us. Moreover, we are always constrained in our choices by the resources available to us.

Rationality   A second basic assumption of positive economics is that people are *rational*—they have an objective and pursue it in a reasonably consistent fashion. When considering *persons*, economists assume that the objective being pursued is *utility maximization*; that is, people are assumed to strive toward the goal of making themselves as happy as they can (given their limited resources). Utility, of course, encompasses both pecuniary and nonpecuniary dimensions.

When considering the behavior of *firms,* which are inherently nonpersonal entities, economists assume that the goal of behavior is *profit maximization.* Profit maximization is really just a special case of utility maximization in which pecuniary gain is emphasized and nonpecuniary factors are ignored.

The assumption of rationality implies a *consistency* of response to general economic incentives and an *adaptability* of behavior when those incentives change. These two characteristics of behavior underlie predictions about how workers and firms will respond to various incentives.[1]

The Models and Predictions of Positive Economics

Behavioral predictions in economics flow more or less directly from the two fundamental assumptions of scarcity and rationality. Workers must continually make choices, such as whether to look for other jobs, accept overtime, move to another area, or acquire more education. Employers must also make choices concerning, for example, the level of output and the mix of machines and labor to use in production. Economists usually assume that, when making these choices, employees and employers are guided by their desires to maximize utility or profit, respectively. However, what is more important to the economic theory of behavior is not the *particular* goal of either employees or employers; rather, it is that economic actors weigh the costs and benefits of various alternative transactions in the context of achieving *some* goal or other.

One may object that these assumptions are unrealistic and that people are not nearly as calculating, as well informed about alternatives, or as amply endowed with choices as economists assume. Economists are likely to reply that if people are not calculating, are totally uninformed, or do not have any choices, then most predictions suggested by economic theory will not be supported by real-world evidence. They thus argue that the theory underlying positive economics should be judged on the basis of its *predictions,* not its assumptions.

The reason we need to make assumptions and create a relatively simple theory of behavior is that the actual workings of the labor market are almost inconceivably complex. Millions of workers and employers interact daily, all with their own sets of motivations, preferences, information, and perceptions of self-interest. What we need to discover are general principles that provide useful insights into the labor market. We hope to show in this text that a few forces are so basic to labor market behavior that they alone can predict or explain many of the outcomes and behaviors observed in the labor market.

Anytime we attempt to explain a complex set of behaviors and outcomes using a few fundamental influences, we have created a *model.* Models are not

---

[1]For articles on rationality and the related issue of preferences, see Gary Becker, "Irrational Behavior and Economic Theory," *Journal of Political Economy* 70, no. 1 (February 1962): 1–13, and three articles in the *Journal of Economic Literature* 36, no. 1 (March 1998): Matthew Rabin, "Psychology and Economics," 11–46; Jon Elster, "Emotions and Economic Theory," 47–74; and Samuel Bowles, "Endogenous Preferences: The Cultural Consequences of Markets and Other Economic Institutions," 75–111. Also see Richard H. Thaler, "From Homo Economicus to Homo Sapiens." *Journal of Economic Perspectives* 14, no. 1 (Winter 2000): 133–141.

EXAMPLE 1.1

Positive Economics: What Does It Mean to "Understand" Behavior?

The purpose of positive economic analysis is to analyze, or understand, the behavior of people as they respond to market incentives. But in a world that is extremely complex, just what does it mean to "understand" behavior? One theoretical physicist put it this way:

> We can imagine that this complicated array of moving things which constitutes "the world" is something like a great chess game being played by the gods, and we are observers of the game. We do not know what the rules of the game are; all we are allowed to do is to watch the playing. Of course, if we watch long enough, we may eventually catch on to a few of the rules. The rules of the game are what we mean by fundamental physics. Even if we know every rule, however ... what we really can explain in terms of those

rules is very limited, because almost all situations are so enormously complicated that we cannot follow the plays of the game using the rules, much less tell what is going to happen next. We must, therefore, limit ourselves to the more basic question of the rules of the game. If we know the rules, we consider that we "understand" the world.*

If the behavior of nature, which does not have a will, is so difficult to analyze, understanding the behavior of people is even more of a challenge. Since people's behavior does not mechanistically follow a set of rules, the goal of positive economics is most realistically stated as trying to discover their behavioral tendencies.

---

* Richard T. Feynman, *The Feynman Lectures on Physics*, V. I, 1963 by Addison Wesley.

intended to capture every complexity of behavior; instead, they are created to strip away random and idiosyncratic factors so that the focus is on general principles. An analogy from the physical sciences may make the nature of models and their relationship to actual behavior clearer.

A Physical Model   Using simple calculations of velocity and gravitational pull, physicists can predict where a ball will land if it is kicked with a certain force at a given angle to the ground. The actual point of landing may vary from the predicted point because of wind currents and any spin the ball might have—factors ignored in the calculations. If 100 balls are kicked, none may ever land exactly on the predicted spot, although they will tend to cluster around it. The accuracy of the model, while not perfect, may be good enough to enable a football coach to decide whether to attempt a field goal or not. The point is that we usually just need to know the *average tendencies* of outcomes for policy purposes. To estimate these tendencies we need to know the important forces at work, but we must confine ourselves to few enough influences so that calculating estimates remains feasible. (A further comparison of physics and positive economics is contained in Example 1.1.)

An Economic Model   To really grasp the assumptions and predictions of economic models, we consider a concrete example. Suppose we begin by asserting that, being subject to resource scarcity, workers will prefer high-paying jobs to low-paying ones *if* all other job characteristics are the same in each job. Thus, they will quit low-paying jobs to take better-paying ones if they believe sufficient improvement is likely. This principle does not imply that workers care only about wages or that all are equally likely to quit. Workers obviously care about a number of employment characteristics, and improvement in any of these on their current job makes turnover less likely. Likewise, some workers are more receptive to change than others. Nevertheless, if we hold other factors constant and increase only wages, we should clearly observe that the probability of quitting will fall.

On the employer side of the market, we can consider a similar prediction. Firms need to make a profit to survive. If they have high turnover, their costs will be higher than otherwise because of the need to hire and train replacements. With high turnover they could not, therefore, afford to pay high wages. However, if they could reduce turnover enough by paying higher wages, it might well be worth incurring the high wage costs. Thus, both the utility-maximizing behavior of employees and the profit-maximizing behavior of firms lead us to expect low turnover to be associated with high wages and high turnover with low wages, other things equal.

We note several important things about the above predictions:

1. The predictions emerge directly from the twin assumptions of scarcity and rationality. Employees and employers, both mindful of their scarce resources, are assumed to be on the lookout for chances to improve their well-being. The predictions are also based on the assumptions that employees are aware of, or can learn about, alternative jobs and that these alternatives are open to them.
2. We made the prediction of a negative relationship between wages and voluntary turnover by holding other things equal. The theory does not deny that job characteristics other than wages matter to employees or that employers can lower turnover by varying policies other than the wage rate. However, holding these other factors constant, our model predicts a negative relationship if the basic assumptions are valid.
3. The *assumptions* of the theory concern *individual* behavior of employers and employees, but the *predictions* are about an *aggregate* relationship between wages and turnover. The prediction is *not* that all employees will remain in their jobs if their wages are increased, but that *enough* will remain for turnover to be cut by raising wages. The test of the prediction thus lies in finding out if the predicted relationship between wages and turnover exists using aggregate data from firms or industries.

Careful statistical studies suggest support for the hypothesis that higher pay reduces voluntary turnover. One study of child care teachers, for example, estimated that a 15 percent increase in wages, holding teacher characteristics constant, reduced their quit rate by two percentage points.[2]

---

[2]Irene Powell, Mark Montgomery, and James Cosgrove, "Compensation Structure and Establishment Quit and Fire Rates," *Industrial Relations* 33, no. 2 (April 1994): 229–248.

Normative Economics

Understanding normative economics begins with the realization that there are two kinds of economic transactions. One kind is entered into voluntarily, because all parties to the transaction gain. If Sally is willing to create blueprints for $15 per hour, for example, and Ace Engineering Services is willing to pay someone up to $16 per hour to do the job, both gain by agreeing to Sally's appointment at an hourly wage between $15 and $16; such a transaction is mutually beneficial. The role of the labor market is to facilitate these voluntary, mutually advantageous transactions. If the market is successful in facilitating *all* possible mutually beneficial transactions, it can be said to have produced a condition economists call *Pareto* (or "economic") *efficiency*.[3] (The word *efficiency* is used by economists in a very specialized sense to denote a condition in which all mutually beneficial transactions have been concluded. This definition of the word is more comprehensive than its normal connotation of cost minimization.) If Pareto efficiency were actually attained, no more transactions would be undertaken voluntarily, because they would not be *mutually* advantageous.

The second kind of transaction is one in which one or more parties *lose*. These transactions often involve the redistribution of income, from which some gain at the expense of others. Transactions that are explicitly redistributional, for example, are not entered into voluntarily unless motivated by charity (in which case the donors gain nonpecuniary satisfaction); otherwise, redistributional transactions are mandated by government through tax and expenditure policies. Thus, while markets facilitate *voluntary* transactions, the job of government is often to make certain transactions *mandatory*.

Any normative statement—a statement about what *ought* to exist—is based on some underlying value. Government policies affecting the labor market are often based on the widely shared, but not universally agreed upon, value that society should try to make the distribution of income more equal. Welfare programs, minimum wage laws, and restrictions on immigration are examples of policies based on *distributional* considerations. Other labor market policies are intended either to change or to overrule the choices workers make in maximizing their utility; the underlying value in these cases is frequently that workers should not be allowed to place themselves or their families at risk of physical or financial harm. The wearing of such personal protective devices as hard hats and earplugs, for example, is seen as so *meritorious* in certain settings that it is required of workers even if they would choose otherwise.

---

[3]Pareto efficiency gets its name from the Italian economist Vilfredo Pareto, who, around 1900, insisted that economic science should make normative pronouncements only about unambiguous changes in social welfare. Rejecting the notion that utility can be measured (and therefore compared across individuals), Pareto argued that we can only know whether a transaction improves social welfare from the testimony or behavior of the affected parties themselves. If they as individuals regard themselves as better off, then the transaction is unambiguously good—even though we are unable to measure *how much* better off they feel.

Policies seeking to redistribute income or force the consumption of meritorious goods are often controversial, because some workers will feel worse off when they are adopted. These transactions must be governmentally mandated because they will not be entered into voluntarily.

Markets and Values   Economic theory, however, reminds us that there is that class of transactions in which there are no losers. Policies or transactions from which all affected parties gain can be said to be *Pareto-improving* because they promote Pareto efficiency. These policies or transactions can be justified on the grounds that they unambiguously enhance social welfare; therefore, they can be unanimously supported. Policies with this justification are of special interest to economists, because economics is largely the study of market behavior—voluntary transactions in the pursuit of self-interest.

A transaction can be unanimously supported when

a. All parties affected by the transaction gain;
b. Some gain and no one else loses; or
c. Some gain and some lose from the transaction, but the gainers fully compensate the losers.

When the compensation in *c* takes place, case *c* is converted to case *b.* In practice, economists often judge a transaction by whether the gains of the beneficiaries exceed the costs borne by the losers, thus making it *possible* that there would be no losers. However, when the compensation of losers is *possible* but does *not* take place, there are in fact losers! Many economists, therefore, argue that compensation *must* take place for a government policy to be justified on the grounds that it promotes Pareto efficiency.

As noted above, the role of the labor market is to facilitate voluntary, mutually advantageous transactions. Hardly anyone would argue against at least some kind of government intervention in the labor market if the market is failing to promote such transactions. Why do markets fail?

Market Failure: Ignorance   First, people may be ignorant of some important facts and thus led to make decisions that are not in their self-interest. For example, a worker who smokes may take a job in an asbestos-processing plant not knowing that the combination of smoking and inhaling asbestos dust substantially increases the risk of disease. Had the worker known this, he or she would probably have stopped smoking or changed jobs, but both transactions were "blocked" by ignorance.

Market Failure: Transaction Barriers   Second, there may be some barrier to the completion of a transaction that could be mutually beneficial. Often such a barrier is created by laws that prohibit certain transactions. For example, as recently as three or four decades ago, many states prohibited employers from hiring women to work more than 40 hours per week. As a consequence, firms that wanted to hire workers for more than 40 hours a week could not transact with those women who wanted to work overtime—to the detriment of both parties. Society as a whole thus suffers losses when transactions that are mutually beneficial are prohibited by government.

Laws can also block transactions in other ways. Consider, for example, a firm that is willing to offer overtime work to its production workers at rates no more than 10 percent above their normal wage. Some workers might be willing to accept overtime at the 10 percent premium. However, this transaction could not legally be completed in most instances because of a law (the Fair Labor Standards Act) requiring production workers to be paid a 50 percent wage premium for overtime. In this case, overtime would not be worked and both parties would suffer.

Another barrier to mutually beneficial transactions may be the expense of completing the transaction. Unskilled workers facing very limited opportunities in one region might desire to move to take better jobs. Alternatively, they might want to enter job-training programs. In either case, they might lack the funds to finance the desired transaction.

Market Failure: Price Distortion   A special barrier to transaction is caused by taxes, subsidies, or other forces that create "incorrect" prices. Prices powerfully influence the incentives to transact, and the prices asked or received in a transaction should reflect the true preferences of the parties to it. When prices become decoupled from preferences, parties may be led to make transactions that are not socially beneficial or to avoid others that would be advantageous. If plumbers charge $15 per hour, but their customers must pay an additional tax of $5 to the government, customers who are willing to pay between $15 and $20 per hour and would hire plumbers in the absence of the tax are discouraged from doing so—to the detriment of both parties.

Nonexistence of Market   A fourth reason why mutually beneficial transactions may not occur voluntarily is that it may not be possible or customary for buyers and sellers of certain resources to transact. As an illustration, assume that a woman who does not smoke works temporarily next to a man who does. She would be willing to pay as much as 50 cents an hour to keep her working environment smoke-free, and he could be induced to give up smoking for as little as 25 cents an hour. Thus, the potential exists for her to give him 35 cents an hour and for both to benefit. However, custom or the transience of their relationship might prevent her from offering him money in this situation, in which case the transaction would not occur.

Normative Economics and Government Policy

The solution to problems that impede the completion of mutually beneficial transactions frequently involves government intervention. When law creates the barrier to a transaction, the "intervention" might be to repeal the law. Laws prohibiting women from working overtime, for example, were repealed as their adverse effects on society became recognized.

In other cases, however, the government might be able to undertake activities to reduce transaction barriers that the private market would not undertake. Below, we cite three examples that relate to the barriers created by lack of information or restrictions on choice. Finally, we conclude with a brief discussion of the trade-off society faces between the goal of a more equitable distribution of income and the goal of achieving Pareto efficiency.

Public Goods   First let us take the case of the dissemination of information. Suppose that workers in noisy factories are concerned about the effects of noise on their hearing, but that ascertaining these effects would require an expensive research program. A union representing sawmill workers considers undertaking such research and financing the project by selling its findings to the many other interested unions or workers. The workers would then have the information they desire—albeit at some cost—which they could use to make more intelligent decisions concerning their jobs.

The hitch in the scheme is that as soon as the union's findings are published to its own members or its first customers, the results can easily become public knowledge—and thus available *free* from newspapers or by word of mouth. Anticipating this problem, the union will probably decide not to undertake the research.

Information in this example is called a *public good*—a good that can be consumed by any number of people at the same time, including those who do not pay for it. Because nonpayers cannot be excluded from consuming the good, no potential customer will have an incentive to pay. The result is that the good never gets produced by a private organization. The government, however, can *compel* payment through its tax system, so it is natural to look to the government to produce public goods. When information on occupational health hazards is to be produced on a large scale, the government is likely to have to be involved.

Capital Market Imperfections   An example of a second type of situation in which the government might have to step in to overcome a transaction barrier is a case in which loans are not available to finance job training or interregional moves, even though such loans might give workers facing a very poor set of choices access to better opportunities. Because such loans are not usually secured by anything other than the debtor's promise to pay them back, banks cannot ordinarily afford to risk making such loans, particularly when the loan recipients are poor. This lack of available loans to finance worthwhile transactions represents a *capital market imperfection*.

The government, however, might be willing to make loans in such situations even if it faced the same risk of default, because enabling workers to move to areas of better economic opportunity could improve overall social welfare and strengthen the economy. In short, because society would reap benefits from encouraging people to enter job-training programs or move to areas where their skills could be better utilized, it might be wise for the government to make the loans itself.

Establishing Market Substitutes   A third situation in which government intervention might be necessary to overcome transaction barriers occurs when a market fails to exist for some reason. Consider again the smoker and nonsmoker who were temporarily working next to each other. Their transitory relationship prevented a mutually beneficial transaction from taking place. A solution in this case might be for the government to impose the same result that a market transaction would have generated—and require the employer to designate that area a nonsmoking area.

In each case, when government does intervene, it must make sure that the transactions it undertakes or imposes on society create more gains for the beneficiaries than they impose in costs on others. Since it is costly to produce information, for example, the government should do it only if the gains are more valuable than the resources used in producing it. Likewise, the government would want to make loans for job training or interregional moves only if these activities enhanced social welfare. Finally, imposing nonsmoking areas would be socially desirable only if the gainers gained more than the losers lost.

Efficiency Versus Equity The social goal of a more equitable distribution of income is often of paramount importance to political decision makers, and disputes can arise over whether equity or economic efficiency should be the prime consideration in setting policy. One source of dispute is rooted in the problem that there is not a unique set of transactions that are Pareto efficient. There are, in fact, a *number* of different sets of transactions that can satisfy our definition of economic efficiency, and questions can arise as to which set is the most equitable.

To understand the multiple sets of efficient transactions that are possible, we return to our example of the woman willing to create blueprints for $15 per hour. If Ace Engineering Services is willing to pay up to $16 per hour for blueprints, and Sally is willing to work for $15, their agreement on her employment at an hourly wage of, say, $15.50 would be beneficial to both parties. However, the same can be said for an agreement on wages of either $15.25 or $15.75 per hour. Which agreement is most equitable?

The second source of dispute over equity and efficiency is rooted in the problem that, to achieve more equity, steps *away* from Pareto efficiency must often be taken.[4] Minimum wage laws, for example, block transactions that parties might be willing to make at a lower wage; thus, some who would have accepted jobs at less than the legislated minimum are not offered any at all because their services are "priced out of the market." Similarly, welfare programs have often been structured so that recipients who find paid work receive, in effect, a zero wage—a price distortion of major proportions, but one that is neither easily nor cheaply avoided (as we will see in chapter 6).

Normative economics tends to stress efficiency over equity considerations, not because it is more important, but because it can be analyzed more scientifically. For a transaction to be mutually beneficial, all that is required is for each party individually to feel better off. Hence studying voluntary transactions (that is, market behavior) is useful when taking economic efficiency into account. Equity considerations, however, always involve comparing the welfare lost by some against the utility gained by others—which, given the impossibility of measuring happiness, cannot be scientifically done. For policy decisions based on considerations of equity, society usually turns to guidance from the political system, not from markets.

---

[4]See Arthur Okun, *Equality and Efficiency: The Big Trade-Off* (Washington, D.C.: Brookings Institution, 1975), for a lucid discussion of the trade-offs between efficiency and equity.

PLAN OF THE TEXT

The study of labor economics is mainly a study of the interplay between employers and employees—or between demand and supply. Chapter 2 presents a quick overview of demand and supply in the labor market, allowing students to see from the outset the interrelationship of the major forces at work shaping labor market behavior. Chapters 3–5 are concerned primarily with the demand for labor. As such, they are devoted to an analysis of employers' incentives and behavior.

Chapters 6–10 contain analyses of various aspects of workers' labor supply behavior. They address issues of whether to work for pay (as opposed to consuming leisure or working at home without pay), the choice of occupations or jobs with very different characteristics, and decisions workers must make about educational and other investments designed to improve their earning capacities. Like the earlier "demand" chapters, these "supply" chapters necessarily incorporate aspects of behavior on the other (here, employer) side of the labor market.

Chapters 11–15 address special topics of interest to labor economists, including the effects of institutional forces in the labor market. Chapter 11 analyzes how the compensation of workers can be structured to create incentives for greater productivity. Chapter 12 analyzes wage differentials associated with race, gender, and ethnicity. The labor market effects of unions are dealt with in chapter 13, and chapter 14 summarizes what economic theory contributes to our understanding of wage differences by looking at the contemporary issue of growing earnings inequality. The final chapter of the text focuses on the topic of unemployment.

At the end of all chapters is a set of review questions that test student understanding; answers to odd-numbered questions are at the back of the book. Selected references and extensive footnotes are provided for those who want to go beyond what can be offered in this text.

REVIEW QUESTIONS

1. Using the concepts of normative economics, when would the labor market be judged to be at a point of optimality? What imperfections might prevent the market from achieving this point?

2. Are the following statements "positive" or "normative"? Why?
   a. Employers should not be required to offer pensions to their employees.
   b. Employers offering pension benefits will pay lower wages than they would if they did not offer a pension program.
   c. If further immigration of unskilled foreigners is prevented, the wages of unskilled immigrants already here will rise.
   d. The military draft compels people to engage in a transaction they would not voluntarily enter into; it should therefore be avoided as a way of recruiting military personnel.
   e. If the military draft were reinstituted, military salaries would probably fall.

3. Suppose the federal government needs workers to repair a levee along a flood-

prone river. From the perspective of normative economics, what difference does it make whether able-bodied citizens are compelled to work (for pay) on the levee or whether a workforce is recruited through the normal process of making job offers to applicants and relying on their voluntary acceptance?

4. What are the functions and limitations of an economic model?

5. In chapter 1 a simple model was developed in which it was predicted that workers employed in jobs paying wages less than they could get in comparable jobs elsewhere would tend to quit and seek the higher-paying jobs. Suppose we observe a worker who, after repeated harassment or criticism from her boss, quits an $8-per-hour job to take another paying $7.50. Answer the three questions below:

a. Is this woman's behavior consistent with the economic model of job quitting outlined in the text?

b. Can we test to see whether this woman's behavior is consistent with the assumption of rationality?

c. Suppose the boss in question had harassed other employees but that this woman was the only one who quit. Can we conclude that economic theory applies to the behavior of some people but not to others?

6. A few decades ago it was common for state laws to prohibit women from working more than 40 hours a week. Using the principles underlying normative economics, evaluate these laws.

7. Child labor laws generally prohibit children from working until age 14 and restrict younger teenagers to certain kinds of work that are not considered dangerous. Reconcile the prohibitions of child labor legislation with the principles underlying normative economic analysis.

8. "Government policies as frequently prevent Pareto efficiency as they enhance it." Comment.

PROBLEMS

1. (Appendix) You have collected the following data (see table below) on 13 randomly selected teenage workers in the fast-food industry. What is the general relationship between age and wage? Plot the data and then construct a linear equation for this relationship.

Age (years)	Wage (dollars per hour)	Age (years)	Wage (dollars per hour)
16	$5.25	18	$6.00
16	$6.00	18	$6.50
17	$5.50	18	$7.50
17	$6.00	19	$6.50
17	$6.25	19	$6.75
18	$5.25	19	$8.00
18	$5.75		

2. (Appendix) Suppose that a least squares regression yields the following estimate:

$$W_i = -1 + 0.3A_i$$

where W is the hourly wage rate (in dollars) and A is the age (in years).

A second regression from another group of workers yields this estimate:

$$W_i = 3 + 0.3A_i - 0.01(A_i)^2$$

a. How much is a 20-year-old predicted to earn based on the first estimate?

b. How much is a 20-year-old predicted to earn based on the second estimate?

3. (Appendix) Suppose that you estimate the following relationship between wages and age:

$$W_i = -1 + 0.3A_i$$
$$(0.1)$$

where the standard error is reported in parentheses. Are you confident that wages actually rise with age?

SELECTED READINGS

Boyer, George R., and Robert S. Smith. "The Development of the Neoclassical Tradition in Labor Economics." *Industrial and Labor Relations Review* 54 (January 2001): 199–223.

Friedman, Milton. *Essays in Positive Economics.* Chicago: University of Chicago Press, 1953.

Hausman, Daniel M. "Economic Methodology in a Nutshell." *Journal of Economic Perspectives* 3 (Spring 1989): 115–128.

McCloskey, Donald. "The Rhetoric of Economics." *Journal of Economic Literature* 21 (June 1983): 481–517.

1A

Statistical Testing of Labor Market Hypotheses

This appendix provides a brief introduction to how labor economists test hypotheses. We will discuss how one might attempt to test the hypothesis presented in chapter 1 that, other things equal, one should expect to observe that the higher the wage a firm pays, the lower will be the voluntary labor turnover among its employees. Put another way, if we define a firm's quit rate as the proportion of its workers who voluntarily quit in a given time period (say, a year), we expect to observe that the higher a firm's wages, the lower will be its quit rate, holding *other* factors affecting quit rates constant.

A UNIVARIATE TEST

An obvious first step is to collect data on the quit rates experienced by a set of firms during a given year and match these data with the firms' wage rates. This type of analysis is called *univariate* because we are analyzing the effects on quit rates of just one other variable (the wage rate); the data are called *cross-sectional* because they provide observations across behavioral units at a point in time.[1] Table 1A.1 contains such information for a hypothetical set of 10 firms located in a single labor market in 1993. For example, firm A is assumed to have paid an average hourly wage of $4 and to have experienced a quit rate of 40 percent in 1993.

The data on wages and quit rates are presented graphically in Figure 1A.1. Each dot in this figure represents a quit-rate/hourly-wage combination for one of the firms in Table 1A.1. Firm A, for example, is represented in the figure by point *A,* which shows a quit rate of 40 percent and an hourly wage of $4, while point *B* shows the comparable data for firm B. From a visual inspection of all 10 data points, it appears from this figure that firms paying higher wages in our hypothetical sample do indeed

---

[1]Several other types of data are also used frequently by labor economists. One could look, for example, at how a given firm's quit rate and wage rate vary over time. Observations that provide information on a single behavioral unit over a number of time periods are called *time-series* data. Sometimes labor economists have data on the behavior of a number of observational units (e.g., employers) for a number of time periods; combinations of cross-sectional and time-series data are called *panel* data.

TABLE 1A.1   Average-Wage and Quit-Rate Data for a Set of
10 Hypothetical Firms in a Single Labor Market in 1993

Firm	Average Hourly Wage Paid	Quit Rate	Firm	Average Hourly Wage Paid	Quit Rate
A	$4	40%	F	$ 8	20%
B	4	30	G	10	25
C	6	35	H	10	15
D	6	25	I	12	20
E	8	30	J	12	10

have lower quit rates. Although the data points in Figure 1A.1 obviously do not lie on a single straight line, their pattern suggests that, on average, there is a linear (straight-line) relationship between a firm's quit rate and its wage rate.

Any straight line can be represented by the general equation

$$Y = a + bX \tag{1A.1}$$

Variable Y is the *dependent variable,* and it is generally shown on the vertical axis of the graph depicting the line. Variable X is the *independent* or *explanatory* variable, which is usually shown on the horizontal axis.[2] The letters "a" and "b" are the *parameters* (the fixed coefficients) of the equation, with "a" representing the intercept and "b" the slope of the line. Put differently, "a" is the value of Y when the line intersects the vertical axis ($X = 0$). The slope, "b," indicates the vertical distance the line travels for each one-unit increase in the horizontal distance. If "b" is a positive number, the line slopes upward (going from left to right); if "b" is a negative number, the line has a downward slope.

If one were to try to draw the straight line that best fits the points in Figure 1A.1, it is clear that the line would slope downward and that it would not go through all 10 points. It would lie above some points and below others, and thus it would "fit" the points only with some error. We could model the relationship between the data points on the graph, then, as follows:

$$Q_i = \alpha_0 + \alpha_1 W_i + \varepsilon_i \tag{1A.2}$$

Here Q_i represents the quit rate for firm i, and it is the dependent variable. The independent or explanatory variable is W_i, firm i's wage rate. α_0 and α_1 are the parameters of the line, with α_0 the intercept and α_1 the slope of the line. The term ε_i is

[2]An exception occurs in the demand and supply curves facing firms, in which the independent variable, price, is typically shown on the vertical axis.

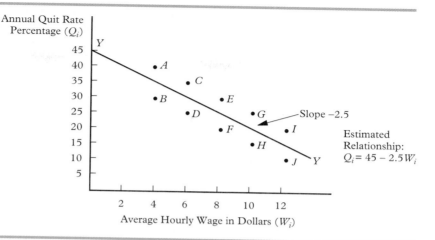

FIGURE 1A.1

Estimated Relationship between Wages and Quit Rates Using Data from Table 1A.1

a random *error term;* it is included in the model because we do not expect that the line (given by $Q_i = \alpha_0 + \alpha_1 W_i$) will connect all the data points perfectly. Behaviorally, we are assuming the presence of random factors unrelated to wage rates that also cause the quit rate to vary across firms.

We seek to estimate what the true values of α_0 and α_1 are. Each pair of values of α_0 and α_1 defines a different straight line, and an infinite number of lines can be drawn that "fit" points *A–J*. It is natural for us to ask, "Which of these straight lines fits the data the best?" Some precise criterion must be used to decide which line fits the best, and the procedure typically used by statisticians and economists is to choose that line for which the sum (in our example, across all firms) of the squared vertical distances between the line and the individual data points is minimized. The line estimated from the data using this method, which is called *least squares regression analysis,* has a number of desirable properties.[3]

Application of this method to the data found in Table 1A.1 yields the following estimated line:[4]

$$Q_i = 45 - 2.5W_i \qquad \qquad (1A.3)$$
$$(5.3)\ \ (0.625)$$

The estimate of α_0, the intercept of the line, is 45, and the estimate of α_1, the slope of the line, is –2.5. Thus, if a firm has a wage rate of $4/hour, we would predict that

---

[3]These properties include that, on average, the correct answer for α_1 is obtained; the estimates are the most precise possible among a certain class of estimators; and the sum of the positive and negative vertical deviations of the data points from the estimated line will be zero. For a more formal treatment of the method of least squares, see any statistics or econometrics text. A good introduction for the reader with no statistical background is Larry D. Schroeder, David L. Sjoquist, and Paula E. Stephan, *Understanding Regression Analysis: An Introductory Guide* (Beverly Hills, Calif.: Sage Publications, 1986).
[4]Students with access to computer software for estimating regression models can easily verify this result.

its annual quit rate would be 45 − 2.5(4), or 35 percent. This estimated quit/wage relationship is drawn in Figure 1A.1 as the line *YY*. (The numbers in parentheses below the equation will be discussed later.)

Several things should be noted about this relationship. First, taken at face value, this estimated relationship implies that firms paying their workers *nothing* (a wage of zero) would be projected to have *only* 45 percent of their workers quit each year (45 − 2.5(0) = 45), while firms paying their workers more than $18 an hour would have negative quit rates.[5] The former result is nonsensical (why should any workers stay if they were paid nothing?), and the latter result is logically impossible (the quit rate cannot be less than zero). As these extreme examples suggest, it is dangerous to use linear models to make predictions that take one outside the range of observations used in the estimation (in the example, wages from $4 to $12). The relationship between wages and quit rates cannot be assumed to be linear (represented by a straight line) for very low and very high values of wages. Fortunately, the linear regression model used in the example can be easily generalized to allow for nonlinear relationships.

Second, the estimated intercept (45) and slope (−2.5) that we obtained are only estimates of the "true" relationship, and there is uncertainty associated with these estimates. The uncertainty arises partly from the fact that we are trying to infer the true values of α_0 and α_1—that is, the values that characterize the wage/quit relationship in the entire population of firms—from a sample of just 10 firms. The uncertainty about each estimated coefficient is measured by its *standard error,* or the estimated standard deviation of the coefficient. These standard errors are reported in parentheses under the estimated coefficients in equation (1A.3); for example, given our data, the estimated standard error of the wage coefficient is 0.625 and that of the intercept term is 5.3. The larger the standard error, the greater the uncertainty about our estimated coefficient's value.

Under suitable assumptions about the distribution of ε, the random error term in equation (1A.2), we can use these standard errors to test hypotheses about the estimated coefficients.[6] In our example, we would like to test the hypothesis that α_1 is negative (which implies, as suggested by theory, that higher wages reduce quits) against the *null hypothesis* that α_1 is zero and there is thus no relationship between wages and quits. One common test involves computing for each coefficient a *t statistic,* which is the ratio of the coefficient to its standard error. A heuristic rule, which can be made precise, is that if the absolute value of the *t* statistic is greater than 2, the hypothesis that the true value of the coefficient equals zero can be rejected. Put another way, if the absolute value of a coefficient is at least twice the size of its standard error, one can be fairly confident that the true value of the coefficient is other than zero. In our example, the *t* statistic for the wage coefficient is −2.5/0.625, or −4.0, which leaves us very confident that the true relationship between wage levels and quit rates is negative.

---

[5]For example, at a wage of $20/hour the estimated quit rate would be 45 − 2.5(20), or −5 percent per year.
[6]These assumptions are discussed in any econometrics text.

MULTIPLE REGRESSION ANALYSIS

The preceeding discussion has *assumed* that the only variable influencing quit rates, other than random (unexplained) factors, is a firm's wage rate. The discussion of positive economics in chapter 1 stressed, however, that the prediction of a negative relationship between wages and quit rates is made holding *all other factors constant*. As we will discuss in chapter 10, economic theory suggests there are many factors besides wages that systematically influence quit rates. These include characteristics both of firms (e.g., employee benefits offered, working conditions, and firm size) and of their workers (e.g., age and level of training). If any of these other variables that we have omitted from our analysis tend to vary across firms systematically with the wage rates that the firms offer, the resulting estimated relationship between wage rates and quit rates will be incorrect. In such cases, we must take these other variables into account by using a model with more than one independent variable. We rely on economic theory to indicate which variables should be included in our statistical analysis and to suggest the direction of causation.

To illustrate this procedure, suppose for simplicity that the only variable affecting a firm's quit rate besides its wage rate is the average age of its workforce. Other things held constant, older workers are less likely to quit their jobs for a number of reasons (as workers grow older, ties to friends, neighbors, and co-workers become stronger, and the psychological costs involved in changing jobs—which often requires a geographic move—grow larger). To capture the effects of both wage rates and age, we assume that a firm's quit rate is given by

$$Q_i = \alpha'_0 + \alpha'_1 W_i + \alpha'_2 A_i + \varepsilon_i \tag{1A.4}$$

A_i is a variable representing the age of firm i's workers. Although A_i could be measured as the average age of the workforce, or as the percentage of the firm's workers older than some age level, for expositional convenience we have defined it as a *dichotomous* variable. A_i is equal to 1 if the average age of firm i's workforce is greater than 40, and it is equal to zero otherwise. Clearly theory suggests that α'_2 is negative, which means that whatever values of α'_0, α'_1, and W_i pertain (that is, holding all else constant), firms with workforces having an average age above 40 years should have lower quit rates than firms with workforces having an average age equal to or below age 40.

The parameters of equation (1A.4)—that is, the values of α'_0, α'_1, and α'_2—can be estimated using *multiple regression analysis,* a method that is analogous to the one described above. This method finds the values of the parameters that define the best straight-line relationship between the dependent variable and the set of independent variables. Each parameter tells us the effect on the dependent variable of a one-unit change in the corresponding independent variable, *holding the other independent variables constant.* Thus, the estimate of α'_1 tells us the estimated effect on the quit rate (Q) of a one-unit change in the wage rate (W), holding the age of a firm's workforce (A) constant.

THE PROBLEM OF OMITTED VARIABLES

If we use a univariate regression model in a situation calling for a multiple regression model—that is, if we leave out an important independent variable—our results may suffer from *omitted variables bias*. We illustrate this bias because it is an important pitfall in hypothesis testing and because it illustrates the need to use economic theory to guide empirical testing.

To simplify our example, we assume that we know the true values of α'_0, α'_1, and α'_2 in equation (1A.4) and that there is no random error term in this model (each ε_i is zero). Specifically, we assume that

$$Q_i = 50 - 2.5W_i - 10A_i \tag{1A.5}$$

Thus, at any level of wages a firm's quit rate will be 10 percentage points lower if the average age of its workforce exceeds 40 than it will be if the average age is less than or equal to 40.

Figure 1A.2 graphically illustrates this assumed relationship between quit rates, wage rates, and workforce average age. For all firms that employ workers whose average age is less than or equal to 40, A_i equals zero and thus their quit rates are given by the line Z_0Z_0. For all firms that employ workers whose average age is greater than 40, A_i equals 1 and thus their quit rates are given by the line Z_1Z_1. The quit-rate schedule for the latter set of firms is everywhere 10 percentage points below the one for the former set. Both schedules indicate, how-

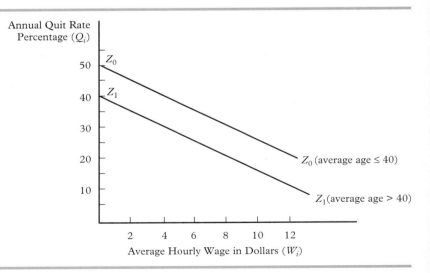

FIGURE 1A.2
True Relationships between Wages and Quit Rates (Equation 1A.5)

TABLE 1A.2   **Hypothetical Average-Wage and Quit-Rate Data for Three Firms That Employ Older Workers and Three That Employ Younger Workers**

	Employ Older Workers ($A_i = 1$)			Employ Younger Workers ($A_i = 0$)	
Firm	Average Hourly Wage	Quit Rate	Firm	Average Hourly Wage	Quit Rate
k	$ 8	20%	p	$4	40%
l	10	15	q	6	35
m	12	10	r	8	30

ever, that a $1 increase in a firm's average hourly wage will reduce its annual quit rate by 2.5 percentage points (that is, both lines have the same slope).

Now suppose a researcher were to estimate the relationship between quit rates and wage rates but ignored the fact that the average age of a firm's workers also affects the quit rate. That is, suppose one were to omit a measure of age and estimate the following equation:

$$Q_i = a_0 + a_1 W_i + \varepsilon_i \qquad (1A.6)$$

Of crucial importance to us is how the estimated value of a_1 will correspond to the true slope of the quit/wage schedule, which we have *assumed* to be −2.5.

The answer depends heavily on how average wages and the average age of employees vary across firms. Table 1A.2 lists combinations of quit rates and wages for three hypothetical firms that employ older workers (average age greater than 40) and three hypothetical firms that employ younger workers. Given the wage each firm pays, the values of its quit rate can be derived directly from equation (1A.5).

It is a well-established fact that earnings of workers tend to increase as they age.[7] On average, then, firms employing older workers are assumed in the table to have higher wages than firms employing younger workers. The wage/quit-rate combinations for these six firms are indicated by the dots on the lines $Z_0 Z_0$ and $Z_1 Z_1$ in Figure 1A.3,[8] which reproduce the lines in Figure 1A.2.

---

[7]Reasons why this occurs will be discussed in chapters 5, 9, and 11.
[8]The fact that the dots fall exactly on a straight line is a graphic representation of the assumption in equation (1A.5) that there is no random error term. If random error is present, the dots would fall around, but not all on, a straight line.

FIGURE 1A.3

Estimated Relationships between Wages and Quit Rates Using Data from Table 1A.2

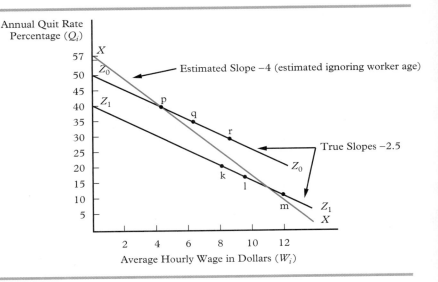

When we estimate equation (1A.6) using these six data points, we obtain the following straight line:

$$Q_i = 57 - 4W_i \qquad (1A.7)$$
$$(5.1)\ (0.612)$$

This estimated relationship is denoted by the line XX in Figure 1A.3. The estimate of a_1, which equals -4, implies that every dollar increase in wages reduces the quit rate by four percentage points, yet we know (by assumption) that the actual reduction is two and a half percentage points. Our estimated response overstates the sensitivity of the quit rate to wages because the estimated equation ignored the effect that age has on quits.

Put differently, quit rates are lower in high-wage firms *both* because the wages they pay are higher *and* because high-wage firms tend to employ older workers, who are less likely to quit. By ignoring age in the analysis, we mistakenly conclude that quit rates are more sensitive to wage changes than they actually are. Therefore, by omitting from our model an important explanatory variable (age) that both affects quit rates and is associated with wage levels, we have obtained a wrong estimate of the effect of wages on quit rates.

This discussion highlights the "other things held equal" nature of most hypotheses in labor economics. In testing hypotheses, we must control for other factors that are expected to influence the variable of interest. Typically this is done by specifying that the dependent variable is a function of a *set* of variables. This specification must be guided by economic theory, and one reason for learning economic theory is that it can guide us in testing hypotheses about human behavior. Without a firm grounding in theory, analyses of behavior can easily fall victim to omitted variables bias.

Having said this, we must point out that it is neither possible nor crucial to have data on all variables that could conceivably influence what is being examined. As emphasized in chapter 1, testing economic models involves looking for *average* relationships and ignoring idiosyncratic factors. Two workers with the same age and the same wage rate may exhibit different quit behaviors because, for example, one wants to leave town to get away from a dreadful father-in-law. This idiosyncratic factor is not important for the testing of an economic model of quit rates, because having a father-in-law has neither a predictable effect on quits (some fathers-in-law are desirable to be around) nor any correlation with one's wage rate. To repeat, omitted variables bias is a problem only if the omitted variable has an effect on the dependent variable (quit rate) *and* is correlated with an independent variable of interest (wages).

2

OVERVIEW OF THE LABOR MARKET

Every society—regardless of its wealth, its form of government, or the organization of its economy—must make basic decisions. It must decide what and how much to produce, how to produce it, and how the output shall be distributed. These decisions require finding out what consumers want, what technologies for production are available, and what the skills and preferences of workers are; deciding where to produce; and coordinating all such decisions so that, for example, the millions of people in New York City and the isolated few in an Alaskan fishing village can each buy the milk, bread, meat, vanilla extract, mosquito repellent, and brown shoe polish they desire at the grocery store. The process of coordination involves creating incentives so that the right amount of labor and capital will be employed at the right place at the required time.

These decisions can, of course, be made by administrators employed by a centralized bureaucracy. The amount of information this bureaucracy must obtain and process to make the millions of needed decisions wisely, and the number of incentives it must create to ensure that these decisions are coordinated, are truly mind-boggling. It boggles the mind even more to consider the major alternative to centralized decision making—the decentralized marketplace. Millions of producers striving to make a profit observe the prices millions of consumers are willing to pay for products and the wages millions of workers are willing to accept for work. Combining these pieces of information with data on various technologies, they decide where to produce, what to produce, whom to hire, and how much to produce. No one is in charge, and while market imperfections impede progress toward achieving the best allocation of resources, millions of people find jobs that enable them to purchase the items they desire each year. The production, employment, and consumption decisions are all made and coordinated by price signals arising through the marketplace.

The market that allocates workers to jobs and coordinates employment decisions is the *labor market*. With over 140 million workers and more than 7 million employers in the United States, thousands of decisions about career choice, hiring, quitting, compensation, and technology must be made and coordinated every day. This chapter will present an overview of what the labor market does and how it works.

THE LABOR MARKET: DEFINITIONS, FACTS, AND TRENDS

Every market has buyers and sellers, and the labor market is no exception: the buyers are employers and the sellers are workers. Some of these participants may not be active at any given moment in the sense of seeking new employees or new jobs, but on any given day thousands of firms and workers will be "in the market" trying to transact. If, as in the case of doctors or mechanical engineers, buyers and sellers are searching throughout the entire nation for each other, we would describe the market as a *national labor market*. If buyers and sellers only search locally, as in the case of data entry clerks or automobile mechanics, the labor market is a *local* one.

When we speak of a particular "labor market"—for taxi drivers, say—we are using the term loosely to refer to the companies trying to hire people to drive their cabs and the people seeking employment as cabdrivers. The efforts of these buyers and sellers of labor to transact and establish an employment relationship constitute the market for cabdrivers. However, neither the employers nor the drivers are confined to this market; both could simultaneously be in other markets as well. An entrepreneur with $100,000 to invest might be thinking of operating either a taxi company or a car wash, depending on the projected revenues and costs of each. A person seeking a cabdriving job might also be trying to find work as an actor. Thus, all the various labor markets that we can define on the basis of industry, occupation, geography, transaction rules, or job character are interrelated to some degree. We speak of these narrowly defined labor markets for the sake of convenience.

Some labor markets, particularly those in which the sellers of labor are represented by a union, operate under a very formal set of rules that partly govern buyer-seller transactions. In the unionized construction trades, for example, employers must hire at the union hiring hall from a list of eligible union members. In other

FIGURE 2.1
Labor Force Status of the
U.S. Adult Civilian Population,
June 2000

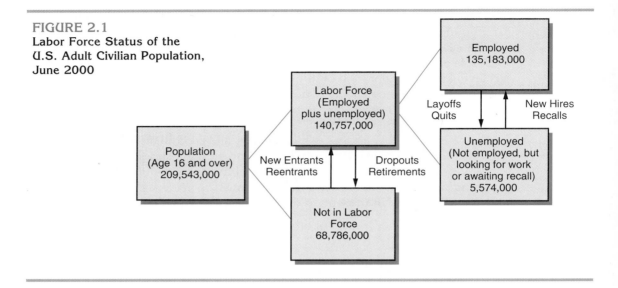

unionized markets, the employer has discretion over who gets hired but is constrained by a union-management agreement in such matters as the order in which employees may be laid off, procedures regarding employee complaints, and promotions. The markets for government jobs and jobs with large nonunion employers also tend to operate under rules that constrain the authority of management and ensure fair treatment of employees. When a formal set of rules and procedures guides and constrains the employment relationship *within* a firm, an *internal labor market* is said to exist[1]

The Labor Force and Unemployment

Figure 2.1 highlights some basic definitions concerning labor market status. The term *labor force* refers to all those over 16 years of age who are either employed, actively seeking work, or expecting recall from a layoff. Those in the labor force who are not employed for pay are the *unemployed*.[2] People who are not employed and are neither looking for work nor waiting to be recalled from layoff by their

---

[1]An analysis of internal labor markets can be found in Michael L. Wachter and Randall Wright, "The Economics of Internal Labor Markets," *University of Pennsylvania Law Review* 29 (Spring 1990): 240–262.
[2]The official definition of unemployment for purposes of government statistics includes those who have been laid off by their employers, those who have been fired or have quit and are looking for other work, and those who are just entering or reentering the labor force but have not found a job as yet. The extent of unemployment is estimated from a monthly survey of some 60,000 households called the Current Population Survey (CPS). Interviewers ascertain whether household members are employed, whether they meet one of the aforementioned conditions (in which case they are considered "unemployed"), or whether they are out of the labor force.

employers are not counted as part of the labor force. The total labor force thus consists of the employed and the unemployed.

The number and identities of people in each labor market category are always changing, and as we shall see in chapter 15, the flows of people from one category to another are sizable. As Figure 2.1 suggests, there are four major flows between labor market states:

1. Employed workers become unemployed by *quitting* voluntarily or *being laid off* (being involuntarily separated from the firm, either temporarily or permanently).
2. Unemployed workers obtain employment by *being newly hired* or *being recalled* to a job from which they were temporarily laid off.
3. Those in the labor force, whether employed or unemployed, can leave the labor force by *retiring* or otherwise deciding against taking or seeking work for pay (*dropping out*).
4. Those who have never worked or looked for a job expand the labor force by *entering* it, while those who have dropped out do so by *reentering* the labor force.

In June 2000 there were more than 140 million people in the labor force, representing a little over 67 percent of the entire population over 16 years of age. An overall *labor force participation rate* (labor force divided by population) of a little over 67 percent is substantially higher than the rates around 60 percent that prevailed prior to the 1980s, as is shown by the data in Table 2.1. This table also indicates

TABLE 2.1 **Labor Force Participation Rates by Gender, 1950–2000**

Year	Total	Men	Women
1950	59.9%	86.8%	33.9%
1960	60.2	84.0	37.8
1970	61.3	80.6	43.4
1980	64.2	77.9	51.6
1990	66.5	76.4	57.5
2000	67.2	74.7	60.2

Sources: 1950–1980: U.S. President, *Employment and Training Report of the President* (Washington, D.C.: U.S. Government Printing Office), transmitted to the Congress 1981, Table A–1.

1990: U.S. Bureau of Labor Statistics, *Employment and Earnings* 45, no. 2 (February 1998), Tables A–1, A–2.

2000: U.S. Bureau of Labor Statistics, *Employment Situation* (News Release, October 2001), Table A–1.

Data and news releases are available online at http://www.bls.gov.

the most important fact about labor force trends in the last 50 years: *labor force participation rates for men are falling while those for women are increasing dramatically.* These trends and their causes will be discussed in detail in chapters 6 and 7.

The ratio of those unemployed to those in the labor force is the *unemployment rate.* While this rate is crude and has several imperfections, it is the most widely cited measure of labor market conditions. When the unemployment rate is around 5 percent in the United States, the labor market is considered *tight,* indicating that jobs in general are plentiful and hard for employers to fill and that most of those who are unemployed will find other work quickly. When the unemployment rate is higher—say, 7 percent or above—the labor market is described as *loose,* in the sense that workers are abundant and jobs are relatively easy for employers to fill. To say that the labor market as a whole is loose, however, does not imply that no shortages can be found anywhere; to say it is tight can still mean that in some occupations or places the number of those seeking work exceeds the number of jobs available at the prevailing wage.

Figure 2.2 shows the overall unemployment rate during the twentieth century (data displayed graphically in Figure 2.2 are contained in a table inside the front cover). The data clearly show the extraordinarily loose labor market during the Great Depression of the 1930s and the exceptionally tight labor market during World War II. However, when we look at long stretches of nonwar years,

FIGURE 2.2
Unemployment Rates for the Civilian Labor Force, 1900–2000 (detailed data in table inside front cover)

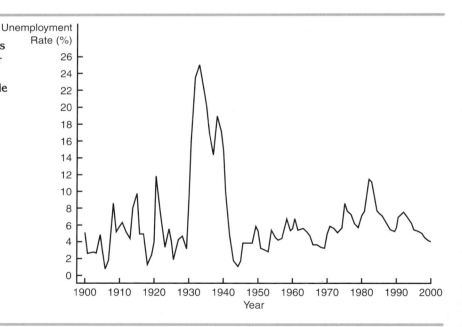

excluding the years of the Great Depression, two interesting patterns emerge. First, the average unemployment rate has clearly risen: it was 4.4 percent in 1900–1914, but in the most recent nonwar periods it was 5.3 percent (1954–1965) and 6.4 percent (1973–2000). Second, in recent years the unemployment rate has fluctuated less than it did in 1900–1914. In the years from 1900 to 1914, the average yearly change in the unemployment rate was 1.9 percentage points; in contrast, from 1954 to 1965 and from 1973 to 2000 it was around 0.8 percentage points. The labor market, then, would appear to be more stable now than it was at the turn of the century, but it operates with proportionately more unemployment. Chapter 15 will present a more detailed analysis of the determinants of the unemployment rate.

Industries and Occupations: Adapting to Change

As we pointed out earlier, the labor market is the mechanism through which workers and jobs are matched. Over the last 100 years, the number of some kinds of jobs has expanded and the number of others has contracted. Both workers and employers have had to adapt to these changes in response to signals provided by the labor market. One way to capture the extent of employment transactions that labor markets must facilitate is to compare the number or distribution of jobs across sectors at different points in time. For example, from 1972 to 1986, roughly 11 percent of all manufacturing jobs were destroyed each year by plant closings and employment contractions, while another 9 percent were newly created yearly by plant expansions and openings.[3]

An examination of the industrial distribution of employment from 1900 to 2000 reveals the kinds of changes the labor market has had to facilitate. Figure 2.3, which graphs data presented in a table inside the front cover, discloses a major shift: *agricultural employment has declined drastically while employment in service industries has expanded.* Goods-producing jobs increased roughly proportionately to the increase in total employment during the first seven decades, but their share fell sharply after 1970. The largest employment increases have been in the service sector. Retail and wholesale trade, which increased from 9.2 percent of employment in 1910 to 22.3 percent in 2000, showed the largest increases in nongovernment services. However, the largest percentage increase has been in government employment, which almost quadrupled its share of total employment over the twentieth century. Some describe this shift in employment from agriculture to services as a shift from the *primary* to the *tertiary* sector (manufacturing being labeled the *secondary* sector). Others describe it as the arrival of the *postindustrial* state.

The combination of shifts in the industrial distribution of jobs and changes in the production technology within each sector has also required that workers

---

[3]Steven J. Davis and John Haltiwanger, "Gross Job Creation, Gross Job Destruction, and Employment Reallocation," *Quarterly Journal of Economics* 107, no. 3 (August 1992): 819–863.

acquire new skills and work in new jobs. Just since 1970, for example, the number of skilled craft and repair jobs has fallen from 13.2 percent to 10.7 percent of total employment, while opportunities for less-skilled operatives and laborers have declined from 22.7 to 14.2 percent of all jobs. Meanwhile, jobs for managers and administrators rose from 8 percent to 14 percent of the total, and those in sales increased from 7 to 11 percent.[4]

The Earnings of Labor

The actions of buyers and sellers in the labor market serve both to allocate and to set prices for various kinds of labor. From a social perspective, these prices act as signals or incentives in the allocation process, a process that relies primarily on individual and voluntary decisions. From the worker's point of view, the price of labor is important in determining income—and hence purchasing power.

Nominal and Real Wages   The *wage rate* is the price of labor per working hour.[5] The *nominal wage* is what workers get paid per hour in current dollars; nominal wages are most useful in comparing the pay of various workers at a given time. *Real wages*, nominal wages divided by some measure of prices, suggest how much can be purchased with workers' nominal wages. For example, if a worker earns $64 a day and a pair of shoes cost $32, we could say the worker earns the equivalent of two pairs of shoes a day (real wage = $64/$32 = 2).

Calculations of real wages are especially useful in comparing the purchasing power of workers' earnings over a period of time when both nominal wages and product prices are changing. For example, suppose we were interested in trying to determine what happened to the real wages of American nonsupervisory workers over the 20-year period from 1980 to 2000. We can note from Table 2.2 that the average hourly earnings of these workers in the private sector were $6.66 in 1980, $10.01 in 1990, and $13.73 in 2000; thus, nominal wage rates were clearly

---

[4]U.S. Bureau of the Census, *Statistical Abstract of the United States* (Washington, D.C.: U.S. Government Printing Office, 1974 and 2000), Table 571 (1974), Table 657 (2000).

[5]In this book we define the hourly wage in the way most workers would if asked to state their "straight-time" wage. It is the money a worker would lose per hour if he or she had an unauthorized absence. When wages are defined in this way, a paid holiday becomes an "employee benefit," as we note below, because leisure time is granted while pay continues. Thus, a worker paid $100 for 25 hours—20 of which are working hours and 5 of which are time off—will be said to earn a wage of $4 per hour and receive time off worth $20.

An alternative is to define the wage in terms of actual hours worked—or as $5 per hour in the above example. We prefer our definition, because if the worker seizes an opportunity to work one less hour in a particular week, his or her earnings would fall by $4, not $5 (as long as the reduction in hours does not affect the hours of paid holiday or vacation time for which the worker is eligible).

FIGURE 2.3
Employment
Distribution
by Major Industrial
Sector, 1900–2000
(detailed data in table
inside front cover)

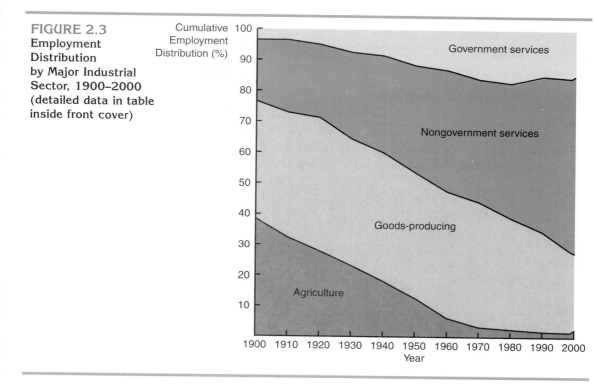

rising over this period. However, the prices such workers had to pay for the items they buy were also rising over this period, so a method of accounting for price inflation must be used in calculating real wages.

The most widely used measure for comparing the prices consumers face over several years is the Consumer Price Index (CPI). Generally speaking, this index is derived by determining what a fixed bundle of consumer goods and services (including food, housing, clothing, transportation, medical care, and entertainment) costs each year. The cost of this bundle in the base period is then set to equal 100, and the index numbers for all other years are set proportionately to this base period. For example, if the bundle's average cost over the 1982–1984 period is considered the base (the average value of the index over this period is set to 100), and if the bundle costs 72 percent more in 2000, then the index for 2000 is equal to 172.0. From the second line in Table 2.2, we can see that with a 1982–1984 base, the CPI was 82.4 in 1980 and 172.0 in 2000—implying that prices had doubled (172.0/82.4 = 2.09) over that period. Put differently, a dollar in 2000 appears to buy about half as much as a 1980 dollar.

TABLE 2.2 Nominal and Real Hourly Earnings, U.S. Nonsupervisory Workers in the Private Sector, 1980–2000

	1980	1990	2000
Average Hourly Earnings	$6.66	$10.01	$13.73
Consumer Price Index (CPI) using 1982–1984 as a base	82.4	130.7	172.0
Average Hourly Earnings, 1982–1984 dollars (using CPI)	$8.08	$7.66	$7.98
Average Hourly Earnings, 2000 dollars (using CPI)	$13.90	$13.17	$13.73
Average Hourly Earnings, 2000 dollars (using CPI inflation less 1 percent per year)	$11.35	$11.96	$13.73

Source: U.S. President, *Economic Report of the President* (Washington D.C.: U.S. Government Printing Office, 2001), 330, 343.

There are several alternative ways to calculate real wages from the information given in the first two rows of Table 2.2. The most straightforward way is to divide the nominal wage by the CPI for each year and multiply by 100. Doing this converts the nominal wage for each year into 1982–1984 dollars; thus, workers paid $6.66 in 1980 could have bought $8.08 worth of goods and services in 1983, while those paid $13.73 in 2000 could have bought $7.98 worth. Alternatively, we could use the table's information to put average hourly earnings into 2000 dollars by multiplying each year's nominal wage rate by the percentage price increase between that year and 2000. Because prices rose by 109 percent between 1980 and 2000, $6.66 in 1980 was equivalent to $13.90 in 2000.

The Consumer Price Index   Our calculations in Table 2.2 suggest that real wages for American nonsupervisory workers fell over the period from 1980 to 2000, and we will see later in this chapter and throughout the text that the downward pressure on wages was especially great for less-skilled workers. A lively debate exists, however, about whether real-wage calculations based on the CPI are accurate indicators of changes in the purchasing power of an hour of work for the ordinary American. The issues are technical and beyond the scope of this text, but they center on two problems associated with using a fixed bundle of goods and services to compare prices from year to year.

One problem is that consumers *change* the bundle of goods and services they actually buy over time, partly in response to changes in prices. If the price of beef rises, for example, consumers may eat more chicken; pricing a fixed bundle may thus understate the purchasing power of current dollars, because it assumes that consumers still purchase the former quantities of beef. For this reason, the bundles used for pricing purposes are updated periodically.

The more difficult issue has to do with the *quality* of goods and services. Suppose that hospital costs rise by 50 percent over a five-year period, but that at the same time new diagnostic equipment and surgical techniques are perfected. Some of the increased price of hospitalization, then, reflects the availability of new services—or quality improvements in previously provided ones—rather than reductions in the purchasing power of a dollar. The problem is that we have not yet found a satisfactory method for feasibly separating the effects of changes in quality.

After considering these problems, some economists believe that the Consumer Price Index has overstated inflation by as much as one percentage point per year.[6] While not everyone agrees that inflation is overstated by this much, it is instructive to recalculate real-wage changes by supposing that it is. Inflation, as measured by the Consumer Price Index, averaged 2.8 percent per year from 1990 to 2000, and in Table 2.2 we therefore estimated that it would take $13.17 in 2000 to buy what $10.01 could have purchased 10 years earlier. Comparing $13.17 with what was actually paid in 2000—$13.73— we would conclude that real wages had risen by 4.3 percent from 1990 to 2000. If the true decline in purchasing power were instead only 1.8 percent per year during that period, then it would have taken a wage of only $11.96 in 2000 to match the purchasing power of $10.01 in 1990. Because workers actually were paid $13.73 in 2000, assuming that true inflation was one percentage point below that indicated by the CPI results in the conclusion that real wage rates rose by 14.8 percent in the decade! Similiar conclusions, based on analogous assumptions and adjustments, hold for real wages over the period from 1980 to 1990. Thus, whether real wages have been rising or falling remains a question that is greatly affected by the accuracy of the CPI in measuring changes in purchasing power over time.

Wages, Earnings, Compensation, and Income   We often apply the term *wages* to payments received by workers who are paid on a salaried basis (monthly, for example) rather than an hourly basis. The term is used this way merely for convenience and is of no consequence for most purposes. It is important, however, to distinguish among wages, earnings, and income, as we do schematically in Figure 2.4. The term *wages* refers to the payment for a *unit* of time, whereas *earnings* refers to wages multiplied by the number of time units (typically hours) worked. Thus, earnings depend on both wages and the length of time the employee works.

Both wages and earnings are normally defined and measured in terms of direct monetary payments to employees (before taxes for which the employee is liable). *Total compensation*, on the other hand, consists of earnings plus *employee benefits*—

---

[6]For fuller discussions, see U.S. President, *Economic Report of the President* (Washington, D.C.: U.S. Government Printing Office, 1992), 253–256; Brent R. Moulton, "Bias in the Consumer Price Index: What Is the Evidence?" *Journal of Economic Perspectives* 10, no. 4 (Fall 1996): 159–177; and several articles in the *Journal of Economic Perspectives* 12, no. 1 (Winter 1998). For a different view, see Alan B. Kreuger and Aaron Siskind, "Using Survey Data to Assess Bias in the Consumer Price Index" *Monthly Labor Review* 121, no. 4 (April 1998): 24–33; and Bruce W. Hamilton, "Using Engel's Law to Estimate CPI Bias," *American Economic Review* 91, no. 3 (June 2001): 619–630. Starting in 1995, several modifications to the CPI were made to reduce inflationary bias; for a summary of these changes, see John B. Carlson and Mark E. Schweitzer, "Productivity Measures and the 'New Economy,'" *Economic Commentary, Federal Reserve Bank of Cleveland* (June 1998). These changes may have cut the inflationary bias in half; see Robert Gordon, "The Boskin Commission and Its Aftermath," working paper no. 7759, National Bureau of Economic Reasearch, Cambridge, Mass., June 2000.

FIGURE 2.4
Relationship between Wages, Earnings, Compensation, and Income

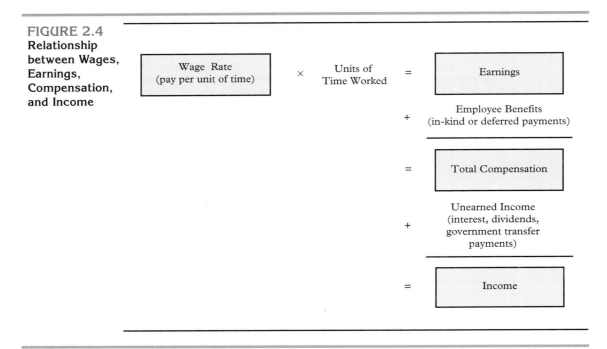

benefits that are either payments in kind or deferred. Examples of *payments in kind* are employer-provided health care and health insurance, where the employee receives a service or an insurance policy rather than money. Paid vacation time is also in this category, since employees are given days off instead of cash.

Deferred payments can take the form of employer-financed retirement benefits, including Social Security taxes, for which employers set aside money now that enables their employees to receive pensions later.

Income—the total command over resources of a person or family during some time period (usually a year)—includes earnings, benefits, and *unearned income,* which includes dividends or interest received on investments and transfer payments received from the government in the form of food stamps, welfare payments, unemployment compensation, and the like.

HOW THE LABOR MARKET WORKS

As shown diagrammatically in Figure 2.5, the labor market is one of three markets in which firms must successfully operate if they are to survive; the other two are the capital market and the product market. The labor and capital markets are the major ones in which firms' inputs are purchased, and the product market is the

FIGURE 2.5
The Markets in Which Firms Must Operate

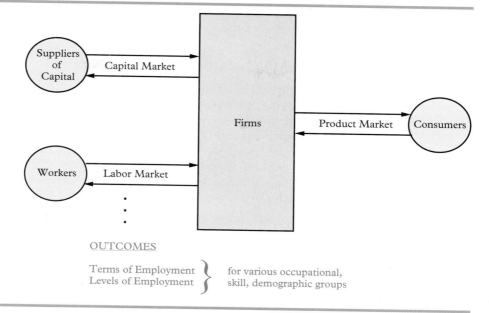

one in which output is sold. In reality, of course, a firm may deal in many different labor, capital, or product markets simultaneously.

Study of the labor market begins and ends with an analysis of the demand for and supply of labor. On the demand side of the labor market are employers, whose decisions about the hiring of labor are influenced by conditions in all three markets. On the supply side of the labor market are workers and potential workers, whose decisions about where (and whether) to work must take into account their other options for how to spend time.

It is useful to remember that the major labor market outcomes are related to (a) the *terms of employment* (wages, compensation levels, working conditions) and (b) the *levels of employment*. In analyzing both these outcomes, one must usually differentiate among the various occupational, skill, or demographic groups that make up the overall labor market. Any labor market outcome is always affected, to one degree or another, by the forces of both demand and supply. To paraphrase economist Alfred Marshall, it takes both demand and supply to determine economic outcomes, just as it takes both blades of a scissors to cut cloth.

In this chapter we present the basic outlines and broadest implications of the simplest economic model of the labor market. In later chapters we shall add some complexities to this basic model and explain assumptions and implications more fully. However, the simple model of demand and supply presented here offers some insights into labor market behavior that can be very useful in the formulation of social policy. Every piece of analysis in this text is an extension or modification of the basic model presented in this chapter.

The Demand for Labor

Firms combine various factors of production—mainly capital and labor—to produce goods or services that are sold in a product market. Their total output and the way in which they combine labor and capital depend on three forces—product demand, the amount of labor and capital they can acquire at given prices, and the choice of technologies available to them. When we study the demand for labor, we are interested in finding out how the number of workers employed by a firm or set of firms is affected by changes in one or more of these three forces. To simplify the discussion, we shall study one change at a time while holding other forces constant.

Wage Changes How does the number of employees (or total labor hours) demanded vary when wages change? Suppose, for example, that we could vary the wages facing a certain industry over a long period of time but keep the technology available, the conditions under which capital is supplied, and the relationship between product price and product demand unchanged. What would happen to the quantity of labor demanded if the wage rate were *increased?*

First, higher wages imply higher costs and, usually, higher product prices. Because consumers respond to higher prices by buying less, employers would tend to reduce their levels of output and employment (other things being equal). This decline in employment is called a *scale effect,* the effect on desired employment of a smaller scale of production.

Second, as wages increase (assuming the price of capital does not change, at least initially), employers have incentives to cut costs by adopting a technology that relies more on capital and less on labor. Desired employment would fall

TABLE 2.3   **Labor Demand Schedule for a Hypothetical Industry**

Wage Rate	Desired Employment Level
$3.00	250
4.00	190
5.00	160
6.00	130
7.00	100
8.00	70

Note: Employment levels can be measured in number of employees or number of labor hours demanded. We have chosen here to use number of employees.

FIGURE 2.6
Labor Demand Curve (based on data in Table 2.3)

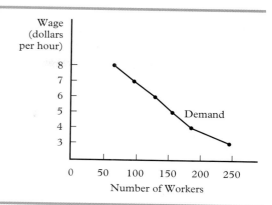

because of a shift toward a more *capital-intensive* mode of production. This second effect is termed a *substitution effect*, because as wages rise, capital is *substituted* for labor in the production process.

The effects of various wages on employment levels might be summarized in a table showing the labor demanded at each wage level. Table 2.3 illustrates such a *demand schedule.* The relationship between wages and employment tabulated in Table 2.3 could be graphed as a *demand curve.* Figure 2.6 shows the demand curve generated by the data in Table 2.3. Note that the curve has a negative slope, indicating that as wages rise, less labor is demanded. (Note also that we follow convention in economics by placing the wage rate on the *vertical* axis despite its being an *independent* variable in the context of labor demand by a firm.) A demand curve for labor tells us how the desired level of employment, measured in either labor hours or number of employees, varies with changes in the price of labor when the other forces affecting demand are held constant.

Changes in Other Forces Affecting Demand   What happens to labor demand when one of the forces other than the wage rate changes?

First, suppose that *demand for the product* of a particular industry were to increase, so that at any output price, more of the goods or services in question could be sold. Suppose in this case that technology and the conditions under which capital and labor are made available to the industry do not change. Output levels would clearly rise as firms in the industry sought to maximize profits, and this *scale* (or *output*) *effect* would increase the demand for labor at any given wage rate. (As long as the relative prices of capital and labor remain unchanged, there is no *substitution effect.*)

How would this change in the demand for labor be illustrated using a demand curve? Since the technology available and the conditions under which capital and labor are supplied have remained constant, this change in product demand would increase the labor desired at any wage level that might prevail. In other words, the entire labor demand curve *shifts* to the right. This rightward shift, shown

FIGURE 2.7
Shift in Demand for Labor Due to Increase in Product Demand

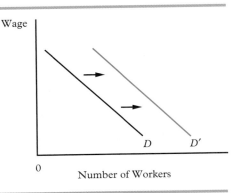

as a movement from D to D' in Figure 2.7, indicates that at every possible wage rate the number of workers demanded has increased.

Second, consider what would happen if the product demand schedule, technology, and labor supply conditions were to remain unchanged, but *the supply of capital* changed so that capital prices fell to 50 percent of their prior level. How would this change affect the demand for labor?

Our method of analyzing the effects on labor demand of a change in the price of *another* productive input is familiar: we must consider the scale and substitution effects. First, when capital prices decline, the costs of producing tend to decline. Reduced costs stimulate increases in production, and these increases tend to raise the level of desired employment at any given wage. The scale effect of a fall in capital prices thus tends to increase the demand for labor at each wage level.

The second effect of a fall in capital prices would be a substitution effect, whereby firms adopt more capital-intensive technologies in response to cheaper capital. Such firms would substitute capital for labor and would use less labor to produce a given amount of output than before. With less labor being desired at each wage rate and output level, the labor demand curve tends to shift to the left.

A fall in capital prices, then, generates *two opposite effects* on the demand for labor. The scale effect will push the labor demand curve rightward, while the substitution effect will push it to the left. As emphasized by Figure 2.8, either effect could dominate. Thus, economic theory does not yield a clear-cut prediction about how a fall in capital prices will affect the demand for labor. (A *rise* in capital prices would generate the same overall ambiguity of effect on the demand for labor, with the scale effect pushing the labor demand curve leftward and the substitution effect pushing it to the right.)

The hypothesized changes in product demand and capital supply just discussed have tended to *shift* the demand curve for labor. It is important to distinguish between a *shift* in a demand curve and *movement along* a curve. A labor

FIGURE 2.8
Possible Shifts in Demand for Labor Due to Fall in Capital Prices

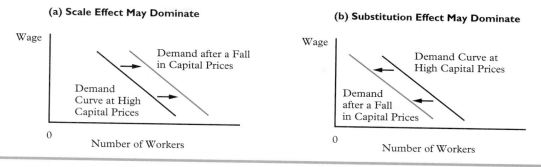

demand curve graphically shows the *labor desired* as a function of the *wage rate*. When the *wage* changes and other forces are held unchanged, one *moves along* the curve. However, when one of the *other forces* changes, the labor demand curve *shifts*. Unlike wages, these forces are not directly shown when the demand curve for labor is drawn. Thus, when they change, a different relationship between wages and desired employment prevails, and this shows up as a shift of the demand curve.

Market, Industry, and Firm Demand   The demand for labor can be analyzed on three levels:

1. To analyze the demand for labor *by a particular firm,* we would examine how an increase in the wage of machinists, say, would affect their employment by a particular aircraft manufacturer.
2. To analyze the effects of this wage increase on the employment of machinists *in the entire aircraft industry,* we would utilize an industry demand curve.
3. Finally, to see how the wage increase would affect the *entire labor market* for machinists, in all industries in which they are used, we would use a market demand curve.

We shall see in chapters 3 and 4 that firm, industry, and market labor demand curves vary in *shape* to some extent because *scale* and *substitution effects* have different strengths at each level. However, it is important to remember that the scale and substitution effects of a wage change work in the same direction at each level, so that firm, industry, and market demand curves *all slope downward.*

Long Run versus Short Run   We can also distinguish between *long-run* and *short-run* labor demand curves. Over very short periods of time, employers find it difficult to substitute capital for labor (or vice versa), and customers may not change their product demand very much in response to a price increase. It takes *time* to fully adjust consumption and production behavior. Over longer periods of time, of course, responses to changes in wages or other forces affecting the demand for labor are larger and more complete.

The Supply of Labor

Having looked at a simple model of behavior on the buyer (or demand) side of the labor market, we now turn to the seller (or supply) side of the market. For the purposes of this chapter, we shall assume that workers have already decided to work and that the question facing them is what occupation and what employer to choose.

Market Supply   To first consider the supply of labor to the entire market (as opposed to the supply to a particular firm), suppose that the market we are considering is the one for secretaries. How will supply respond to changes in the wages secretaries might receive? In other words, what does the supply schedule of secretaries look like?

If the salaries and wages in *other* occupations are held constant and the wages of secretaries rise, we would expect to find more people wanting to become secretaries. For example, suppose that each of 100 people in a high school graduating class has the option of becoming an insurance agent or a secretary. Some of these 100 people will prefer to be insurance agents even if secretaries are better paid, because they like the challenge and sociability of selling. Some would want to be secretaries even if the pay were comparatively poor, because they hate the pressures of selling. Many, however, could see themselves doing either job; for them the compensation in each occupation would be the major factor in their decision.

Thus, the supply of labor to a particular market is positively related to the wage rate prevailing in that market, holding other wages constant. That is, if the wages of insurance agents are held constant and the secretary wage rises, more people will want to become secretaries because of the relative improvement in compensation (as shown graphically in Figure 2.9).

FIGURE 2.9
Market Supply Curve for Secretaries

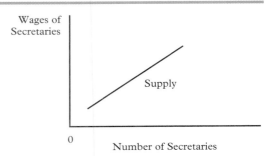

FIGURE 2.10

**Shift in Market Supply Curve for Secretaries
as Salaries of Insurance Agents Rise**

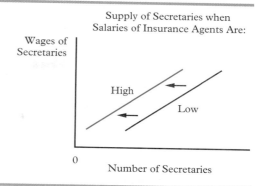

As with demand curves, each supply curve is drawn holding other prices and wages constant. If one or more of these other prices or wages were to change, it would cause the supply curve to *shift*. As the salaries of insurance agents *rise*, some people will change their minds about becoming secretaries and choose to become insurance agents. In graphical terms (see Figure 2.10), increases in the salaries of insurance agents would cause the supply curve of secretaries to shift to the left.

Supply to Firms   Having decided to become a secretary, the individual would then have to decide which offer of employment to accept. If all employers were offering secretarial jobs that were more or less alike, the choice would be based entirely on compensation. Any firm unwise enough to attempt paying a wage below what others were paying would find it could not attract any employees (or at least none of the caliber it wanted). Conversely, no firm would be foolish enough to pay more than the going wage, because it would be paying more than it would have to pay to attract a suitable number and quality of employees. Supply curves to a firm, then, are horizontal, as shown in Figure 2.11, indicating that at the going wage, a firm could get all the secretaries it needs. If the secretarial wage paid by

FIGURE 2.11

**Supply of Secretaries to a Firm
at Alternative Market Wages**

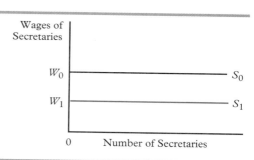

others in the market is W_0, then the firm's labor supply curve is S_0; if the wage falls to W_1, the firm's labor supply curve becomes S_1.

The difference in slope between the market supply curve and the supply curve to a firm is directly related to the type of choice facing workers. In deciding whether to enter the secretarial labor market, workers must weigh both the compensation *and* the job requirements of alternative options (such as being an insurance agent). If wages of secretaries were to fall, not everyone would withdraw from the market, because the jobs of insurance agent and secretary are not perfect substitutes. Some people would remain secretaries after a wage decline because they dislike the job requirements of insurance agents.

Once the decision to become a secretary had been made, however, the choice of which employer to work for would be a choice among alternatives in which the job requirements were nearly the *same.* Thus, the choice would have to be made on the basis of compensation alone. If a firm were to lower its wage offers below those of other firms, it would lose all its applicants. The horizontal supply curve is, therefore, a reflection of supply decisions made among alternatives that are perfect substitutes for each other.

We have argued that firms wishing to hire secretaries must pay the going wage or lose all applicants. While this may seem unrealistic, it is not. If a firm offers jobs *comparable* to those offered by other firms but at a lower level of total compensation, it might be able to attract a few applicants of the quality it desires because a few people will be unaware of compensation elsewhere. Over time, however, knowledge of the firm's poor relative pay would become more widespread, and the firm would find it had to rely solely on less-qualified people to fill its jobs. It could secure quality employees at below-average pay only if it offered *noncomparable* jobs (more pleasant working conditions, longer paid vacations, and so forth). This factor in labor supply will be discussed in chapter 8. For now, we will assume that individual firms, like individual workers, are usually *wage takers*; that is, the wages they pay to their workers must be pretty close to the going wage if they face competition in the labor market. Neither individual workers nor firms can set a wage much different from the going wage and still hope to transact. (Exceptions to this general proposition will be developed in later chapters.)

The Determination of the Wage

The wage that prevails in a particular labor market is heavily influenced by labor demand and supply, regardless of whether the market involves a labor union or other nonmarket forces. In this section we analyze how the interplay of demand and supply in the labor market affects wages.

The Market-Clearing Wage   Recall that the market demand curve indicates how many workers employers would want at each wage rate, holding capital prices and the product demand schedule constant. The market supply curve indicates how many workers would enter the market at each wage level, holding the wages in other occupations constant. These curves can be placed on the same graph to reveal some interesting information, as shown in Figure 2.12.

For example, suppose the market wage were set at W_1. At this low wage, Figure 2.12 indicates that demand *exceeds* supply. Employers will be competing for the few workers in the market and a shortage of workers would exist. The desire of firms to attract more employees would lead them to increase their wage offers, thus driving up the overall level of wage offers in the market. As wages rose, two things would happen. First, more workers would choose to enter the market and look for jobs (a movement along the supply curve); second, increasing wages would induce employers to seek fewer workers (a movement along the demand curve).

If wages were to rise to W_2, supply would exceed demand. Employers would desire fewer workers than the number available, and not all those desiring employment would be able to find jobs, resulting in a surplus of workers. Employers would have long lines of eager applicants for any opening, and would find that they could fill their openings with qualified applicants even if they offered lower wages. Further, if they could pay lower wages, they would want to hire more employees. Some employees would be more than happy to accept the lower wages if they could just find a job. Others would leave the market and look for work elsewhere as wages fell. Thus, demand and supply would become more equal as wages fell from the level of W_2.

The wage rate at which demand equals supply is the *market-clearing* or *market equilibrium* wage. At W_e in Figure 2.12, employers can fill the number of openings they have, and all employees who want jobs in this market can find them. At W_e there is no surplus and no shortage. All parties are satisfied, and no forces exist that would alter the wage. The market is in equilibrium in the sense that the wage will remain at W_e.

The market-clearing wage, W_e, thus becomes the *going wage* that individual employers and employees must face. In other words, wage rates are determined by the market and "announced" to individual market participants. Figure 2.13

FIGURE 2.12
Market Demand and Supply

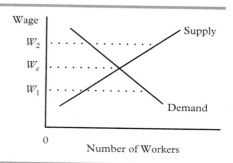

FIGURE 2.13
Demand and Supply at the "Market" and "Firm" Level

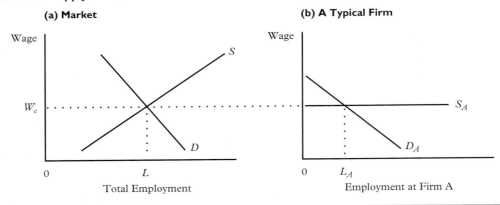

graphically depicts market demand and supply in panel (a), along with the demand and supply curves for a typical firm (firm A) in that market in panel (b). All firms in the market pay a wage of W_e, and total employment of L equals the sum of employment in each firm.

Disturbing the Equilibrium   What could happen to change the market equilibrium wage once it has been reached? Changes could arise from shifts in either the demand or the supply curve. Suppose, for example, that the increase in paperwork accompanying greater government regulation of industry caused firms to demand more secretarial help (at any given wage rate) than before. Graphically, as in Figure 2.14, this greater demand would be represented as a rightward shift

FIGURE 2.14
New Labor Market Equilibrium after Demand Shifts Right

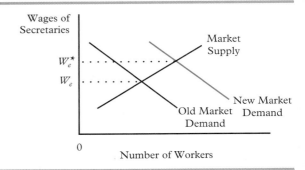

FIGURE 2.15
New Labor Market Equilibrium after Supply Shifts Left

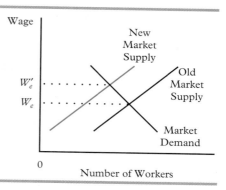

of the demand curve. If W_e were to persist, there would be a labor shortage in the secretarial market (because demand would exceed supply). This shortage would induce employers to improve their wage offers. Eventually, the secretarial wage would be driven up to W_e^*. Notice that in this case, the equilibrium level of *employment* will also rise.

The market wage can also increase if the labor supply curve shifts to the left. As shown in Figure 2.15, such a shift creates a labor shortage at the old equilibrium wage of W_e, and as employers scramble to fill their job openings, the market wage is bid up to W_e'. In the case of a leftward-shifting labor supply curve, however, the increased market wage is accompanied by a decrease in the equilibrium level of employment. (See Example 2.1 for an analysis of the labor market effects of the leftward shift in labor supply accompanying the Black Death in 1348–1351.)

If a leftward shift in labor supply is accompanied by a rightward shift in labor demand, the market wage can rise dramatically. Such a condition occurred in Egypt during the early 1970s. Lured by wages over six times higher in Saudi Arabia and other oil-rich Arab countries, roughly half of Egypt's construction workers left the country just as a residential building boom in Egypt got under way. The combination of a leftward-shifting labor supply curve and a rightward-shifting labor demand curve drove the real wages of Egyptian construction workers up by 373 percent in just seven years![7] (This notable wage increase was accompanied by a net employment *increase* in Egypt's construction industry. The student will be asked, in the first review question on page 54, to analyze these events graphically.)

A fall in the market equilibrium wage rate would occur if there were increased supply or reduced demand. An increase in supply would be represented by a rightward shift of the supply curve, as more people entered the market at each wage

---

[7]Bent Hansen and Samir Radwan, *Employment Opportunities and Equity in Egypt* (Geneva: International Labour Office, 1982), p. 74.

EXAMPLE 2.1

The Black Death and the Wages of Labor

An example of what happens to wages when the supply of labor suddenly shifts occurred when plague—the Black Death—struck England (among other European countries) in 1348–1351. Estimates vary, but it is generally agreed that plague killed between 17 and 40 percent of the English population in that short period of time. This shocking loss of life had the immediate effect of raising the wages of laborers. As the supply curve shifted to the left, a shortage of workers was created at the old wage levels, and competition among employers for the surviving workers drove the wage level dramatically upward.

Reliable figures are hard to come by, but many believe wages rose by 50–100 percent over the three-year period. A thresher, for example, earning $2\frac{1}{2}$ pence per day in 1348 earned $4\frac{1}{2}$ pence in 1350, and mowers receiving 5 pence per acre in 1348 were receiving 9 pence in 1350. Whether the overall rise in wages was this large or not, there was clearly a labor shortage and an unprecedented increase in wages. A royal proclamation commanding landlords to share their scarce workers with neighbors and threatening workers with imprisonment if they refused work at the pre-plague wage was issued to deal with this shortage, but it was ignored. The

shortage was too severe and market forces were simply too strong for the rise in wages to be thwarted.

The discerning student might wonder at this point about the demand curve for labor. Did it not also shift to the left as the population—and the number of consumers—declined? It did, but this leftward shift was not as pronounced as the leftward shift in supply. While there were fewer customers for labor's output, the customers who remained consumed greater amounts of goods and services per capita than before. The money, gold and silver, and durable goods that had existed prior to 1348 were divided among many fewer people by 1350, and this rise in per capita wealth was associated with a widespread and dramatic increase in the level of consumption, especially of luxury goods. Thus, the leftward shift in labor demand was dominated by the leftward shift in supply, and the predictable result was a large increase in wages.

Data from: Harry A. Miskimin, *The Economy of Early Renaissance Europe, 1300–1460* (Englewood Cliffs, N.J.: Prentice-Hall, 1969); George M. Modlin and Frank T. deVyver, *Development of Economic Society* (Boston: D.C. Heath, 1946); Douglass C. North and Robert Paul Thomas, *The Rise of the Western World* (Cambridge, England: Cambridge University Press, 1973); Philip Ziegler, *The Black Death* (New York: Harper & Row, 1969).

(see Figure 2.16). This rightward shift would cause a surplus to exist at the old equilibrium wage (W_e) and lead to behavior that reduced the wage to W_e'' in Figure 2.16. Note that the equilibrium employment level has increased. A decrease (leftward shift) in labor demand would also cause a decrease in the market equilibrium wage, although such a shift would be accompanied by a *fall* in employment.

Disequilibrium and Nonmarket Influences   That a market-clearing wage exists in theory does not imply that it is reached—or reached quickly—in practice. Because labor services cannot be separated from the worker, and because labor income is by far the most important source of spending power for ordinary people, the labor market is subject to forces that impede the adjustment of both wages and employment to changes in demand or supply. Some of these barriers to adjustment are themselves the result of economic forces that will be discussed later in the text. For example, changing jobs often requires an employee to invest in new skills (see chapter 9) or bear costs of moving (chapter 10). On the employer side of the

FIGURE 2.16
New Labor Market Equilibrium after Supply Shifts Right

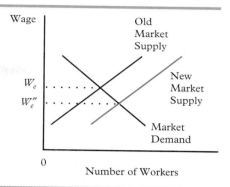

market, hiring workers can involve an initial investment in search and training (chapter 5), while firing them or cutting their wages can be perceived as unfair and therefore have consequences for the productivity of those who remain (chapter 11).

Other barriers to adjustment are rooted in *nonmarket* forces: laws, customs, or institutions constraining the choices of individuals and firms. Although forces keeping wages *below* their equilibrium levels are not unknown, nonmarket forces usually serve to keep wages *above* market levels. Minimum wage laws (discussed in chapter 4) and unions (chapter 13) are examples of influences explicitly designed to raise wages beyond those dictated by the market. Likewise, if there is a widespread belief that cutting wages is unfair, laws or customs may arise that prevent wages from falling in markets experiencing leftward shifts in demand or rightward shifts in supply.

It is commonly believed that labor markets adjust more quickly when market forces are calling for wages to rise as opposed to pressuring them to fall. If this is so, then those markets observed to be in disequilibrium for long periods will tend to be ones with above-market wages. The existence of above-market wages implies that the supply of labor exceeds the number of jobs being offered (refer to the relative demand and supply at wage W_2 in Figure 2.12); therefore, if enough markets are experiencing this kind of disequilibrium, the result will be widespread *unemployment*. In fact, as we will see in the chapter-closing section on international differences in unemployment, these differences can sometimes be used to identify where market forces are most constrained by nonmarket influences.

APPLICATIONS OF THE THEORY

Although this simple model of how a labor market functions will be refined and elaborated upon in the following chapters, it can explain many important phenomena, including the issues of when workers are overpaid or underpaid and what explains international differences in unemployment.

Who Is Underpaid and Who Is Overpaid?

People tend to judge the wages paid or received against some notion of what they "need," but there is no universally accepted standard of need. A worker may "need" more income to buy a larger home or finance a recreational vehicle. An employer may "need" greater profits to pay for sending a child to college. In general, almost all of us feel we "need" more income!

Despite the difficulties of assessing needs, there are still important reasons for defining "overpaid" and "underpaid." For example, the public utilities commissions in every state must consider and approve rate increases requested by the gas and electric companies. These companies desire increases partly to keep up with production costs, which the companies obviously want to pass on to consumers. Suppose, however, that a public utilities commission observed that the *level* of wages paid by these companies or the *increases* in such wages were "excessive." In the interests of holding down consumer prices, it might want to consider adopting a policy whereby excessive labor costs could not be passed on to consumers in the form of rate increases. Obviously, such a policy would require a definition of what constitutes overpayment.

We pointed out in chapter 1 that a fundamental value of normative economics is that, as a society, we should strive to complete all those transactions that are mutually beneficial. Another way of stating this value is to say that we must strive to use our scarce resources as effectively as possible, which implies that output should be produced in the least-costly manner so that the most can be obtained from such resources. This goal, combined with the labor market model outlined in this chapter, suggests how we can define what it means to be overpaid.

Above-Equilibrium Wages   We shall define workers as *overpaid* if their wages are higher than the market equilibrium wage for their job. Because a labor surplus exists for jobs that are overpaid, a wage above equilibrium has two implications (see Figure 2.17). First, employers are paying more than necessary to produce

---

FIGURE 2.17
Effects of an Above-Equilibrium Wage

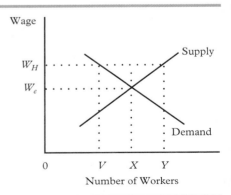

their output (they pay W_H instead of W_e); they could cut wages and still find enough qualified workers for their job openings. In fact, if they did cut wages, they could expand output and make their product cheaper and more accessible to consumers. Second, more workers want jobs than can find them (Y workers want jobs, and only V openings are available). If wages were reduced a bit, more of these disappointed workers could find work. A wage above equilibrium thus causes consumer prices to be higher and output to be smaller than is possible, and it creates a situation in which not all workers who want the jobs in question can get them.

With this definition of overpayment, the public utilities commission in question could look to employee behavior for signs of above-market wages. If wages were above those for comparable jobs, current employees would be *very* reluctant to quit because they would know their chances of doing better were small. Likewise, the number of applicants for job openings would be unusually large.

An interesting example of above-equilibrium wages was seen in Houston's labor market in 1988. Bus cleaners working for the Houston Metropolitan Transit Authority received $10.08 per hour, or 83 percent more than the $5.94 received by cleaners working for private bus companies in Houston. One (predictable) result of this overpayment is that the quit rate among Houston's Transit Authority cleaners was only *one-seventh* as great as the average for cleaners nationwide.[8]

To better understand the social losses attendant on overpayment, let us return to the principles of normative economics. Can reducing overpayment create a situation in which the gainers gain more than the losers lose? Suppose in the case of Houston's Transit Authority cleaners that *only* the wage of *newly hired* cleaners was reduced—to $6.40, say. Current cleaners thus would not lose, but many others who were working elsewhere at $5.94 would jump at the chance to earn a higher wage. Taxpayers, realizing that transit services could now be expanded at lower cost than before, would increase their demand for such services, thus creating jobs for these additional workers. Some workers would gain while no one lost— and social well-being would clearly be enhanced.[9] The wage reduction, in short, would be *Pareto-improving* (see chapter 1).

Below-Equilibrium Wages   Employees can be defined as *underpaid* if their wage is below market equilibrium. At below-equilibrium wages, employers have difficulty finding workers to meet the demands of consumers, and a labor shortage thus exists. They also have trouble keeping the workers they do find. If wages were increased, output would rise and more workers would be attracted to the market. Thus, an increase would benefit the people in society in *both* their consumer

---

[8]William J. Moore and Robert J. Newman, "Government Wage Differentials in a Municipal Labor Market: The Case of Houston Metropolitan Transit Workers," *Industrial and Labor Relations Review* 45, no. 1 (October 1991): 145–153.

[9]If the workers who switched jobs were getting paid approximately what they were worth to their former employers, these employers would lose $5.94 in output but save $5.94 in costs—and their welfare would thus not be affected. The presumption that employees are paid what they are worth to the employer is discussed at length in chapter 3.

FIGURE 2.18

Effects of a Below-Equilibrium Wage

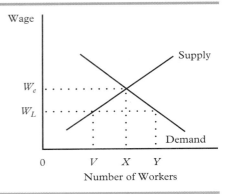

and their worker roles. Figure 2.18 shows how a wage increase from W_L to W_e would increase employment from V to X (at the same time wages were rising).

Wages in the U.S. Army illustrate how the market adjusts to below-equilibrium wages. Prior to 1973, when the military draft was eliminated, the government could pursue a policy of paying below-market wages to military recruits, because the resultant gap between supply and demand could be filled by conscription (see Example 2.2). Not surprisingly, when comparing wages in the late 1970s with those in the last decade of the military draft, we find that the average military cash wages paid to enlisted personnel rose 19 percent more than those of comparable civilian workers.

Economic Rents   The concepts of underpayment and overpayment have to do with the *social* issue of producing desired goods and services in the least-costly way; therefore, we compared wages paid with the *market-clearing wage*. At the level of *individuals*, however, it is often useful to compare the wage received in a job with one's *reservation wage,* the wage below which the worker would refuse (or quit) the job in question. The amount by which one's wage exceeds one's reservation wage in a particular job is the amount of his or her *economic rent.*

Consider the labor supply curve to, say, the military. As shown in Figure 2.19, if the military is to hire L_1 people, it must pay W_1 in wages. These relatively low wages will attract to the military those who most enjoy the military culture and are least averse to the risks of combat. If the military is to be somewhat larger and to employ L_2 people, then it must pay a wage of W_2. This higher wage is required to attract those who would have found a military career unattractive at the lower wage. If W_2 turns out to be the wage that equates demand and supply, and if the military pays that wage, everyone who would have joined up for less would be receiving an economic rent!

Put differently, the supply curve to an occupation or industry is a schedule of reservation wages that indicates the labor forthcoming at each wage level. The difference between the wage actually paid and workers' reservation wages—the

FIGURE 2.19
**Labor Supply to the Military:
Different Preferences Imply
Different "Rents"**

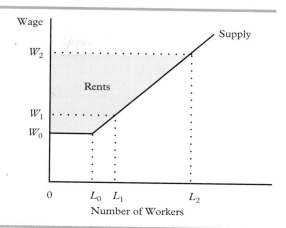

shaded area in Figure 2.19—is the amount of the rent. Since each worker potentially has a different reservation wage, rents may well differ for each worker in the market. In Figure 2.19, the greatest rents are received by those L_0 individuals who would have joined the military even if the wage were only W_0. They collect an economic rent of $W_2 - W_0$.

Why don't employers reduce the wage of each employee down to his or her reservation level? While capturing employee rents would seem to be lucrative, since by definition it could be done without the workers' quitting, attempting to do so would create resentment and such a policy would be extremely costly, if not impossible, to implement. Employers do not know the true reservation wages of each employee or applicant, and finding it would involve experiments in which the wage offers to each worker either started high and were cut or started low and were raised. This would be costly, and if workers realized the firm was *experimenting*, they would attempt to disguise their true reservation wages and adopt the strategic behavior associated with bargaining (bluffing, for example). Therefore, firms usually pay according to the job, one's level of experience or longevity with the employer, and considerations of merit—but not according to preferences. An exception to this general rule is the two-tier wage schedule that has arisen in a few cases in which the market is calling for a wage decrease and the firm does not want to cut wages for its current workers; in these cases, lower wages are paid to the firm's new entrants than were paid to its current workers when they were new. Thus, rents are extracted from new workers but no attempt is made to extract them from current employees.

International Differences in Unemployment

We noted earlier that labor markets are often influenced by nonmarket forces that keep wages above market-clearing levels. Because these nonmarket forces generally take the form of laws, government programs, customs, or institutions (labor

EXAMPLE 2.2

Ending the Conscription of Young American Men: The Role of Economists

Before 1973, American men in their late teens and early 20s were liable to be drafted into the Army for a period of two years. The U.S. Navy, Marine Corps, and Air Force all relied solely on voluntary enlistments, but it was widely believed that the draft was necessary to supplement voluntary enlistments in the Army. The decision to end the draft, which had been in place since World War II, was both momentous and controversial—and it was one in which economists played a central role.

Normative economics provided the philosophical underpinnings of the push for an all-volunteer military. The 1970 report of the President's Commission on an All-Volunteer Armed Force, which contained the policy blueprint for ending conscription, had an introductory chapter entitled "Conscription Is a Tax." This chapter reflected the normative standard of Pareto efficiency, which rests on the proposition that we can be assured a transaction is mutually beneficial only if it is voluntary:

> Under the present system, first-term servicemen must bear a disproportionately large share of the defense burden. Draftees and draft-induced volunteers are paid less than they would require to volunteer. The loss they suffer is a tax-in-kind....
>
> Conscription also imposes social and human costs by distorting the personal life and career plans of the young.

Positive economics also provided crucial input to the policy debate. Questions naturally arose concerning whether the Army could attract enough high-quality volunteers and how high pay would have to rise to do so. The answers were provided by a careful estimate of the military labor supply curve, which suggested that to maintain the size and quality of the military in 1970 would require the basic pay of first-term enlisted personnel to rise by 50 percent, the pay of first-term officers to rise by 28 percent, and the pay of second-term enlistees to rise by an average of 9 percent.

Data from: President's Commission on an All-Volunteer Armed Force, *Report of the President's Commission on an All-Volunteer Armed Force* (Washington, D.C.: U.S. Government Printing Office, February 1970). For a recent review, see John T. Warner and Beth J. Asch, "The Record and Prospects of the All-Volunteer Military in the United States," *Journal of Economic Perspectives* 15 (Spring 2001): 169–192.

unions, for example), their strength typically varies across countries. Can we form some conclusions about the countries in which they are most pronounced?

Theory presented in this chapter suggests that if wages are above market-clearing levels, unemployment will result (the number of people seeking work will exceed the number of available jobs). Further, if wages are held above market-clearing levels and the labor demand curve *shifts to the left*, unemployment will rise to even higher levels (you should be able to show this by drawing a graph with an unchanging supply curve, a fixed wage rate, and a leftward-shifting demand curve). Moreover, above-market wages deter the growth of *new* jobs, so wages "stuck" above market-clearing levels also can cause those who suffer a spell of unemployment to remain in that status for a long time. Thus, measures of the incidence and duration of unemployment—which, fortunately, are comparably defined and estimated in several advanced economies—can sometimes be used to infer the relative strength of non-market forces across countries. Consider, for example, what happened to unemployment rates in Europe and North America in the 1980s and 1990s.

One phenomenon characterizing the 1980s was an acceleration of technological change, associated primarily with computerization, in the advanced

TABLE 2.4   Unemployment and Long-Term Unemployment, Selected European and North American Countries, 2000

	Unemployment: Overall Rate	Percent of Unemployed Out of Work > One Year	Unemployment: Long-Term Rate
Belgium	7.0%	56.3%	3.9%
Canada	6.8	11.2	0.8
Denmark	4.7	20.0	0.9
France	9.5	42.5	4.0
Germany	8.1	51.5	4.2
Netherlands	2.8	32.7	0.9
Norway	3.5	5.0	0.2
Sweden	5.9	26.4	1.6
United Kingdom	5.5	28.0	1.5
United States	4.0	6.0	0.2

Source: OECD, *Employment Outlook* (Paris: OECD, 2001), Tables A and G.

economies of the world. These changes led to a fall in the demand for less-skilled, less-educated, lower-paid workers. In Canada and the United States, the decline in demand for low-skilled workers led to a fall in their real wages throughout the 1980s; despite that, the unemployment rate for less-educated workers rose over that decade—from 7.2 percent to 8.5 percent in the United States, and from 6.3 percent to 9.3 percent in Canada. In the two European countries for which we have data on wages and unemployment by skill level, however, the real wages of low-paid workers *rose* over the decade, with the consequence that increases in unemployment for the less educated were much more pronounced. In France, real wages among the lowest-paid workers rose 1 percent per year, and their unemployment rate increased from 4.6 percent to 10.7 percent over the decade. In Germany, where the pay of low-wage workers rose an average of 5 percent per year, unemployment rates among these workers went from 4.4 percent to 13.5 percent.[10]

Evidence that nonmarket forces are probably stronger in Europe than in North America is seen in Table 2.4, which compares unemployment rates across countries. While overall rates are not systematically different, the percentages unemployed for longer than one year are generally much greater in Europe. Later, we will identify some of the nonmarket forces that might be responsible.[11]

---

[10]Earnings data for all four countries are for workers in the lowest decile (lowest 10%) of their country's earnings distribution. These data are found in Organisation for Economic Co-operation and Development (OECD), *Employment Outlook: July 1993* (Paris: OECD, 1993), Table 5.3. Data on unemployment rates are from Federal Reserve Bank of Kansas City, *Reducing Unemployment: Current Issues and Policy Options* (Kansas City, Mo.: Federal Reserve Bank of Kansas City, 1994), 25.

[11]For a discussion of this issue, see Horst Siebert, "Labor Market Rigidities: At the Root of Unemployment in Europe," and Stephen Nickell, "Unemployment and Labor Market Rigidities: Europe versus North America," both in *Journal of Economic Perspectives* 11, no. 3 (Summer 1997): 37–74.

REVIEW QUESTIONS

1. As discussed on page 45, in the early 1970s Egypt experienced a dramatic outflow of construction workers, seeking higher wages in Saudi Arabia, at the same time that the demand for their services rose within Egypt. Graphically represent these two shifts of supply and demand, and then use the graph to predict the direction of change in wages and employment within Egypt's construction sector during that period.

2. Analyze the impact of the following changes on wages and employment in a given occupation:
   a. A decrease in the danger of the occupation.
   b. An increase in product demand.
   c. Increased wages in alternative occupations.

3. What would happen to the wages and employment levels of engineers if government expenditures on research and development programs were to fall? Show the effect graphically.

4. Suppose a particular labor market were in market-clearing equilibrium. What could happen to cause the equilibrium wage to fall? If all money wages rose with inflation each year, how would this market adjust?

5. Assume that you have been hired by a company to do a salary survey of its arc welders, who the company suspects are overpaid. Given the company's expressed desire to maximize profits, what definition of "overpaid" would you apply in this situation and how would you identify whether arc welders were, in fact, overpaid?

6. How will a fall in the civilian unemployment rate affect the supply of recruits for the volunteer army? What will be the effect on military wages?

7. Unions can raise wages paid to their members in two ways: (i) Unions can negotiate a wage rate that lies above the market-clearing wage. While management cannot pay below that rate, management does have the right to decide how many workers to hire. (ii) Construction unions often have agreements that require management to hire only union members, but they also have the power to control entry into the union. Hence they can raise wages by restricting labor supply.
   a. Graphically depict method (i) above using a labor demand and a labor supply curve. Show the market-clearing wage as W_e, the market-clearing employment level as L_e, the (higher) negotiated wage as W_u, the level of employment associated with W_u as L_u, and the number of workers wanting to work at W_u as L_s.
   b. Graphically depict method (ii) above using a labor demand and a labor supply curve. Show the market-clearing wage as W_e, the market-clearing employment level as L_e, the number of members the union decides to have as L_u (which is less than L_e), and the wage associated with L_u as W_u.

8. Suppose that the Consumer Product Safety Commission issues a regulation requiring an expensive safety device to be attached to all power lawnmowers. This device does not increase the efficiency with which the lawnmower operates. What, if anything, does this regulation do to the demand for labor of firms manufacturing power lawnmowers? Explain.

9. Suppose the Occupational Safety and Health Administration were to mandate that all punch presses be fitted with a very expensive device to prevent injuries to workers. This device does not improve the efficiency with which punch presses operate. What does this requirement do to the demand curve for labor? Explain.

10. Suppose we observe that employment levels in a certain region suddenly decline as a result of (i) a fall in the region's demand for labor, and (ii) wages that are fixed in the short run. If the *new* labor demand curve remains unchanged for a long period and the region's labor supply curve does not shift, is it likely that employment in the region will recover? Explain.

PROBLEMS

1. Suppose that the adult population is 210 million, and there are 130 million who are employed and 5 million who are unemployed. Calculate the unemployment rate and the labor force participation rate.
2. Suppose that the supply curve for schoolteachers is $L_S = 20,000 + 350W$ and the demand curve for schoolteachers is $L_D = 100,000 - 150W$, where L = the number of teachers and W = the daily wage.
   a. Plot the demand and supply curves.
   b. What are the equilibrium wage and employment level in this market?
   c. Now suppose that at any given wage 20,000 more workers are willing to work as schoolteachers. Plot the new supply curve and find the new wage and employment level. Why doesn't employment grow by 20,000?
3. Have the real average hourly earnings for production and nonsupervisory workers in the United States risen during the past 12 months? Go online to the Bureau of Labor Statistics Web site (http://www.bls.gov) to find the numbers needed to answer the question.

SELECTED READINGS

Organisation for Economic Co-operation and Development. *Employment Outlook*. Chapter 1, "Labour Market Trends and Prospects in the OECD Area," 1–31. Paris: OECD, July 1990.

President's Commission on an All-Volunteer Armed Force. *Report of the President's Commission on an All-Volunteer Armed Force*. Chapter 3, "Conscription Is a Tax," 23–33. Washington, D.C.: U.S. Government Printing Office, February 1970.

Rottenberg, Simon. "On Choice in Labor Markets." *Industrial and Labor Relations Review* 9, no. 2 (January 1956): 183–199. Robert J. Lampman. "On Choice in Labor Markets: Comment." *Industrial and Labor Relations Review* 9, no. 4 (July 1956): 636–641.

3

THE DEMAND FOR LABOR

The demand for labor is a derived demand, in that workers are hired for the contribution they can make toward producing some good or service for sale. However, the wages workers receive, the employee benefits they qualify for, and even their working conditions are all influenced, to one degree or another, by the government. There are minimum wage laws, pension regulations, restrictions on firing workers, safety requirements, immigration controls, and government-provided pension and unemployment benefits that are financed through employer payroll taxes. All these requirements and regulations have one thing in common: they increase employers' costs of hiring workers.

We explained in chapter 2 that both the scale and the substitution effects accompanying a wage change suggest that the demand curve for labor is a *downward-sloping function of the wage rate.* If this rather simple proposition is true, then policies that mandate increases in the costs of employing workers will have the undesirable side effect of reducing their employment opportunities. If the reduction is large enough, lost job opportunities actually could undo any help provided to workers by the regulations. Understanding the characteristics of labor demand curves, then, is absolutely crucial to anyone interested in public policy. To a great extent, how one feels about many labor market regulatory programs is a function of one's beliefs about labor demand curves!

This chapter and the next will address economic theory as it relates to the essential nature of labor demand curves. The current chapter will identify *assumptions* underlying the proposition that labor demand is a downward-sloping function of the wage rate. As we proceed, we will also analyze how changes in these assumptions affect the basic characteristics of the labor demand curve. Chapter 4 will take the downward-sloping nature of labor demand curves as given, addressing instead why, in the face of a given wage increase, declines in demand might be large in some cases and barely perceptible in others.

PROFIT MAXIMIZATION

The fundamental assumption of labor demand theory is that firms—the employers of labor—seek to maximize profits (or, in the case of not-for-profit employers, some measure of services rendered, net of costs). In doing so, firms are assumed to continually ask, "Can we make changes that will improve profits?" Two things should be noted about this constant search for enhanced profits. First, a firm can make changes only in variables that are within its control. Because the price a firm can charge for its product and the prices it must pay for its inputs are largely determined by others (the "market"), profit-maximizing decisions by a firm mainly involve the question of *whether, and how, to increase or decrease output.*

Second, because the firm is assumed to constantly search for profit-improving possibilities, our theory must address the *small* ("marginal") changes that must be made almost daily. Really major decisions of whether to open a new plant or introduce a new product line, for example, are relatively rare; once having made them, the employer must approach profit maximization incrementally through the trial-and-error process of small changes. We therefore need to understand the basis for these incremental decisions, paying particular attention to when an employer *stops* making changes in output levels or in its mix of inputs.

(With respect to the employment of inputs, it is important to recognize that analyzing marginal changes implies considering a small change in one input *while holding employment of other inputs constant.* Thus, when analyzing the effects of adjusting the labor input by one unit, for example, we will do so on the assumption that capital is held constant. Likewise, marginal changes in capital will be considered assuming the labor input is held constant.)

In incrementally deciding on its optimal level of *output,* the profit-maximizing firm will want to expand output by one unit if the added revenue from selling that unit is greater than the added cost of producing it. As long as the marginal revenue from an added unit of output exceeds its marginal cost, the firm will continue to expand output. Likewise, the firm will want to contract output whenever the marginal cost of production exceeds marginal revenue. Profits are maximized (and the firm stops making changes) when output is such that marginal revenue equals marginal cost.

A firm can expand or contract output, of course, only by altering its use of *inputs.* In the most general sense, we will assume that a firm produces its output by combining two types of inputs, or *factors of production: labor and capital*. Thus, the rules stated above for deciding whether to marginally increase or reduce output have important corollaries with respect to the employment of labor and capital:

    a. If the income generated by one more unit of an input exceeds the additional expense, then add a unit of that input;

    b. If the income generated by one more unit of input is less than the additional expense, reduce employment of that input;

    c. If the income generated by one more unit of input is equal to the additional expense, no further changes in that input are desirable.

Decision rules (a) through (c) state the profit-maximizing criterion in terms of *inputs* rather than output; as we will see, these rules are useful guides to deciding *how*— as well as *whether*—to marginally increase or decrease output. Let us define and examine the components of these decision rules more closely.

Marginal Income from an Additional Unit of Input

Employing one more unit of either labor or capital generates additional income for the firm because of the added output that is produced and sold. Similarly, reducing the employment of labor or capital reduces a firm's income flow because the output available for sale is reduced. Thus, the marginal income associated with a unit of input is found by multiplying two quantities: the change in physical output produced (called the input's *marginal product*) and the *marginal revenue* generated per unit of physical output. We will therefore call the marginal income produced by a unit of input the input's *marginal revenue product*. For example, if the presence of a tennis star increases attendance at a tournament by 20,000 spectators, and the organizers net $25 from each additional fan, the marginal income produced by this star is equal to her marginal product (20,000 fans) times the marginal revenue of $25 per fan. Thus, her marginal revenue product equals $500,000. (For an actual calculation of marginal revenue product in college football, see Example 3.1.)

Marginal Product   Formally, we will define the *marginal product of labor*, or MP_L, as the change in physical output (ΔQ) produced by a change in the units of labor (ΔL), holding capital constant:[1]

$$MP_L = \Delta Q/\Delta L \quad \text{(holding capital constant)} \tag{3.1}$$

Likewise, the marginal product of capital (MP_K) will be defined as the change in output associated with a one-unit change in the stock of capital (ΔK), holding labor constant:

$$MP_K = \Delta Q/\Delta K \quad \text{(holding labor constant)} \tag{3.2}$$

---

[1]The symbol Δ (the uppercase Greek letter delta) is used to signify "a change in."

EXAMPLE 3.1

The Marginal Revenue Product of College Football Stars

Calculating a worker's marginal revenue product is often very complicated due to lack of data and the difficulty of making sure that everything else is being held constant and only *additions* to revenue are counted. Perhaps for this reason, economists have been attracted to the sports industry, which generates so many statistics on player productivity and team revenues.

Football is a big-time concern on many campuses, and some star athletes generate huge revenues for their colleges, even though they are not paid—except by receiving a free education. Robert Brown collected revenue statistics for 47 Division I-A college football programs for the 1988–1989 season—including revenues retained by the school from ticket sales, donations to the athletic department, and television and radio payments. (Unfortunately, this leaves out some other potentially important revenue sources, such as parking and concessions at games and donations to the general fund.)

Next, he examined variation in revenues due to market size, strength of opponents, national ranking, and the number of players on the team who were so good that they were drafted into professional football (the NFL). He found that each additional player drafted into the NFL was worth about $540,000 in extra revenue to his team. Over a four-year college career, a premium player could therefore generate over $2 million in revenues for his team!

Data from: Robert W. Brown, "An Estimate of the Rent Generated by a Premium College Football Player," *Economic Inquiry* 31, no. 4 (October 1993), 671–684.

Marginal Revenue   The definitions in (3.1) and (3.2) reflect the fact that a firm can expand or contract its output only by increasing or decreasing its use of either labor or capital. The marginal revenue (*MR*) that is generated by an extra unit of output depends on the characteristics of the product market in which that output is sold. If the firm operates in a purely competitive product market, and therefore has many competitors and no control over product price, the marginal revenue per unit of output sold is equal to product price (*P*). If the firm has a differentiated product, and thus has some degree of monopoly power in its product market, extra units of output can be sold only if product price is reduced (because the firm faces the *market* demand curve for its particular product); students will recall from introductory economics that in this case marginal revenue is less than price ($MR < P$).[2]

Marginal Revenue Product   Combining the definitions presented in this subsection, the firm's marginal revenue product of labor, or MRP_L, can be represented as

$$MRP_L = MP_L \cdot MR \quad \text{(in the general case)} \tag{3.3a}$$

---

[2]A competitive firm can sell added units of output at the market price because it is so small relative to the entire market that its output does not affect price. A monopolist, however, *is* the supply side of the product market, so to sell extra output it must lower price. Because it must lower price on *all* units of output, and not just on the extra units to be sold, the marginal revenue associated with an additional unit is below price.

or as

$$MRP_L = MP_L \cdot P \quad \text{(if the product market is competitive)} \qquad (3.3b)$$

Likewise, the firm's marginal revenue product of capital (MRP_K) can be represented as $MP_K \cdot MR$ in the general case, or as $MP_K \cdot P$ if the product market is competitive.

Marginal Expense of an Added Input

Employing added units of either labor or capital, of course, will add to the firm's total costs. Likewise, reducing the units of labor or capital employed will reduce the firm's costs. If the firm competes with many other firms to hire its inputs, it has no control over the prices of these inputs and must therefore pay the market price. In this case, the marginal expense of an input is simply equal to its unit price. To avoid unnecessary complications at this point, we will regard the wage rate (W) as the expense of hiring one unit of labor for one time period (an hour, for example). The price of capital will be represented in our analyses as C, which we will define as the expense of renting a unit of capital for one time period. (The specific calculation of C need not concern us here, but clearly it depends on the purchase price of the capital asset, its expected useful life, the rate of interest on borrowed funds, and even special tax provisions regarding capital.)

If firms have some control over the wages they pay to their workers, they are said to hire labor under *monopsonistic* conditions. As we will explain later, the monopsonistic employer of labor does not simply pay the wage presented to it by the market (as in Figure 2.13). Because it is the only employer in its labor market, if it wants to increase employment it must attract workers from other markets, not just from similar employers in the same labor market. We will thoroughly explain the implications of monopsony later in this chapter; as we will see, when conditions in a firm's labor market are monopsonistic, the marginal expense associated with an added unit of labor (ME_L) is greater than W.

THE SHORT-RUN DEMAND FOR LABOR WHEN BOTH PRODUCT AND LABOR MARKETS ARE COMPETITIVE

The simplest way to understand how the profit-maximizing behavior of firms generates a labor demand curve is to analyze the firm's behavior over a period of time so short that the firm cannot vary its stock of capital. This period is what we will call the *short run*, and of course the time period involved will vary from firm to firm (an accounting service might be able to order and install a new computing system for the preparation of tax returns within three months, whereas it may take an oil refinery five years to install a new production process). What is simplifying about the short run is that, with capital fixed, a firm's choice of output level and its choice of employment level are two aspects of the very same decision. Put differently, in the short run the firm needs only to decide *whether* to alter its output level; *how* to increase or decrease output is not an issue, because only the employment of labor can be adjusted.

A Critical Assumption: Declining MP_L

We defined the marginal product of labor (MP_L) as the change in the (physical) output of a firm when it changes its employment of labor by one unit, holding capital constant. Since the firm can vary its employment of labor, we must consider how increasing or reducing labor will affect labor's marginal product. Consider Table 3.1, which illustrates a hypothetical car dealership with sales personnel who are all equally hardworking and persuasive. With no sales staff the dealership is assumed to sell zero cars, but with one salesperson it will sell 10 cars per month. Thus, the marginal product of the first salesperson hired is 10. If a second person is hired, total output is assumed to rise from 10 to 21, implying that the marginal product of a second salesperson is 11. If a third equally persuasive salesperson is hired, sales rise from 21 to 26 ($MP_L = 5$), and if a fourth is hired sales rise from 26 to 29 ($MP_L = 3$).

Table 3.1 assumes that adding an extra salesperson increases output (cars sold) in each case. As long as output *increases* as labor is added, labor's marginal product is *positive*. In our example, however, the marginal product of labor increased at first (from 10 to 11), but then fell (to 5 and eventually to 3). Why?

The initial rise in marginal product occurs *not* because the second salesperson is better than the first; we ruled out this possibility by our assumption that the salespeople were equally capable. Rather, the rise could be the result of cooperation between the two in generating promotional ideas or helping each other out in some way. Eventually, however, as more salespeople are hired, the marginal product of labor must fall. A fixed building (remember that capital is held constant) can

TABLE 3.1   The Marginal Product of Labor in a Hypothetical Car Dealership (capital held constant)

Number of Salespersons	Total Cars Sold	Marginal Product of Labor
0	0	
		10
1	10	
		11
2	21	
		5
3	26	
		3
4	29	

contain only so many cars and customers, and thus each additional increment of labor must eventually produce progressively smaller increments of output. This law of *diminishing marginal returns* is an empirical proposition that derives from the fact that as employment expands, each additional worker has a progressively smaller share of the capital stock to work with. For expository convenience, we shall assume that the marginal product of labor is always decreasing.[3]

From Profit Maximization to Labor Demand

From the profit-maximizing decision rules discussed earlier, it is clear that the firm should keep increasing its employment of labor as long as labor's marginal revenue product exceeds its marginal expense. Conversely, it should keep reducing its employment of labor as long as the expense saved is greater than the income lost. *Profits are maximized, then, only when employment is such that any further one-unit change in labor would have a marginal revenue product equal to marginal expense:*

$$MRP_L = ME_L \qquad (3.4)$$

Under our current assumptions of competitive product and labor markets, we can symbolically represent the profit-maximizing level of labor input as that level at which

$$MP_L \cdot P = W \qquad (3.5)$$

Clearly, equation (3.5) is stated in terms of some *monetary* unit (dollars, for example).

Alternatively, however, we can divide both sides of equation (3.5) by product price, P, and state the profit-maximizing condition for hiring labor in terms of *physical quantities:*

$$MP_L = W/P \qquad (3.6)$$

We defined MP_L as the change in physical output associated with a one-unit change in labor, so it is obvious that the left-hand side of equation (3.6) is in physical quantities. To understand that the right-hand side is also in physical quantities, note that the numerator (W) is the dollars per unit of labor and the denominator (P) is the dollars per unit of output. Thus, the ratio W/P has the dimension of physical units. For example, if a woman is paid $10 per hour and the output she produces sells for $2 per unit, from the firm's viewpoint she is paid five units of output per hour ($10 \div 2$). From the perspective of the firm these five units represent her "real wage."

---

[3]We lose nothing by this assumption, because we show later in this section that a firm will never be operated at a point where its marginal product of labor is increasing.

FIGURE 3.1
Demand for Labor
in the Short Run (Real Wage)

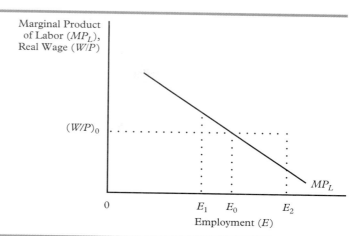

Labor Demand in Terms of Real Wages   The demand for labor can be analyzed in terms of either *real* or *money* wages. Which version of demand analysis is used is a matter of convenience only. In this and the following subsection, we give examples of both.

Figure 3.1 shows a marginal product of labor schedule (MP_L) for a representative firm. In this figure the marginal product of labor is tabulated on the vertical axis and the number of units of labor employed on the horizontal axis. The negative slope of the schedule indicates that each additional unit of labor employed produces a progressively smaller (but still positive) increment in output. Because the real wage and the marginal product of labor are both measured in the same dimension (units of output), we can also plot the real wage on the vertical axis of Figure 3.1.

Given any real wage (by the market), the firm should thus employ labor to the point at which the marginal product of labor just equals the real wage (equation 3.6). In other words, *the firm's demand for labor in the short run is equivalent to the downward-sloping segment of its marginal product of labor schedule.*[4]

To see that this is true, pick any real wage—for example, the real wage denoted by $(W/P)_0$ in Figure 3.1. We have asserted that the firm's demand for labor is equal to its marginal product of labor schedule and consequently that the firm would employ E_0 employees. Now suppose that a firm initially employed E_2 workers as indicated in Figure 3.1, where E_2 is *any* employment level greater than E_0. At the employment level E_2, the marginal product of labor is less than the real wage rate; the marginal real cost of the last unit of labor hired is therefore greater than its marginal product. As a result, profit could be increased by reducing the level of

---

[4]We should add here, "provided that the firm's revenue exceeds its labor costs." Above some real wage level this may fail to occur, and the firm will go out of business (employment will drop to zero).

employment. Similarly, suppose instead that a firm initially employed E_1 employees, where E_1 is *any* employment level less than E_0. Given the specified real wage $(W/P)_0$, the marginal product of labor is greater than the real wage rate at E_1—and consequently the marginal additions to output of an extra unit of labor exceed its marginal real cost. As a result, a firm could increase its profit level by expanding its level of employment.

Hence, to maximize profits, given any real wage rate, a firm should stop employing labor at the point at which any additional labor would cost more than it would produce. This profit-maximization rule implies two things. First, the firm should employ labor up to the point at which its real wage equals the marginal product of labor—but not beyond that point.

Second, its profit-maximizing level of employment lies in the range where its marginal product of labor is *declining*. If $W/P = MP_L$ but MP_L is *increasing*, then adding another unit of labor will create a situation in which marginal product *exceeds* W/P. As long as adding labor causes MP_L to exceed W/P, the profit-maximizing firm will continue to hire labor. It will stop hiring only when an extra unit of labor would reduce MP_L below W/P, which will happen only when MP_L is declining. Thus, the only employment levels that could possibly be consistent with profit maximization are those in the range where MP_L is decreasing.

Labor Demand in Terms of Money Wages   In some circumstances, labor demand curves are more readily conceptualized as downward-sloping functions of *money* wages. To make the analysis as concrete as possible, in this subsection we analyze the demand for department store detectives.

At a business conference one day, a department store executive boasted that his store had reduced theft to 1 percent of total sales. A colleague shook her head and said, "I think that's too low. I figure it should be about 2 percent of sales." How can more shoplifting be better than less? The answer is based on the fact that reducing theft is costly in itself. A profit-maximizing firm will not want to take steps

TABLE 3.2   Hypothetical Schedule of Marginal Revenue Productivity of Labor for Store Detectives

Number of Detectives on Duty during Each Hour Store Is Open	Total Value of Thefts Prevented per Hour	Marginal Value of Thefts Prevented per Hour (MRP_L)
0	$ 0	$—
1	50	50
2	90	40
3	110	20
4	115	5
5	117	2

FIGURE 3.2

Demand for Labor in the Short Run (Money Wage)

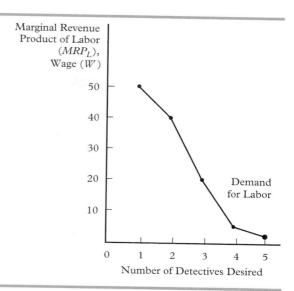

to reduce shoplifting if the added costs it must bear in so doing exceed the value of the savings such steps will generate.

Table 3.2 shows a hypothetical marginal revenue product of labor (MRP_L) schedule for department store detectives. Hiring one detective would, in this example, save $50 worth of thefts per hour. Two detectives could save $90 worth of thefts each hour, or $40 more than hiring just one. The MRP_L of hiring a second detective is thus $40. A third detective would add $20 more to thefts prevented each hour.

The MRP_L does *not* decline from $40 to $20 because the added detectives are incompetent; in fact, we shall assume that all are equally alert and well trained. MRP_L declines, in part, because surveillance equipment (capital) is fixed; with each added detective, there is less equipment per person. However, the MRP_L also declines because it becomes progressively harder to generate savings. With just a few detectives, the only thieves caught will be the more-obvious, less-experienced shoplifters. As more detectives are hired, it becomes possible to prevent theft by the more-expert shoplifters, but they are harder to detect and fewer in number. Thus, MRP_L falls because theft prevention becomes more difficult once all those who are easy to catch are apprehended.

To draw the demand curve for labor, we need to determine how many detectives the store will want to employ at a given wage. For example, at a wage of $50 per hour, how many detectives will the store want? Using the $MRP_L = W$ criterion (equation 3.5), it is easy to see that the answer is "one." At $40 per hour, the store would want to hire two, and at $20 per hour the number demanded would be three. The labor demand curve that summarizes the store's profit-maximizing employment of detectives is shown in Figure 3.2.

Figure 3.2 illustrates a fundamental point: the labor demand curve in the short run slopes downward because it *is* the MRP_L curve—and the MRP_L curve slopes downward because of labor's diminishing marginal product. The demand curve and the MRP_L curve coincide; this could be demonstrated by graphing the MRP_L schedule in Table 3.2, which would yield exactly the same curve as in our graph. When one detective is hired, MRP_L is \$50; when two are hired, MRP_L is \$40; and so forth. Since MRP_L always equals W for a profit maximizer who takes wages as given, the MRP_L curve and labor demand curve (expressed as a function of the money wage) must be the same.

An implication of our example is that there is some level of shoplifting the store finds more profitable to tolerate than to eliminate. This level will be higher at high wages for store detectives than at lower wages. To say the theft rate is "too low" thus implies that the marginal costs of crime reduction exceed the marginal savings generated, and the firm is therefore failing to maximize profits.

Finally, we must emphasize that the marginal product of an individual is *not* a function solely of his or her personal characteristics. As stressed above, the marginal product of a worker depends upon the number of similar employees the firm has already hired. An individual's marginal product also depends upon the size of the firm's capital stock; increases in the firm's capital stock shift the entire marginal product of labor schedule up. It is therefore incorrect to speak of an individual's productivity as an immutable factor that is associated only with his or her characteristics, independent of the characteristics of the other inputs he or she has to work with.

Market Demand Curves The demand curve (or schedule) for an individual firm indicates how much labor that firm will want to employ at each wage level. A *market demand curve* (or schedule) is just the *summation* of the labor demanded by all firms in a particular labor market at each level of the *real* wage.[5] If there are three firms in a certain labor market, and if at a *given* real wage firm A wants 12 workers, firm B wants 6, and firm C wants 20, then the market demand at that real wage is 38 employees. More important, because market demand curves are so closely derived from firm demand curves, they too will *slope downward* as a function of the real wage. When the real wage falls, the number of workers that existing firms want to employ increases. In addition, the lower real wage may make it profitable for new firms to enter the market. Conversely, when the real wage increases, the number of workers that existing firms want to employ decreases, and some firms may be forced to cease operations completely.

Objections to the Marginal Productivity Theory of Demand Two kinds of objections are sometimes raised to the theory of labor demand introduced

---

[5]If firms' demand curves are drawn as a function of the money wage, they represent the downward-sloping portion of the firms' marginal revenue product of labor curves. In a competitive industry, the price of the product is given to the firm by the market, and thus at the firm level the marginal revenue product of labor has imbedded in it a given product price. When aggregating labor demand to the *market* level, product price can no longer be taken as given, and the aggregation is no longer a simple summation.

in this section. The first is that almost no employer can ever be heard uttering the words "marginal revenue product of labor," and that the theory assumes a degree of sophistication that most employers do not have. Employers, it is also argued, are unable in many situations to accurately measure the output of individual workers.

These first objections can be answered as follows: Whether employers can verbalize the profit-maximizing conditions, or whether they can explicitly measure the marginal revenue product of labor, they must at least *intuit* them to survive in a competitive environment. Competition will "weed out" employers who are not good at generating profits, just as competition will weed out pool players who do not understand the intricacies of how speed, angles, and spin affect the motion of bodies through space. Yet one could canvass the pool halls of America and probably not find one player who could verbalize Newton's laws of motion! The point is that employers can *know* concepts without being able to verbalize them. Those that are not good at maximizing profits will not last very long in competitive markets.

The second objection is that in many cases it seems that adding labor while holding capital constant would not add to output at all. For example, one secretary and one computer can produce output, but it might seem that adding a second secretary while holding the number of word processors constant could produce nothing extra, since that secretary would have no machine on which to work.

The answer to this second objection is that the two secretaries could take turns using the computer, so that neither became fatigued to the extent that mistakes increased and typing speeds slowed down. The second secretary could also answer the telephone and in other ways expedite work. Thus, even with technologies that seem to require one machine per person, labor will generally have a marginal product greater than zero if capital is held constant.

THE DEMAND FOR LABOR IN COMPETITIVE MARKETS WHEN OTHER INPUTS CAN BE VARIED

An implication of our theory of labor demand is that, because labor can be varied in the short run—that is, at any time—the profit-maximizing firm will always operate so that labor's marginal revenue product equals the wage rate (which is labor's marginal expense in a competitive labor market). What we must now consider is how the firm's ability to adjust *other* inputs affects the demand for labor. We first analyze the implications of being able to adjust capital in the long run, and we then turn our attention to the case of more than two inputs.

Labor Demand in the Long Run

To maximize profits in the long run, the firm must adjust both labor and capital so that the marginal revenue product of each equals its marginal expense. Using the definitions discussed earlier in this chapter, profit maximization requires that the following two equalities be satisfied:

$$MP_L \cdot P = W \quad \text{(a restatement of equation 3.5)} \tag{3.7a}$$
$$MP_K \cdot P = C \quad \text{(the profit-maximizing condition for capital)} \tag{3.7b}$$

Both (3.7a) and (3.7b) can be rearranged to isolate P, so these two profit-maximizing conditions also can be expressed as

$$P = W/MP_L \quad \text{(a rearrangement of equation 3.7a)} \tag{3.8a}$$
$$P = C/MP_K \quad \text{(a rearrangement of equation 3.7b)} \tag{3.8b}$$

Further, because the right-hand sides of both (3.8a) and (3.8b) equal the same quantity, P, profit maximization therefore requires that

$$W/MP_L = C/MP_K \tag{3.8c}$$

The economic meaning of equation (3.8c) is key to understanding how the ability to adjust capital affects the firm's demand for labor. Consider the left-hand side of (3.8c): the numerator is the cost of a unit of labor, while the denominator is the extra output produced by an added unit of labor. Therefore, the ratio W/MP_L turns out to be the added cost of producing an added unit of output using labor.[6] Analogously, the right-hand side is the marginal cost of producing an extra unit of output using capital. What equation (3.8c) suggests is that, to maximize profits, *the firm must adjust its labor and capital inputs so that the marginal cost of producing an added unit of output using labor is equal to the marginal cost of producing an added unit of output using capital.* Why is this condition a requirement for maximizing profits?

To maximize profits a firm must be producing its chosen level of output in the least-cost manner. Logic suggests that as long as the firm can expand output more cheaply using one input than the other, it cannot be producing in the least-cost way. For example, if the marginal cost of expanding output by one unit using labor were $10, and the marginal cost using capital were $12, the firm could keep output constant and lower its costs of production! How? It could reduce its capital by enough to cut output by one unit (saving $12), and then add enough labor to restore the one-unit cut (costing $10). Output would be the same, but costs would have fallen by $2. Thus, for the firm to be maximizing profits, it must be operating at the point such that further marginal changes in both labor and capital would neither lower costs nor otherwise add to profits.

With equations (3.8a) to (3.8c) in mind, what would happen to the demand for labor in the long run if the wage rate (W) facing a profit-maximizing firm were

---

[6]Because $MP_L = \Delta Q/\Delta L$, the expression W/MP_L can be rewritten as $W \cdot \Delta L/\Delta Q$. Since $W\Delta L$ represents the added cost from employing one more unit of labor, the expression $W\Delta L/\Delta Q$ equals the cost of an added unit of output when that unit is produced by added labor.

to rise? First, as we discussed in the section on the short-run demand for labor, the rise in W disturbs the equality in (3.8a), and the firm will want to cut back on its use of labor even before it can adjust capital. Because the marginal product of labor is assumed to rise as employment is reduced, any cuts in labor will raise MP_L.

Second, because each unit of capital now has less labor working with it, the marginal product of capital (MP_K) falls, disturbing the equality in (3.8b). By itself, this latter inequality will cause the firm to want to reduce its stock of capital.

Third, the rise in W will initially end the equality in (3.8c), meaning that the marginal cost of production using labor now exceeds the marginal cost using capital. If the above cuts in labor are made in the short run, the associated increase in MP_L and decrease in MP_K will work toward restoring equality in (3.8c); however, if it remains more costly to produce an extra unit of output using labor than using capital, the firm will want to substitute capital for labor in the long run. Substituting capital for labor means that the firm will produce its profit-maximizing level of output (which is clearly reduced by the rise in W) in a more capital-intensive way. The act of substituting capital for labor also will serve to increase MP_L and reduce MP_K, thereby reinforcing the return to equality in (3.8c).

In the end, the increase in W will cause the firm to reduce its desired employment level for two reasons. The firm's profit-maximizing level of output will fall, and the associated reduction in required inputs (both capital and labor) is an example of the *scale effect*. The rise in W also causes the firm to substitute capital for labor, so that it can again produce in the least-cost manner; changing the mix of capital and labor in the production process is an example of the *substitution effect*. The scale and substitution effects of a wage increase will have an ambiguous effect on the firm's desired stock of *capital*, but both effects serve to reduce the demand for *labor*. Thus, the long-run ability to adjust capital lends further theoretical support to the proposition that the labor demand curve is a downward-sloping function of the wage rate.

More than Two Inputs

Thus far we have assumed that there are only two inputs in the production process: capital and labor. In fact, labor can be subdivided into many categories; for example, labor can be categorized by age, educational level, and occupation. Other inputs that are used in the production process include materials and energy. If a firm is seeking to minimize costs, in the long run it should employ all inputs up until the point that the marginal cost of producing an added unit of output is the same regardless of which input is increased. This generalization of equation (3.8c) leads to the somewhat obvious result that the demand for *any* category of labor will be a function of its own wage rate *and* (through the scale and substitution effects) the wage or prices of all other categories of labor, capital, and supplies.

If Inputs Are Substitutes in Production   The demand curve for each category of labor will be a downward-sloping function of the wage rate paid to workers in that category, for the reasons discussed earlier, but how is it affected by wage or price changes for *other* inputs? If two inputs are *substitutes in production* (that is, if the greater use of one in producing output can compensate for reduced use of the other), then increases in the price of the *other* input may shift the entire demand curve for a *given* category of labor either to the right or to the left, depending on the relative strength of the substitution and scale effects. If an increase in the price of one input shifts the demand for *another* input to the left, as in panel (a) of Figure 3.3, the scale effect has dominated the substitution effect and the two inputs are *gross complements;* if the increase shifts the demand for the other input to the right, as in panel (b) of Figure 3.3, the substitution effect has dominated and the two inputs are *gross substitutes.*

If Inputs Are Complements in Production   If, instead, the two inputs are *complements in production,* which means they must be used together, then reduced use of one implies reduced use of the other. In this case, there is no substitution effect, only a scale effect, and the two inputs must be gross complements.

Examples   Consider an example of a snow-removal firm in which skilled and unskilled workers are substitutes in production—snow can be removed using either unskilled workers (with shovels) or skilled workers driving snowplows. Let us focus on demand for the skilled workers. Other things equal, an increase in the wage of skilled workers would cause the firm to employ fewer of them; their demand curve would be a downward-sloping function of their wage. If only the wage of *unskilled* workers increased, however, the employer would want fewer unskilled workers than before, and more of the now relatively less expensive skilled

FIGURE 3.3
Effect of Increase in the Price of One Input (k) on Demand for Another Input (j), Where Inputs Are Substitutes in Production

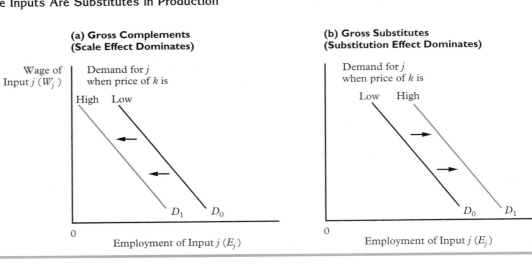

workers, to remove any *given amount of snow*. To the extent that this substitution effect dominated over the scale effect, the demand for skilled workers would shift to the right. In this case, skilled and unskilled workers would be gross substitutes. In contrast, if the reduction in the scale of output caused employment of skilled workers to be reduced, even though skilled workers were being substituted for unskilled workers in the production process, skilled and unskilled workers would be considered gross complements.

In the above firm, snowplows and skilled workers are complements in production. If the price of snowplows went up, the employer would want to cut back on their use, which would result in a reduced demand at each wage for the skilled workers who drove the snowplows. As noted above, inputs that are complements in production are always gross complements.

LABOR DEMAND WHEN THE PRODUCT MARKET IS NOT COMPETITIVE

Our analysis of the demand for labor, in both the short and the long run, has so far taken place under the assumption that the firm operates in competitive product and labor markets. This is equivalent to assuming that the firm is both a price taker and a wage taker; that is, that it takes both P and W as given and makes decisions only about the levels of output and inputs. We complete our theoretical analysis of labor demand by exploring the effects of noncompetitive markets. In this section we assume that the product market is monopolistic; in the next, we assume that the labor market is monopsonistic.

Maximizing Monopoly Profits

As explained earlier in footnote 2 and the surrounding text, product market monopolies are subject to the *market* demand curve for their output, and they therefore do not take output price as given. They can expand their sales only by reducing product price, which means that their marginal revenue (MR) from an extra unit of output is less than product price (P). Using the general definition of marginal revenue product in equation (3.3a), and applying the usual profit-maximizing criteria outlined in equation (3.4) to a monopoly that searches for workers in a competitive *labor* market (so that $ME_L = W$), the monopolist would hire workers until its marginal revenue product of labor (MRP_L) equals the wage rate:

$$MRP_L = MR \cdot MP_L = W \tag{3.9}$$

Now we can express the demand for labor in the short run in terms of the real wage by dividing equation (3.9) by the firm's product price, P, to obtain

$$\frac{MR}{P} \cdot MP_L = \frac{W}{P} \tag{3.10}$$

Since marginal revenue is always less than a monopoly's product price, the ratio MR/P in equation (3.10) is less than one. Therefore, the labor demand curve for a firm that has monopoly power in the output market will lie below and to the left of the labor demand curve for an *otherwise identical* firm that takes product price as given. Put another way, just as output is lower under monopoly than it is under competition, other things equal, so is the level of employment.

The *wage* rates that monopolies pay, however, are not necessarily different from competitive levels even though *employment* levels are. An employer with a product market monopoly may still be a very small part of the market for a particular kind of employee, and thus be a *price taker* in the labor market. For example, a local utility company might have a product market monopoly, but it would have to compete with all other firms to hire secretaries and thus would have to pay the going wage.

Do Monopolies Pay Higher Wages?

There are circumstances, however, in which economists suspect that product market monopolies might pay wages that are *higher* than competitive firms would pay.[7] The monopolies that are legally permitted to exist in the United States are regulated by governmental bodies in an effort to prevent them from exploiting their favored status and earning monopoly profits. This regulation of profits, it can be argued, gives monopolies incentives to pay higher wages than they would otherwise pay for two reasons.

First, regulatory bodies allow monopolies to pass the costs of doing business on to consumers. Thus, while unable to maximize profits, the managers of a monopoly can enhance their *utility* by paying high wages and passing the costs along to consumers in the form of higher prices. The ability to pay high wages makes a manager's life more pleasant by making it possible to hire people who might be more attractive or personable or have other characteristics managers find desirable.

Second, monopolies that are as yet unregulated may not want to attract attention to themselves by earning the very high profits usually associated with monopoly. Therefore they, too, may be induced to pay high wages in a partial effort to "hide" their profits. The excess profits of monopolies, in other words, may be partly taken in the form of highly preferred workers—paid a relatively high wage rate—rather than in the usual monetary form.

The evidence on monopoly wages, however, is not very clear as yet. Some studies suggest that firms in industries with relatively few sellers *do* pay higher wages than competitive firms for workers with the same education and experience.

---

[7]For a full statement of this argument, see Armen Alchian and Reuben Kessel, "Competition, Monopoly, and the Pursuit of Money," in *Aspects of Labor Economics,* ed. H. G. Lewis (Princeton, N.J.: Princeton University Press, 1962).

Other studies of regulated monopolies, however, have obtained mixed results on whether wages tend to be higher for comparable workers in these industries.[8]

MONOPSONY IN THE LABOR MARKET

When only one firm is the buyer of labor in a particular labor market, such a firm is called a *monopsonist*. Because the firm is the only demander of labor in this market, it can influence the wage rate. Rather than being a *wage taker* and facing the horizontal labor supply curve that competitive firms are confronted with, monopsonists face an upward-sloping labor supply curve. The supply curve confronting them, in other words, is the *market* supply curve. To expand its workforce, a monopsonist must increase its wage rate to attract workers from other labor markets. (In contrast, a competitive firm can expand its workforce while paying the prevailing market wage, because there are many employers with similar jobs from which workers can be attracted.)

Profit Maximization

The unusual aspect of a firm's being confronted with an upward-sloping labor supply curve is that the *marginal expense of hiring labor exceeds the wage*. If a competitive firm wants to hire 10 workers instead of 9, the hourly cost of the additional worker is equal to the wage rate. If a monopsonist hires 10 instead of 9, it must pay a higher wage to all workers *in addition to* paying the bill for the added worker. For example, suppose that a monopsonist could get 9 workers if it paid $7 per hour but that if it wished to hire 10 workers it would have to pay a wage of $7.50. The labor cost associated with 9 workers would be $63 per hour (9 × $7), but the labor cost associated with 10 workers would be $75 per hour (10 × $7.50). Hiring the additional worker would cost $12 per hour—far more than the $7.50 wage rate![9]

The fact that the marginal expense of hiring labor is above the wage rate affects the labor market behavior of monopsonists. To maximize profits, we know that any firm should hire labor until the point at which the marginal revenue product of labor (MRP_L) equals labor's marginal expense. Hence, the monopsonist

---

[8]Ronald Ehrenberg, *The Regulatory Process and Labor Earnings* (New York: Academic Press, 1979); Barry T. Hirsch, "Trucking Regulation, Unionization, and Labor Earnings," *Journal of Human Resources* 23 (Summer 1988): 296–319; S. Nickell, J. Vainiomaki, and S. Wadhwani, "Wages and Product Market Power," *Economica* 61, no. 244 (November 1994): 457–473; and Marianne Bertrand and Sendhil Mullainathan, "Is There Discretion in Wage Setting? A Test Using Takeover Legislation," *RAND Journal of Economics* 30, no. 3 (Autumn 1999): 535–554.

[9]We assume here that the monopsonist does not know which workers it can hire for $7 per hour and which workers could only be hired at $7.50. All it knows is that if it wants to hire 10 workers it must pay $7.50, whereas if it wants to hire 9 it can pay only $7. Therefore, all workers get paid the same wage.

FIGURE 3.4
The Effects of Monopsony

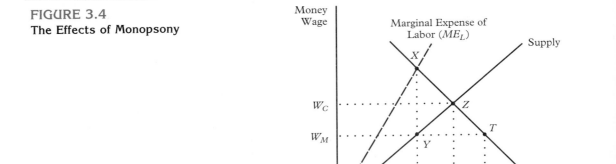

should hire workers up to the point at which MRP_L equals the marginal expense of hiring additional workers (ME_L):

$$MRP_L = ME_L \qquad (3.11)$$

The profit-maximizing level of employment for a monopsonist is shown in Figure 3.4. The firm has a conventional MRP_L curve, but its labor supply curve is upward-sloping. As usual, this supply curve depicts that amount of labor available to the firm at each wage rate. What is different about monopsony is that the *marginal* expense of hiring labor exceeds the wage; hence, the (dashed) ME_L curve lies above the labor supply curve. With the marginal expense of hiring labor along the dashed curve, the firm's profit-maximizing level of employment is found where the ME_L and MRP_L curves intersect (at point X). Thus, the monopsonist will want to hire E_M workers. The wage rate necessary to attract E_M workers to the firm—which can be read off the supply curve—is W_M (see point Y). Thus for a profit-maximizing monopsonist, MRP_L is *above*, not equal to, the wage rate.

If the market depicted in Figure 3.4 were competitive, each firm in the market would hire labor until labor's marginal revenue product equaled the wage, and the marginal revenue product schedule would be the demand curve for labor. Thus, the wage rate would be W_C and the employment level would be E_C. Note that in a labor market that is monopsonized, wages and employment levels are *below* W_C and E_C. (For an example of how monopsony keeps wages below competitive levels, see Example 3.2.)

EXAMPLE 3.2

Monopsony and Competition in Major-League and Negro-League Baseball

Between World War I and the mid-1970s, Major-League Baseball built one of the most powerful monopsonies in the history of American labor markets. Owners agreed not to compete among themselves (except when signing amateur players), and they inserted the "reserve clause" into player contracts that bound each player to a single team. This meant that players had very limited bargaining power. When offered a contract extension by his employer, a player had the choice of either taking it or leaving the major leagues. If he didn't agree to the new contract, no other major league team would bid on his services, and if he took an offer to play baseball outside the country (in the Mexican League, for example), he was banned from ever playing in the major leagues again.

Unlike the major leagues, which barred African-American players, Negro-League teams had little monopsony power. Players could take outside offers because the club owners could not enforce any agreement to suspend players who did so. Their lack of monopsony power can be seen in the career of the great pitcher, Leroy "Satchel" Paige. In 1937, Paige refused to report to work after the Negro League's Pittsburgh Crawfords sold his contract to the Newark Eagles. When he jumped to a league in the Dominican Republic, Negro-League owners retaliated with a three-year suspension—but they could not enforce it. After a year, Paige returned, but when his club tried again to send him to Newark, he decided to play in Mexico. Finally, the Negro League's Kansas City Monarchs signed Paige to a lucrative contract and created a traveling farm team that enabled him to earn additional money in the off season. By 1942, Paige was the highest-paid player in professional baseball, earning some four times the average pay in the all-white major leagues!

Data from: Robert F. Burk, *Much More Than a Game: Players, Owners and American Baseball since 1921* (Chapel Hill: University of North Carolina Press, 2001), and Don Rogosin, *Invisible Men: Life in Baseball's Negro Leagues,* New York: Atheneum, 1983.

Examples of pure monopsony in the labor market are difficult to cite. Isolated coal-mining towns or sugar plantations, where the mines or sugar companies are literally the only employers, are increasingly rare. And there is little evidence that these employers ever enjoyed much monopsony power, as shown later in Example 10.5. However, the monopsony model is still useful for analyzing labor markets in which there is only one major employer of an *occupational* group (for example, registered nurses in a labor market with only one hospital).[10] Moreover, the really critical aspect of the monopsony model is that *individual employers face an upward-sloping labor supply curve.* There are several conditions that could cause an employer's labor supply curve to slope upward, even if there are many other employers competing with it in the labor market,[11] and we will

[10]For studies of monopsony in the market for nurses, see Barry T. Hirsch and Edward J. Schumacher, "Monopsony Power and Relative Wages in the Labor Market for Nurses," *Journal of Health Economics* 14 (1995): 443–476.

[11]See William M. Boal and Michael Ransom, "Monopsony in the Labor Market," *Journal of Economic Literature* 35, no. 1 (March 1997): 86–112, for a review of the literature on this topic.

examine them later in the context of labor mobility (chapter 10), supervising employees (chapter 11), and discrimination (chapter 12).

How Do Monopsonists Respond to Supply Shifts and Mandated Wage Increases?

The central theme of this chapter is that, with competitive labor markets (that is, each firm is a wage taker) the demand curve for labor is downward-sloping. Thus, if market labor supply curves shift to the left, or if wages are mandated to rise above their market-clearing levels, employment will decline as wages rise. We now inquire whether, under monopsonistic conditions (that is, with upward-sloping labor supply curves to firms), similar employment declines will accompany leftward shifts in labor supply curves or the imposition of above-market wages.

With monopsony, the firm does not have a labor demand curve! Labor demand curves for a firm are essentially derived from sequentially asking, "If the market wage were at some level ($5, say), what would be the firm's profit-maximizing level of employment? If, instead, the wage were $6, what would be the firm's desired level of employment?" With monopsony, the firm is not a wage taker, so asking hypothetical questions about the level of wages facing the firm is meaningless. Given the firm's labor supply curve and its schedule of marginal revenue product (MRP_L at various levels of employment), there is only one profit-maximizing level of employment and only one associated wage rate, both of which are chosen by the firm.

Shifts in Labor Supply That Increase ME_L   Consider the short-run and long-run effects on a monopsonistic firm's desired level of employment if the supply curve facing the firm shifts (but remains upward-sloping). Suppose, for example, that the labor supply curve were to shift to the left, reflecting a situation in which fewer people are willing to work at any given wage level. With the competitive model of labor demand, a leftward shift of a market supply curve would cause the market wage to increase and the level of employment to fall, as employers moved to the left along their labor demand curves. Will these changes in wages and employment occur with monopsony?

In Figure 3.5, the MRP_L curve is fixed (we are in the short run) and the leftward shift of the labor supply curve is represented by a movement to curve S' from the original curve, S. With a supply curve of S, the firm's marginal expense of labor curve was ME_L, and it chose to hire E workers and pay them a wage of W. When the supply curve shifts to S', the firm's marginal labor expenses shift to a higher curve, ME_L'. Therefore, its new profit-maximizing level of employment falls to E', and its new wage rate increases to W'. Thus, with monopsony just as with the competitive model, a leftward shift in labor supply increases ME_L, raises wages, and reduces firms' desired levels of employment in the short run.

In the long run, labor's increased marginal expense will induce the substitution of capital for labor as firms seek to find the cost-minimizing mix of capital

FIGURE 3.5

The Monopsonist's Short-Run Response to a Leftward Shift in Labor Supply: Employment Falls and Wage Increases

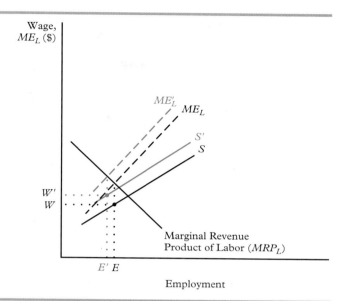

and labor. You will recall that the cost-minimizing conditions for capital and labor under *competitive* conditions were given in equation (3.8c), in which the wage rate was treated as the marginal expense of labor. In a noncompetitive labor market, ME_L exceeds W, so the left-hand side of equation (3.8c) must be written in its general form:

$$ME_L/MP_L = C/MP_K \qquad (3.12)$$

Clearly, if a monopsonist is minimizing its costs of production and its ME_L is increased, it will want to restore equality to condition (3.12) by substituting capital for labor. Thus, employment decreases even more in the long run than in the short run.

Effects of a Mandated Wage   Let us next consider what would happen if some nonmarket force were to compel the firm to pay a particular wage rate that was higher than the one it was paying. Would the firm's desired level of employment decline? For the monopsonist's short-run response, refer to Figure 3.6, where a monopsonistic firm initially equates MRP_L and ME_L at point A and chooses to hire E_0 workers, which requires it to pay a wage of W_0.

Suppose now that a mandated wage of W_m is set in Figure 3.6. This mandate prevents the firm from paying a wage less than W_m and effectively creates a

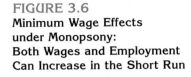

FIGURE 3.6
Minimum Wage Effects under Monopsony: Both Wages and Employment Can Increase in the Short Run

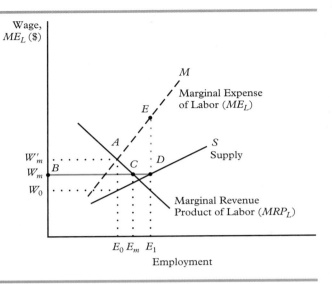

horizontal portion (*BD*) in the labor supply curve facing the firm (which is now *BDS*). The firm's marginal expense of labor curve is now *BDEM*, because up to employment level E_1 the marginal costs of labor are equal to W_m. The firm, which maximizes profits by equating marginal revenues with marginal costs (which equality is now at point *C*), will hire E_m workers. Even though wages have risen from W_0 to W_m, employment rises from E_0 to E_m.

For a monopsonist, then, a mandated wage can simultaneously increase the *average* cost of labor (that is, the wages paid to workers) and reduce labor's *marginal* expense. It is the decrease in *marginal* expense that induces the firm to expand output and employment in the short run. Thus, because an upward-sloping supply curve is converted to one that is horizontal, at least for employment near the current level, it is possible that both wages and employment can increase with the imposition of a mandated wage on a monopsonist. This possibility is subject to two qualifications, however.

First, in the context of Figure 3.6, employment will increase only if the mandated wage is set between W_0 and W'_m. A mandated wage above W'_m would increase ME_L above its current level and cause the profit-maximizing level of employment to fall below E_0. (The student can verify this by drawing a horizontal line from any point above W'_m on the vertical axis and noting that it will intersect the MRP_L curve to the left of E_0.)

Second, Figure 3.6, with its fixed MRP_L curve, depicts only the short-run response to a mandated wage. In the long run, two (opposing) effects on employment are possible. With a mandated wage that is *not too high,* a monopsonist's ME_L

is reduced, causing a substitution of labor for capital in the long run. While the monopsonist's *marginal* cost of labor may have fallen, however, labor's *average* cost has increased. It is now more expensive to produce even the same scale of output as before; thus, profits will decline. A firm may have monopsony power in the labor market, but it also may have many competitors in its product market. If it is in a competitive product market, its initial profit level will be normal for that market, so the decline will push its profits below normal. Some owners will get out of the market, putting downward pressure on employment. If this latter (scale) effect is large enough, employment in monopsonistic sectors could fall in the long run if a mandated wage were imposed.

In summary, then, the presence of monopsony introduces uncertainty into how employment will respond to the imposition of a mandated wage *if* the new wage reduces the firm's marginal expense of labor. Any shift in the supply of labor curve that *increases* the marginal expense of labor, of course, will unambiguously reduce employment.

POLICY APPLICATION: THE LABOR MARKET EFFECTS OF EMPLOYER PAYROLL TAXES AND WAGE SUBSIDIES

Having carefully examined the theory of labor demand, we turn now to an application of this theory to the phenomena of *employer* payroll taxes and wage subsidies. Governments widely finance certain social programs through taxes that require employers to remit payments based on their total payroll costs. As we will see, new or increased payroll taxes levied on the employer raise the cost of hiring labor, and they might therefore be expected to reduce the demand for labor. Conversely, it can be argued that if the government were to subsidize the wages paid by employers, the demand for labor would increase; indeed, wage subsidies for particular disadvantaged groups in society are sometimes proposed as a way to increase their employment. In this section we will analyze the effects of payroll taxes and subsidies.

Who Bears the Burden of a Payroll Tax?

In the United States, social insurance programs for workers commonly are financed at least in part by *payroll* taxes levied on *employers.* These taxes require employers to pay the government a certain percentage of their employees' earnings, often up to some maximum amount. Unemployment insurance, as well as Social Security retirement, disability, and Medicare programs, are prominent examples. Does taxing employers to generate revenues for these programs relieve *employees* of a financial burden that would otherwise fall on them?

Suppose that only the employer is required to make payments and that the tax is a fixed amount (X) per labor hour, rather than a percentage of payroll. Now consider the market demand curve D_0 in Figure 3.7, which is drawn in such a way that desired employment is plotted against the wage *employees receive*. Prior to the imposition of the tax, the wage employees receive is the same as the wage employers pay. Thus, if D_0 were the demand curve before the tax was imposed, it would have the conventional interpretation of indicating how much labor firms would be willing to hire at any given wage. However, *after* imposition of the tax, employer wage costs would be X above what employees received.

Shifting the Demand Curve   If employees received W_0, employers would now face costs of $W_0 + X$. They would no longer demand E_0 workers; rather, because their costs were $W_0 + X$, they would demand E_2 workers. Point A (where W_0 and E_2 intersect) would lie on a new market demand curve, formed when demand shifted down because of the tax (remember, the wage on the vertical axis of Figure 3.7 is the wage *employees receive*, not the wage employers pay). Only if employee wages fell to $W_0 - X$ would firms want to continue hiring E_0 workers, for then *employer* costs would be the same as before the tax. Thus, point B would also be on the new, shifted demand curve. Note that, with a tax of X, the new demand curve (D_1) is parallel to the old one and the vertical distance between the two is X.

Now, the tax-related shift in the market demand curve to D_1 implies that there would be an excess supply of labor at the previous equilibrium wage of W_0. This surplus of labor would create downward pressure on the *employee* wage, and this downward pressure would continue to be exerted until the employee wage fell to W_1, the point at which the quantity of labor supplied just equaled the quantity demanded. At this point, employment would also have fallen to E_1. Thus, *employees* bear a burden in the form of *lower wage rates and lower employment levels*. The lesson is clear: *employees* are not exempted from bearing costs when the government chooses to generate revenues through a payroll tax on *employers*.

FIGURE 3.7
The Market Demand Curve and Effects of an Employer-Financed Payroll Tax

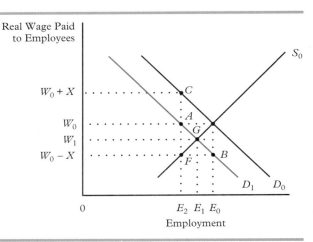

FIGURE 3.8

Payroll Tax with a Vertical Supply Curve

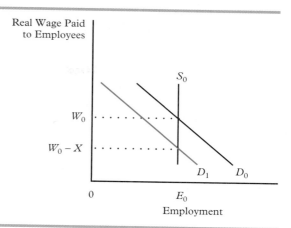

Figure 3.7 does suggest, however, that employers may bear at least *some* of the tax, because the wages received by employees do not fall by the full amount of the tax ($W_0 - W_1$ is smaller than X, which is the vertical distance between the two demand curves). This occurs because, with an upward-sloping labor market supply curve, employees withdraw labor as their wages fall, and it becomes more difficult for firms to find workers. If wages fell to $W_0 - X$, the withdrawal of workers would create a labor shortage that would drive wages to some point (W_1 in our example) between W_0 and $W_0 - X$. Only if the labor market supply curve were *vertical*—meaning that lower wages have no effect on labor supply—would the *entire amount of the tax* be shifted to workers in the form of a decrease in their wages by the amount of X, as shown by supply curve S_0 in Figure 3.8.

Effects of Labor Supply Curves   The extent to which the labor market *supply* curve is sensitive to wages affects the proportion of the employer payroll tax that gets shifted to employees' wages. The less responsive labor supply is to changes in wages, the fewer the employees who withdraw from the market and the higher the proportion of the tax that gets shifted to workers in the form of a wage decrease (compare the outcomes in Figures 3.7 and 3.8). It must also be pointed out, however, that to the degree employee wages do *not* fall, employment levels *will*; when employee wages do not fall much in the face of an employer payroll-tax increase, employer labor costs are increased—and this increase reduces the quantity of labor employers demand.

A number of empirical studies have sought to ascertain what fraction of employers' payroll-tax costs are actually passed on to employees in the form of lower wages (or lower wage increases). Although the evidence is somewhat ambiguous, a comprehensive review of these studies led to at least a tentative conclusion that most of a payroll tax is eventually shifted to wages, with little long-run effect on employment.[12]

Are Payroll Taxes Responsible for European Unemployment?

Most developed countries, and many developing nations, have a variety of social programs designed to compensate workers who have retired or who are sick, injured, permanently disabled, or unemployed. In addition, such countries typically provide their citizens with general health insurance in some form or other. These various social insurance programs are most often financed by employer payroll taxes or by employer payments to private insurers that are based on payroll. Table 3.3 displays these employer taxes and payments as a percentage of payroll (for manufacturing industries) in the United States, Canada, and several European countries.

Two facts are immediately apparent from Table 3.3. First, payroll-based taxes and payments required of employers in the countries shown are a substantial percentage of employee earnings: 16 percent in Canada, 21 percent in the United States, and over 25 percent in Belgium, Germany, France, and Sweden. Second, the rates displayed in the table are generally higher in Europe than in North America. In commenting on European unemployment relative to that in North America during the 1980s, one economist called European payroll taxes "mass job-killers."[13] Another report on the unemployment problems facing Europe stated the issue in this way:

> One particular policy concern is that taxes imposed on the wage bill may reduce employment, either through making production unprofitable, or through encouraging the use of more capital-intensive methods of production.[14]

As noted above, one would not expect employment to be especially correlated with employer payroll-tax rates if the bulk of those taxes were shifted to employee wages. Indeed, comparing international data on unemployment (Table 2.4) with the employer payroll-tax rates in Table 3.3 presents a somewhat murky picture. On the one hand, the four countries with the highest current payroll-tax rates in Table 3.3 (Belgium, France, Germany, and Sweden) also have the highest long-term unemployment rates in Table 2.4. On the other hand, three countries have lower payroll-tax rates than Norway and the United States, which have by far the lowest rates of long-term unemployment among the 10 countries shown in Table 2.4. It will be obvious from our discussion of unemployment in chapter 15 that payroll

[12]Daniel S. Hamermesh, *Labor Demand* (Princeton, N.J.: Princeton University Press, 1993), 169–173; Jonathan Gruber, "The Incidence of Payroll Taxation: Evidence from Chile," *Journal of Labor Economics* 15, no. 3, pt. 2 (July 1997): S72–S101; and Patricia M. Anderson and Bruce D. Meyer, "The Effects of the Unemployment Insurance Payroll Tax on Wages, Employment, Claims and Denials," *Journal of Public Economics* 78 (October 2000): 81–106.

TABLE 3.3   **Payroll-Related Taxes and Other Mandated Expenses as a Percent of Hourly Compensation, Manufacturing Production Workers, 1980 and 1999**

Country	1980	1999
Belgium	23.2%	28.1%
Canada	10.6	16.0
Denmark	4.4	6.3
France	27.3	31.8
Germany	21.0	25.1
Netherlands	24.1	22.6
Norway	19.6	17.3
Sweden	27.4	28.1
United Kingdom	18.0	12.9
United States	19.1	20.7

Source: U.S. Bureau of Labor Statistics, "International Comparisons of Hourly Compensation Costs for Production Workers in Manufacturing, 1975–1999," USDL 00–254, September 7, 2000, Table 13.

taxes are certainly not the only potential factor affecting unemployment rates, so not much weight can be placed on these simple comparisons. However, a survey of research on European unemployment problems did not find payroll taxes to be a major contributor.[15]

Employment Subsidies as a Device to Help the Poor

The opposite of a payroll tax on employers is a government subsidy of employers' payrolls. In Figure 3.7, for example, if instead of *taxing* each hour of labor by X the government *paid* the employer X, the market labor demand curve would shift *upward* by a vertical distance of X. This upward movement of the demand curve would create pressures to increase employment and the wages received by employees; as with a payroll tax, whether the eventual effects would be felt more on employment or on wage rates depends on the shape of the labor market supply curve.

---

[13]Edmund S. Phelps, "Commentary: Past and Prospective Causes of High Unemployment," in *Reducing Unemployment: Current Issues and Policy Options* (Kansas City, Mo.: Federal Reserve Bank of Kansas City, 1994), 85.

[14]Organisation for Economic Co-operation and Development, *Employment Outlook* (Paris: OECD, July 1990), 153.

[15]Charles R. Bean, "European Unemployment: A Survey," *Journal of Economic Literature* 32 (June 1994): 573–619.

(Students should test their understanding in this area by drawing labor demand curves that reflect a new payroll subsidy of X per hour, and then analyzing the effects on employment and employee wages with market supply curves that are, alternatively, upward-sloping and vertical. *Hint:* The outcomes should be those that would be obtained if demand curve D_1 in Figures 3.7 and 3.8 were shifted to curve D_0.)

Payroll subsidies to employers can take many forms. They can be in the form of cash payments, as implied by the above hypothetical example, or they can be in the form of tax credits. These credits might directly reduce a firm's payroll-tax rate, or they might reduce some other tax by an amount proportional to the number of labor hours hired; in either case, the credit has the effect of reducing the cost of hiring labor.

Further, wage subsidies can apply to a firm's employment *level*, to any *new* employees hired after a certain date (even if they just replace workers who have left), or only to new hires that serve to *increase* the firm's level of employment. Finally, subsidies can be either *general* or *selective*. A general subsidy is not conditional on the characteristics of the people hired, whereas a selective, or *targeted*, plan makes the subsidy conditional on hiring people from certain target groups (such as the disadvantaged).

The beneficial effects on wages and employment that are expected to derive from payroll-tax subsidies have led to their proposed use as a policy to help alleviate poverty. One economist concerned about unemployment and earnings levels among low-wage workers recently wrote:

> What to do? The solution for which I have pleaded the past five years: a low-wage employment subsidy. It would best take the form of a tax credit that employers could use to offset the payroll taxes they owe from their employment of low-wage workers. Lower unemployment and better pay would result at the low end of the labor market—the less of the one, the more of the other.[16]

Experience in the United States with targeted wage subsidies, such as the one proposed above, has been modest. The Targeted Jobs Tax Credit (TJTC) program, which began in 1979 and was changed slightly over the years until it was finally discontinued in 1995, targeted disadvantaged youth, the handicapped, and welfare recipients, providing their employers with a tax credit that lasted for one year. In practice, the average duration of jobs under this program was six months, and the subsidy reduced employer wage costs by about 15 percent for jobs of this duration.

One problem that limited the effectiveness of the TJTC program was that the eligibility requirements for many of its participants were stigmatizing; that is, being eligible (on welfare, for example) was often seen by employers as a negative indicator of productivity. Nevertheless, one recent evaluation found

---

[16]Phelps, "Commentary: Past and Prospective Causes of High Unemployment," 89. For his book on this topic, see Edmund S. Phelps, *Rewarding Work* (Cambridge, Mass.: Harvard University Press, 1997).

that the employment of disadvantaged youth was enhanced by the TJTC. Specifically, it found that when 23- to 24-year-olds were removed from eligibility for the TJTC by changes in 1989, employment of disadvantaged youths of that age fell over 7 percent.[17]

---

[17]Lawrence F. Katz, "Wage Subsidies for the Disadvantaged," in *Generating Jobs: How to Increase Demand for Less-Skilled Workers,* ed. Richard B. Freeman and Peter Gottschalk (New York: Russell Sage Foundation, 1998), 21–53.

REVIEW QUESTIONS

1. In a statement during the 1992 presidential campaign, one organization attempting to influence the political parties argued that the wages paid by U.S. firms in their Mexican plants were so low that they "have no relationship with worker productivity." Comment on this statement using the principles of profit maximization.

2. Suppose that the U.S. military is having difficulty recruiting volunteers and is considering one of two options: raising pay or reinstating the draft system. Analyze the opportunity costs of lost civilian production when volunteers are used as compared with those associated with drafting civilians using some random method of choice.

3. The Occupational Safety and Health Administration promulgates safety and health standards. These standards typically apply to machinery (capital), which is required to be equipped with guards, shields, and the like. An alternative to these standards is to require the employer to furnish personal protective devices to employees (labor)—such as earplugs, hard hats, and safety shoes. *Disregarding* the issue of which alternative approach offers greater protection from injury, what aspects of each alternative must be taken into account when analyzing the possible *employment* effects of the two approaches to safety?

4. Suppose that prisons historically have required inmates to perform, *without pay,* various cleaning and food preparation jobs within the prison. Now suppose that prisoners are offered paid work in factory jobs within the prison walls, and that the cleaning and food preparation tasks are now performed by nonprisoners hired to do them. Would you expect to see any differences in the *technologies* used to perform these tasks? Explain.

5. Several years ago Great Britain adopted a program that placed a tax—to be collected from employers—on wages in *service* industries. Wages in manufacturing industries were not taxed. Discuss the wage and employment effects of this tax policy.

6. Suppose the government were to subsidize the wages of all women in the population by paying their *employers* 50 cents for every hour they work. What would be the effect on the wage rate women received? What would be the effect on the net wage employers paid? (The net wage would be the wage women received less 50 cents.)

7. In the last decade or two the United States has been subject to huge increases in the illegal immigration of workers from Mexico, most of them unskilled, and the government has recently considered ways to reduce the flow. One policy that has been

considered is to impose larger financial penalties on employers who are discovered to have hired illegal immigrants.

What effect would this policy have on the employment of unskilled illegal immigrants? What effect would it have on the demand for skilled "native" labor?

8. In 1999, the U.S. Bureau of Labor Statistics reported that hourly compensation costs per U.S. manufacturing worker were $19.20, while those in Mexico were $2.12. Recognizing that the analysis leading up to equation (3.8c) can be used to understand the choices firms make between *any* two factors of production, explain why a growing firm with facilities in both Mexico and the United States might still expand its output using U.S. workers. (*Hint:* Consider U.S. and Mexican workers to be substitute factors of production.)

PROBLEMS

1. An experiment conducted in Tennessee found that the scores of second and third graders on standardized tests for reading, math, listening, and word study skills were the same in small classrooms (13 to 17 students) as in regular classrooms (22 to 25 students). Suppose that there is a school that had 90 third graders taught by four teachers and that added two additional teachers to reduce the class size. If the Tennessee study can be generalized, what is the marginal product of labor of these two additional teachers?

2. The marginal revenue product of labor in the local sawmill is $MRP_L = 20 - 0.5L$, where L = the number of workers. If the wage of sawmill workers is $10 per hour, then how many workers will the mill hire?

3. Suppose that the supply curve for lifeguards is $L_S = 20$ and the demand curve for lifeguards is $L_D = 100 - 20W$, where L = the number of lifeguards and W = the hourly wage. Graph both the demand and supply curves. Now suppose that the government imposes a tax of $1 per hour per worker on companies hiring lifeguards. Draw the new (after-tax) demand curve in terms of the employee wage. How will this tax affect the wage of lifeguards and the number employed as lifeguards?

4. The output of workers at a factory depends on the number of supervisors hired (see table below). The factory sells its output for $0.50 each, it hires 50 production workers at a wage of $100 per day, and it needs to decide how many supervisors to hire. The

Supervisors	Output (units per day)
0	11,000
1	14,800
2	18,000
3	19,500
4	20,200
5	20,600

daily wage of supervisors is $500, but output rises as more supervisors are hired, as shown below. How many supervisors should it hire?

5. (Appendix) The Hormsbury Corporation produces yo-yos at its factory. Both its labor and capital markets are competitive. Wages are $12 per hour and yo-yo making equipment (a computer-controlled plastic extruding machine) rents for $4 per hour. The production function is $q = 40K^{0.25}L^{0.75}$, where q = boxes of yo-yos per week, K = hours of yo-yo equipment used, and L = hours of labor. Therefore, $MP_L = 30K^{0.25}L^{-0.25}$ and $MP_K = 10K^{-0.75}L^{0.75}$. Determine the cost-minimizing capital-labor ratio at this firm.

SELECTED READINGS

Blank, Rebecca M., ed. *Social Protection versus Economic Flexibility: Is There a Trade-Off?* Chicago: University of Chicago Press, 1994.

Hamermesh, Daniel. *Labor Demand.* Princeton, N.J.: Princeton University Press, 1993.

Katz, Lawrence F. "Wage Subsidies for the Disadvantaged." In *Generating Jobs: How to Increase Demand for Less-Skilled Workers,* ed. Richard B. Freeman and Peter Gottschalk. New York: Russell Sage Foundation, 1998, pp. 21–53.

3A

Graphical Derivation of a Firm's Labor Demand Curve

C hapter 3 described verbally the derivation of a firm's labor demand curve. This appendix will present the *same* derivation graphically. This graphical representation permits a more rigorous derivation, but our conclusion that demand curves slope downward in both the short and the long run will remain unchanged.

THE PRODUCTION FUNCTION

Output can generally be viewed as being produced by combining capital and labor. Figure 3A.1 illustrates this production function graphically and depicts several aspects of the production process.

Consider the convex curve labeled $Q = 100$. Along this line, every combination of labor (L) and capital (K) produces 100 units of output (Q). That is, the combination of labor and capital at point A (L_a, K_a) generates the same 100 units of output as the combinations at points B and C. Because each point along the $Q = 100$ curve generates the same output, that curve is called an *isoquant* (*iso* = "equal"; *quant* = "quantity").

Two other isoquants are shown in Figure 3A.1 ($Q = 150$, $Q = 200$). These isoquants represent higher levels of output than the $Q = 100$ curve. The fact that these isoquants indicate higher output levels can be seen by holding labor constant at L_b (say) and then observing the different levels of capital. If L_b is combined with K_b in capital, 100 units of Q are produced. If L_b is combined with K_b', 150 units are produced (K_b' is greater than K_b). If L_b is combined with even more capital (K_b'', say), 200 units of Q could be produced.

Note that the isoquants in Figure 3A.1 have *negative* slopes, reflecting an assumption that labor and capital are substitutes. If, for example, we cut capital from K_a to K_b, we could keep output constant (at 100) by increasing labor from L_a

FIGURE 3A.1
A Production Function

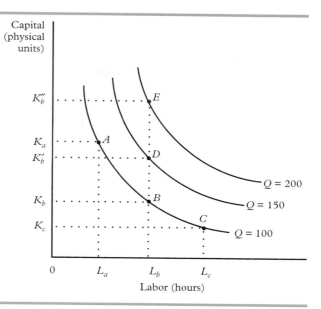

to L_b. Labor, in other words, could be substituted for capital to maintain a given production level.

Finally, note the *convexity* of the isoquants. At point A, the $Q = 100$ isoquant has a steep slope, suggesting that to keep Q constant at 100, a given decrease in capital could be accompanied by a *modest* increase in labor. At point C, however, the slope of the isoquant is relatively flat. This flatter slope means that the same given decrease in capital would require a much *larger* increase in labor for output to be held constant. The decrease in capital permitted by a given increase in labor while output is being held constant is called the *marginal rate of technical substitution* (*MRTS*) between capital and labor. Symbolically, the *MRTS* can be written as

$$MRTS = \frac{\Delta K}{\Delta L} \,|\, \overline{Q} \tag{3A.1}$$

where Δ means "change in" and $|\,\overline{Q}$ means "holding output constant." The *MRTS* is *negative*, because if L is increased, K must be reduced to keep Q constant.

Why does the absolute value of the marginal rate of technical substitution diminish as labor increases? When labor is highly used in the production process and capital is not very prevalent (point C in Figure 3A.1), there are many jobs that capital can do. Labor is easy to replace; if capital is increased, it will be used as a substitute for labor in parts of the production process where it will have the highest payoff. As capital becomes progressively more utilized and labor less so, the few remaining workers will be doing jobs that are hardest for a machine to do, at which point it will take a lot of capital to substitute for a worker.[1]

DEMAND FOR LABOR IN THE SHORT RUN

Chapter 3 argued that firms will maximize profits in the short run (K fixed) by hiring labor until labor's marginal product (MP_L) is equal to the real wage (W/P). The reason for this decision rule is that the real wage represents the *cost* of an added unit of labor (in terms of output), while the marginal product is the *output* added by the extra unit of labor. As long as the firm, by increasing labor (K fixed), gains more in output than it loses in costs, it will continue to hire employees. The firm will stop hiring when the marginal cost of added labor exceeds MP_L.

The requirement that $MP_L = W/P$ in order for profits to be maximized means that the firm's labor demand curve in the short run (in terms of the *real* wage) is identical to its marginal product of labor schedule (refer to Figure 3.1). Remembering that the marginal product of labor is the extra output produced by one-unit increases in the amount of labor employed, holding capital constant, consider the production function displayed in Figure 3A.2. Holding capital constant at K_a, the firm can produce 100 units of Q if it employs labor equal to L_a. If labor is increased to L_a', the firm can produce 50 more units of Q; if labor is increased from L_a' to L_a'', the firm can produce an additional 50 units. Notice, however, that the required increase in labor to get the latter 50 units of added output, $L_a'' - L_a'$, is larger than the extra labor required to produce the first 50-unit increment ($L_a' - L_a$). This difference can only mean that as labor is increased when K is held constant, each successive labor hour hired generates progressively smaller increments in output. Put differently, Figure 3A.2 graphically illustrates the diminishing marginal productivity of labor.

Why does labor's marginal productivity decline? Chapter 3 explained that labor's marginal productivity declines because, with K fixed, each added worker has less capital (per capita) with which to work. Is this explanation proven in Figure 3A.2? The answer is, regrettably, no. Figure 3A.2 is drawn *assuming* diminishing marginal productivity. Renumbering the isoquants could produce a different set of marginal productivities. (To see this, change $Q = 150$ to $Q = 200$, and change $Q = 200$ to $Q = 500$. Labor's marginal productivity would then rise.) However, the logic that labor's marginal product must eventually fall as labor is increased, holding buildings, machines, and tools constant, is compelling. Further, as chapter 3 pointed out, even if MP_L rises initially, the firm will stop hiring labor only in the range where MP_L is declining; as long as MP_L is above W/P and *rising*, it will pay to continue hiring.

The assumptions that MP_L declines eventually and that firms hire until $MP_L = W/P$ are the bases for the assertion that a firm's short-run demand curve

---

[1]Here is one example. Over time, telephone operators (who used to place long-distance calls) were replaced by a very capital-intensive direct-dialing system. Those operators who remain employed, however, perform tasks that are the most difficult for a machine to perform—handling collect calls, dispensing directory assistance, and acting as troubleshooters when problems arise.

FIGURE 3A.2
The Declining Marginal Productivity of Labor

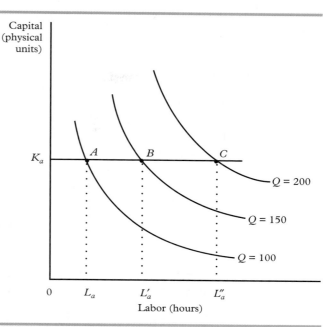

for labor slopes downward. The graphical, more rigorous derivation of the demand curve in this appendix confirms and supports the verbal analysis in the chapter. However, it also emphasizes more clearly than a verbal analysis can that the downward-sloping nature of the short-run labor demand curve is based on an *assumption*—however reasonable—that MP_L declines as employment is increased.

DEMAND FOR LABOR IN THE LONG RUN

Recall that a firm maximizes its profits by producing at a level of output (Q^*) where marginal cost equals marginal revenue. That is, the firm will keep increasing output until the addition to its revenues generated by an extra unit of output just equals the marginal cost of producing that extra unit of output. Because marginal revenue, which is equal to output *price* for a competitive firm, is not shown in our graph of the production function, the profit-maximizing level of output cannot be determined. However, continuing our analysis of the production function can illustrate some important aspects of the demand for labor in the long run.

Conditions for Cost Minimization

In Figure 3A.3, profit-maximizing output is assumed to be Q^*. How will the firm combine labor and capital to produce Q^*? It can maximize profits only if it produces Q^* in the least expensive way; that is, it must minimize the costs of producing Q^*.

FIGURE 3A.3

Cost Minimization in the Production of Q* (Wage = $10 per Hour; Price of a Unit of Capital = $20)

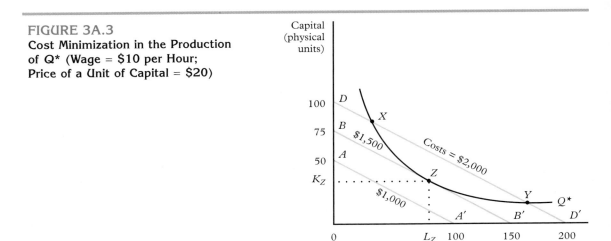

To better understand the characteristics of cost minimization, refer to the three *isoexpenditure* lines—*AA'*, *BB'*, *DD'*—in Figure 3A.3. Along any one of these lines the costs of employing labor and capital are equal.

For example, line *AA'* represents total costs of $1,000. Given an hourly wage (*W*) of $10 per hour, the firm could hire 100 hours of labor and incur total costs of $1,000 if it used no capital (point *A'*). In contrast, if the price of a unit of capital (*C*) is $20, the firm could produce at a total cost of $1,000 by using 50 units of capital and no labor (point *A*). All the points between *A* and *A'* represent combinations of *L* and *K* that, at *W* = $10 and *C* = $20, cost $1,000 as well.

The problem with the isoexpenditure line of *AA'* is that it does not intersect the isoquant *Q**, implying that *Q** cannot be produced for $1,000. At prices of *W* = $10 and *C* = $20, the firm cannot buy enough resources to produce output level *Q** and hold total costs to $1,000. The firm can, however, produce *Q** for a total cost of $2,000. Line *DD'*, representing expenditures of $2,000, intersects the *Q** isoquant at points *X* and *Y*. The problem with these points, however, is that they are not cost-minimizing; *Q** can be produced for less than $2,000.

Since isoquant *Q** is convex, the cost-minimizing combination of *L* and *K* in producing *Q** will come at a point where an isoexpenditure line is *tangent* to the isoquant (that is, just barely touches isoquant *Q** at only one place). Point *Z*, where labor equals *L_Z* and capital equals *K_Z*, is where *Q** can be produced at minimal cost, *given* that *W* = $10 and *C* = $20. No lower isoexpenditure curve touches the isoquant, meaning that *Q** cannot be produced for less than $1,500.

An important characteristic of point *Z* is that the slope of the isoquant at point *Z* and the slope of the isoexpenditure line are the same (the slope of a curve at a given point is the slope of a line tangent to the curve at that point). The slope of the isoquant at any given point is the *marginal rate of technical substitution* as defined in equation (3A.1). Another way of expressing equation (3A.1) is

$$MRTS = \frac{-\Delta K / \Delta Q}{\Delta L / \Delta Q} \tag{3A.2}$$

Equation (3A.2) directly indicates that the *MRTS* is a ratio reflecting the reduction of capital required to *decrease* output by one unit if enough extra labor is hired so that output is tending to *increase* by one unit. (The ΔQs in equation (3A.2) cancel each other and keep output constant.) Pursuing equation (3A.2) one step further, the numerator and denominator can be rearranged to obtain the following:[2]

$$MRTS = \frac{-\Delta K / \Delta Q}{\Delta L / \Delta Q} = -\frac{\Delta Q / \Delta L}{\Delta Q / \Delta K} = -\frac{MP_L}{MP_K} \tag{3A.3}$$

where MP_L and MP_K are the marginal productivities of labor and capital, respectively.

The slope of the *isoexpenditure line* is equal to the negative of the ratio W/C (in Figure 3A.3, W/C equals 10/20, or 0.5).[3] Thus, at point Z, where Q^* is produced in the minimum-cost fashion, the following equality holds:

$$MRTS = -\frac{MP_L}{MP_K} = -\frac{W}{C} \tag{3A.4}$$

Equation (3A.4) is simply a rearranged version of equation (3.8c) in the text.[4]

The economic meaning, or logic, behind the characteristics of cost minimization can most easily be seen by stating the *MRTS* as $-\dfrac{\Delta K / \Delta Q}{\Delta L / \Delta Q}$ (see equation 3A.2) and equating this version of the *MRTS* to $-\dfrac{W}{C}$:

$$-\frac{\Delta K / \Delta Q}{\Delta L / \Delta Q} = -\frac{W}{C} \tag{3A.5}$$

or

$$\frac{\Delta K}{\Delta Q} \cdot C = \frac{\Delta L}{\Delta Q} \cdot W \tag{3A.6}$$

Equation (3A.6) makes it plain that to be minimizing costs, the cost of producing an extra unit of output by adding only labor must equal the cost of producing that extra unit by employing only additional capital. If these costs differed, the

---

[2]This is done by making use of the fact that dividing one number by a second one is equivalent to *multiplying* the first by the *inverse* of the second.
[3]Note that 10/20 = 75/150, or 0B/0B′.
[4]The negative signs on each side of equation (3A.4) cancel each other and can therefore be ignored.

company could reduce total costs by expanding its use of the factor with which output can be increased more cheaply and cutting back on its use of the other factor. Any point where costs can still be reduced while Q is held constant is obviously not a point of cost minimization.

The Substitution Effect

If the wage rate, which was assumed to be $10 per hour in Figure 3A.3, goes up to $20 per hour (holding C constant), what will happen to the cost-minimizing way of producing output of Q^*? Figure 3A.4 illustrates the answer that common sense would suggest: total costs rise, and more capital and less labor are used to produce Q^*. At $W = \$20$, 150 units of labor can no longer be purchased if total costs are to be held to $1,500; in fact, if costs are to equal $1,500, only 75 units of labor can be hired. Thus, the isoexpenditure curve for $1,500 in costs shifts from BB' to BB'' and no longer is tangent to isoquant Q^*. Q^* can no longer be produced for $1,500, and the minimum-cost way of producing Q^* will rise. In Figure 3A.4 we assume that it rises to $2,250 (isoexpenditure line EE' is the one tangent to isoquant Q^*).

Moreover, the increase in the cost of labor relative to capital induces the firm to use more capital and less labor. Graphically, the old tangency point of Z is replaced by a new one (Z'), where the marginal productivity of labor is higher relative to MP_K, as our discussions of equations (3.8c) and (3A.4) explained. Point Z' is reached (from Z) by adding more capital and reducing employment of labor. The movement from L_Z to L'_Z is the *substitution effect* generated by the wage increase.

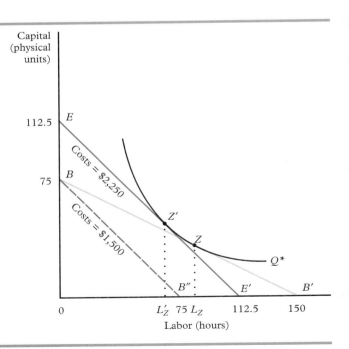

FIGURE 3A.4
Cost Minimization in the Production of Q^* (Wage = $20 per Hour; Price of a Unit of Capital = $20)

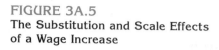

FIGURE 3A.5
The Substitution and Scale Effects of a Wage Increase

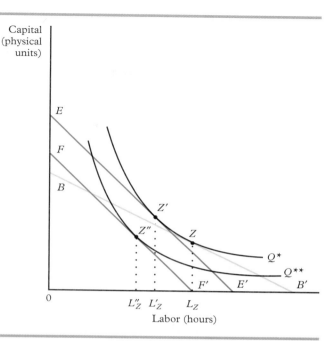

The Scale Effect

The fact that Q^* can no longer be produced for $1,500, but instead involves at least $2,250 in costs, will generally mean that it is no longer the profit-maximizing level of production. The new profit-maximizing level of production will be less than Q^* (how much less cannot be determined unless we know something about the product demand curve).

Suppose that the profit-maximizing level of output falls from Q^* to Q^{**}, as shown in Figure 3A.5. Since all isoexpenditure lines have the new slope of -1 when $W = 20 and $C = 20, the cost-minimizing way to produce Q^{**} will lie on an isoexpenditure line parallel to EE'. We find this cost-minimizing way to produce Q^{**} at point Z'', where an isoexpenditure line (FF') is tangent to the Q^{**} isoquant.

The *overall* response in the employment of labor to an increase in the wage rate has been a fall in labor usage from L_Z to L''_Z. The decline from L_Z to L'_Z is called the substitution effect, as we have noted. It results because the *proportions* of K and L used in production change when the ratio of wages to capital prices (W/C) changes. The *scale effect* can be seen as the reduction in employment from L'_Z to L''_Z, wherein the usage of both K and L is cut back solely because of the reduced *scale* of production. Both effects are simultaneously present when wages increase and capital prices remain constant, but as Figure 3A.5 emphasizes, the effects are conceptually distinct and occur for different reasons. Together, these effects lead us to assert that the long-run labor demand curve slopes downward.

4

LABOR DEMAND ELASTICITIES

I n 1995 a heated debate broke out among economists and policymakers about the employment effects of minimum wage laws. Clearly, the standard theory developed in chapter 3 predicts that if wages are raised above their market level by a minimum wage law, employment opportunities will be reduced as firms move up (and to the left) along their labor demand curves. Two prominent labor economists, however, after reviewing previous work on the subject and doing new studies of their own, published a 1995 book in which they concluded that the predicted job losses associated with increases in the minimum wage simply could not be observed to occur, at least with any regularity.[1] On one level, the findings in this book raised a controversy about the usefulness of standard labor demand theory. Those who found the book and related research persuasive called for the use of new labor demand models (especially ones that are monopsony-like in character), while others argued that the new

---

[1]David Card and Alan B. Krueger, *Myth and Measurement: The New Economics of the Minimum Wage* (Princeton, N.J.: Princeton University Press, 1995).

studies in this book were flawed and confidently asserted that appropriately executed studies would yield the results predicted by standard theory.[2]

On another level, however, the 1995 book simply triggered a highly charged discussion of a long-standing question: just how responsive is employment demand to given changes in wages? Hardly anyone doubts that jobs would be lost if mandated wage increases were huge, but how many are lost with modest increases? One economist framed the issue in this way:

> Economists ... are divided into two basic groups. On one side are those who believe that responses to price incentives are usually large—the Big Responders (BRs). On the other side are those who believe that responses to price incentives are generally small—Small Responders (SRs).... Logic tells us that massive changes in prices ... will have large effects on quantities.... But *whether the BR or SR perspective applies to minimum wages in the range observed in the United States is a purely empirical question*.[3]

The focus of this chapter is on the degree to which employment responds to changes in wages. Put in the context of the above quotation, this chapter will analyze both theory and evidence in the Big Responder–Small Responder debate.

The responsiveness of labor demand to a change in wage rates is normally measured as an *elasticity,* which is the percentage change in employment brought about by a 1 percent change in wages. We begin our analysis by defining, analyzing, and measuring *own-wage* and *cross-wage* elasticities. We then apply these concepts to analyses of minimum wage laws and the employment effects of technological innovations. (Because the effects of free trade on the demand for labor are qualitatively similar to those of technological change, we analyze the employment effects of free trade in the appendix to this chapter.)

THE OWN-WAGE ELASTICITY OF DEMAND

The *own-wage elasticity of demand* for a category of labor is defined as the percentage change in its employment (E) induced by a 1 percent increase in its wage rate (W):

$$\eta_{ii} = \frac{\%\Delta E_i}{\%\Delta W_i} \tag{4.1}$$

---

[2]Six reviews of Card and Krueger, *Myth and Measurement,* appear in the book review section of the July 1995 issue of *Industrial and Labor Relations Review* 48, no. 4. These reviews give an excellent overview of the range of responses to the Card and Krueger book. A more recent review of findings and issues surrounding them can be found in Richard V. Burkhauser, Kenneth A. Couch, and David C. Wittenburg, "A Reassessment of the New Economics of the Minimum Wage Literature with Monthly Data from the Current Population Survey," *Journal of Labor Economics* 18, no. 4 (October 2000): 653–680.

[3]Richard Freeman, "Comment," *Industrial and Labor Relations Review* 48, no. 4 (July 1995): 830–831.

In equation (4.1), we have used the subscript i to denote category of labor i, the Greek letter η (eta) to represent elasticity, and the notation %Δ to represent "percentage change in." Since the previous chapter showed that labor demand curves slope downward, an increase in the wage rate will cause employment to decrease; the own-wage elasticity of demand is therefore a negative number. What is at issue is its magnitude. The larger its *absolute value* (its magnitude, ignoring its sign), the larger will be the percentage decline in employment associated with any given percentage increase in wages.

Labor economists often focus on whether the absolute value of the elasticity of demand for labor is greater than or less than 1. If it is greater than 1, a 1 percent increase in wages will lead to an employment decline of greater than 1 percent; this situation is referred to as an *elastic* demand curve. In contrast, if the absolute value is less than 1, the demand curve is said to be *inelastic:* a 1 percent increase in wages will lead to a proportionately smaller decline in employment. If demand is elastic, aggregate earnings (defined here as the wage rate times the employment level) of individuals in the category will decline when the wage rate increases, because employment falls at a faster rate than wages rise. Conversely, if demand is inelastic, aggregate earnings will increase when the wage rate is increased. If the elasticity just equals –1, the demand curve is said to be *unitary elastic,* and aggregate earnings will remain unchanged if wages increase.

Figure 4.1 shows that the flatter of the two demand curves graphed (D_1) has greater elasticity than the steeper (D_2). Beginning with any wage (W, for example), a given wage change (to W', say) will yield greater responses in employment with demand curve D_1 than with D_2. To judge the different elasticities of response brought about by the same percentage wage increase, compare $(E_1 - E'_1)/E_1$ with $(E_2 - E'_2)/E_2$. Clearly, the more elastic response occurs along D_1.

To speak of a demand curve as having "an" elasticity, however, is technically incorrect. Given "specific demand curves" will generally have elastic and inelastic ranges—and while we are usually interested only in the elasticity of demand in

FIGURE 4.1
Relative Demand Elasticities

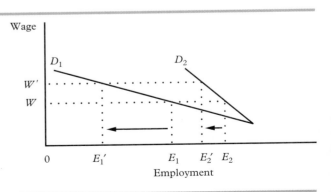

the range around the current wage rate in any market, we cannot fully understand elasticity without comprehending that it can vary along a given demand curve.

To illustrate, suppose we examine the typical straight-line demand curve that we have used so often in chapters 2 and 3 (see Figure 4.2). One feature of a straight-line demand curve is that, at *each* point along the curve, a unit change in wages induces the *same* response in terms of units of employment. For example, at any point along the demand curve shown in Figure 4.2, a $2 decrease in wages will increase employment by 10 workers.

However, the same responses in terms of *unit* changes along the demand curve do *not* imply equal *percentage* changes. To see this point, look first at the upper end of the demand curve in Figure 4.2 (the end where wages are high and employment is low). A $2 decrease in wages when the base is $12 represents a 17 percent reduction in wages, while an addition of 10 workers when the starting point is also 10 represents a 100 percent increase in demand. Demand at this point is clearly *elastic*. However, if we look at the same unit changes in the lower region of the demand curve (low wages, high employment), demand there is inelastic. A $2 reduction in wages from a $4 base is a 50 percent reduction, while an increase of 10 workers from a base of 50 is only a 20 percent increase. Since the percentage increase in employment is smaller than the percentage decrease in wages, demand is seen to be inelastic at this end of the curve.

Thus, the upper end of a straight-line demand curve will exhibit greater elasticity than the lower end. Moreover, a straight-line demand curve will actually be elastic in some ranges and inelastic in others (as shown in Figure 4.2).

FIGURE 4.2
Different Elasticities along a Demand Curve

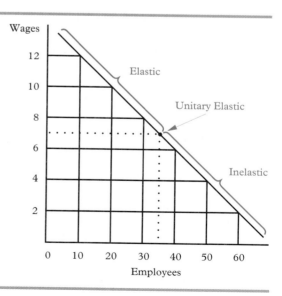

The Hicks-Marshall Laws of Derived Demand

The factors that influence own-wage elasticity can be summarized by the Hicks-Marshall laws of derived demand—four laws named after the two distinguished British economists, John Hicks and Alfred Marshall, who are closely associated with their development.[4] These laws assert that, other things equal, the own-wage elasticity of demand for a category of labor is high under the following conditions:

1. When the price elasticity of demand for the product being produced is high;
2. When other factors of production can be easily substituted for the category of labor;
3. When the supply of other factors of production is highly elastic (that is, usage of other factors of production can be increased without substantially increasing their prices); and
4. When the cost of employing the category of labor is a large share of the total costs of production.

Not only are these laws generally valid as an empirical proposition, but the first three can be shown to always hold. There are conditions, however, under which the final law does not hold.

In seeking to explain why these laws hold, it is useful to act as if we could divide the process by which an increase in the wage rate affects the demand for labor into two steps: First, an increase in the wage rate increases the relative cost of the category of labor in question and induces employers to use less of it and more of other inputs (the *substitution effect*). Second, when the wage increase causes the marginal costs of production to rise, there are pressures to increase product prices and reduce output, causing a fall in employment (the *scale effect*). The four laws of derived demand each deal with substitution or scale effects.

Demand for the Final Product   We noted above that wage increases cause production costs to rise and tend to result in product price increases. The greater the price elasticity of demand for the final product, the larger will be the decline in output associated with a given increase in price—and the greater the decrease in output, the greater the loss in employment (other things equal). Thus, *the greater the elasticity of demand for the product, the greater the elasticity of demand for labor will be.*

One implication of this first law is that, other things equal, the demand for labor at the *firm* level will be more elastic than the demand for labor at the *industry*, or market, level. For example, the product demand curves facing *individual* carpet-manufacturing companies are highly elastic because the carpet of company X is a very close substitute for the carpet of company Y. Compared with price increases at the *firm* level, however, price increases at the *industry* level will not have

---

[4]John R. Hicks, *The Theory of Wages,* 2d ed. (New York: St. Martin's Press, 1966), 241–247; and Alfred Marshall, *Principles of Economics,* 8th ed. (London: Macmillan, 1923), 518–538.

as large an effect on demand because the closest substitutes for carpeting are hardwood, ceramic, or some kind of vinyl floor covering—none a very close substitute for carpeting. (For the same reasons, the labor demand curve for a monopolist is less elastic than for an individual *firm* in a competitive industry. Monopolists, after all, face *market* demand curves for their product because they are the only seller in the particular market.)

Another implication of this first law is that *wage elasticities will be higher in the long run than in the short run.* The reason for this is that price elasticities of demand in product markets are higher in the long run. In the short run there may be no good substitutes for a product, or consumers may be locked into their current stock of consumer durables. After a period of time, however, new products that are substitutes may be introduced and consumers will begin to replace durables that have worn out.

Substitutability of Other Factors   As the wage rate of a category of labor increases, firms have an incentive to try to substitute other, now relatively cheaper, inputs for the category. Suppose, however, that there were no substitution possibilities; a given number of units of the type of labor *must* be used to produce one unit of output. In this case, there is no reduction in employment due to the substitution effect. In contrast, when substitution possibilities do present themselves, a reduction in employment owing to the substitution effect will accompany whatever reductions are caused by the scale effect. Hence, other things equal, *the easier it is to substitute other factors of production, the higher the wage elasticity of labor demand will be.*

Limitations on substitution possibilities need not be solely technical ones. For example, as we shall see in chapter 13, unions often try to limit substitution possibilities by including specific work rules in their contracts (e.g., minimum crew size for railroad locomotives). Alternatively, the government may legislate limitations by specifying minimum employment levels for safety reasons (e.g., each public swimming pool in New York State must always have a lifeguard present). Such restrictions make the demand for labor less elastic, but substitution possibilities that are not feasible in the short run may well become feasible over longer periods of time. For example, if the wages of railroad workers went up, companies could buy more powerful locomotives and operate with larger trains and fewer locomotives. Likewise, if the wages of lifeguards rose, cities might build larger, but fewer, swimming pools. Both adjustments would occur only in the long run, which is another reason why the demand for labor is more elastic in the long run than in the short run.

The Supply of Other Factors   Suppose that, as the wage rate increased and employers attempted to substitute other factors of production for labor, the prices of these inputs were bid up substantially. This situation might occur, for example, if we were trying to substitute capital equipment for labor. If producers of capital equipment were already operating their plants near capacity, so that taking on new orders would cause them substantial increases in costs because they would have to work their employees overtime and pay them a wage premium, they would accept new orders only if they could charge a higher price for their equipment. Such a price increase would dampen firms' "appetites" for capital and thus limit the substitution of capital for labor.

For another example, suppose an increase in the wages of unskilled workers caused employers to attempt to substitute skilled employees for unskilled employees. If there were only a fixed number of skilled workers in an area, their wages would be bid up by employers. As in the prior example, the incentive to substitute alternative factors would be reduced, and the reduction in unskilled employment due to the substitution effect would be smaller. In contrast, if the prices of other inputs did not increase when employers attempted to increase their use, other things equal, the substitution effect—and thus the wage elasticity of demand—would be larger.

Note again that prices of other inputs are less likely to be bid up in the long run than in the short run. In the long run, existing producers of capital equipment can expand their capacity and new producers can enter the market. Similarly, in the long run more skilled workers can be trained. This observation is an additional reason why the demand for labor will be more elastic in the long run.

The Share of Labor in Total Costs   Finally, the share of the category of labor in total costs is crucial to the size of the elasticity of labor demand. If the category's initial share were 20 percent, a 10 percent increase in the wage rate, other things equal, would raise total costs by 2 percent. In contrast, if its initial share were 80 percent, a 10 percent increase in the wage rate would increase total costs by 8 percent. Since employers would have to increase their product prices by more in the latter case, output and employment would fall more in that case. *Thus, the greater the category's share in total costs, the higher the wage elasticity of demand will tend to be.*[5]

Estimates of Own-Wage Labor Demand Elasticities

We now turn to the results of studies that estimate own-wage demand elasticities for labor as a generic input (that is, labor undifferentiated by skill level). The estimates we discuss are based on studies that utilize wage, output, and employment data from firms or narrowly defined industries. Thus, the employment responses being estimated approximate those that would be expected to occur in a firm that had to raise wages to remain competitive in the labor market. These estimates are

---

[5]An exception to the law occurs when it is easier for employers to substitute other factors of production for the category of labor than it is for customers to substitute other products for the product being produced; in this case the law is reversed. An example illustrates this exception. Suppose we classify the carpenters who build houses by their race/ethnicity. For example, we might divide carpenters into African-, Asian-, German-, Hispanic-, Irish-, and Italian-American carpenters. Suppose further that carpenters from each group are perfect substitutes for each other. If any one group's wages rose, construction contractors could easily substitute employment of other carpenters for the group's members. Thus, the demand for any one group of carpenters would be highly elastic despite its small share in total cost. In contrast, the demand for all carpenters (taken together) would be less elastic, as long as the price elasticity of the demand for houses was not high. Put another way, even a relatively small share in total cost cannot "protect" inputs with very good substitutes; their wage elasticities of demand will tend to be elastic. See George J. Stigler, *The Theory of Price*, 4th ed. (New York: Macmillan, 1987), 254.

TABLE 4.1   **Components of the Own-Wage Elasticity of Demand for Labor: Empirical Estimates Using Plant-Level Data**

	Estimated Elasticity
Short-Run Scale Effect	
British manufacturing firms, 1974–1982	−0.53
Substitution Effect	
32 studies using plant or narrowly defined industry data	Average: −0.45 (Typical range: −0.15 to −0.75)
Overall Labor Demand Elasticity	
British plants, 1984	−0.93
British coal mines, 1950–1980	−1.0 to −1.4

Source: Daniel S. Hamermesh, *Labor Demand* (Princeton, N.J.: Princeton University Press, 1993), 94–104.

suggestive of what might be a "typical" response, but of course are not indicative of what would happen with any particular firm.

As our analysis has indicated, employers' labor demand responses to a wage change can be broken down into two components: a scale effect and a substitution effect. These two effects can themselves be expressed as elasticities, and their sum is the own-wage labor demand elasticity. In Table 4.1 we display the results of estimates of (a) the short-run scale effect, (b) the substitution effect, and (c) the overall elasticity of demand for labor in the long run.

The scale effect (expressed as an elasticity) is defined as the percentage change in employment associated with a given percentage change in the wage, *holding production technology constant;* that is, it is the employment response that occurs without a substitution effect. By definition, the *short-run* labor demand elasticity includes *only* the scale effect, although we noted earlier that the scale effect is likely to be greater in the long run than it is in the short run (owing to greater possibilities for *product market* substitutions in the long run). Therefore, estimates of short-run labor demand elasticities will be synonymous with the short-run scale effect, which may approximate the long-run scale effect if product market substitutions are relatively swift. A study using data from British manufacturing plants estimated the short-run, own-wage labor demand elasticity to be −0.53 (see Table 4.1). The short-run labor demand curve for a typical firm or narrowly defined sector, therefore, would appear to be inelastic.

The substitution effect, when expressed as an elasticity, is the percentage change in employment associated with a given percentage change in the wage rate, *holding output constant.* That is, it is a measure of how employers change their production techniques in response to wage changes, even if output does not change (that is, even if the scale effect is absent). It happens that substitution effects are easier to credibly estimate, so there are many more studies of these effects. One careful summary of 32 studies estimating substitution-effect elasticities placed the average estimated elasticity at –0.45 (which is what is displayed in Table 4.1), with most estimates falling into the range of –0.15 to –0.75.[6]

With the short-run scale elasticity and the substitution elasticity each very close to –0.5, it is not surprising that estimates of the long-run overall elasticity of demand for labor are close to unitary in magnitude. Table 4.1 indicates that a study of plants across several British industries estimated an own-wage elasticity of –0.93, whereas another of British coal mines placed the elasticity of demand for labor in the range of –1.0 to –1.4. Thus, these estimates suggest that if the wages a firm must pay rise by 10 percent, the firm's employment will shrink by close to 10 percent in the long run, other things being equal (that is, unless something else occurs that also affects the demand for labor).

Applying the Laws of Derived Demand: Inferential Analysis

Because empirical estimates of demand elasticities that may be required for making particular decisions are often lacking, it is frequently necessary to guess what these elasticities are likely to be. In making these guesses, we can apply the laws of derived demand to predict at least relative magnitudes for various types of labor. Consider first the demand for unionized New York City garment workers. As we shall discuss in chapter 13, because unions are complex organizations, it is not always possible to specify what their goals are. Nevertheless, it is clear that most unions value both wage *and* employment opportunities for their members. This observation leads to the simple prediction that, other things equal, the more elastic the demand for labor, the smaller will be the wage gain that a union will succeed in winning for its members. The reason for this prediction is that the more elastic the demand curve, the greater will be the percentage employment decline associated with any given percentage increase in wages. As a result, we can expect the following:

1. Unions would win larger wage gains for their members in markets with inelastic labor demand curves;
2. Unions would strive to take actions that reduce the wage elasticity of demand for their members' services; and
3. Unions might first seek to organize workers in markets in which labor demand curves are inelastic (because the potential gains to unionization are higher in these markets).

Because of foreign competition, the price elasticity of demand for the clothing produced by New York City garment workers is extremely high. Furthermore, employers can easily find other inputs to substitute for these workers—namely, lower-paid nonunion garment workers in the South (this substitution would require moving the plant to the South, a strategy that many manufacturers have followed).

---

[6]Daniel Hamermesh, *Labor Demand* (Princeton, N.J.: Princeton University Press, 1993), 103.

These facts lead one to predict that the wage elasticity of demand for New York City unionized garment workers is very high. Consequently, its wage demands historically have been moderate. It has also sought to reduce the elasticity of product demand by supporting policies that reduce foreign competition, and it has pushed for higher federal minimum wages in order to reduce employers' incentives to move their plants to the South. (For another illustration of how an elastic *product* demand inhibits union wage increases, see Example 4.1.)

Next, consider the wage elasticity of demand for unionized airplane pilots in the United States. Only a small share of the costs of operating large airplanes goes to pay pilots' salaries; such salaries are dwarfed by fuel and capital costs. Furthermore, substitution possibilities are limited; there is little room to substitute unskilled labor for skilled labor (although airlines can substitute capital for labor by reducing the number of flights they offer while increasing the size of airplanes). In addition, before the deregulation of the airline industry in 1978, many airlines faced no competition on many of their routes or were prohibited from reducing their prices to compete with other airlines that flew the same routes. These factors all suggest that the wage elasticity of demand for airline pilots was quite low (inelastic). As one might expect, pilots' wages were also quite high because their union could push for large wage increases without fear that these increases would substantially reduce pilots' employment levels. However, after airline deregulation, competition among airline carriers increased substantially, leading to a more elastic labor demand for pilots. As a result, many airlines "requested," and won, reduced wages from their pilots.

THE CROSS-WAGE ELASTICITY OF DEMAND

Because firms may employ several categories of labor and capital, the demand for any one category can be affected by price changes in the others. For example, if the wages of carpenters rose, more people might build brick homes and the demand for *masons* might increase. An increase in carpenters' wages might decrease the overall level of home building in the economy, however, which would decrease the demand for *plumbers*. Finally, changes in the price of *capital* could increase or decrease the demand for workers in all three trades.

The direction and magnitude of the above effects can be summarized by examining the elasticities of demand for inputs with respect to the prices of *other* inputs. The *elasticity of demand for input j with respect to the price of input k* is the percentage change in the demand for input j induced by a 1 percent change in the price of input k. If the two inputs are both categories of labor, these *cross-wage elasticities of demand* are given by

$$\eta_{jk} = \frac{\%\Delta E_j}{\%\Delta W_k} \tag{4.2}$$

and

$$\eta_{kj} = \frac{\%\Delta E_k}{\%\Delta W_j}$$

EXAMPLE 4.1

Why Are Union Wages So Different in Two Parts of the Trucking Industry?

The trucking industry's "general freight" sector, made up of motor carriers that handle nonspecialized freight requiring no special handling or equipment, is split into two distinct segments. One type of general freight carrier exclusively handles full truckloads, taking them directly from a shipper to a destination. The other type of carrier handles less-than-truckload shipments, which involve multiple shipments on each truck and an intricate coordination of pickups and deliveries. These two segments of the general freight industry have vastly different *elasticities of product demand,* and thus the union that represents truck drivers has a very different ability to raise wages (without suffering unacceptable losses of employment) in each segment.

The full-truckload (TL) part of the industry has a product market that is very competitive, because it is relatively easy for firms or individuals to enter the market; one needs only a truck, the proper driver's license, and access to a telephone (to call a freight broker, who matches available drivers with shipments needing delivery). Because this part of the industry has many competing firms, with the threat of even more if prices rise, each firm faces a relatively elastic product demand curve.

Firms specializing in less-than-truckload (LTL) shipments must have a complex system of coordinated routes running between and within cities, and they must therefore be sufficiently large to support their own terminals for storing and transferring shipments from one route to another. The LTL segment of the industry is not easily entered and thus is partially monopolized. From 1980 to 1995—a time period over which the number of TL carriers tripled—virtually the only new entrants into the LTL market were regional subsidiaries of preexisting national carriers! To contrast competition in the two product markets somewhat differently, in 1987 the four largest LTL carriers accounted for 37 per-

cent of total LTL revenues, while the four largest TL carriers accounted for only 11 percent of TL revenues.

The greater extent of competition in the TL part of the industry implies that, at the firm level, *product* demand is more elastic there than in the LTL sector; other things being equal, then, we would expect the *labor* demand curve also to be more elastic in the TL sector. Because unions worry about potential job losses when negotiating with carriers about wages, we would expect to find that union wages are lower in the TL than in the LTL part of the industry. In fact, a 1991 survey revealed that the union mileage rates (drivers are typically compensated on a cents-per-mile basis) were dramatically different in the two sectors:

TL sector

Average union rate: 28.4 cents per mile
Ratio, union to nonunion rate: 1.23

LTL sector

Average union rate: 35.8 cents per mile
Ratio, union to nonunion rate: 1.34

The above data support the theoretical implication that a union's power to raise wages is greater when product (and therefore labor) demand is relatively inelastic. In the less-competitive LTL segment of the trucking industry, union drivers' wages are higher, both absolutely and relative to nonunion wages, than they are in the more competitive TL sector.

Data from: Michael H. Belzer, "Collective Bargaining after Deregulation: Do the Teamsters Still Count?" *Industrial and Labor Relations Review* 48, no. 4 (July 1995): 636–655; and Michael H. Belzer, *Paying the Toll: Economic Deregulation of the Trucking Industry* (Washington, D.C.: Economic Policy Institute, 1994).

where, again, the Greek letter η is used to represent the elasticity. If the cross-elasticities are positive (with an increase in the price of one "category" increasing the demand for the other), the two are said to be *gross substitutes*. If these cross-elasticities are negative (and an increase in the price of one "category" reduces the demand for the other), the two are said to be *gross complements* (refer back to Figure 3.3).

It is worth restressing that whether two inputs are gross substitutes or gross complements depends on the relative sizes of the scale and substitution effects. To see this, suppose we assume that adults and teenagers are substitutes in production. A decrease in the teenage wage will thus have opposing effects on adult employment. On the one hand, there is a substitution effect: for a given level of output, employers will now have an incentive to substitute teens for adults in the production process and reduce adult employment. On the other hand, there is a scale effect: a lower teenage wage provides employers with an incentive to increase employment of all inputs, including adults.

If the scale effect proves to be smaller than the substitution effect, adult employment will move in the same direction as teenage wages and the two groups will be gross substitutes. In contrast, if the scale effect is larger than the substitution effect, adult employment and teenage wages will move in opposite directions and the two groups will be gross complements. Knowing that two groups are substitutes in production, then, is not sufficient to tell us whether they are gross substitutes or gross complements.[7]

Because economic theory cannot indicate in advance whether two given inputs will be gross substitutes or gross complements, the major policy questions about cross-wage elasticities of demand relate to the issue of their *sign*; that is, we often want most to know whether a particular cross-elasticity is positive or negative. Before turning to a review of actual findings, we analyze underlying forces that determine the signs of cross-elasticities.

Can the Laws of Derived Demand Be Applied to Cross-Elasticities?

The Hicks-Marshall laws of derived demand are based on four technological or market conditions that determine the size of *own-wage* elasticities. Each of the four conditions influences the substitution or the scale effect and, as noted above, the relative strengths of these two effects are also what determine the sign of *cross-elasticities*. The laws that apply to own-wage elasticities cannot be applied directly to cross-elasticities, because with cross-elasticities the substitution effect (if there is one) and the scale effect work in opposite directions. The same underlying considerations, however, are basic to an analysis of cross-elasticities.

As we discuss these four considerations in the context of cross-elasticities, it will be helpful to have an example in mind. Let us return, therefore, to the question of what might happen to the demand for adult workers if the wages of teenage workers were to fall. As noted above, the answer depends on the relative strengths of the scale and substitution effects. What determines the strength of each?

---

[7]As noted in chapter 3, if two groups are complements in production, a decrease in the price of one should lead to increased employment of the other. Complements in production are always gross complements.

The Scale Effect   The most immediate effect of a fall in the wages of teenagers would be reduced production costs for those firms that employ them. Competition in the product market would ensure that lower costs are followed by price reductions, which should stimulate increases in both product demand and the level of output. Increased levels of output will tend to cause increases in employment of all kinds of workers, including adults. This chain of events obviously describes behavior underlying the scale effect, and we now investigate what conditions are likely to make for a strong (or weak) scale effect.

The initial cost (and price) reductions would be greater among those employers for whom teenage wages constituted a higher proportion of total costs. Other things equal, greater price reductions would result in greater increases in both product demand and overall employment. Thus, *the share of total costs devoted to the productive factor whose price is changing* will influence the size of the scale effect. The larger this share is, other things equal, the greater will be the scale effect (and the more likely it is that gross complementarity will exist). This tendency is analogous to the fourth Hicks-Marshall law discussed earlier; the difference is that with cross-elasticities, the factor whose *price* is changing is not the same as the one for which *employment* changes are being analyzed.

The other condition that greatly influences the size of the scale effect is product demand elasticity. In the above case of teenage wage reductions, the greater the increase in product demand when firms reduce their prices, the greater will be the tendency for employment of all workers, including adults, to increase. More generally, *the greater the price elasticity of product demand, other things equal, the greater will be the scale effect (and thus the greater the likelihood of gross complementarity).* The effects of product demand elasticity are thus similar for both own-wage and cross-wage elasticities.

The Substitution Effect   After teenage wages fall, firms will also have incentives to alter their production techniques so that teenagers are more heavily used. Whether the greater use of teenagers causes an increase or some loss of adult jobs partially depends on a technological question: are teenagers and adults substitutes or complements in production? If they are complements in production, the effect on adults of changing productive techniques will reinforce the scale effect and serve to unambiguously increase adult employment (meaning, of course, that adults and teenagers would be gross complements). If they are substitutes in production, however, then changing productive techniques involves using a higher ratio of teenagers to adults, and the question then becomes whether this substitution effect is large or small relative to the scale effect.

A technological condition affecting the size of the substitution effect is a direct carryover from the second Hicks-Marshall law discussed previously: *the substitution effect will be greater when the category of labor whose price has changed is easily substituted for other factors of production.* When analyzing the effects on adult employment of a decline in the teenage wage, it is evident that when teenagers are more easily substituted for adults, the substitution effect (and therefore the chances of gross substitutability between the two categories of labor) will be greater.

Another condition influencing the size of the substitution effect associated with a reduction in the teenage wage relates to the labor supply curve of adults. If the adult labor supply curve were upward-sloping and rather steep, then adult wages would tend to fall as teenagers were substituted for adults and the demand curve for adults shifted left. This fall would blunt the substitution effect, because adults would also become cheaper to hire. Conversely, if the adult labor supply curve were relatively flat, adult wages would be less affected by reduced demand and the substitution effect would be less blunted. As in the case of own-wage elasticities, *more-elastic supply curves of substitute inputs also lead to a greater substitution effect, other things equal, in the case of cross-wage elasticities.*[8]

Estimates Relating to Cross-Elasticities

Estimating at least the sign of cross-wage labor demand elasticities is useful for evaluating public policies, because a policy aimed at one group can have unintended consequences for other groups. For example, a policy to subsidize the wages of teenagers could reduce employers' demand for adult workers. Thus, it is important to know which categories of labor and capital are substitutes for or complements with each other in the production process. Also, we would like to know whether particular categories of labor exhibit *gross* substitutability or complementarity with each other or with capital.

Most of the cross-wage empirical studies to date have focused on the issue of whether two factors are substitutes or complements in production. These studies estimate the employment response for one category of labor to a wage or price change elsewhere, *holding output constant* (which in effect allows us to focus just on changes in the *mix* of factors used in production). The factors of production paired together for analysis in these studies are numerous and the results are not always clear-cut; nevertheless, the findings taken as a whole offer at least a few generalizations:[9]

1. Labor and energy are clearly substitutes in production, although their degree of substitutability is small. Labor and materials are probably substitutes in production, with the degree of substitutability again being small.
2. Skilled and unskilled labor are probably substitutes in production.[10]

---

[8]The share of the teenage wage bill in total costs influences the substitution effect as well as the scale effect in the example we are analyzing. For example, if teenage labor costs were a very large fraction of total costs, the possibilities for further substitution of teenagers for adults would be rather limited (this can be easily seen by considering an example in which teenagers constituted 100 percent of all production costs). Thus, while a larger share of teenagers in total cost would make for a relatively large scale effect, it also could reflect a situation in which the possibilities of substituting teenagers for adults are smaller than they would otherwise be.

[9]Hamermesh, *Labor Demand*, 105–127.

[10]James D. Adams, "The Structure of Firm R & D, the Factor Intensity of Production, and Skill Bias," *Review of Economics and Statistics* 81, no. 3 (August 1999): 499–510.

3. We are not certain whether either skilled or unskilled labor is a substitute for or a complement with capital in the production process. What does appear to be true is that skilled (or well-educated) labor is more likely to be complementary with capital than is unskilled labor—and that if they are both substitutes for capital, the degree of substitutability is smaller for skilled labor.[11]

4. The finding summarized in 3 above suggests that skilled labor is more likely than unskilled labor to be a *gross* complement with capital. This finding is important to our understanding of recent trends in the earnings of skilled and unskilled workers (see chapter 14), because the prices of computers and other high-tech capital goods have fallen dramatically in the past decade or two.

5. The finding in 3 above also implies that if the wages of both skilled and unskilled labor were to rise by the same percentage, the magnitude of any employment loss associated with the substitution effect (as capital is substituted for labor) will be greater for the unskilled. Thus, we expect that, other things equal, *own-wage* labor demand elasticities will be larger in magnitude for unskilled than for skilled workers.

POLICY APPLICATION: EFFECTS OF MINIMUM WAGE LAWS

History and Description

The Fair Labor Standards Act of 1938 was the first major piece of protective labor legislation adopted at the national level in the United States. Among its provisions were a minimum wage rate, below which hourly wages could not be reduced, an overtime-pay premium for workers who worked long workweeks, and restrictions on the use of child labor. When initially adopted, the minimum wage was set at $0.25 an hour and covered roughly 43 percent of all nonsupervisory wage and salary workers—primarily those employed in larger firms involved in interstate commerce (manufacturing, mining, and construction). Both the basic minimum wage and coverage under the minimum wage have expanded over time. Indeed, after September 1997, the minimum wage was set at $5.15 an hour and over 70 percent of all nonsupervisory workers were covered by its provisions.

---

[11]Evidence has been offered that the degree of substitutability depends on the age of capital equipment. Specifically, Ann Bartel and Frank Lichtenberg, "Technology: Some Empirical Evidence," *Review of Economics and Statistics* 69 (February 1987): 1–11, present evidence that the relative demand for highly educated workers vis-à-vis less-educated workers declines as the capital stock ages. They attribute this to the comparative advantage that highly educated workers have with respect to learning and implementing new technologies; thus as the capital stock ages, the complementarity of these workers with capital declines.

FIGURE 4.3

Federal Minimum Wage: Level, and Relative to Wages in Manufacturing, 1938-2000

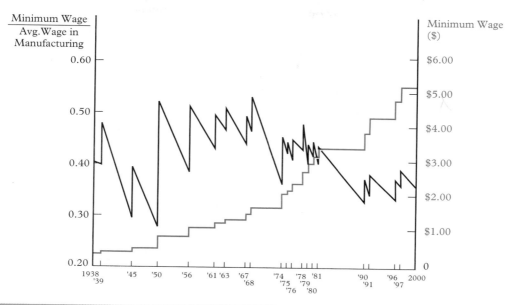

It is important to emphasize that the minimum wage rate is specified in *nominal* terms and not in terms *relative* to some other wage or price index. As illustrated by Figure 4.3, the nominal wage rate usually has been raised only once every few years. Until the early 1980s, newly legislated minimum wage rates were typically at least 45 percent of the average hourly wage in manufacturing. During the years between legislation, productivity growth and inflation caused manufacturing wages to rise, with the result that the minimum wage has often fallen by 10 or more percentage points relative to the manufacturing wage before being raised again. In the last two decades, even the newly legislated minimums have been below 40 percent of the average manufacturing wage.

Employment Effects: Theoretical Analysis

Since the minimum wage was first legislated, a concern has been that it will reduce employment, especially among the groups it is intended to benefit. In the face of downward-sloping labor demand curves, a policy that compels firms to raise the wages paid to all low-wage workers can be expected to *reduce employment opportunities* for the least skilled or least experienced. Further, if the percentage loss of employment among low-wage workers is greater than the percentage increase in their wages—that is, if the demand curve for low-wage workers is *elastic*—then the *aggregate* earnings of low-wage workers could be made smaller by an increase in the minimum wage.

In evaluating the findings of research on the employment effects of minimum wages, we must keep in mind that good research has to be guided by good theory. Theory provides us with a road map that directs our explorations into the real world, and it suggests several issues that must be addressed by any research study of the minimum wage.

Nominal versus Real Wages   Minimum wage levels in the United States have been set in nominal terms and adjusted by Congress only sporadically. The result is that general price inflation gradually lowers the real minimum wage during the years between congressional action, so what appears to be a fixed minimum wage turns out to have constantly changing incentives for employment. Recall that the demand for labor is a downward-sloping function of real wages, so as the real minimum wage falls from the point when it is newly enacted to just before it is raised again, its adverse effects on employment can be expected to decline.

Also, the federal minimum wage in the United States is uniformly applied to a large country characterized by regional differences in prices. Taking account of regional differences in prices or wages, we find that the real minimum wage in Alaska (where wages and prices are very high) is lower than it is in Mississippi. Recognizing that there are regional differences in the real minimum wage leads to the prediction that employment effects of a uniformly applied minimum wage law generally will be most adverse in regions with the lowest costs of living. (Researchers must also take into account the fact that many states have their own minimum wage laws, some having minimums that exceed the federal minimum.)

Holding Other Things Constant   Predictions of job loss associated with higher minimum wages are made *holding other things constant*. In particular, the prediction grows out of what is expected to happen to employment as we move up and to the left along a *fixed* labor demand curve. If the labor demand curve were to shift at the same time that a new minimum becomes effective, the employment effects of the shift could be confounded with those of the new minimum.

Consider, for example, Figure 4.4, where for simplicity we have omitted the labor supply curve and focused on only the demand side of the market. Suppose that D_0 is the demand curve for low-skilled labor in year 0, in which year the real wage is W_0/P_0 and the employment level is E_0. Further assume that in the absence of any change in the minimum wage, the money wage and the price level would both increase by the same percentage over the next year, so that the real wage in year 1 (W_1/P_1) would be the same as that in year 0.

Now suppose that in year 1, two things happen. First, the minimum wage rate is raised to W_2, which is greater than W_1, so that the real wage increases to W_2/P_1. Second, because the economy is expanding, the demand for low-skilled labor shifts out to D_1. The result of these two changes is that employment increases from E_0 to E_1.

FIGURE 4.4
Minimum Wage Effects:
Growing Demand Obscures
Job Loss

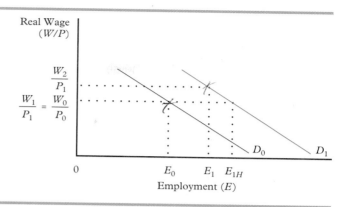

Comparisons of observed employment levels at two points of time have led some investigators to conclude that minimum wage increases had no adverse employment effects. However, this simple before/after comparison is *not* the correct one if labor demand has shifted, as in Figure 4.4. Rather, we should ask, "How did the actual employment level in period 1 compare with the level that *would have prevailed* in the absence of the increase in the minimum wage?" Since demand grew between the two periods, this hypothetical employment level would have been E_{1H}. E_{1H} is greater than E_1, the actual level of employment in period 1, so that $E_{1H} - E_1$ represents the loss of jobs caused by the minimum wage. In a growing economy, then, the expected effect of a one-time increase in the minimum wage is to reduce the rate of growth of employment. Controlling for all the "other things" besides wages that affect labor demand turns out to be the major difficulty in measuring employment changes caused by the minimum wage.

Effects of Uncovered Sectors   The federal minimum wage law, like many governmental regulations, has an *uncovered* sector. Coverage has increased over the years, but the law still does not apply to about 30 percent of nonsupervisory workers (mainly those in government and in small firms in the retail trade and service industries). Also, with millions of employers and limited resources for governmental enforcement, *noncompliance* with the law may be widespread, creating another kind of noncoverage.[12] The existence of uncovered sectors significantly affects how the overall employment of low-wage workers will respond to increases in the minimum wage.

Consider the labor market for unskilled, low-wage workers that is depicted in Figure 4.5. The market has two sectors. In one, employers must pay wages equal

[12]Orley Ashenfelter and Robert Smith, "Compliance with the Minimum Wage Law," *Journal of Political Economy* 87 (April 1979): 335–350.

FIGURE 4.5

Minimum Wage Effects: Incomplete Coverage Causes Employment Shifts

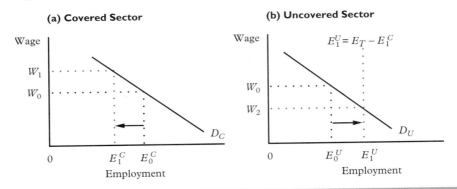

(a) Covered Sector

(b) Uncovered Sector

to at least the minimum wage of W_1; wages in the uncovered sector are free to vary with market conditions. While the total labor supply to both markets taken as a whole is fixed at E_T (that is, the total labor supply curve is vertical), workers can freely move from one sector to the other seeking better job offers. Free movement between sectors suggests that, in the absence of minimum wage regulations, the wage in each sector will be the same. Referring to Figure 4.5, let us assume that this "pre-minimum" wage is W_0 and that total employment of E_T is broken down into E_0^C in the covered sector plus E_0^U in the uncovered sector.

If a minimum wage of W_1 is imposed on the covered sector, all unskilled workers will prefer to work there. However, the increase in wages in that sector, from W_0 to W_1, reduces demand, and covered-sector employment will fall from E_0^C to E_1^C. Some workers who previously had, or would have found, jobs in the covered sector must now seek work in the uncovered sector. Thus, to the E_0^U workers formerly working in the uncovered sector are added $E_0^C - E_1^C$ other workers seeking jobs there. Thus, all unskilled workers in the market who are not lucky enough to find "covered jobs" at W_1 must now look for work in the uncovered sector,[13] and the (vertical) supply curve to that sector becomes $E_1^U [= E_0^U + (E_0^C - E_1^C) = E_T - E_1^C]$. The increased supply of workers to that sector drives down the wage there from W_0 to W_2.

The presence of an uncovered sector thus suggests the possibility that employment among unskilled workers will be rearranged, but not reduced, by an increase

---

[13]Under some circumstances it may be rational for these unemployed workers to remain unemployed for a while and to search for jobs in the covered sector. We shall explore this possibility—which is discussed by Jacob Mincer in "Unemployment Effects of Minimum Wage Changes," *Journal of Political Economy* 84 (August 1976): S87–S104—in chapter 13. At this point we simply note that if it occurs, unemployment will result.

in the minimum wage. In the above example, all E_T workers remained employed after the minimum was imposed. Rather than reducing overall employment of the unskilled, then, a partially covering minimum wage law might serve to shift employment out of the covered to the uncovered sector, with the further result that wages in the uncovered sector would be driven down.

The magnitude of any employment shift from the covered to the uncovered sector, of course, depends on the size of the latter; the smaller it is, the lower are the chances that job losers from the covered sector will find employment there. Whatever the size of the uncovered sector, however, its very presence means that the *overall* loss of employment is likely to be less than the loss of employment in the covered sector.

Intersectoral Shifts in Product Demand   The employment effects of a wage change are the result of scale and substitution effects. Substitution effects stem from changes in how firms choose to produce, while scale effects are rooted in consumer adjustments to changes in product prices. Recall that, faced with a given increase (say) in the minimum wage, firms' increases in costs will generally be greater when the share of low-wage labor in total costs is greater; thus, the same increase in the minimum wage can lead to rather different effects on product prices among different parts of the covered sector. Further, if these subsectors compete with each other for customers, it is possible that scale effects of the increased wage will serve to *increase* employment among some firms in the covered sector.

Suppose, for example, that convenience stores sell items that supermarkets also carry, and that a minimum wage law raises the wages paid to low-skilled workers in both kinds of stores. If low-skilled labor costs are a higher fraction of total costs in convenience stores than they are in supermarkets, then other things equal, the minimum wage law would raise costs in convenience stores by a greater percentage. With prices of items increasing more in convenience stores than in supermarkets, consumers would tend to shift some of their convenience-store purchases to supermarkets. Thus, the minimum wage increase could have an ambiguous effect on employment in supermarkets. On the one hand, increased costs of unskilled workers in supermarkets would create scale and substitution effects that cause employment to decline. On the other hand, because they may pick up business formerly going to convenience stores, supermarkets may experience a scale effect that could work to increase their demand for labor.

Employment Effects: Empirical Estimates

While the initial employment effects of adopting a minimum wage in the United States were readily observed (see Example 4.2), the effects of more recent increases are not as obvious—and must therefore be studied using sophisticated statistical techniques. The demographic group for which the effects of minimum wages are expected to be most visible are teenagers—a notoriously low-paid group!—but studies of how mandated wage increases have affected their employment have produced no consensus.

EXAMPLE 4.2

The Employment Effects of the First Federal Minimum Wage

When the federal minimum wage first went into effect, on October 24, 1938, it was expected to have a substantial impact on the economy of the South, where wages were much lower than in the rest of the country. An examination of one of the largest manufacturing industries in the South, seamless hosiery, verifies these predictions.

It is readily apparent that the new minimum wage was binding in the seamless hosiery industry. By 1940, nearly one-third of the labor force earned within 2.5 cents per hour of the minimum wage (which was then 32.5 cents per hour). A longitudinal survey of 97 firms shows that employment, which had been rising, reversed course and started to fall, even though overall demand for the product and production levels were rising. Employment fell by 5.5 percent in southern mills but rose by 4.9 percent in northern mills. Even more strikingly, employment fell by 17 percent in mills that had previously paid less than the new minimum wage, while it stayed virtually the same at higher-wage mills.

Before the passage of the minimum wage, there had been a slow movement from the use of hand-transfer to converted-transfer knitting machines. (A converted-transfer machine had an attachment to enable automated production for certain types of work.) The minimum wage seems to have accelerated this trend. In the first two years of the law's existence, there was a 23 percent decrease in the number of hand-transfer machines, a 69 percent increase in converted-transfer machines, and a 10 percent increase in fully automatic machines. In addition, the machines were used more intensively than before. A night shift was added at many mills, and these workers did not receive extra pay for working this undesirable shift. Finally, total imports of seamless hosiery surged by about 27 percent within two years of the minimum wage's enactment.

Data from: Andrew J. Seltzer, "The Effects of the Fair Labor Standards Act of 1938 on the Southern Seamless Hosiery and Lumber Industries," *Journal of Economic History* 57, no. 2 (June 1997): 396–415.

Widely reviewed and replicated studies of employment changes in the fast-food industry, for example, disagree on whether employment was affected at all by minimum-wage increases in the early 1990s.[14] Recent research on the United States that reviews and updates earlier studies of *overall* teenage employment, however, finds that there have been negative employment effects associated with increases in minimum wages. It estimates that the elasticity of demand for teenagers with respect to minimum-wage changes is in the range of −0.20 to −0.60.[15] A study that

[14]See David Neumark and William Wascher, "Minimum Wages and Employment: A Case Study of the Fast-Food Industry in New Jersey and Pennsylvania: Comment," and David Card and Alan B. Krueger, "Minimum Wages and Employment: A Case Study of the Fast-Food Industry in New Jersey and Pennsylvania: Reply," both in *American Economic Review* 90, no. 5 (December 2000): 1362–1420. These studies contain references to earlier studies and reviews on this topic.

[15]Burkhauser, Couch, and Wittenburg (see footnote 2). This paper also contains very complete references to (and reviews of) previous research. The elasticity of total teenage *hours worked* may be somewhat larger than the elasticity of teenage *employment levels;* see Kenneth A. Couch and David C. Wittenburg, "The Response of Hours of Work to Increases in the Minimum Wage," *Southern Economic Journal* 68, no. 1 (July 2001): 171–177.

compared how minimum-wage changes affected teenage employment in France and the United States estimated that mandated wage increases of, say, 10 percent would reduce teenage employment by 1–2 percent in both countries, but a follow-up study of increased minimum wages that did not focus just on teenagers found employment reductions in France but not the United States.[16]

It is interesting that in the studies finding the expected negative employment effects, the estimated elasticities of teenage employment with respect to changes in the minimum wage (of −0.20 to −0.60) are smaller than the roughly unitary elasticity of demand reported from the studies summarized in Table 4.1. Given what we know about substitution effects among unskilled workers, one would expect that the demand for *teenage* labor would be *more* (not less) elastic than average! The smaller elasticity with respect to *mandated* wage changes may suggest that there is at least some degree of monopsony power in the labor market.

As we saw in chapter 3, one feature of the monopsony model is that it generates ambiguous predictions about how employment might be expected to respond to modest increases in the minimum wage, especially in the short run. Remember that the ambiguity concerns only the response of employment to *mandated* wage increases, which flatten the labor supply curve, not to those wage changes generated by shifts in labor supply curves that still leave them upward-sloping. Thus, the monopsony model might help account for the differences in labor demand elasticities based on minimum-wage changes and the larger elasticities cited earlier, which were estimated using wage changes generated under different conditions.[17]

Does the Minimum Wage Fight Poverty?

As noted above, the short-run response of low-wage employment to changes in the minimum wage is widely believed to be inelastic. Thus, we expect that an increase in the minimum would serve to increase the total earnings going to low-wage workers as a whole. Can it be said, then, that minimum wage laws are effective weapons in the struggle to reduce poverty?

Identifying those who are considered to be living in poverty is done by comparing the income of each family with the poverty line set for families of its particular size; thus, *family* income and family size are the critical variables for defining poverty. Teenagers earning below the minimum, for example, may benefit if their

---

[16]John M. Abowd, Francis Kramarz, Thomas Lemieux, and David N. Margolis, "Minimum Wages and Youth Employment in France and the United States," in *Youth Employment and Joblessness in Advanced Countries,* ed. David G. Blanchflower and Richard B. Freeman (Chicago: University of Chicago Press, 1999), 427–472; and John M. Abowd, Francis Kramarz, David N. Margolis, and Thomas Philippon, "The Tale of Two Countries: Minimum Wages and Employment in France and the United States," School of Industrial and Labor Relations, Cornell University, September 2000.

[17]For a study of monopsony in labor markets in which tips play an important role in compensation, see Walter J. Wessels, "Minimum Wages and Tipped Servers," *Economic Inquiry* 35, no. 2 (April 1997): 334–349.

wages are raised by a legislated increase, but if these teenagers mostly live in non-poor families, then the increased overall income among teenagers may do very little to reduce poverty.

One study of the 1990–1991 increases in the minimum wage found that, of those who earned between the old and new minimums (that is, between $3.35 and $4.24), only 22 percent lived in poor families. Conversely, of those workers in 1990 who lived in poverty, only 26 percent earned between the old and new minimums. All told, assuming no employment effects, only 19 percent of the estimated earnings increases associated with the 1990 and 1991 minimum wage increases went to poor families.[18] Thus, the minimum wage is a relatively blunt instrument with which to reduce poverty. A study that directly estimated the effects of minimum-wage increases on poverty rates among both teenagers and junior high dropouts found reductions associated with wage increases in the early 1990s but not with the changes legislated in the 1980s.[19]

APPLYING CONCEPTS OF LABOR DEMAND ELASTICITY TO THE ISSUE OF TECHNOLOGICAL CHANGE

Technological change, which can encompass the introduction of new products and production techniques as well as changes in technology that serve to reduce the cost of capital (for example, increases in the speed of computers), is frequently viewed as a blessing by some and a curse by others. Those who view it positively point to the enormous gains in the standard of living made possible by new technology, while those who see technological change as a threat often stress its adverse consequences for workers. Are the concepts underlying the elasticity of demand for labor useful in making judgments about the effects of technological change?

There are two aspects of technological change that affect the demand for labor. One is product demand. *Shifts* in product demand curves will tend to shift labor demand curves in the same direction, and changes in the *elasticity* of product demand with respect to product price will tend to cause qualitatively similar changes in the own-wage elasticity of labor demand. The invention of new products (personal computers, for example) that serve as substitutes for old ones (typewriters) will tend to

---

[18]In 1990, the poverty line for a single individual under age 65 was $6,800, while for a family of three it was $10,419 and for a family of four it was $13,359 (see U.S. Bureau of the Census, *Poverty in the United States: 1990*, Series P–60, no. 175, August 1991). The percentages in this paragraph are based on Richard V. Burkhauser, Kenneth A. Couch, and David C. Wittenburg, "'Who Gets What' from Minimum Wage Hikes: A Re-Estimation of Card and Kreuger's Distributional Analysis in *Myth and Measurement: The New Economics of the Minimum Wage*," *Industrial and Labor Relations Review* 49, no. 3 (April 1996): 547–552. Also see Card and Kreuger, *Myth and Measurement*, chapter 9 (see footnote 1); and David Neumark and William Wascher, "Do Minimum Wages Fight Poverty?" working paper no. 6127, National Bureau of Economic Research, Cambridge, Mass., August 1997.

[19]John T. Addison and McKinley L. Blackburn, "Minimum Wages and Poverty," *Industrial and Labor Relations Review* 52, no. 3 (April 1999): 393–409.

shift the labor demand curve in the older sector to the left, causing loss of employment in that sector. If greater product substitution possibilities are also created by these new inventions, the introduction of new products can increase the *elasticity* of product—and labor—demand. This increases the amount of job loss associated with collectively bargained wage increases, and it reduces the power of unions to secure large wage increases in the older sector. While benefiting consumers and providing jobs in the new sectors, the introduction of new products does necessitate some painful changes in established industries as workers, unions, and employers must all adjust to a new environment.

A second aspect of technological change is often associated with automation, or the substitution of capital for labor. For purposes of analyzing its effects on labor demand, this second aspect of technological change should be thought of as reducing the cost of capital. In some cases—the mass production of personal computers is one example—a fall in capital prices is what literally occurs. In other cases of technological change—the miniaturization of computer components, for example, which has made possible new production techniques—an invention makes completely new technologies available. When something is unavailable, it can be thought of as having an infinite price (it is not available at any price); therefore, the availability of a new technique is equivalent to observing a decline in its price to some finite number. In either case, with a decline in its cost, capital tends to be substituted for labor in the production process.

The *sign* of the cross-elasticity of demand for a given category of labor with respect to a fall in the price of capital depends on whether capital and the category of labor are gross substitutes or gross complements. If a particular category of labor is a substitute in production for capital, *and* if the scale effect of the reduced capital price is relatively weak, then capital and the category of labor are gross substitutes and automation reduces demand for workers in this category. For categories of labor that are not close substitutes for the new technology, however, the scale effect may dominate and the two can be gross complements. Thus, the effect of automation on the demand for *particular* categories of labor can be either positive or negative.

Clearly, whether capital and a given type of labor are gross substitutes depends on several factors, all of which are highly specific to particular industries and production processes. Perhaps the most that can be said generally is that unskilled labor and capital are more likely to be substitutes in production than are skilled labor and capital, which some studies have identified as complements in production. Because factors of production that are complementary must be gross complements, technological change is more likely to increase the demand for skilled than for unskilled labor.[20]

Before concluding that technological change is a threat to the unskilled, however, we must keep three things in mind. First, even factors that are substitutes in production can be gross complements (if scale effects are large enough). Second,

---

[20]See David Autor, Lawrence Katz, and Alan Krueger, "Computing Inequality: Have Computers Changed the Labor Market?" *Quarterly Journal of Economics* 113, no. 4 (November 1998): 1169–1213.

substitution of capital for labor can destroy some unskilled jobs, but accompanying scale effects can create others, sometimes in the same industry.

Finally, although the fraction of all workers who are unskilled laborers has declined over the course of the last 100 years, this decline is not in itself convincing evidence of gross substitutability between capital and unskilled labor. The concepts of elasticity and cross-elasticity refer to changes in labor demand caused by changes in wages or capital prices, *holding all else constant.* That is, labor demand elasticities focus on the labor demand curve at a particular point in time. Actual employment outcomes over time are also influenced by labor *supply* behavior of workers. Thus, from simple observations of employment levels over time it is impossible to tell anything about own-wage demand elasticities or about the signs or magnitudes of cross-elasticities of labor demand.

The effects of technological change on *total* employment and on society in general are less ambiguous. Technological change permits society to achieve better consumption possibilities, and it leads to scale effects that both enlarge and change the mix of output. As the productive mix changes, some sectors decline or are eliminated (see the data inside the front cover, which show declining employment shares in agriculture and goods-producing industries). Other sectors of the economy—the services, for example—expand. While these dislocations can create pockets of unemployment as some workers must seek new jobs or acquire new skills, there is no evidence that, by itself, technological change leads to permanent problems of unemployment.

REVIEW QUESTIONS

1. Suppose that the government raises the minimum wage by 20 percent. Thinking of the four Hicks-Marshall laws of derived demand as they apply to a particular industry, analyze the conditions under which job loss among teenage workers in that industry would be smallest.

2. Union A faces a demand curve in which a wage of $4 per hour leads to demand for 20,000 person-hours and a wage of $5 per hour leads to demand for 10,000 person-hours. Union B faces a demand curve in which a wage of $6 per hour leads to demand for 30,000 person-hours, whereas a wage of $5 per hour leads to demand for 33,000 person-hours.

a. Which union faces the *more* elastic demand curve?

b. Which union will be more successful in increasing the total income (wages times person-hours) of its membership?

3. The federal government, in an effort to stimulate job growth, passes a law that gives a tax credit to employers who invest in new machinery and other capital goods. Applying the concepts underlying cross-elasticities, discuss the conditions under which employment gains in a particular industry will be largest.

4. Clerical workers represent a substantial share of the U.S. workforce—over 15 percent in recent years. Concern has been

expressed that computerization and office automation will lead to a substantial decline in white-collar employment and increased unemployment of clerical workers. Is this concern well founded?

5. Many employers provide health insurance for their employees, but others—primarily small employers—do not. Suppose that the government wants to ensure that all employees are provided with health insurance coverage that meets or exceeds some standard. Suppose also that the government wants employers to pay for this coverage and is considering two options:

Option A: An employer not voluntarily offering its employees acceptable coverage would be required to pay a tax of *X* cents per hour for each labor hour employed. The funds collected would support government-provided health coverage.

Option B: Same as option A, except that the government-provided coverage would be financed by a tax collected as a fraction of the employer's total revenues.

Compare and contrast the labor market effects of each of the two options.

6. In 1942 the government promulgated regulations that prohibited the manufacture of many types of garments by workers who did the sewing, stitching, and knitting in their homes. If these prohibitions are repealed, so that clothing items may now be made either by workers in factories or by independent contractors doing work in their homes, what effect will this have on the labor demand curve for *factory workers* in the garment industry?

7. Briefly explain how the following programs would affect the elasticity of demand for labor in the steel industry:
   a. An increased tariff on steel imports;
   b. A law making it illegal to lay off workers for economic reasons;
   c. A boom in the machinery industry (which uses steel as an input)—causing production in that industry to rise;
   d. A decision by the owners of steel mills to operate each mill longer than has been the practice in the past;
   e. An increase in the wages paid by employers in the steel industry;
   f. A tax on each ton of steel produced.

PROBLEMS

1. Suppose that the demand for dental hygienists is $L_D = 5,000 - 20W$, where L = the number of dental hygienists and W = the daily wage. What is the own-wage elasticity of demand for dental hygienists when $W = \$100$ per day? Is the demand curve elastic or inelastic at this point? What is the own-wage elasticity of demand when $W = \$200$ per day? Is the demand curve elastic or inelastic at this point?

2. Professor Pessimist argues before Congress that reducing the size of the military will have grave consequences for the typ-

ical American worker. He argues that if 1 million individuals were released from the military and were instead employed in the civilian labor market, average wages in the civilian labor market would fall dramatically. Assume that the demand curve for civilian labor does not shift when workers are released from the military. *First,* draw a simple diagram depicting the effect of this influx of workers from the military. *Next,* using your knowledge of (i) the definition of the own-wage elasticity of labor demand, (ii) the magnitude of this elasticity for the economy as a whole, and (iii) the size of civilian employment in comparison with this flood from the military, graph these events and estimate the magnitude of the reduction in wages for civilian workers as a whole. Do you concur with Professor Pessimist?

3. Suppose that the demand for burger flippers at fast-food restaurants in a small city is $L_D = 300 - 20W$, where L = the number of burger flippers and W = the wage in dollars per hour. The equilibrium wage is $4 per hour, but the government puts in place a minimum wage of $5 per hour.

   a. Assuming that none of the firms has any monopsony power, how does the minimum wage affect employment in these fast-food restaurants? Draw a graph to show what has happened, and estimate the effects on employment in the fast-food sector.

   b. Suppose that in the city above, there is an uncovered sector where $L_S = -100 + 80W$ and $L_D = 300 - 20W$, before the minimum wage is put in place. Suppose that all the workers who lose their jobs as burger flippers due to the introduction of the minimum wage seek work in the uncovered sector. What happens to wages and employment in that sector? Draw a graph to show what happens, and analyze the effects on both wages and employment in the uncovered sector.

4. (Appendix) The production possibilities curve for the United States is linear and allows the country to produce a maximum of 500 million units of clothing or 300 million units of food. The production possibilities curve for France is also linear and allows it to produce a maximum of 250 million units of clothing or 150 million units of food. Which good will the United States export to France?

SELECTED READINGS

Card, David, and Alan B. Krueger. *Myth and Measurement: The New Economics of the Minimum Wage.* Princeton: N.J.: Princeton University Press, 1995.

Hamermesh, Daniel. *Labor Demand.* Princeton, N.J.: Princeton University Press, 1993.

Kennan, John. "The Elusive Effects of Minimum Wages." *Journal of Economic Literature* 33, no. 4 (December 1995), pp. 1950–1965.

"Review Symposium: *Myth and Measurement: The New Economics of the Minimum Wage,* by David Card and Alan B. Krueger." *Industrial and Labor Relations Review* 48, no. 4 (July 1995).

APPENDIX 4A

International Trade and the Demand for Labor: Can High-Wage Countries Compete?

The question of how international trade affects labor demand in the long run has been highlighted recently by the increasing importance of exports and imports in the U.S. economy. As late as 1970, imports represented only slightly less than 6 percent of gross domestic purchases, while exports were less than 6 percent of gross domestic product. By the year 2000, however, imports had more than doubled, to almost 16 percent of purchases, and exports had grown to about 12 percent of gross domestic product.[1]

The public is often inclined to support laws restricting free trade on the grounds that lower wages and living standards in other countries inevitably cause employment losses among American workers—losses that could be mitigated only by a large decline in American living standards. This section will show that the effects of international trade on the demand for labor are analogous to the effects of technological change, that they do not depend on relative living standards, and that two countries will generally find trade mutually beneficial regardless of their respective wage rates. To keep things simple, we assume in what follows that goods and services can be traded across countries but that capital and labor are immobile (international mobility of labor is discussed in chapter 10).[2]

---

[1]U.S. President, *Economic Report of the President* (Washington, D.C.: U.S. Government Printing Office, 2001), Tables B-25, B-26.

[2]The model presented here is necessarily simplified. More-complex models and a discussion of the conditions under which free trade may not be in a country's best interests are found in Robert E. Baldwin, "Are Economists' Traditional Trade Policy Views Still Valid?" *Journal of Economic Literature* 30 (June 1992): 804–829.

PRODUCTION IN THE UNITED STATES
WITHOUT INTERNATIONAL TRADE

Suppose that the available supplies of labor and capital in the United States can be combined to produce two goods, food and clothing. (To allow a graphical presentation, the analysis will be in the context of just two goods; however, the results are applicable to more.) If all inputs were devoted to food production, 200 million units of food could be produced; similarly, if all available resources were devoted to the production of clothing, 100 million units of clothing could be produced. If 15 percent (say) of the resources were devoted to food and 85 percent to clothing, 30 million units of food and 85 million units of clothing could be produced. All the possible combinations of food and clothing that could be produced in the United States are summarized graphically by line XY in Figure 4A.1, which is called a *production possibilities curve.*

Two things should be noted about the production possibilities curve in Figure 4A.1. It is negative in slope, indicating that if more of one good is produced, less of the other can be produced. It has a slope of −0.50, symbolizing the real cost of producing food: if the country chooses to produce 1 more unit of food, it must forgo 0.50 units of clothing. (Conversely, if it wants to produce 1 more unit of clothing, it must give up 2 units of food.)[3]

The ultimate mix of food and clothing produced depends on consumer preferences. If the United States is assumed to have 100 million workers and chooses to allocate 15 percent to the production of food, incomes would average 0.30 units of food and 0.85 units of clothing per worker.

Suppose an inventor were to come along with a device that could increase the efficiency of inputs in the production of clothing, so that if all inputs were devoted to clothing, 180 million units could be produced. The production possibilities curve would shift out to the colored line (YZ) in Figure 4A.1, and per capita real incomes in the United States would rise (it is possible to produce more of both food and clothing with the resources available, as can be seen at point L). After this innovation, only 1.11 (200/180) units of food would have to be given up to obtain 1 unit of clothing.

(Note that when the real cost of clothing falls from 2 to 1.11 units of food, the *real cost* of food is *automatically* increased from 0.50 to 0.90 units (180/200) of clothing. The reason for this food cost increase is straightforward: if a given set of inputs can now produce more clothing but the same amount of food, diverting enough from the production of clothing to produce 1 more unit of food will now result in a larger decline in clothing output than before. It is this decline in clothing output that is the real cost, or *opportunity cost,* of producing a unit of food.)

---

[3]The production possibilities "curve" in Figure 4A.1 is a straight line, which reflects the simplifying assumption that the ratio at which food can be "transformed" into clothing, and vice versa, never changes. This assumption is not necessary to the argument but does make it a bit easier to grasp initially.

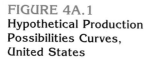

FIGURE 4A.1
Hypothetical Production Possibilities Curves, United States

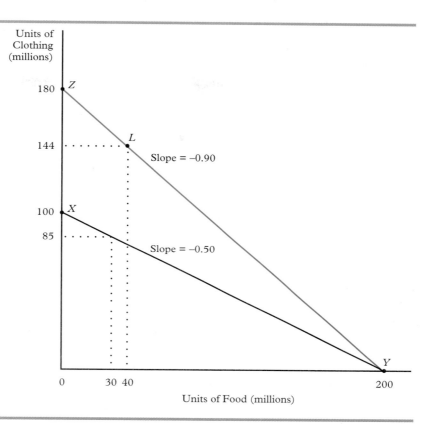

PRODUCTION IN A FOREIGN COUNTRY WITHOUT INTERNATIONAL TRADE

It would be an amazing coincidence if the rates at which food and clothing could be traded off were equal in all countries. Land quality differs, as do the quality and quantity of capital and labor. Therefore, let us assume that a country—call it China—can produce either 300 million units of food, or 500 million units of clothing, or any other combination of food and clothing along the production possibilities curve, *AB*, in Figure 4A.2.

If 40 percent of its productive inputs were devoted to farming, China could produce 120 million units of food and 300 million units of clothing. With a population of, say, 500 million workers, China's average income per worker would be 0.24 units of food and 0.60 units of clothing. Clearly, then, living standards (real wage rates) are lower in China than in the United States (since the average consumption per worker of *both* food and clothing is lower in China).

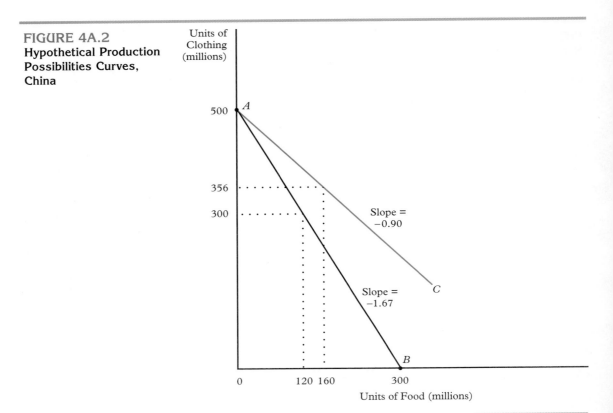

FIGURE 4A.2
Hypothetical Production Possibilities Curves, China

After analyzing China's production possibilities curve (*AB* in Figure 4A.2), it can be calculated that the real cost of a unit of food within China is 1.67 (500/300) units of clothing; to produce 1 more unit of food means that 1.67 fewer units of clothing can be produced. Conversely, the real price of a unit of clothing in China is 0.60 (300/500) units of food.

THE MUTUAL BENEFITS OF INTERNATIONAL TRADE

In the absence of innovation in the clothing industry, discussed earlier, the price of food within the United States is 0.50 units of clothing and the price of clothing is 2 units of food. In contrast, the price of food in China is 1.67 units of clothing and the price of clothing is 0.60 units of food. These prices are summarized in columns (a) and (b) of Table 4A.1. Because the real internal cost of food is lower in the United States than in China, while the real internal cost of clothing is higher, economists therefore say that the United States has a *comparative advantage* in producing food and China has a *comparative advantage* in producing clothing.

It is important to note that the real costs of each good in the two countries depend *only* on the *internal trade-offs* between food and clothing output. Despite the assumed fact, for example, that real wages in China are lower than in the United States, food is much more costly in the former country than in the latter! Further, despite the generally more productive inputs in the United States, the real cost of clothing is lower in China.

The costs listed in columns (a) and (b) of Table 4A.1 make it plain that both countries could benefit from trade. China would be willing to buy food from the United States as long as it had to give up something less than 1.67 units of clothing per unit of food (its internal real cost of production). The United States would be willing to trade away a unit of food as long as it could obtain something more than 0.50 units of clothing in return (0.50 units represents what the United States can now obtain internally if it gives up 1 unit of food). The divergent internal values placed on food and clothing make it possible for mutually beneficial trades to take place.

With a lower-bound price of 0.50 units of clothing per unit of food, and an upper-bound price of 1.67, the ultimate price at which the two countries would trade is not predictable. Trade at any price in between these two bounds would benefit both countries and be preferable to each over no trade at all; however, the

TABLE 4A.1 **Hypothetical Costs and Quantities of Food and Clothing in the United States and China, before and after Trade**

	Before Trade		After Trade	
Good	*(a) United States*	*(b) China*	*(c) United States*	*(d) China*
Food costs	0.50 units of clothing	1.67 units of clothing	0.90 units of clothing	0.90 units of clothing
Clothing costs	2 units of food	0.60 units of food	1.11 units of food	1.11 units of food
Assumed food consumption:				
Total	30 million	120 million	40 million	160 million
Per capita	0.30	0.24	0.40	0.32
Assumed clothing consumption:				
Total	85 million	300 million	144 million	356 million
Per capita	0.85	0.60	1.44	0.71
World production of food	150 million		200 million	
World production of clothing	385 million		500 million	

closer the price of food is to 0.50 units of clothing the less the United States gains and the more China benefits.

Let us assume that the bargaining strengths of the two countries are such that units of food are traded by the United States to China in return for 0.90 units of clothing. From the perspective of the United States, 1 unit of food can now be transformed into 0.90 units of clothing instead of just 0.50 units. In this example, trade will therefore accomplish exactly what the previously discussed technological innovation in clothing production did: it will move the production possibilities curve out and give the country a greater command over resources. In terms of Figure 4A.1, trade by itself could move the production possibilities curve from XY to YZ. This outward shift allows the United States to consume more food *and* more clothing.

From the Chinese perspective, trading 0.90 units of clothing for 1 unit of food is equivalent to allowing the transformation of 1 unit of clothing into 1.11 units of food (up from 0.60 units of food). This increase represents an outward shift in the Chinese production possibilities curve (see curve AC in Figure 4A.2), and the output that can be consumed by each Chinese worker clearly increases.

To obtain a sense of how trade could affect per capita consumption in our example, let us suppose that the United States specialized in food production and that China specialized in the production of clothing.[4] The United States would produce 200 million units of food, and if it consumed 40 million units, the remaining 160 million units could be traded to China for 144 million units of clothing (0.9×160 million). China would produce 500 million units of clothing, exporting 144 million, so that its total internal consumption of clothing would equal 356 million units. China, of course, would consume 160 million units of food under these assumptions. As can be seen from Table 4A.1, where the pre- and post-trade units of production and consumption are compared, per capita real incomes rise in both countries as a result of trade. Conversely, when trade is restricted, consumers in both countries can lose.[5]

LABOR MARKET IMPLICATIONS

International trade is driven by the relative internal (real) costs of producing various goods. Conclusions from our two-good analysis of trade between the United

---

[4]Complete specialization in production will occur in one or both countries if the production possibilities curves are straight lines; in these cases the internal rate of transformation between the two goods is unchanging. Specialization may not be total when the production possibilities curves are concave from below. A concave curve implies that the real costs of food production, say, rise with food output, so that at some point the United States could lose its comparative advantage.

[5]For a review of empirical studies on this issue, see Sebastian Edwards, "Openness, Trade Liberalization, and Growth in Developing Countries," *Journal of Economic Literature* 31 (September 1993): 1358–1393; and Mary E. Burfisher, Sherman Robinson, and Karen Thierfelder, "The Impact of NAFTA on the United States," *Journal of Economic Perspectives* 15, no. 1 (Winter 2001): 125–144.

States and China are not at all affected by the assumptions about living standards (real wages) in the two countries. If the production possibilities curves remained the same but the assumed populations of the two countries had been reversed—and living standards were posited to be higher in China—trade would still have taken place, and the United States would still have traded food for Chinese-made clothing.

The general conclusion we can reach from this simple model of trade is that the advent of free trade between two countries will tend to cause each to specialize in producing goods for which it has a comparative advantage and to reduce its production of goods for which its real internal costs are relatively high. Trade, just like an important technological improvement in a given industry, will tend to *shift* employment from one industry to another.[6] However, there is no reason to believe that the advent of free trade will create a permanent loss of employment in the country with higher real wages. It is the production possibilities curves, not real-wage rates, that drive international trade.

If the average wages for production workers in, say, Haiti are 20 percent of the average wages in the United States, why can't Haiti undersell American producers in every product line? How can American workers hope to remain employed at high wages when faced with such low-wage competitors?

Haiti has labor and capital resources that are fixed at any moment. It cannot produce *everything!* If, for example, several thousand Haitian workers are employed sewing garments for export to the United States, they are thus not available for (say) the growing and harvesting of agricultural produce. Thus, while there may be a benefit to Haiti when jobs in the garment trades open up, there is also a cost in terms of forgone output that must now be purchased from the United States (the place where dollars received from the export of clothes to the United States must ultimately be spent). Haiti will benefit from increasing the labor it devotes to garment exports *only* if it can replace its forgone production of food more cheaply.

To make the above concepts more concrete, suppose that shirts costing $10 to sew in the United States can be produced in Haiti for $2. Will American garment workers lose their jobs to foreign exports? If the food production forgone in Haiti when one additional shirt is made cannot be purchased from the United States for $2 or less, neither Haitian workers nor their country as a whole will be better off by taking the new jobs. In this case, American workers—despite their higher wages—would not lose jobs to Haitians.

---

[6]For studies of the labor market effects of increased foreign trade, see John Abowd and Thomas Lemieux, "The Effects of International Trade on Collective Bargaining Outcomes: A Comparison of the United States and Canada," in *Immigration, Trade, and the Labor Market*, ed. John Abowd and Richard Freeman (Chicago: University of Chicago Press, 1991), 343–369; Ana L. Revenga, "Exporting Jobs: The Impact of Import Competition on Employment and Wages in U.S. Manufacturing," *Quarterly Journal of Economics* 107 (February 1992): 255–284; and Lael Brainard and David Riker, "Are U.S. Multinationals Exporting U.S. Jobs?" in *Globalization and Labor Markets*, ed. David Greenaway and Douglas Nelson (Northhampton, Mass.: Edward Elgar Publishing, 2001), forthcoming.

If, however, the food production forgone when a shirt is produced can be purchased from the United States for $2 or less, American jobs in the garment trades will tend to be lost to Haitians. However, it is equally true that Haitian agricultural jobs are thereby lost to the much higher paying agricultural sector in the United States!

International trade can cause employment to shift across industries, and these shifts may well be accompanied by unemployment if workers, employers, or market wages are slow in adapting to change. However, there is no reason to believe that the transitional unemployment associated with international trade will become permanent; trade does not condemn jobs in high-wage countries to extinction.

5

QUASI-FIXED LABOR COSTS AND THEIR EFFECTS ON DEMAND

To this point in our detailed discussion of the demand for labor, we have treated all labor costs as *variable*—that is, as being strictly proportional to the length of time the employee works. Variable labor costs, such as the hourly wage rate, recur every period and, of course, can be reduced if the hours of work are reduced. Many labor costs, however, are *quasi-fixed*, in that they are not strictly proportional to hours of work. Such costs are borne by the firm on a *per-worker* basis that is largely independent of the hours each employee works. This chapter traces the effects these quasi-fixed costs have on the demand for labor.

Because quasi-fixed labor costs are generally *nonwage*, the first section discusses the nature and magnitude of nonwage labor costs. Included in our discussion are the costs to firms of hiring and training new employees, the costs of legally required social insurance programs (such as Social Security and unemployment compensation), and the costs of privately negotiated employee benefits (such as health insurance, vacation and sick-leave pay, and private pensions).

One important effect that quasi-fixed costs have on the demand for labor is the choice firms have between hiring more (or fewer) workers and employing those already on the payroll for longer (or shorter) hours. We will discuss, in the second section of this chapter, why some employers decide to regularly work their

131

employees overtime at legally required premium wage rates rather than increasing the level of employment.

The third section looks at the consequences of one important type of quasi-fixed labor cost: *investments* by firms in the hiring and training of their employees. Investments involve a current outlay of funds with a future payback, so investments in workers cause firms' employment decisions to extend over multiple periods. Thus, this section discusses two critical issues: the ways current costs and future returns can be meaningfully compared, and the multiperiod criterion for profit maximization in the hiring of labor. Application of these concepts to the issue of *training* investments is made in the fourth section, and in the final section we discuss *hiring* investments.

NONWAGE LABOR COSTS

Although simple textbook models of the labor market often refer to the hourly wage rate paid to workers as the cost of labor, substantial *nonwage* labor costs have important implications for labor market behavior. In general, such costs fall into two categories: hiring and training costs and employee benefits.

Hiring and Training Costs

Firms incur substantial costs in hiring and training new employees. *Hiring costs* include all costs involved in advertising positions, screening applicants to evaluate their qualifications, and processing successful applicants who have been offered jobs. One might also include in this category of costs the overhead costs of maintaining employees on the payroll once they have been employed; these costs would include recordkeeping costs, the costs of computing and issuing paychecks, and the costs of providing forms to the government (such as W-2 forms to the Internal Revenue Service) giving information on employees' earnings.

New employees typically undergo formal or informal training and orientation programs. These programs may teach new skills, such as how to use a machine, that directly increase the employees' productive abilities. Alternatively, orientation programs may simply provide newcomers with background information on how the firm is structured, such as who to call if a machine breaks down or how to requisition supplies. Such information, while not changing skill levels, does increase productivity by enabling workers to make more efficient use of time. Firms incur at least three types of *training costs:*

1. The *explicit* monetary costs of employing individuals to serve as trainers and the costs of materials used up during the training process;
2. The *implicit* or opportunity costs of using capital equipment and experienced employees to do the training in less-formal training situations (for example, an experienced employee demonstrating to a new recruit how he or she does a job may work at a slower pace than normal); and

TABLE 5.1   Hours Devoted by Firms to Training a New Worker during First Three Months on Job, 1992

Activity	Average Hours
Hours of formal instruction by training personnel	19
Hours spent by management in orientation, informal training, extra supervision	59
Hours spent by co-workers in informal training	34
Hours spent by new worker watching others do work	41
Total	153

Source: John Bishop, "The Incidence of and Payoff to Employer Training," working paper 94–17, Cornell University Center for Advanced Human Resource Studies, July 1994, 11.

3. The *implicit* or opportunity costs of the trainee's time (individuals undergoing training are not producing as much output as they would if all of their time were devoted to production activities).

Since a large share of employers' hiring and training costs are implicit, quantifying their dollar magnitudes is difficult. However, two surveys of employers that asked about the hours spent recruiting and training a new employee yield at least some idea of hourly magnitudes. A 1982 survey, weighted toward employers hiring less-skilled workers, found that almost 22 hours were spent screening and interviewing applicants for a vacancy if these applicants were recruited through newspaper ads. If an employment agency was used to find applicants, the hours spent by the employer on these hiring activities were reduced to around 15.[1]

More recent information on hours spent training new workers comes from a 1992 survey that asked employers about training activities in a worker's first three months on the job. These data, summarized in Table 5.1, indicate that, of the roughly 520 hours each employee was at work during the three months, 153 hours (almost 30 percent) were spent in some form of training. Very little of this training was formal classroom-type instruction; most took place informally at the workstation.[2]

---

[1]John Bishop, "Improving Job Matches in the U.S. Labor Market," *Brookings Papers on Economic Activity: Microeconomics* (1993), 379.

[2]Corroborating evidence is found in Jonathan R. Veum, "Sources of Training and Their Impact on Wages," *Industrial and Labor Relations Review* 48, no. 4 (July 1995): 812–826, which cites a survey of workers in their 20s. For other studies and related references, see H. Frazis, M. Gittleman, M. Horrigan, and M. Joyce, "Results from the 1995 Survey of Employer-Provided Training," *Monthly Labor Review* 121, no. 6 (June 1998): 3–13; and John M. Barron, Mark C. Berger, and Dan A. Black, "Job Training of the Newly Hired in Small and Large Firms," in *Advances in the Study of Entrepreneurship, Innovation, and Economic Growth: Critical Social and Technological Factors Affecting Entrepreneurial Midsize Firms*, vol. 9, ed. Gary D. Libecap (JAI Press: Greenwich, Conn., 1997), 83–122.

Because of the cost of recruiting and training workers, employers must decide on an overall hiring strategy. Firms choosing a *high-wage* strategy generate many applicants for each opening and can be selective, taking only trained, experienced workers. By paying high wages they avoid the explicit and implicit costs of hiring the inexperienced. Firms choosing a *low-wage* strategy can attract only inexperienced applicants, and they must be prepared not only to undertake a period of training but to sustain the risks later on of losing to higher-wage employers the workers they have trained. Thus, low-wage employers save on hourly costs but must incur higher training and recruiting expenses.

Employee Benefits

Employee benefits include *legally required* social insurance contributions and *privately provided* benefits. Examples of legally required benefits are payroll-based payments employers must make to fund programs that compensate workers for unemployment (unemployment insurance), injury (workers' compensation), and retirement (old-age, survivors', disability, and health insurance—Social Security). Examples of privately provided benefits are holiday pay, vacation and sick leave, private pensions, and private health and life insurance.

Table 5.2 gives some idea of employee benefits as a percentage of total compensation, at least among the large firms responding to a recent U.S. Chamber of Commerce survey. The data indicate that nonwage benefits constitute about 27 percent of total compensation, with the largest categories being pay for time not worked (7.7%), insurance (6.4%), legally required payments (6.1%), and retirement (6.3%). These nonwage benefits have grown over time, although in the last decade their growth has slowed and even reversed a bit.

The Quasi-Fixed Nature of Many Nonwage Costs

The distinction between wage and nonwage costs of employment is important because many nonwage costs are *costs per worker* rather than *costs per hour worked*. That is, many nonwage costs do not vary at the margin with the number of hours an employee works. Economists thus refer to them as *quasi-fixed*, in the sense that once an employee is hired the firm is committed to a cost that does not vary with his or her hours of work.

It should be obvious that hiring and training costs are quasi-fixed; they are associated with each new employee, not with the hours he or she works after the training period. Many benefit costs, however, are also quasi-fixed. For example, most life and medical insurance policies are paid on a per-worker basis, as is pay for time not worked (breaks, holidays, vacation, and sick leave). Some pension costs are proportional to hours worked, because some employers (those with *defined contribution* plans) agree to contribute a certain percentage of employee pay to a pension fund. However, many private sector pension plans promise benefits that are a function of years of service rather than hours of work; the costs of these *defined benefit* plans are quasi-fixed in most cases.

TABLE 5.2 Employee Benefits as a Percent of Total Compensation, 1999 (Average Yearly Cost in Parentheses)		
Legally required payments	**6.1**	**($3,220)**
Social Security	5.0	($2,621)
Workers' compensation	0.7	($371)
*Unemployment insurance and other	0.4	($228)
Retirement	**6.3**	**($3,244)**
*Employment costs based on benefit formulas (defined benefit plans)	2.4	($1,327)
Employer costs proportional to earnings (defined contribution plans)	2.5	($1,368)
*Other (including insurance, annuities, and administrative costs)	1.4	($549)
***Insurance** (medical, life)	**6.4**	**($3,668)**
***Paid rest** (coffee breaks, meal periods, set-up and wash-up time)	**1.2**	**($620)**
***Paid vacations, holidays, sick leave**	**6.5**	**($3,600)**
***Miscellaneous** (discounts on products bought, employee meals, child care)	**0.4**	**($302)**
Total	**26.9**	**($14,654)**

*Category of costs believed by authors to be largely *quasi-fixed* (see discussion in the text).
Source: U.S. Chamber of Commerce, *The 1999 Employee Benefits Study* (Washington, D.C.: U.S. Chamber of Commerce, 1999), Table 1.

In the category of legally required benefits, workers' compensation costs are strictly proportional to hours worked, because they are levied as a percentage of payroll, and Social Security taxes are proportional for most employees.[3] However, the unemployment insurance payroll-tax liability is specified to be a percentage (the tax rate) of each employee's earnings up to a maximum earnings level (the taxable wage base), which in 1999 was between $7,000 and $12,000 in over two-thirds of all states.[4] Since most employees earn more than $12,000 per year, having an

---

[3]The Social Security payroll-tax liability of employers is specified as a percentage of each employee's earnings up to a maximum taxable wage base. In 2001, this tax was 6.20 percent of earnings up to $80,400 for retirement and disability insurance, and 1.45 percent on all earnings for Medicare. Because the maximum earnings base exceeded the annual earnings of most workers, the employer's payroll-tax liability *is* increased when a typical employee works an additional hour per week.
[4]National Foundation for Unemployment Compensation and Workers' Compensation, *Highlights of State Unemployment Compensation Laws: January 2001* (Washington, D.C., 2001).

employee work an additional hour per week will *not* cause any increase in the employer's payroll-tax liability. Therefore, unemployment insurance costs are a quasi-fixed cost to most employers.

In Table 5.2 we have indicated (by an asterisk) which nonwage costs are usually of a quasi-fixed nature. The data suggest that around 19 percent of total compensation (over two-thirds of nonwage costs) is quasi-fixed. These quasi-fixed costs averaged roughly $10,300 per employee in 1999. The quasi-fixed nature of many nonwage labor costs has important effects on employer hiring and overtime decisions. These effects are discussed below.

THE EMPLOYMENT/HOURS TRADE-OFF

The simple model of the demand for labor presented in the preceding chapters spoke to the quantity of labor demanded, making no distinction between the number of individuals employed by a firm and the average length of its employees' workweek. Holding all other inputs constant, however, a firm can produce a given level of output with various combinations of the number of employees hired and the number of hours worked per week. Presumably increases in the number of employees hired will allow for shorter workweeks, whereas longer workweeks will allow for fewer employees, other things equal.

In chapter 3 we defined the marginal product of labor (MP_L) as the change in output generated by an added unit of labor, holding capital constant. Once we distinguish between the *number* of workers hired (which we will denote by M) and the *hours* each works on average (H), we must think of two marginal products of labor. MP_M is the added output associated with an added worker, holding both capital and average hours per worker constant. MP_H is the added output generated by increasing average hours per worker, holding capital and the number of employees constant. As with MP_L, we assume that both MP_M and MP_H are positive, but that they decline as M and H (respectively) increase.[5]

How does a firm determine its optimal employment/hours combination? Is it ever rational for a firm to work its existing employees overtime on a regularly scheduled basis, even though it must pay them a wage premium, rather than hiring additional employees?

Determining the Mix of Workers and Hours

The fact that certain labor costs are not hours-related and others are makes it important to examine the marginal expense (ME_M) an employer faces when employing an additional *worker* for whatever length workweek its other employees are working. This marginal expense will be a function of the quasi-fixed labor costs plus the

---

[5]When the number of employees is increased, the decline in MP_M may be due to the reduced quantity of capital now available to each individual employee. When the hours each employee works per week are increased, the decline in MP_H may occur because after some point fatigue sets in.

weekly wage and variable (with hours) employee-benefit costs for the specified length of workweek. Similarly, it is important to examine the marginal expense (ME_H) a firm faces when it seeks to increase the *average workweek* of its existing workforce by one hour. This marginal expense will equal the per-hour wage and variable employee-benefit costs multiplied by the number of employees in the workforce. Of course, if the employer is in a situation in which an overtime premium (such as time and a half or double time) must be paid for additional hours, that higher rate is the relevant wage rate to use in the latter calculation.

Viewed in this way, a firm's decision about its optimal employment/hours combination is no different from its decision about the use of any two factors of production, which was discussed in chapter 3 (see equation 3.8c). Specifically, to minimize the cost of producing any given level of output, a firm should adjust both its employment level and its average workweek so that the costs of producing an added unit of output are equal for each:

$$\frac{ME_M}{MP_M} = \frac{ME_H}{MP_H} \tag{5.1}$$

Thus, if ME_M rises relative to ME_H, for example, a profit-maximizing firm will want to substitute *hours* for *workers* by hiring fewer employees but having each work more hours per week. Conversely, if ME_H rises relative to ME_M, the employer will want to produce its profit-maximizing level of output with a higher ratio of workers to average hours per worker.

The Fair Labor Standards Act (FLSA) requires that all employees covered by the legislation receive an overtime-pay premium of at least 50 percent of their regular hourly wage (time and a half) for each hour per week they work in excess of 40 hours.[6] A large proportion of overtime hours are worked because of disequilibrium phenomena—rush orders, seasonal demand, mechanical failures, and absenteeism, for example. (Example 5.1 discusses how the presence of quasi-fixed costs affects the market for temporary workers, who offer firms another way to meet these needs.) A substantial amount of overtime, however, appears to be regularly scheduled; equation (5.1) indicates why this scheduling of overtime may occur. Although overtime hours require premium pay, they also enable an employer to avoid the quasi-fixed employment costs associated with employing an additional worker. This point can be illustrated by considering what would happen if the overtime-pay premium were to be increased.

Policy Analysis: The Overtime-Pay Premium

Periodically proposals have been introduced in Congress to raise the overtime premium to double time. The argument made to support such an increase is that there

---

[6]The major categories of excluded employees are executive, administrative, and professional personnel, outside salespersons, and agricultural workers.

EXAMPLE 5.1

"Renting" Workers as a Way of Coping with Hiring Costs

One indication that the quasi-fixed costs of hiring are substantial can be seen in the growth of temporary-help agencies. Temporary-help agencies specialize in recruiting workers who are then put to work in client firms that need temporary workers. The temporary-help agency bills its clients, and its hourly charges are generally above the wage the client would pay if it hired workers directly—a premium the client is willing to pay because it is spared the investment costs associated with hiring. Because obtaining jobs through the temporary-help agency also saves employees repeated investment costs associated with searching and applying for available temporary openings, its employees are willing to take a wage less than they otherwise would receive. The difference between what its clients are charged and what its employees are paid permits the successful temporary-help agency to cover its quasi-fixed costs.

How anxious are firms and workers to avoid the costs of search and hiring? Some 2 million workers were employed by tempory-help services in 1995, and growth in this industry has been so rapid that it accounted for one-fourth of all employment growth in the United States during the mid-1990s.

Data from: Lewis M. Segal and Daniel G. Sullivan, "The Growth of Temporary Services Work," *Journal of Economic Perspectives* 11, no. 2 (Spring 1997): 117–136.

has been a growing share in total compensation of hiring and training costs, employee benefits, and government-mandated insurance premiums. As already noted, many of these costs are *quasi-fixed*, and thus do not vary with overtime hours of work. An increase in these costs increases employers' marginal expense of hiring new employees relative to the expense of working their existing workforces overtime. It is claimed, therefore, that the growth of quasi-fixed costs has been at least partly responsible for the greater use of overtime hours and that an increase in the overtime premium is required to better "spread the work" and increase employment.

Would an increase in the overtime premium prove to be an effective way of increasing employment and reducing unemployment? Although the overtime premium is legislatively fixed at a point in time, ME_M and ME_H vary across employers, depending on their quasi-fixed and hourly-wage costs. The first step in estimating the effects on employment of increasing the overtime premium is to find out whether the use of overtime actually increases as ME_M rises relative to ME_H. Several studies do indicate that, as summarized in Figure 5.1, firms with quasi-fixed costs that are high relative to their hourly labor costs schedule more overtime.[7]

If the number of overtime hours is sensitive to the ratio ME_M/ME_H, then an increase in the overtime premium to double time should lower the ratio and induce employers to cut back on the use of overtime (from H_0 to H_1 in Figure 5.1).

---

[7]For a recent study that references earlier empirical work on overtime hours, see Dora L. Costa, "Hours of Work and the Fair Labor Standards Act: A Study of Retail and Wholesale Trade, 1938–1950," *Industrial and Labor Relations Review* 53, no. 4 (July 2000): 648–664.

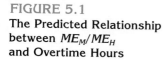

FIGURE 5.1

The Predicted Relationship between ME_M/ME_H and Overtime Hours

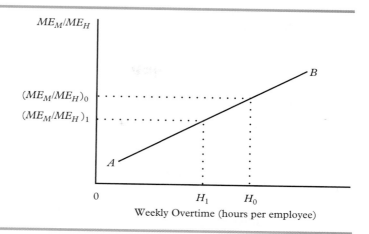

Will all these overtime hours be converted to added employment, thereby reducing unemployment?

Effects on Labor Costs   First, an increase in the overtime premium raises the average cost of labor even if all overtime is eliminated! The reason for this increase is that firms eliminating overtime and increasing employment must bear the quasi-fixed costs of employment discussed earlier. Firms using overtime *before* the imposition of the double-time premium *could* have hired more workers and reduced overtime usage earlier; the fact that they did not make this choice suggests it was a more costly one. If the double-time premium now induces this more costly choice, their labor costs will clearly rise. This increase may cause the total hours of labor hired to decrease as firms shift to more capital-intensive modes of production.

Effects on Scale   Second, even if the firms that used overtime prior to the double-time premium were to shift to more capital-intensive modes of production, their unit costs of output would tend to increase (they could have chosen to substitute capital for labor *before* but decided not to—presumably because of the higher cost). If this cost increase were passed on to consumers in the form of higher prices, a reduction in the quantity of output would occur. This scale effect should also lead to a decline in the number of labor hours purchased by employers.

Substitutability of New Workers   Third, the degree of substitutability between those who work overtime and those who are unemployed may be low. If, for example, those working overtime are skilled while those who are unemployed are unskilled, it might be difficult to convert overtime hours to added jobs for the unemployed.

Adjustment of Wages   Finally, it is possible that employers and employees mutually agree on a "package" of weekly hours and total compensation. Firms that regularly schedule overtime hours might respond to a legislated increase in the overtime premium by reducing the straight-time hourly wage by a sufficient amount to leave total compensation per worker unchanged. The original package of weekly hours and total compensation that both employers and employees had agreed upon might therefore remain unchanged. Empirical evidence suggests that straight-time hourly wages do adjust partially to changes in the overtime premium.[8] These adjustments further moderate the job-creation effects of any increase in the overtime premium.

Policy Analysis: Part-Time Employment and Mandated Employee Benefits

Overtime is one example of how employers can adjust their mix of workers and hours per worker; part-time employment is another. Part-time employment has grown as a share of total employment in most European countries and in the United States in recent years. For example, between 1955 and 2000 the percentage of employees in U.S. nonagricultural industries who were employed part-time (defined as less than 35 hours per week) rose from 10.5 to 22.7.[9] Explanations for this growth have focused mainly on the supply side of the labor market and on the changing industrial composition of employment. The growing shares of married women with children in the labor force (see chapter 6), of older workers phasing into retirement, and of students who need to work to finance their educations are all thought to have increased the number of workers willing to work part-time. On the demand side of the market, growth in the share of service-sector employment (Figure 2.3) has increased the number of jobs in which part-time workers can be easily employed.

Substitution Effects   Recently, however, attention has shifted to the role that relative costs play in the growth of part-time employment. Assuming that part-time workers and full-time workers are substitutes in production, if the hourly labor costs or the quasi-fixed costs of part-time workers fall relative to those of full-time workers, part-time employment should expand relative to full-time employment.

One study showed that employment of part-time workers in Great Britain expanded most rapidly during periods when they were covered by relatively few social insurance programs and protective regulations. Specifically, Britain's passage of the Employment Protection Act of 1975, which increased the eligibility of part-time employees for job separation payments and maternity benefits (both of which increase quasi-fixed costs), seemed to be associated with a slowdown in its

---

[8]Stephen J. Trejo, "The Effects of Overtime Pay Regulation on Worker Compensation," *American Economic Review* 81 (September 1991): 719–739. Noncompliance with the FLSA is also a phenomenon that could reduce employment growth; see Ronald G. Ehrenberg and Paul L. Schumann, "Compliance with the Overtime Pay Provisions of the Fair Labor Standards Act," *Journal of Law and Economics* 25 (April 1982): 159–181; and Brigitte Sellekaerts and Stephen Welch, "Noncompliance with the Fair Labor Standards Act: Evidence and Policy Implications," *Labor Studies Journal* 8 (Fall 1983): 124–136.

[9]U.S. Department of Labor, *Monthly Labor Review* 121 (June 1998), Table 5; and U.S. Bureau of Labor Statistics, *Monthly Labor Review* 124 (September 2001), Table 5. These reports are available at http://www.bls.gov in the *Monthly Labor Review Online* Archives.

part-time employment growth.[10] Studies that used U.S. data at a point in time have also documented that across industries in the United States, the part-time/full-time employment ratio is negatively related to the part-time/full-time wage ratio. Thus, holding other factors constant, in industries in which part-time workers' wages are lower relative to full-time workers' wages, usage of part-time employees is higher relative to that of full-time employees.[11]

Quasi-Fixed Costs   A recurrent policy proposal aimed at expanding health insurance coverage of American citizens is to require employers to provide medical insurance to *all* employees. Health insurance costs are quasi-fixed, and mandating employer-provided health insurance for all employees is predicted to disproportionately reduce the demand for part-time workers, on two accounts. First, relatively few part-time workers are currently provided with health insurance by their employers, so firms that heavily use part-time workers would face the greatest cost increases, other things equal. Second, mandated health insurance would raise the quasi-fixed costs of hiring workers relative to employing fewer workers for longer hours, thus increasing the costs of hiring part-time workers relative to full-time employees. Indeed, one study estimated that requiring firms to provide health insurance to their employees would cause a sizable reduction in the demand for part-time workers.[12] (Similarly, reductions in employment relative to hours worked can be expected to result when *firing* workers becomes more costly; see Example 5.2.)

FIRMS' LABOR INVESTMENTS AND THE DEMAND FOR LABOR

The models of the demand for labor given in chapters 3 and 4 were static in the sense that they considered only *current* marginal productivities and *current* labor costs. If all of a firm's labor costs are variable each year, then it will employ labor *each period* to the point at which labor's marginal revenue product equals the wage. Once we begin to consider hiring and training costs, however, the analysis changes somewhat.

Hiring and training costs are usually heavily concentrated in the initial periods of employment and do not recur. Later on, however, these early investments in hiring and training raise the productivity of employees. Once the investments are made, it is cheaper for the firm to *continue* using its current workers than to hire,

---

[10] R. Disney and E. M. Szyszczak, "Protective Labor Legislation and Part-Time Employment in Great Britain," *British Journal of Industrial Relations* 22 (March 1984): 78–100.

[11] Ronald G. Ehrenberg, Pamela Rosenberg, and Jeanne Li, "Part-Time Employment in the United States," in *Employment, Unemployment, and Labor Utilization,* ed. Robert A. Hart (Boston: Unwin Hyman, 1988), 256–281.

[12] Mark Montgomery and James Cosgrove, "The Effect of Employee Benefits on the Demand for Part-Time Workers," *Industrial and Labor Relations Review* 47, no. 1 (October 1993): 87–98. Also see Michael Lettau and Thomas C. Buchmueller, "Comparing Benefit Costs for Full- and Part-Time Workers," *Monthly Labor Review* 122, no. 3 (March 1999): 30–35.

EXAMPLE 5.2

Do Unjust Dismissal Policies Reduce Employment?

In most European nations, workers have some protection against "unjust dismissals." Typically their legislation mandates the use of labor courts or industrial tribunals to resolve disputes, and often severance pay is required. In contrast, the doctrine of *employment-at-will*, under which employers have the right to terminate the employment relationship at any time, for any reason, has historically prevailed in the United States. (Those not subject to this doctrine in the United States have included unionized workers with contract provisions governing discharges, tenured teachers, and workers under some civil service systems.)

A number of state courts, however, have adopted exceptions to this doctrine. Some exceptions prevent an employee from being discharged for an action that is consistent with public policy (e.g., reporting an employer for failing to pay the minimum wage), while others prevent discharges "without cause" if an employer's oral statements, established past practices, or statements in a personnel manual implicitly promise such protection.

Relaxation of the employment-at-will doctrine effectively increases the costs of both terminating and hiring workers (employers are likely to respond by expending more resources to screen out undesirable job applicants).

Economic theory suggests that these increased hiring and firing costs provide firms with an incentive to reduce employment and substitute additional hours per worker.

Is it the case that policies designed to protect jobs actually serve to reduce employment? Studies of employment in the U.S. have found that states with legal exceptions to the employment-at-will doctrine had lower levels of employment, other factors held constant. In Europe, countries with stricter employment protection laws also appear to have reduced employment levels, especially among younger workers and women (adult men may benefit from greater job protection). Thus, employment protection may help save jobs that *now* exist, but they appear to reduce the number of *new* job opportunities.

References: James M. Dertouzos and Lynn A. Karoly, "Employment Effects of Worker Protection: Evidence from the United States," and Daniel Hamermesh, "Employment Protection: Theoretical Implications and Some U.S. Evidence," in *Employment Security and Labor Market Behavior*, ed. Christoph F. Buechtermann (Ithaca, N.Y.: ILR Press, 1993); Alan B. Krueger, "The Evolution of Unjust Dismissal Legislation in the United States," *Industrial and Labor Relations Review* 44 (July 1991): 644–660; and Organisation for Economic Co-operation and Development, "Employment Protection and Labour Market Performance," *OECD Employment Outlook: June 1999*, 49–132.

at the same wage rate, new ones (who would have to be trained). Likewise, with an investment required for all *new* workers, employers have to consider not only *current* marginal productivity and labor cost but also *future* marginal productivity and labor costs in deciding whether (and how many) to hire. In short, the presence of investment costs—hiring and training expenses—means that hiring decisions must take into account past, present, and future factors.

To illustrate the hiring decision in the face of labor-investment costs, let us consider a firm that is seeking to determine its employment level over a two-period horizon. To keep the discussion simple, we shall ignore employee-benefit costs and the decision about how many hours employees will work; all workers employed in a period will be assumed to work for the entire period. We shall also assume that the firm is in a competitive product market and therefore takes its product price as given. Finally, firms that invest in their workers do so in the initial period (period 0) and reap their returns in the final period (period 1).

FIGURE 5.2
Effects of Training
on Marginal Product Schedules

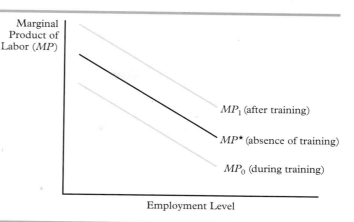

We will assume, with reference to Figure 5.2, that in the absence of training the firm's marginal product of labor schedule is MP^*. If the firm decides to invest in training during period 0, however, the marginal product of labor schedule during this period is reduced to MP_0. After training (that is, in period 1), the schedule of labor's marginal product rises to MP_1, where MP_1 exceeds both MP_0 and MP^*.[13]

We will also assume that the direct outlays on training the firm would have to make during period 0 are Z per worker in real terms (dollar costs divided by product price). Further, it will be assumed that the real wage it pays during the training period is W_0 and that the post-training wage is W_1; for now, we take these wages as given, although we shall shortly examine how they are determined.

The Concept of Present Value

In determining its optimal employment level over the two periods, the firm clearly must consider the costs of employing workers in both periods and their marginal products in both periods. A *naive* approach would be to simply add up the costs $(W_0 + W_1 + Z)$, add up the marginal products $(MP_0 + MP_1)$, and then stop hiring when the sum of the marginal products that the last worker produces over the two periods is just equal to the sum of his or her real wages and training costs. This approach is naive because it ignores the fact that revenues accruing in the future are worth less to the firm than an equal level of revenues that accrue now. Similarly, costs that occur in the future are less burdensome to the firm than equal dollar costs that occur in the present.

Why should this be the case? The answer hinges on the role of interest rates. A dollar of revenue earned by a firm today can be invested at some market rate

---

[13]In the remainder of this chapter, the subscript L is omitted from the algebraic representation of labor's marginal product. The subscripts used designate time period; the L is omitted to avoid clutter.

of interest so that by the next period it will be worth more than a dollar. Hence, faced with a choice of employing a worker whose marginal product is 5 in period 0 and 2 in period 1, or a worker whose marginal product is 2 in period 0 and 5 in period 1, the firm would prefer the former (if wages for the two workers were equal in each period). The sooner the product is produced and sold, the more quickly the firm can gain access to the funds, invest them, and earn interest. Similarly, faced with the option of paying $100 today or $100 next period, the firm should prefer the second option. It could invest and earn interest on the $100 now, make the payment in the next period, and have the interest left over. If the firm makes the payment now, it cannot earn interest income on the $100.

These examples illustrate why firms prefer benefit streams in which the benefits occur as early as possible and cost streams in which the costs occur as late as possible. But how do we compare different benefit and cost streams when benefits and costs occur in more than one period? Economists rely on the concept of *present value*, which we define to be the value *now* of an entire stream of future benefits or costs.

Suppose a firm receives the sum of B_0 in the current period and will receive nothing in the next period. How much money could it have in the next period if it invested B_0 at a rate of interest that equals r? It would have its original sum, B_0, plus the interest it earned, rB_0:

$$B_1 = B_0 + rB_0 = B_0(1 + r) \tag{5.2}$$

Since assets of B_1 can be automatically acquired by investing B_0 at the market rate of interest, B_0 *now and* B_1 *next period are equivalent values*. That is, a person who is offered B_0 now or B_1 in one year would regard the offers as exactly the same as long as $B_1 = B_0(1 + r)$.

Following this line of reasoning, suppose that the firm knows it will receive B_1 in the next period. What is the *current* value of that sum? Receiving B_1 in one year is equivalent to receiving a smaller amount (call it X) *now* and investing it so that it equals B_1 in a year. That is, the firm would need to have amount X now in order to invest it and wind up with principal plus interest equal to B_1 in the next period:

$$X(1 + r) = B_1 \tag{5.3}$$

Dividing both sides by $(1 + r)$:

$$X = \frac{B_1}{1 + r} \tag{5.4}$$

The quantity X in equation (5.4) is called the *discounted value* of B_1 earned one period in the future.

The *present value* of the firm's earnings over two periods is equal to its earnings in the initial period plus the discounted value of its earnings in the next period.[14] Returning to our two-period hiring decision example given at the start of this section, the *present value* of marginal productivity (*PVP*) can now be seen as

$$PVP = MP_0 + \frac{MP_1}{1 + r} \qquad (5.5)$$

That is, the value *now* of a worker's marginal productivity over two periods is the marginal productivity in the current period (MP_0) plus the marginal productivity in the next period *discounted* by $(1 + r)$. Likewise, the present value of the real marginal expense of labor (*PVE*) is equal to

$$PVE = W_0 + Z + \frac{W_1}{1 + r} \qquad (5.6)$$

where r is the market rate of interest. W_0 and Z are not discounted because they are incurred in the current period. However, W_1 is discounted by $(1 + r)$ because it is incurred one year in the future.

The present-value calculation reduces a stream of benefits or costs to a single number that summarizes a firm's entire stream of revenues or liabilities over different time periods. For example, the *PVE* can be thought of as the answer to the question, "Given that a firm incurs costs per worker of $W_0 + Z$ this period and W_1 next period, how much does it have to set aside today to be able to cover both periods' costs?" The *PVE* is *less* than $W_0 + Z + W_1$ because W_1 is not owed until the latter period and any funds set aside to cover W_1 can be invested now. If the firm sets aside $W_1/(1 + r)$ to cover its labor cost in the next period and invests this amount earning a rate of return r, the interest, $r[W_1/(1 + r)]$, plus principal, $W_1/(1 + r)$, available in the next period will just equal W_1.

Similarly, the *PVP* can be thought of as the answer to the question, "Given that a worker's marginal product will be MP_0 in this period and MP_1 next period, what is the value of that output stream to the employer today?" The *PVP* is less than $MP_0 + MP_1$ because if the firm were to attempt to borrow against the employee's future marginal product, it could borrow at most $MP_1/(1 + r)$ today and still afford to repay this principal plus the interest, $r[MP_1/(1 + r)]$, out of earnings in the next period.[15]

---

[14]Earnings in the initial period are not discounted because they are received *now*, not in the future.

[15]More generally, if the firm expects to receive benefits of $B_0, B_1, B_2, ..., B_n$ dollars over the current and next n periods, and if it faces the same interest rate, r, in each period, its present value of benefits (*PVB*) is given by

$$PVB = B_0 + \frac{B_1}{1 + r} + \frac{B_2}{(1 + r)^2} + \frac{B_3}{(1 + r)^3} + \cdots + \frac{B_n}{(1 + r)^n}$$

An analogous expression exists for the present value of costs. The reader should make sure that he or she understands why the denominator of B_2 is $(1 + r)^2$, the denominator of B_3 is $(1 + r)^3$, and so forth. If one thinks in terms of a series of one-period loans or investments, it should become obvious. For example, X_0 invested for one period yields $X_0(1 + r)$ at the end of the period. Let us call $X_0(1 + r) = X_1$. Now X_0 invested for two periods is equal to its value after one period (X_1) multiplied by $(1 + r)$—or $X_2 = X_1(1 + r)$. But $X_1 = X_0(1 + r)$, so $X_2 = X_0(1 + r)^2$. To find the present value of X_2 we divide by $(1 + r)^2$, so $X_0 = X_2/(1 + r)^2$.

FIGURE 5.3
**Multiperiod Demand
for Labor**

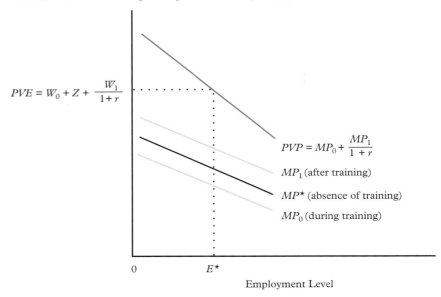

Marginal Product of Labor (*MP*)
Present Value of Marginal Product of Labor (*PVP*)
Present Value of Real Marginal Expense of Labor (*PVE*)

$$PVE = W_0 + Z + \frac{W_1}{1+r}$$

$$PVP = MP_0 + \frac{MP_1}{1+r}$$

MP_1 (after training)

$MP^\star$ (absence of training)

MP_0 (during training)

0            $E^\star$

Employment Level

The Multiperiod Demand for Labor

The concept of present value can help clarify what determines the labor demand function in our two-period model. Rather than focusing on the marginal product of labor schedule for each period separately, the firm must consider them jointly by considering their present values. Thus, the present value of schedules MP_0 and MP_1 in Figure 5.3 is shown as curve *PVP*. Similarly, rather than focusing on the hiring and training costs and the wage rates in each period separately, an employer must consider the *present value* of the marginal expense of labor (*PVE*).

Multiperiod Profit Maximization   To maximize its present value of profits, a firm should employ labor up until the point that adding an *additional* employee yields as much as it costs (when both yields and costs are stated as present values). That is, the profit-maximizing condition in our two-period example is

$$PVP = PVE \tag{5.7a}$$

or

$$MP_0 + \frac{MP_1}{1+r} = W_0 + Z + \frac{W_1}{1+r} \tag{5.7b}$$

Given the particular values of W_0, W_1, Z, and r that are specified in Figure 5.3, profits are maximized at employment level E^*.

Now, equation (5.7b) merely states the familiar profit-maximizing condition, that marginal returns should equal marginal costs, in a multiperiod context. If Z were zero, for example, equation (5.7b) implies that profits could be maximized when labor is hired so that $MP_0 = W_0$ and $MP_1/(1 + r) = W_1/(1 + r)$, or, since $1 + r$ is the denominator on both sides of the equation, $MP_1 = W_1$. Thus, when there are no hiring or training costs ($Z = 0$), the conditions demonstrated in chapter 3 are sufficient to guarantee profit maximization in the multiperiod context. However, when Z is positive, which means that firms make initial investments in their workers, the conditions for maximizing profits change.

Recouping Investment Costs   To understand the change in profit-maximizing conditions suggested by equation (5.7b), suppose that in the initial period the real wage an additional worker receives (W_0) plus the firm's direct investment outlays (Z) exceed the worker's output (MP_0). We can call this difference the *net expense* to the firm of hiring an additional worker in the initial period (NE_0):

$$NE_0 = W_0 + Z - MP_0 > 0 \qquad (5.8)$$

In order for the firm to maximize the present value of its profit stream, it must thus get a net *surplus* in the subsequent period. If it does not, the firm will not have any incentive to hire the additional worker.

The discounted value of the subsequent period's surplus (G) is defined as

$$G = \frac{MP_1}{1 + r} - \frac{W_1}{1 + r} = \frac{MP_1 - W_1}{1 + r} \qquad (5.9)$$

From equations (5.7b), (5.8), and (5.9), we see that, if the firm is to maximize profits, labor must be hired until the discounted value of the subsequent-period surplus equals the net expense (NE_0) in the initial period:

$$W_0 + Z - MP_0 = \frac{MP_1 - W_1}{1 + r} \qquad (5.10)$$

A subsequent-period surplus can exist *only* if real wages in that period (W_1) lie *below* marginal product (MP_1). This surplus makes up for the fact that the employer's labor costs in the initial period ($W_0 + Z$) were above the worker's marginal product (MP_0).

Summarizing   To this point we have established two things. First, equation (5.7b) has shown that in a multiperiod model of labor demand, the firm's demand curve is the same as the curve representing the *present value* of labor's marginal product over the periods of hire. Thus, the firm maximizes profits when the present value of its marginal labor expense equals the present value of labor's marginal product. Second, we demonstrated in equation (5.10) that maximizing profits when the firm's labor costs in the initial period exceed the worker's initial-period marginal product requires real wages in the subsequent period to be below marginal product in that period (so that a surplus is generated). The only times when a subsequent-period surplus is not necessary to induce the hiring of an additional employee are when investment costs (Z) are zero in the initial period, or when investment costs of Z exist but the initial-period real wage is decreased to such an extent that it equals $MP_0 - Z$. (In the latter case, employees pay for their own training by accepting a wage in the initial period that is decreased by the direct costs of training.)

Constraints on Multiperiod Wage Offers

In the single-period model of labor demand introduced in chapter 3, a firm in a competitive labor market takes the market wage as given and adjusts its hiring of labor so that labor's marginal product is equal to this wage. Our discussion above, however, implies that a profit-maximizing firm employing its workers for more than one period has some choice about its wage stream over these periods; it can pay more than marginal product in some periods and less in others. While such choice potentially does exist, it is constrained by the need to make a multiperiod "package" of wage offers that is competitive with the offers being made by other employers in the market. Just as the concept of present value was useful in expressing the profit-maximizing conditions in a multiperiod context, the concept is also useful in summarizing the constraints on a firm's stream of wage offers.

Alternative Wage Streams   To take a very simple example, suppose that the market wage for firms offering single-period jobs is W^*; that is, assume that workers can always find a job paying W^*. Suppose, further, that firm X wants to offer its job applicants a written, two-period employment contract, guaranteeing a wage of W_0 in the first period and W_1 in the second. It would *not* have to pay its workers W^* in both periods! It could pay wages in one period that were below W^* as long as its wages in the other period were enough above W^* that the following condition was met:

$$W_0 + \frac{W_1}{1 + r} \geq W^* + \frac{W^*}{1 + r} \tag{5.11}$$

Condition (5.11) states that, with a market wage of W^* in each period, firm X could select a W_0 and a W_1 that varied from W^* as long as the *present value of its wages over the two periods were at least as large as the present value of wages the workers could obtain elsewhere.* If, for example, $W^* = \$100$, firm X could make several offers of W_0 and W_1 that yielded present values equivalent to receiving $100 in both periods. A few of these alternative wage streams are shown in Table 5.3, which assumes a discount rate (r) of 6 percent. We can see from the table that, given our assumption, if firm X wished to pay its workers $81 in the first period, for instance, it must pay them at least $120 in the second period to be competitive in the labor market.

Rejection of Streams   Does the fact that all five alternative wage streams in Table 5.3 have equal present values mean that all are equally attractive to firm X and its potential workers? *If a two-period employment contract were legally binding*

TABLE 5.3 **Alternative Two-Period Wage Streams That Have Equal Present Values Using a 6 Percent Discount Rate**

Alternative	W_0	W_1	Present Value
A	$128	$ 70	$194
B	100	100	194
C	81	120	194
D	62	140	194
E	43	160	194

on both the firm and its employees, and if both used the same 6 percent discount rate, then all five wage streams would indeed be equally attractive to both parties. Generally speaking, however, written employment contracts are legally binding only on the *employer,* which means that employees are free to quit at any time. Alternative A is therefore unattractive to the employer, because employees could take the $128 offered in the first period and then, when wages are cut to $70, quit to take an always-available $100 job elsewhere in the second period.

If instead of offering its workers a written (*formal*) contract of employment, firm X were offering a set of promises about employment and wages over two periods that were not legally enforceable (often called an *informal* or *implicit* contract), it would face further constraints. Specifically, with implicit contracts, alternatives C, D, and E are unattractive to employees. With these alternatives, workers would fear that the firm might profit from paying a wage less than $100 in the first period and then fire them in the second period, when their wages were due to rise above what they could obtain elsewhere.

Attractive Alternatives If firm X always rules out alternative A and, in the absence of a formal contract, its employees rule out alternatives C, D, and E, is there any practical choice other than paying the market wage in each period? If the firm wants to offer a wage stream that departs from paying W^* in both periods, it must offer a stream whose present value is *above* that of a stream paying W^* in each period. In terms of Table 5.3, if firm X, in the absence of a formal contract, wants to pay wages below $100 in the first period, it must alter alternatives C, D, or E by increasing either W_0 or W_1 so that the present value of its offer rises above $194. Only by so doing can firm X induce at least some workers to take the risk that the firm will renege on its promises and fire them in the second period.

How, then, can a firm offering multiperiod employment afford to pay its workers a wage stream whose present value is above the market? One way is to train its workers so that their marginal product is increased beyond that of untrained workers. The other, which is useful when workers differ in their abilities, is to carefully select applicants so that only the best are hired. We therefore turn our attention to training and hiring investments to see just how it is that firms can profit from them.

GENERAL AND SPECIFIC TRAINING

It is useful to conceptually distinguish between two types of training: *general training* that increases an individual's productivity *to many employers* equally, and *specific training* that increases an individual's productivity *only at the firm* offering the training.[16] Pure general training might include teaching an applicant basic reading skills or how to use a word-processing program. Pure specific training might include teaching a worker how to use a machine that is unique to a single employer. The distinction is primarily a conceptual one because most training contains aspects of both types; however, the distinction does yield some interesting insights.

Suppose, continuing our two-period model, that a firm offers *general* training to its employees, who have a marginal product of MP^* (and can obtain wage offers of $W^* = MP^*$ elsewhere). Suppose, too, that the firm incurs an initial-period net cost of training equal to NE_0 of equation (5.8). This training increases employee marginal product to MP_1 ($> MP^*$) in the subsequent period, and the firm scales its wages (W_1) in the subsequent period so that there is a surplus in that period whose present value (G) equals NE_0. What will happen?

The trained employee is worth MP_1 to several other firms, but is getting paid less than MP_1 by the firm doing the training (so that it can obtain the required surplus). The employee can thus get *more* from some other employer, who did not incur training costs and thus will not demand a surplus, than he or she can get from the employer offering the training. This situation is likely to induce the employee to quit after training and seek work elsewhere. Assuming all other conditions of employment are the same, the firm would have to pay its employees MP_1 after general training to keep them from quitting. One exception arises when the employer can offer the worker a valuable credential for staying during the second period. This occurs in the case of apprenticeships and is discussed in Example 5.3.

If firms must pay a wage equal to MP_1 after training, they will not be willing to pay for general training of their employees. Either they will not offer it, or they will force trainees to bear the full cost of their training by paying wages that are less than marginal product in the period of training by an amount equal to the direct training costs (that is, NE_0 must equal zero).

In contrast, consider an individual who receives *specific training* that increases marginal productivity with the *current* employer to MP_1 in the subsequent period. Since the training is firm-specific, the trainee's marginal product in *other* firms remains at its pre-training level of MP^*; therefore, the most the employee can obtain elsewhere is still W^*. The firm that trains the worker in firm-specific skills *will* have an incentive to offer (and at least partially pay for) the job training because it can pay a wage above W^* but below MP_1 in the subsequent period. We explain below.

---

[16]Gary Becker, *Human Capital*, 2d ed. (New York: National Bureau of Economic Research, 1975), was first to formalize this distinction. A refinement can be found in Margaret Stevens, "A Theoretical Model of On-the-Job Training with Imperfect Competition," *Oxford Economic Papers* 46, no. 4 (October 1994): 537–562.

EXAMPLE 5.3

Apprenticeship in the United States and Elsewhere

Apprenticeship is very rare in the United States, where it accounts for about 0.3 percent of civilian employment, mostly in the building trades. In contrast, in Britain, Australia, and New Zealand, apprenticeship accounts for 1.9 to 2.7 percent of civilian employment and is the principal means of training for skilled manual trades. In Germany, Austria, and Switzerland, apprenticeship covers 5 to 6 percent of civilian employees and one-third to one-half of workers aged 15 to 18.

When apprenticeship works as it is designed, it allows employers to supply employees with general human capital. The young apprentices agree to work with an employer for a set period of time, after which the apprentice receives a credentialed status. In the early period, when most of the training occurs, their total compensation is generally higher than the value of their output to the employer. In the later part of the apprenticeship, the trained workers are generally paid less than the value of their output. The length of the apprenticeship is set so that underpayments in the second period offset overpayments in the first period. Apprentices have incentives to stay through the later period because the credential allows them access to future jobs at better pay.

Data from: Bernard Elbaum, "Why Apprenticeship Persisted in Britain but Not in the United States," *Journal of Economic History* 49, no. 2 (June 1989), 337–349.

Specific Training and the Wage Profile

With regard to specific training investments, firms have two related decisions to make: how much to invest in training their employees and, if they offer training, how to structure wages during and after training so that they can recoup their investment. How much training to offer any group of employees is affected by how much their productivity can be enhanced and by how likely they are to remain with the firm after being trained; clearly, firms are more likely to offer training to workers who learn efficiently and are less inclined to quit. While some workers are more likely to quit than others in any given situation, firms can also adopt pay policies that reduce their workers' quit rates, as we will see in a moment.

To help understand how a firm offering specific training decides on the wage stream it will offer, refer to the two-period example summarized in Figure 5.4. The firm's workers come to it with a marginal product of MP^*, and they can obtain a wage of W^* ($= MP^*$) elsewhere. If they receive specific training in the first period of employment, their marginal product with the firm is reduced to MP_0 during the training period but rises to MP_1 ($> MP^*$) in the post-training period. How will the firm set wages in the training and post-training periods?

In selecting its stream of wage offers, the firm must meet three conditions. First, it must not incur wage and training expenses whose present value is larger than that of its workers' marginal products; that is, in maximizing profits, it must satisfy equation (5.7b). Second, it must offer a wage stream whose present value is at least as large as that of alternative employers, as indicated by equation (5.11). Third, it must

FIGURE 5.4

A Two-Period Wage Stream Associated with Specific Training

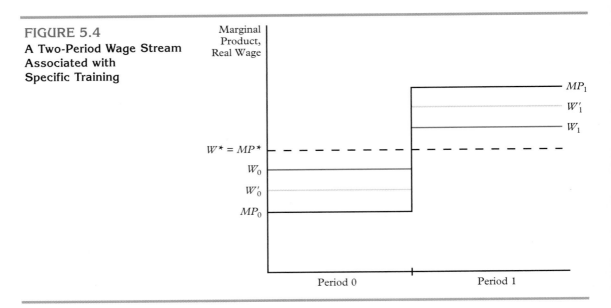

offer a post-training wage that is high enough to discourage its trained workers from quitting right after training, for if they do, the firm's training investments will be lost. Clearly, these conditions imply that the post-training wage will lie above W^* (to discourage quits) but below MP_1 (to allow the firm to recoup investment costs).

Effects of Quit Rates   If the firm believes that its workers will find it relatively costly to quit after training, then it could offer a wage stream similar to (W_0, W_1) in Figure 5.4, in which W_1 is only slightly more than W^* and W_0 is only slightly less. W_1 need not be much above W^* to induce those workers to stay with the firm in the post-training period, which means that the firm can (and must) pay a wage closer to W^* during training. Note that the higher W_0 is relative to MP_0 during training, the greater are the training costs borne by the firm.

   If its workers have lower costs of job changing and are therefore more likely to quit in the post-training period, then the firm will want to force them to bear more of any training costs by paying a relatively low wage during the training period. This will allow (and require) them to pay a relatively high post-training wage, which will have the benefit of reducing their workers' likelihood of quitting. Firms, then, are less willing to invest in groups of workers who are more quit-prone, and specific training, if offered, is associated with a more steeply rising wage profile, such as the one labeled W_0', W_1' in Figure 5.4.[17]

---

[17]See Lisa M. Lynch and Sandra E. Black, "Beyond the Incidence of Employer-Provided Training," *Industrial and Labor Relations Review* 52, no. 1 (October 1998): 64–81; and Elizabeth Becker and Cotton Lindsay, "Sex Differences in Tenure Profiles: Effects of Shared Firm-Specific Investment," *Journal of Labor Economics* 12, no. 1 (January 1994): 98–118.

Protecting Investments   From the perspective of employees, if they are paid a wage below W^* during the training period, they too have an investment to protect in the post-training period. Just as employers can reduce employees' incentives to quit by paying a post-training wage that is higher relative to W^*, workers can obtain more protection from being fired after training by accepting a post-training wage lower relative to MP_1. If *employees* bore all the costs of specific training and received all the returns (by receiving a post-training wage equal to MP_1), then employers would have no investment of their own to protect, would receive no post-training surplus from their employees, and would not be inhibited from firing employees after training. If *employers* bore all the costs, they might not be able to pay their employees enough in the subsequent period to guard against their quitting. It is in the *mutual* interest of both employers and employees, then, to share the costs of specific training and thereby foster a long-term employment relationship.

Actual Wage Profiles   Empirical studies measuring the wage profiles associated with on-the-job training in the United States suggest that employers bear much of the costs and reap most of the returns. There is evidence that wages are not depressed enough initially to offset employers' direct costs of training,[18] and there is corresponding evidence that subsequent wage increases are much smaller than productivity increases. A survey of employers, summarized in Figure 5.5, estimated that productivity increases, which generally rose with the hours of initial on-the-job training, were far larger than wage increases over a worker's first two years with an employer. Other studies that directly link the wage profiles of American workers with the amount of training they have received find that post-training wage increases are relatively modest.[19]

Implications of the Theory

Layoffs   One major implication of the provision of specific training is the above-mentioned reluctance of firms to lay off workers in whom they have invested. We have seen that in the post-training period, wages must be less than marginal productivity if the firm is to have any incentive at all to bear some initial training costs. This gap between MP_1 and W_1 provides protection against employee layoffs, even in a recession.

---

[18]John Bishop, "The Incidence of and Payoff to Employer Training," Cornell University Center for Advanced Human Resource Studies Working Paper 94-17, July 1994, 41; and Margaret Stevens, "An Investment Model for the Supply of General Training by Employers," *Economic Journal* 104 (May 1994): 556–570.

[19]David Blanchflower and Lisa Lynch, "Training at Work: A Comparison of U.S. and British Youths," in *Training and the Private Sector: International Comparisons*, ed. Lisa Lynch (Chicago: University of Chicago Press for the National Bureau of Economic Research, 1994), 233–260; Veum, "Sources of Training and Their Impact on Wages" (see footnote 2); and Alan Krueger and Cecilia Rouse, "The Effect of Workplace Education on Earnings, Turnover, and Job Performance," *Journal of Labor Economics* 16, no. 1 (January 1998): 61–94. Also see Judith K. Hellerstein and David Neumark, "Are Earnings Profiles Steeper than Productivity Profiles? Evidence from Israeli Firm-Level Data," *Journal of Human Resources* 30, no. 1 (Winter 1995): 89–112.

FIGURE 5.5

Productivity and Wage Growth, First Two Years on Job, by Occupation and Initial Hours of Employer Training

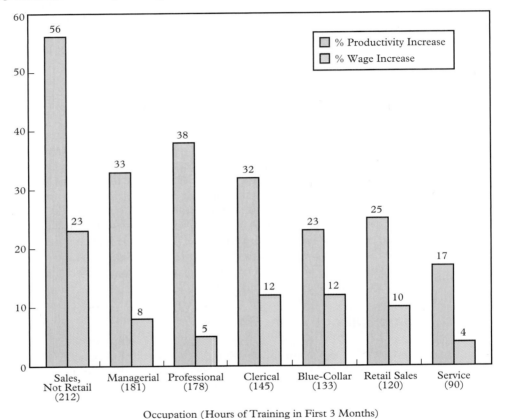

Source: John Bishop, "The Incidence of and Payoff to Employer Training," Cornell University Center for Advanced Human Resource Studies Working Paper 94-17, July 1994, Table 1.

Suppose a recession were to occur and cause product demand to fall. The marginal productivity associated with each employment level would fall (from *MP'* to *MP"* in Figure 5.6). For workers whose wage was equal to marginal productivity before the recession, this fall would reduce their marginal productivity to *below* their wage—and profit-maximizing employers would reduce employment, as shown in panel (a) of Figure 5.6, in order to maximize profits under the changed market conditions. In terms of Figure 5.6a, employment would fall from *E'* to *E"*.

FIGURE 5.6
The Effect of a Decline in Demand on Employment with General and Specific Training

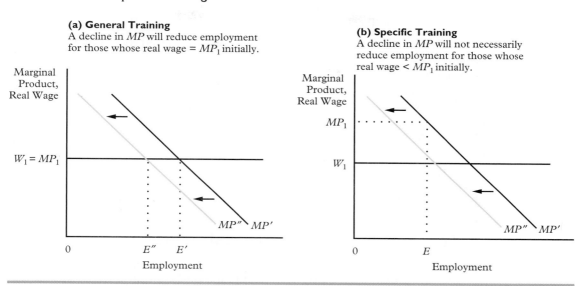

(a) General Training
A decline in *MP* will reduce employment for those whose real wage = MP_1 initially.

Marginal Product, Real Wage

$W_1 = MP_1$

MP'' MP'

0   E'' E'

Employment

(b) Specific Training
A decline in *MP* will not necessarily reduce employment for those whose real wage < MP_1 initially.

Marginal Product, Real Wage

MP_1

W_1

MP'' MP'

0   E

Employment

For a worker whose wage was *less* than marginal productivity, owing to past specific training, the decline in marginal productivity might *still* leave such productivity *above* the wage. Firms would not be making enough surplus in the post-training period to earn back the net labor costs they incurred during the training period. However, these costs have already been spent and the firms cannot get them back. They will not hire and train *new* workers, but neither will they fire the ones they have trained. After all, these trained workers are still generating more than the company is paying them, and to lay them off would only reduce profits further. Thus, as panel (b) of Figure 5.6 shows, workers in whom their employers have invested are shielded to some extent from being laid off in business downturns. Of course, if marginal productivity fell to the point where it was below the wage, even trained workers might be laid off.[20]

Thus, this model suggests that during an economic downturn firms have an incentive to lay off workers with either no training or general training, but that it may prove profitable for firms to retain workers who have specific training. Although it is difficult to estimate the extent to which workers have specific

[20]If the downturn is expected to be short and if marginal productivity is not too much below the wage, firms might not lay off workers and chance losing them. Why any adjustment would come in the form of layoff, rather than by temporarily reducing wages or hours of work, is discussed in chapter 15.

training "imbedded" in them, there is some evidence that layoffs are lower for workers with higher skill levels, holding all other things, including their wage rates, constant.[21] Since the divergence between skill (productivity) and wages during the post-training period can be taken as a measure of the extent of specific training, this finding provides some support for the theory.

Labor Productivity   A second phenomenon our revised theory of demand can help explain is the fall in average productivity—output per labor hour—that occurs in the early stages of a recession. As demand and output start to fall, firms that have invested in specific training respond by maintaining their specifically trained workers on their payrolls. Such *labor hoarding* causes measured productivity to fall. Of course, the converse of this is that when demand picks up, firms can increase their output levels without proportionately increasing their employment levels because, in effect, they have maintained an *inventory* of skilled labor. Labor hoarding due to specific investments in human capital thus causes average productivity to increase in the early stages of a cyclical expansion and decrease in the early stages of a recession.

Do Employers Ever Pay for General Training?

Our theory suggests that the costs of general training must be borne by employees, because any attempts by employers to obtain a post-training surplus will be met with an exodus of already-trained workers seeking higher wages elsewhere. Despite this clear implication of theory there is a growing body of evidence that firms in the United States *do* offer (and pay for) general training among their workers.[22] Why?

Sometimes employees who receive general training can be tied to their employer by a contract requiring them to pay back the costs of educational programs if they quit within, say, two years of completing them. Such legal barriers to quitting, however, are rare. More often, mobility is inhibited only by various costs employees naturally must bear in switching employers: time must be spent interviewing, travel and relocation costs must be borne, and there are costs of leaving a familiar environment for the unknown. These mobility costs, which we will analyze more fully in chapter 10, may generate monopsonistic

---

[21]For a recent paper on this topic, see Hilary Hoynes, "The Employment, Earnings, and Income of Less Skilled Workers over the Business Cycle," in *Finding Jobs: Work and Welfare Reform*, ed. Rebecca Blank and David Card (New York: Russell Sage Foundation, 2000): pp. 23–71.

[22]Daron Acemoglu and Jörn-Steffen Pischke, "Beyond Becker: Training in Imperfect Labour Markets," *Economic Journal* 109 (February 1999): F112–F142; Mark A. Loewenstein and James R. Spletzer, "General and Specific Training: Evidence and Implications," *Journal of Human Resources* 34, no. 4 (Fall, 1999): 710–733; and Laurie J. Bassi and Jens Ludwig, "School-to-Work Programs in the United States: A Multi-Firm Case Study of Training, Benefits, and Costs," *Industrial and Labor Relations Review* 53, no. 2 (January 2000): 219–239.

EXAMPLE 5.4

Why Do Temporary-Help Firms Provide Free General Skills Training?

Temporary-help agencies employ about one in thirty-five workers. They hire workers who are, in effect, "rented out" to client firms—making their money by charging clients an hourly fee that exceeds what they pay their employees by 35 to 65 percent. Most provide their employees with nominally free training (temp workers are paid during training days), which is given "up-front" with no requirement of continued employment. The training is *general*, focusing on word processing and other computer skills. Training periods average only eleven hours, but the skills are clearly valuable—one leading company charges $150 per worker per day to provide similar training to its clients' non-temporary workers. Why do these temp agencies give valuable general training to workers who could take their new skills and run?

A recent study explains this phenomenon by noting that providing training allows the temp agencies to attract lower-paid workers who may lack certain skills, but have an aptitude for, and place a value on, learning. The training allows temp agencies to screen such workers and learn about their abilities. How can these agencies capitalize on the information they generate about their trainees?

Many client firms use temp agencies to acquire information on applicants for permanent jobs without having to put much into the quasi-fixed costs of hiring and firing—and, of course, many temp workers are looking for permanent jobs. Indeed, about 15 percent of temporary-help workers are hired directly by client firms each month. Temp agencies have thus become a means of providing and auditioning potential permanent workers to their clients, and they are paid primarily as information brokers. Client firms are willing to pay a premium for this information without themselves having to risk an investment, temp workers are willing to take a lower wage for the opportunity to audition for permanent work, and the audition period is long enough to recoup training costs because it takes some time for client firms to make their own evaluations.

Data from: David Autor, "Why Do Temporary Help Firms Provide Free General Skills Training?" *Quarterly Journal of Economics* 116, no. 4 (November 2001): 1409–1448.

conditions in many labor markets and thereby enable firms to pay a real wage less than marginal product.

In addition to training employees, firms must also evaluate them when making hiring, placement, and promotion decisions. They may therefore find that training programs—even ones with a "general" component—can be used to help discover the learning abilities, work habits, and motivation levels of new employees (see Example 5.4).[23] Thus, some of what appears to be general training may actually represent an investment in firm-specific information about employees that will be useful later on in making assignments and deciding on promotions. We conclude this chapter with a section that analyzes hiring and screening investments in greater detail.

---

[23]Margaret Stevens, "An Investment Model for the Supply of General Training by Employers." Also see W. R. Bowman and Stephen L. Mehay, "Graduate Education and Employee Performance: Evidence from Military Personnel," *Economics of Education Review* 18, no. 4 (October 1999): 453–463.

HIRING INVESTMENTS

We have noted that firms often incur significant costs in recruiting and selecting employees. These costs cause them to adopt standards or conventions in hiring and promoting workers that can be explained using the concepts we have discussed. The implications of hiring costs are the subject of this section.

The Use of Credentials

Since firms often bear the costs of hiring and training workers, it is in their interest to make these costs as low as possible. Other things equal, firms should prefer to obtain a workforce of a given quality at the least possible cost. Similarly, they should prefer to hire workers who are fast learners because such workers could be trained at less cost. Unfortunately, it may prove expensive for firms to extensively investigate the background of every individual who applies for a job to ascertain his or her skill level and ability to undertake training.

One way to reduce these costs is to rely on *credentials*, or *signals*, in the hiring process, rather than intensively investigating the qualities of individual applicants.[24] For example, if *on average* college graduates are more productive than high school graduates, an employer might specify that a college degree is a requirement for the job. Rather than interviewing and testing all applicants to try to ascertain the productivity of each, the firm may simply select its new employees from the pool of applicants who meet this educational standard.

Such forms of *statistical discrimination*, judging individuals by *group* characteristics, have obvious costs. On the one hand, for example, some high school graduates may be fully qualified to work for a firm that insists on college graduates. Excluding them from the pool of potential applicants imposes costs on them (they do not get the job); however, it also imposes costs on the employer *if* other qualified applicants cannot be readily found. On the other hand, there may be some unproductive workers among the group of college graduates, and an employer who hires them may well suffer losses while they are employed. However, if the reduction in hiring costs that arises when *signals* (such as educational credentials, marital status, or age) are used is large, it may prove profitable for an employer to use them even if an occasional unsatisfactory worker sneaks through.

Internal Labor Markets

One of the difficulties in hiring employees is that such personal attributes as dependability, motivation, honesty, and flexibility are difficult to judge from interviews, employment tests, or even the recommendations of former employers. This difficulty has led many larger firms to create an *internal labor market*, in which workers

---

[24]See Michael Spence, "Job Market Signaling," *Quarterly Journal of Economics* 87 (August 1973): 355–374. Refer to chapter 9 for a more detailed discussion of signaling.

are hired into relatively low-level jobs, and higher-level jobs are filled only from within the firm. This policy gives employers a chance to observe *actual* productive characteristics of the employees hired, and this information is then used to determine who stays with the firm and how fast and how high employees are promoted.

The *benefits* of using an internal labor market to fill vacancies are that the firm knows a lot about the people working for it. Hiring decisions for upper-level jobs in either the blue-collar or the white-collar workforces will thus offer few surprises to the firm. The *costs* of using the internal labor market are associated with the restriction of competition for the upper-level jobs to those in the firm. Those in the firm may not be the best employees available, but they are the only ones the firm considers for these jobs. Firms most likely to decide that the benefits of using an internal labor market outweigh the costs are those whose upper-level workers must have a lot of firm-specific knowledge and training that can best be attained by on-the-job learning over the years.[25]

As noted earlier, firms that pay for *training* will want to ensure that they obtain employees who can learn quickly and will remain with them long enough for the training costs to be recouped through the post-training surplus. For these firms, the internal labor market offers two attractions. First, it allows the firm to observe workers on the job, and thus make better decisions about which workers will be the recipients of later, perhaps very expensive, training. Second, the internal labor market tends to foster an attachment to the firm by its employees. They know that they have an inside track on upper-level vacancies because outsiders will not be considered. If they quit the firm, they would lose this privileged position. They are thus motivated to become long-term employees of the firm. The full implications of internal labor markets for wage policies within the firm will be discussed in chapter 11.

How Can the Employer Recoup Its Hiring Investments?

Whether a firm invests in training its workers or in selecting them, it will do so only if it believes it can generate an acceptable rate of return on its investment. For a labor investment to be worthwhile, an employer must be able to benefit from a situation in which workers are paid less than their marginal value to the firm in the postinvestment period. How can employers generate a postinvestment surplus from their *hiring* investments?

Suppose that applicants for a job vacancy have either average, below-average, or above-average productivity, but that the employer cannot tell which without making some kind of investment in acquiring that information. If the firm does not make this investment, it must assume that any particular applicant is of average ability

---

[25]For a detailed discussion of internal labor markets, see Paul Osterman, ed., *Internal Labor Markets* (Cambridge, Mass.: MIT Press, 1984); and George Baker and Bengt Holmstrom, "Internal Labor Markets: Too Many Theories, Too Few Facts," *American Economic Review* 85, no. 2 (May 1995): 255–259.

and pay accordingly. If the firm makes an investment in acquiring information about its applicants, however, it could then hire *only* those whose productivity is above average. The surplus required to pay back its investment costs would then be created by paying these above-average workers a wage less than their true productivity.

Would the firm pay its new workers the average wage even though they are above average in productivity, thereby obtaining the full surplus? As with the case of training, the firm would probably decide to pay a wage greater than the average, but still below workers' actual productivity, to increase the likelihood that the workers in whom it has invested will remain. If its workers quit, the firm would have to invest in acquiring information about their replacements.

While the self-interest of employers would drive them to pay an above-average wage to above-average workers, two things could allow the screening firm to pay a wage that is still lower than workers' full productivity. One is the presence of mobility costs among employees, which we just discussed in the context of general training. The other is that information one employer finds out through a costly screening process may not be observable by other employers without an investment of their own. Either of these conditions would inhibit employees from obtaining wage offers from competing firms that could afford to pay full-productivity wages because they had no screening expenses to recoup.

REVIEW QUESTIONS

1. Both low-skilled workers and high-paid college professors have high rates of voluntary quits. What do they have in common that leads to a high quit rate?

2. When plants close, firms usually must incur various costs associated with laying off their workers, including processing necessary forms, helping them find other jobs, and paying them severance allowances. Suppose that industry X finds itself in a much more competitive product market than it used to face, and that firms in the industry now have a greater probability of closing than they used to have. How might this change affect (a) the number of employees hired in the industry, and (b) their average hours of work?

3. For decades, most large employers bought group health insurance from insurers who charged them premiums on a *per-worker* basis. In 1993, a proposal for a national

health insurance plan contained a provision requiring group health insurers to charge premiums based on *payroll* (in effect, financing health insurance by a payroll "tax"). Assuming the *total* premiums paid by employers remain the same, what are the labor market implications of this proposed change in the way in which health insurance is financed?

4. Workers in a certain job are trained by the company, and the company calculates that to recoup its investment costs the workers' wages must be $5 per hour below their marginal productivity. Suppose that after training, wages are set at $5 below marginal productivity, but that developments in the product market quickly (and permanently) reduce marginal productivity by $2 per hour. If the company does not feel it can lower wages or employee benefits, how will its employment level be affected in the

short run? How will its employment level be affected in the long run? Explain, being sure to define what you mean by the short run and the long run!

5. In recent years, many plants have closed, forcing thousands of workers out of their jobs and into new ones. Studies of wage loss suffered by these displaced workers find that, *among groups of workers with exactly the same skills and types of training*, workers who had been with the firm for many years and were in the 55–64 age range had greater wage losses than those in the 25–34 age range. Is it possible that the presence of employer-provided specific training (among the new employers of these displaced workers) could cause this outcome?

6. Suppose that the United States adopts a policy requiring employers to offer 600 hours of paid leave for mothers of newly born babies. Assuming wages remain the same, analyze the labor demand effects of mandated paid child-care leave on women of childbearing age and on women past childbearing age.

7. In recent years there has been discussion of taxing employees for the nonwage benefits they receive. (At present, most benefits—medical and life insurance, for example—are not subject to the personal income tax.) If benefits such as insurance are taxed, they will become less attractive to employees, who may prefer to obtain increases in compensation in the form of wage increases rather than increases in nonwage benefits. Should this happen, what would be the likely effect on hours of work per employee per week?

8. Major league baseball teams scout and hire younger players whom they then train in the minor leagues for a period of three to five years. Very few of their trainees (perhaps 5 percent) actually make it to the major leagues, but if they do they are bound to the team that owns their contract for a period of six years. After six years, the player can become a *free agent* and choose any major league team on which to play. Keeping in mind that the major league teams pay the costs of, but derive no revenues from, their minor league teams, what would be the most important predictable effects of allowing players to become free agents immediately upon their entry into the major leagues?

PROBLEMS

1. Suppose that a worker's alternative wage, W^*, is $200 in every period. A firm offers the worker a three-period contract that pays $180 in the first period and $200 in the second period. Assuming that the discount rate is 10 percent, how much must the firm offer in the third period to attract the worker?

2. Suppose that a firm is considering training a worker. The worker's MP_L is $100 during the training period, but rises to $200 in the post-training period. The worker's wage is $100 during the training period, the cost of training is $50, and the discount rate is 10 percent. What is the most that a profit-maximizing firm can afford to pay the worker in the second period?

3. A firm is considering hiring a worker and providing the worker with general training. The training costs $1,000 and the worker's MP_L during the training period is $3,000. If the worker can costlessly move to another employer in the post-training period and that employer will pay a wage equaling the new MP_L, how much will the training firm pay the worker in the training period?

SELECTED READINGS

Becker, Gary. *Human Capital.* 2d ed. New York: National Bureau of Economic Research, 1975.

Ehrenberg, Ronald G., and Paul L. Schumann. *Longer Hours or More Jobs? An Investigation of Amending Hours Legislation to Create Employment.* Ithaca, N.Y.: ILR Press, 1982.

Hart, Robert. *Working Time and Employment.* London: Allen and Unwin, 1986.

Lynch, Lisa, ed. *Training and the Private Sector: International Comparisons.* Chicago: University of Chicago Press, 1994.

Osterman, Paul, ed. *Internal Labor Markets.* Cambridge, Mass.: MIT Press, 1984.

Parsons, Donald. "The Firm's Decision to Train." In *Research in Labor Economics* 11, ed. Lauri J. Bassi and David L. Crawford. Greenwich, Conn.: JAI Press, 1990. Pp. 53–75.

Williamson, Oliver, et al. "Understanding the Employment Relation: The Analysis of Idiosyncratic Exchange." *Bell Journal of Economics* 16 (Spring 1975): 250–280.

6

SUPPLY OF LABOR TO THE ECONOMY:
The Decision to Work

T his and the next four chapters will focus on issues of *worker* behavior. That is, chapters 6–10 will discuss and analyze various aspects of *labor supply* behavior. Labor supply decisions can be roughly divided into two categories. The first, which is addressed in this chapter and the next, includes decisions about whether to work at all and, if so, how long to work. Questions that must be answered include whether to participate in the labor force, whether to seek part-time or full-time work, and how long to work both at home and for pay. The second category of decisions, which is addressed in chapters 8–10, deals with the questions that must be faced by a person who has decided to seek work for pay: the occupation or general class of occupations in which to seek offers (chapters 8–9) and the geographical area in which offers should be sought (chapter 10).

This chapter begins with some basic facts concerning labor force participation rates and hours of work. We then develop a theoretical framework that can be used in the analysis of decisions to work for pay. This framework is also useful for analyzing the structure of various income maintenance programs.

TRENDS IN LABOR FORCE PARTICIPATION AND HOURS OF WORK

When a person actively seeks work, he or she is, by definition, in the *labor force.* As pointed out in chapter 2, the *labor force participation rate* is the percentage of a given population that either has a job or is looking for one. Thus, one clear-cut statistic important in measuring people's willingness to work outside the home is the labor force participation rate.

Labor Force Participation Rates

Perhaps the most revolutionary change taking place in the labor market today is the tremendous increase in the proportion of women, particularly married women, working outside the home. Table 6.1 shows the dimensions of this change in the United States. As recently as 1950 only 21.6 percent of married women were in the labor force. By 1960 this percentage had risen to 31.9 percent, and recently it has reached over 60 percent—over two and a half times what it was in 1950. Our interest in this chapter is in understanding the factors that have influenced this fundamental change in the propensity of women to seek work outside the home.

TABLE 6.1   **Labor Force Participation Rates of Females in the United States over 16 Years of Age, by Marital Status, 1900–1999 (percent)**

Year	All Females	Single	Widowed, Divorced	Married
1900	20.6	45.9	32.5	5.6
1910	25.5	54.0	34.1	10.7
1920	24.0			9.0
1930	25.3	55.2	34.4	11.7
1940	26.7	53.1	33.7	13.8
1950	29.7	53.6	35.5	21.6
1960	37.7	58.6	41.6	31.9
1970	43.3	56.8	40.3	40.5
1980	51.5	64.4	43.6	49.8
1990	57.5	66.7	47.2	58.4
1999	60.0	68.7	49.1	61.2

Sources: 1900–1950: Clarence D. Long, *The Labor Force under Changing Income and Employment* (Princeton, N.J.: Princeton University Press, 1958), Table A–6.

1960–1999: U.S. Department of Labor, Bureau of Labor Statistics, *Handbook of Labor Statistics,* Bulletin 2340 (Washington, D.C.: U.S. Government Printing Office, 1989), Table 6; and Eva E. Jacobs, ed., *Handbook of U.S. Labor Statistics* (Lanham, Md.: Bernan Press, 2001), 11, 18.

A second major trend in labor force participation is the decrease in length of careers for males, as can be seen in Table 6.2. The overall labor force participation rate of men has been falling, especially among the young and the old. The most substantial decreases in the United States have been among those 65 and over—from 68.3 percent in 1900 down to 16.9 percent by 1999. Participation rates for men of "prime age" have declined only slightly, although among 45- to 64-year-olds there were sharp decreases in the 1930s and 1970s. Clearly, men are starting their careers later and ending them earlier than they were at the beginning of this century.

The trends in American labor force participation rates have been observed in other industrialized countries as well. In Table 6.3 we display, for countries with comparable data, the trends in participation rates for women in the 25–54 age group and for men near the age of early retirement (55 to 64 years old). Typically, the fraction of women in the labor force rose from half or less in 1965 to roughly three-quarters some thirty years later. Among men between the ages of 55 and 64, participation fell markedly in each country except Japan, although the declines were much larger in some countries (France, for example) than others (Sweden). Thus, while there are some differences in trends across the countries, it is likely that common forces are influencing labor supply trends in the industrialized world.

TABLE 6.2 **Labor Force Participation Rates for Males in the United States, by Age, 1900–1999 (percent)**

Year	*Age Groups*					
	14–19	*16–19*	*20–24*	*25–44*	*45–64*	*Over 65*
1900	61.1		91.7	96.3	93.3	68.3
1910	56.2		91.1	96.6	93.6	58.1
1920	52.6		90.9	97.1	93.8	60.1
1930	41.1		89.9	97.5	94.1	58.3
1940	34.4		88.0	95.0	88.7	41.5
1950	39.9	63.2	82.8	92.8	87.9	41.6
1960	38.1	56.1	86.1	95.2	89.0	30.6
1970	35.8	56.1	80.9	94.4	87.3	25.0
1980		60.5	85.9	95.4	82.2	19.0
1990		55.7	84.4	94.8	80.5	16.3
1999		52.9	81.9	93.0	80.7	16.9

Sources: 1900–1950: Clarence D. Long, *The Labor Force under Changing Income and Employment* (Princeton, N.J.: Princeton University Press, 1958), Table A–2.

1960: U.S. Department of Commerce, Bureau of the Census, *Census of Population, 1960: Employment Status*, Subject Reports PC(2)–6A, Table 1.

1970: U.S. Department of Commerce, Bureau of the Census, *Census of Population, 1970: Employment Status and Work Experience*, Subject Reports PC(2)–6A, Table 1.

1980–1999: Eva E. Jacobs, ed., *Handbook of U.S. Labor Statistics* (Lanham, Md.: Bernan Press, 2001), 24, 33.

TABLE 6.3   Labor Force Participation Rates of Women and Older Men, Selected Countries, 1965–1999

| Country | Women, aged 25 to 54 | | | |
	1965	1973	1983	1999
Canada	33.9	44.0	65.1	78.2
France	42.8	54.1	67.0	78.4
Germany	46.1	50.5	58.3	75.7
Japan	—	53.0*	59.5	66.4
Sweden	56.0	68.9	87.0	85.7
United States	45.1	52.0	67.1	76.8
	Men, aged 55 to 64			
Canada	86.4	81.3	72.3	60.7
France	76.0	72.1	53.6	42.6
Germany	84.6	73.4	63.1	55.1
Japan	—	86.3*	84.7	85.2
Sweden	88.3	82.7	77.0	72.3
United States	82.9	76.9	69.4	67.9

*Data are for 1974 (earlier data not comparable).
Source: Organisation for Economic Co-operation and Development, *Labor Force Statistics* (Paris: OECD, various dates).

Hours of Work

Because data on labor force participation include both the employed and those who want a job but do not have one, they are a relatively pure measure of labor supply. In contrast, the weekly or yearly hours of work put in by the typical employee are often thought to be determined only by the demand side of the market. After all, don't employers, in responding to the factors discussed in chapter 5, set the hours of work expected of their employees? They do, of course, but hours worked are also influenced by *employee* preferences on the supply side of the market, especially in the long run.

Even though employers set work schedules, employees can exercise their preferences regarding hours of work through their choice of part-time or full-time work, their decisions to work at more then one job,[1] or their selection of occupations and employers. For example, women managers who work full-time average more hours of work per week than full-time clerical workers, and male sales

---

[1]Some 20 percent of men, and 12 percent of women, hold more than one job at some time during a year. See Christina H. Paxon, and Nachum Sicherman, "The Dynamics of Dual Job Holding and Job Mobility," *Journal of Labor Economics* 14, no. 3 (July 1996): 357–393; and Karn Smith Conway and Jean Kimmel, "Male Labor Supply Estimates and the Decision to Moonlight," *Labour Economics* 5 (1998): 135–166.

workers work more hours per week than their full-time counterparts in skilled craft jobs. Moreover, different employers offer different mixes of full- and part-time work, require different weekly work schedules, and have different policies regarding vacations and paid holidays.

Employer offers regarding both hours and pay are intended to enhance their profits, but they must also satisfy the preferences of current and prospective employees. For example, if employees receiving an hourly wage of $X for 40 hours per week really wanted to work only 30 hours at $X per hour, some enterprising employer (presumably one with relatively lower quasi-fixed costs) would eventually seize on their dissatisfaction and offer jobs with a 30-hour workweek, ending up with a more satisfied, productive workforce in the process.

While the labor supply preferences of employees must be satisfied in the long run, most of the short-run changes in hours of work seem to emanate from the *demand* side of the market.[2] Workweeks typically vary over the course of a business cycle, for example, with longer hours worked in periods of robust demand. In analyzing trends in hours of work, then, we must carefully distinguish between the forces of demand and supply.

In the first part of the twentieth century, workers in U.S. manufacturing plants typically worked 55 hours per week in years with strong economic activity; in the last two decades American manufacturing workers have worked, on average, less than 40 hours per week during similar periods. In 1988 and 1995, when the unemployment rate was roughly 5.5 percent and falling, manufacturing workers averaged 38.4 (in 1988) and 39.3 (in 1995) hours per week.[3] In general, the decline in weekly hours of manufacturing work in the United States occurred prior to 1950, and since then hours of work have shown no tendency to decline.

A THEORY OF THE DECISION TO WORK

Can labor supply theory help us to understand the long-run trends in labor force participation and hours of work noted above? Because labor is the most abundant factor of production, it is fair to say that any country's well-being in the long run depends heavily on the willingness of its people to work. Leisure and other ways of spending time that do not involve work for pay are also important in

---

[2]See, for example, Joseph G. Altonji and Christina H. Paxon, "Job Characteristics and Hours of Work," in *Research in Labor Economics*, vol. 8, ed. Ronald Ehrenberg (Greenwich, Conn.: JAI Press, 1986); Orley Ashenfelter, "Macroeconomic Analyses and Microeconomic Analyses of Labor Supply," *Carnegie-Rochester Conference Series on Public Policy* 21 (1984): 117–156; and John C. Ham, "On the Interpretation of Unemployment in Empirical Labour Supply Analysis," in *Unemployment, Search, and Labour Supply*, ed. Richard Blundell and Ian Walker (Cambridge, Eng.: Cambridge University Press, 1986), 121–142. Altonji and Paxon show, for example, that hours of work fluctuate much more over time for individuals who change employers than they do for individuals who remain with the same employer.

[3]The averages cited in this paragraph refer to *actual* hours of work (obtained from the *Census of Manufacturers*), not the more commonly available "hours paid for," which include paid time off for illness, holidays, and vacations.

generating well-being; however, any economy relies heavily on goods and services produced for market transactions. Therefore, it is important to understand the *work-incentive* effects of higher wages and incomes, different kinds of taxes, and various forms of income maintenance programs.

The decision to work is ultimately a decision about how to spend time. One way to use our available time is to spend it in pleasurable leisure activities. The other major way in which people use time is to work.[4] We can work around the home, performing such *household production* as raising children, sewing, building, or even growing food. Alternatively, we can work for pay and use our earnings to purchase food, shelter, clothing, and child care.

Because working for pay and engaging in household production are two ways of getting the same jobs done, we shall initially ignore the distinction between them and treat work activities as working for pay. We shall therefore be characterizing the decision to work as a choice between leisure and working for pay. Most of the crucial factors affecting work incentives can be understood in this context, but insight into labor supply behavior can be enriched by a consideration of household production as well; this we do in chapter 7.

If we regard the time spent eating, sleeping, and otherwise maintaining ourselves as more or less fixed by natural laws, then the discretionary time we have (16 hours a day, say) can be allocated to either work or leisure. It is most convenient for us to begin our analysis of the work/leisure choice by analyzing the *demand for leisure hours*.

Some Basic Concepts

Basically, the demand for a good is a function of three factors:

1. The *opportunity cost* of the good (which is often equal to *market price*),
2. One's level of *wealth*, and
3. One's set of *preferences*.

For example, consumption of heating oil will vary with the *cost* of such oil; as that cost rises, consumption tends to fall unless one of the other two factors intervenes. As *wealth* rises, people generally want larger and warmer houses that obviously require more oil to heat.[5] Even if the price of energy and the level of personal wealth were to remain constant, the demand for energy could rise if a falling birthrate and lengthened life span resulted in a higher proportion of the population being aged and therefore wanting warmer houses. This change in the

---

[4]Another category of activity is to spend time acquiring skills or doing other things that enhance future earning capacity. These activities will be discussed in chapters 9 and 10.
[5]When the demand for a good rises with wealth, economists say the good is a *normal good.* If demand falls as wealth rises, the good is said to be an *inferior good* (traveling or commuting by bus is sometimes cited as an example of an inferior good).

composition of the population amounts to a shift in the overall *preferences* for warmer houses and thus leads to a change in the demand for heating oil. (Economists usually assume that preferences are given and not subject to immediate change. For policy purposes, changes in prices and wealth are of paramount importance in explaining changes in demand because these variables are more susceptible to change by government or market forces.)

Opportunity Cost of Leisure   To apply this general analysis of demand to the demand for leisure, we must first ask, "What is the opportunity cost of leisure?" The cost of spending an hour watching television is basically what one could earn if one had spent that hour working. Thus, the opportunity cost of an hour of leisure is equal to one's *wage rate*—the *extra earnings* a worker can take home from an *extra hour of work*.[6]

Wealth and Income   Next, we must understand and be able to measure wealth. Naturally, wealth includes a family's holdings of bank accounts, financial investments, and physical property. Workers' skills can also be considered assets, since these skills can be, in effect, rented out to employers for a price. The more one can get in wages, the larger is the value of one's human assets. Unfortunately, it is not usually possible to directly measure people's wealth. It is much easier to measure the *returns* from that wealth, because data on total *income* are readily available from government surveys. Economists often use total income as an indicator of total wealth, since the two are conceptually so closely related.[7]

Defining the Income Effect   Theory suggests that if income increases while wages and preferences are held constant, the number of leisure hours demanded will rise. Put differently, *if income increases, holding wages constant, desired hours of work will go down.* (Conversely, if income is reduced while the wage rate is held constant, desired hours of work will go up.) Economists call the response of desired hours of leisure to changes in income, with wages held constant, the *income effect.* The income effect is based on the simple notion that as incomes rise, holding leisure's opportunity cost constant, people will want to consume more leisure (which means working less).

Because we have assumed that time is spent either in leisure or in working for pay, the income effect can be expressed in terms of the *supply of working hours* as well as the demand for leisure hours. Because the ultimate focus of this chapter is labor supply, we choose to express this effect in the context of supply.

---

[6]This assumes that individuals can work as many hours as they want at a fixed wage rate. While this assumption may seem overly simplistic, it will not lead to wrong conclusions with respect to the issues analyzed in this chapter. More rigorously, it should be said that leisure's marginal opportunity cost is the marginal wage rate (the wage one could receive for an extra hour of work).

[7]The best indicator of wealth is permanent, or long-run potential, income. Current income may differ from permanent income for a variety of reasons (unemployment, illness, unusually large amounts of overtime work, etc.). For our purposes here, however, the distinction between current and permanent income is not too important.

Using algebraic notation, we define the income effect as the change in hours of work (ΔH) produced by a change in income (ΔY), holding wages constant ($\overline{W}$):

$$\text{Income Effect} = \frac{\Delta H}{\Delta Y} \bigg|_{\overline{W}} < 0 \qquad (6.1)$$

We say the income effect is *negative* because the *sign* of the *fraction* in equation (6.1) is *negative*. If income goes up (wages held constant), hours of work fall. If income goes down, hours of work increase. The numerator (ΔH) and denominator (ΔY) in equation (6.1) move in opposite directions, giving a negative sign to the income effect.

Defining the Substitution Effect   Theory also suggests that *if income is held constant, an increase in the wage rate will raise the price and reduce the demand for leisure, thereby increasing work incentives.* (Likewise, a decrease in the wage rate will reduce leisure's opportunity cost and the incentives to work, holding income constant.) This *substitution effect* occurs because as the cost of leisure changes, income held constant, leisure and work hours are substituted for each other.

In contrast to the income effect, the substitution effect is *positive*. Because this effect is the change in hours of work (ΔH) induced by a change in the wage (ΔW), holding income constant ($\overline{Y}$), the substitution effect can be written as

$$\text{Substitution Effect} = \frac{\Delta H}{\Delta W} \bigg|_{\overline{Y}} > 0 \qquad (6.2)$$

Because numerator (ΔH) and denominator (ΔW) always move in the same direction, at least in theory, the substitution effect has a positive sign.

Observing Income and Substitution Effects Separately   At times it is possible to observe situations or programs that create only one effect or the other. (Laboratory experiments can also create separate income and substitution effects; one on pigeons, discussed in Example 6.1, suggests that labor supply theory can even be generalized beyond humans!) Usually, however, both effects are simultaneously present, often working against each other.

Receiving an inheritance offers an example of the income effect by itself. The bequest enhances wealth (income) *independent* of the hours of work. Thus, income is increased *without* a change in the compensation received from an hour of work. In this case, the income effect induces the person to consume more leisure, thereby reducing the willingness to work. (Some support for this theoretical prediction can be seen later in Example 6.2.)

Observing the substitution effect by itself is rare, but one example comes from the 1980 presidential campaign, when candidate John Anderson proposed a program aimed at conserving gasoline. His plan consisted of raising the gasoline tax but offsetting this increase by a reduced Social Security tax payable by individuals on their earnings. The idea was to raise the price of gasoline without reducing people's overall spendable income.

EXAMPLE 6.1

The Labor Supply of Pigeons

Economics has been defined as "the study of the allocation of scarce resources among unlimited and competing uses." Stated this way, the tools of economics can be used to analyze the behavior of animals, as well as humans. In a classic study, Raymond Battalio, Leonard Green, and John Kagel describe an experiment in which they estimated income and substitution effects (and thus the shape of the labor supply curve) for animals.

The subjects were male White Carneaux pigeons. The job task consisted of pecking at a response key. If the pigeons pecked the lever enough times, their payoff was access to a food hopper containing mixed grains. "Wages" were changed by altering the average number of pecks per payoff. Pecking requirements varied from as much as 400 pecks per payoff (a very low wage) to as few as 12.5 pecks. In addition, "unearned income" could be changed by giving the pigeons free access to the food hopper without the need for pecking. The environment was meant to observe the tradeoff between key pecking ("work") and the pigeons' primary alternative activities of preening themselves and walking around ("leisure"). The job task was not awkward or difficult for pigeons to perform, but it did require effort.

Battalio, Green, and Kagel found that pigeons' actions were perfectly consistent with economic theory. In the first stage of the experiment, they cut the wage rate (payoff per peck) but added enough free food to isolate the substitution effect. In almost every case the birds reduced their labor supply and spent more time on leisure activities. In the second stage of the experiment, they took away the free food to isolate the income effect. They found that every pigeon increased its pecking (cutting its leisure) as its income was cut. Thus, leisure is a normal good for pigeons. Additionally, both income and substitution effects got smaller in absolute value as wages increased, but the substitution effect decreased relatively more than the income effect. The authors concluded that "income-leisure tradeoffs of pigeons are in many respects similar to those of humans."

Data from: Raymond C. Battalio, Leonard Green, and John H. Kagel, "Income-Leisure Tradeoffs of Animal Workers," *American Economic Review* 71, no. 4 (September 1981): 621–632.

For our purposes, this plan is interesting because it would have created only a substitution effect on labor supply. Social Security revenues are collected by a tax on earnings, so reductions in the tax are, in effect, increases in the wage rate for most workers. For the average person, however, the increased wealth associated with this wage increase would have been exactly offset by increases in the gasoline tax.[8] Hence, wages would have been increased while income was held more or less constant. This program would have created a substitution effect that induced people to work more hours.

Both Effects Occur when Wages Rise   While the above examples illustrate situations in which the income or the substitution effect is present by itself, *normally*

---

[8]An increase in the price of gasoline will reduce the income people have left for expenditures on non-gasoline consumption only if the demand for gasoline is inelastic. In this case, the percentage reduction in gasoline consumption is smaller than the percentage increase in price: total expenditures on gasoline would thus rise. Our analysis assumes this to be the case.

both effects are present, often working in opposite directions. The presence of both effects working in opposite directions creates ambiguity in predicting the overall labor supply response in many cases. Consider the case of a person who receives a wage increase.

The labor supply response to a simple wage increase will involve *both* an income effect and a substitution effect. The *income effect* is the result of the worker's enhanced wealth (or potential income) after the increase. For a given level of work effort, he or she now has a greater command over resources than before (because more income is received for any given number of hours of work). The *substitution effect* results from the fact that the wage increase raises the opportunity costs of leisure. Because the actual labor supply response is the *sum* of the income and substitution effects, we cannot predict the response in advance; theory simply does not tell us which effect is stronger.

If the *income* effect is stronger, the person will respond to a wage increase by decreasing his or her labor supply. This decrease will be *smaller* than if the same change in wealth were due to an increase in *nonlabor* wealth, because the substitution effect is present and acts as a moderating influence. However, when the *income* effect dominates, the substitution effect is not large enough to prevent labor supply from *declining*. It is entirely plausible, of course, that the *substitution* effect will dominate. If so, the actual response to wage increases will be to *increase* labor supply.

Should the substitution effect dominate, the person's labor supply curve—relating, say, desired hours of work to wages—will be *positively sloped*. That is, labor supplied will increase with the wage rate. If, in contrast, the income effect dominates, the person's labor supply curve will be *negatively sloped*. Economic theory cannot say which effect will dominate, and in fact individual labor supply curves could be positively sloped in some ranges of the wage and negatively sloped in others. In Figure 6.1, for example, the person's desired hours of work increase (substitution effect dominates) when wages go up as long as wages are low (below W^*). At higher wages, however, further increases result in reduced hours of work (the income effect dominates); economists refer to such a curve as *backward-bending.*

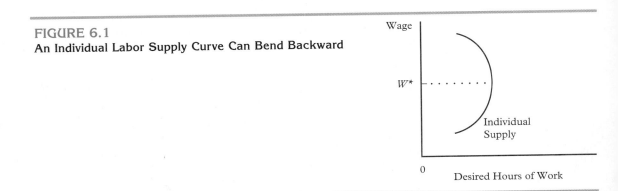

FIGURE 6.1
An Individual Labor Supply Curve Can Bend Backward

Analysis of the Labor/Leisure Choice

This section introduces indifference curves and budget constraints—visual aids that make the theory of labor supply easier to understand and to apply to complex policy issues. These graphical aids visually depict the basic factors underlying the demand for leisure (supply of labor) discussed above.

Preferences   Let us assume that there are two major categories of goods that make people happy—leisure time and the goods people can buy with money. If we take the prices of goods as fixed, then they can be compressed into one index that is measured by money income (with prices fixed, more money income means it is possible to consume more goods). Using two categories, leisure and money income, allows our graphs to be drawn in two-dimensional space.

Since both leisure and money can be used to generate satisfaction (or *utility*), these two goods are to some extent substitutes for each other. If forced to give up some money income—by cutting back on hours of work, for example—some increase in leisure time could be substituted for this lost income to keep a person as happy as before.

To understand how preferences can be graphed, suppose a thoughtful consumer/worker were asked to decide how happy he or she would be with a daily income of $64 combined with 8 hours of leisure (point *a* in Figure 6.2). This level of happiness could be called utility level A. Our consumer/worker could name *other combinations* of money income and leisure hours that would *also* yield utility level A. Assume that our respondent named five other combinations. All six combinations

FIGURE 6.2
**Two Indifference Curves
for the Same Person**

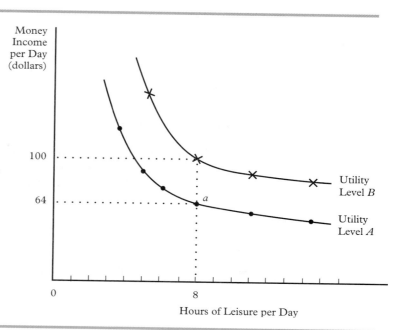

of money income and leisure hours that yield utility level *A* are represented by heavy dots in Figure 6.2. The curve connecting these dots is called an *indifference curve,* a curve connecting the various combinations of money income and leisure that yield equal utility. (The term *indifference curve* is derived from the fact that, since each point on the curve yields equal utility, a person is truly indifferent about where on the curve he or she will be.)

Our worker/consumer could no doubt achieve a higher level of happiness if he or she could combine the 8 hours of leisure with an income of $100 per day, instead of just $64 a day. This higher satisfaction level could be called utility level *B*. The consumer could name other combinations of money income and leisure that would also yield *this* higher level of utility. These combinations are denoted by the ×'s in Figure 6.2 that are connected by a second indifference curve.

Indifference curves have certain specific characteristics that are reflected in the way they are drawn:

1. Utility level *B* represents more happiness than level *A*. Every level of leisure consumption is combined with a higher income on *B* than on *A*. Hence our respondent prefers all points on indifference curve *B* to any point on curve *A*. A whole *set* of indifference curves could be drawn for this one person, each representing a different utility level. Any such curve that lies to the northeast of another one is preferred to any curve to the southwest because the northeastern curve represents a higher level of utility.

2. Indifference curves *do not intersect*. If they did, the point of intersection would represent one combination of money income and leisure that yielded two different levels of satisfaction. We assume our worker/consumer is not so inconsistent in stating his or her preferences that this could happen.

3. Indifference curves are *negatively sloped*, because if either income or leisure hours are increased, the other is reduced in order to preserve the same level of utility. If the slope is steep, as at segment *LK* in Figure 6.3, a given loss of income need not be accompanied by a large increase in leisure hours to keep utility constant.[9] When the curve is relatively flat, however, as at segment *MN* in Figure 6.3, a given decrease in income must be accompanied by a large increase in the consumption of leisure to hold utility constant. Thus, when indifference curves are relatively steep, people do not value money income as highly as when such curves are relatively flat; when they are flat, a loss of income can only be compensated for by a large increase in leisure if utility is to be kept constant.

---

[9]Economists call the change in money income needed to hold utility constant when leisure hours are changed by one unit the *marginal rate of substitution* between leisure and money income. This marginal rate of substitution can be graphically understood as the slope of the indifference curve at any point. At point *L*, for example, the slope is relatively steep, so economists would say that the marginal rate of substitution at point *L* is relatively high.

FIGURE 6.3

An Indifference Curve

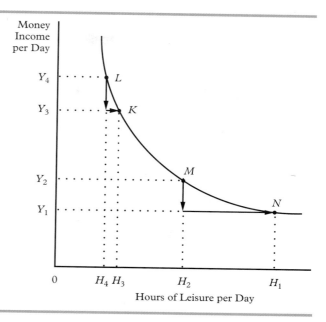

4. Indifference curves are *convex*—steeper at the left than at the right. This shape reflects the assumption that when money income is relatively high and leisure hours are relatively few, leisure is more highly valued than when leisure is abundant and income relatively scarce. At segment *LK* in Figure 6.3, a great loss of income (from Y_4 to Y_3, for example) can be compensated for by just a little increase in leisure, whereas a little loss of leisure time (from H_3 to H_4, for example) would require a relatively large increase in income to maintain equal utility. What is relatively scarce is more highly valued.

5. Conversely, when income is low and leisure is abundant (segment *MN* in Figure 6.3), income is more highly valued. Losing income (by moving from Y_2 to Y_1, for example) would require a huge increase in leisure for utility to remain constant. To repeat, what is relatively scarce is assumed to be more highly valued.

6. Finally, different people have different sets of indifference curves. The curves drawn in Figures 6.2 and 6.3 were for *one person*. Another person would have a completely different set of curves. People who value leisure more highly, for example, would have had indifference curves that were generally steeper (see Figure 6.4a). People who do not value leisure highly would have relatively flat curves (see Figure 6.4b). Thus, individual preferences can be portrayed graphically.

FIGURE 6.4
Indifference Curves for Two Different People

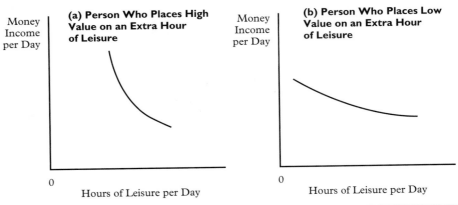

Income and Wage Constraints   Now, everyone would like to maximize his or her utility, which would be ideally done by consuming every available hour of leisure combined with the highest conceivable income. Unfortunately, the resources anyone can command are limited. Thus, all that is possible is to do the best one can, given limited resources. To see these resource limitations graphically requires superimposing constraints on one's set of indifference curves to see which combinations of income and leisure are available and which are not.

Suppose the person whose indifference curves are graphed in Figure 6.2 had no source of income other than labor earnings. Suppose, further, that he or she could earn $8 per hour. Figure 6.5 includes the two indifference curves shown in Figure 6.2 as well as a straight line (*DE*) connecting combinations of leisure and income that are possible for a person with an $8 wage and no outside income. If 16 hours per day are available for work and leisure[10] and if this person consumes all 16 in leisure, then money income will be zero (point *D* in Figure 6.5). If 5 hours a day are devoted to work, income will be $40 per day (point *M*), and if 16 hours a day are worked, income will be $128 per day (point *E*). Other points on this line—for example, the point of 15 hours of leisure (1 hour of work) and $8 of income—are also possible. This line, which reflects the combinations of leisure and income that are possible for the individual, is called the *budget constraint*. Any combination to the

---

[10]Our assumption that 8 hours per day are required for sleeping and other "maintenance" activities is purely for ease of exposition. These activities themselves are a matter of economic choice, at least to some extent; see for example, Jeff E. Biddle and Daniel Hamermesh, "Sleep and the Allocation of Time," *Journal of Political Economy* 98, no. 5, pt. 1 (October 1990): 922–943. Modeling a three-way choice between work, leisure, and maintenance activities would complicate our analysis without changing the essential insights theory can offer about the labor/leisure choice workers must make.

FIGURE 6.5

Indifference Curves and Budget Constraint

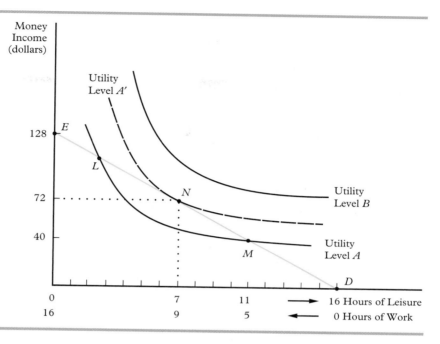

right of the budget constraint is not achievable; the person's command over resources simply is not sufficient to attain these combinations of leisure and money income.

The *slope* of the budget constraint is a graphical representation of the wage rate. One's wage rate is properly defined as the increment in income (ΔY) derived from an increment in hours of work (ΔH):

$$\text{Wage Rate} = \frac{\Delta Y}{\Delta H} \tag{6.3}$$

Now, $\Delta Y/\Delta H$ is exactly the slope of the budget constraint (in absolute value).[11] Figure 6.5 shows how the constraint rises $8 for every one-hour increase in work: if the person works zero hours, income per day is zero; if the person works 1 hour, $8 in income is received; if he or she works 5 hours, $40 in income is achieved. The constraint rises $8 because the wage rate is $8 per hour. If the person could earn $16 per hour, the constraint would rise twice as fast and therefore be twice as steep.

---

[11]The vertical change for a one-unit change in horizontal distance is the definition of *slope. Absolute value* refers to the magnitude of the slope, disregarding whether it is positive or negative. The budget constraint drawn in Figure 6.5 is a straight line (and thus has a constant slope). In economic terms, a straight-line budget constraint reflects the assumption that the wage rate at which one can work is fixed, and that it does not change with the hours of work. However, the major theoretical implications derived from using a straight-line constraint would be unchanged by employing a concave one, so we are using the fixed-wage assumption for ease of exposition.

It is clear from Figure 6.5 that our consumer/worker cannot achieve utility level *B*. He or she can achieve *some* points on the indifference curve representing utility level *A*—specifically, those points between *L* and *M* in Figure 6.5. However, if our consumer/worker is a utility maximizer, he or she will realize that a utility level *above A* is possible. Remembering that an infinite number of indifference curves can be drawn between curves *A* and *B* in Figure 6.5, one representing each possible level of satisfaction between *A* and *B*, we can draw a curve (*A′*) that is northeast of curve *A* and just *tangent* to the budget constraint at point *N*. Any movement along the budget constraint *away* from the tangency point places the person on an indifference curve lying *below A′*.

Workers who face the same budget constraint, but who have different preferences for leisure, will make different choices about hours of work. If the person whose preferences were depicted in Figure 6.5 had placed lower values on leisure time—and therefore had indifference curves that were comparatively flatter, such as the one shown in Figure 6.4b—then the point of tangency with constraint *ED* would have been to the left of point *N* (indicating more hours of work). Conversely, if he or she had steeper indifference curves, signifying that leisure time was more valuable (see Figure 6.4a), then the point of tangency in Figure 6.5 would have been to the right of point *N*, and fewer hours of work would have been desired. Indeed, some people will have indifference curves so steep (that is, preferences for leisure so strong) that there is no point of tangency with *ED*. For these people, as is illustrated by Figure 6.6, utility is maximized at the "corner" (point *D*); they desire no work at all and therefore are not in the labor force.

FIGURE 6.6

The Decision Not to Work Is a "Corner Solution"

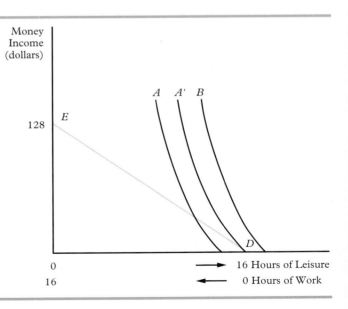

FIGURE 6.7
Indifference Curves and Budget Constraint (with an increase in nonlabor income)

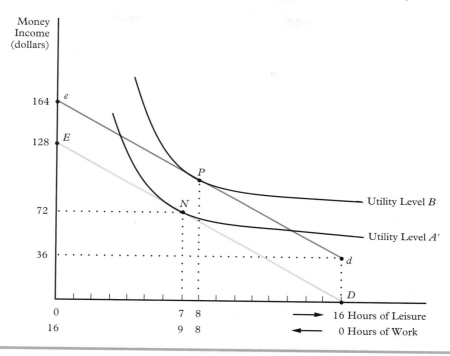

0	7 8	16 Hours of Leisure
16	9 8	0 Hours of Work

The Income Effect   Suppose now that the person depicted in Figure 6.5 receives a source of income independent of work. Suppose, further, that this *nonlabor* income amounts to about $36 per day. Thus, even if this person worked zero hours per day, his or her daily income would be $36. Naturally, if the person worked more than zero hours, his or her daily income would be equal to $36 plus earnings (the wage multiplied by the hours of work).

Our person's command over resources has clearly increased, as can be shown by drawing a new budget constraint to reflect the nonlabor income. As shown by the darker green line in Figure 6.7, the endpoints of the new constraint are point *d* (zero hours of work and $36 of money income) and point *e* (16 hours of work and $164 of income—$36 in nonlabor income plus $128 in earnings). Note that the new constraint is *parallel* to the old one. Parallel lines have the same slope; since the slope of each constraint reflects the wage rate, we can infer that the increase in nonlabor income has not changed the person's wage rate.

We have just described a situation in which a pure *income effect* should be observed. Income (wealth) has been increased, but the wage rate has remained

FIGURE 6.8
Wage Increase with Substitution Effect Dominating

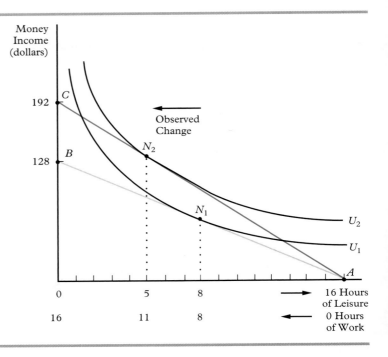

unchanged. The previous section noted that if wealth *increased* and the opportunity cost of leisure remained constant, the person would consume more leisure and work *less*. We thus concluded that the income effect was negative, and this negative relationship is illustrated graphically in Figure 6.7.

When the old budget constraint (*DE*) was in effect, the person's highest level of utility was reached at point *N*, working 9 hours a day. With the new constraint (*de*), the optimum hours of work are 8 per day (point *P*). The new source of income, because it does not alter the wage, has caused an income effect that results in one less hour of work per day. Statistical analyses of people who received large inheritances (Example 6.2) or who won large lottery prizes[12] support the prediction that labor supply is reduced when unearned income rises.

Income and Substitution Effects with a Wage Increase   Suppose that, instead of increasing one's command over resources by receiving a source of non-labor income, the wage rate were to be increased from $8 to $12 per hour. This increase, as noted earlier, would cause *both* an income effect and a substitution effect; workers would be wealthier *and* face a higher opportunity cost of leisure. Theory tells

[12]Guido W. Imbens, Donald B. Rubin, and Bruce I. Sacerdote, "Estimating the Effects of Unearned Income on Labor Earnings, Savings, and Consumption: Evidence from a Survey of Lottery Players," *American Economic Review* 91, no. 4 (Septmeber 2001): 778–794.

FIGURE 6.9

Wage Increase with Income Effect Dominating

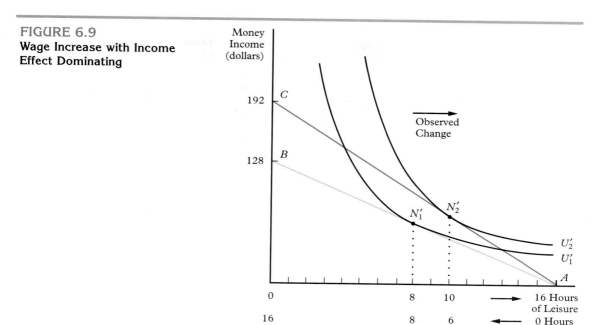

us in this case that the substitution effect pushes them toward more hours of work and the income effect toward fewer, but cannot tell us which effect will dominate.

Figures 6.8 and 6.9 illustrate the possible effects of the above wage change on a person's labor supply, which we now assume is initially 8 hours per day. Figure 6.8 illustrates the case in which the observed response by a worker is to increase the hours of work; in this case the substitution effect is stronger than the income effect. Figure 6.9 illustrates the case in which the income effect is stronger and the response to a wage increase is to reduce the hours of work. The difference between the two figures lies *solely* in the shape of the indifference curves that might describe a person's preferences; the budget constraints, which reflect wealth and the wage rate, are exactly the same.

Figures 6.8 and 6.9 both show the old constraint, *AB,* the slope of which reflects the wage of $8 per hour. They also show the new one, *AC,* which reflects the $12 wage. Because we assume workers have no source of nonlabor income, both constraints are anchored at point *A,* where income is zero if a person does not work. Point *C* on the new constraint is now at $192 (16 hours of work times $12 per hour).

With the worker whose preferences are depicted in Figure 6.8, the wage increase makes utility level U_2 the highest that can be reached. The tangency point at N_2 suggests that 11 hours of work is optimum. When the old constraint was in effect, the utility-maximizing hours of work were 8 per day (point N_1). Thus, the wage increase would cause this person's desired hours of work to increase by 3 per day.

With the worker whose preferences are depicted in Figure 6.9, the wage increase would make utility level U_2' the highest one possible (the prime emphasizes that workers' preferences differ, and that utility *levels* in Figures 6.8 and 6.9 cannot be compared). Utility is maximized at N_2', at 6 hours of work per day. Thus, with preferences like those in Figure 6.9, working hours fall from 8 to 6 as the wage rate increases.

Isolating Income and Substitution Effects   We have graphically depicted the income effect by itself (Figure 6.7) and the two possible outcomes of an increase in wages (Figures 6.8 and 6.9), which combines the income and substitution effects. Is it possible to graphically isolate the substitution effect? The answer is yes, and the most meaningful way to do this is to return to the context of a wage change, such as the one depicted in Figures 6.8 and 6.9. We arbitrarily choose to analyze the response shown in Figure 6.8.

Figure 6.10 has three panels. Panel (a) repeats Figure 6.8; it shows the final, overall effect of a wage increase on the labor supply of the person whose preferences are depicted. As we saw earlier, the effect of the wage increase in this case is to raise the person's utility from U_1 to U_2 and to induce this worker to increase desired hours of work from 8 to 11 per day. Imbedded in this overall effect of the wage increase, however, is an income effect pushing toward less work and a substitution effect pushing toward more. These effects are graphically separated in panels (b) and (c).

Panel (b) of Figure 6.10 shows the income effect that is imbedded in the overall response to the wage change. By definition, the income effect is the change in desired hours of work brought on by increased wealth, holding the wage rate constant. To reveal this imbedded effect, we ask a hypothetical question: "What would have been the change in labor supply if the person depicted in panel (a) had reached the new indifference curve (U_2) with a change in *nonlabor* income instead of a change in his or her wage rate?"

We begin to answer this question graphically by moving the old constraint to the northeast, which depicts the greater command over leisure time and goods—and hence the higher level of utility—associated with greater wealth. The constraint is shifted outward while maintaining its original slope (reflecting the old $8 wage), which holds the wage constant. The dashed line in panel (b) depicts this hypothetical movement of the old constraint, and it results in a tangency point at N_3. This tangency suggests that had the person received nonlabor income, with no change in the wage, sufficient to reach the new level of utility, he or she would have *reduced* work hours from 8 (N_1) to 7 (N_3) per day. This shift is graphical verification that the income effect is negative, assuming that leisure is a normal good.

The substitution effect is the effect on labor supply of a change in the wage rate, holding wealth constant. It can be seen in panel (c) of Figure 6.10 as the difference between where the person actually ended up on indifference curve U_2 (tangency at N_2) and where he or she would have ended up with a pure income effect (tangency at N_3). Comparing tangency points on the *same* indifference curve is a graphical approximation to holding wealth constant. Thus, *with* the wage change, the person represented in Figure 6.10 ended up at point N_2, working 11 hours a day. *Without* the wage change, the person would have chosen to work 7 hours a day (point N_3). The wage change *by itself*, holding utility (or real wealth) constant,

FIGURE 6.10
Wage Increase with Substitution Effect Dominating: Isolating Income and Substitution Effects

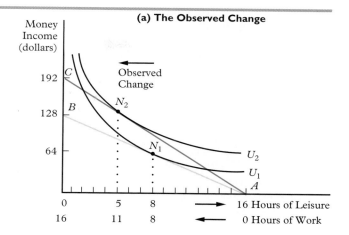

(a) The Observed Change

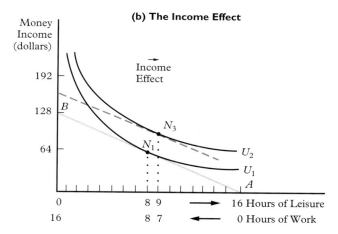

(b) The Income Effect

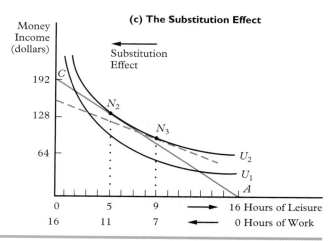

(c) The Substitution Effect

EXAMPLE 6.2

Do Large Inheritances Induce Labor Force Withdrawal?

Do large bequests of unearned income reduce people's incentives to work? A recent study allows us to divide people who received inheritances in 1982–1983 into two groups: those who received small bequests (averaging $7,700) and those who received bequests averaging $346,200. The study then analyzed changes in the labor force participation behavior of the two groups between 1982 and 1985. Not surprisingly, those who received the larger inheritances were more likely to drop out of the labor force. Specifically, during a period in which the labor force participation rate among the small-bequest group rose from 76 to 81 percent, the rate in the large-bequest group fell from 70 to 65 percent. Somewhat more surprising was the fact that, perhaps in anticipation of the large bequest, the labor force participation rate among the people in the latter group was lower to begin with!

Data from: Douglas Holtz-Eakin, David Joulfaian, and Harvey S. Rosen, "The Carnegie Conjecture: Some Empirical Evidence," *Quarterly Journal of Economics* 108, no. 2 (1993): 413–435. The findings reported above hold up even after controlling for such factors as age and earnings.

caused work hours to increase by 4 per day.[13] This increase demonstrates that the substitution effect is positive.

To summarize, the observed effect of raising wages from $8 to $12 per hour increased the hours of work in Figure 6.10 from 8 to 11 per day. This observed effect, however, is the *sum* of two component effects. The income effect, which operates because a higher wage increases one's real wealth, tended to *reduce* the hours of work from 8 to 7 per day. The substitution effect, which captures the pure effect of the change in leisure's opportunity cost, tended to push the person toward 4 more hours of work per day. The end result was an increase of 3 in the hours worked each day.

Which Effect Is Stronger?   Suppose that a wage increase changes the budget constraint facing a worker from *CD* to *CE* in Figure 6.11. If the worker had a relatively flat set of indifference curves, the initial tangency along *CD* might be at point *A*, implying a relatively heavy work schedule. If the person had more steeply sloped indifference curves, the initial tangency might be at point *B*, where hours at work are fewer.

One important influence on the size of the income effect is the extent of the northeast movement of the new constraint: the more the constraint shifts outward, the greater the income effect will tend to be. For a person with an initial tangency at point *A*, for example, the northeast movement is larger than for a person whose initial tangency is at point *B*. Put in words, the increased command over

---

[13]In our initial definition of the substitution effect we held *money income* constant, while in the graphical analysis we held *utility* constant. These slightly different approaches were followed for explanatory convenience, and they represent (respectively) the theoretical analyses suggested by Evgeny Slutsky and John Hicks. For an easy-to-follow explanation of the two approaches, see Heinz Kohler, *Intermediate Microeconomics* (Glenview, Ill.: Scott, Foresman & Co., 1986), 76–81.

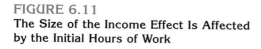

FIGURE 6.11
The Size of the Income Effect Is Affected
by the Initial Hours of Work

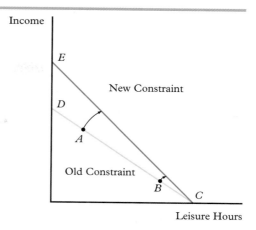

resources made possible by a wage increase is only attainable if one works, and the more work-oriented the person is, the greater will be his or her increase in resources. Other things equal, people who are working longer hours will exhibit greater income effects when wage rates change.

To take this reasoning to the extreme, suppose a person's indifference curves were so steep that the person was initially out of the labor force (that is, when the budget constraint was *CD* in Figure 6.11, his or her utility was maximized at point *C*). The wage increase and the resultant new constraint, *CE*, can induce only two outcomes: the person will either begin to work for pay or remain out of the labor force. *Reducing* the hours of paid employment is not possible. For those who are out of the labor force, then, the decision to *participate* as wage offers rise clearly reflects a dominant substitution effect. Conversely, if someone currently working decides to change his or her participation decision and drop out of the labor force when wages fall, the substitution effect has again dominated. Thus, the labor force *participation* decisions brought about by wage changes exhibit a dominant substitution effect. We turn now to a more detailed analysis of the decision whether to join the labor force.

The Reservation Wage   An implication of our labor supply theory is that if people who are not in the labor force place a value of $X on the marginal hour of leisure, then they would be unwilling to take a job unless the offered wage were greater than $X. Because they will "reserve" their labor unless the wage is $X or more, economists say that they have a *reservation wage* of $X. The reservation wage, then, is the wage below which a person will not work, and in the labor/leisure context it represents the value placed on an hour of lost leisure time.[14]

---

[14]See Hans G. Bloemen and Elena G. F. Stancanelli, "Individual Wealth, Reservation Wages, and Transitions into Employment," *Journal of Labor Economics* 19, no. 2 (April 2001): 400–439, for a recent study of reservation wages.

Looking back at Figure 6.6, which graphically depicted a person choosing not to work, the reason there was no tangency between an indifference curve and the budget constraint—and the reason the person remained out of the labor force—was that the wage was everywhere lower than his or her marginal value of leisure time. (See Example 6.3 for how reservation wages affect participation when pay varies daily.)

Often, people are thought to behave as if they have both a reservation wage *and a certain number of work hours* that must be offered before they will consider taking a job. The reasons are not difficult to understand and are illustrated by Figure 6.12. Suppose that taking a job entails two hours of commuting time (round-trip) per day. These hours, of course, are unpaid, so the worker's budget constraint must reflect that, if a job is accepted, two hours of leisure are given up before there is any increase in income. These fixed costs of working are reflected in Figure 6.12 by segment *AB*. Segment *BC*, of course, reflects the earnings that are possible (once at work), and the slope of *BC* represents the person's wage rate.

Is the wage underlying *BC* great enough to induce the person to work? Consider indifference curve U_1, which represents the highest level of utility this person can achieve, given budget constraint *ABC*. Utility is maximized at point *A*, and the person chooses not to work. It is clear from this choice that the offered wage (given the two-hour commute) is below the person's reservation wage, but can we show the latter wage graphically?

To take work with a two-hour commute, the person depicted in Figure 6.12 must find a job able to generate a combination of earnings and leisure time that

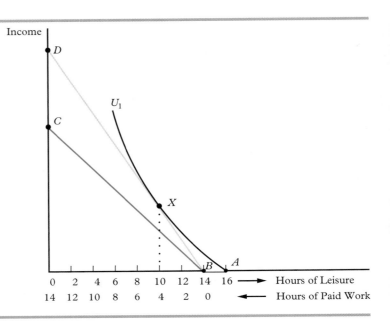

FIGURE 6.12
Reservation Wage with Fixed Time Costs of Working

EXAMPLE 6.3

Daily Labor Supply at the Ballpark

The theory of labor supply rests in part on the assumption that when workers' offered wages climb above their reservation wages they will decide to participate in the labor market. An implication of this theory is that in jobs for which hiring is done on a daily basis, and for which wages fluctuate widely from day to day, we should observe daily fluctuations in participation! These expectations are supported by the daily labor supply decisions of vendors at major-league baseball games.

A recent study examined the individual labor supply behavior of vendors in one ballpark over the course of the 1996 major-league baseball season. Vendors walk through the stands selling food and drinks, and their earnings are completely determined by the sales they are able to make each day. The vendors studied could freely choose whether to work any given game, and the data collected by this study clearly suggests they made their decisions by weighing their opportunity cost of working against their expected earnings during the

course of the game. (Expected earnings, of course, are related to a number of factors, including how many fans were likely to attend the game.)

The study was able to compare the actual amount earned by each vendor at each game with the number of vendors who had decided to work. The average amount earned by vendors was $43.81, with a low of $26.55 for one game and a high of $73.15 for another—and about 45 vendors worked the typical game at this ballpark. The study found that an increase in average earnings of $10 (which represents about a one standard deviation increase from the mean of $43.81) lured about six extra vendors to the stadium.

Clearly, then, vendors behaved as if they had reservation wages that they compared to expected earnings when deciding whether to work particular games.

Data from: Gerald Oettinger, "An Empirical Analysis of the Daily Labor Supply of Stadium Vendors," *Journal of Political Economy* 107, no. 2 (April 1999): 360–392.

yields a utility level equal to, or greater than, U_1. This is possible only if the person's budget constraint is equal to (or to the right of) *ABD,* which is tangent to U_1 at point *X.* The person's reservation wage, then, is equal to the slope of *BD,* and you can readily note that in this case the slope of *BD* exceeds the slope of *BC,* which represents the offered wage. Moreover, to bring utility up to the level of U_1 (the utility associated with not working), the person shown in Figure 6.12 must be able to find a job at the reservation wage that offers 4 hours of work per day. Put differently, at this person's reservation wage, he or she would want to consume 10 hours of leisure daily, and with a two-hour commute this implies 4 hours of work.

Empirical Findings on the Income and Substitution Effects

Labor supply theory suggests that the choices workers make concerning their desired hours of work depend on their wealth and the wage rate they can command, in addition to their preferences. In particular, this theory suggests the existence of a negative income effect and a positive substitution effect. Empirical tests of labor supply theory generally attempt to determine if these two effects can be observed, if they operate in the expected directions, and what their relative magnitudes are. Data used for these tests are generally of two kinds:

1. *Cross-sectional* data can be used to analyze the patterns of labor supply across individuals at a given point in time.
2. *Time-series* data can be used to look at *trends* in labor force participation and hours of work over a period of several years. (Cross-sectional and time-related data can also be combined, as illustrated in Example 6.4.)

Cross-Sectional Data   Numerous studies of labor supply behavior have relied on cross-sectional data. These studies basically analyze labor force participation or annual hours of work as they are affected by wage rates and income, holding other influences (age, for example) constant. The most reliable and informative studies are those done on large samples of men, primarily because the labor supply behavior of women has been complicated by child-rearing and household work arrangements for which data are sketchy at best.

The cross-sectional studies of male labor supply behavior, especially for men between the ages of 25 and 55, generally conclude that both income and substitution effects are small—perhaps even zero. Probably because responses to wage changes are so small, the results of studies that attempt to isolate income and substitution effects are highly dependent on the statistical methods used.[15]

Cross-sectional estimates of the labor supply behavior among married women generally find a greater responsiveness to wage changes than is found among men. The studies also commonly find that the substitution effect dominates the income effect. Recent studies, however, suggest that the response of working women's *hours* of work to wage changes are about like those of men (that is, very small); it may be the labor force *participation* decision that is most distinctive for married women.[16] As noted in our discussion of Figure 6.11, participation decisions have a dominant substitution effect.

---

[15]See Thomas MaCurdy, David Green, and Harry Paarsch, "Assessing Empirical Approaches for Analyzing Taxes and Labor Supply," *Journal of Human Resources* 25 (Summer 1990): 415–490, for a reference to prior work and an explanation of some methodological issues. This entire issue of the *Journal of Human Resources* is devoted to estimates of the effects, in five countries, of income taxation on labor supply. Also see Finis Welch, "Wages and Participation," *Journal of Labor Economics* 15, no. 1, pt. 2 (January 1997): S77–S103; and Robert A. Moffitt and Mark Wilhem, "Taxation and the Labor Supply Decisions of the Affluent," in *Does Atlas Shrug? The Economic Consequences of Taxing the Rich*, ed. Joel B. Slemrod (New York: Russell Sage Foundation; Cambridge, Mass.: Harvard University Press, 2000).

[16]See Thomas A. Mroz, "The Sensitivity of an Empirical Model of Married Women's Hours of Work to Economic and Statistical Assumptions," *Econometrica* 55, no. 4 (July 1987): 765–800. Articles on women's labor supply in the United States and 11 other countries appear in the *Journal of Labor Economics,* January 1985 supplement. Mark Killingsworth, *Labor Supply,* Cambridge Surveys of Economic Literature (Cambridge, Eng.: Cambridge University Press, 1983), offers a very comprehensive review of "first- and second-generation" estimates of income and substitution effects. For more recent contributions, see John H. Pencavel, "The Market Work Behavior and Wages of Women: 1975–94," *Journal of Human Resources* 33, no. 4 (Fall 1998): 771–804; and Nada Eissa and Hilary Hoynes, "Labor Supply Response to the Earned Income Tax Credit," *Quarterly Journal of Economics* 111, no. 2 (May 1996): 605–637.

EXAMPLE 6.4

Labor Supply Effects of Income Tax Cuts

In 1986, Congress changed the personal income tax system in the United States by drastically reducing tax rates on upper levels of income. Before this change, for example, families paid a 50 percent tax rate on taxable incomes over $170,000; after the change, this tax rate was reduced to 28 percent. The tax rate on taxable incomes over $50,000 was also set at 28 percent, down from about 40 percent. Lower income tax rates have the effect of increasing take-home earnings, and they therefore act as an increase in wage rates. Because lower rates generate an income and a substitution effect that work in opposite directions, they have an ambiguous anticipated effect on labor supply. Can we find out which effect is stronger in practice?

The 1986 changes served as a *natural experiment* (abrupt changes in only one variable, the sizes of which vary by group). The changes were sudden, large, and very different for families of different incomes. For married women in families that, without their earnings, had incomes at the 99th percentile of the income distribution (that is, the upper 1 percent), the tax rate cuts meant a 29 percent increase in their take-home wage rates. For women in families with incomes at the 90th percentile, the smaller tax rate cuts meant a 12 percent increase in take-home wages. It turns out that married women at the 99th and 90th percentiles of family income are similar in age, education, and occupation—and increases in

their labor supply had been similar prior to 1986. Therefore, comparing their responses to very different changes in their after-tax wage rates should yield insight into how the labor supply of married women responds to tax rate changes.

One study compared labor supply increases, from 1984 to 1990, for married women in the 99th and 90th percentiles. It found that the labor force participation rate for women in the 99th percentile rose by 19.4 percent and that, if working, their hours of work rose by 12.7 percent during that period. In contrast, both labor force participation and hours of work for women at the 90th percentile rose only by about 6.5 percent. The data from this natural experiment, then, suggest that women who experienced larger increases in their take-home wages desired greater increases in their labor supply—which implies that the substitution effect dominated the income effect for these women. Also, consistent with both theory and the results from other studies (discussed in the text), the dominance of the substitution effect was more pronounced for labor force participation decisions than it was for hours-of-work decisions.

Data from: Nada Eissa, "Taxation and Labor Supply of Married Women: The Tax Reform Act of 1986 as a Natural Experiment," working paper no. 5023, National Bureau of Economic Research, Cambridge, Mass., February 1995.

Time-Series Data This chapter began with tables that indicated some significant trends in labor force participation and hours of work in the United States and elsewhere. Economists have attempted to explain these trends through the use of labor supply theory, but the use of time-series data to test the theory presents some problems. One problem is that over a period of any given length, there will be years in which labor market disequilibrium causes many workers to work fewer hours than they really want to.

Another problem in trying to relate labor supply trends to changes in income (or wealth) and wage rates is that, over long periods of time, *other* factors that affect desired participation and hours of work can also change. For example, the growth of pensions has affected the labor supply of older workers, and the labor supply of married women has been affected by the growing availability of time-saving devices around the home (washing machines and microwave ovens, for example) and changing attitudes about working wives.

If the other factors that affect labor supply change at the same time that incomes and real wages change, it is difficult to isolate the separate effects of each. Nevertheless, studies that have made serious efforts to control for these other factors have found evidence that the income and substitution effects are indeed important in explaining labor supply behavior. One comprehensive analysis of the labor supply trends of married women concluded that income and substitution effects worked in their expected directions throughout the twentieth century, with the substitution effect clearly dominant after 1950. There is evidence, however, that the *magnitudes* of both effects became smaller over the last forty years, with the result that the substitution effect for married women is now less dominant and their labor supply behavior is thus becoming less responsive to changes in wages.[17]

An empirical analysis of the labor force participation behavior of older men concludes that their trend toward earlier retirement also suggests a dominant substitution effect.[18] This study finds that the sharp rise in early retirement (mostly at age 62) is primarily among men with lower levels of education, for whom demand has fallen in recent years. As demand has fallen for men of less education (we will discuss this decline in chapter 14), wages for many workers have been pushed below the level of their reservation wage. Apparently, then, a dominant substitution effect has been responsible for the declining participation rates of older men (a subject we will return to in chapter 7).

POLICY APPLICATIONS

Many income maintenance programs create budget constraints that increase income while reducing the take-home wage rate (thus causing the income and substitution effects to work in the same direction). Therefore, using labor supply theory to analyze the work-incentive effects of various social programs is both instructive and important. We characterize these programs by the budget constraints they create for their recipients.

Budget Constraints with "Spikes"

Some social insurance programs compensate workers who are unable to work because of a temporary work injury, a permanent disability, or a layoff. Workers' compensation insurance replaces most of the earnings lost when workers are hurt on the job, and private or public disability programs do the same for workers who

---

[17]Claudia Goldin, *Understanding the Gender Gap* (New York: Oxford University Press, 1990), chapter 5.
[18]Franco Peracchi and Finis Welch, "Trends in the Labor Force Transitions of Older Men and Women," *Journal of Labor Economics* 12, no. 2 (April 1994): 210–242. For a companion study, see Chinhui Juhn, Kevin M. Murphy, and Finis Welch, "Why Has the Natural Rate of Unemployment Increased over Time?" *Brookings Papers on Economic Activity* 2 (1991): 75–126.

FIGURE 6.13
**Budget Constraint
with a "Spike"**

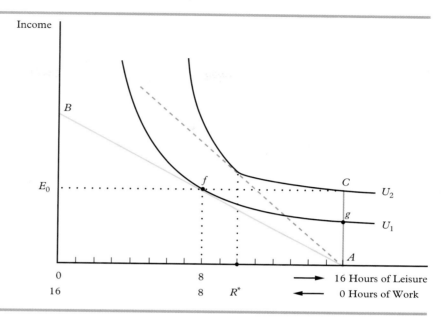

become physically or emotionally unable to work for other reasons. Unemployment compensation is paid to those who have lost a job and have not been able to find another. While exceptions can be found in the occasional jurisdiction,[19] it is generally true that these *income replacement* programs share a common characteristic: they pay benefits only to those who are not working.

To understand the consequences of paying benefits only to those who are not working, let us suppose that a workers' compensation program is structured so that, after injury, workers receive their preinjury earnings for as long as they are off work. Once they work even one hour, however, they are no longer considered disabled and cannot receive further benefits. The effects of this program on work incentives are analyzed in Figure 6.13, in which it is assumed that the preinjury budget constraint was AB and preinjury earnings were $E_0 (=AC)$. Further, we assume that the worker's "market" budget constraint (that is, the constraint in the absence of a workers' compensation program) is unchanged, so that after recovery the preinjury wage can again be earned. Under these conditions, the postinjury budget constraint is BAC, and the person maximizes utility at point C—a point of no work.

Note that constraint BAC contains the segment AC, which looks like a spike. It is this spike that creates severe work-incentive problems, for two reasons. First, the returns associated with the first hour of work are *negative*. That is, a person at

---

[19]Unemployment insurance and workers' compensation programs in the United States are run at the state level and thus vary in their characteristics to some extent.

point C who returns to work for one hour would find his or her income to be considerably reduced by working. Earnings from this hour of work would be more than offset by the reduction in benefits, which creates a negative "net wage."[20] The substitution effect associated with this program characteristic clearly discourages work.

Second, our assumed no-work benefit of AC is equal to E_0, the preinjury level of earnings. If the worker values leisure at all (as is assumed by the standard downward slope of indifference curves), being able to receive the old level of earnings while also enjoying more leisure clearly enhances utility. The worker is better off at point C than at point f, the preinjury combination of earnings and leisure hours, because he or she is on indifference curve U_2 rather than U_1. Allowing workers to reach a higher utility level without working generates a strong income effect that discourages, or at least slows, the return to work.[21]

Indeed, the program we have assumed raises a worker's reservation wage above his or her preinjury wage, meaning that a return to work is possible only if the worker qualifies for a higher-paying job. To see this graphically, observe the dashed green line in Figure 6.13 that begins at point A and is tangent to indifference curve U_2 (the level of utility made possible by the social insurance program). The slope of this line is equal to the person's reservation wage, because if the person can obtain the desired hours of work at this or a greater wage, utility will be at least equal to that associated with point C. Note also that, for labor force participation to be induced, the reservation wage must be received for at least R^* hours of work.

Given that the work-incentive aspects of income replacement programs often quite justifiably take a backseat to the goal of making unfortunate workers "whole" in some economic sense, creating programs that avoid work disincentives is not easy. With the preferences of the worker depicted in Figure 6.13, a benefit of slightly less than Ag would ensure minimal loss of utility while still providing incentives to return to work as soon as physically possible (work would allow indifference curve U_1 to be attained—see point f—while not working and receiving a benefit of less than Ag would not). Unfortunately, workers differ in their preferences, so the optimal benefit—one that would provide work incentives yet ensure only minimal loss of utility—differs for each individual.

With programs that create "spikes," the best policymakers can do is set a no-work benefit as some fraction of previous earnings and then use administrative means to encourage the return to work among any whose utility is greater when not working. Unemployment insurance, for example, replaces something like half

---

[20]For recent empirical evidence, see Jonathan Gruber, "Disability Insurance Benefits and Labor Supply," *Journal of Political Economy* 108, no. 6 (December 2000): 1162–1183. In graphical terms, the budget constraint contains a vertical spike, and the slope of this vertical segment is infinitely negative. In economic terms, the implied infinitely negative (net) wage arises from the fact that even one minute of work causes a person to lose his or her entire benefit.

[21]We are assuming here that the psychic costs of injury or layoff are small. It could be argued that complete income replacement is justified on the grounds that it compensates for large psychic losses, but our analysis of work-incentive effects would be unchanged.

EXAMPLE 6.5

Staying Around One's Kentucky Home: Workers' Compensation Benefits and the Return to Work

Workers injured on the job receive workers' compensation insurance benefits while away from work. These benefits differ across states, but they are calculated for most workers as some fraction (normally two-thirds) of weekly, pretax earnings. For high-wage workers, however, weekly benefits are typically capped at a maximum, which again varies by state.

On July 15, 1980, Kentucky raised its maximum weekly benefit by 66 percent. It did not alter benefits in any other way, so this change effectively granted large benefit increases to high-wage workers without awarding them to anyone else. Because those injured before July 15 were ineligible for the increased benefits, even if they remained off work *after* July 15, this policy change created a nice natural experiment: one group of injured workers was able to obtain higher benefits, while another group was not. Did the group receiving higher benefits show evidence of reduced labor supply, as suggested by theory?

The effects of increased benefits on labor supply were unmistakable. High-wage workers ineligible for the new benefits typically stayed off the job for four weeks, but those injured after July 15 stayed away for five weeks—25 percent longer! No increases in the typical time away from work were recorded among lower-paid injured workers, who were unaffected by the changes in benefits.

Data from: Bruce D. Meyer, W. Kip Viscusi, and David L. Durbin, "Workers' Compensation and Injury Duration: Evidence from a Natural Experiment," *American Economic Review* 85, no. 3 (June 1995): 322–340.

---

of lost earnings for the typical U.S. worker, but the program puts an upper limit on the weeks each unemployed worker can receive benefits. Workers' compensation replaces two-thirds of lost earnings for the average worker but must rely on doctors—and sometimes judicial hearings—to determine whether a worker continues to be eligible for benefits. (For evidence that more-generous workers' compensation benefits do indeed induce longer absences from work, see Example 6.5.)

Programs with Net Wage Rates of Zero

The programs just discussed were intended to confer benefits on those who are unable to work, and the budget-constraint spike was created by the eligibility requirement that to receive benefits, one must not be working. Other social programs, such as welfare, have different eligibility criteria and calculate benefits differently. These programs factor income needs into their eligibility criteria and then pay benefits based on the difference between one's actual earnings and one's needs. We will see that paying people the difference between their earnings and their needs creates a net wage rate of zero; thus, the work-incentive problems associated with these welfare programs result from the fact that they increase the income of program recipients while also drastically reducing the price of leisure.

Nature of Welfare Subsidies   Welfare programs have historically taken the form of a guaranteed annual income, under which a welfare worker determines the

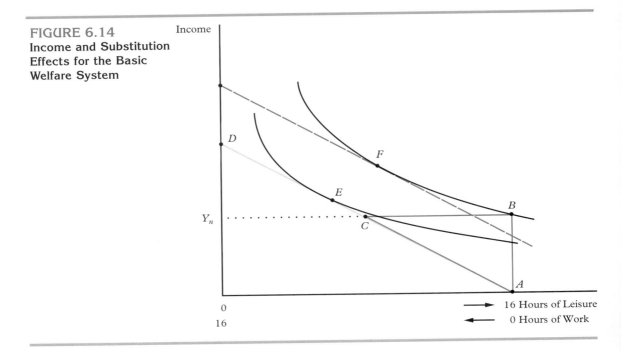

FIGURE 6.14
Income and Substitution Effects for the Basic Welfare System

income needed by an eligible person (Y_n in Figure 6.14) based on family size, area living costs, and local welfare regulations. Actual earnings are then subtracted from this needed level, and a check is issued to the person each month for the difference. If the person does not work, he or she receives a subsidy of Y_n. If the person works, and if earnings cause dollar-for-dollar reductions in welfare benefits, then a budget constraint like *ABCD* in Figure 6.14 is created. The person's income remains Y_n as long as he or she is subsidized. If receiving the subsidy, then, an extra hour of work yields *no* net increase in income, because the extra earnings result in an equal reduction in welfare benefits. The net wage of a person on the program—and therefore his or her price of leisure—is zero, which is graphically shown by the segment of the constraint having a slope of zero (*BC*).[22]

Thus, a welfare program like the one summarized in Figure 6.14 increases the income of the poor by moving the lower end of the budget constraint out from *AC* to *ABC*; as indicated by the dashed hypothetical constraint in Figure 6.14, this shift creates an *income effect* tending to reduce labor supply from the hours associated with point *E* to those associated with point *F*. However, it *also* causes the wage to effectively drop to zero: every dollar earned is matched by a dollar

---

[22]Gary Burtless, "The Economist's Lament: Public Assistance in America," *Journal of Economic Perspectives* 4 (Winter 1990): 57–78, summarizes a variety of public assistance programs in the United States prior to 1990. This article suggests that, in actual practice, benefits usually were reduced by something less than dollar for dollar (perhaps by 80 or 90 cents per dollar of earnings).

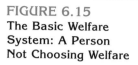

FIGURE 6.15
The Basic Welfare System: A Person Not Choosing Welfare

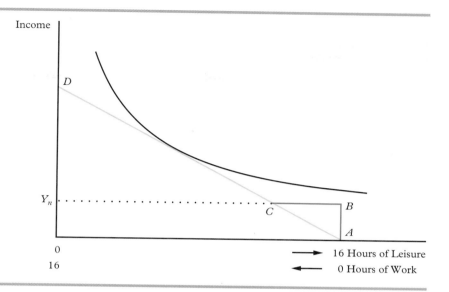

reduction in welfare benefits. This dollar-for-dollar reduction in benefits induces a huge *substitution effect,* causing those accepting welfare to reduce their hours of work to zero (point *B*). Of course, if a person's indifference curves were sufficiently flat so that the curve tangent to segment *CD* passed *above* point *B* (see Figure 6.15), then that person's utility would be maximized by choosing work instead of welfare.[23]

Welfare Reform   In light of the disincentives for work built into traditional welfare programs, the United States enacted the Personal Responsibility and Work Opportunity Reconciliation Act in 1996, which limited and restricted the ways that states could use federal welfare funds. This act addressed several issues related to those on welfare, but the two most directly related to labor supply incentives were a five-year (lifetime) time limit placed on the receipt of welfare benefits and a requirement that, after two years on welfare, recipients work at least 30 hours a week. While both kinds of reforms theoretically increase work incentives,[24] the effects of a minimum work requirement can be better understood by a bit more analysis.

Figure 6.16 illustrates the budget constraint associated with a minimum work requirement of five hours a day (30 hours per week). If the person fails to work the required five hours a day, no welfare benefits are received, and he or she will

---

[23]See Robert Moffitt, "Incentive Effects of the U.S. Welfare System: A Review," *Journal of Economic Literature* 30, no. 1 (March 1992): 1–61, for a summary of the literature on labor supply effects of the welfare system.

[24]For a study of the time limit, see Jeffrey Grogger, "The Effects of Time Limits and Other Policy Changes on Welfare Use, Work, and Income among Female-Headed Families," working paper no. 8153, National Bureau of Economic Research, Cambridge, Mass., March 2001.

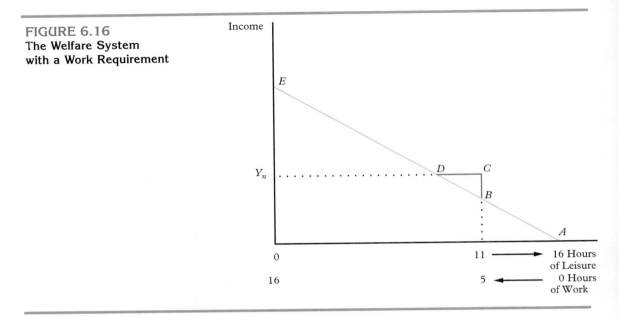

FIGURE 6.16
The Welfare System with a Work Requirement

be along segment *AB* of the constraint. If the work requirement is met, but earnings are less than Y_n, welfare benefits of *BC* are received. If the work requirement is exceeded, income (earnings plus benefits) remains at Y_n—the person is along *CD*—until earnings rise above needed income and the person is along segment *DE* of the constraint and no longer economically eligible for welfare benefits.

The work-incentive effects of this *work requirement* can be seen from studying Figure 6.16. If indifference curves are steep enough so that utility is maximized at point *C*, those on welfare will desire to work five hours a day, but no more than that. If indifference curves are flat enough so that the curve tangent to segment *DE* passes *above* point *C*, then the person would choose not to receive welfare. Thus, the effect of the work requirement is to induce welfare recipients to work, but as long as they are on welfare they will have incentives to work only the minimum hours needed to qualify. Above the required hours of work, a program recipient's effective wage is still zero. (For labor supply responses to different forms of a work requirement—requisitions of food from farmers during wartime—see Example 6.6.)

Subsidy Programs with Positive Net Wage Rates

So far we have analyzed the work-incentive effects of income maintenance programs that create net wage rates for program recipients that are either negative or zero (that is, they create constraints that have either a spike or a horizontal

EXAMPLE 6.6

Wartime Food Requisitions and Agricultural Work Incentives

Countries at war often adopt "work requirement" policies to obtain needed food supplies involuntarily from their farming populations. Not surprisingly, the way in which these requisitions are carried out can have enormous effects on the work incentives of farmers. Two alternative methods are contrasted in this example: one was used by the Bolshevik government during the civil war that followed the Russian revolution, and the other by Japan during World War II.

From 1917 to 1921, the Bolsheviks requisitioned from farmers all food in excess of the amounts needed for the farmers' own subsistence; in effect, the surplus was confiscated and given to soldiers and urban dwellers. Graphically, this policy created a budget constraint for farmers like ACY_s in diagram (a) below. Because farmers could keep their output until they reached the subsistence level of income (Y_s), the market wage prevailed until income of Y_s was reached. After that, their net wage was zero (on segment CY_s), because any extra output went to the government. Thus, a prewar market constraint of AB was converted

to ACY_s, with the consequence that most farmers maximized utility near point C. Acreage planted dropped by 27 percent from 1917 to 1921, while harvested output fell by 50 percent!

Japan, during World War II, handled its food requisitioning policy completely differently. It required a quota to be delivered by each farmer to the government at very low prices, but it allowed farmers to sell any produce above the quota at higher (market) prices. This policy converted the prewar constraint of AB to one much like EFG in diagram (b). In effect, farmers had to work AE hours for the government at lower than market pay (EF), but were allowed to earn the market wage after that. This preserved farmers' work incentives and apparently created an income effect that increased the total hours of work by Japanese farmers, for despite war-induced shortages of capital and labor, rice production was greater in 1944 than in 1941!

Data from: Jack Hirshleifer, *Economic Behavior in Adversity* (Chicago: University of Chicago Press, 1987), 16–21, 39–41.

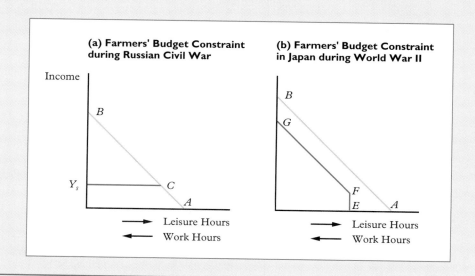

(a) Farmers' Budget Constraint during Russian Civil War

(b) Farmers' Budget Constraint in Japan during World War II

segment). Programs can be devised, however, that create positive net wages for those who are eligible. Do these programs offer a solution to the problem of work incentives? We will answer this question by analyzing a relatively recent and rapidly growing program, the Earned Income Tax Credit (EITC).

The EITC program makes income tax credits available to low-income families with at least one worker. A tax credit of one dollar reduces a person's income taxes by one dollar, and in the case of the EITC, if the tax credit for which workers qualify exceeds their total income tax liability, the government will mail them a check for the difference. Thus, the EITC functions as an earnings subsidy, and because the subsidy goes only to those who work, the EITC is seen by many as an income maintenance program that preserves work incentives. This view led Congress to vastly expand the EITC under President Clinton, and it is now the largest cash subsidy program directed at low-income households with children.

The tax credits offered by the EITC program vary with one's earnings and the number of dependent children. For purposes of our analysis, which is intended to illustrate the work-incentive effects of the EITC, we will focus on the credits in

FIGURE 6.17
Earned Income Tax Credit (One Child), 2000

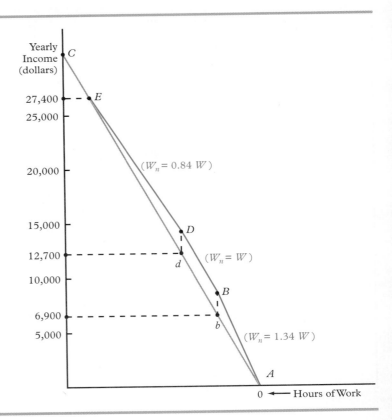

the year 2000 offered to workers with one child. Figure 6.17 graphs the relevant program characteristics for a worker with one child who could earn a "market" (unsubsidized) wage reflected by the slope of AC. As we will see below, for such a worker, the EITC created a budget constraint of $ABDEC$.

For workers with earnings of $6,900 or less, the tax credit was calculated at 34 percent of earnings. That is, for every dollar earned, a tax credit of 34 cents was also earned; thus, for those with earnings of under $6,900, net wages ($W_n$) were 34 percent higher than market wages (W). Note that this tax credit is represented by segment AB on the EITC constraint in Figure 6.17, and that the slope of AB *exceeds the slope of the market constraint, AC.*

The maximum tax credit allowed for a worker with one child was $2,353. Workers who earned between $6,900 and $12,700 per year qualified for this maximum tax credit. Because these workers experienced no increases or reductions in tax credits per added dollar of earnings, for them the net wage was equal to the market wage. The constraint facing workers with $6,900 to $12,700 of earnings is represented by segment BD in Figure 6.17, which has a slope equal to that of segment AC.

For earnings above $12,700, the tax credit was gradually phased out, so that when earnings reached $27,400 the tax credit was zero. Because after $12,700 in earnings, each dollar earned *reduced* the tax credit, the net wage of anyone earning between $12,700 and $27,400 was *below* one's market wage; this segment of the constraint is shown by DE in Figure 6.17, which has a flatter slope than AC.

Inspection of Figure 6.17 will disclose that, among workers eligible for the EITC, work-incentive effects are different in three earnings zones. The *incomes* of workers in all three zones are enhanced, which means that all EITC recipients experience an income effect that pushes them in the direction of less work. However, the program creates quite different net wage rates in the zones, and therefore the substitution effect differs across zones.

For workers with earnings below $6,900, the net wage is greater than the market wage (by 34 percent), so along segment AB workers experience an increase in the price of leisure. Workers with earnings below $6,900, then, experience a substitution effect that pushes them in the direction of more work. With an income effect and a substitution effect that push in opposite directions, it is uncertain which effect will dominate. What we can predict, though, is that some of those who would have been out of the labor force in the absence of the EITC program will now decide to seek work (earlier we discussed the fact that, for nonparticipants in the labor force, the substitution effect dominates).

Segments BD and DE represent two other zones, in which theory predicts that labor supply will *fall.* Along BD the net wage is equal to the market wage, so the price of leisure in this zone is unchanged while income is enhanced. Workers in this zone experience a pure income effect. Along segment DE the net wage is actually below the market wage, so in this zone *both* the income and the substitution effects push in the direction of reduced labor supply.

Labor supply theory, then, suggests that workers in two of the three earnings zones will reduce their labor supply in response to the EITC; the responses of those in the other zone are not predictable, except we can anticipate that some who were previously out of the labor force will now seek work. Empirical studies of labor supply responses suggest that expansion of the EITC did induce more *single* mothers to join the labor market, while it reduced labor supply among *married* mothers in families qualifying for the program (single women were more likely to be along segment *AB* of Figure 6.17, while married women were more likely to have family incomes along *BD* or *DE*).[25]

---

[25]Bruce D. Meyer and Dan T. Rosenbaum, "Welfare, the Earned Income Tax Credit, and the Labor Supply of Single Mothers," *Quarterly Journal of Economics* 116, no. 3 (August 2001): 1063–1114; and David T. Ellwood, "The Impact of the Earned Income Tax Credit and Social Policy Reforms on Work, Marriage, and Living Arrangements," *National Tax Journal* 53, no. 4 (December 2000): 1063–1105. The latter issue of the *National Tax Journal* is a special issue devoted to the EITC.

REVIEW QUESTIONS

1. Referring to the definitions in footnote 5, is the following statement true, false, or uncertain: "Leisure must be an inferior good for an individual's labor supply curve to be backward-bending." Explain your answer.

2. Evaluate the following quote: "Higher take-home wages for any group should increase the labor force participation rate for that group."

3. Suppose a government is considering several options to ensure that legal services are provided to the poor:

   Option A: All lawyers would be required to devote 5 percent of their work time to the poor, free of charge.

   Option B: Lawyers would be required to provide 100 hours of work, free of charge, to the poor.

   Option C: Lawyers who earn over $50,000 in a given year would have to donate $5,000 to a fund that the government would use to help the poor.

   Discuss the likely effects of each option on the hours of work among lawyers. (It would help to draw the constraints created by each option.)

4. The way the workers' compensation system works now, employees permanently injured on the job receive a payment of $X each year whether they work or not. Suppose the government were to implement a new program in which those who did not work at all got $0.5X but those who did work got $0.5X plus workers' compensation of 50 cents *for every hour worked* (of course, this subsidy would be in addition to the wages paid by their employers).

   What would be the change in work incentives associated with this change in the way workers' compensation payments were calculated?

5. A firm wants to offer paid sick leave to its workers, but it wants to encourage them not to abuse it by being unnecessarily absent. The firm is considering two options:

   a. Ten days of paid sick leave per year; any unused leave days at end of year are converted to cash at the worker's daily wage rate.

   b. Ten days of paid sick leave per year; if no sick days are used for two consecutive years, the company agrees to buy the worker a $100,000 life insurance policy.

Compare the work-incentive effects of the two options, both immediately and in the long run.

6. Suppose the Social Security disability insurance (DI) program was structured so that otherwise eligible recipients lost their *entire* disability benefit if they had any labor market earnings at all. Suppose, too, that Congress was concerned about the *work disincentives* inherent in this program, and that the relevant committee was studying two alternatives for increasing work incentives among those disabled enough to qualify for it. One alternative was to *reduce* the benefits paid to all DI recipients but make no other changes in the program. The other was to maintain the old benefit levels (for those who received them) but allow workers to earn $300 per month and still keep their benefits; those who earned over $300 per month would lose all DI benefits.

Analyze the work-incentive effects of both alternatives. (The use of graphical analyses will be of great help to you.)

7. Suppose there is a proposal to provide poor people with housing subsidies that are tied to their income levels. These subsidies will be in the form of vouchers the poor can turn over to their landlords in full or partial payment of their housing expenses. The yearly subsidy will equal $2,400 as long as earnings do not exceed $8,000 per year. The subsidy is to be reduced 60 cents for every dollar earned in excess of $8,000; that is, when earnings reach $12,000, the person is no longer eligible for rent subsidies.

Draw an arbitrary budget constraint for a person assuming that he or she receives no government subsidies. Then draw in the budget constraint that arises from the above housing subsidy proposal. After drawing in the budget constraint associated with the proposal, analyze the effects of this proposed housing subsidy program on the labor supply behavior of various groups in the population.

8. The Tax Reform Act of 1986 was designed to reduce the marginal tax rate (the tax rate on the last dollars earned) while eliminating enough deductions and loopholes so that total revenues collected by the government could remain constant. Analyze the work-incentive effects of tax reforms that lower marginal tax rates while keeping total tax revenues constant.

PROBLEMS

1. When the Fair Labor Standards Act began to mandate paying 50 percent more for overtime work, many employers tried to avoid it by cutting hourly pay, so that total pay and hours remained the same.

   a. Assuming that this 50 percent overtime-pay premium is newly required for all work beyond eight hours per day, draw a budget constraint that pictures a strategy of cutting hourly pay so that, at the original hours of work, total earnings remain the same.

   b. Suppose that an employer initially paid $11 per hour and had a 10-hour workday. What hourly base wage will the employer offer so that the total pay for a 10-hour workday will stay the same?

   c. Will employees who used to work 10 hours per day want to work more or fewer than 10 hours in the new environment (which includes the new wage rate and the mandated overtime premium)?

2. Nina is able to select her weekly work hours. When a new bridge opens up, it cuts one hour off Nina's total daily commute to work. If both leisure and income are normal goods, what is the effect of the shorter commute on Nina's work time?

SELECTED READINGS

Card, David E., and Rebecca M. Blank, eds. *Finding Jobs: Work and Welfare Reform.* New York: Russell Sage Foundation, 2000.

Ellwood, David T. *Poor Support: Poverty in the American Family.* New York: Basic Books, 1988.

Keeley, Michael C. *Labor Supply and Public Policy: A Critical Review.* New York: Academic Press, 1981.

Killingsworth, Mark R. *Labor Supply.* Cambridge, Eng.: Cambridge University Press, 1983.

Linder, Staffan B. *The Harried Leisure Class.* New York: Columbia University Press, 1970.

Moffitt, Robert. "Incentive Effects of the U.S. Welfare System: A Review," *Journal of Economic Literature* 30 (March 1992): 1–62.

Pencavel, John. "Labor Supply of Men: A Survey." In *Handbook of Labor Economics*, ed. Orley Ashenfelter and David Card. Amsterdam, New York: Elsevier, 1999.

7

LABOR SUPPLY:
Household Production, the Family, and the Life Cycle

I n chapter 6 the theory of labor supply focused on the simple case in which individuals decide how to allocate their time between labor and leisure. This chapter elaborates on this simple labor supply model by taking account of three issues. First, much of the time spent at home is given to work activities (cooking and child care, for example), not leisure. Second, for those who live with partners, decisions about work for pay, household work, and leisure are usually made in a way that takes account of the activities and income of other household members. Third, just as time at paid work is substitutable with time at home, time spent working for pay in one part of the life cycle is substitutable with time later on. These refinements of our simple model do not alter the fundamental considerations or predictions of labor supply theory, but they do add useful richness to it.

THE THEORY OF HOUSEHOLD PRODUCTION

In this chapter we analyze a model of labor supply that is built on the assumption that household work, not leisure, is the alternative to working for pay.[1] Such a model

---

[1]Continuing our analysis of the choice between just two time-use alternatives allows the theory to be summarized graphically. For more on the theory of household production, see Reuben Gronau, "The Theory of Home Production: The Past Ten Years," *Journal of Labor Economics* 15, no. 2 (April 1997): 197–205.

assumes that household time and purchased goods (made possible by paid work and any nonlabor income) are combined to produce commodities that are then consumed. Food and energy are combined with preparation time to produce meals, for example, while books, toys, and supervision time contribute to the development of children. Thus, household time is viewed as an *input* to the production of household commodities, not as an item that is directly consumed. It is the *commodities* that are ultimately consumed and that generate utility for household members.

Graphing the Model

To obtain a sense of how we can model the production of household commodities, let us consider a household with just one decision maker: a single mother, Sally, who derives satisfaction (utility) from raising her children.[2] Her objective is to maximize utility for herself and her children, and this she will do by allocating available time to both working for pay and working at home in a way that best satisfies her preferences. In making this allocation, as we will see, she will be deciding simultaneously on how much to work for pay *and* how to accomplish her child-rearing duties.

Equal satisfaction from child-rearing can be generated in a number of different ways. Sally can minimize the use of goods and services purchased outside the household by staying home to supervise the children, prepare their meals, and even make some of their clothing. A very different approach would rely heavily on purchased goods or services, and less on her input of household time, by working for pay and then, for example, purchasing the services of a babysitter, serving prepared foods, and buying all clothing. Because various combinations of household time and purchased goods or services potentially generate equally satisfactory results, we could plot a curve that represents all the time/goods combinations that produce equal utility for Sally. Such a curve can be called a utility *isoquant*, where *iso* means "equal" and *quant* means "quantity" (of utility). Two utility isoquants are depicted in Figure 7.1 as M_0 and M_1.

Note several things about the isoquants in Figure 7.1. First, along M_0 the utility provided by child-rearing is constant. The utility produced by the time/goods combinations along M_1 is also constant, but it is greater than the utility represented by M_0 because Sally can do more for her children (that is, the child-rearing process involves more parental time and more, or higher-quality, purchased goods or services).

Second, the isoquants M_0 and M_1 are both negative in slope and convex (as viewed from below) in shape. The negative slope reflects an assumption that household time and purchased goods or services are substitutes in the "production" of child-rearing. If Sally's household time is reduced, child-rearing affording equal satisfaction can be produced by increasing the purchases of goods or services outside the home.

The convexity of the isoquants reflects an assumption that as household time devoted to child-rearing progressively falls, it becomes increasingly difficult to make

---

[2]Sally would also derive utility from other things, of course, but to keep things simple we focus just on one activity for now.

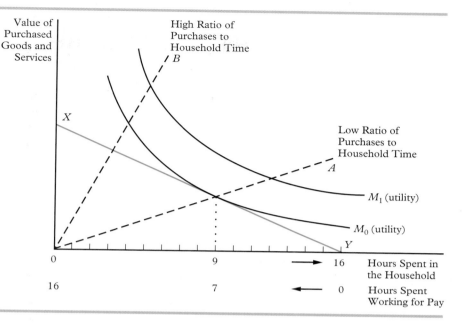

FIGURE 7.1
**The Production
of Child Care**

up for it with purchased goods or services and still hold utility constant. If Sally spends a lot of time at home (making clothes, for example), it is relatively easy to replace some of that time with just a few purchased goods (store-bought clothing) and maintain equal levels of satisfaction. However, when her household time is very short to begin with, a further cut in such time may be very difficult to absorb and still keep utility constant (it may take a large increase in the quality of child-care services to replace an hour of parental time if a parent is already out of the home for, say, 10 hours a day).

The slope of the utility isoquants, therefore, reflects the trade-offs a person, in this case Sally, is willing to make between household time and purchased goods or services in the production of household commodities. When isoquants are steeply sloped, it is relatively difficult to satisfactorily substitute purchased goods or services for the loss of an hour of household time; as a result, the marginal hour of such time is highly valued. A flatter slope depicts a situation in which it is easier to substitute for household time, and in this case it can be said that an extra hour of household time is less highly valued.

Finally, along any ray (*A* or *B*, for example) emanating from the origin of Figure 7.1, the ratio of purchased goods and services to household time in the production of child-rearing is constant. When household time and purchased goods or services are used in the combinations along ray *A*, Sally accomplishes child-rearing by using a relatively low ratio of purchases to household time. Along ray *B*, her child-rearing process uses a higher ratio of purchased goods and services to household time.

Because we have assumed that the only two uses of time are paid (or "market") work and household work, deciding on the utility-maximizing mode of child-rearing is the same as deciding on the utility-maximizing supply of hours to the labor market. This decision is influenced by Sally's utility isoquants, discussed above, and her budget constraint. Just as in chapter 6, a budget constraint—like *XY* in Figure 7.1—reflects the combinations of purchases and household time that are possible for Sally. Also as before, the slope of the budget constraint reflects Sally's wage rate, because it indicates the increased value of purchases made possible by an additional hour of paid work.

Implications of the Model

Given the isoquants and the constraint *XY* in Figure 7.1, Sally's utility is maximized by spending 7 hours working for pay and 9 hours working at home each day. If Sally faced the same budget constraint as in Figure 7.1 but had isoquants with a generally flatter slope—indicating that in her view purchased goods or services could more easily substitute for an hour of her own parental time—then the utility-maximizing point of tangency would have been further to the left along *XY* and she would have decided to work more hours outside the home.

Note that the utility-maximization process depicted in Figure 7.1 looks just like the graphical depictions in chapter 6, even though the models assume different uses of household time. In both models the budget constraints reflect the combinations of purchased goods or services and household time (whether for leisure or for household work) that can be attained by the person. In both models the slope of the budget constraint indicates the person's wage rate. In both models, convex isoquants reflect the trade-offs in utility between purchased goods or services and household time. In both, steeply sloped isoquants represent a person who highly values an added hour at home. And in both, a person with steeply sloped isoquants will have a tangency point toward the lower end of the budget constraint, therefore spending relatively few hours in paid work.

Thus, whether household time is conceived of as work or as leisure time, the resulting theory of labor supply is unchanged. Supply of hours to paid work is a function of income, the wage rate, and the trade-offs a person is willing to make between household time and money income (which can be used to purchase goods and services) in the generation of utility. If, for example, Sally were to receive unearned income in a way that did not alter her wage rate, shown in Figure 7.1, her new budget constraint would lie to the northeast of *XY* (and be parallel to it). Because the added income would allow a greater command over resources, she would now be able to increase her utility by doing more for (or with) her children. She would tend to purchase more, or higher-quality, goods and services, and she would also spend more time at home. Thus, there is an *income effect* that operates just as it did in chapter 6; in this case, the *added* income would tend to *reduce* labor supply to the market.

Likewise, if Sally's *wage* were to rise, there would be an income effect *and* a substitution effect. The income effect would serve to reduce labor supply, but it would be offset to some extent by the fact that the higher wage increases the cost of spending an extra hour at home. In short, there would be a *substitution effect* associated with the wage increase that would push Sally in the direction of more paid work (and, at the same time, would push her toward a mode of child-rearing that relies more on purchased goods or services). As we also found in chapter 6, theory cannot tell us whether, if wages increase, it is the income or the substitution effect that will dominate; that will depend on the shape of the utility isoquants.

THE TRIPARTITE CHOICE: MARKET WORK, HOUSEHOLD WORK, AND LEISURE

While the household production model of labor supply does not change our conclusions in chapter 6 about the influence of income and substitution effects, consideration of household production does introduce the notion that there is really a *tripartite* choice of how to spend time. That is, people can choose to spend time in market work (for pay), in household work, or in leisure activities. Explicit recognition of this tripartite choice enriches our understanding of how people allocate their time.

Time Use by Women and Men

Consider data from time-use diaries in Table 7.1, which summarizes how men and women in the United States allocated their weekly hours in 1965 and 1981.[3] From the table we can see reflections of the previously discussed trends in hours of paid work: weekly hours of market work were up for women and down for men (primarily because of changes in labor force participation rates) over the 1965–1981 period. While

TABLE 7.1   **Weekly Hours Spent in Work and Leisure by Men and Women, Ages 25–64, in the United States, 1965–1981**

	Men		*Women*	
	1965	*1981*	*1965*	*1981*
Paid work (including commuting)	51.6	44.0	18.9	23.9
Household work	11.5	13.8	41.8	30.5
Leisure	36.7	41.8	35.4	41.9
Personal care	68.2	68.2	71.9	71.6

Source: F. Thomas Juster and Frank P. Stafford, "The Allocation of Time: Empirical Findings, Behavioral Models, and Problems of Measurement," *Journal of Economic Literature* 29, no. 2 (June 1991): Table 3.

---

[3]Diary-based estimates of market work hours included commuting time, hours of job search, hours at a second job, and unpaid time spent at the workplace before and after work; thus, these data are not fully comparable to the hours data discussed at the beginning of chapter 6. F. Thomas Juster and Frank P. Stafford, "The Allocation of Time: Empirical Findings, Behavioral Models, and Problems of Measurement," *Journal of Economic Literature* 29 (June 1991): 471–522, argue that the diary-based measures are superior to conventional interview data.

EXAMPLE 7.1

Work and Leisure: Past versus Present

In 1880 the typical adult male had very little free time. Averaged over the course of a typical week during his working life, a male worker spent 66.5 hours working for pay and traveling to and from work; 14 hours doing household chores; and 75 hours on sleep, meals, hygiene, and other maintenance activities. This left about 12.5 hours per week—only 1.8 hours per day—for leisure. Historical calculations for women are much more difficult, but evidence suggests that women enjoyed about 2 hours less of leisure each week than men. Looking at Table 7.1, one can see that by 1981, men's weekly hours of work (including commuting time) had dropped to 44, their household work time had stayed at 14, and their leisure time had risen to almost 42 hours per week. While women's work for pay has increased, time spent on household chores has fallen so much that women's weekly leisure hours are now approximately equal to those of men.

In addition to these gains in leisure for people in the labor force, leisure time has increased because the average age of entering the labor force is about 5 years later today than it was in 1880, and the average period of retirement for those who live to age 50 is about 11 years longer today than it was in 1880. Pulling all these estimates together implies that while lifetime discretionary time (the 14 hours per day that is not used for sleeping, eating, and hygiene) has risen from 225,000 hours to 298,500 hours, lifetime leisure hours have increased from 43,800 hours to 176,100 hours. In the bad old days, market and household work occupied 80 percent of discretionary time for the typical adult, and leisure's share was a mere 20 percent. Today leisure is king. Market and household work consume about 40 percent of discretionary time and leisure's share is nearly 60 percent!

Data from: Robert W. Fogel, "Catching Up with the Economy," *American Economic Review* 89, no. 1 (March 1999): 1–21.

women still average more than twice as many hours in household chores as men, their hours of household work are falling while those of men are rising. Finally, both men and women experienced substantial increases in leisure time over the period. (Example 7.1 discusses changes in work and leisure over a much longer period.)

Two Substitution Effects

In chapter 6 we noted that the substitution effect has tended to dominate the income effect in the labor supply of women. As women's labor force participation has increased, the dominance of the substitution effect for women has appeared to fade, and the relative size of the two effects for men and women has begun to converge. The historical differences in the substitution effects for men and women, and their apparently growing convergence, can be at least partly understood by the presence of *two* substitution effects: one between market and household work, and the other between market work and leisure. We argue below that the magnitudes of these two effects differ depending upon one's role in household production.

Recall from Figure 6.10 that the substitution effect is graphically depicted by changing the slope of the budget constraint, keeping it tangent to the same indifference curve. You can see from comparing the two panels in Figure 7.2 that the substitution effect is larger if the isoquant is gently bent (panel a), as opposed to abruptly bent (panel b). What can cause these isoquants to bend differently?

FIGURE 7.2
Large versus Small Substitution Effects Attendant to a Wage Increase

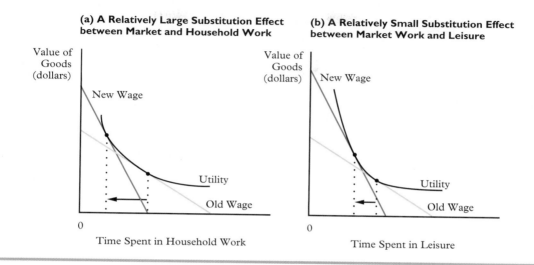

(a) A Relatively Large Substitution Effect between Market and Household Work

(b) A Relatively Small Substitution Effect between Market Work and Leisure

Both panels of Figure 7.2 place the value of goods (and services) used in producing utility on the vertical axis; thus, the vertical axis depicts the goods that can be purchased with the money derived from market work. Panel (a), however, shows the trade-offs between these goods and household *work* time that keep utility constant, while panel (b) shows the goods/*leisure* trade-off. The gradual bend in panel (a) implies that reductions in hours of household work can be easily compensated for by purchasing more goods; that is, reduced time devoted to such household chores as cooking, cleaning, and child care can be easily replaced through the purchase of a microwave oven, prepared foods, an electric dishwasher, or the services of a babysitter.

The steeper bend in the goods/leisure indifference curve (panel b) reflects the greater difficulty in substituting goods for *leisure* time without loss of utility.[4] Leisure activities normally include time as an essential input, and the possibilities for economizing on time are thus limited. A television show can be taped and watched more quickly later by fast-forwarding through commercials, and one can listen to a Beethoven symphony while doing other things, such as

---

[4]To prove this to yourself, ask, "If an hour of time at home is given up, what amount of goods will have to be added to keep utility constant?" When it is difficult to substitute goods for time, it will take many goods to keep utility constant, and the indifference curve will rise steeply. You should be able to convince yourself that the limiting case in which no substitution is possible involves an indifference curve that is L-shaped; in this case no change in the wage rate will change the optimum mix of inputs.

driving or jogging. These examples, however, highlight how difficult it is to substitute satisfactorily for time in leisure activities.

Married women have traditionally been—and remain today, judging by Table 7.1—the primary household producers in most families. Therefore, as wages have risen, the (stronger) market/household-work substitution effect shown in panel (a) of Figure 7.2 probably has been of greater importance for women than for men. Moreover, as women have increased their hours of paid work markedly over recent decades, they have undoubtedly substituted many purchased goods for household-work time—with the result that further substitutions now may be more difficult. In short, many households now may be at a more steeply sloped point on the trade-off curve in panel (a) than they were several years ago. The historical dominance of the substitution effect for women, and the apparent fall in this dominance, thus may at least partially reflect the prominent role of women in household production and the adjustments in household production made over the years as their labor force participation has increased.

JOINT LABOR SUPPLY DECISIONS WITHIN THE HOUSEHOLD

The models depicted in chapter 6 and so far in this chapter have been for a single decision maker, who was assumed to be trying to maximize his or her own utility. For those who live with partners, however, some kind of *joint* decision-making process must be used to allocate the time of each and to agree on who does what in the household. This process is complicated by emotional relationships between the partners, and their decisions about market and household work are also heavily influenced by custom.[5] Nevertheless, economic theory may help provide insight into at least some of the forces that shape the decisions all households must make.

Just how to model the different decision-making processes that can be used by households is a question economists have only begun to study. The formal models of decision making among married couples that have been developed, all of which are based on principles of utility maximization, fall into three general categories.[6] The simplest models extend the assumption of a single decision maker to marriage partners, either by assuming they both have exactly the same preferences or by assuming that one makes all the decisions. A second type of model assumes that the partners engage in a bargaining process in making household decisions; each is assumed to have resources that affect their bargaining power. Finally, some models assume that the partners act independently to max-

---

[5]See Julie A. Nelson, "I, Thou, and Them: Capabilities, Altruism, and Norms in the Economics of Marriage," *American Economic Review* 84, no. 2 (May 1994): 126–131; and Claire Brown, "An Institutional Model of Wives' Work Decisions," *Industrial Relations* 24, no. 2 (Spring 1985): 182–204.

[6]See Shelly Lundberg and Robert A. Pollak, "Bargaining and Distribution in Marriage," *Journal of Economic Perspectives* 10, no. 4 (Fall 1996): 139–158.

imize their own utility, but each does so by considering the likely actions, and reactions, of the other.

Whatever process partners use to decide on the allocation of their time, and it may be different in different households, there are certain issues that nearly all households must face. We turn now to a brief analysis of some joint decisions that affect labor supply.

Specialization of Function

Partners often find it beneficial to specialize to some extent in the work that needs to be done, both in the market and in the household. Often, one or the other partner will bear primary responsibilities for meal planning, shopping, home maintenance, or child-rearing. It may also be the case that, when both work for pay, one or the other of the partners will be more available for overtime, for job-related travel, or for cutting short a workday if an emergency arises at home. What factors are weighed in deciding who specializes in what?

Theory   Consider a couple trying to decide which spouse, if either, will take primary responsibility for child-rearing by staying at home (say) or by taking a job that has a less-demanding schedule or a shorter commute. Because the person with primary child-care duties will probably end up spending more hours in the household, the couple needs to answer two questions: Who is relatively more productive at home? Who is relatively more productive in market work?

For example, a couple deciding whether one partner should stay home more and perform most of the child-rearing would want to consider what gains and losses are attendant on either the husband or the wife assuming this responsibility. The losses from staying home are related to the market wage of each, while the gains depend on their enjoyment of, and skill at, child-rearing. (Since enjoyment of the parenting process increases utility, we can designate both higher levels of enjoyment *and* higher levels of skill as indicative of greater "productivity" in child-rearing.) Wage rates for women, for reasons discussed in later chapters, typically have been below those for men. It is also likely that, because of socialization, wives have been historically more productive than husbands in child-rearing. If a given woman's wage rate is lower than her husband's and the woman is more productive in child-rearing, the family gives up less in market goods and gains more in child-rearing if the wife takes primary responsibility in this area.

Implications for the Future   Modeling the choice of who handles most of some household duty as influenced by relative household and market productivities is not meant to imply that customs are unimportant in shaping preferences or in limiting choices concerning household production; clearly they are. What the theory of household production emphasizes is that the distribution of household work may well change as wages, incomes, and home productivities change. One study has found that, when both spouses work outside the home, the weekly hours that each spends in household work are affected by their relative wage rates. That is, as wives' wages rise relative to those of their husbands, the household work done by husbands appears to increase, while the work done by wives decreases.[7]

Do Both Partners Work for Pay?

It is clearly not necessary, of course, that either partner stay at home full-time. Many household chores, from cooking and cleaning to child care, can be hired out or otherwise performed in a goods-intensive manner. The considerations underlying the decision about whether both should work can be best understood by looking at Figure 7.3. The utility isoquants there (U_1 and U_2) represent the various combinations of household time and goods that can be used to generate family (or individual) utility of two levels (level 1 and level 2).

As long as an extra hour of market work by both partners creates the ability to buy more goods than are required to make up for the hour of lost home time, both can enhance household resources if they work for pay that extra hour. In terms of Figure 7.3, if a person spending H_0 hours at home decides to work an extra hour for pay, so that H_1 hours are now spent at home, he or she will gain BD in goods.[8] Since an increase of only BC in goods is required to compensate for the lost hour of home production to keep utility constant, household resources are clearly increased if the person works for pay. In other words, at point A the person is relatively more productive in the marketplace than at home. Thus, decisions about household labor supply must be made in full consideration of the market and household productivities of both partners.

The Joint Decision and Cross-Effects

We have seen that family labor supply decisions are enhanced by jointly considering the household and market productivities of each partner. However, one partner's productivity in both production and consumption at home is affected by the *other* partner's labor supply to the market, so that modeling the joint decision is quite complex. On the one hand, if a married woman decides to increase her hours worked outside the home, her husband's marginal productivity for a given number of hours at home may rise as he takes over chores she once performed. Thus, if both wife and husband are *substitutes* in the household production of commodities, one spouse's increased labor supply to the market may tend to decrease the labor supply of the other.

On the other hand, both spouses may be *complementary* in the *consumption* of household commodities. That is, if the woman above takes a job that involves working until 8:00 P.M. each night, her husband may decide that dinners at 6:00

---

[7]Joni Hersch and Leslie S. Stratton, "Housework, Wages, and the Division of Household Time for Employed Spouses," *American Economic Review* 84, no. 2 (May 1994): 120–125. Hersch and Stratton also suggest that wages are themselves affected (negatively) by increased household work time; see their "Household, Fixed Effects, and Wages of Married Workers," *Journal of Human Resources* 32, no. 2 (Spring 1997): 285–307.
[8]We are talking here of after-tax spending power. The value of what one produces at home is not taxed, but earnings in the marketplace are—a difference that forces us to focus here on wages and earnings *net* of taxes.

FIGURE 7.3

Home versus Market Productivities

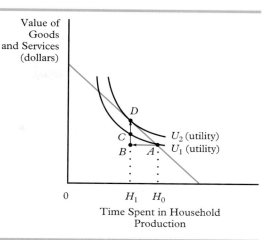

P.M. have less utility than before, and as a result, he might decide that the benefits of working later outweigh the utility lost by so doing. In this case, one spouse's decision to increase hours worked for pay may induce the other spouse to likewise increase labor supply. (See Example 7.2 for a case in which the comsumption of household time by spouses was *not* complementary.)

Theory cannot predict whether the spouses are substitutes or complements in household production and consumption; similarly, it is impossible to say which cross-effect will dominate if their signs conflict. There is as yet no real consensus on the sizes and signs of these cross-effects for husbands and wives.[9]

Labor Supply in Recessions: The "Discouraged" versus the "Additional" Worker

Changes in one partner's productivity, either at home or in market work, can alter the family's basic labor supply decision. Consider, for example, a "traditional" family in which market work is performed by the husband and in which the wife is employed full-time in the home. What will happen if a recession causes the husband to become unemployed?

Added-Worker Effect The husband's market productivity declines, at least temporarily. The drop in his market productivity relative to his household productivity

---

[9]For reviews of these issues, see Mark Killingsworth, *Labor Supply* (Cambridge, Eng.: Cambridge University Press, 1983); Marjorie B. McElroy, "Appendix: Empirical Results from Estimates of Joint Labor Supply Functions of Husbands and Wives," in *Research in Labor Economics*, vol. 4, ed. Ronald Ehrenberg (Greenwich, Conn.: JAI Press, 1981), 53–64; Shelly Lundberg, "Labor Supply of Husbands and Wives: A Simultaneous Equations Approach," *Review of Economics and Statistics* 70 (May 1988): 224–234; and Joni Hersch and Leslie S. Stratton, "Housework, Wages, and the Division of Household Time for Employed Spouses."

EXAMPLE 7.2

Husbands, Wives, Neighbors and the End of the Six-Hour Workday at Kellogg's

Economic theory suggests that the supply of work hours depends, in part, upon the value people place on household time, including leisure. This point is illustrated quite clearly by the workers at Kellogg's, the cereal maker. During the Great Depression, Kellogg's gained the national spotlight by dropping its standard eight-hour workday and adopting a workday of only six hours. Workers willingly "shared the work" with the unemployed, accepting lower earnings for more leisure.

During World War II, the company switched to a 48-hour workweek, but promised to revert to six-hour shifts after the emergency ended. In mid-1946, employees reaffirmed their desire for the shorter workday, with 87 percent of women and 71 percent of men voting for six hours. By 1957, however, most departments had opted to switch back to the eight-hour work day—so that only about one-quarter of the work force, mostly women, retained the six-hour shift.

What happened between the end of World War II and the late 1950s that caused workers, especially men, to change their minds about how much to work? Interviews of these workers suggest that one of the most important factors was a clash in spouses' perceptions of how household time should be used. Many men complained about the friction that resulted when they spent too much time around the house: "The wives didn't like the men underfoot all day," and "The wife always found something for me to do if I hung around," were typical responses.

In addition, these men paid attention to what their neighbors did and thought. Without the rationale of sharing work with the unemployed or returning war veterans, they became embarrassed about working shorter shifts than other men. Spending too much time at home came to be seen as abnormal or unmanly, and even though their incomes were rising, these men felt that longer hours were needed buy the material possessions being acquired by their neighbors. The utility of household time, then, was influenced not only by personal tastes, but also by household interactions and societal pressures.

Data from: Benjamin Kline Hunnicutt, *Kellogg's Six-Hour Day,* Philadelphia: Temple University Press, 1996.

(which is unaffected by the recession) makes it more likely that the family will find it beneficial for him to engage in household production. If the wage his wife can earn in paid work is not affected, the family *may* decide that, to try to maintain the family's prior level of utility (which might be affected by both consumption and *savings* levels), *she* should seek market work and *he* should substitute for her in home production for as long as the recession lasts. He may remain a member of the labor force as an unemployed worker awaiting recall, and as she begins to look for work, she becomes an added member of the labor force. Thus, in the face of falling family income, the number of family members seeking market work may increase. This potential response is akin to the *income effect* in that, as family income falls, fewer commodities are consumed—and less time spent in consumption tends to be matched by more desired hours of work for pay.

Discouraged-Worker Effect   At the same time, however, we must look at the *wage rate* someone without a job can *expect* to receive if he or she looks for work. This expected wage, denoted by $E(W)$, can actually be written as a precise statistical concept:

$$E(W) = \pi W \tag{7.1}$$

where W is the wage rate of people who have the job and π is the probability of obtaining the job if out of work. For someone without a job, the opportunity cost of staying home is $E(W)$. The reduced availability of jobs that occurs when the unemployment rate rises causes the *expected wage of those without jobs to fall* sharply for two reasons. First, an excess of labor supply over demand tends to push down real wages (for those with jobs) during recessionary periods. Second, the chances of getting a job fall in a recession. Thus, both W and π fall in a recession, causing $E(W)$ to decline.

Noting the *substitution effect* that accompanies a falling expected wage, some have argued that people who would otherwise have been looking for work become discouraged in a recession and tend to remain out of the labor market. Looking for work has such a low expected payoff for them that such people decide that spending time at home is more productive than spending time in job search. The reduction of the labor force associated with discouraged workers in a recession is a force working against the added-worker effect—just as the substitution effect works against the income effect.

Which Effect Dominates?   It is possible, of course, for both the added-worker and the discouraged-worker effects to coexist, because "added" and "discouraged" workers will be different groups of people. Which group predominates, however, is the important question. If the labor force is swollen by added workers during a recession, the published unemployment rate will likewise become swollen (the added workers will increase the number of people looking for work). If workers become discouraged and drop out of the labor market after having been unemployed, the decline in people seeking jobs will depress the unemployment rate. Knowledge of which effect predominates is needed in order to make accurate inferences about the actual state of the labor market from the published unemployment rate.

We know that the added-worker effect does exist, although it tends to be rather small. The added-worker effect is confined to the relatively few families whose sole breadwinner loses a job, and there is some evidence that it may be reduced by the presence of unemployment insurance benefits; further, as more and more women become regularly employed for pay, the added-worker effect will tend to both decline and become increasingly confined to teenagers.[10] In contrast, the fall in expected real wages occurs in nearly *every* household, and since the substitution effect is relatively strong for married women, it is not surprising that studies have consistently found the discouraged-worker effect to be large and dominant.[11] Other things equal, *the labor force tends to shrink during recessions and grow during periods of economic recovery.*

Hidden Unemployment   The dominance of the discouraged-worker effect creates what some call the *hidden* unemployed—people who would like to work but believe jobs are so scarce that looking for work is of no use. Because they are not

---

[10]Julie Berry Cullen and Jonathan Gruber, "Does Unemployment Insurance Crowd Out Spousal Labor Supply?" *Journal of Labor Economics* 18, no. 3 (July 2000): 546–572; and Shelly Lundberg, "The Added Worker Effect," *Journal of Labor Economics* 3, no. 1 (January 1985): 11–37.

[11]For recent studies, see Luca Benati, "Some Empirical Evidence on the 'Discouraged Worker' Effect," *Economics Letters* 70, no. 3 (March 2001): 387–395; and Paul Bingley and Ian Walker, "Household Unemployment and the Labour Supply of Married Women," *Economica* 68 (May 2001): 157–185.

looking for work, they are not counted as unemployed in government statistics. Focusing on the period from February 2001 to February 2002, when the overall official unemployment rate rose from 4.2 percent to 5.5 percent, can give some indication of the size of hidden unemployment.

In February 2001, an average of 5.9 million people (4.2 percent of the labor force) were counted as unemployed. In addition, 289,000 people indicated that they wanted work but were not seeking it because they felt jobs were unavailable to them; this group constituted 0.4 percent of those adults not in the labor force. By February 2002, some 7.9 million people (5.5 percent of the labor force) were officially counted as unemployed, but there were 371,000 others among the group not seeking work because they felt jobs were unavailable. Coincident with reduced job opportunities, the number of "discouraged workers" had grown to 0.5 percent of those adults not in the labor force. If discouraged workers were counted as unemployed members of the labor force, the unemployment rate would have been 4.5 percent in February 2001 and 6.1 percent by February 2002; thus, while the official unemployment rate went up 1.3 percentage points, the rate that includes discouraged workers went up 1.6 percentage points.[12]

LIFE-CYCLE ASPECTS OF LABOR SUPPLY

Because market productivity (wages) and household productivity vary over the life cycle, people vary the hours they supply to the labor market over their lives. In the early adult years relatively fewer hours are devoted to work than in later years, and more time is devoted to schooling. In the very late years people fully or partially retire, though at varying ages. In the middle years (say, 25 to 50) most males are in the labor force continuously, but for married women labor force participation rates rise with age. While the issue of schooling is dealt with in chapter 9, expanding the model of household production discussed in this chapter to include life-cycle considerations can enrich our understanding of labor supply behavior in several areas, three of which are discussed below.

The Labor Force Participation Patterns of Married Women

When one examines married women's labor force participation rates using cross-sectional data—data on women of different ages at a point in time—it appears that married women have falling labor force participation during their 20s and rising participation rates from ages 30 to 50. However, a study that followed separate birth cohorts of women (women born in the same years) found that cross-sectional data may be misleading if we want to describe the participation patterns of the "typical" married woman over her life cycle. Following cohorts of married

---

[12]To say that including discouraged workers would change the published unemployment rate does not imply that it should be done. For a summary of the arguments for and against counting discouraged workers as unemployed, see the final report of the National Commission on Employment and Unemployment Statistics, *Counting the Labor Force* (NCEUS: Washington, D.C., 1979), 44–49.

FIGURE 7.4
Household Productivity Can Change over the Life Cycle

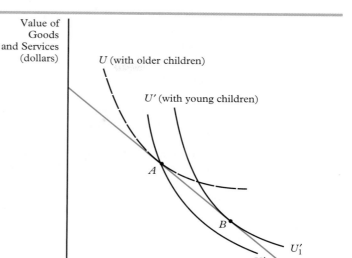

women throughout each decade of the life cycle suggests that labor force participation rates rise in each decade of life, with the increases after age 30 typically being
much greater than those from ages 20 to 30.[13] Can household production theory
help to explain these more steeply rising participation rates after age 30?

The basic premise of the household production model is that people are productive in two places: in the home and in a "market" job. Their decisions about
whether to seek market work and for how many hours are a function of their *relative* productivities in both places.

Home productivity of at least one parent is relatively higher when young
children are present, and it probably falls as children become older (see Example
7.3). Higher household productivity can be represented by a steeper tilt to the
utility isoquants, as shown by the U' curves in Figure 7.4. The U' "family" of isoquants implies that the parent who is the primary caregiver (historically the
mother) will have a tangency point near B with relatively less time in market work
and more time at home. As children grow older, the isoquants take on a flatter
slope, as shown by the dashed curve U in Figure 7.4 (to see the flatter slope, compare the slopes of U and U' at a common point, A). The flatter slope of the dashed
isoquant results in a tangency point to the left of point B, implying reduced time
at home by the primary caregiver and more time in market work.

---

[13]Claudia Goldin, *Understanding the Gender Gap* (New York: Oxford University Press, 1990), 21–26. A
study by David Shapiro and Frank L. Mott, "Long-Term Employment and Earnings of Women in Relation to Employment Behavior Surrounding First Birth," *Journal of Human Resources* 29, no. 2 (Spring
1994): 248–275, found that women most "attached" to the labor force returned to work almost immediately after childbirth. It is among those less attached that we observe the rising labor force participation rates as children age.

EXAMPLE 7.3

The Value of a Homemaker's Time

The services performed by homemakers are not sold in the marketplace, but this does not imply they are not valuable. For purposes of settling claims involving the permanent injury or wrongful death of a homemaker, and often in cases in which property must be divided upon divorce, it is important to place a value on homemakers' services. There are three approaches that can be taken.

Market-Price Approach. One method is to measure how much a homemaker's services (cooking, child care, recordkeeping, etc.) would cost if they were to be individually purchased in the marketplace. The problem with this approach is that in cases in which the services are available but not purchased, the family must believe such services are not worth their cost; for these households, the value assigned by the market-price approach overstates the value of the homemaker's services.

Opportunity-Cost Approach. A second method is to estimate what the homemaker would have been able to earn, after taxes, if she (or he) had worked for pay. Of course, some homemakers do not work at all, which implies they value the services they provide at home at more than their potential market earnings. Using the forgone wage to place a value on each hour of household work thus results in an underestimate of the value of a homemaker's services.

Self-Employment Approach. A third method is to treat homemakers as self-employed individuals who can either increase hours at home if their marginal household productivity (*MHP*) exceeds their market wage (*W*) or reduce hours at home if *W* exceeds *MHP*. If *MHP* exceeds *W* even when hours of paid work are zero, the homemaker works full-time at home; if *W* exceeds *MHP* even when working full-time for pay, the person works full-time outside the home. If a person is at home part of the time and also works part-time for pay, we can infer that *MHP* and *W* must be equal. It is from part-time workers, then, that we obtain estimates of marginal household productivities, and from these estimates it is possible to derive a relationship between hours at home and the total value of household services.

Estimated Values. The first two approaches above, while less theoretically satisfactory, are computationally more feasible. Studies that estimate time spent on various household services from diary data have estimated the value of household services under both the market-price and opportunity-cost approaches. The estimated yearly values for full-time homemakers are as follows (year 2000 dollars):

	Market Price	Opportunity Cost
With children ages 2–5	$26,092	$23,172
Youngest child aged 6–14	23,481	19,999
No children	18,940	18,812

Data from: William H. Gauger and Kathryn E. Walker, *The Dollar Value of Household Work* (Ithaca, N.Y.: College of Human Ecology, 1979); W. Keith Bryant, Cathleen D. Zick, and Hyoshin Kim, *Household Work: What's It Worth and Why?* (Ithaca, N.Y.: Cornell Cooperative Extension, 1992); and Carmel Ullman Chiswick, "The Value of a Housewife's Time," *Journal of Human Resources* 16 (Summer 1982): 412–425.

The Substitution Effect and When to Work over a Lifetime

Just as joint decisions about market and household work involve comparing market and home productivities of the two partners, deciding *when* to work over the course of one's life involves comparing market and home productivities *over time*. The basic idea here is that people will tend to perform the most market work when their earning capacity is high relative to home productivity. Conversely, they will engage in household production when their earning capacity is relatively low.

Suppose a sales representative working on a commission basis knows that her potential income is around $60,000 in a certain year, but that July's income potential will be twice that of November's. Would it be rational for her to schedule her vacation (a time-intensive activity) in November? The answer depends on her market productivity relative to her household productivity for the two months. Obviously her market productivity (her wage rate) is higher in July than November, which means that the opportunity costs of a vacation are greater in July. However, if she has children who are free to vacation only in July, she may decide that her household productivity (in terms of utility) is so much greater in July than November that the benefits of vacationing in July outweigh the costs. If she does not have children of school age, the utility generated by a November vacation may be sufficiently close to that of a July vacation that the smaller opportunity costs make a November vacation preferable.

Similar decisions can be made over longer periods of time, even one's entire life. As chapter 9 will show, market productivity (reflected in the wage) starts low in the young adult years, rises rapidly with age, then levels off and even falls in the later years, as shown in panel (a) of Figure 7.5. This general pattern occurs within each of the broad educational groupings of workers, although the details of the wage trajectories differ. With an *expected* path of wages over their lives, workers can generate rough predictions of two variables critical to labor supply decisions: lifetime wealth and the costs of leisure or household time they will face at various ages. Thus, if home productivity is more or less constant as they age, workers who make labor supply decisions by taking expected lifetime wealth into account will react to *expected* (life-cycle) wage increases by unambiguously increasing their labor supply. Such wage increases raise the cost of leisure and household time but do not increase expected lifetime wealth; these wage increases, then, are accompanied only by a substitution effect.

FIGURE 7.5
Life-Cycle Allocation of Time

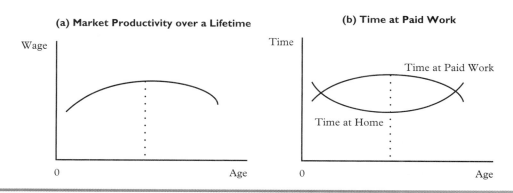

Introducing life-cycle considerations into labor supply theory yields a prediction that the profiles of time spent at, and away from, market work will resemble those shown in panel (b) of Figure 7.5; that is, workers will spend more time at paid work activities in their (relatively high-wage) middle years. Similarly, life-cycle considerations suggest that the consumption of very time-intensive leisure activities will occur primarily in one's early and late years. (That travelers abroad are predominantly young adults and the elderly is clearly related to the fact that, for these groups, opportunity costs of time are lower.)

If workers make labor supply decisions with the life cycle in mind, they will react differently to expected and unexpected wage changes. Expected wage changes will generate only a substitution effect, because estimates of lifetime wealth will remain unchanged. *Unexpected* wage changes, however, will cause them to revise their estimates of lifetime wealth, and these changes will be accompanied by both substitution and income effects. Empirical tests of the life-cycle model of labor supply are relatively recent; to date, they suggest that life-cycle considerations are at best of modest importance in the labor supply decisions of most workers.[14]

The Choice of Retirement Age

A multiyear perspective is also required to more fully model workers' retirement decisions, because *yearly* retirement benefits, expected *lifetime* benefits, and lifetime earnings are all influenced by the date of retirement. The purpose of this section is to explore some of the economic factors that affect the age of retirement. For the sake of illustration, we discuss the retirement incentives facing a 62-year-old male who has earned, and can continue to earn, $32,700 per year as shown in Table 7.2. To further simplify our discussion, we assume this man has no pension other than that provided by Social Security and that, for him, retirement means the cessation of all paid work.

The retirement incentives facing this worker are related to three basic factors: (a) the present value of income available to him over his remaining life expectancy if he retires at age 62; (b) the *change* in this sum if retirement is delayed; and (c) preferences regarding household time and the goods one can buy with money. As we will show below, in terms of the labor supply analyses in this chapter and chapter 6, factor (a) is analogous to nonlabor income, and factor (b) is analogous to the wage rate.

Graphing the Budget Constraint   Table 7.2 summarizes the present value now (at age 62) of pension and earned income available to our hypothetical worker at each possible retirement age, up to age 70. If he retires at age 62, the present value of income over his remaining life expectancy is $149,422. If he delays retirement until

---

[14]For studies that refer to earlier work, see Jean Kimmel and Thomas J. Kniesner, "The Intertemporal-Substitution Hypothesis Is Alive and Well (but Hiding in the Data)," staff working paper no. 93–19, W. E. Upjohn Institute for Employment Research, May 1993; and Peter Rupert, Richard Rogerson, and Randall Wright, "Homework in Labor Economics: Household Production and Intertemporal Substitution," *Journal of Monetary Economics* 46, no. 3 (December 2000): 557–579.

TABLE 7.2   Assumed Social Security Benefits and Earnings for a Hypothetical Male, Aged 62 (yearly wage = $32,700; discount rate = 2%; life expectancy = 17 years)

Age of Retirement	Yearly Soc. Sec. Benefit	Present Value* of Remaining Lifetime:		
		Earnings	Soc. Sec. Benefits	Total
62	$10,455	$ 0	$149,422	$149,422
63	11,326	32,059	150,766	182,825
64	12,197	63,489	150,637	214,126
65	13,068	94,303	149,080	243,383
66	13,852	124,513	145,226	269,739
67	14,636	154,130	140,190	294,320
68	15,420	183,167	134,007	317,174
69	16,204	211,634	126,713	338,347
70	16,988	239,543	118,345	357,888

*Present values calculated as of age 62. All dollar values are as of the current year.

age 63, the present value of his remaining lifetime income rises by $33,403, to $182,825. Note from the second and third columns that delaying retirement from age 62 to 63 increases the present value of both his lifetime earnings *and* Social Security benefits. Delays after age 63, however, are implicitly penalized by reductions in lifetime Social Security benefits; yearly pension benefits rise, but not by enough to offset the reduced number of years such benefits will be received. For example, despite causing a $784 increase in yearly pension benefits, the present value of Social Security benefits falls by $3,854 if he delays retirement from age 65 to 66.

The data in the last column of Table 7.2 are presented graphically in Figure 7.6 as budget constraint *ABJ*. Segment *AB* represents the present value of lifetime income if our worker retires at age 62 and, as such, represents nonlabor income. The slope of segment *BC* represents the $33,403 increase in lifetime income (to $182,825) if retirement is delayed to age 63, and the slopes of the other segments running from points *B* to *J* similarly reflect the increases in discounted lifetime income associated with delaying retirement by a year. These slopes, therefore, represent the yearly *net wage*. The slight concavity of *BJ* reflects the successively smaller increments to lifetime income from delaying retirement after age 63.

Changes in the Constraint   Given preferences summarized by curve U_1, the optimum age of retirement for our hypothetical worker is age 64. How would his optimum age of retirement change if Social Security benefits were increased?[15] The

---

[15]The analysis in this section borrows heavily from Olivia S. Mitchell and Gary S. Fields, "The Effects of Pensions and Earnings on Retirement: A Review Essay," *Research in Labor Economics*, vol. 5, ed. Ronald Ehrenberg (Greenwich, Conn.: JAI Press, 1982), 115–155.

answer depends on how the increases are structured. If the benefit increases were such that a fixed amount was unexpectedly added to lifetime benefits at each retirement age, the constraint facing our 62-year-old male would shift up (and out) to $AB'J'$. The slopes along the segments between B' and J' would remain parallel to those along BJ; thus, there would be an income effect with no substitution effect (that is, no change in the yearly net wage). The optimum age of retirement would be unambiguously reduced, as shown in Figure 7.6.

Alternatively, if Social Security benefits were to be increased by removing the implicit penalties for delaying retirement, so that the segments between B and the vertical axis became more steeply sloped, both an income effect and a substitution effect would be present. Greater lifetime wealth would move our hypothetical worker in the direction of earlier retirement, but a higher net wage from working an extra year would push toward delay. As noted in chapter 6, however, we expect the substitution effect to dominate in labor force *participation* decisions, so if retirement is defined as withdrawal from the labor force, then we would expect a higher net yearly wage to result in delayed retirement.[16]

Our graphical model of the retirement decision emphasizes that this decision is a function of both preferences for household time and the budget constraint facing an individual over his or her remaining lifetime. Changes in Social Security benefits, of course, alter the budget constraint, but there are two other factors that have had important effects on older (especially male) workers' lifetime budget constraints in recent years. First, as we will discuss in chapter 14, the labor demand for men with modest educational backgrounds has fallen in the past two decades, with the result that the real wages of such workers have been reduced. This development, by itself, tends to flatten the budget constraint and induce earlier withdrawal from labor force participation.[17]

Second, perhaps because of the fall in labor demand noted above and employers' related desire to induce older workers to leave, the present value of *private* pension benefits associated with early retirement changed after 1975.[18] In particular, the present value of benefits typically associated with *early* retirement was raised relative to that of retiring at the normal age of (usually) 65, which, in terms of Figure 7.6, lengthened segment AB while it flattened the slope of BJ. The combination of these effects can be confidently predicted to lower the age of retirement.

[16]For recent empirical studies on retirement, see Andrew A. Samwick, "New Evidence on Pensions, Social Security, and the Timing of Retirement," *Journal of Public Economics* 70 (November 1998): 207–236; and Patricia M. Anderson, Alan L. Gustman, and Thomas L. Steinmeier, "Trends in Male Labor Force Participation and Retirement: Some Evidence on the Role of Pensions and Social Security in the 1970s and 1980s," *Journal of Labor Economics* 17, no. 4 (October 1999): 757–783.

[17]Franco Peracchi and Finis Welch, "Trends in the Labor Force Transitions of Older Men and Women," *Journal of Labor Economics* 12, no. 2 (April 1994): 210–242.

[18]Edward P. Lazear, "Pensions as Severance Pay," in *Financial Aspects of the United States Pension System*, ed. Zvi Bodie and John B. Shoven, National Bureau of Economic Research Project Report (Chicago: University of Chicago Press, 1983), 57–90; and Richard Ippolito, "Toward Explaining Earlier Retirement after 1970", *Industrial and Labor Relations Review* 43, no. 5 (July 1990): 556–569.

FIGURE 7.6

Choice of Optimum Retirement Age for Hypothetical Worker (based on data in Table 7.2)

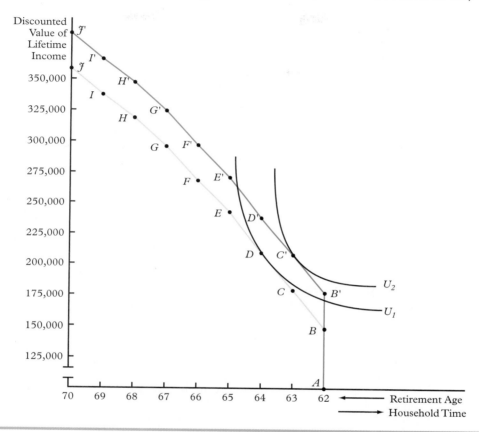

POLICY APPLICATION: CHILD CARE AND LABOR SUPPLY

For many families, a critical element of what we have called household production is the supervision and nurture of children. Most parents are concerned about providing their children with quality care, whether this care is produced mostly in the household or is purchased to a great extent outside the home. Society at large also has a stake in the quality of care parents provide for their children. There are many forms such programs take, from tax credits for child-care services purchased by working parents to governmental subsidies for day care, school lunches, and health care. The purpose of this section is to consider the labor market implications of programs to support the care of children.

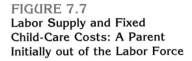

FIGURE 7.7
Labor Supply and Fixed Child-Care Costs: A Parent Initially out of the Labor Force

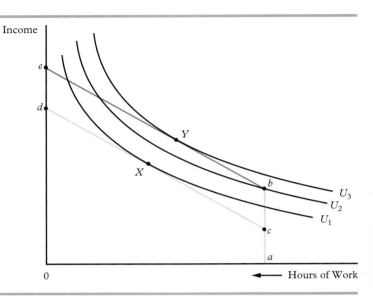

Child-Care Subsidies

Roughly 40 percent of American families pay for child care, and on average their costs represent 7 percent of family income—although the percentages are higher for those with lower incomes.[19] Child-care costs obviously rise with the hours of care, but part of these costs appear to be fixed: one study found that child-care costs per hour of work were three times greater for women who worked fewer than 10 hours per week than for those who worked more.[20] In the last decade, however, federal spending on child-care subsidies has tripled, and the purpose of this section is to analyze the effects of these greater subsidies on the labor supply of parents.

Reducing the Fixed Costs of Care   Suppose for a moment that child-care costs are purely fixed, so that without a subsidy working parents must pay a certain amount per day no matter how many hours their children are in care. Figures 7.7 and 7.8 illustrate how a subsidy that covers the entire cost of child care affects the labor supply incentives of a mother who has daily unearned income equal to *ab*.

Consider first the case of a mother who is not now working (Figure 7.7). If she decides to work, she must choose from points along the line *cd*, with the distance *bc* representing the fixed costs of child care. The slope of *cd*, of course, represents

[19]Patricia M. Anderson and Phillip B. Levine, "Child Care and Mothers' Employment Decisions," in *Finding Jobs: Work and Welfare Reform*, ed. David E. Card and Rebecca M. Blank (New York: Russell Sage Foundation, 2000), 426.
[20]David C. Ribar, "A Structural Model of Child Care and the Labor Supply of Married Women," *Journal of Labor Economics* 13, no. 3. (July 1995): 558–597.

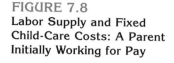

FIGURE 7.8
Labor Supply and Fixed
Child-Care Costs: A Parent
Initially Working for Pay

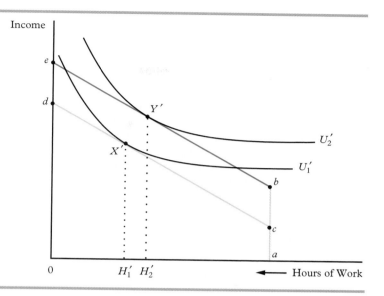

her wage rate. Given her preferences and the constraint depicted in Figure 7.7, this woman receives more utility from not working (at point b) than she would from working (point X). If the fixed cost were reduced to zero, so her constraint were now abe, her utility would be maximized at point Y on curve U_3, and she would now find it beneficial to work. *Thus, child-care subsidies that reduce or remove the fixed cost of child care will encourage work among those previously out of the labor force.* (Such subsidies do not guarantee that all of those out of the labor force would now join it, because some people will have such steep indifference curves that work will still not be utility-maximizing.)

Now consider the case, represented in Figure 7.8, of a woman who is already working when the subsidy is adopted. Before the subsidy, her utility was maximized at point X' on indifference curve U_1'—a point at which H_1' hours are worked. When the subsidy generates the constraint abe, her utility now will be maximized at point Y' (on U_2'), and she will reduce her hours of work to H_2'. *Thus, for those already working, removing the fixed cost of child care has an income effect that pushes them toward fewer hours of work.* (Note, however, that the woman depicted in Figure 7.8 remains in the labor force.)

Reducing the Hourly Costs of Care   Now let us take a case in which the costs of child care are purely hourly and have no fixed component. If such costs, say, are $3 per hour, they simply reduce the hourly take-home wage rate of a working parent by $3. If a government subsidy were to reduce the child-care costs to zero, the parent would experience an increase in the take-home wage, and the labor supply effects would be those of a wage increase. For those already working, the subsidy would create an income effect and a substitution effect that work in opposite directions on the desired hours of work. For those not in the labor force, the increased take-home wage would make it more likely they would join the labor force (the substitution effect dominates in participation decisions).

Observed Responses to Child-Care Subsidies   Our analysis above suggests that child-care subsidies, which in actuality reduce *both* the fixed and the hourly cost of care, would have a theoretically ambiguous effect on the hours of work among those already in the labor force. The effect on labor force participation, however, is theoretically clear: child-care subsidies should increase the labor force participation rates among parents, especially mothers. Empirical studies of the relationship between child-care costs and labor force participation are consistent with this latter prediction: when costs go down, labor force participation goes up. Further, it appears that the greatest increases are among those with the lowest incomes.[21]

Child Support Assurance

The vast majority of children who live in poor households have an absent parent. The federal government has taken several steps to ensure, for families receiving welfare, that absent parents contribute adequately to their children's upbringing. Greater efforts to collect child support payments are restricted in their effectiveness by the lack of resources among some absent parents, deliberate noncompliance by others, and the lack of court-awarded child support obligations in many more cases of divorce. To enhance the resources of single-parent families, some have proposed the creation of child support assurance programs. The essential feature of these programs is a guaranteed child support benefit that would be paid by the government to the custodial parent in the event the absent parent does not make payments. If the absent parent makes only a portion of the required support payment, the government would make up the remainder.[22]

A critical question to ask about such a program is how it would affect the labor supply of custodial parents. The answer provided by economic theory is not completely straightforward.

Consider a single mother who has two options for supporting herself and her children. One option is to work outside the home with no support from the absent father or from the welfare system. In Figure 7.9, we assume that the budget constraint provided by this option can be graphed as *AB,* which has a slope that represents her wage rate. The mother's other option is to apply for welfare benefits, which we assume would guarantee her an income of *AC.* Recall from chapter 6 that welfare payments typically are calculated by subtracting from a family's "needed" level of income (*AC*) its actual income from other sources, including earnings. Thus,

---

[21]See Anderson and Levine, "Child Care and Mothers' Employment Decisions," for a summary of empirical work on how the cost of child care affects mothers' decisions to work.

[22]Irwin Garfinkel, Philip K. Robins, Pat Wong, and Daniel R. Meyer, "The Wisconsin Child Support Assurance System: Estimated Effects on Poverty, Labor Supply, Caseloads, and Costs," *Journal of Human Resources* 25, no. 1 (Winter 1990): 1–31.

FIGURE 7.9

**Budget Constraints Facing
a Single Parent before and after
Child Support Assurance
Program Adopted**

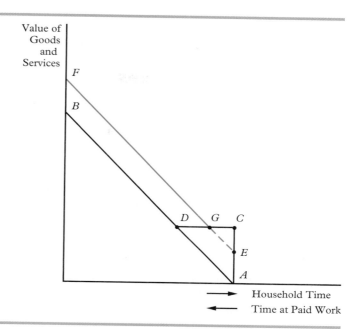

the welfare constraint is *ACDB*, and it can be seen that segment *CD* is reflective of a take-home wage rate equal to zero.

If the mother's utility isoquants are steeply sloped (meaning, of course, that she is less able or less willing to substitute for her time at home), her utility is maximized at point *C*; she applies for welfare and does not work for pay. If her utility isoquants are relatively flat, her utility will be maximized along segment *DB*, and in this case she works for pay and does not rely on welfare benefits to supplement her income.

Suppose, now, that a child support assurance program is adopted that guarantees support payments of *AE* to the mother, regardless of her income. If she works, the effect of the new program would be to add the amount *AE* (= *BF*) to her earnings. If she does not work and remains on welfare, her *welfare* benefits are reduced by *AE*; thus, her child support benefits *plus* her welfare benefits continue to equal *AC*. After the child support assurance program is implemented, then, her budget constraint is *ACGF*.

How will the new child support programs affect the mother's time in the household and her hours of paid work? There are three possibilities. First, some mothers will have isoquants so steeply sloped that they will remain out of the labor force and spend all their time in the household (they will remain at point *C* in Figure 7.9). These mothers would receive child support payments of *AE* and welfare benefits equal to *EC*.

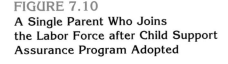

FIGURE 7.10

**A Single Parent Who Joins
the Labor Force after Child Support
Assurance Program Adopted**

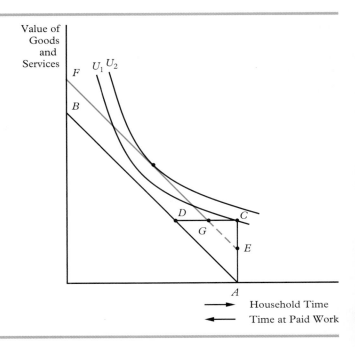

Second, for those who worked for pay before, and were therefore along segment *DB*, the new program produces a pure income effect. These mothers will continue to work for pay, but their utility is now maximized along *GF* and they can be expected to reduce their desired hours of work outside the home.

Third, some women, like the one whose isoquants (U_1 and U_2) are shown in Figure 7.10, will move from being on welfare to seeking paid work; for these women, the supply of labor to market work increases. These women formerly maximized utility at point *C*, but the new possibility of working *and* still being able to receive an income subsidy now places their utility-maximizing hours of paid work along segment *GF*.

On balance, then, the hypothetical child support assurance program discussed above can be expected to *increase the labor force participation rate* among single mothers (and thus reduce the numbers on welfare), while *reducing the desired hours of paid work* among those who have jobs. Studies that analyze the labor market effects of child support payments (from absent fathers) have found that the labor supply responses among single mothers are consistent with theoretical expectations.[23]

[23]John W. Graham and Andrea H. Beller, "The Effect of Child Support Payments on the Labor Supply of Female Family Heads," *Journal of Human Resources* 24, no. 4 (Fall 1989): 664–688; and Wei-Yin Hu, "Child Support, Welfare Dependency, and Women's Labor Supply," *Journal of Human Resources* 34, no. 1 (Winter 1999): 71–103.

REVIEW QUESTIONS

1. Suppose that 5 percent unemployment is defined as "full employment" and currently unemployment is 7 percent. Suppose further that we have the following information:

Unemployment Rate	Labor Force	Unemployment	Employment
5 percent	6,000	300	5,700
7 percent	5,600	392	5,208

   a. What is the amount of "hidden" unemployment when the unemployment rate is 7 percent?

   b. If the population is 10,000, what change occurs in the participation rate as a result of the marginal change in the unemployment rate?

   c. What is the economic significance of hidden unemployment? Should measured and hidden unemployment be added to obtain a "total unemployment" figure?

2. A recent study of the labor force participation rates of women in the post–World War II period notes:

   > Over the long run women have joined the paid labor force because of a series of changes affecting the nature of work. Primary among these was the rise of the clerical and professional sectors, the increased education of women, labor-saving advances in households, declining fertility rates, and increased urbanization.

   Relate each of these factors to the household production model of labor supply outlined in chapter 7.

3. In a debate in the 1976 U.S. presidential campaign, candidate Jimmy Carter argued, "While it is true that much of the recent rise in employment is due to the entrance of married women and teenagers into the labor force, this influx of people into the labor force is itself a sign of economic decay. The reason these people are now seeking work is because the primary breadwinner in the family is out of work and extra workers are needed to maintain the family income." Comment.

4. Is the following statement true, false, or uncertain? Why? "If a married woman's husband gets a raise, she tends to work less, but if *she* gets a raise, she tends to work more."

5. Suppose day-care centers charge working parents for each hour their children spend at the centers (no fixed costs of care). Suppose, too, that the federal government passes subsidy legislation so that the hourly cost per child now borne by the parents is cut in half. Would this policy cause an increase in the labor supply of parents with small children?

6. Several studies have indicated that for prime-age males, the income effect of a wage increase tends to dominate the substitution effect. Other recent studies point out that hourly wages tend to rise over the early stages of the life cycle (the young receive lower wages than the middle-aged) *and* that young males tend to work fewer hours than middle-aged males, other things equal. Employing a theory of life-cycle allocation of time, explain the apparent discrepancy.

7. Suppose that, as the ratio of the working population to the retired population continues to fall, the voters approve a change in the way Social Security benefits are calculated— a way that effectively reduces every retired person's benefits by half. This change affects everyone in the population, no matter what their age or current retirement status, and it is accompanied by a 50 percent reduction in payroll taxes. What would be the labor supply effects on those workers who are very close to the typical age of retirement (62 to 65)? What would be the labor supply effects on those workers just beginning their careers (workers in their 20s, for example)?

8. Suppose that, under state law, the financial settlement in a divorce case that does not involve dependent children depends upon the economic contribution each marriage partner made up to the date of divorce. Thus, if the wife earned an income equal to her husband's throughout the years, she would be determined to qualify for half of the assets at the date of divorce. Based on what you have learned in chapter 7, how could an equitable settlement be determined in the case of a woman who stayed home, raised the family's children, and never worked for pay?

9. Teenagers under age 18 in New York State are prohibited from working more than 8 hours a day, except if they work as golf caddies, babysitters, or farmworkers. Consider a 16-year-old whose primary household work in the summer is studying for college entrance exams and practicing a musical instrument, but who also has two options for paid work. She can work for $6 per hour with a catering service (limited to 8 hours per day), or work for $5 per hour as a babysitter (with no limitations on hours worked).

   a. First, draw the daily budget constraints for each of her paid-work options (assume she can work either for the catering service or as a babysitter, but cannot do both).

   b. Next, analyze the possible labor supply decisions this 16-year-old can make, making special reference to the effects of the state law restricting most paid work to 8 hours a day.

SELECTED READINGS

Becker, Gary. "A Theory of the Allocation of Time." *Economic Journal* 75 (September 1965): 493–517.

Fields, Gary S., and Olivia S. Mitchell. *Retirement, Pensions, and Social Security.* Cambridge, Mass.: MIT Press, 1984.

Ghez, Gilbert R., and Gary S. Becker. *The Allocation of Time and Goods over the Life Cycle.* New York: Columbia University Press, 1975. Chapter 3.

Gronau, Reuben. "The Measurement of Output of the Nonmarket Sector: The Evaluation of Housewives' Time." In *The Measurement of Economic and Social Performance*, ed. Milton Moss. New York: National Bureau of Economic Research, 1973. Pp. 163–189.

Layard, Richard, and Jacob Mincer, eds. *Journal of Labor Economics* 3 (January 1985, pt. 2).

"Special Issue on Child Care." *Journal of Human Resources* 27, no. 1 (Winter 1992).

8

COMPENSATING WAGE DIFFERENTIALS AND LABOR MARKETS

C hapters 6 and 7 analyzed workers' decisions about *whether to seek employment* and *how long to work*. Chapters 8 and 9 will analyze workers' decisions about the industry, occupation, or firm in which they will work. This chapter will emphasize the influence on job choice of such daily, *recurring* job characteristics as the work environment, the risk of injury, and the generosity of employee benefits. The following chapter will analyze the effects of required educational *investments* on occupational choice.

JOB MATCHING: THE ROLE OF WORKER PREFERENCES AND INFORMATION

One of the major functions of the labor market is to provide the signals and the mechanisms by which workers seeking to maximize their utility can be matched to employers trying to maximize profits. Matching is a formidable task, because workers have varying skills and preferences and because employers offer jobs that differ in requirements and working environment. The process of finding the worker–employer pairings that are best for each is truly one of trial and error, and whether the process is woefully deficient or reasonably satisfactory is an important policy issue that can be analyzed using economic theory in its normative mode.

The assumption that workers are attempting to maximize utility implies that they are interested in both the pecuniary and the nonpecuniary aspects of their jobs.

On the one hand, we expect that higher compensation levels in a job (holding job tasks constant) would attract more workers to it. On the other hand, it is clear that pay is not all that matters; occupational tasks and how workers' preferences mesh with those tasks are critical elements in the matching process. The focus of this chapter is on how the labor market accommodates worker preferences.

If all jobs in a labor market were *exactly alike* and located in the *same place*, an individual's decision about where to seek work would be a simple matter of choosing the job with the highest compensation. Any differences in the pay offered by employers would cause movement by workers from low- to high-paying firms. If there were no barriers inhibiting this movement, the market would force offers of all employers into equality.

All jobs are not the same, however. Some jobs are in clean, modern spaces, and others are in noisy, dusty, or dangerous environments. Some permit the employee discretion over the hours or the pace of work, while others allow less flexibility. Some employers offer more generous employee-benefit packages than others, and different *places* of employment involve different commuting distances and neighborhood characteristics. We discuss below the ways that differences in job characteristics influence individual choice and observable market outcomes.

Individual Choice and Its Outcomes

Suppose several unskilled workers have received offers from two employers. Employer X pays $8 per hour and offers clean, safe working conditions. Employer Y also pays $8 per hour but offers employment in a dirty, noisy factory. Which employer would the workers choose? Most would undoubtedly choose employer X, because the pay is the same while the job is performed under more agreeable conditions.

Clearly, however, $8 is not an equilibrium wage in both firms.[1] Because firm X finds it easy to attract applicants at $8, it will hold the line on any future wage increases. Firm Y, however, must clean up the plant, pay higher wages, or do both if it wants to fill its vacancies. Assuming it decides not to alter working conditions, it must pay a wage *above* $8 to be competitive in the labor market. The *extra* wage it must pay to attract workers is called a *compensating wage differential* because the higher wage is paid to compensate workers for the undesirable working conditions. If such a differential did not exist, firm Y could not attract the unskilled workers that firm X can obtain.

An Equilibrium Differential   Suppose that firm Y raises its wage offer to $8.50 while the offer from X remains at $8.00. Will this 50-cent-per-hour differential— an extra $1,000 per year—attract *all* the workers in our group to firm Y? If it did attract them all, firm X would have an incentive to raise its wages and firm Y

---

[1]A few people may be indifferent to noise and dirt in the workplace. We assume here that these people are so rare, or firm Y's demand for workers is so large, that Y cannot fill all its vacancies with just those who are totally insensitive to dirt and noise.

might want to lower its offers a bit; the 50-cent differential in this case would *not* be an equilibrium differential.

More than likely, however, the higher wage in firm Y would attract only *some* of the group to firm Y. Some people are not bothered much by dirt and noise, and they may decide to take the extra pay and put up with the poorer working conditions. Those who are very sensitive to noise or dust may decide that they would rather be paid less than expose themselves to such working conditions. If both firms could obtain the quantity and quality of workers they wanted, the 50-cent differential *would* be an equilibrium differential, in the sense that there would be no forces causing the differential to change.

The desire of workers to avoid unpleasantness or risk, then, should force employers offering unpleasant or risky jobs to pay higher wages than they would otherwise have to pay. This wage differential serves two related, socially desirable ends. First, it serves a *social* need by giving people an incentive to voluntarily do dirty, dangerous, or unpleasant work. Second, at an *individual* level, it serves as a reward to workers who accept unpleasant jobs by paying them more than comparable workers in more pleasant jobs.

The Allocation of Labor   A number of jobs are unavoidably nasty or would be very costly to make safe and pleasant (coal mining, deep-sea diving, and police work are examples). There are essentially two ways to recruit the necessary labor for such jobs. One is to compel people to do these jobs (the military draft is the most obvious contemporary example of forced labor). The second way is to induce people to do the jobs voluntarily.

Most modern societies rely mainly on incentives, compensating wage differentials, to recruit labor to unpleasant jobs voluntarily. Workers will mine coal, bolt steel beams together fifty stories off the ground, or agree to work at night because, compared to alternative jobs for which they could qualify, these jobs pay well. Night work, for example, can be stressful because it disrupts normal patterns of sleep and family interactions; however, employers often find it efficient to keep their plants and machines in operation around the clock. The result is that nonunion employees working night shifts are paid about 4 percent more than they would receive if they worked during the day.[2]

Compensation for Workers   Compensating wage differentials also serve as *individual* rewards by paying those who accept bad or arduous working conditions more than they would otherwise receive. In a parallel fashion, those who opt for more pleasant conditions have to "buy" them by accepting lower pay. For example, if a person takes the $8.00-per-hour job with firm X, he or she is giving up

---

[2]Peter F. Kostiuk, "Compensating Differentials for Shift Work," *Journal of Political Economy* 98, no. 5, pt. 1 (October 1990): 1054–1075. Compensating wage differentials of almost 12 percent have been estimated for registered nurses who work at night; see Edward J. Schumacher and Barry T. Hirsch, "Compensating Differentials and Unmeasured Ability in the Labor Market for Nurses: Why Do Hospitals Pay More?" *Industrial and Labor Relations Review* 50, no. 4 (July 1997): 557–579.

the $8.50-per-hour job with less pleasant conditions in firm Y. The better conditions are being bought, in a very real sense, for 50 cents per hour.

Thus, compensating wage differentials become the prices at which good working conditions can be purchased by, or bad ones accepted by, workers. Contrary to common assertions, a monetary value *can* often be attached to events or conditions whose effects are primarily psychological in nature. Compensating wage differentials provide the key to the valuation of these nonpecuniary aspects of employment.

For example, how much do workers value a work schedule that permits them to enjoy leisure activities and sleep at the usual times? If we know that night-shift workers earn 4 percent—or about $1,000 per year for a typical worker—more than they otherwise would earn, the reasoning needed to answer this question is straightforward. Those who have difficulty sleeping during the day, or whose favorite leisure activities require the companionship of family or friends, are not likely to be attracted to night work for only $1,000 extra per year; they are quite willing to forgo a $1,000 earnings premium to obtain a normal work schedule. Others, however, are less bothered by the unusual sleep and leisure patterns, and they are willing to work at night for the $1,000 premium. While some of these latter workers would be willing to give up a normal work schedule for *less* than $1,000, others find the decision to work at night a close call at the going wage differential. If the differential were to marginally fall, a few working at night would change their minds and refuse to continue, while if the differential rose a bit above $1,000 a few more could be recruited to night work. Thus, the $1,000 yearly premium represents what those *at the margin* (the ones closest to changing their minds) are willing to pay for a normal work schedule.[3]

Assumptions and Predictions

We have seen how a simple theory of job choice by individuals leads to the *prediction* that compensating wage differentials will be associated with various job characteristics. Positive differentials (higher wages) will accompany "bad" characteristics, while negative differentials (lower wages) will be associated with "good" ones. However, it is very important to understand that this prediction can *only* be made *holding other things equal.*

Our prediction about the existence of compensating wage differentials grows out of the reasonable assumption that if an informed worker has a choice between a job with "good" working conditions and a job of equal pay with "bad" working conditions, he or she will choose the "good" job. If the employee is an unskilled laborer, he or she may be choosing between an unpleasant job spreading hot asphalt or a more comfortable job in an air-conditioned warehouse. In either case, he or she

---

[3]Daniel Hamermesh, "The Timing of Work over Time," *Economic Journal* 109, no. 452 (January 1999): 37–66, finds evidence that as people become more wealthy, they increasingly want to avoid working at night.

is going to receive something close to the wage rate unskilled workers typically receive. However, our theory would predict that this worker would receive *more* from the asphalt-spreading job than from the warehouse job.

Thus, the predicted outcome of our theory of job choice is *not* simply that employees working under "bad" conditions receive more than those working under "good" conditions. The prediction is that, *holding worker characteristics constant,* employees in bad jobs receive higher wages than those working under more pleasant conditions. The characteristics that must be held constant include all the other things that influence wages: skill level, age, experience, race, gender, union status, region of the country, and so forth. Three assumptions have been used to arrive at this prediction.

Assumption 1: Utility Maximization

Our first assumption is that workers seek to maximize their *utility*, not their income. Compensating wage differentials will arise only if some people do *not* choose the highest-paying job offered, preferring instead a lower-paying but more pleasant job. This behavior allows those employers offering lower-paying, pleasant jobs to be competitive. Wages do not equalize in this case. Rather, the *net advantages*—the overall utility from the pay and the psychic aspects of the job—tend to equalize for the marginal worker.

Assumption 2: Worker Information

The second assumption implicit in our analysis is that workers are aware of the job characteristics of potential importance to them. Whether they know about them before they take the job or find out about them soon after taking it is not too important. In either case, a company offering a "bad" job with no compensating wage differential would have trouble recruiting or retaining workers, trouble that would eventually force it to raise its wage.

It is quite likely, of course, that workers would quickly learn of danger, noise, rigid work discipline, job insecurity, and other obvious bad working conditions. It is equally likely that they would *not* know the *precise* probability of being laid off, say, or of being injured on the job. However, even with respect to these probabilities, their own direct observations or word-of-mouth reports from other employees could give them enough information to evaluate the situation with some accuracy. For example, the proportions of employees considering their work dangerous have been shown to be closely related to the actual injury rates published by the government for the industries in which they work.[4] This finding illustrates that, while workers probably cannot state the precise probability of being injured, they do form accurate judgments about the relative risks of several jobs.

---

[4]W. Kip Viscusi, "Labor Market Valuations of Life and Limb: Empirical Evidence and Policy Implications," *Public Policy* 26 (Summer 1978): 359–386. W. Kip Viscusi and Michael J. Moore, "Worker Learning and Compensating Differentials," *Industrial and Labor Relations Review* 45 (October 1991): 80–96, suggest that the accuracy of risk perceptions rises with job tenure. For an analysis of how well people estimate the risk of death, see Daniel K. Benjamin and William R. Dougan, "Individuals' Estimates of the Risk of Death: Part II—New Evidence," *Journal of Risk and Uncertainty* 22, no. 1 (January 2001): 35–57.

Where predictions may disappoint us, however, is with respect to *very* obscure characteristics. For example, while we now know that asbestos dust is highly damaging to worker health, this fact was not widely known forty years ago. One reason information on asbestos dangers in plants was so long in being generated is that it takes more than twenty years for asbestos-related disease to develop. Cause and effect were thus obscured from workers and researchers alike, creating a situation in which job choices were made in ignorance of this risk. Compensating wage differentials for this danger thus could not possibly have arisen at that time. Our predictions about compensating wage differentials, then, hold only for job characteristics that workers know about.

Assumption 3: Worker Mobility   The final assumption implicit in our theory is that workers have a range of job offers from which to choose. Without a range of offers, workers would not be able to select the combination of job characteristics they desire or avoid the ones to which they do not wish exposure. A compensating wage differential for risk of injury, for example, simply could not arise if workers were able to obtain only dangerous jobs. It is the act of choosing safe jobs over dangerous ones that forces employers offering dangerous work to raise wages.

One manner in which this choice can occur is for each job applicant to receive several job offers from which to choose. However, another way in which choice could be exercised is for workers to be (at least potentially) highly mobile. In other words, workers with few concurrent offers could take jobs and continue their search for work if they thought an improvement could be made. Thus, even with few offers at any *one* time, workers could conceivably have relatively wide choice over a *period* of time, which would eventually allow them to select jobs that maximized their utility.

Job mobility among workers in the United States is high enough that in the year 2000 almost one-third of workers in the 25 to 34 age group had been with their current employers less than a year. Among those whose ages were 35 to 44, about one in five were in that category.[5] While some of this mobility is voluntary and some is initiated by employers, what is of significance is that a large fraction of the labor force is "in the market" at any given time.

Empirical Tests for Compensating Wage Differentials

The prediction that there are compensating wage differentials for undesirable job characteristics is over two hundred years old. Adam Smith, in his *Wealth of Nations*, published in 1776, proposed five "principal circumstances which … make up for a small pecuniary gain in some employments, and counterbalance a great one in others." One of these, the *constancy of employment*, is discussed in the appendix to

---

[5]U.S. Department of Labor, Bureau of Labor Statistics, "Employee Tenure Summary," news release USDL 00–245 (http://stats.bls.gov/newsrels.htm), August 29, 2000: Table 3.

this chapter. Another two will be discussed in other chapters: the *difficulty of learning the job* (chapter 9) and the *probability of success* (chapter 11). Our discussion in this chapter, while it could draw upon any of Smith's "principal circumstances" to illustrate the concept of compensating wage differentials, will focus on his assertion that "*the wages of labour vary with the ease or hardship, the cleanliness or dirtiness, the honourableness or dishonourableness of the employment.*"[6]

There are two difficulties in actually estimating compensating wage differentials. First, we must be able to create data sets that allow us to match, at the level of individual workers, their relevant job characteristics with their personal characteristics (age, education, union status, and so forth) that also influence wages. Second, we must be able to specify in advance those job characteristics that are generally regarded as disagreeable (for example, not everyone may regard outdoor work or repetitive tasks as undesirable).

The most extensive testing for the existence of compensating wage differentials has been done with respect to the risks of injury or death on the job, primarily because higher levels of such risks are unambiguously "bad." These studies generally, but not always, support the prediction that wages will be higher whenever risks on the job are higher. One review of studies done up through the early 1990s estimates that wages tend to be 1–2 percent higher for workers facing twice the average risk of a job-related fatality than for comparable workers facing the average level of risk (the average yearly risk is 1 in 20,000).[7]

Many other studies of compensating wage differentials have been done, but because they are spread thinly across a variety of job characteristics, judging the strength of their support for the theory is problematic. Nonetheless, positive wage premiums have been related, holding other influences constant, to such disagreeable characteristics as night work,[8] an inflexible work schedule, having to stand a lot, and working in a noisy environment[9] (see Example 8.1 for less formal data on another "bad" working condition: working away from home). Similarly, wage rates appear higher, other things equal, when job security is lower; however, as discussed in the appendix to this chapter, the relationship between wages and the probability of layoff is complex.

---

[6]See Adam Smith, *Wealth of Nations* (New York: Modern Library, 1937), Book 1, Chapter 10. The fifth "principal circumstance" is "the small or great trust which be reposed in the workmen"; on this, see Joel Waldfogel, "The Effect of Criminal Conviction on Income and the 'Trust Reposed in the Workmen,'" *Journal of Human Resources* 29, no. 1 (Winter 1994): 62–81.

[7]W. Kip Viscusi, "The Value of Risks to Life and Health," *Journal of Economic Literature* 31, no. 4 (December 1993): 1912–1946. For a study that cites more recent work, see G. R. Arabsheibani and A. Marin, "Stability of Estimates of the Compensation for Danger," *Journal of Risk and Uncertainty* 20, no. 3 (May 2000): 247–269.

[8]Refer back to footnote 2 of this chapter.

[9]Christophe Daniel and Catherine Sofer, "Bargaining, Compensating Wage Differentials, and Dualism of the Labor Market: Theory and Evidence for France," *Journal of Labor Economics* 16, no. 3 (July 1998): 546–575.

EXAMPLE 8.1

Working on the Railroad: Making a Bad Job Good

While compensating wage differentials are difficult to measure with precision, the theory in this chapter can often find general support in everyday discussions of job choice. This example is based on a newspaper article about the exclusive use of Navajos by the Santa Fe Railway to repair and replace its 9,000 miles of track between Los Angeles and Chicago.

The 220 Navajos are organized into two "steel gangs." Workers do what machines cannot: pull and sort old spikes, weld the rails together, and check the safety of the new rails. The grueling work is intrinsically unappealing: jobs last for only five to eight months per year; much of the work is done in sweltering desert heat; workers must live away from their families and are housed in bunk cars with up to sixteen other workers; and the remote locations can render the off-hours boring and lonely.

Two hypotheses about jobs such as these can be derived from the theory in this chapter. These hypotheses are listed below, along with supporting quotations or facts from the newspaper article.

Hypothesis 1. Companies offering unappealing jobs find it difficult to recruit and retain employees. Workers who take these jobs are the ones for whom the conditions are least disagreeable.

> They had tried everyone. The Navajos were the only ones willing to be away from home, to do the work, and to do a good job.
>
> [A Santa Fe recruiter]

> Lonely? No, I never get lonely. There is nothing but Navajo here....We speak the same language and understand one another.... It's a good job.
>
> [A steel gang worker with 16 years' experience]

Hypothesis 2. The jobs are made appealing to the target group of workers by raising wages well above those of their alternatives.

> I wish I could stay home all the time and be with my family. It's just not possible. Where am I going to find a job that pays $900 every two weeks?
>
> [A steel gang veteran of 11 years]

(Steel gang wages in the early 1990s ranged between $12 and $17 per hour, well above the national average of about $10 per hour for "handlers and laborers.")

Data from: Paula Moñarez, "Navajos Keep Rail Lines Safe," *Long Beach Independent Press-Telegram*, May 14, 1992, D1.

HEDONIC WAGE THEORY AND THE RISK OF INJURY

We now turn to a graphic presentation of the theory of compensating wage differentials, which has become known as *hedonic* wage theory.[10] The graphic tools used permit additional insights into the theory and greatly clarify the normative analysis of important regulatory issues. In this section we analyze the theory of compensating wage differentials for a *negative* job characteristic, the risk of injury, and apply the concepts to a normative analysis of governmental safety regulations.

Job injuries are an unfortunate characteristic of the workplace, and injury rates vary considerably across occupations and industries. For example, while we noted that the average yearly rate of fatal injury in the American workplace is about

---

[10]The philosophy of hedonism is usually associated with Jeremy Bentham, a philosopher of the late eighteenth century who believed people always behaved in ways that they thought would maximize their happiness. The analysis that follows is adapted primarily from Sherwin Rosen, "Hedonic Prices and Implicit Markets," *Journal of Political Economy* 82 (January/February 1974): 34–55.

one in 20,000, the rates for construction workers and truck drivers are three and four times higher, respectively. Roughly 3 percent of American workers are injured seriously enough each year that they lose at least a day of work, but even in just the manufacturing sector these rates vary from 2 percent in chemical plants, for example, to over 7 percent in food processing.[11]

To simplify our analysis of compensating wage differentials for the risk of injury, we shall assume that compensating differentials for every *other* job characteristic have already been established. This assumption allows us to see more clearly the outcomes of the job selection process, and since the same analysis could be repeated for every other dimension, our conclusions are not obscured by it. To obtain a complete understanding of the job selection process and the outcomes of that process, it is necessary, as always, to consider both the employer and the employee sides of the market.

Employee Considerations

Employees, it may safely be assumed, dislike the risk of being injured on the job. A worker who is offered a job for $8 per hour in a firm in which 3 percent of the workforce is injured each year would achieve a certain level of utility from that job. If the risk of injury were increased to 4 percent, holding other job characteristics constant, the job would have to pay a higher wage to produce the same level of utility (except in the unlikely event that the costs of wage loss, medical treatment, and suffering caused by the added injuries were completely covered by the firm or its insurance company after the fact).[12]

Other combinations of wage rates and risk levels could be devised that would yield the same utility as the $8/hour–3 percent risk offer. These combinations can be connected on a graph to form an indifference curve (for example, the curve U_2 in Figure 8.1). Unlike the indifference curves drawn in chapters 6 and 7, those in Figure 8.1 slope upward because risk of injury is a "bad" job characteristic, not a "good" (such as leisure). In other words, if risk increases, wages must rise if utility is to be held constant.

As in the previous chapters, there is one indifference curve for each possible level of utility. Because a higher wage at a given risk level will generate more utility, indifference curves lying to the northwest represent higher utility.[13] Thus, all

---

[11]U.S. Bureau of Labor Statistics, "National Census of Fatal Occupational Injuries, 1997," USDL–98–336, August 12, 1998; and U.S. Bureau of Labor Statistics, "Workplace Injuries and Illnesses in 1999," USDL–00–357, December 12, 2000.

[12]Compensating wage differentials provide for *ex ante*—"before the fact"—compensation related to injury risk. Workers can also be compensated (to keep utility constant) by *ex post*—or after-injury—payments for damages. Workers' compensation insurance provides for *ex post* payments, but these payments typically offer incomplete compensation for all the costs of injury.

[13]When a "bad" is on the horizontal axis (as in Figure 8.1) and a "good" on the vertical axis, people with more of the "good" and less of the "bad" are unambiguously better off, and this combination is achieved by moving in a northwest direction on the graph.

FIGURE 8.1

**A Family of Indifference Curves
between Wages and Risk of Injury**

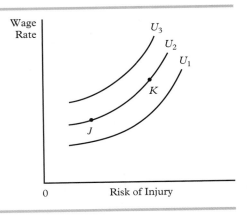

points on curve U_3 in Figure 8.1 are preferred to those on U_2, and those on U_2 are preferred to U_1. The fact that each indifference curve is convex (when viewed from below) reflects the normal assumption of diminishing marginal rates of substitution. At point K of curve U_2, the person receives a relatively high wage and faces a high level of risk. He or she will be willing to give up a lot in wages to achieve a given reduction in risk because risk levels are high enough to place one in imminent danger, and the consumption level of the goods that are bought with wages is already high. However, as risk levels and wage rates fall (to point J, say), the person becomes less willing to give up wages in return for the given reduction in risk; the danger is no longer imminent, and consumption of other goods is not as high.

   People differ, of course, in their aversion to the risk of being injured. Those who are very sensitive to this risk will require large wage increases for any increase

FIGURE 8.2

**Representative Indifference Curves
for Two Workers Who Differ
in Their Aversion to Risk of Injury**

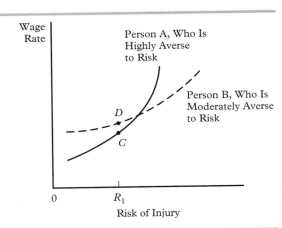

in risk, while those who are less sensitive will require smaller wage increases to hold utility constant. The more-sensitive workers will have indifference curves that are steeper at any level of risk, as illustrated in Figure 8.2. At risk level R_1, the slope at point C is steeper than at point D. Point C lies on the indifference curve of worker A, who is highly sensitive to risk, while point D lies on an indifference curve of a worker (B) who is less sensitive. Of course, each person has a whole family of indifference curves that are not shown in Figure 8.2, and each will attempt to achieve the highest level of utility possible.

Employer Considerations

Employers are faced with a wage/risk trade-off of their own that derives from three assumptions. First, it is presumably costly to reduce the risk of injury facing employees. Safety equipment must be placed on machines, production time must be sacrificed for safety training sessions, protective clothing must be furnished to workers, and so forth. Second, competitive pressures will presumably force many firms to operate at *zero profit* (that is, at a point at which all costs are covered and the rate of return on capital is about what it is for similar investments).[14] Third, all *other* job characteristics are presumably given or already determined. The consequence of these three assumptions is that, if a firm undertakes a program to reduce the risk of injury, it must reduce wages to remain competitive.

Thus, forces on the employer side of the market tend to cause low risk to be associated with low wages and high risk to be associated with high wages, *holding other things constant*. These "other things" may be employee benefits or other job characteristics; assuming they are given will not affect the validity of our analysis (even though it may seem at first unrealistic). The major point is that if a firm spends *more on safety*, it must spend *less on other things* if it is to remain competitive. The term *wages* can thus be thought of as shorthand for "terms of employment" in our theoretical analyses.

The employer trade-offs between wages and levels of injury risk can be graphed through the use of *isoprofit curves,* which show the various combinations of risk and wage levels that yield a given level of profits (*iso-* means "equal"). Thus, all the points along a given curve, such as those depicted in Figure 8.3, are wage/risk combinations that yield the *same* level of profits. Curves to the southeast represent higher profit levels because with all other items in the employment contract given, each risk level is associated with a *lower* wage level. Curves to the northwest represent, conversely, lower profit levels.

Note that the isoprofit curves in Figure 8.3 are concave (from below). This concavity is a graphic representation of our assumption that there are diminishing

---

[14]If returns are permanently below normal, it would benefit the owners to close down the plant and invest their funds elsewhere. If returns are above normal, other investors will be attracted to the industry and profits will eventually be driven down by increased competition.

marginal returns to safety expenditures. Suppose, for example, that the firm is operating at point M in Figure 8.3, a point where the risk of injury is high. The first expenditures by the firm to reduce risk will have a relatively high return, because the firm will clearly choose to attack the safety problem by eliminating the most obvious and cheaply eliminated hazards. Because the risk (and accompanying cost) reductions are relatively large, the firm need not reduce wages by very much to keep profits constant. Thus, the isoprofit curve at point M is relatively flat. At point N, however, the curve is steeply sloped, indicating that wages will have to be reduced by quite a bit if the firm is to maintain its profits in the presence of a program to reduce risk. This large wage reduction is required because, at this point, further increases in safety are very costly.

We also assume that employers differ in the ease (cost) with which they can eliminate hazards. We have just indicated that the cost of reducing risk levels is reflected in the *slope* of the isoprofit curve. In firms where injuries are costly to reduce, large wage reductions will be required to keep profits constant in the face of a safety program; the isoprofit curve in this case will be steeply sloped. The isoprofit curve of one such firm is shown as the dashed curve YY' in Figure 8.4. The isoprofit curves of firms where injuries are easier to eliminate are flatter. Note that the solid curve XX' in Figure 8.4 is flatter at each level of risk than YY'; this indicates that firm X can reduce risk more cheaply than firm Y.

The Matching of Employers and Employees

The aim of employees is to achieve the highest possible utility from their choice of a job. If they receive two offers at the same wage rate, they will choose the lower-risk job. If they receive two offers in which the risk levels are equal, they will accept the offer with the higher wage rate. More generally, they will choose the offer that falls on the highest, or most northwest, indifference curve.

In obtaining jobs, employees are constrained by the offers they receive from employers. Employers, for their part, are constrained by two forces. On the one hand, they cannot make outrageously lucrative offers because they will be driven out of business by firms whose costs are lower. On the other hand, if their offered terms of employment are very low, they will be unable to attract employees (who will choose to work for other firms). These two forces compel firms in competitive markets to operate on their zero-profit isoprofit curves.

To better understand the offers firms make, refer to Figure 8.4, where two different firms are depicted. Firm X, the firm that can cheaply reduce injuries, can make higher wage offers at low levels of risk (left of point R') than can firm Y. Because it can produce safety more cheaply, it can pay higher wages at low levels of risk and still remain competitive. Any point along segment XR' will be preferred by employees to any point along YR' because, for given levels of risk, higher wages are paid.

At higher levels of risk, however, firm Y can outbid firm X for employees. Firm X does not save much money if it permits the risk level to rise above R,

FIGURE 8.3

A Family of Isoprofit Curves for an Employer

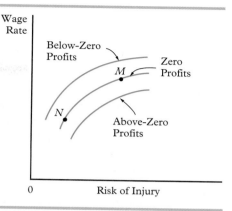

because risk reduction is so cheap. Because firm Y *does* save itself a lot by operating at levels of risk beyond R, it is willing to pay relatively high wages at high risk levels. For employees, offers along $R'Y'$ will be preferable to those along $R'X'$, so those employees working at high-risk jobs will work for Y.

Graphing worker indifference curves and employer isoprofit curves together can show which workers choose which offers. Figure 8.5 contains the zero-profit curves of two employers (X and Y) and the indifference curves of two employees (A and B). Employee A maximizes utility (along A_2) by working for employer X at wage W_{AX} and risk level R_{AX}, while person B maximizes utility by working for employer Y at wage W_{BY} and risk level R_{BY}.

Looking at A's choice more closely, we see that if he or she took the offer B accepted—W_{BY} and R_{BY}—the level of utility achieved would be A_1, which is less

FIGURE 8.4

The Zero-Profit Curves of Two Firms

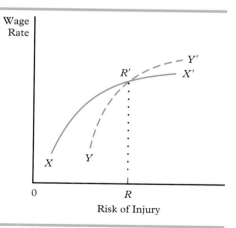

EXAMPLE 8.2

Parenthood, Occupational Choice, and Risk

The theory of compensating wage differentials is built on the assumption that, among workers in a given labor market, those with the stronger aversions to risk will select themselves into safer (but lower paying) jobs. It is difficult to test the implications of this assumption because measuring risk aversion is not generally possible. However, one study did perform a test on workers and found that the relative strength of aversion to injury risk could be logically inferred.

It is well known that women are found in safer jobs than men. In the mid-1990s, for example, men made up 54 percent of all workers, but constituted 92 percent of workers killed on the job! What is not so well known is that, among each gender group, there is an equally striking pattern—*men and women who are single parents choose to work in safer jobs.*

This study argues that workers who are raising children feel a greater need to avoid risk on the job because they have loved ones who depend on them, and of course this should be especially true for single parents. Indeed, the study found that married women without children worked in jobs with a greater risk of death than married women with children, but that single mothers chose to work in even safer jobs.

It was found that, among men, those who are single parents worked in safer jobs than married men, but married men with children apparently did not behave much differently than those without. The study argues that, because married men are typically not in the role of caregiver to their children, they may feel they can take higher-paying, riskier jobs but adequately protect their children through buying life insurance. Married women, in contrast, do not find life insurance as effective in protecting children, because it provides only money, which cannot replace the care and nurturing that mothers give.

Data from: Thomas DeLeire and Helen Levy, "Gender, Occupation Choice and the Risk of Death at Work," National Bureau of Economic Research Working Paper no. 8574 (November 2001).

than A_2. Person A values safety very highly, and wage W_{BY} is just not high enough to compensate for the high level of risk. Person B, whose indifference curves are flatter (signifying he or she is less averse to risk), finds the offer of W_{BY} and R_{BY} on curve B_2 superior to the offer A accepts. Person B is simply not willing to take a cut in pay to W_{AX} in order to reduce risk from R_{BY} to R_{AX}, because that would place him or her on curve B_1.

The matching of A with firm X and B with firm Y is not accidental or random. Since X can "produce" safety more cheaply than Y, it is logical that X will be a low-risk producer who attracts employees, like A, who value safety highly. Likewise, employer Y generates a lot of cost savings by operating at high risk levels and can thus afford to pay high wages and still be competitive. Y attracts people like B, who have a relatively strong preference for money wages and a relatively weak preference for safety. (For a study of how aversion to risk affects job choice, see Example 8.2.)

The Offer Curve   The above job-matching process, of course, can be generalized beyond the case of two employees and two employers. To do this it is helpful to note that in Figures 8.4 and 8.5, the only offers of jobs to workers with a chance of being accepted lie along $XR'Y'$. The curve $XR'Y'$ can be called an *offer curve,*

FIGURE 8.5

Matching Employers and Employees

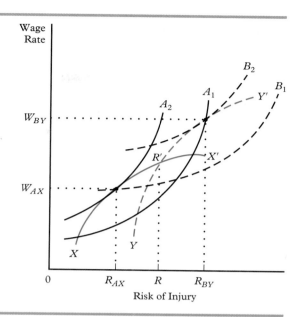

because only along $XR'Y'$ will offers that employers can afford to make be potentially acceptable to employees. The concept of an offer curve is useful in generalizing our discussion beyond two firms, because a single offer curve can summarize the potentially acceptable offers any number of firms in a particular labor market can make.

Consider, for example, Figure 8.6, which contains the zero-profit isoprofit curves of firms L through Q. We know from our discussions of Figures 8.4 and 8.5 that employees will accept offers along only the most northwest segments of this set of curves; to do otherwise would be to accept a lower wage at each level of risk. Thus, the potentially acceptable offers will be found along the darkened curve of Figure 8.6, which we shall call the offer curve. The more types of firms there are in a market, the smoother this offer curve will be; however, it will always slope upward because of our twin assumptions that risk is costly to reduce and that employees must be paid higher wages to keep their utility constant if risk is increased. In some of the examples that follow, the offer curve is used to summarize the feasible, potentially acceptable offers employers are making in a labor market, because using an offer curve saves our diagrams from becoming cluttered with the isoprofit curves of many employers.

Major Behavioral Insights   From the perspective of "positive economics," our hedonic model generates two major insights. The first is that wages rise with risk, other things equal. According to this prediction, there will be compensating wage

FIGURE 8.6
An Offer Curve

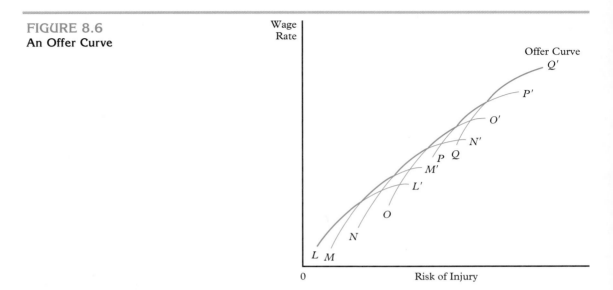

differentials for job characteristics that are viewed as undesirable by workers whom employers must attract (see Example 8.3). Second, workers with strong preferences for safety will tend to take jobs in firms where safety can be generated most cheaply. Workers who are not as averse to accepting risk will seek out and accept the higher-paying, higher-risk jobs offered by firms that find safety costly to "produce."[15] The second insight, then, is that the job-matching process—if it takes place under the conditions of knowledge and choice—is one in which firms and workers offer and accept jobs in a fashion that makes the most of their strengths and preferences.

Normative Analysis: Occupational Safety and Health Regulation

The hedonic analysis of wages in the context of job safety can be normatively applied to government regulation of workplace safety. In particular, we now have the conceptual tools to analyze such questions as the *need* for regulation and, if needed, what the *goals* of the regulation should be.

Are Workers Benefited by the Reduction of Risk?   In 1970 Congress passed the Occupational Safety and Health Act, which directed the U.S. Department of

---

[15]There is evidence that workers with fewer concerns about off-the-job risk (smokers, for example) also choose higher-risk jobs; for an analysis of this issue, see W. Kip Viscusi and Joni Hersch, "Cigarette Smokers as Job Risk Takers," *Review of Economics and Statistics* 83, no. 2 (May 2001): 269–280.

EXAMPLE 8.3

Compensating Wage Differentials in 19th-Century Britain

English mill towns in the mid–1800s were often beset by violence and unhealthy living conditions. Infant deaths, a common indicator of health conditions, averaged over 200 per 1,000 live births in English towns, a rate well above those that typically prevail today in the poorest countries. Violence was also a common part of life, and corporal punishment was often used by factory supervisors against child laborers.

It is interesting, however, that the conditions varied from town to town and factory to factory. Infant mortality rates ranged from 110 to 344 per 1,000 live births in English towns in 1834, and not all factories used corporal punishment as a means of industrial discipline. These differences in conditions have led economic historians to wonder whether workers' *information* and *choices* back then were sufficient to generate compensating wage differentials for the more unpleasant or unhealthy sectors of employment.

More specifically, workers were leaving rural areas to work in towns during this era, and the towns and factories in which conditions were unhealthy would have been less attractive to potential migrants. If workers had reasonably good information on health conditions and could have obtained work in several places, they would have gravitated toward the more pleasant places. Factories in the more squalid towns, and those

that used corporal punishment, would have had to offer higher wages to compete for migrants.

While data from the 1800s are such that research results are probably only suggestive, two intriguing findings have emerged. First, it appears that once the cost of living and regional wage differences are accounted for, in areas where infant mortality rates were 10 percent greater than average, the unskilled wage was 2–3 percent higher than average. It also appears that boys who worked in factories where corporal punishment was used received wages some 16–18 percent higher than boys of the same age, experience, and literacy who worked in plants where violence was not used. (Because workers receive compensating wage differentials only if employers are willing to pay them, we must entertain the notion that the threat, and use, of corporal punishment raised productivity by 16–18 percent.)

Data from: Jeffrey G. Williamson, "Was the Industrial Revolution Worth It? Disamenities and Death in 19th-Century British Towns," *Explorations in Economic History* 19 (1982): 221–245; Clark Nardinelli, "Corporal Punishment and Children's Wages in Nineteenth Century Britain," *Explorations in Economic History* 19 (1982): 283–295. For an analysis of compensating differentials in the United States around 1900, see Price V. Fishback, "Operations of 'Unfettered' Labor Markets: Exit and Voice in American Labor Markets at the Turn of the Century," *Journal of Economic Literature* 36, no. 2 (June 1998): 722–765.

Labor to issue and enforce safety and health standards for all private employers. Safety standards are intended to reduce the risk of traumatic injury, while health standards address worker exposure to substances thought to cause disease. The stated goal of the act was to ensure the "highest degree of health and safety protection for the employee."

Despite the *ideal* that employees should face the minimum possible risk in the workplace, implementing this ideal as social *policy* is not necessarily in the best interests of workers. Our hedonic model can show that reducing risk in some circumstances will lower the workers' utility levels. Consider Figure 8.7.

Suppose a labor market is functioning about like our textbook models, in that workers are well informed about dangers inherent in any job and are mobile

FIGURE 8.7

The Effects of Government Regulation in a Perfectly Functioning Labor Market

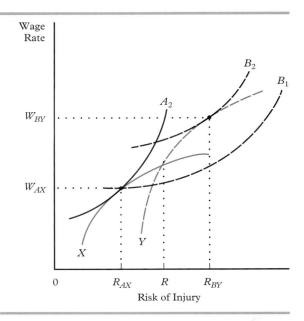

enough to avoid risks they do not wish to take. In these circumstances, wages will be positively related to risk (other things equal), and workers will sort themselves into jobs according to their preferences. This market can be modeled graphically in Figure 8.7, where, for simplicity's sake, we have assumed there are two kinds of workers and two kinds of firms. Person A, who is very averse to the risk of injury, works at wage W_{AX} and risk R_{AX} for employer X. Person B works for employer Y at wage W_{BY} and risk R_{BY}.

Now suppose the Occupational Safety and Health Administration (OSHA), the Department of Labor agency responsible for implementing the federal safety and health program, promulgates a standard that makes risk levels above R_{AX} illegal. The effects, although unintended and perhaps not immediately obvious, would be detrimental to employees like B. Reducing risk is costly, and the best wage offer a worker can obtain at risk R_{AX} is W_{AX}. For B, however, wage W_{AX} and risk R_{AX} generate *less utility* than did Y's offer of W_{BY} and R_{BY}.

When the government mandates the reduction of risk in a market where workers are compensated for the risks they take, it penalizes workers like B, who are not terribly sensitive to risk and appreciate the higher wages associated with higher risk. The critical issue, of course, is whether workers have the knowledge and choice necessary to generate compensating wage differentials. Many people believe that workers are uninformed, unable to comprehend different risk levels, or immobile, and thus that most do not choose risky jobs voluntarily. If this belief were true, government regulation *could* make workers better off. Indeed, while the evidence of a positive relationship between wages and risk of fatal injury should challenge the notion that information and mobility are *generally* insufficient to create compensating differentials, there are specific areas in which problems obviously exist. For example, the introduction each year of new workplace chemicals whose health effects on humans may be unknown for two or more decades (owing to the long gestation periods for most cancers and lung diseases) clearly presents substantial informational problems to affected labor market participants.

To say that worker utility *can* be reduced by government regulation does not, then, imply that it *will* be reduced. The outcome depends on how well the unregulated market functions and how careful the government is in setting its standards for risk reduction. The following section will analyze a government program implemented in a market that has *not* generated enough information about risk for employees to make informed job choices.

How Strict Should OSHA Standards Be?   Consider a labor market, like that mentioned previously for asbestos workers, in which ignorance or worker immobility hinders labor market operation. Let us suppose also that the government becomes aware of the health hazard involved and wishes to set a standard regulating worker exposure to this hazard. How stringent should this standard be?

The crux of the problem in standard-setting is that reducing hazards is costly; the greater the reduction, the more it costs. While businesses bear these costs initially, they ultimately respond to them by cutting costs elsewhere and raising prices (to the extent that cutting costs is not possible). Since labor costs constitute the largest cost category for most businesses, it is natural for firms facing large government-mandated hazard reduction costs to hold the line on wage increases or to adopt policies that are the equivalent of reducing wages: speeding up production, being less lenient with absenteeism, reducing employee benefits, and so forth. It is also likely, particularly in view of any price increases (which, of course, tend to reduce product demand), that employment will be cut back. Some of the job loss will be in the form of permanent layoffs that force workers to find other jobs—jobs they presumably could have had before the layoff but chose not to accept. Some of the loss will be in the form of cutting down on hiring new employees who would have regarded the jobs as their best employment option.

Thus, whether in the form of smaller wage increases, more difficult working conditions, or inability to obtain or retain one's first choice in a job, the costs of compliance with health standards will fall on employees. A graphic example can be used to make an educated guess about whether worker utility will be enhanced or not as a result of the increased protection from risk mandated by an OSHA health standard.

Figure 8.8 depicts a worker who believes she has taken a low-risk job when in fact she is exposing herself to a hazard that has a relatively high probability of damaging her health in twenty years. She receives a wage of W_1 and *believes* she

FIGURE 8.8
A Worker Accepting Unknown Risk

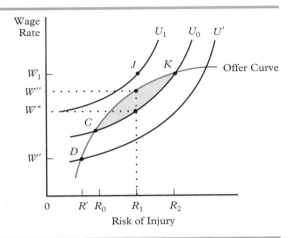

is at point J, where the risk level is R_1 and the utility level is U_1. Instead, she is in fact at point K, receiving W_1 for accepting (unknowingly) risk level R_2; she would thus experience lower utility (indifference curve U_0) if she knew the extent of the risk she was taking.

Suppose now that the government discovers that her job is highly hazardous. The government could simply inform the affected workers and let them move to other work. However, if it has little confidence in the ability of workers to understand the information or to find other work, the government could pass a standard that limits employee exposure to this hazard. But what level of protection should this standard offer?

If OSHA forced the risk level down to R', the best wage offer the worker in our example could obtain is W' (at point D on the offer curve). Point D, however, lies on indifference curve U', which represents a lower level of utility than she is in fact getting now (U_0). She would be worse off with the standard. On the other hand, if the government forced risk levels down to a level between R_0 and R_2, she would be better off because she would be able to reach an indifference curve above U_0 (within the shaded area of Figure 8.8). To better understand this last point, we will briefly explain the concepts underlying *benefit-cost analysis*, the technique economists recommend for estimating which government mandates will improve social welfare.

Benefit-Cost Analysis   The purpose of benefit-cost analysis in the labor market is to weigh the likely costs of a government regulation against the value that workers place on its expected benefits (as measured by what workers would be willing to pay for these benefits). In the terms of Figure 8.8, the per-worker *costs* of achieving reduced risk under the OSHA standard are reflected along the offer curve, which indicates the wage cuts that firms would have to make to keep profits constant. For example, if OSHA mandated that risk levels fall from R_2 to R_1, employer costs would require that wage offers fall to W''. The per worker cost of this standard therefore would be ($W_1 - W''$).

Conceptually, the *benefits* of the OSHA standard can be measured by the wage reductions that workers would be willing to take if they could get the reduced risk. In Figure 8.8, the worker depicted would be willing to take a wage as low as W^* if risk is cut to R_1, because at that wage and risk level her utility is the same as it is now (recall she is actually at point K on curve U_0). Thus, the *most* she would be willing to pay for this risk reduction is $(W_1 - W^*)$. If wages were forced below W^* she would be worse off (on a lower indifference curve), and if wages were above W^* she would be better off than she is now.

In the example graphed by Figure 8.8, a mandated risk level of R_1 would produce benefits that outweigh costs. That is, the amount that workers would be willing to pay $(W_1 - W^*)$ would exceed the costs $(W_1 - W'')$. If employers could get the wage down to W^* they would be more profitable than they are now, and workers would have unchanged utility. If the wage were W'' workers would be better off and employers would have unchanged profits, and a wage between W^* and W'' would make both parties better off. All these possible options would be Pareto-improving (at least one party would be better-off and neither would be worse-off).

In Figure 8.8, mandated risk levels between R_0 and R_2 would produce benefits greater than costs. These risk levels could be accompanied by wage rates that place the parties in the shaded zone, which illustrates all the Pareto-improving possibilities. Risk levels below R_0 would impose costs on society that would be greater than the benefits.

Moving away from textbook graphs, how can we estimate, in a practical way, the wage reductions workers would be willing to bear in exchange for a reduction in risk? The answer lies in estimating compensating wage differentials in markets that appear to work. Suppose, in a properly functioning market, that workers are estimated to accept wage cuts of $900 per year for reductions in the yearly death rate of 1 in 10,000. These workers appear to feel that, other things equal, $900 is a price they are willing to pay for this reduction in risk. The use of such differentials should not be oversold, because the difficulties of establishing which markets are properly functioning are considerable. However, estimating compensating wage differentials is probably the best way of finding out what value workers attach to various job characteristics.

HEDONIC WAGE THEORY AND EMPLOYEE BENEFITS

In Table 5.2 we saw that employee benefits are roughly 30 percent of total compensation for workers in larger firms. Over half of such benefits relate to pensions and medical insurance, both of which have grown in importance over the past thirty years and have attracted the attention of policymakers. In this section we use hedonic theory to analyze the labor market effects of employee benefits.

Employee Preferences

The distinguishing feature of most employee benefits is that they compensate workers in a form *other* than currently spendable cash. In general, there are two broad categories of such benefits. First are *payments in kind*—that is, compensation in the form of such commodities as employer-provided insurance or paid vacation time.[16] The second general type of employee benefit is *deferred compensation,* compensation that is earned now but will be paid in the form of money later on. Employer contributions to employee pension plans make up the largest proportion of these benefits.

Payments in Kind   It is a well-established tenet of economic theory that, *other things equal,* people would rather receive $X in cash than a commodity that costs $X. The reason is simple. With $X in cash the person can choose to buy the particular commodity or choose instead to buy a variety of other things. Cash is thus the form of payment that gives the recipient the most discretion and the most options in maximizing utility.

As might be suspected, however, "other things" are not equal. Specifically, such in-kind payments as employer-provided health insurance offer employees a sizable tax advantage because, for the most part, they are not taxable under current income tax regulations. The absence of a tax on important in-kind payments is a factor that tends to offset their restrictive nature. A worker may prefer $1,000 in cash to $1,000 in some in-kind payment, but if his or her income tax and payroll-tax rates total 25 percent, the comparison is really between $750 in cash and $1,000 in the in-kind benefit.

Deferred Compensation   Like payments in kind, deferred compensation schemes are restrictive but enjoy a tax advantage over current cash payments. In the case of pensions, for example, employers contribute currently to a pension fund, but employees do not obtain access to this fund until they retire. However, neither the pension fund *contributions* made on behalf of employees by employers nor the *interest* that compounds when these funds are invested is subject to the personal income tax. Only when the retirement benefits are received does the ex-worker pay taxes.

Indifference Curves   Two opposing forces are therefore at work in shaping workers' preferences for employee benefits. On the one hand, these benefits are accorded special tax treatment, a feature of no small significance when one considers that income and Social Security taxes come to well over 20 percent for most workers. On the other hand, benefits involve a loss of discretionary control over one's total compensation. The result is that if we graph worker preferences regarding cash compensation (the wage rate) and employee benefits, we would come up with indifference curves shaped generally like the one shown in Figure 8.9. When cash earnings are relatively high and employee benefits are small (point *J*), workers are willing to give up a lot in terms of cash earnings to obtain the tax advantages of employee benefits. However, once compensation is heavily weighted toward such benefits (point *K*), further increases in benefits reduce discretionary

---

[16]A woman earning $15,000 per year for 2,000 hours of work can have her hourly wage increased from $7.50 to $8.00 by either a straightforward increase in current money payments or a reduction in her working hours to 1,875 with no reduction in yearly earnings. If she receives her raise in the form of paid vacation time, she is in fact being paid in the form of a commodity: leisure time.

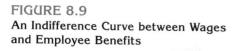

FIGURE 8.9

An Indifference Curve between Wages and Employee Benefits

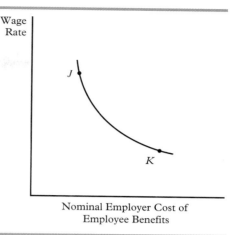

Wage Rate

J

K

Nominal Employer Cost of Employee Benefits

earnings so much that the tax advantages seem small; at point *K*, then, the indifference curve is flatter. Hence, indifference curves depicting preferences between cash earnings and employee benefits are shaped like those in chapters 6 and 7.[17]

Employer Preferences

Employers also have choices to make in the mix of cash compensation and employee benefits offered to their workers. Their preferences about this mix can be graphically summarized through the use of isoprofit curves.

Isoprofit Curves with a Unitary Slope   The best place to start our analysis of the trade-offs employers are willing to offer workers between cash compensation and employee benefits is to assume they are totally indifferent about whether to spend $X on wages or $X on benefits. Both options cost the same, so why would they prefer one option to the other?

If firms were indifferent about the mix of cash and benefits paid to workers, their only concern would be with the *level* of compensation. If a certain type of job commands $X in total compensation to attract workers, firms would be willing to pay $X in wages, $X in benefits, or adopt a mix of the two totaling $X in cost. These equally attractive options are summarized along the zero-profit isoprofit curve shown in Figure 8.10. Note that this curve is drawn with a slope of −1, indicating that to keep profits constant, every extra dollar the firm puts into the direct cost of employee benefits must be matched by payroll reductions of a dollar.

---

[17]As noted in footnote 13, the indifference curves in the prior section were *upward*-sloping because a "bad," not a "good," was on the horizontal axis.

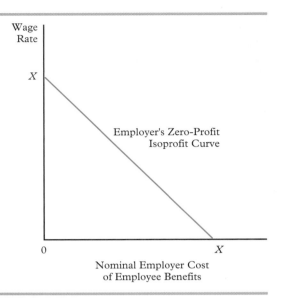

FIGURE 8.10

An Isoprofit Curve Showing the Wage/Benefit Offers a Firm Might Be Willing to Make to Its Employees: A Unitary Trade-off

Isoprofit Curves with a Flatter Slope   The trade-offs that employers are willing to make between wages and employee benefits are not always one-for-one. Some benefits produce employer tax savings when compared to paying workers in cash. For example, Social Security taxes employers must pay are levied on cash payroll, not on employee benefits, so compensating workers with in-kind or deferred benefits instead of an equal amount of cash reduces their tax liabilities.

Moreover, offering benefits that are more valued by one group of prospective workers than another can be a clever way to save on the costs of screening applicants. The key here is to offer benefits that will attract applicants with certain characteristics the firm is searching for and will discourage applications from others. For example, deferred compensation will generally be more attractive to workers who are more future-oriented, and offering tuition assistance will be attractive only to those who place a value on continued education. Applicants who are present-oriented or do not expect to continue their schooling will be discouraged from even applying, thus saving employers who offer these two benefits (instead of paying higher wages) the costs of screening applicants they would not hire anyway.

When employee benefits have tax or other advantages to the firm, the isoprofit curve is flattened (see curve *A* in Figure 8.11). This flatter curve indicates that benefits nominally costing $300, say, might save enough in other ways that only a $280 decrease in wages would be needed to keep profits constant.

Isoprofit Curves with a Steeper Slope   Employee benefits can also increase employer costs in other areas and thus end up being more expensive than pay-

FIGURE 8.11

Alternative Isoprofit Curves Showing the Wage/Benefit Offers a Firm Might Be Willing to Make to Its Employees: Nonunitary Trade-offs

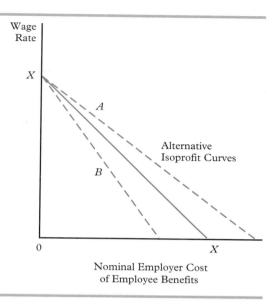

ing in cash. The value of life and health insurance provided by employers, for example, is typically unaffected by the hours of work (as long as employees are considered "full-time"). Increasing insurance benefits rather than wage rates, then, will produce an *income effect* without a corresponding increase in the price of leisure. Increasing compensation in this way will push workers in the direction of reduced work hours, possibly through greater levels of absenteeism.[18] If employee benefits increase costs in other areas, the isoprofit curve will steepen (see curve *B* in Figure 8.11)—indicating that to keep profits constant, wages would have to drop by more than $300 if benefits nominally costing $300 are offered.

The Joint Determination of Wages and Benefits

The offer curve in a particular labor market can be obtained by connecting the relevant portions of each firm's zero-profit isoprofit curve. When all firms have isoprofit curves with a slope of −1, the offer curve is a straight line with a negative and unitary slope. One such offer curve is illustrated in Figure 8.12, and the only difference between this curve and the zero-profit isoprofit curve in Figure 8.10 is that the latter traced out *hypothetical* offers *one* firm could make, while this one

---

[18]See Steven G. Allen, "Compensation, Safety, and Absenteeism: Evidence from the Paper Industry," *Industrial and Labor Relations Review* 34 (January 1981): 207–218, and also his "An Empirical Model of Work Attendance," *Review of Economics and Statistics* 63 (February 1981): 77–87. For evidence on teacher absenteeism, see Ronald G. Ehrenberg et al., "School District Leave Policies, Teacher Absenteeism, and Student Achievement," *Journal of Human Resources* 26 (Winter 1991): 72–105.

FIGURE 8.12
**Market Determination of the Mix
of Wages and Benefits**

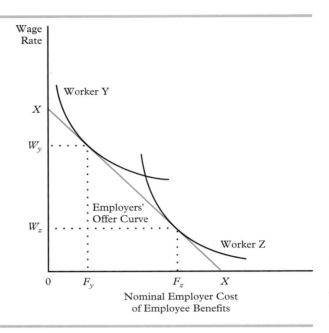

traces out the *actual* offers made by *all* firms in this labor market. Of course, if firms have isoprofit curves whose slopes are different from −1, the offer curve will not look exactly like that depicted in Figure 8.12. Whatever its shape or the absolute value of its slope at any point, however, it will slope downward.

Employees, then, face a set of wage and employee-benefit offers that imply the necessity for making trade-offs. Those employees (like worker Y in Figure 8.12) who attach relatively great importance to the availability of currently spendable cash will choose to accept offers in which total compensation is largely in the form of wages. Employees who may be less worried about current cash income but more interested in the tax advantages of benefits will accept offers in which employee benefits form a higher proportion of total compensation (see the curve for worker Z in Figure 8.12). Thus, employers will tailor their compensation packages to suit the preferences of the workers they are trying to attract. If their employees tend to be young or poor, for example, their compensation packages may be heavily weighted toward wages and include relatively little in the way of pensions and insurance. Alternatively, if they are trying to attract people in an area where family incomes are high and hence employee benefits offer relatively large tax savings, firms may offer packages in which benefits constitute a large proportion of the total.

Figure 8.12 shows that workers receiving more generous benefits pay for them by receiving lower wages, other things being equal. Further, if employer isoprofit curves have a unitary slope, a benefit that costs the employer $1 to provide will cost workers $1 in wages. In other words, economic theory suggests that workers pay for their own benefits.

Actually observing the trade-off between wages and employee benefits is not easy. Because firms that pay high wages usually also offer very good benefits packages, it often appears to the casual observer that wages and employee benefits are *positively* related. Casual observation in this case is misleading, however, because it does not allow for the influences of *other factors*, such as the demands of the job and the quality of workers involved, that influence total compensation. The other factors are most conveniently controlled for statistically, and the few statistical studies on this subject tend to support the prediction of a negative relationship between wages and benefits.[19] The policy consequences of a negative wage/benefits trade-off are enormously important, because government legislation designed to improve employee benefits might well be paid for by workers in the form of lower future wage increases.

---

[19]See Edward Montgomery and Kathryn Shaw, "Pensions and Wage Premia," *Economic Inquiry* 35, no. 3 (July 1997): 510–522, for a paper that references earlier work on compensating wage differentials for pensions. For a paper on wages and mandated insurance coverage, see Jonathan Gruber, "The Incidence of Mandated Maternity Benefits," *American Economic Review* 84, no. 3 (June 1994): 622–641.

REVIEW QUESTIONS

1. Building the oil pipeline across Alaska required the use of many construction workers recruited from the continental United States, who lived in dormitories and worked in an inhospitable climate. Discuss the creation of a compensating wage differential for these jobs using ordinary supply and demand concepts.

2. Statement 1: "Business executives are greedy profit maximizers, caring only for themselves." Statement 2: "It has been established that workers doing filthy, dangerous work receive higher wages, other things equal." Can both of these statements be generally true? Why?

3. "There are three methods of allocating labor across a spectrum of jobs that may differ substantially in working conditions. One is the use of force, one is the use of trickery, and one is the use of compensating wage differentials." Comment.

4. Suppose highway workers in a certain city are required to give the Supervisor of Highways an under-the-table payment of $X per year. Would you expect wages paid to highway workers by this city to be higher or lower than the market wage? Would you expect the salary paid by the city to its Supervisor of Highways to be above or below market? Explain.

5. Is the following true, false, or uncertain: "Certain occupations, such as coal mining, are inherently dangerous to workers' health and safety. Therefore, unambiguously, the most appropriate government policy is the establishment and enforcement of rigid safety and health standards." Explain your answer.

6. Suppose that Congress were to mandate that all employers had to offer their employees a life insurance policy worth at least $50,000 in the event of death. Use economic theory, both positively and normatively, to analyze the effects of this mandate on employee well-being.

7. The U.S. government passed a law in 1942 that prohibited garment makers from employing independent contractors working out of their homes. The reason was that those working at home made less money, and policymakers believed they were being exploited. Comment on the assertion that the difference in pay between factory workers and home workers doing the same tasks constitutes a measure of exploitation.

8. "The concept of compensating wage premiums for dangerous work does not apply to industries like the coal industry, where the union has forced all wages and other compensation items to be the same. Because all mines must pay the same wage, compensating differentials cannot exist." Is this statement correct? (Assume wages and other forms of pay must be equal for dangerous and nondangerous work and consider the implications for individual labor supply behavior.)

9. In 1991 Germany proposed that the European Community countries collectively agree that no one be allowed to work on Sundays (exceptions could be made for Muslims, Jews, and other religious groups celebrating the Sabbath on a day other than Sunday). Use economic theory both *positively* and *normatively* to assess, as completely as you can, the effects of prohibiting work on Sundays.

PROBLEMS

1. A researcher estimates the following wage equation for underwater construction workers, $W_i = 10 + .5D_i$ where W = the wage in dollars per hour and D = the depth underwater at which workers work, in meters. Based on this information, draw the offer curve and possible indifference curves for two workers, A and B: A works at a depth of 3 meters and B works at 5 meters. At their current wages and depths, what is the tradeoff (keeping utility constant) between hourly wages and a 1-meter change in depth that each worker is willing to make? Which worker has a greater willingness to pay for reduced depth at 3 meters of depth?

2. Consider the conditions of work in perfume factories. In New York perfume factories, workers dislike the smell of perfume, while in California plants, workers appreciate the smell of perfume, provided that the level does not climb above S^*. (If it rises above S^*, they start to dislike it.) Suppose that there is no cost for firms to reduce or eliminate the smell of perfume in perfume factories, and assume that the workers have an alternative wage, W^*.

Draw a diagram using isoprofit and indifference curves that depicts the situation. (The New York and California isoprofit curves are the same, but their indifference curves differ.) What level of perfume smell is there in the New York factories? In the California factories? Is there a wage differential between the California and New York workers?

3. (Appendix). Thomas's utility function is $U = \sqrt{Y}$, where Y = annual income. He has two job offers. One is in an industry in which there are no layoffs and the annual pay is $40,000. In the other industry, there is uncertainty about layoffs. Half the years are bad years and layoffs push Thomas's annual pay down to $22,500. The other years are good years. How much must Thomas earn in the good years in this job to compensate him for the high risk of layoffs?

SELECTED READINGS

Duncan, Greg, and Bertil Holmlund. "Was Adam Smith Right After All? Another Test of the Theory of Compensating Wage Differentials." *Journal of Labor Economics* 1 (October 1983): 366–379.

Fishback, Price V. "Operations of 'Unfettered' Labor Markets: Exit and Voice in American Labor Markets at the Turn of the Century." *Journal of Economic Literature* 36, no. 2 (June 1998): 722–765.

Rosen, Sherwin. "Hedonic Prices and Implicit Markets." *Journal of Political Economy* 82 (January–February 1974): 34–55.

———. "The Theory of Equalizing Differences." In *Handbook of Labor Economics,* ed. Orley Ashenfelter and Richard Layard (New York: North-Holland, 1986): 641–692.

Smith, Robert S. "Compensating Wage Differentials and Public Policy: A Review." *Industrial and Labor Relations Review* 32 (April 1979): 339–352.

Viscusi, W. Kip. "The Value of Risks to Life and Health." *Journal of Economic Literature* 31, no. 4 (December 1993): 1912–1946.

8A

Compensating Wage Differentials and Layoffs

A s mentioned in the chapter text, one of the circumstances identified by Adam Smith under which compensating wage differentials would arise relates to the "constancy or inconstancy of employment." While there is evidence, as we shall see, to support this prediction, the relationship of wages to layoff probabilities is by no means as simple as Smith thought. In particular, there are three issues relevant to the analysis, all of which we shall discuss briefly.[1]

UNCONSTRAINED CHOICE OF WORK HOURS

Suppose that, in the spirit of chapters 6 and 7, employees are free to choose their hours of work in a labor market that offers an infinite choice of work hours. Given the wage a particular worker can command and his or her nonwage income, the utility-maximizing choice of working hours would be selected. For the person depicted in Figure 8A.1, the utility-maximizing choice of work hours is H^*, given his or her offered wage rate (W^*) and level of nonwage income (assumed here to be zero).

If H^* is thought of in terms of yearly work hours, it is easy to understand that a worker may *prefer* a job involving layoff! Suppose H^* is 1,500 hours per year, or essentially three-quarters of the typical "full-time" job of 2,000 hours. One could work 6 hours a day, 5 days a week, for 50 weeks a year, or one could work 8 hours a day, 5 days a week, for 9 months and agree to be laid off for 3 months. Which alternative holds more appeal to any given individual depends on his or her preferences with respect to large blocks of leisure or household time, but it is clear that many peo-

---

[1]The analysis in this appendix draws heavily on John M. Abowd and Orley Ashenfelter, "Anticipated Unemployment, Temporary Layoffs, and Compensating Wage Differentials," in *Studies in Labor Markets*, ed. Sherwin Rosen (Chicago: University of Chicago Press, 1981), 141–170.

FIGURE 8A.1
Choice of Hours of Work

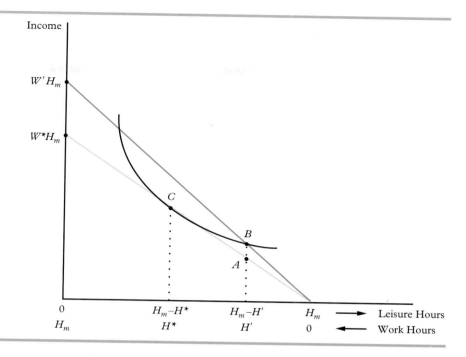

ple value such large blocks. Teachers, for example, typically work full-time during a 9-month school year, and then some of them vacation during the summer. Many other jobs, from the construction trades to work in canning factories, involve predictable seasonal layoffs, and workers in these jobs may have chosen them because they value the leisure or household production time accompanying the layoffs.

Putting the point differently, the theory of compensating wage differentials suggests they will be positive only when a job characteristic is regarded as bad by the marginal worker. Predictable blocks of leisure or household time accompanying seasonal layoffs may not be regarded as bad by the marginal worker. In fact, workers in some markets may see layoffs as a mechanism through which they can best achieve their desired yearly hours of work.

CONSTRAINED HOURS OF WORK

Suppose that the worker depicted in Figure 8A.1 is offered a choice between a job offering wage W^* and hours H^*, and one offering fewer hours than desired because of a predictable layoff each year that reduces hours of work to H'. Clearly, if the wage for the latter job remains at W^*, the worker's utility will be reduced by taking the job offering H' hours because he or she will be on an indifference curve passing through point A. The job offering W^* and H^* is thus clearly preferred.

However, suppose that H' is offered at a wage of W', where W' exceeds W^* by enough so that point B can be reached. Point B, where the wage is W' and hours of work are H', is on the *same* indifference curve as point C (the utility-maximizing point when W^* is the offered wage). Point B is not a point of utility maximization[2] at a wage offer of W', but if the worker is offered an unconstrained choice of hours at wage rate W^*, or a wage of W' where working hours are *constrained* to equal H', he or she would be indifferent between the two job offers.

In the above example, $(W' - W^*)$ is the compensating wage differential that would have to arise for the worker to consider a job where hours of work were constrained to lie below those otherwise desired. Many people view layoffs as an event that prevents workers from working the number of hours they would otherwise desire to work. If this is the case, and if these layoffs are predictable and known with certainty, such as layoffs accompanying model changeovers in the auto industry, then compensating wage differentials associated with the predictable, certain layoff rate would arise in a well-functioning labor market (that is, one where workers are informed and mobile).[3]

THE EFFECTS OF UNCERTAIN LAYOFFS

In the above section, we assumed that layoffs were predictable and known with certainty. In most cases, however, they are not. While we might expect layoff rates to be higher in some industries than in others, they are in fact often subject to considerable random fluctuation *within* industries over the years. This *uncertainty* of layoffs is itself another aspect of affected jobs that is usually thought to be a negative feature and for which a compensating wage differential might arise.

Suppose that utility is measurable and is a function only of income, so that it can be graphed against income (Y), as in Figure 8A.2.[4] Suppose also that the person depicted is offered a job for which a wage of W' and yearly hours of H' are known *with certainty*. The utility associated with these H' hours, $U(H')$, is a function of his or her income at H' hours of work: $W'H'$ (again assuming no nonwage income).

Now suppose there is another job paying W' in which the *average* hours of work per year are H' but half of the time H_h is worked and half of the time H_l is

---

[2]It is not a point of tangency; that is, at a wage of W' the worker depicted in Figure 8A.1 would prefer to work more than H' hours if he or she were free to choose work hours. We have assumed in the discussion that the choice is constrained so that hours cannot exceed H'.

[3]A similar argument can be used to predict that workers will receive compensating wage differentials if they are forced to work longer hours than they would otherwise prefer. For the argument and evidence in support of it, see Ronald G. Ehrenberg and Paul L. Schumann, "Compensating Wage Differentials for Mandatory Overtime," *Economic Inquiry* 22 (December 1984).

[4]Although economists typically work with *ordinal* utility functions, which specify the relative ranking of alternatives without assigning each alternative a numerical value of utility, the analysis of choice under uncertainty requires the use of *cardinal* utility functions (ones in which each alternative is assigned a specific numerical value of utility).

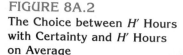

FIGURE 8A.2

The Choice between H' Hours with Certainty and H' Hours on Average

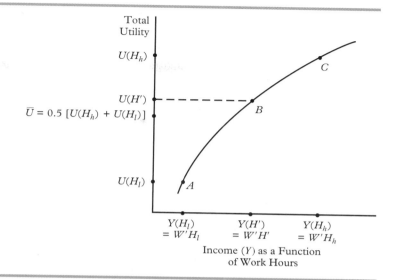

worked. Although we have assumed that $0.5 H_h + 0.5 H_l = H'$, so that over the years the person averages H' hours of work, it turns out that with the concave utility function we have drawn, the person's average utility is *below* $U(H')$. To understand this we must look closely at Figure 8A.2.

When the person's working hours are H_h, which is half the time, he or she earns $W'H_h$, and this income yields a utility of $U(H_h)$. Thus, half the time the worker will be at point C enjoying utility level $U(H_h)$. The other half of the time, however, the person will be working H_l hours, earning $W'H_l$ in income, and be at point A enjoying utility of $U(H_l)$. His or her average utility is thus $\overline{U}$, which is $\overline{U} = 0.5 U(H_h) + 0.5 U(H_l)$. Note that $\overline{U}$, which is midway between $U(H_h)$ and $U(H_l)$ in our example, lies *below* $U(H')$—the utility derived from a job paying W' and employing the person for H' hours *with certainty* every year.

Why is $\overline{U} < U(H')$ even though H' hours are worked on *average* in both cases? The answer lies in the concavity of the utility function, which economists define as exhibiting *risk aversion*. Moving from $Y(H')$ to $Y(H_h)$ covers the same absolute distance on the horizontal axis as moving from $Y(H')$ to $Y(H_l)$, but the changes in *utility* are not the same in magnitude. In particular, moving from $Y(H')$ to $Y(H_h)$ (points B to C) in the good years adds *less* to utility than moving from $Y(H')$ to $Y(H_l)$ (points B to A) in the bad years takes away. Put differently, the concavity of the total utility curve in Figure 8A.2 implies diminishing marginal utility of income. Thus, in the unlucky years, when hours are below H', there is a relatively big drop in utility (as compared to the utility associated with H' hours), while in the lucky years the added income increases utility by a relatively small amount.

The upshot of this discussion is that when workers are averse to risk—that is, when their utility functions are concave so that they in essence place a larger value on negative changes from a given level of income than they do on positive changes of equal dollar magnitude—they would prefer a job paying W' and offering H' hours with certainty to one paying W' and offering H' hours only on average. Thus, to compensate them for the loss in utility associated with *risk aversion,* they would require a wage above W' for the job offering H' hours only on average.

THE OBSERVED WAGE/LAYOFF RELATIONSHIP

The discussion above centered on worker preferences regarding layoffs. For compensating wage differentials to arise, of course, employers must be willing to pay them. That is, employers must profit from being able to lay off workers, and if we are to observe firms pursuing a high-wage/high-layoff strategy, their gains from layoff must exceed their costs of higher wages.

The discussion above also neglected unemployment insurance (UI) payments to laid-off workers. This topic is discussed in some detail in chapter 15. Here we need note only that if UI payments fully compensate laid-off workers for their lost utility, compensating wage differentials will not arise. Compensating wage differentials will arise only if UI payments do not fully compensate laid-off workers.

One study that looked very carefully at the relationship between wages and layoffs suggests that the compensating wage differential for an average probability of layoff is around 4 percent of wages, with over 80 percent of this differential related to the aversion to risk associated with the variability (uncertainty) in layoff rates facing workers over time. Workers in the high-layoff industries of automobile manufacturing and construction received estimated compensating wage differentials ranging over the early 1970s from 6 to 14 percent and 6 to 11 percent, respectively.[5] A study of farm workers around 1990 found that those who risked unemployment by working seasonally were paid from 9 to 12 percent more per hour than those who held permanent jobs in farming.[6]

---

[5]These estimates are from the Abowd and Ashenfelter article in footnote 1 of this appendix. Similar evidence for the late 1970s can be found in Robert H. Topel, "Equilibrium Earnings, Turnover, and Unemployment: New Evidence," *Journal of Labor Economics* 2, no. 4 (October 1984): 500–522. For those interested in how UI benefits affect wages, see David A. Anderson, "Compensating Wage Differentials and the Optimal Provision of Unemployment Insurance," *Southern Economic Journal* 60, no. 3 (January 1994): 644–656.

[6]Enrico Moretti, "Do Wages Compensate for Risk of Unemployment? Parametric and Semiparametric Evidence from Seasonal Jobs," *Journal of Risk and Uncertainty* 20, no. 1 (January 2000): 45–66.

9

INVESTMENTS IN HUMAN CAPITAL:
Education and Training

Many labor supply choices require a substantial initial *investment* on the part of the worker. Recall that investments, by definition, entail an initial cost that one hopes to recoup over some period of time. Thus, for many labor supply decisions, *current* wages and working conditions are not the only deciding factors. Modeling investment decisions requires developing a framework that incorporates a *lifetime* perspective.

Workers undertake three major kinds of labor market investments: education and training, migration, and search for new jobs. All three investments involve an initial cost, and all three are made in the hope and expectation that the investment will pay off well into the future. To emphasize the essential similarity of these investments to other kinds of investments, economists refer to them as investments in *human capital,* a term that conceptualizes workers as embodying a set of skills that can be "rented out" to employers. The knowledge and skills a worker has—which come from education and training, including the learning that experience yields—generate a certain *stock* of productive capital. The *value* of this productive capital is derived from how much these skills can earn in the labor market. Job search and migration are activities that increase the value of one's human capital by increasing the price (wage) received for a given stock of skills.

EXAMPLE 9.1

War and Human Capital

We can illustrate the relative importance of physical and human capital by noting some interesting facts about severely war-damaged cities. The atomic attack on Hiroshima destroyed 70 percent of its buildings and killed about 30 percent of the population. Survivors fled the city in the aftermath of the bombing, but within three months two-thirds of the city's surviving population had returned. Because the air-burst bomb left the city's underground utility networks intact, power was restored to surviving areas in one day. Through railway service began again in two days, and telephone service was restarted in a week. Plants responsible for three-quarters of the city's industrial production (many were located on the outskirts of the city and undamaged) could have begun normal operations within 30 days.

In Hamburg, Germany, a city of around 1.5 million in the summer of 1943, Allied bombing raids over a ten-day period in July and August destroyed about half of the buildings in the city and killed about 3 percent of the city's population. Although there was considerable damage to the water supply system, electricity and gas service were adequate within a few days after the last attack, and within four days the telegraph system was again operating. The central bank was reopened and business had begun to function normally after one week, and postal service was resumed within twelve days of the attack. The Strategic Bombing Survey reported that within five months, Hamburg had recovered up to 80 percent of its former productivity.

The speed and success of recovery from these disasters has prompted one economist to offer the following two observations:

(1) the fraction of the community's real wealth represented by visible material capital is small relative to the fraction represented by the accumulated knowledge and talents of the population, and (2) there are enormous reserves of energy and effort in the population not drawn upon in ordinary times but which can be utilized under special circumstances such as those prevailing in the aftermath of disaster.

Data from: Jack Hirshleifer, *Economic Behavior in Adversity* (Chicago: University of Chicago Press, 1987), pp. 12–14, 78–79.

Society's total wealth is a combination of human and nonhuman capital. Human capital includes accumulated investments in such activities as education, job training, and migration, whereas nonhuman capital includes society's stock of natural resources, buildings, and machinery. Total per capita wealth in North America, for example, was around $379,000 in 1994, 76 percent of which ($289,000) was in the form of human capital. Indeed, in worldwide regions outside the resource-rich Middle East, over 60 percent of estimated national wealth in 1994 was derived from investments in human capital.[1] (Example 9.1 illustrates the overall importance of human capital in another way.)

Investment in the knowledge and skills of workers takes place in three stages. First, in early childhood, the acquisition of human capital is largely determined by the decisions of others. Parental resources and guidance, plus our cultural environment

---

[1]World Bank, *Expanding the Measure of Wealth: Indicators of Environmentally Sustainable Development* (Washington, D.C.: World Bank, 1997), Table 3.3. The wealth estimates for 1994 are expressed in dollars as of the year 2000.

and early schooling experiences, help to influence basic language and mathematical skills, attitudes toward learning, and general health and life expectancy (which themselves affect the ability to work). Second, teenagers and young adults go through a stage in which they acquire knowledge and skills as full-time students in a high school, college, or vocational training program. Finally, after entering the labor market, workers' additions to their human capital generally take place on a part-time basis, through on-the-job training, night school, or participation in relatively short, formal training programs. In this chapter we focus on the latter two stages.

One of the challenges of any behavioral theory is to explain why people faced with what appears to be the same environment make different choices. We will see in this chapter that individuals' decisions about investing in human capital are affected by the ease and speed with which they learn, their aspirations and expectations about the future, and their access to financial resources.

HUMAN CAPITAL INVESTMENTS: THE BASIC MODEL

Like any other investment, an investment in human capital entails costs that are borne in the near term with the expectation that benefits will accrue in the future. Generally speaking, we can divide the *costs* of adding to human capital into three categories:

1. *Out-of-pocket* or *direct* expenses, including tuition costs and expenditures on books and other supplies.
2. *Forgone earnings* that arise because during the investment period it is usually impossible to work, at least not full-time.
3. *Psychic losses* that occur because learning is often difficult and tedious.

In the case of educational and training investments by workers, the expected *returns* are in the form of higher future earnings, increased job satisfaction over their lifetime, and a greater appreciation of nonmarket activities and interests. Calculating the benefits of an investment over time requires us to progressively discount benefits lying further into the future (see chapter 5). Benefits that are received in the future are worth less to us now than an equal amount of benefits received today, for two reasons. First, if people plan to consume their benefits, they prefer to consume earlier. (We are relatively sure of being able to enjoy such consumption now, for example, but the uncertainties of life make future enjoyment problematic.) Second, if people plan to invest the monetary benefits rather than use them for consumption, they can earn interest on the investment and enlarge their funds in the future. Thus, no matter how people intend to use their benefits, they will discount future receipts to some extent.

As chapter 5 explained, the present value of a stream of yearly benefits ($B_1, B_2,...$) over time (T) can be calculated as follows:

$$\text{Present Value} = \frac{B_1}{1+r} + \frac{B_2}{(1+r)^2} + \frac{B_3}{(1+r)^3} + \cdots + \frac{B_T}{(1+r)^T} \tag{9.1}$$

where the interest rate (or discount rate) is r. As long as r is positive, benefits into the future will be progressively discounted. For example, if $r = 0.06$, benefits payable in 30 years would receive a weight that is only 17 percent of the weight placed on benefits payable immediately ($1.06^{30} = 5.74$; $1/5.74 = 0.17$). The smaller r is, the greater the weight placed on future benefits; for example, if $r = 0.02$, a benefit payable in 30 years would receive a weight that is 55 percent of the weight given to an immediate benefit.

Our model of human capital investment assumes that people are utility maximizers and take a lifetime perspective when making choices about education and training. They are therefore assumed to compare the near-term investment costs (C) with the present value of expected future benefits when making a decision, say, about additional schooling. Investment in additional schooling is attractive if the present value of future benefits exceeds costs:

$$\frac{B_1}{1 + r} + \frac{B_2}{(1 + r)^2} + \cdots + \frac{B_T}{(1 + r)^T} > C \tag{9.2}$$

Utility maximization, of course, requires that people continue to make additional human capital investments as long as condition (9.2) is met, and that they stop only when the benefits of additional investment are equal to or less than the additional costs.

There are two ways we can measure whether the criterion in (9.2) is met. Using the *present-value method*, we can specify a value for the discount rate, r, and then determine how the present value of benefits compares to costs. Alternatively, we can adopt the *internal rate of return method*, which asks, "How large could the discount rate be and still render the investment profitable?" Clearly, if the benefits are so large that even a very high discount rate would render investment profitable, then the project is worthwhile. In practice, we calculate this internal rate of return by setting the present value of benefits equal to costs, solving for r and then comparing r to the rate of return on other investments.

Some basic implications of the model embedded in expression (9.2) are illustrated graphically in Figure 9.1, which depicts human capital decisions in terms of marginal costs and marginal benefits (focus for now on the black lines in the figure). The marginal costs, MC, of each additional unit of human capital (the tuition, supplies, forgone earnings, and psychic costs of an additional year of schooling, say) are assumed to be constant. The present value of the marginal benefits, MB, is shown as declining, because each added year of schooling means fewer years over which benefits can be collected. The utility-maximizing amount of human capital (HC^*) for any individual is shown as that amount for which $MC = MB$.

Those who find learning to be especially arduous will implicitly attach a higher marginal psychic cost to acquiring human capital. As shown by the green line, MC', in Figure 9.1a, individuals with higher marginal costs will acquire lower levels of human capital (compare HC' with HC^*). Similarly, those who expect smaller future benefits from additional human capital investments (the green line, MB'', in Figure 9.1b) will acquire less human capital.

FIGURE 9.1
The Optimum Acquisition of Human Capital

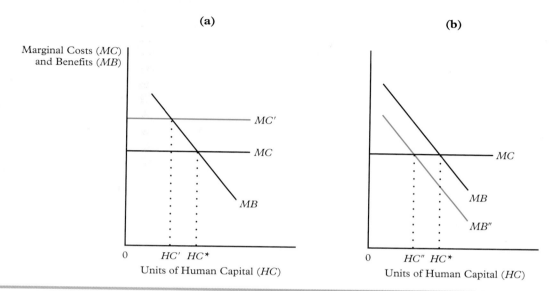

This straightforward theory yields some interesting insights about the behavior and earnings of workers. Many of these insights can be discovered by analyzing the decision confronting young adults about whether to invest full-time in college after leaving high school.

THE DEMAND FOR A COLLEGE EDUCATION

The demand for a college education, as measured by the percentage of graduating high school seniors who enroll in college, is surprisingly variable. For males, enrollment rates went from 55.2 percent in 1970, down to 46.7 percent in 1980, and back up to 61.4 percent by 1999. The comparable enrollment rates for women started lower, at 48.5 percent in 1970, and rose slowly during the 1970s, quickly during the 1980s, and again more slowly during the 1990s—reaching 64.4 percent in 1999. Why have enrollment rates followed these patterns?

Weighing the Costs and Benefits of College

Clearly, people attend college when they believe they will be better off by so doing. For some, at least part of the benefits may be short-term—they like the courses

FIGURE 9.2
Alternative Earnings Streams

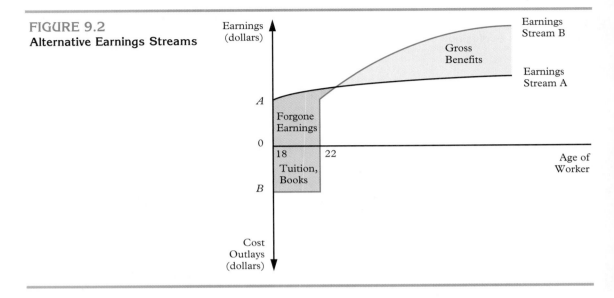

or the lifestyle of a student—and to this extent college is at least partially a *consumption* good. The consumption benefits of college, however, are unlikely to change much over the course of a decade, so changes in college attendance rates over relatively short periods of time probably reflect changes in marginal costs or benefits associated with the *investment* aspects of college attendance.

A person considering college has, in some broad sense, a choice between two streams of earnings over his or her lifetime. Stream A begins immediately but does not rise very high; it is the earnings stream of a high school graduate. Stream B (the college graduate) has a negative income for the first four years (owing to college tuition costs), followed by a period when the salary may be less than the high school graduate makes, but then it takes off and rises above stream A. Both streams are illustrated in Figure 9.2. (Why these streams are differentially *curved* will be discussed later in this chapter.) The streams shown in the figure are stylized so that we can emphasize some basic points. Actual earnings streams will be shown in Figures 9.3 and 9.4.

Obviously, the earnings of the college graduate would have to rise above those of the high school graduate to induce someone to invest in a college education (unless, of course, the consumption-related returns were large). The gross benefits, the difference in earnings between the two streams, must total much more than the costs because such returns are in the future and are therefore discounted. For example, suppose it costs $25,000 per year to obtain a four-year college education and the real interest rate (the nominal rate less the rate of inflation) is 2 percent. The after-tax returns—if they were the same each year—must be $3,652 in constant-dollar terms (that is, after taking away the effects of inflation) each year for 40 years in order to justify the investment on purely monetary grounds. These returns must be $3,652 because $100,000 invested at a 2 percent interest rate can provide a payment (of interest and principal) totaling $3,652 a year for 40 years.[2]

Predictions of the Theory

In deciding whether to attend college, no doubt few students make the very precise calculations suggested in expression (9.2). Nevertheless, if they make less formal estimates that take into account the same factors, we can make four predictions concerning the demand for college education:

1. Present-oriented people are less likely to go to college than forward-looking people (other things equal).
2. Most college students will be young.
3. College attendance will decrease if the costs of college rise (other things equal).
4. College attendance will increase if the gap between the earnings of college graduates and high school graduates widens (again, other things equal).

Present-Orientedness   Though we all discount the future somewhat with respect to the present, psychologists use the term *present-oriented* to describe people who do not weight future events or outcomes very heavily. In terms of expressions (9.1) and (9.2), a present-oriented person is one who uses a very high discount rate (r).

Suppose we were to calculate investment returns using the *present-value method*. If r is large, the present value of benefits associated with college will be lower than if r is smaller. Thus, a present-oriented person would impute smaller benefits to college attendance than one who is less present-oriented, and those who are more present-oriented are less likely to attend college. Using the *internal rate of return method* for evaluating the soundness of a college education, we would arrive at the same result. If a college education earns an 8 percent rate of return but the individuals in question are so present-oriented that they would insist on a 25 percent rate of return before investing, they would likewise decide not to attend.

---

[2]This calculation is made using the annuity formula:

$$Y = X \ \frac{1 - [1/(1 + r)^n]}{r}$$

where Y = the total investment ($100,000 in our example), X = the yearly payment ($3,652), r = the rate of interest (0.02), and n = the number of years (40). In this example, we treat the costs of a college education as being incurred all in one year rather than being spread out over four, a simplification that does not alter the magnitude of required returns much at all.

The prediction that present-oriented people are less likely to attend college than forward-looking ones is difficult to substantiate because the rates of discount that people use in making investment decisions can rarely be quantified.[3] However, the model does suggest that people who have a high propensity to invest in education will also engage in other forward-looking behavior. Certain medical statistics tend to support this prediction.

In the United States there is a strong statistical correlation between education and health status.[4] People with more years of schooling have lower mortality rates, fewer symptoms of disease (such as high blood pressure, high cholesterol levels, abnormal X-rays), and a greater tendency to report themselves to be in good health. This effect of education on health is independent of income, which appears to have no effect of its own on health status except at the lowest poverty levels. Is this correlation between education and health a result of better use of medical resources by the well-educated? It appears not. Better-educated people undergoing surgery choose the same doctors, enter the hospital at the same stage of disease, and have the same length of stay as less-educated people of equal income.

What *may* cause this correlation is a more forward-looking attitude among those who have obtained more education. People with lower discount rates will be more likely to attend college, and they will *also* be more likely to adopt forward-looking habits of health. They may choose healthier diets, be more aware of health risks, and make more use of preventive medicine. This explanation for the correlation between education and health is not the only plausible one, but it receives some direct support from American data on cigarette smoking.[5] From 1966 to 1987, the proportion of male college graduates who smoked fell by 50 percent, while it was unchanged among male high school dropouts. It is unlikely that the less-educated group was uninformed of smoking dangers; it is more likely that they were less willing to give up a present source of pleasure for a distant benefit. Thus, we have at least some evidence that people who invest in education also engage in *other* forward-looking behavior.

Age   Given similar *yearly* benefits of going to college, young people have a larger present value of *total* benefits than older workers simply because they have a longer

---

[3]A recent study infers personal discount rates from the choices of separation-pay options made by members of the military being separated for budget reasons. It finds that those officers with graduate degrees had lower discount rates than officers without, and that college-educated officers had lower discount rates than enlisted personnel (who generally do not have college educations). See John T. Warner and Saul Pleeter, "The Personal Discount Rate: Evidence from Military Downsizing Programs," *American Economic Review* 91, no. 1 (March 2001): 33–53.

[4]The analysis of the correlation between education and health status is taken from Victor Fuchs, "The Economics of Health in a Post-Industrial Society," *The Public Interest* (Summer 1979): 3–20.

[5]It could be, for example, that healthy people, with longer life spans, are more likely to invest in human capital because they expect to experience a longer payback period. Alternatively, we could argue that the higher incomes of college graduates later in life mean they have more to lose from illness than do non-college graduates. Data on smoking are from U.S. Department of Health and Human Services, Public Health Service, *Smoking Tobacco and Health*, DHHS publication no. (CDC)87–8397, October 1989, 5.

remaining work life ahead of them. In terms of expression (9.2), T is greater for younger people than for older ones. We would therefore expect younger people to have a greater propensity than older people to obtain a college education or engage in other forms of training activity. This prediction is parallel to the predictions in chapter 5 about which workers employers will decide to invest in when they make decisions about hiring or specific training.

Costs   A third prediction of our model is that human capital investments are more likely when costs are lower. The major monetary costs of college attendance are forgone earnings and the direct costs of tuition, books, and fees. (Food and lodging are not always opportunity costs of going to college because some of these costs would have to be incurred in any event.) Thus, if forgone earnings or tuition costs fall, other things equal, we would expect a rise in college enrollments.[6]

The costs of college attendance are an additional reason why older people are less likely to attend than younger ones. As workers age, their greater experience and maturity result in higher wages and therefore greater opportunity costs of college attendance. Interestingly, however, as suggested by Example 9.2, college attendance by military veterans (who are older than the typical college student) has been responsive to the educational subsidies for which they are eligible.[7]

The subject of cost raises an interesting question: just who is *most* responsive to cost considerations? Economic theory postulates that, in any set of market transactions, some people are *at the margin*—meaning that they are close to the point of not transacting. Who are those for whom the decision to attend college is a close call? Our theoretical considerations suggest that, facing given monetary costs and post-college earnings, students with lower achievement levels (for whom learning is more difficult) or higher discount rates are more likely to be at the margin. Interestingly, studies looking at how the cost advantage of a hometown college affects college-attendance decisions find that the effects are largest for those who would be otherwise least likely to attend.[8]

Earnings Differentials   The fourth prediction of human capital theory is that the demand for education is positively related to the increases in lifetime earnings that a college education allows. Strictly speaking, it is the benefits one *expects* to receive that are critical to this decision, and the expected benefits

---

[6]See Orley Ashelfelter and Cecilia Rouse, "Income, Schooling, and Ability: Evidence from a New Sample of Identical Twins," *Quarterly Journal of Economics* 113, no. 1 (February 1998): 253–284, for evidence that lower costs of schooling among abler students drive them to obtain more schooling.

[7]Also see Joshua D. Angrist, "The Effect of Veterans' Benefits on Education and Earnings," *Industrial and Labor Relations Review* 46, no. 4 (July 1993): 637–652.

[8]C. A. Anderson, M. J. Bowman, and B. Tinto, *Where Colleges Are and Who Attends* (New York: McGraw-Hill, 1972); and David Card, "Using Geographic Variation in College Proximity to Estimate the Return to Schooling," in *Aspects of Labour Market Behavior: Essays in Honour of John Vanderkamp*, ed. L. N. Christofides, E. K. Grant, and R. Swindinsky (Toronto: University of Toronto Press, 1995).

EXAMPLE 9.2

Did the G.I. Bill Increase Educational Attainment for Returning World War II Vets?

Veterans returning from service in World War II were eligible to receive unprecedented federal support through the G.I. Bill if they chose to attend college. Benefits under the G.I. Bill substantially subsidized the costs of a college education, covering the tuition charged by almost all private and public universities and providing monthly stipends ranging from roughly 50 to 70 percent of the median income in the United States at the time. After the war, many veterans enrolled in college—and total college enrollments jumped by more than 50 percent from their pre-war levels. Over 2.2 million veterans attended college under the bill, accounting for about 70 percent of the male student body at the peak of the bill's usage. Because of these effects, Senator Ralph Yarborough called the World War II G.I. Bill "one of the most beneficial, far-reaching programs ever instituted in American life."

Did the G.I. Bill really have a big effect, or did it merely subsidize returning veterans who would have gone to college anyway? A recent article helps to answer this question by comparing the college attendance of male veterans to otherwise similar individuals. It finds that among high school graduates, World War II veterans completed an average of about 0.3 more years of college than did non-veterans, and that they had a 6 percentage-point greater college completion rate. Similar estimates were obtained when comparing those eligible for war service and G.I. Bill subsidies with those born too late to serve in the war.

The conclusions of this study are that the responses of veterans to the G.I. Bill's subsidies were quite similar to the contemporary responses of students to changes in tuition costs. In both cases, a 10 percent reduction in the cost to students of attending college resulted in a 4 or 5 percent increase in college attendance and completion.

Data from: John Bound and Sarah Turner, "Going to War and Going to College: Did the G.I. Bill Increase Educational Attainment?" *Journal of Labor Economics,* forthcoming, and Keith W. Olson, *The G.I. Bill, the Veterans, and the Colleges* (Lexington: University Press of Kentucky, 1974).

for any individual are rather uncertain. Future earnings can never be perfectly foretold, and in addition, many students are uncertain about their later occupational choice.[9] As a first approximation, however, it is reasonable to conjecture that the *average* returns received by recent college graduates have an important influence on students' decisions.

Dramatic changes in the average monetary returns to a college education over the past three decades are at least partially, if not largely, responsible for the changes in college enrollment rates noted earlier. It can be seen from the first and third columns of Table 9.1, for example, that the decline in male enrollment rates dur-

---

[9]For a study that incorporates uncertainty into the formal model of choice, see Joseph G. Altonji, "The Demand for and Return to Education When Education Outcomes Are Uncertain," *Journal of Labor Economics* 10 (January 1993): 48–83. For studies on the accuracy of students' knowledge about the salaries in various fields, or at various ages, see Julian R. Betts, "What Do Students Know about Wages? Evidence from a Survey of Undergraduates," and Jeff Dominitz and Charles F. Manski, "Eliciting Student Expectations of the Returns to Schooling," both in *Journal of Human Resources* 31, no. 1 (Winter 1996): 1–56.

TABLE 9.1 Changes in College Enrollments and the College/High School Earnings Differential, by Gender, 1970–1999

Year	College Enrollment Rates of New High School Graduates		Ratios of Mean Earnings of College to High School Graduates, Ages 25–34, Prior Year[a]	
	Male	*Female*	*Male*	*Female*
1970	55.2%	48.5%	1.38	1.42
1980	46.7	51.8	1.19	1.29
1990	57.8	62.0	1.48	1.59
1999	61.4	64.4	1.62	1.60

[a]For year-round, full-time workers. Data for the first two years are for personal income, not earnings; however, in the years for which both income and earnings are available, the ratios are essentially equal.

Sources: U.S. Department of Education, *Digest of Education Statistics 2000* (January 2001), Table 185; U.S. Bureau of the Census, *Money Income of Families and Persons in the United States,* Current Population Reports P–60, no. 66 (Table 41), no. 129 (Table 53), no. 174 (Table 29), no. 209 (Table 9).

ing the 1970s was correlated with a decline in the college/high school earnings differential, while the higher enrollment rates after 1980 were associated with larger earnings differentials.

The second and fourth columns of Table 9.1 document changes in enrollment rates and earnings differentials for women. Unlike enrollment rates for men, those for women rose throughout the three decades; however, it is notable that they rose most in the 1980s, when the college/high school earnings differential rose most sharply. Why did enrollment rates among women increase in the 1970s when the earnings differential fell? It is quite plausible that, despite the reduced earnings differential, the expected returns to education for women actually rose because of increases in their intended labor force attachment and hours of work outside the home (both of which increase the period over which the earnings differential will be received).[10]

While changes in average earnings differentials are a useful indicator of relative labor market conditions, individuals must assess their *own* probabilities of success in specific fields or occupations. Recent studies have pointed to the

---

[10]For evidence that women with "traditional" views of their economic roles receive lower rates of return on, and invest less in, human capital, see Francis Vella, "Gender Roles and Human Capital Investment: The Relationship between Traditional Attitudes and Female Labour Market Performance," *Economica* 61, no. 242 (May 1994): 191–211. For an interesting analysis of historical trends in female college attendance, see Claudia Goldin, "Career and Family: College Women Look to the Past," in *Gender and Family Issues in the Workplace*, ed. Francine D. Blau and Ronald G. Ehrenberg (New York: Russell Sage Foundation, 1997): 20–58.

importance of friends, ethnic affiliation, and neighborhoods in the human capital decisions of individuals, even after controlling for the effects of parental income or education.[11] The educational and occupational choices of friends and acquaintances appear to have a significant effect on an individual's human capital decisions, perhaps because the presence of role models helps to reduce the uncertainty that inevitably surrounds estimates of future success in specific areas.

Market Responses to Changes in College Attendance

Like other market prices, the returns to college attendance are determined by the forces of both employer demand and employee supply. If more high school students decide to attend college when presented with higher returns to such an investment, market forces are put into play that will tend to lower these returns in the future. Increased numbers of college graduates put downward pressure on the wages observed in labor markets for these graduates, other things equal, while a smaller number of high school graduates will tend to raise wages in markets for less-educated workers.

Thus, adding to uncertainties about expected payoffs to an investment in college is the fact that current returns may be an unreliable estimate of future returns. A high return now might motivate an individual to opt for college, but it will also cause many *others* to do likewise. An influx of college graduates in four years could put downward pressure on returns at that time, which reminds us that all investments—even human-capital ones—involve outlays now and uncertain returns in the future. (For an analysis of how the labor market might respond when workers behave as if the returns observed currently will persist into the future, see Appendix 9A.)

EDUCATION, EARNINGS, AND POSTSCHOOLING INVESTMENTS IN HUMAN CAPITAL

The preceding section used human capital theory to analyze the decision to undertake a formal educational program (college) on a full-time basis. We now turn to an analysis of workers' decisions to acquire training at work. The presence of on-the-job training is difficult for the economist to directly observe; much of it is informal and not publicly recorded. We can, however, use human capital theory and certain patterns in workers' lifetime earnings to draw inferences about their demand for this type of training.

Figures 9.3 and 9.4 graph the 1999 earnings of men and women of various ages with different levels of education. These figures reveal four notable characteristics:

---

[11]For a recent study, see Ira N. Gang and Klaus F. Zimmermann, "Is Child Like Parent? Educational Attainment and Ethnic Origin," *Journal of Human Resources* 35, no. 3 (Summer 2000): 550–569.

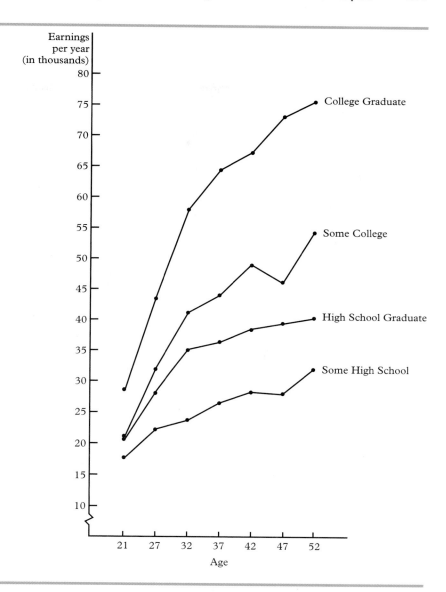

FIGURE 9.3
Money Earnings (Mean), for Full-Time, Year-Round Male Workers, 1999

Earnings per year (in thousands)

College Graduate

Some College

High School Graduate

Some High School

Age

Source: See footnote 12.

1. Average earnings of full-time workers rise with the level of education.
2. The most rapid increase in earnings occurs early, thus giving a concave shape to the age/earnings profiles of both men and women.
3. Age/earnings profiles tend to fan out, so that education-related earnings differences later in workers' lives are greater than those early on.

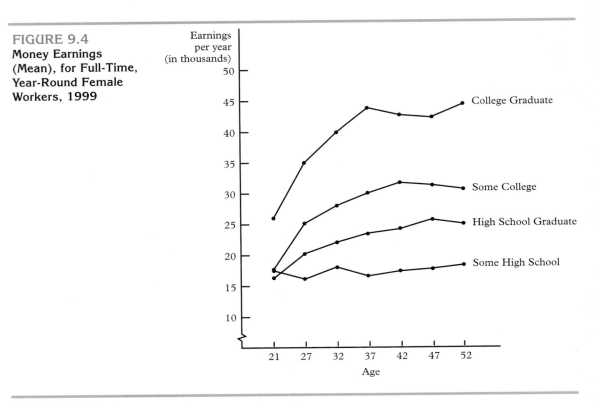

FIGURE 9.4

Money Earnings (Mean), for Full-Time, Year-Round Female Workers, 1999

Source: See footnote 12.

4. The age/earnings profiles of men tend to be more concave and to fan out more than those for women.

Can human capital theory help explain the above empirical regularities?

Average Earnings and Educational Level

Our *investment* model of educational choice implies that earnings rise with the level of education, for if they did not, the incentives for students to invest in more education would disappear. It is thus not too surprising to see in Figures 9.3 and 9.4 that the average earnings of more-educated workers exceed those of less-educated workers.

Remember, however, that *earnings* are influenced by both wage rates and hours of work. Data on *wage rates* are probably most relevant when we look at the returns to an educational investment, because they indicate pay per unit of time at work. Wage data, however, are less widely available than earnings data. A crude, but readily available, way to control for working hours when using earnings data is to focus on full-time, year-round workers—which we do in Figures 9.3 and 9.4. More careful statistical analyses, however, which control for hours of work and factors other than education that can increase wage rates, come to the same conclusion suggested by Figures 9.3 and 9.4: namely, that more education is associated with higher pay. (A more rigorous theoretical analysis of the association between education and pay can be found in Appendix 9B, which presents the analysis in the context of hedonic wage theory.)

On-the-Job Training and the Concavity of Age/Earnings Profiles

The age/earnings profiles in Figures 9.3 and 9.4 typically rise steeply early on, then tend to flatten.[12] In fact, the early increases are so steep relative to those later on that a study of men's wage rates found that two-thirds of their *career* wage growth occurred in their first ten years of work![13] While in the next two chapters we will encounter other potential explanations for why earnings rise in this way with age, human capital theory explains the concavity of these profiles in terms of *on-the-job training*.[14]

Training Declines with Age   Training on the job can occur through learning by doing (skills improving with practice), through formal training programs at or away from the workplace, or by informally working under the tutelage of a more experienced worker. All forms entail reduced productivity among trainees during the learning process, and both formal and informal training also involve a commitment of time by those who serve as trainers or mentors. Training costs are either shared by workers and the employer, as with specific training, or are borne mostly by the employee (in the case of general training).

From the perspective of workers, training depresses wages during the learning period but allows them to rise with enhanced productivity afterwards. Thus, workers who opt for jobs that require a training investment are willing to accept

---

[12]Data in these figures are from U.S. Bureau of the Census, *Money Income in the United States*, Current Population Reports P-60, no. 209, Table 9; they match average earnings with age and education in a given year and do not follow individuals through time. For a study using longitudinal data on specific individuals, see Richard W. Johnson and David Neumark, "Wage Declines and Older Men," *Review of Economics and Statistics* 78, no. 4 (November 1996): 740–748.

[13]Kevin M. Murphy and Finis Welch, "Empirical Age–Earnings Profiles," *Journal of Labor Economics* 8 (April 1990): 202–229.

[14]For discussions of the relative importance of the human capital explanation for rising age/earnings profiles, see Ann P. Bartel, "Training, Wage Growth, and Job Performance: Evidence from a Company Database," *Journal of Labor Economics* 13, no. 3 (July 1995): 401–425; Charles Brown, "Empirical Evidence on Private Training," in *Research in Labor Economics*, vol. 11, ed. Lauri J. Bassi and David L. Crawford (Greenwich, Conn.: JAI Press, 1990), 97–114; and Jacob Mincer, "The Production of Human Capital and the Life Cycle of Earnings: Variations on a Theme," *Journal of Labor Economics* 15, no. 1, pt. 2 (January 1997): S26–S47.

FIGURE 9.5

Investment in On-the-Job Training over the Life Cycle

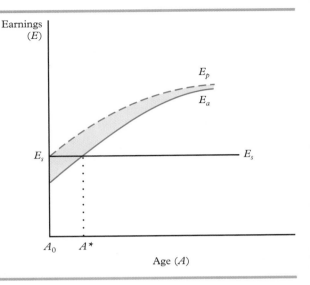

lower wages in the short run to get higher pay later on. As with other human-capital investments, returns are generally larger when the post-investment period is longer, so we would expect workers' investments in on-the-job training to be greatest at younger ages and to fall gradually as they grow older.

Figure 9.5 graphically depicts the life-cycle implications of human capital theory as it applies to on-the-job training. The individual depicted has completed full-time schooling and is able to earn E_s at age A_0. Without further training, if the knowledge and skills the worker possesses do not depreciate over time, earnings would remain at E_s over the life cycle. If the worker chooses to invest in on-the-job training, his or her future earnings potential can be enhanced, as shown by the (dashed) curve E_p in the figure. Investment in on-the-job training, however, has the near-term consequence that actual earnings are below potential; thus, in terms of Figure 9.5, actual earnings (E_a) lie below E_p as long as the worker is investing. In fact, the gap between E_p and E_a equals the worker's investment costs.

Figure 9.5 is drawn to reflect the theoretical implication, noted above, that human capital investments decline with age. With each succeeding year, actual earnings become closer to potential earnings; further, because workers become less willing to invest in human capital as they age, the yearly *increases* in potential earnings become smaller and smaller. Thus, curve E_p takes on a concave shape, quickly rising above E_s but flattening later in the life cycle. Curve E_a (which is what we observe in Figures 9.3 and 9.4) takes on its concave shape for the same reasons.

The "Overtaking" Age   For those who invest in on-the-job training, actual earnings start below E_s, approach it near age A^*, and continue to rise above it afterwards. Age A^* is called the *overtaking age*, and it is the age at which workers with the same level of schooling have equivalent earnings regardless of whether they have invested in on-the-job training. The concept of an overtaking age has an interesting empirical implication.

We can observe educational levels workers possess, but we cannot observe workers' E_p or the time they have spent in on-the-job training. Thus, when we use statistical methods to analyze earnings differences across individuals, the correlation between earnings and education will be strongest at A^*, where $E_a = E_s$. Why? The correlation between schooling and earnings is weakened both before and after A^* by the presence of on-the-job training, which we cannot measure and for which we cannot therefore statistically control. Interestingly, we find that educational and earnings levels correlate most strongly at about ten years after labor market entry.[15] This finding offers support for the human-capital explanation of age-earnings profiles based on job training.

The Fanning Out of Age/Earnings Profiles

Earnings differences across workers with different educational backgrounds tend to become more pronounced as they age. This phenomenon is also consistent with what human capital theory would predict.

Investments in human capital tend to be more likely when the expected earnings differentials are greater, when the initial investment costs are lower, and when the investor has either a longer time to recoup the returns or a lower discount rate. The same can be said of people who have the ability to learn more quickly. The ability to learn rapidly shortens the training period, and fast learners probably also experience lower psychic costs (lower levels of frustration) during training.

Thus, people who have the ability to learn quickly are those most likely to seek out, and be presented by employers with, training opportunities. But who are these fast learners? They are most likely the people who, because of their abilities, were best able to reap benefits from formal schooling! Thus, human capital theory leads us to expect that workers who invested more in schooling will also invest more in postschooling job training.[16]

The tendency of the better-educated workers to invest more in job training explains why their age/earnings profiles start low, rise quickly, and keep rising after the profiles of their less-educated counterparts have leveled off. Their earnings rise more quickly because they are investing more heavily in job training,

---

[15]See Jacob Mincer, *Schooling, Experience, and Earnings* (New York: Columbia University Press for National Bureau of Economic Research, 1974), 57. For other evidence consistent with the human capital model summarized in Figure 9.5, see David Neumark and Paul Taubman, "Why Do Wage Profiles Slope Upward? Tests of the General Human Capital Model," *Journal of Labor Economics* 13, no. 4 (October 1995): 736–761.

[16]For studies showing that on-the-job training is positively correlated with both educational level and ability, see Joseph G. Altonji and James R. Spletzer, "Worker Characteristics, Job Characteristics, and the Receipt of On-the-Job Training," *Industrial and Labor Relations Review* 45 (October 1991): 58–79; and Joseph Hight, "Younger Worker Participation in Post-School Education and Training," *Monthly Labor Review* 121, no. 6 (June 1998): 14–21.

and they rise for a longer time for the same reason. In other words, people with the ability to learn quickly select the ultimately high-paying jobs where much learning is required and thus put their abilities to greatest advantage.

Women and the Acquisition of Human Capital

A comparison of Figures 9.3 and 9.4 discloses immediately that the earnings of women who work full-time year-round are lower than for men of equivalent age and education, and that women's earnings within each educational group rise less steeply with age. The purpose of this section is to analyze these differences in the context of human capital theory (a more complete analysis of male/female wage differentials is presented in chapter 12).

A major difference in the incentives of men and women to make human capital investments has historically been in the length of work life over which the costs of a human capital investment can be recouped. Chapters 6 and 7 clearly showed how rapidly working for pay has increased among women in recent decades, and this fact obviously should have made human capital investments more lucrative for women. Nevertheless, Table 9.2 shows it is still the case that, on average, women can be expected to work (for pay) fewer years than men. In addition, Table 9.2 indicates that within the occupations shown—all of which require the acquisition of skills—women average fewer hours of work per week than do men.

To the extent that there is a shorter expected work life for women than for men, it is caused primarily by the role women have historically played in child-rearing and household production. This traditional role, while undergoing significant change, has caused many women to drop out of the labor market for a period of time in their childbearing years. Thus, female workers often have not had the continuity of experience that their male counterparts accumulate. If this historical experience causes younger women who are making important human capital decisions to expect a discontinuity in their own labor force participation, they might understandably avoid occupations or fields of study in which their skills depreciate during the period out of the labor market.[17] Moreover, historical experience could cause employers to avoid hiring women for jobs requiring much on-the-job training—a practice that itself will reduce the returns women can expect from a human capital investment. Human capital theory, however, *also* predicts that recent changes in the labor force participation of women, especially married women of childbearing age, are causing dramatic changes in the acquisition of schooling and training by women. We turn now to a discussion of recent changes in these two areas.

---

[17]For a discussion of the wage losses facing women who interrupt their labor force attachment at childbirth, see Jane Waldfogel, "Understanding the 'Family Gap' in Pay for Women with Children," *Journal of Economic Perspectives* 12, no. 1 (Winter 1998): 137–156. Losses were also suffered by men who involuntarily withdrew from their careers by being drafted into military service during the Vietnam War; see Joshua D. Angrist, "Lifetime Earnings and the Vietnam Era Draft Lottery: Evidence from Social Security Administrative Records," *American Economic Review* 80 (June 1990): 313–336.

TABLE 9.2 Average Work Life and Hours of Work, by Gender		
Remaining Expected Years of Paid Work at Age 25[a]:	*Male*	*Female*
High school graduates	33.4 (years)	27.3 (years)
Some college	34.5	29.5
College graduates	35.8	31.7
Average Weekly Hours of Paid Work for Those Working Full-Time in 2000:		
Executive, administrative, managerial workers	47.7 (hours)	43.3 (hours)
Professional specialty workers	45.8	42.1
Technicians and related support workers	43.9	40.6
Sales workers	46.6	41.8
Precision production, craft, and repair workers	43.4	41.4

[a]Data relate to nondisabled individuals in 1994.
Sources: Anthony M. Gamboa, "The New Worklife Expectancy Tables," Vocational Econometrics, Louisville, Kentucky (1995); U.S. Bureau of Labor Statistics, *Employment and Earnings* 48 (January 2001), Table 23.

Women and Job Training   There is little doubt that women receive less on-the-job training than men, although the gap is probably narrowing. The most recent survey of employer-provided training found that, during a six-month period in 1995, women reported receiving 41.5 hours of both formal and informal training, while men received 47.6 hours; differences were mainly in the area of informal training.[18] To the extent that on-the-job training causes age/earnings profiles to be concave, an explanation for the flatter age/earnings profiles of women may be rooted in their lower levels of such training.

This human capital explanation for the flatter age/earnings profiles among women does not directly address whether the lower levels of job training emanate from the employer or the employee side of the market, but both possibilities are theoretically plausible. If employers expect women workers to have shorter work

---

[18]H. Frazis, M. Gittleman, M. Horrigan, and M. Joyce, "Results from the 1995 Survey of Employer-Provided Training," *Monthly Labor Review* 121, no. 6 (June 1998): 3–13.

FIGURE 9.6
**The Increased
Concavity
of Women's
Age/Earnings Profiles**

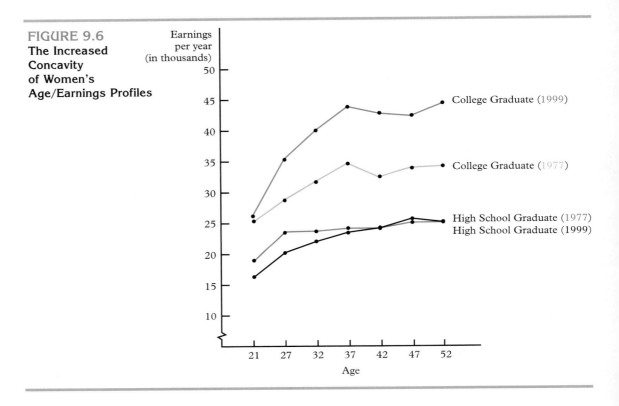

lives, they are less likely to provide training to them. Alternatively, if women themselves expect shorter work lives, they will be less inclined to seek out jobs requiring high levels of training. Finally, if women expect employers to bar them from occupations requiring a lot of training or experience, incentives to enter these occupations will be diminished.[19]

While human capital theory predicts that the traditional role of women in child-rearing will lead to reduced incentives for training investments, it also suggests that as this role changes, the incentives for women to acquire training will change. We should thus expect to observe a growing concavity in women's age/earnings profiles over the past decades, and Figure 9.6 indicates that this expectation is generally supported.

The darker lines in Figure 9.6 are the 1999 profiles for college and high school graduates that appeared in Figure 9.4. The lighter lines indicate the comparable

---

[19]Francine D. Blau and Marianne A. Ferber, "Career Plans and Expectations of Young Women and Men," *Journal of Human Resources* 26 (Fall 1991): 581–607, found that female college seniors, who expected starting salaries equal to those expected by men, expected much lower salaries later in their careers.

TABLE 9.3 Percentages of Women among College and University Graduates, by Degree and Field of Study, 1971 and 1998

Percentage of Women among:	Bachelor's Degree		Master's Degree	
	1971	*1998*	*1971*	*1998*
Total	43.4%	56.1%	40.1%	57.1%
Business majors	9.1	48.5	3.9	38.6
Computer science majors	13.6	26.7	10.3	29.0
Education majors	74.5	75.2	56.2	76.4
Engineering majors	0.8	18.5	1.1	19.8
English majors	66.7	66.8	61.0	66.1
Health professionals	77.1	82.1	55.9	77.7
First professional degree[a]			6.3	42.9

[a]Degrees in this category are largely doctor's degrees in law, medicine, and dentistry.
Sources: U.S. National Center for Education Statistics, *Digest of Education Statistics 1993* (1993), Tables 235, 269, 271–273, 275, 278; *Digest of Education Statistics 2000* (2001), Tables 266, 269, 274.

profiles for 1977 (adjusted to 1999 dollars using the Consumer Price Index). A visual comparison reveals that the earnings profiles for both high school and college graduates have become steeper for women in their 20s and 30s, especially among the college educated. This faster earnings growth among women at the early stages of their careers suggests that they may be receiving more on-the-job training than they did two decades ago.

Women and Formal Schooling As Table 9.1 suggested, there have been dramatic changes in the level of formal education received by women in recent years. Their fields of study have also changed markedly. These changes undoubtedly reflect the increased returns to human capital investments arising from women's increased attachment to the labor force and longer expected work lives. Table 9.3 outlines some of the magnitudes of these changes.

Women, who traditionally were less likely than men to graduate from college, now represent well over half of both bachelor's and master's graduates. There also have been dramatic shifts in the fields in which women major, most notably in the areas of business (graduate and undergraduate), law, and medicine—where women have gone from under 10 percent of all majors to roughly 40 percent or more. While still underrepresented in computer science and engineering, women have posted gains in these areas as well.[20] What the data in Table 9.3 suggest is that

---

[20]A study that measures gender changes in undergraduate majors differently, however, concludes that, aside from business majors, changes since the 1970s have not been dramatic. See Sarah E. Turner and William G. Bowen, "Choice of Major: The Changing (Unchanging) Gender Gap," *Industrial and Labor Relations Review* 52, no. 2 (January 1999): 289–313.

women's expected labor force attachment has grown so fast that investing in technical degrees has become more attractive over the last three decades.

IS EDUCATION A GOOD INVESTMENT?

The question whether more education would be a good investment is one that concerns both individuals and government policymakers. Individuals ask, "Will I increase my monetary and psychic income enough to justify the costs of additional education?" Governments must decide if the expected social benefits of enhanced productivity outweigh the opportunity costs of investing more social resources in the educational sector. We pointed out earlier that these questions can be answered using either the *present-value* method (an illustration of which is in Example 9.3) or the *internal rate of return* method. The latter is primarily used in the subsections that follow.

Is Education a Good Investment for Individuals?

Individuals about to make an investment in a college education are typically committing themselves to costs of at least $18,000 per year. Is there evidence that this investment pays off for the typical student? Several studies have tried to answer this question by calculating the internal rates of return to educational investments. While the methods and data used vary, these studies normally estimate benefits by calculating earnings differentials at each age from age/earnings profiles such as those in Figures 9.3 and 9.4. (*Earnings* are usually used to measure benefits because higher wages and more stable jobs are both payoffs to more education.) All such studies have analyzed only the monetary, not the psychic, costs of and returns on educational investments.

The rates of return to education typically estimated for the average American worker fall into the range of 5–12 percent (after adjusting for inflation), although they may vary across individuals with such factors as parental background, school quality, and even the level of education (as will be seen later in Example 9.4).[21] These findings are interesting because most other investments generate returns in the same range. Thus, it appears, at least at first glance, that an investment in education is about as good as an investment in stocks, bonds, or real estate. This conclusion must be qualified, however, by recognizing that there are potential biases in the estimated rates of return to education. These biases, which are of unknown size, work in opposite directions.

The Upward Bias   The typical estimates of the rate of return on further schooling may overstate the gain an individual student could obtain by investing in education because they do not distinguish between the contribution that *ability*

---

[21]See David Card, "The Causal Effect of Education on Earnings," in *Handbook of Labor Economics*, ed. Orley Ashenfelter and David Card (New York: Elsevier, 1999), pp. 1802–1863, for a comprehensive review of recent estimates of the rates of return to educational investments.

EXAMPLE 9.3

Valuing a Human Asset:
The Case of the Divorcing Doctor

State divorce laws typically provide for the assets acquired during marriage to be divided in some equitable fashion. Among the assets to be divided is often the value of human capital investments made by either spouse during marriage. How these acquired human capital values are estimated can be illustrated by the following example.

Dr. Doe married right after he had acquired a license to practice as a general practitioner. Instead of opening a general (family) practice, however, Dr. Doe undertook specialized training to become a surgeon. During his training (residency) period, the income of Dr. Doe and his wife was much lower than it would have been had he been working as a general practitioner. Thus both spouses were investing, albeit to different degrees, in Dr. Doe's human capital.

Shortly after his residency was completed and he had acquired board certification as a general surgeon, Dr. Doe and his wife decided to divorce. She sued him for an equitable division of the asset value of his certification as a general surgeon. How can this asset value be estimated?

The asset value of Dr. Doe's certificate as a general surgeon is the present value of his estimated *increase in lifetime earnings* this certificate made possible. The most reasonable estimate of his increase in yearly earnings is calculated by subtracting from what the typical general surgeon earns the average earnings of general practitioners (which is an estimate of what Dr. Doe could have earned in the absence of his training as a surgeon).

In 1997, the median earnings of general surgeons were $217,000 and those of general practitioners were $132,000. Thus, assuming Dr. Doe is an "average" doctor, obtaining his certificate as a surgeon increased his earnings capacity by $85,000 per year in 1997 dollars.* Assuming a remaining work life of 25 years and a real interest rate (which takes account of what inflation will do to the earnings differential) of 2 percent, the present value of the asset Dr. Doe acquired as the result of his surgical training comes to $1,658,000. (It would then be up to the court to divide this asset equitably between the two divorcing spouses.)

---

*Earnings data are from U.S. Department of Labor, Bureau of Labor Statistics, *Occupational Outlook Handbook, 2000–01 Edition* (Government Printing Office, 2000), p. 195. The formula used to calculate present value is the one given in footnote 2 of this chapter, where $X = \$85,000$, $r = 0.02$, and $n = 25$.

---

makes to higher earnings and the contribution made by *schooling*.[22] The problem is that (*a*) people who are smarter, harder-working, and more dynamic are likely to obtain more schooling, and (*b*) such people might be more productive, and hence earn higher-than-average wages, even if they did not complete more years of schooling than others. When measures of true ability are not observed or accounted for, the studies attribute *all* the earnings differentials associated with college to college itself and none to ability, even though *some* of the added

---

[22]If investments in education have a rate of return comparable to alternative investments people could make, they will raise wages more than overall wealth—which (recalling chapters 6 and 7) should cause hours of work to rise. Thus, some of the increased earnings from more education could be associated with reduced leisure, which would constitute another source of upward bias. This point is made by C. M. Lindsay, "Measuring Human Capital Returns," *Journal of Political Economy* 79 (November/December 1971): 1195–1215.

earnings college graduates typically receive may have been received by an equally able high school graduate who did not attend college.

Recent studies that attempt to control for *ability bias* in estimating rates of return to schooling have utilized several strategies. Some have estimated the separate effects of schooling and aptitude-test scores on earnings. Others have estimated how much the earnings of people are affected when a random event, not ability, affects their level of schooling. Still others analyze differences among family members, who have the same family background, and even among identical twins, who share the same inherited characteristics. These studies generally conclude that the problem of ability bias in conventional estimates is small.[23]

The Downward Bias There are three reasons to believe that conventionally estimated rates of return to educational investments may be downward biased. First, some benefits of college attendance are not necessarily reflected in higher productivity, but rather in an increased ability to understand and appreciate the behavioral, historical, and philosophical foundations of human existence. Second, most rate-of-return studies fail to include employee benefits; they measure money earnings, not total compensation. Because employee benefits as a percentage of total compensation tend to rise as money earnings rise, ignoring benefits tends to create a downward bias in the estimation of rates of return to education.

Third, some of the job-related rewards of college are captured in the form of psychic or nonmonetary benefits. Jobs in the executive or professional occupations are probably more interesting and pleasant than the more routine jobs typically available to people with less education. While executive and professional jobs do pay more than others, the total benefits of these jobs may be understated when only earnings differences are analyzed.

Selection Bias A third source of bias in the standard estimates of rates of return on education arises from the *selectivity* problem. Briefly put, a person who decides to go to college and become a manager, rather than terminate schooling with high school and become a mechanic, may do so in part because he or she has very little mechanical aptitude; thus, becoming a mechanic might yield this person *less* income than is earned by those who actually become mechanics. Likewise, those who become mechanics rather than go to college and become managers might not have aptitudes that would allow them to earn much as managers.

To understand the potential selectivity biases in the conventionally calculated returns to a college education, keep in mind that these returns are usually based on differences between the actual earnings of college and high school graduates. For people who graduated from college, the rate-of-return calculation thus assumes that, in the absence of a college education, their earnings would have been equal to those of the average high school graduate. If, instead, their earnings would have

[23]See Card, "The Causal Effect of Education on Earnings," for a comprehensive review of studies that attempt to correct for ability bias.

been *less* than those of the high school graduate, the conventional calculation *understates* their gains from a college investment.

Does the conventionally calculated rate of return to college indicate the yield mechanics would have obtained had they gone to college to become managers? It does not, because this calculation assumes that they would have been able to earn as much as the average manager. Thus, while the conventional calculations underestimate the returns for those who actually go to college, they overestimate the returns that would have been received by those who decided not to go.

Fortunately, the selectivity bias in estimated rates of return to schooling appears to be small.[24] Nevertheless, raising the selectivity issue does serve to remind us that the principle of comparative advantage is potentially important in making choices about schooling and occupations.

Is Education a Good Social Investment?

The issue of education as a social investment has been of heightened interest in the United States during the past decade, especially because of three related developments. First, product markets have become more global, increasing the elasticity of both product and labor demand. As a result, American workers are now facing more competition from workers in other countries. Second, the growing availability of high-technology capital has created new products and production systems that may require workers to have greater cognitive skills and to be more adaptable, efficient learners.[25] Third, American elementary and secondary school students have scored poorly relative to students elsewhere in language proficiency, scientific knowledge, and (especially) mathematical skills.[26]

The combination of these three developments has led to concern about the productivity of America's future workforce, relative to workers elsewhere, and to a series of questions about our educational system. Are we devoting enough resources to educating our current and future workforce? Should the resources we devote to education be reallocated in some way? Should we demand more of students in elementary and secondary schools?

---

[24]The discussion in this subsection is based on Robert J. Willis and Sherwin Rosen, "Education and Self-Selection," *Journal of Political Economy* 87 (October 1979): S7–S36. For discussion of how selectivity based on discount rate affects the measured rates of return to education, see David Card, "Estimating the Return to Schooling: Progress on Some Persistent Econometric Problems," *Econometrica* 69, no. 5 (September 2001): 1127–1160.

[25]For recent studies on the earnings of those with greater cognitive skills, see Richard J. Murnane, John B. Willett, and Frank Levy, "The Growing Importance of Cognitive Skills in Wage Determination," *Review of Economics and Statistics* 77, no. 2 (May 1995): 251–266; and John Cawley, James Heckman, and Edward Vytlacil, "Understanding the Role of Cognitive Ability in Accounting for the Recent Rise in the Economic Return to Education," in *Meritocracy and Economic Inequality*, ed. Kenneth Arrow, Samuel Bowles, and Steven Durlauf (Princeton: Princeton University Press, 2000).

[26]National Center for Education Statistics, *The Condition of Education 1998* (NCES 98-013, October 1998), p. 76.

TABLE 9.4   **International Comparisons of Schooling, 1997–1998**

Country	Expenditures per Pupil, Secondary Level (in U.S. $)	% of Those, Ages 25–44, Who Have Completed	
		Secondary School	*University*
France	6,564	75%	15%
Germany	6,149	88	14
Japan	5,917	94	24
United Kingdom	4,609	63	17
United States	7,230	88	28

Source: National Center for Education Statistics, *The Condition of Education 2001* (NCES 2001-072), pp. 52, 178.

The Social Cost   As Table 9.4 indicates, the United States devotes at least as many resources to elementary and secondary education as do other developed countries. In terms of dollars per student, the United States ranks first among the five countries shown, and in terms of the percentages of the population completing secondary school, it ranks in the upper middle. Moreover, the percentage of the population completing college is higher than in every comparison country. Thus, with about 7 percent of its gross domestic product devoted to the direct costs of formal education (elementary, secondary, and college), and with forgone earnings (especially of college students) adding another 3 or 4 percent, the United States devotes a substantial fraction of its available resources to formal schooling.[27] Whether this huge social investment pays off and whether its returns can be enhanced are important questions. In beginning to answer them, we must try to understand how education and productivity are related.

The Social Benefit   The view that increased educational investments increase worker productivity is a natural outgrowth of the observation that such investments enhance the earnings of individuals who undertake them. However, this view that the educational investment is what *causes* productivity to rise is not the only possible interpretation for the positive relationship between earnings and schooling. Another interpretation is that the educational system provides society with a screening device that sorts people by their (predetermined) ability. As discussed below, this alternative view, in its extreme form, sees the educational system as a means of *finding out* who is productive, not of enhancing worker productivity.

---

[27]The forgone earnings of high school and college students have been estimated to equal 60 percent of the *direct* cost outlays at those schooling levels. See Theodore Schultz, *The Economic Value of Education* (New York: Columbia University Press, 1963).

The Signaling Model   An employer seeking to hire workers is never completely sure of the actual productivity of any applicant, and in many cases the employer may remain unsure long after an employee is hired. What an employer *can* observe are certain indicators that firms believe to be correlated with productivity: age, experience, education, and other personal characteristics. Some indicators, such as age, are immutable. Others, like formal education, can be *acquired* by workers. Indicators that can be acquired by individuals can be called *signals;* our analysis here will focus on the signaling aspect of formal education.

Let us suppose that firms wanting to hire new employees for particular jobs know that there are two groups of applicants that exist in roughly equal proportions. One group has a productivity of 2, let us say, and the other has a productivity of 1. Further, suppose that these productivity levels cannot be changed by education and that employers cannot readily distinguish which applicants are from which group. If they were unable to make such distinctions, firms would be forced to assume that all applicants are "average"; that is, they would have to assume that each had a productivity of 1.5 (and would offer them wages of up to 1.5).

While workers in this simple example would be receiving what they were worth on *average,* any firm that could devise a way to distinguish between the two groups (at little or no cost) could enhance its profits. When wages equal 1.5, workers with productivities equal to 1 are receiving more than they are worth. If these applicants could be discovered, and either rejected or placed into lower-paying jobs, the firm could obviously increase its profits. It turns out that using educational attainment as a hiring standard can increase profits even if education does not enhance productivity. We can illustrate this with a simple example.

An Illustration of Signaling   To illustrate the use of educational signaling, suppose that employers come to believe that applicants with at least e^* years of education beyond high school are the ones with productivity 2, and that those with less than e^* are in the lower-productivity group. With this belief, workers with less than e^* years would be rejected for any job paying a wage above 1, while those with at least e^* would find that competition among employers drives their wages up to 2. This simple wage structure is illustrated in Figure 9.7.[28] If additional schooling does not enhance productivity, can requiring the signal of e^* really distinguish between the two groups of applicants? The answer is yes *if the costs to the worker of acquiring the added schooling are negatively related to his or her on-the-job productivity.*

If workers with at least e^* years of education beyond high school can obtain a wage of 2, while those with less can earn a wage of only 1, all workers would want to acquire the signal of e^* if it were costless for them to do so. As we argued earlier, however, schooling costs are both large and different for different individuals. In particular, the psychic costs of education are probably inversely related to ability: those who learn easily can acquire the educational signal (of e^* in this case)

---

[28]This analysis is based on Michael Spence, "Job Market Signaling," *Quarterly Journal of Economics* 87 (August 1973): 205–221.

FIGURE 9.7
The Benefits to Workers of Educational Signaling

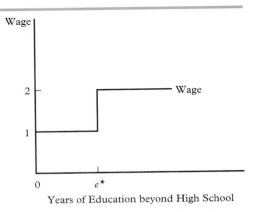

more cheaply than others. *If*—and this is critical—those who have *lower* costs of acquiring education are *also* more productive on the job, then requiring educational signals can be useful for employers.

To understand the role of costs in signaling, refer to Figure 9.8, in which the reward structure from Figure 9.7 is expressed in terms of the present value of life-time earnings (at a wage of 1 their discounted lifetime earnings sum to PVE_1, while at a wage of 2 they sum to PVE_2). Now assume that each year of education costs C for those with less productivity and $C/2$ for those with greater productivity.

Workers will choose the level of schooling at which the difference between their discounted lifetime earnings and their total educational costs is maximized. For those with yearly educational costs of C, the difference between lifetime earnings and total educational costs is maximized at zero years of education beyond high school. For these workers, the net benefit of an additional e^* years (distance BD) is less than the net benefit of zero additional years (distance $A0$). For them, the benefits of acquiring the signal of e^* years is not worth the added costs.

For those whose costs are $C/2$, it can be seen that the net benefits of invest-ing in e^* (distance BF) exceed the net benefits of other schooling choices. Therefore, only those with costs of $C/2$—the workers with productivities of 2—find it advan-tageous to acquire e^* years of schooling. In this example, then, schooling attainment signals productivity.

Some Cautions about Signaling   Our simple example demonstrated how edu-cation could have value even if it did not directly enhance worker productivity. It is necessary to stress, though, that for education to have signaling value in this case, on-the-job productivity and the costs of education must be *negatively* related. If the higher costs reflected along line C were associated with lower cognitive ability or a distaste for learning, then it is conceivable that these costs could be indicative of lower productivity. If, however, those with costs along C have higher costs only because of lower family wealth (and therefore smaller contributions from others

FIGURE 9.8

The Lifetime Benefits and Costs of Educational Signaling

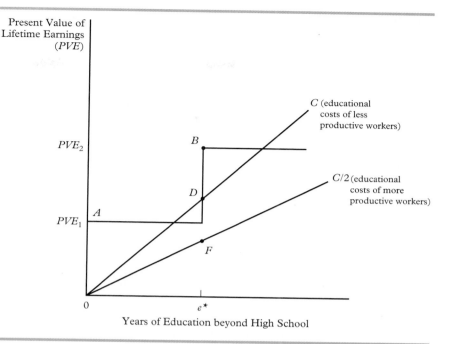

toward their schooling costs), then they may be no less productive on the job than those along line $C/2$. In this latter case, signaling would fail, because it would only indicate those with low family wealth, not lower productivity.

Even when educational signaling is a useful way to predict future productivity, there is an *optimum* signal beyond which society would not find it desirable to go. Suppose, for example, that employers now requiring e^* years for entry into jobs paying a wage of 2 were to raise their hiring standards to e' years, as shown in Figure 9.9. Those with educational costs along C would still find it in their best interests to remain at zero years of schooling beyond high school, and those with costs along $C/2$ would find it profitable to invest in the required signal of e' (because distance $B'F'$ is greater than $A0$). Requiring more schooling of those who are selected for high-wage jobs, however, is more costly for those workers (and thus for society as a whole). While the new required signal would distinguish between the two groups of workers, it would do so at increased (and unnecessary) costs to individuals, which cannot be socially optimal.

It clearly can be beneficial for individuals to invest in educational signals, but if schooling *only* has signaling value, is it a worthy investment for society to make? If the only purpose of schools is to provide signals, why encourage investments in the expansion or qualitative upgrading of schooling? If forty years ago being a high school graduate signaled above-average intelligence and work discipline, why

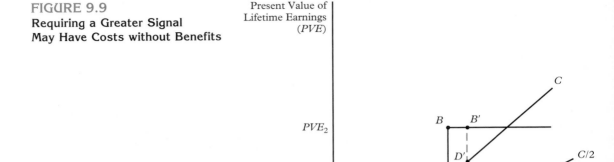

FIGURE 9.9

Requiring a Greater Signal May Have Costs without Benefits

incur the enormous costs of expanding college attendance only to find out that now these qualities are signaled by having a bachelor's degree? The issue is of even more importance in less-developed countries, where mistakes in allocating extremely scarce capital resources could be disastrous (see Example 9.4). Before attempting to decide if schooling has social value when all it produces are signals, let's first turn to the more basic question of whether we can figure out if schooling enhances, or merely signals, human capital.

Signaling or Human Capital?   Direct evidence on the role schooling plays in society is difficult to obtain. Advocates of the signaling viewpoint, for example, might point to the higher rates of return for college graduates than for college dropouts as evidence that schooling is a signaling device.[29] They argue that what is learned in school is proportional to the time spent there and that an added bonus (rate of return) just for a diploma is proof of the signaling hypothesis. Advocates of the view that schooling enhances human capital would counter that those who

---

[29]Dropouts naturally have lower earnings than graduates, but because they have also invested less, it is not clear that their *rates of return* should be lower. For further discussion and evidence, see David A. Jaeger and Marianne E. Page, "Degrees Matter: New Evidence on Sheepskin Effects in the Returns to Education," *Review of Economics and Statistics* 78, no. 4 (November 1996): 733–740. Thomas J. Kane and Cecilia Elena Rouse, "Comment on W. Norton Grubb: 'The Varied Economic Returns to Postsecondary Education: New Evidence from the Class of 1972'," *Journal of Human Resources* 30, no. 1 (Winter 1995): 205–221, calls into question the benefits of graduation independent of the number of *credits* taken.

EXAMPLE 9.4
The Socially Optimal Level of Educational Investment

In addition to asking whether schooling is a good social investment, we could also ask: What is the socially optimal *level* of schooling? The general principle guiding our answer to this question is that society should increase or reduce its educational investments until the marginal rate of return (to society) equals the marginal rate of return on other forms of capital investment (investment in physical capital, for example).

The rationale for the above principle is that if society has some funds it wants to invest, it will desire to invest them in projects yielding the highest rates of return. If an investment in physical capital yields a 20 percent rate of return and the same funds invested in schooling yield (all things considered) only a 10 percent return, society will clearly prefer to invest in physical capital. As long as the two rates of return differ, society could be made better off by reducing its investments in low-yield projects and increasing them in those with higher rates of return.

The text has discussed many of the difficulties and biases inherent in estimating rates of return to school-

ing. However, the general principle of equating the rates of social return on all forms of investments is still a useful one to consider. It suggests, for example, that capital-poor countries should invest in additional schooling only if the returns are very high—higher, in all probability, than the rates of return required for optimality in more-capital-rich countries.

Indeed, the rates of return to both secondary schooling and higher education appear to be generally higher in less-developed countries than in developed countries. One review estimated that the rate of return on secondary schooling investment was 10 percent for a developed country (on average), while for a less-developed country it was 13 to 15 percent. Comparable rates of return on investments in higher education were 8 percent and 11 percent, respectively.

Data from: George Psacharopoulos, "Returns to Investment in Education: A Global Update," *World Development* 22, no. 9 (1994): 1325–1343.

---

graduate after four years have learned more than four times what the freshman dropout has learned. They argue that dropouts are more likely to be poorer students—the ones who overestimated their returns on schooling and quit when they discovered their mistake. Thus, their relatively low rate of return is associated not with their dropping out but with their *reason* for dropping out.

To take another example, proponents of the human capital view could argue that the fact that earnings differentials between college and high school graduates grow with age supports their view. If schooling were just a signaling device, employers would rely on it *initially*, but as they accumulated direct information from experience with their employees, schooling would play a smaller role in determining earnings. Signaling advocates could counter that continued growth in earnings differentials only illustrates that educational attainment was a *successful* signaling device.[30]

---

[30]Attempts to distinguish between the two views include Joseph Altonji, "The Effects of High School Curriculum on Education and Labor Market Outcomes," *Journal of Human Resources* 30, no. 3 (Summer 1995): 409–438; Andrew Weiss, "Human Capital vs. Signaling Explanations of Wages," *Journal of Economic Perspectives* 9, no. 4 (Fall 1995): 133–154; Wim Groot and Hessel Oosterbeek, "Earnings Effects of Different Components of Schooling: Human Capital versus Screening," *Review of Economics and Statistics* 76, no. 2 (May 1994): 317–321; and Kelly Bedard, "Human Capital versus Signaling Models: University Access and High School Dropouts," *Journal of Political Economy* 109, no. 4 (August 2001): 749–775.

School Quality Given the difficulty of generating predictions of labor market outcomes that can directly distinguish the signaling from the human capital hypothesis, you may wonder if there are other ways to resolve the debate. A research strategy with some potential grows out of issues related to school quality.

As mentioned earlier, concerns have been raised about the cognitive achievement of American students. If schooling performs primarily a signaling function, by helping to *discover* people's cognitive abilities, we would not necessarily look to the educational system to remedy the problem of low cognitive achievement. However, if schooling can enhance the kinds of skills that pay off in the labor market, then increased investment in the quality of the nation's schools could be warranted.

Proponents of the signaling and human capital views of education can agree that people of higher cognitive ability are likely to be more productive; where they disagree is on whether better schools can enhance worker productivity by improving cognitive skills. Advocates of the signaling viewpoint cite a substantial literature suggesting it is difficult to demonstrate a relationship between schooling expenditures and student performance on *tests of cognitive skill*.[31] Advocates of the human capital view, however, find support in studies of *earnings* and school quality. These studies generally indicate that students attending higher-quality schools (that is, ones with greater resources per student) have higher subsequent earnings, other things equal.[32]

Clearly, assessments of the social returns to schooling that examine the role of school quality have so far yielded somewhat ambiguous results. Better schools may enhance labor market earnings, but evidence that they enhance measured cognitive abilities is relatively weak. One possibility, of course, is that better schools enhance productivity by teaching useful problem-solving skills or better work habits—characteristics that may be valued in the labor market but not captured especially well by standardized tests of cognitive achievement. Another possibility, however, is that better schools give students better information about their own interests and abilities, thus helping them to make more successful career choices. Some important questions, then, remain unanswered.

Does the Debate Matter? In the end, perhaps the debate between advocates of the signaling and human capital views of schooling is not terribly important. The fact is that schooling investments offer *individuals* monetary rates of return that are comparable to those received from other forms of investment. For individuals to recoup their human capital investment costs requires willingness on the part of employers to pay higher wages to people with more schooling; and for

---

[31]Eric A. Hanushek and Dennis D. Kimko, "Schooling, Labor Force Quality, and the Growth of Nations," *American Economic Review* 90, no. 5 (December 2000): 1184–1208. For a dissenting view, see Alan B. Krueger and Diane M. Whitmore, "Would Smaller Classes Help Close the Black-White Achievement Gap?" working paper no. 451, Industrial Relations Section, Princeton University, March 2001.

[32]For summaries of the lively debate on the effects of school quality on both cognitive skills and earnings, see the following symposium issues: *Federal Reserve Bank of New York Economic Policy Review* 4, no. 1 (March 1998); *Journal of Economic Perspectives* 10, no. 4 (Fall 1996); and *Review of Economics and Statistics* 78, no. 4 (November 1996).

employers to be willing to do this, schools must be providing a service that they could not perform more cheaply themselves.

For example, we argued earlier that to profit from an investment of $100,000 in a college education, college graduates must be paid at least $3,652 more per year than they would have received otherwise. Naturally, this requires that they find employers who are willing to pay them the higher yearly wage. If college merely helps *reveal* who is more productive, employers who believe they could find this out for less than a yearly cost of $3,652 per worker would clearly have incentives to adopt their own methods of screening workers.

The fact that employers continue to emphasize (and pay for) educational requirements in the establishment of hiring standards suggests one of two things. Either more education *does* enhance worker productivity, or it is a *less expensive* screening tool than any other that firms could use. In either case, the fact that employers are willing to pay a high price for an educated workforce seems to suggest that education produces social benefits.[33]

Is Public Sector Training a Good Social Investment?

Policymakers should also ask whether government job training programs can be justified based on their returns. During the past four decades, the federal government has funded a variety of these programs that primarily targeted disadvantaged men, women, and youth. Some programs have served trainees who applied voluntarily, and others have been mandatory programs for public assistance recipients (who stood to lose benefits if they did not enroll). Some of these programs have provided relatively inexpensive help in searching for work, while others have directly provided work experience or (in the case of the Job Corps) comprehensive services associated with living away from home. Over these decades, however, roughly half of those enrolled received classroom training at vocational schools or community colleges, and another 15 percent received in-plant training. The per-student costs of these latter two types of programs have been in the range of $3,500 to $7,000 (in 2000 dollars).[34]

Evaluating these programs requires comparing their costs to an estimate of the present value of their benefits, which are measured by calculating the increase in wages made possible by the training program. Calculating the benefits involves estimating what trainees would have earned in the absence of training, and there are several thorny issues the researcher must successfully confront. Nevertheless, summaries of credible studies done to date have concluded that adult women are the only group among the disadvantaged that clearly benefits from these training programs; adult men and youth show no consistent earnings increases across studies. Moreover,

---

[33]Kevin Lang, "Does the Human Capital/Educational Sorting Debate Matter for Development Policy?" *American Economic Review* 84, no. 1 (March 1994): 353–358, comes to a similar conclusion through a more formal argument.

[34]Robert J. LaLonde, "The Promise of Public Sector–Sponsored Training Programs," *Journal of Economic Perspectives* 9, no. 2 (Spring 1995): 149–168, gives a brief history of federally sponsored training programs and summarizes several issues relevant to evaluating their efficacy.

the average increase in earnings for women in voluntary training programs is roughly $1,500 per year, while it is less than half that for the mandatory training associated with welfare programs.[35] Were these increases large enough to justify program costs?

The programs had direct costs of $3,500 to $7,000 per trainee, but they also had opportunity costs in the form of forgone output. The typical trainee was in her program for 16 weeks, and while many of the trainees had been on welfare prior to training, the opportunity costs of their time surely were not zero. Recall from chapter 7 that a person can be productive in the home as well as the workplace. If we place a value on time at home equal to $20,000 per year (see Example 7.3 in chapter 7), spending one-third of a year in training had opportunity costs of roughly $6,700. Thus, the total costs of training were probably in the range of $10,000 to $14,000 per woman.

If benefits of $1,500 per year were received annually for 20 years after *voluntary* training, and if the appropriate discount rate is 2 percent, the present value of benefits comes to $24,500. Benefits of this magnitude are clearly in excess of costs. Indeed, the present value of benefits for voluntary training would still be in excess of $14,000 even if the yearly earnings increases lasted for just more than 10 years. The returns to *mandatory* training for women, as noted above, are less than half of those for voluntary training, so even if benefits were to last for 20 years, they are not too likely to cover costs.[36]

---

[35]Daniel Friendlander, David H. Greenberg, and Philip K. Robins, "Evaluating Government Training Programs for the Economically Disadvantaged," *Journal of Economic Literature* 35, no. 4 (December 1997): 1809–1855, and Robert LaLonde, "The Promise of Public Sector–Sponsored Training Programs," Table 1.

[36]Paul Lengermann, "How Long Do the Benefits of Training Last? Evidence of Long Term Effects Across Current and Previous Employers," *Research in Labor Economics* 18 (1999): 439–461, found that the gains from formal and company training last at least nine years. For a discussion of the social returns to investments by the Job Corps, see Alan B. Krueger, "Economic Scene: A Study Backs Up What George Forman Already Said, the Job Corps Works," *New York Times* (March 30, 2000), p. C2. For reference to studies of vocational education, see Paul Ryan, "The School-to-Work Transition: A Cross-National Perspective," *Journal of Economic Literature* 29, no. 1 (March 2001): 34–92.

REVIEW QUESTIONS

1. Women receive lower wages, on average, than men of equal age. What concepts of human capital help to explain this phenomenon? Explain. Why does the discrepancy between earnings for men and women grow with age?

2. "The vigorous pursuit by a society of tax policies that tend to equalize wages across skill groups will frustrate the goal of optimum resource allocation." Comment.

3. A few years ago, a prominent medical college inadvertently accepted more applicants than it could accommodate in its first-year class. Not wanting to arbitrarily delay the entrance date of the students admitted, it offered them one year of free tuition if they would delay their medical studies by one year. Discuss the factors entering into a student's assessment of whether he or she should take this offer.

4. When Plant X closed, Employer Y (which offers no training to its workers) hired many of X's employees after they had completed a lengthy, full-time retraining program offered by a local agency. The city's Equal Opportunity Commission noticed that the workers Employer Y hired from X were all young, and it launched an age-discrimination investigation. During this investigation, Employer Y claimed that it hired *all* of the applicants from X who had successfully completed the retraining program, without regard to age. From what you know of human capital theory, does Y's claim sound credible? Explain.

5. Why do those who argue that more education "signals" greater ability believe that the most able people will obtain the most education?

6. Suppose that the government, in an effort to upgrade the quality of mechanics, promulgates legislation requiring all new mechanics to take three years of post–high school training and to pass a competency test. Those who are currently mechanics will not be subjected to these requirements. What are the likely labor market effects of this legislation? Which labor and consumer groups would gain and which would lose?

7. In many countries higher education is heavily subsidized by the government (that is, university students do not bear the full cost of their college education). While there may be good reasons for heavily subsidizing university education, there are also some dangers in it. Using human capital theory, explain what these dangers are.

8. Many crimes against property (burglary, for example) can be thought of as acts that have immediate gains but run the risk of long-run costs. If imprisoned, the criminal loses income from both criminal and noncriminal activities. Using the framework for occupational choice in the long run, analyze what kinds of people are most likely to engage in criminal activities. What can society do to reduce crime?

PROBLEMS

1. Becky works in sales but is considering quitting work for two years to earn an MBA. Her current job pays $40,000 per year (after taxes), but she could earn $55,000 per year (after taxes) if she had a master's degree in business administration. Tuition is $10,000 per year and the cost of an apartment near campus is equal to the $10,000 per year she is currently paying. Becky's discount rate is 6 percent per year. She just turned 48 and plans to retire when she turns 60, whether or not she gets her MBA. Based on this information, should she go to school to earn her MBA? Explain carefully.

2. (Appendix). Suppose that the supply curve for optometrists is given by $L_S = -6 + 0.6W$, while the demand curve is given by $L_D = 50 - W$, where W = annual earnings in thousands of dollars per year and L = thousands of optometrists.

   a. Find the equilibrium wage and employment levels.

   b. Now suppose that the demand for optometrists increases and the new demand curve is $L_{D'} = 66 - W$. Assume that this market is subject to cobwebs because it takes about three years to produce people who specialize in optometry. While this adjustment is taking place, the short-run supply of optometrists is fixed. Calculate the wage and employment levels in each of the first three rounds and find the new long-run equilibrium. Draw a graph to show these events.

SELECTED READINGS

Becker, Gary. *Human Capital*. New York: National Bureau of Economic Research, 1975.

Borjas, George J. "Earnings Determination: A Survey of the Neoclassical Approach." In *Three Worlds of Labor Economics*, ed. Garth Mangum and Peter Philips. Armonk, N.Y.: M. E. Sharpe, 1988.

Card, David. "The Causal Effect of Education on Earnings." In *Handbook of Labor Economics*, ed. Orley Ashenfelter and David Card. New York: Elsevier, 1999.

Clotfelter, Charles T., Ronald G. Ehrenberg, Malcolm Getz, and John Siegfried. *Economic Challenges in Higher Education*. Chicago: University of Chicago Press, 1991.

Freeman, Richard B. *The Overeducated American*. New York: Academic Press, 1976.

Friendlander, Daniel, David H. Greenberg, and Philip K. Robins, "Evaluating Government Training Programs for the Economically Disadvantaged." *Journal of Economic Literature* 35, no. 4 (December 1997): 1809–1855.

Krueger, Alan B., and Mikael Lindahl, "Education for Growth: Why and for Whom?" *Journal of Economic Literature* 39, no. 4 (December 2001): 1101–1136.

Mincer, Jacob. *Schooling, Experience, and Earnings*. New York: National Bureau of Economic Research, 1974.

Schultz, Theodore. *The Economic Value of Education*. New York: Columbia University Press, 1963.

Spence, Michael. "Job Market Signaling." *Quarterly Journal of Economics* 87 (August 1973): 355–374.

A "Cobweb" Model
of Labor Market Adjustment

The adjustment of college enrollments to changes in the returns to education is not always smooth or rapid, particularly in special fields, like engineering and law, that are highly technical. The problem is that if engineering wages (say) were to go up suddenly in a given year, the supply of graduate engineers would not be affected until three or four years later (owing to the time it takes to learn the field). Likewise, if engineering wages were to fall, those students enrolled in an engineering curriculum would understandably be reluctant to immediately leave the field. They have already invested a lot of time and effort and may prefer to take chances in engineering rather than devote more time and money to learning a new field.

The failure of supply to respond immediately to changed market conditions can cause *boom-and-bust cycles* in the market for highly technical workers. If educational planners in government or the private sector are unaware of these cycles, they may seek to stimulate or reduce enrollments at times when they should be doing exactly the opposite, as illustrated below.

AN EXAMPLE OF "COBWEB" ADJUSTMENTS

Suppose the market for engineers is in equilibrium, where the wage is W_0 and the number of engineers is N_0 (see Figure 9A.1). Let us now assume that the demand curve for engineers shifts from D_0 to D_1. Initially, this increase in the demand for engineers does *not* induce the supply of engineers to increase beyond N_0, because it takes a long time to become an engineer once one has decided to do so. Thus, while the increased demand for engineers causes more people to decide to enter the field, the number available for employment *at the moment* is N_0. These N_0 engineers, therefore, can *currently* obtain a wage of W_1 (in effect, there is a vertical supply curve, at N_0, for a few years until the supply of engineering graduates is increased).

FIGURE 9A.1
The Labor Market for Engineers

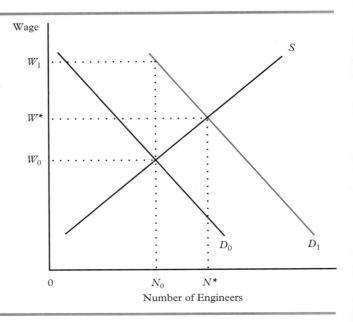

Now W_1, the *current* engineering wage, is above W^*, the new *long-run* equilibrium wage caused by the intersection of D_1 and S. The market, however, is unaware of W^*, observing only W_1. If people are myopic and assume W_1 is the new equilibrium wage, N_1 people will enter the engineering field (see Figure 9A.2). When these N_1 all graduate, there will be a *surplus* of engineers (remember that W_1 is *above* long-run equilibrium).

With the supply of engineers now temporarily fixed at N_1, the wage will fall to W_2. This fall will cause students and workers to shift *out* of engineering, but that effect will not be fully felt for a few years. In the meantime, note that W_2 is below long-run equilibrium (still at W^*). Thus, when supply *does* adjust, it will adjust too much—all the way to N_2. Now there will be another shortage of engineers, because after supply adjusts to N_2, demand exceeds supply at a wage rate of W_2. This causes wages to rise to W_3, and the cycle repeats itself. Over time, the swings become smaller, and eventually equilibrium is reached. Because the adjustment path in Figure 9A.2 looks somewhat like a cobweb, the adjustment process described above is sometimes called a *cobweb model*.

WORKER EXPECTATIONS OF FUTURE WAGES

Critical to cobweb models is the assumption that workers form myopic expectations about the future behavior of wages. In our example, they first assume that W_1

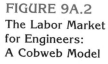

FIGURE 9A.2
The Labor Market
for Engineers:
A Cobweb Model

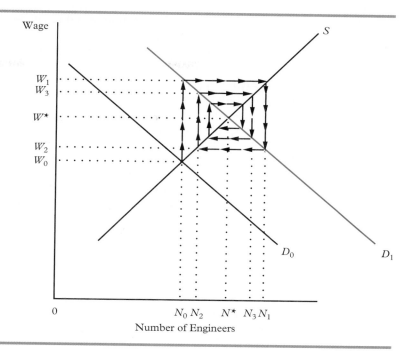

will prevail in the future and ignore the possibility that the occupational choice decisions of others will, in four years, drive the wage below W_1. Just how workers (and other economic actors, such as investors and taxpayers) form expectations about future wage (price) levels is very important to the understanding of many key issues affecting the labor market.[1]

Adaptive Expectations

The simplest and most naive way to predict future wage levels is to assume that what is observed today is what will be observed in the future; this naive assumption, as noted above, underlies the cobweb model. A more sophisticated way to form predictions about the future is with an *adaptive expectations* approach. Adaptive expectations are formed by setting future expected wages equal to a weighted average of

---

[1]Also critical to cobweb models is that the demand curve be flatter than the supply curve; if it is not, the cobweb *explodes* when demand shifts and an equilibrium wage is never reached. An exploding cobweb model is an example from economics of the phenomenon of *chaos*. For a general introduction to this fascinating topic, see James Gleick, *Chaos* (New York: Penguin Books, 1987). For an article on chaos theory in the economic literature, see William J. Baumol and Jess Benhabib, "Chaos: Significance, Mechanism, and Economic Applications," *Journal of Economic Perspectives* 3, no. 1 (Winter 1989): 77–106.

current and past wages. While more weight may be given to current than past wages in forecasting future wage levels, changes in those levels prior to the current period are not ignored; thus, it is likely that wage expectations formed adaptively do not alternatively overshoot and undershoot the equilibrium wage as much as those formed using the naive approach. If, however, adaptive expectations also lead workers to first overpredict and then underpredict the equilibrium wage, cobweblike behavior of wages and labor supply will still be observed (although the fluctuations will be of a smaller magnitude if the predictions are closer to the mark than those made naively).

Rational Expectations

The most sophisticated way to predict future market outcomes is to use a full-blown model of the labor market. Those who believe in the *rational expectations* method of forming predictions about future wages assume that workers do have such a model in their heads, at least implicitly. Thus, they will realize that a marked increase in the earnings of engineers (say) is likely to be temporary, because supply will expand and eventually bring the returns to an investment in engineering skills in line with those for other occupations. Put differently, the rational expectations model assumes workers behave as if they have taken (and mastered!) a good course in labor economics and that they will not be fooled into over- or underpredicting future wage levels.

Clearly, how people form expectations is an important empirical issue. In the case of engineers, lawyers, and dentists, periodic fluctuations in supply that characterize the cobweb model have been found.[2] Whether these fluctuations are the result of naive expectations or not, the lesson to be learned from cobweb models should not be lost on government policymakers. If the government chooses to take an active role in dealing with labor shortages and surpluses, it must be aware that, because supply adjustments are slow in highly technical markets, wages in those markets tend to *over*adjust. In other words, to the extent possible, governmental predictions and market interventions should be based on rational expectations. For example, at the initial stages of a shortage, when wages are rising toward W_1 (in our example), the government should be pointing out that W_1 is likely to be *above* the long-run equilibrium. If instead it attempts to meet the current shortage by *subsidizing* study in that field, it will be encouraging an even greater *surplus* later on. The moral of the story is that a complete knowledge of how markets adjust to changes in demand or supply is necessary before we can be sure that government intervention will do more good than harm.

---

[2]See Richard B. Freeman, "A Cobweb Model of the Supply and Starting Salary of New Engineers," *Industrial and Labor Relations Review* 29 (January 1976): 236–246, and Michael G. Finn and Joe G. Baker, "Future Jobs in Natural Science and Engineering: Shortage or Surplus?" *Monthly Labor Review* 116, no. 2 (February 1993): 54–61. Gary Zarkin, "Occupational Choice: An Application to the Market for Public School Teachers," *Quarterly Journal of Economics* 100 (May 1985): 409–446, and Peter Orazem and Peter Mattila, "Human Capital, Uncertain Wage Distributions, and Occupational and Educational Choices," *International Economic Review* 32 (February 1991): 103–122, use rational expectations models of occupational choice.

A Hedonic Model of Earnings and Educational Level

Chapter 9 employed human capital theory to explore the demand for education and the relationship between education and pay. This appendix uses the hedonic theory of wages to more formally explore the factors underlying the positive association between wage and educational levels. Thus, it treats the higher pay associated with a higher education level as a compensating wage differential.

Unless education is acquired purely for purposes of consumption, people will not undertake an investment in education or training without the expectation that, by so doing, they can improve their stream of lifetime earnings or psychic rewards. In order to obtain these higher benefits, however, *employers* must be willing to pay for them. Therefore, it is necessary to examine both sides of the market to fully understand the prediction made over two hundred years ago by Adam Smith that wages rise with the "difficulty and expense" of learning the job.[1]

SUPPLY (WORKER) SIDE

Consider a group of people who have chosen selling as a desired career. These salespersons-to-be have a choice of how much education or training to invest in, given their career objectives. In making this choice they will have to weigh the returns against the costs. Crucial to this decision is how the *actual* returns compare with the returns each would *require* in order to invest.

Figure 9B.1 shows the indifference curves between yearly earnings and education for two workers, A and B. To induce A or B to acquire X years of educa-

---

[1]See Adam Smith, *Wealth of Nations,* book 1, ch. 10. The five "principal circumstances" listed by Smith as affecting wages were first discussed in this text in chapter 8.

FIGURE 9B.1
Indifference Curves for Two Different Workers

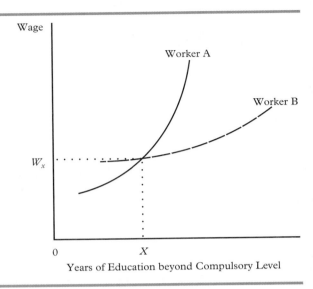

tion would require the assurance of earning W_x after beginning work. However, to induce A to increase his or her education beyond X years (holding utility constant) would require a larger salary increase than B would require. A's greater aversion to making educational investments could be explained in several ways. Person A could be older than B, thus having higher forgone earnings and fewer years over which to recoup investment costs. Person A could be more present-oriented and thus more inclined to discount future benefits heavily, or could have less ability in classroom learning or a greater dislike of schooling. Finally, A may find it more difficult to finance additional schooling. Whatever the reason, this analysis points up the important fact that people differ in their propensity to invest in schooling.

DEMAND (EMPLOYER) SIDE

On the demand side of the market, employers must consider whether they are willing to pay higher wages for better-educated workers. If they are, they must also decide how much to pay for each additional year. Figure 9B.2 illustrates employers' choices about the wage/education relationship. Employers Y and Z are *both* willing to pay more for better-educated sales personnel (to continue our example) because they have found that better-educated workers are more productive.[2]

---

[2]Whether schooling causes workers to be more productive or simply reflects—or *signals*—higher productivity is not important at this point.

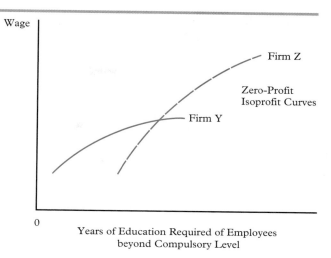

FIGURE 9B.2
Isoprofit Curves for Two Different Firms

Thus, they can achieve the same profit level by paying either lower wages for less-educated workers or higher wages for more-educated workers. Their isoprofit curves are thus upward-sloping (see chapter 8 for a description of isoprofit curves). The isoprofit curves in Figure 9B.2 have three important characteristics:

1. For each firm the curves are concave; that is, they get flatter as education increases. This concavity results from the assumption that, at some point, the added benefits to the employer of an additional year of employee schooling begin to decline. In other words, we assume that schooling is subject to diminishing marginal productivity.
2. The isoprofit curves are the *zero-profit curves*. Neither firm can pay higher wages for each level of education than those indicated on the curves; if they did so, their profits would be negative and they would cease operations.
3. The added benefits from an extra year of schooling are smaller in firm Y than in firm Z, causing Y to have a flatter isoprofit curve. Firm Y, for example, may be a discount department store in which "selling" is largely a matter of working a cash register. While better-educated people may be more productive, they are not *too* much more valuable than less-educated people; hence, firm Y is not willing to pay them much more. Firm Z, on the other hand, may sell technical instruments for which a knowledge of physics and of customer engineering problems is needed. In firm Z, additional education adds a relatively large increment to worker productivity.

MARKET DETERMINATION
OF THE EDUCATION/WAGE RELATIONSHIP

Putting both sides of the market for educated workers together, it is clear that the education/wage relationship will be positive, as indicated in Figure 9B.3. Worker A will work for Y, receiving a wage equal to W_{AY} and obtaining X_1 years of education. The reason for this matching is simple. Firm Z cannot pay higher wages (for each level of education) than those shown on the isoprofit curve in Figure 9B.3, for the reasons noted above. Clearly, then, worker A could never derive as much utility from Z as he or she could from Y; working for firm Z would involve a loss of utility to worker A. For similar reasons, worker B will accept work with firm Z, obtain X_2 years of schooling, and receive higher pay (W_{BZ}).

When examined from an overall social perspective, the positive wage/education relationship is the result of a very sensible sorting of workers and employers performed by the labor market. Workers with the greatest aversion to investing in education (A) will work for firms where education adds least to employee productivity (Y). People with the least aversion to educational investment (B) are hired by those firms most willing to pay for an educated workforce (Z).

Given the assertion by the critics of the human capital view of education that education adds nothing to worker productivity, it is interesting to consider the implications of an unwillingness by employers to pay higher wages to workers with more education. If employers were unwilling to pay higher wages for more-

FIGURE 9B.3
The Education/Wage Relationship

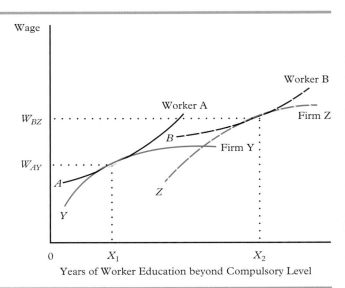

FIGURE 9B.4
Unwillingness of a Firm to Pay for More Education of Employees

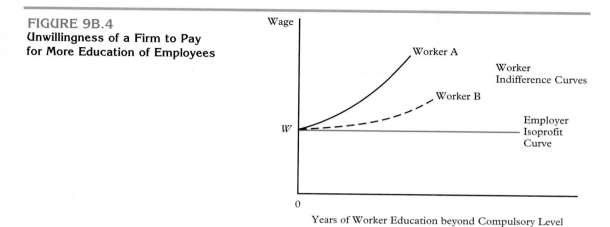

educated workers, no education-related differentials would exist and employer iso-profit curves would be horizontal. Without a positive education/wage relationship, employees would have no incentive to invest in an education (see Figure 9B.4). The fact that educational wage differentials exist and that workers respond to them when making schooling decisions suggests that, for some reason or other, employers *are* willing to pay higher wages to more-educated workers.

10

WORKER MOBILITY: Migration, Immigration, and Turnover

Worker mobility plays a critical role in market economies. Because the job of any market is to promote voluntary exchange, society relies on the free movement of workers among employers to allocate labor in a way that achieves maximum satisfaction for both workers and consumers. The flow (either actual or threatened) of workers from lower-paying to higher-paying jobs, for example, is what forces firms that are paying below-equilibrium wages to increase their wage offers. The existence of compensating wage differentials, to take another example, also depends on the ability of informed workers to exercise choice among employment opportunities in the search for enhanced utility.

Mobility, however, is costly. Workers must take time to seek out information on other jobs, and for at least some workers, job search is most efficient if they quit their current job first (to look for work in a new geographic area, for example). Severing ties with the current employer means leaving friends and familiar surroundings, and it may mean giving up valuable employee benefits or the inside track on future promotions. Once a new job is found, workers may well face *monetary*, and will almost certainly face *psychic*, costs of moving to new surroundings. In short, workers who move to new employers bear costs in the near term so that utility can be enhanced later on. Therefore, the human capital model introduced in chapter 9 can be used to analyze mobility investments by workers.

THE DETERMINANTS OF WORKER MOBILITY

The human capital model views mobility as an investment in which costs are borne in some early period in order to obtain returns over a longer period of time. If the present value of the benefits associated with mobility exceeds the costs, both monetary and psychic, we assume that people will decide to change jobs or move, or both. If the discounted stream of benefits is not as large as the costs, then people will decide against such a change.

What determines the present value of the net benefits of mobility—that is, the benefits minus the costs—determines the mobility decision. These factors can be better identified by writing out the formula to use if we were to precisely calculate these net benefits:

$$\text{Present Value of Net Benefits} = \sum_{t=1}^{T} \frac{B_{jt} - B_{ot}}{(1 + r)^t} - C \tag{10.1}$$

where:

B_{jt} = the utility derived from the new job (j) in the year t
B_{ot} = the utility derived from the old job (o) in the year t
T = the length of time (in years) one expects to work at job j
r = the rate of discount
C = the utility lost in the move itself (direct and psychic costs)
Σ = a summation—in this case the summation of the yearly discounted net benefits over a period running from year 1 to year T

Clearly, the present value of the net benefits of mobility will be larger the greater is the utility derived from the new job, the less happy one is in the job of origin, the smaller are the immediate costs associated with change, and the longer is one's horizon (that is, the greater is T and the lower is r). These observations lead to some clear-cut predictions about which groups in society will be most mobile and about the *patterns* of mobility we would expect to observe.

GEOGRAPHIC MOBILITY

Mobility of workers among countries, and among regions within a country, is an important fact of economic life. Roughly 100 million people in the world live in a country different from the one in which they were born, and Table 10.1 indicates that for the world's larger economies, immigrants typically constitute from 5 to 20 percent of the labor force. One study indicated that of the people who migrated to another country from 1975 to 1980, two-thirds went to the United States, Canada, or Australia.[1]

---

[1]Rachel M. Friedberg and Jennifer Hunt, "The Impact of Immigrants on Host Country Wages, Employment, and Growth," *Journal of Economic Perspectives* 9, no. 2 (Spring 1995): 23–44.

TABLE 10.1   Immigrants as a Percentage of the Labor Force, Selected Countries, 1995–1998

Country	Immigrants as a Percentage of Labor Force
Australia	24.8
Canada	19.2
France	6.1
Germany	9.1
Italy	1.7
Japan	0.2
Sweden	5.1
United Kingdom	3.9
United States	11.7

Source: Organisation for Economic Co-Operation and Development, *Trends in International Migration,* Annual Report 2000 (OECD, 2001), Table A.2.3.

Within the United States during a recent one-year period (1999–2000), almost 5 million workers—3.7 percent of all those employed—moved out of state, and almost half of those moved to a different *region* (the South experienced the largest net influx, while the Northeast had the largest net outflow).[2] When asked about their reasons for moving, 70 to 85 percent of workers cite economic reasons. Roughly one-third of those moving among states stay with their current employers, but taking account of those whose move is motivated by economic factors *and* who change employers, about half of all interstate moves are precipitated by a change in employment.[3] This emphasis on job change suggests that human capital theory can help us understand which workers are most likely to undertake investments in geographic mobility and the directions in which mobility flows will take place.

The Direction of Migratory Flows

Human capital theory predicts that migration will flow from areas of relatively poor earnings possibilities to places where opportunities are better. Studies of migratory flows support this prediction. In general, the results of such studies suggest that the *pull* of good opportunities in the areas of destination are stronger than the *push* of poor opportunities in the areas of origin. In other words, while people are

---

[2]U.S. Bureau of the Census, *Geographic Mobility: March 1999 to March 2000,* www.census.gov; then go to "subjects" and "migration," Tables 8, 18.
[3]Ann P. Bartel, "The Migration Decision: What Role Does Job-Mobility Play?" *American Economic Review* 69 (December 1979): 775–786. See also Larry Schroeder, "Interrelatedness of Occupational and Geographical Labor Mobility," *Industrial and Labor Relations Review* 29 (April 1976): 405–411.

more attracted to places where earnings are expected to be better, they do not necessarily come from areas where opportunities are poorest.

The most consistent finding in these detailed studies is that people are attracted to areas where the real earnings of full-time workers are highest. Studies find no consistent relationship, however, between unemployment and in-migration, perhaps because the number of people moving with a job already in hand is three times as large as the number moving *to look* for work. If one already has a job in a particular field, the area's unemployment rate is irrelevant.[4]

Most studies have found that, contrary to what we might expect, the characteristics of the place of origin do not appear to have much net influence on migration. While those in the poorest places have the greatest *incentives* to move, the very poorest areas also tend to have people with lower levels of wealth, education, and skills—the very people who seem least *willing* (or able) to move. To understand this phenomenon, we must turn from the issue of *where* people go to a discussion of *who* is most likely to move. (In addition, there is the issue of *when* people move. See Example 10.1, which pulls together the issues of who, where, and when in analyzing one of the most momentous internal migrations in the history of the United States—the Great Migration of blacks from the South to the North in the first half of the twentieth century.)

Personal Characteristics of Movers

Migration is highly selective in the sense that it is not an activity in which all people are equally likely to be engaged. To be specific, mobility is much higher among the young and the better-educated, as human capital theory would suggest.

Age   Age is the single most important factor in determining who migrates. The peak years for mobility are the ages 20–24; 15 percent of this age group migrates across county or state lines each year. By age 32 this rate of migration is roughly 10 percent, and by age 47 it is only 5 percent.

There are two explanations for the fact that migration is an activity primarily for the young. First, the younger one is, the longer the period over which benefits from an investment can be obtained, and the larger the present value of these benefits.

Second, a large part of the costs of migration are psychic, the losses associated with giving up friends, community ties, and the benefits of knowing one's way around. As we grow older, our ties to the community become stronger and the losses associated with leaving loom larger.

Education   While age is probably the best predictor of who will move, education is the single best indicator of who will move *within* an age group. As can be seen

---

[4]The level of *new hires* in an area appears to explain migration flows much better than the unemployment rate; see Gary Fields, "Place to Place Migration: Some New Evidence," *Review of Economics and Statistics* 61, no. 1 (February 1979): 21–32. Robert H. Topel, "Local Labor Markets," *Journal of Political Economy* 94, no. 3, pt. 2 (June 1986): S111–S143, contains an analysis of how permanent and transitory shifts in an area's demand affect migration and wages.

EXAMPLE 10.1

The Great Migration: Southern Blacks Move North

Our model predicts that workers will move whenever the present value of the net benefits of migration is positive. After the Civil War and emancipation, a huge wage gap opened up between the South and the North, with northern wages often twice as high as those in the South. Yet black migration out of the South was very low—only 68,000 during the 1870s.

During World War I, however, the Great Migration began, and over half a million blacks moved out of the South in the 1910s. Black migration during the 1920s was almost twice this high, and it exceeded 1.5 million during the 1940s, so that by 1950 over 20 percent of southern-born blacks had left the region.

Why did this migration take so long to get going? One important factor was low education levels, which made obtaining information about outside opportunities very difficult. In 1880 more than 75 percent of African Americans over age ten were illiterate, but this figure fell to about 20 percent by 1930. One study finds that in 1900 literate adult black males were three times more likely to have migrated than those who were illiterate. In 1940, blacks who had attended high school were twice as likely to have migrated than those with zero to four years of schooling. However, rising literacy alone cannot explain the sudden burst of migration.

The outbreak of World War I seems to have triggered the migration in two ways. First, it caused labor demand in northern industry to soar. Second, it brought the collapse of immigration inflows from abroad. Before World War I, growing northern industries had relied heavily on immigrants from Europe as a source of labor. With the immigration flood slowing to a trickle, employers began to hire black workers—even sending agents to recruit in the South. Job opportunities for blacks in the North finally opened up and many responded by moving.

A study using census data from 1870 to 1950 finds that, as expected, northern states in which wages were highest attracted more black migrants, as did those in which manufacturing growth was more rapid. Reduced European immigration seems to have spurred black migration, and it is estimated that if European immigration had been completely restricted at the turn of the century, the Great Migration would have started much sooner.

Data from: William J. Collins, "When the Tide Turned: Immigration and the Delay of the Great Black Migration," *Journal of Economic History* 57, no. 3 (September 1997), 607–632; Robert A. Margo, *Race and Schooling in the South, 1880–1950* (Chicago: University of Chicago Press, 1990).

from Table 10.2, which presents U.S. migration rates for people ages 30–34, more education does make one more likely to move between states.

One cost of migration is that of ascertaining *where* opportunities are and *how good* they are likely to be. If one's occupation has a national labor market, as is the case for many college graduates, it is relatively easy to find out about opportunities in distant places. Jobs are advertised in national newspapers, recruiters from all over visit college campuses and employment agencies make nationwide searches.

However, if the relevant labor market for one's job is localized, it is difficult to find out where opportunities might be better. For a janitor in Beaumont, Texas, finding out about employment opportunities in the north-central region, say, is difficult and may require quitting Beaumont and moving north to mount an effective search.

The Role of Distance

Human capital theory clearly predicts that as migration costs rise, the flow of migrants will fall. The costs of moving increase with distance for two reasons. First,

---

TABLE 10.2   U.S. Migration Rates for People Age 30–34, by Educational Level, 1999–2000, (in percentages)

Educational Level (in Years)	Moving between Counties within States	Moving out of State
9–11	6.0	3.8
12	3.7	4.1
13–15	4.5	4.7
16	4.6	6.1
17 or more	6.1	7.7

Source: U.S. Bureau of the Census, *Geographical Mobility: March 1999 to March 2000,* www.census.gov, then go to "subjects" and "migratory" Table 6.

---

acquiring trustworthy *information* on opportunities elsewhere is easier when employment prospects are closer to home. Second, the time and money cost of a move and for trips back to see friends and relatives, and hence the psychic costs of the move, rise with distance. Thus, we would clearly expect to find that people are more likely to move short distances than long distances.

In general, this expectation is borne out by the statistics. Of the 23 million employed Americans who changed their place of residence during the March 1999–March 2000 period, 57 percent moved to a different house in the same county, 21 percent moved to a different county in the same state, 12 percent changed states within the same region, and 9 percent moved to a different region.[5]

Interestingly, lack of education appears to be a bigger deterrent to long-distance migration than does age (other influences held constant), a fact that can shed some light on whether information costs or psychic costs are the primary deterrent. As suggested by our arguments in the previous subsection, the age deterrent is closely related to psychic costs, while educational level and ease of access to information are closely linked. The apparently larger deterrent of educational level suggests that information costs may have more influence than psychic costs on the relationship between migration and distance.[6]

Skills, the Earnings Distribution, and International Migration

To this point, our examples of factors that influence geographic mobility have related to domestic migration, but the influences of age, access to information,

---

[5]U.S. Bureau of the Census, *Geographical Mobility: March 1999–March 2000,* www.census.gov; then go to "subjects" and "migration," Table 8.

[6]Aba Schwartz, "Interpreting the Effect of Distance on Migration," *Journal of Political Economy* 81 (September/October 1973): 1153–1167.

EXAMPLE 10.2

Migration and One's Time Horizon

Economic theory suggests that those with longer time horizons are more likely to make human-capital investments. Can we see evidence of this theoretical implication in the horizons of people who are most likely to migrate? A recent paper explores the possibility that people who give greater weight to the welfare of their children and grandchildren have a higher propensity to bear the considerable costs of immigration.

Before 1989, the Soviet Union made it difficult, though not impossible, for Jews to emigrate. After applying for emigration, which itself involved heavy fees, the applicant's property was often confiscated and his or her right to work was often suspended. However, after the collapse of the Soviet Union in 1989, these hassles were eliminated. The monetary benefits of migrating were approximately the same before and after 1989, but the costs fell considerably.

How did migrants from the earlier period—who were willing to bear the very high costs—differ from those who only emigrated when the costs were reduced? The study finds evidence that Jewish women who migrated to Israel during the earlier period brought with them larger families (on average, 0.4 to 0.8 more children) than otherwise-similar migrants in the later period. This suggests that the benefits of migration to children were a decisive factor in the decision to migrate during the pre-1989 period.

Likewise, a survey of women aged 51 to 61 shows that grandmothers who had immigrated to the United States spend over 200 more hours per year with their grandchildren than American-born grandmothers. They are also more likely to report that they consider it important to leave an inheritance (rather than spending all their wealth on themselves).

Thus, there is evidence consistent with the theoretical implication that those who invest in immigration have longer time horizons (in the sense of putting greater weight on the welfare of their children and grandchildren) than those who do not.

Data from: Eli Berman and Zaur Rzakhanov, "Fertility, Migration and Altruism," National Bureau of Economic Research working paper no. 7545 (February 2000).

the potential gains in earnings, and distance are all relevant to international migration as well. Additionally, because immigrants are self-selected and the costs of immigration are so high, personal discount rates and the horizon over which benefits are calculated are critical and likely to be very different for immigrants and nonmigrants—as illustrated by Example 10.2.

One aspect of the potential gains from migration that is uniquely important when analyzing international flows of labor is the distribution of earnings in the sending as compared with the receiving country. The relative distribution of earnings can help us predict which skill groups within a sending country are most likely to emigrate.

Some countries have a more compressed (equal) earnings distribution than is found in the United States. In these countries, the average earnings differential between skilled and unskilled workers is smaller, implying that the returns to human capital investments are lower than in the United States. Skilled and professional workers from these countries (northern European countries are most notable in this regard) have the most to gain from emigration to the United States. Unskilled workers in countries with more equality of earnings are well paid compared to unskilled workers here and thus have less incentive to move. Immigrants to the United States from these countries therefore tend to be more skilled than the average worker who does not emigrate.

In countries with a less equal distribution of earnings than is found in the United States, skilled workers do relatively well, but there are large potential gains to the unskilled from emigrating to the United States. These unskilled workers may be blocked from making human capital investments within their own countries (and thus from taking advantage of the high returns to such investments that are implied by the large earnings differentials). Instead, their human capital investment may take the form of emigrating and seeking work in the United States. Less-developed countries tend to have relatively unequal earnings distributions, so it is to be expected that immigrants from these countries (and especially Mexico, which is closest) will be disproportionately unskilled.[7]

The Returns to International and Domestic Migration

We have seen that migrants generally move to places that allow them greater earnings opportunities. How great these earnings increases are for individual migrants depends on the reasons and preparation for the move—as vividly illustrated in Example 10.3, which compares the earnings of *political* and *economic* immigrants.

Internal Migration for Economic Reasons The largest gains from migration can be expected among those whose move is motivated by a better job offer and who have obtained this offer through a job-search process undertaken before quitting their prior jobs. A study of men and women in their 20s who were in this category found that, for moves in the 1979–1985 period, earnings increased 14–18 percent more than earnings of nonmigrants. Even those who quit voluntarily and migrated for economic reasons *without* a prior job search earned 6–9 percent more than if they had stayed put.[8] The returns for women and men who migrated for economic reasons were very similar.

Family Migration Most of us live in families, and if there is more than one employed person in a family the decision to migrate is likely to have different earnings effects on the members. You will recall from chapter 7 that there is more than one plausible model for how those who live together actually make joint labor-supply decisions, but with migration a decision to move might well be made if the *family as a whole* experiences a net increase in total earnings. Total family earnings, of course, could be increased even if one partner's earnings were

---

[7]For a more thorough discussion of this issue, see George J. Borjas, *Friends or Strangers* (New York: Basic Books, 1990), especially chs. 1 and 7.
[8]Kristen Keith and Abagail McWilliams, "The Returns to Mobility and Job Search by Gender," *Industrial and Labor Relations Review* 52, no. 3 (April 1999): 460–477.

EXAMPLE 10.3
Economic vs. Political Immigrants

Individuals who immigrate to a country like the United States presumably do so because they believe they will be improving their well-being. For some the decision is motivated primarily by economic considerations, and the timing of the move is both voluntary and planned. These individuals may be referred to as *economic* migrants. Others, however, may be forced to flee their countries because of *political* upheavals, and for these individuals the decision may not be planned as far in advance.

What differences might we expect in the economic success of the two groups in the United States? On the one hand, we might expect that economic migrants would initially earn more than political migrants, who were less prepared for the move. On the other hand, members of the latter group do not have the option of ultimately returning to their homelands as the economic migrants do. Because return migration is precluded for political migrants, they have stronger incentives than economic migrants to make human capital investments that have payoffs only in the United

States. In addition, political migrants often leave all their physical or financial assets behind when they flee their homelands; as a result, they may prefer to concentrate a greater share of their subsequent investments in human (rather than physical) capital. For both reasons, we might expect political migrants to have steeper earnings profiles—more rapid earnings growth with years in the United States—than economic migrants.

One recent study found that political refugees coming in the late 1970s earned 11 percent less than economic immigrants in 1980, but by 1990 they earned 24 percent more. The political refugees were more likely to attend school, improve their English skills, and apply for citizenship.

Data from: Kalena E. Cortes, "Are Refugees Different from Economic Immigrants? Some Empirical Evidence on the Heterogeneity of Immigrant Groups in the United States," working paper no. 41, Center for Labor Economics, University of California, Berkeley (September 2001); and George Borjas, "The Economic Status of Male Hispanic Migrants and Natives in the U.S.," in *Research in Labor Economics*, vol. 6, ed. Ronald Ehrenberg (Greenwich, Conn.: JAI Press, 1984), 65–122.

to fall as a result of the move, as long as the other partner experienced relatively large gains. Considering family migration decisions raises the issue of *tied movers*—those who agree to move for family reasons, not necessarily because the move improves their own earnings.

Among those in their 20s who migrated in the 1979–1985 period, quitting jobs and moving for *family* reasons caused earnings to decrease by an average of 10–15 percent—although searching for a new job before moving apparently held wage losses to zero.[9] Clearly, migrating as a tied mover can be costly to an individual. Women move more often than men for family reasons, but as more complete college or graduate school and enter careers, their willingness to move for family reasons may fall. The growing preference among college-educated couples for living in large urban areas, where both have access to many opportunities without moving, reflects the costs of migrating as a tied mover.[10]

[9]Keith and McWilliams, "The Returns to Mobility and Job Search by Gender."
[10]Dora L. Costa and Matthew E. Kahn, "Power Couples: Changes in the Locational Choice of the College Educated, 1940–1990," *Quarterly Journal of Economics* 115, no. 4 (November 2000): 1287–1315.

TABLE 10.3	Ratio of Wages, Immigrant to Native-Born Men, 1970–1990		
A. Comparison with All Native-Born Men, Ages 25–64			
Immigrants Arriving in	*1970*	*1980*	*1990*
1965–1969	**0.834**	0.922	1.011
1975–1979	—	**0.724**	0.822
1985–1989	—	—	**0.683**
B. Comparison with Ethnically Similar Natives, Ages 25–34 in Years Shown: Asians			
1965–1969	**0.824**	1.091	1.085
1975–1979	—	**0.803**	0.898
1985–1989	—	—	**0.757**
C. Comparison with Ethnically Similar Natives, Ages 25–34 in Years Shown: Mexicans			
1965–1969	**0.735**	0.835	0.805
1975–1979	—	**0.662**	0.705
1985–1989	—	—	**0.661**

Source: George Borjas, "The Economics of Immigration," *Journal of Economic Literature* 32, no. 4 (December 1994), Tables 3, 7.

Returns to Immigration   Comparing the earnings of *international* immigrants with what they would have earned had they not emigrated is generally not feasible, owing to a lack of data on earnings in the home country.[11] Thus, studies of the returns to immigration have focused on comparisons with native-born workers in the host country. Most of the published research has been done on the United States, and Table 10.3 contains data from different time periods on the wages, relative to those for native-born Americans, of three cohorts of male immigrants: those who came in the late 1960s, the late 1970s, and late 1980s.

We can observe three phenomena from Table 10.3. First, as can be seen from looking at the ratios printed in boldface type, immigrants earn substantially less than natives (including those who are ethnically similar) when they first arrive. Second, if we look along the rows for the 1965–1969 and 1975–1979 cohorts, it is clear that relative wages increase from their initially low levels, which means that wages of immigrants rise faster than those of natives during at least the immigrants' first

---

[11]Barry R. Chiswick, *Illegal Aliens: Their Employment and Employers* (Kalamazoo, Mich.: W.E. Upjohn Institute for Employment Research, 1988), mentions two studies that compared the earnings or living standards of Mexican immigrants with the conditions under which they lived before they left. In one study it was found that living conditions, as indexed by the availability of running water and electricity, rose substantially. The other study reported that the earnings of Mexican apple harvesters in Oregon, even after deducting the costs of migration, were triple what they would have been in Mexico.

decade in this country. Increases in the second decade are generally smaller and less certain to be above those for natives. Third, from comparing the initial (bold-face) ratios across the three cohorts, we see that each cohort of immigrants did less well at entry than its predecessor.

Immigrants' Initial Earnings   That immigrants initially earn substantially less than natives is hardly surprising. Even after controlling for the effects of age and education (the typical immigrant is younger and less educated than the typical native), immigrants earn less owing to their difficulties with English, their unfamiliarity with American employment opportunities, and their lack of an American work history (and employers' consequent uncertainties about their productivity).

The fall in the initial earnings of successive immigrant groups relative to U.S. natives has been widely studied in recent years. It appears to reflect the fact that immigrants to the United States are coming increasingly from countries with relatively low levels of educational attainment, and they are therefore arriving in America with less and less human capital.[12]

Immigrants' Earnings Growth   Earnings of immigrants rise relatively quickly, which no doubt reflects their high rates of investment in human capital after arrival. After entry, immigrants typically invest in themselves by acquiring work experience and improved proficiency in English, and these investments raise the wages they can command. For example, a recent study found that English fluency raises immigrant earnings by an average of 17 percent in the United States, 12 percent in Canada, and 9 percent in Australia. Of course, not all immigrants have the same incentives to become proficient in English. Those who live in enclaves where business is conducted in their native tongue, those who expect to return to their homeland, and those who immigrated for other than economic reasons are less likely to invest time and money in learning English.[13]

Earnings Growth and Return Migration   In Table 10.3, the earnings growth immigrants experience relative to natives is measured by comparing the relative earnings of immigrants who have been in the United States for ten years, say, with their relative earnings upon entry a decade earlier. This method of measuring growth, however, may *overstate* the growth individual immigrants can expect when they arrive, because those who have difficulty finding or keeping a job, learning English, or improving their earnings for some other reason are more likely than other immigrants to return to their country of origin. If only those who are "successful" remain in the United States for as long as ten years, the data underlying

---

[12]George Borjas, "The Economics of Immigration," *Journal of Economic Literature* 32, no. 4 (December 1994): 1667–1717, and George Borjas, *Heaven's Door: Immigration Policy and the American Economy* (Princeton: Princeton University Press, 1999).

[13]Barry R. Chiswick and Paul W. Miller, "The Endogeneity between Language and Earnings: International Analyses," *Journal of Labor Economics* 13, no. 2 (April 1995): 246–288; and Barry R. Chiswick and Paul W. Miller, "Language Skills and Earnings among Legalized Aliens," *Journal of Population Economics* 12, no. 1 (February 1999): 63–91.

Table 10.3 do not reflect those whose migration investment turned sour and who left, say, after five years.

Return migration is not inconsequential. About 20 percent of all moves are back to a place where one previously lived, and various analyses suggest that those most likely to move back are the ones for whom the original move did not work out well.[14] One study also found that those who return are the ones who were *closest to the margin* (expected the least net gains) when they first decided to come.[15] Recent research on earnings growth has used difficult-to-get longitudinal data, which permit us to follow the earnings of individual immigrants through time and thus capture data on the less successful before they leave. The findings of this research confirm that the rate at which entering immigrants can expect their earnings to rise toward those of ethnically similar natives is slower than is implied by looking along the rows in Table 10.3—and that the relative earnings of non-Hispanic whites may even fall.[16]

POLICY APPLICATION: RESTRICTING IMMIGRATION

Nowhere are the analytical tools of the economist more important than in the area of immigration policy; the lives affected by immigration policy number in the millions each year. After a brief outline of the history of U.S. immigration policy, this section will analyze in detail the consequences of illegal immigration, a phenomenon currently attracting widespread attention.

U.S. Immigration History

The United States is a rich country whose wealth and high standard of living make it an attractive place for immigrants from nearly all parts of the world. For the first 140 years of its history as an independent country, the United States followed a policy of essentially unrestricted immigration (the only major immigration restrictions were placed on Asians and on convicts). The flow of immigrants was especially large after 1840, when U.S. industrialization and political and economic upheavals in Europe made immigration an attractive investment for millions. Officially recorded

---

[14]John Vanderkamp, "Migration Flows, Their Determinants and the Effects of Return Migration," *Journal of Political Economy* 79 (September/October 1971): 1012–1031; Fernando A. Ramos, "Outmigration and Return Migration of Puerto Ricans," in *Immigration and the Work Force,* ed. George J. Borjas and Richard B. Freeman (Chicago: University of Chicago Press, 1992); and Borjas, "The Economics of Immigration," 1691–1692.

[15]George J. Borjas and Bernt Bratsberg, "Who Leaves? The Outmigration of the Foreign-Born," *Review of Economics and Statistics* 78, no.1 (February 1996): 165–176.

[16]Wei-Yin Hu, "Immigrant Earnings Assimilation: Estimates from Longitudinal Data," *American Economic Review* 90, no. 2 (May 2000): 368–372; and Darren Lubotsky, "Chutes or Ladders? A Longitudinal Analysis of Immigrant Earnings," working paper no. 445, Industrial Relations Section, Princeton University, August 2000.

immigration peaked in the first decade of the twentieth century, when the *yearly* flow of immigrants was more than 1 percent of the population (see Table 10.4).

Restrictions   In 1921, Congress adopted the Quota Law, which set annual quotas on immigration on the basis of nationality. These quotas had the effect of reducing immigration from eastern and southern Europe. This act was followed by other laws in 1924 and 1929 that further restricted immigration from southeastern Europe. These various revisions in immigration policy were motivated, in part, by widespread concern over the alleged adverse effect on native employment of the arrival of unskilled immigrants from eastern and southern Europe.

In 1965, the passage of the Immigration and Nationality Act abolished the quota system based on national origin that so heavily favored northern and western Europeans. Under this law, as amended in 1990, overall immigration is formally restricted to 675,000 people per year, with 480,000 spots reserved for family-reunification purposes, 140,000 reserved mostly for immigrants with exceptional skills who are coming for employment purposes, and 55,000 for "diversity" immigrants (from countries that have not recently provided many immigrants to the United States). Political refugees, who must meet certain criteria relating to persecution in their home countries, are admitted without numerical limit. The fact that immigration to the United States is a very worthwhile investment for many more people than can legally come, however, has created incentives for people to live in the country illegally.

Illegal Immigrants   Illegal immigration can be divided into two categories of roughly equal size: immigrants who enter legally but overstay or violate the provisions of their visas, and those who enter the country illegally. Over 30 million

TABLE 10.4   Officially Recorded Immigration: 1901 to 1998

Period	Number (in thousands)	Annual Rate (per thousand of U.S. population)	Year	Number (in thousands)	Annual Rate (per thousand of U.S. population)
1901–1910	8,795	10.4	*1990	1,536	6.1
1911–1920	5,736	5.7	*1991	1,827	7.3
1921–1930	4,107	3.5	*1992	974	3.8
1931–1940	528	0.4	*1993	904	3.5
1941–1950	1,035	0.7	*1994	804	3.1
1951–1960	2,515	1.5	1995	593	2.3
1961–1970	3,322	1.7	1996	916	3.5
1971–1980	4,389	2.0	1997	798	2.8
1981–1990	7,338	3.1	1998	660	2.4

*Includes illegal immigrants granted amnesty under the Immigration Reform and Control Act of 1986.
Source: U.S. Immigration and Naturalization Service, *1998 Statistical Yearbook*, Table 1.

people enter the United States each year under nonimmigrant visas, usually as students or visitors. Once here, the foreigner can look for work, although it is illegal to work at a job under a student's or visitor's visa. If the student or visitor is offered a job, he or she can apply for an "adjustment of status" to legally become a permanent resident, although the chances for approval as an employment-based immigrant are slim for the ordinary worker.

The other group of illegal immigrants enter the country without a visa. Immigrants from the Caribbean often enter through Puerto Rico, whose residents are U.S. citizens and thus are allowed free entry to the mainland. Others walk across the Mexican border. Still others are smuggled into the United States or use false documents to get through entry stations. For obvious reasons, it is difficult to establish the number of illegal immigrants who have come to the United States; however, the flow of illegals is believed to be 275,000 per year, and the total number residing in the United States in 1996 was estimated at 5 million.[17]

By the 1980s, illegal immigration had become a very prominent policy issue. The Secretary of Labor estimated in late 1979 that if only *half* of the jobs held by illegal aliens were given to U.S. citizens, the unemployment rate would drop from 6 percent to 3.7 percent. Similar beliefs led Congress to pass the Immigration Reform and Control Act of 1986, which imposed penalties on *employers* who knowingly hire illegal aliens (previously, the only penalty for illegal employment was deportation). The sanctions against employers included fines ranging from $250 to $10,000 per illegal worker, with penalties escalating throughout that range for repeated offenses. Jail terms were prescribed for "pattern and practice" offenders.

The policies people advocate are based on their beliefs about the consequences of immigration for employers, consumers, taxpayers, and workers of various skill levels and ethnicities. Nearly everyone with an opinion on this subject has an economic model implicitly or explicitly in mind when addressing these consequences; the purpose of this section is to make these economic models explicit and to evaluate them.

Naive Views of Immigration

There are two opposing views of illegal immigration that can be considered naive. One view is that every illegal immigrant deprives a citizen or legal resident of a job. For example, a Department of Labor official told a House committee studying immigration, "I think it is logical to conclude that if they are actually employed, they are taking a job away from one of our American citizens."[18] According to this view, if *x* illegal aliens are deported and others kept out, the number of unemployed Americans would decline by *x*.

---

[17]U.S. Immigration and Naturalization Service, *1998 Statistical Yearbook of the Immigration and Naturalization Service,* ch. 7, p. 199.

[18]Elliott Abrams and Franklin S. Abrams, "Immigration Policy—Who Gets In and Why?" *Public Interest* 38 (Winter 1975): 25.

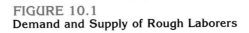

FIGURE 10.1
Demand and Supply of Rough Laborers

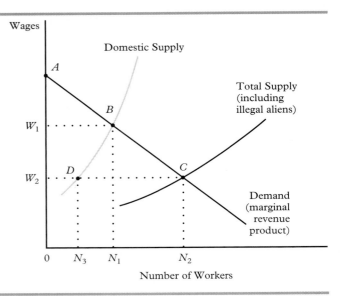

At the opposite end of the policy spectrum is the equally naive argument that the illegals perform jobs no American citizen would do:

> You couldn't conduct a hotel in New York, you couldn't conduct a restaurant in New York…if you didn't have rough laborers. We haven't got the rough laborers any-more….Where are we going to get the people to do that rough work?[19]

Both arguments are simplistic because they ignore the slopes of the demand and supply curves. Consider, for example, the labor market for the job of "rough laborer"—any job most American citizens find distasteful. Without illegal immigrants, the restricted supply of Americans to this market would imply a relatively high wage (W_1 in Figure 10.1). N_1 citizens would be employed. If illegal aliens entered the market, the supply curve would shift outward and perhaps flatten (implying that immigrants were more responsive to wage increases for rough laborers than citizens were). The influx of illegals would drive the wage down to W_2, but employment would increase to N_2.

Are Americans unwilling to do the work of rough laborers? Clearly, at the market wage of W_2, many more immigrants are willing to work at the job than U.S. citizens are. Only N_3 citizens would want these jobs at this low wage, while the remaining supply ($N_2 - N_3$) is made up entirely of immigrants. If there were no immigrants, however, N_1 Americans would be employed at wage W_1 as rough laborers. Wages would be higher, as would the prices of the goods or services produced with this labor,

---

[19]Abrams and Abrams, 26.

FIGURE 10.2

Demand and Supply of Rough Laborers with a Minimum Wage

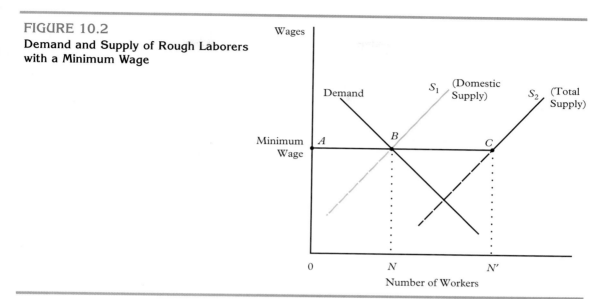

but the job would get done. The only shortage of American citizens is at the low wage of W_2; at W_1 there is no shortage (review chapter 2 for a discussion of labor shortages).

Would deporting those illegal immigrants working as rough laborers create the same number of jobs for U.S. citizens? The answer is clearly no. If the $N_2 - N_3$ immigrants working as laborers were deported and all other illegal immigrants were kept from the market, the number of Americans employed as laborers would rise from N_3 to N_1 and their wages would rise from W_2 to W_1 (Figure 10.1). $N_2 - N_1$ jobs would be destroyed by the rising wage rate associated with deportation. Thus, while deportation would increase the employment and wage levels of Americans in the market for laborers, it would certainly not increase employment on a one-for-one basis.

There is, however, one condition in which deportation *would* create jobs for American citizens on a one-for-one basis: when the federal minimum wage law creates a surplus of labor. Suppose, for example, that the supply of American laborers is represented by ABS_1 in Figure 10.2 and the total supply is represented by ACS_2. Because an artificially high wage has created a surplus, only N of the N' workers willing to work at the minimum wage can actually find employment. If some of them are illegal immigrants, sending them back—coupled with successful efforts to deny other immigrants access to these jobs—would create jobs for a comparable number of Americans. However, the demand curve would have to intersect the domestic supply curve (ABS_1) at or to the left of point B to prevent the wage level from rising (and thus destroying jobs) after deportation.

The analyses above ignore the possibility that if low-wage immigrant labor is prevented from coming to the jobs, employers may transfer the jobs to countries with abundant supplies of low-wage labor. Thus, it may well be the case that unskilled American workers are in competition with foreign unskilled workers anyway, whether those workers are employed in the United States or elsewhere. However, not all unskilled jobs can be moved abroad, because not all outputs can be imported (most unskilled services, for example, must be performed at the place of consumption); therefore, our analyses will continue to focus on situations in which the "export" of unskilled jobs is infeasible or very costly.

An Analysis of the Gainers and Losers

The claim that immigration is harmful to American workers is often based on a single-market analysis like that contained in Figure 10.1, where only the effects on the market for rough labor are examined. As far as it goes, the argument is plausible. When immigration increases the supply of rough laborers, both the wages and the employment levels of American citizens working as laborers are reduced. The total wage bill paid to American laborers falls from $W_1 0 N_1 B$ in Figure 10.1 to $W_2 0 N_3 D$. Some American workers leave the market in response to the reduced wage, and those who stay earn less. Even if the immigration of unskilled labor were to adversely affect domestic laborers, however, it would be a mistake to conclude that it is necessarily harmful to Americans as a *whole*.

Consumers   Immigration of "cheap labor" clearly benefits consumers using the output of this labor. As wages are reduced and employment increases, the goods and services produced by this labor are increased in quantity and reduced in price.

Employers   Employers of rough labor (to continue our example) are obviously benefited, at least in the short run. In Figure 10.1, profits are increased from $W_1 A B$ to $W_2 A C$. This rise in profitability will have two major effects. By raising the returns to capital, it will serve as a signal for investors to increase investments in plant and equipment. Increased profits will also induce more people to become employers. The increases in capital and the number of employers will eventually drive profits down to their normal level, but in the end the country's stock of capital is increased and opportunities are created for some workers to become owners.

Scale and Substitution Effects   Our analysis of the market for laborers assumed that the influx of immigrants had no effect on the demand curve (which was held fixed in Figure 10.1). This is probably not a bad assumption when looking at just one market, because the fraction of earnings immigrant laborers spend on the goods and services produced by rough labor may be small. However, immigrants do spend money in the United States, and this added demand creates job opportunities for others (see Figure 10.3). Thus, workers who are not close substitutes for unskilled immigrant labor may benefit from immigration because of the increase in consumer demand attendant on this addition to our working population.

Recall from chapter 3 that if the demand for skilled workers increases when the wage of unskilled labor falls, the two grades of labor are *gross complements*. Assuming skilled and unskilled labor are substitutes in the production process, the only way they could be gross complements is if the *scale effect* dominated the substitution effect. In the case of immigration we may suppose the scale effect to be very large, because as the working population rises, aggregate demand is increased. While theoretical

FIGURE 10.3
Market for All Labor Except Unskilled

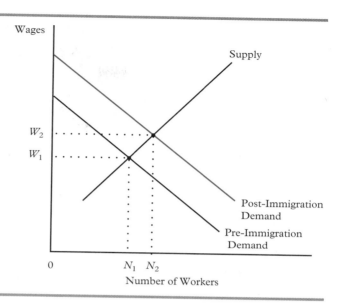

analysis cannot *prove* that the demand for skilled workers is increased by the immigration of unskilled labor if the two grades of labor are substitutes in the production process, it can offer the observation that an increase in demand for skilled workers remains a distinct possibility. Of course, any type of labor that is *complementary* with unskilled labor in the production process—supervisory workers, for example—can expect to gain from an influx of unskilled immigrants.

Most studies that attempt to actually measure the strength of substitution and scale effects use local labor markets as units of observation. Comparisons can be made of native wage and employment levels in the same area before and after an increase in immigration (as in Example 10.4); or comparisons can be made for a given year among areas with very different immigrant compositions. While there is some evidence that low-skilled immigrants are substitutes in production for natives with less than a high school education, these studies generally find very small effects of immigration on the wages and employment levels of resident workers.[20]

---

[20]David Card, "Immigrant Inflows, Native Outflows, and the Local Labor Market Impacts of Higher Immigration," *Journal of Labor Economics* 19, no. 1 (January 2001): 22–64; Cordelia W. Reimers, "Unskilled Immigration and Changes in the Wage Distributions of Black, Mexican American, and Non-Hispanic White Male Dropouts," and Kristin F. Butcher, "An Investigation of the Effect of Immigration on the Labor-Market Outcomes of African Americans," both in *Help or Hindrance? The Economic Implications of Immigration for African Americans*, ed. Daniel S. Hamermesh and Frank D. Bean (New York: Russell Sage Foundation, 1998), 107–181; James P. Smith and Barry Edmonston, eds., *The New Americans: Economic, Demographic, and Fiscal Effects of Immigration* (Washington, D.C.: National Academy Press, 1997); George J. Borjas, "The Economic Benefits from Immigration," *Journal of Economic Perspectives* 9, no. 2 (Spring 1995): 3–22; Friedberg and Hunt, "The Impact of Immigrants on Host Country Wages, Employment, and Growth"; and Borjas, "The Economics of Immigration."

EXAMPLE 10.4

The Mariel Boatlift and Its Effects on Miami's Wage and Unemployment Rates

Between May and September of 1980, some 125,000 Cubans were allowed to emigrate to Miami from the port of Mariel in Cuba. These immigrants, half of whom permanently settled in Miami, increased Miami's overall labor force by 7 percent in under half a year. Because two-thirds of "the Mariels" had not completed high school, and because unskilled workers made up about 30 percent of Miami's workforce, it is likely that the number of *unskilled* workers in Miami increased by 16 percent or more during this short period! Such a marked and rapid increase in labor market size is highly unusual, but it provides an interesting "natural experiment" on the consequences of immigration for a host area.

If immigration has negative effects on wages in the receiving areas, we would expect to observe that the wages of Miami's unskilled workers fell relative to the wages of its skilled workers *and* relative to the wages of unskilled workers in otherwise comparable cities. Neither relative decline occurred; in fact, the wages of unskilled black workers in Miami actually rose relative to wages of unskilled blacks in four comparison cities (Atlanta, Los Angeles, Houston, and Tampa).

Similarly, the unemployment rate among low-skilled blacks in Miami improved, on average, relative to that in other cities during the five years following the boatlift. Among Hispanic workers, there was a predictable increase in Miami's unemployment rate relative to that in the other cities in 1981, but from 1982 to 1985 the Hispanic unemployment rate in Miami fell faster than in the comparison cities.

What accounts for the absence of adverse pressures on the wages and unemployment rates of unskilled workers in the Miami area? First, concurrent rightward shifts in the demand curve for labor probably tended to offset the rightward shifts in labor supply curves.

Second, it also appears that some residents left Miami in response to the influx of immigrants and that other potential migrants went elsewhere; the rate of Miami's population growth after 1980 slowed considerably relative to that of the rest of Florida, so that by 1986 its population was roughly equal to what it was projected to be by 1986 *before* the boatlift. For locational adjustments of residents and potential immigrants to underlie the lack of wage and unemployment effects, these adjustments would have to have been very rapid. Their presence reinforces the theoretical prediction, made earlier in this chapter, that migration flows are sensitive to economic conditions in both sending and receiving areas.

Data from: David Card, "The Impact of the Mariel Boatlift on the Miami Labor Market," *Industrial and Labor Relations Review* 43, no. 2 (January 1990): 245–257. For similar studies, see Jennifer Hunt, "The Impact of the 1962 Repatriates from Algeria on the French Labor Market," *Industrial and Labor Relations Review* 45, no. 3 (April 1992): 556–572, and William Carrington and Pedro De Lima, "The Impact of the 1970s Repatriates from Africa on the Portuguese Labor Market," *Industrial and Labor Relations Review* 49, no. 2 (January 1996): 330–347.

Do the Overall Gains from Immigration Exceed the Losses?

So far, we have used economic theory to analyze the likely effects of immigration on various groups of natives, including consumers, owners, and skilled and unskilled workers. Theory suggests that some of these groups should be clear-cut gainers; among these are owners, consumers, and workers who are complements in production with immigrants. Native workers whose labor is highly substitutable in production with immigrant labor are the most likely losers from immigration, while the gains or losses for other groups of native workers are theoretically unpredictable owing to potentially offsetting influences of the substitution and scale effects. Further, the estimated effects on the above groups are quite small, although the actual effects still must be classified as uncertain.

In this subsection, we use economic theory to analyze a slightly different question: What does economic theory say about the *overall* effects of immigration on the host country? Put in the context of the *normative* criteria presented in chapter 1, this subsection asks, "If there are both gainers and losers from immigration among natives in the host country, is it likely that the gainers would be able to compensate the losers and still feel better off?" The answer to this question will be yes if immigration increases the aggregate disposable income of natives.

What Do Immigrants Add?   Immigrants are both consumers and producers, so whether their influx makes those already residing in the host country richer or poorer, in the aggregate, depends on how much the immigrants *add* to overall production as compared to how much they *consume*. Let us take a simple example of elderly immigrants allowed into the country to reunite with their adult children. If these immigrants do not work, and if they are dependent on their children or on American taxpayers for their consumption, then clearly the overall per capita disposable income among natives must fall. (This fall, of course, could well be offset by the increased utility of the reunited families, in which case it would be a price the host country might be willing to pay.)

If immigrants *work* after their arrival, our profit-maximizing models of employer behavior suggest that they are paid no more than the value of their marginal product. Thus, if they rely only on their own earnings to finance their consumption, immigrants who work do not reduce the per capita disposable income of natives in the host country. Moreover, if immigrant earnings are less than the *full* value of the output they add to the host country, then the total disposable income of natives will increase.[21]

Immigrants and Public Subsidies   Most host countries (including the United States) have government programs that may distribute benefits to immigrants. If the taxes paid by immigrants are sufficient to cover the benefits they receive from such programs, then the presence of these immigrants does not threaten the per capita disposable income of natives. Indeed, some government programs, such as national defense, are true *public goods* (whose costs are not increased by immigration), and any taxes paid by immigrants help natives defray the expenses of these programs. However, if immigrants are relatively high users of government support services, and if the taxes they pay do not cover the value of their benefits, then it is possible that the fiscal burden of immigration could be large enough to reduce the aggregate income of natives.

---

[21]Economic theory suggests this will be the case if the shift in labor supply is large enough to significantly lower the marginal revenue product of labor in the immigrants' labor market. If so, wages will fall, output will expand, and the *profits from the added output* are captured by owners, who are presumably natives.

Given the declining skills of recent immigrant cohorts, and given that many government programs (public health, welfare, and unemployment insurance, for example) are aimed at subsidizing the poor, there is growing concern that recent immigration to the United States may be harmful to natives. One study found that recent (legal) immigrants are relatively high users of welfare programs (including food stamps and medical and housing subsidies), although another found that they are much less likely than natives to become institutionalized for crime or mental disorders.[22]

A study of the net fiscal effects of recent legal immigraton suggests that these effects—measured over the lifetimes of the immigrants and their descendants—are *positive*. That is, immigrants and their descendants typically pay more in taxes than they receive in government benefits, with the present value of the surplus averaging $80,000 per immigrant. The study estimates that net fiscal effects are more likely to be positive if immigrants come as *young adult workers* and if they are *better educated*. For example, immigrants with more than a high school education are estimated to have a positive net fiscal effect averaging $198,000, while those with a high school education average a positive effect of $51,000. For legal immigrants with less than a high school education, the net fiscal effects are estimated to be a *negative* $13,000.[23]

Illegal Immigration   Illegal immigration has been the major focus of immigration policy in recent years, so it is interesting to consider how it, in particular, is likely to affect the overall disposable incomes of American citizens (and other legal residents). While the exact answer is unknown, three considerations suggest that *illegal immigration may be more likely to increase native incomes than legal immigration!*

First, illegal immigrants come mainly to work, not for purposes of family reunification.[24] Therefore, they clearly add to the production of domestic goods and services. Second, while they tend to be poor, they are ineligible for many programs (welfare, food stamps, Social Security, unemployment insurance) that transfer resources to low-income citizens. Third, despite their wish to hide from the government, immigrants cannot avoid paying most taxes (especially payroll, sales, and property taxes); indeed, one study indicated that 75 percent of illegal immigrants had income taxes withheld but that relatively few filed for a refund.[25]

---

[22]George Borjas and Lynette Hilton, "Immigration and the Welfare State: Immigrant Participation in Means-Tested Entitlement Programs," *Quarterly Journal of Economics* 111, no. 2 (May 1996): 575–604; and Kristin F. Butcher and Anne Morrison Piehl, "Recent Immigrants: Unexpected Implications for Crime and Incarceration," *Industrial and Labor Relations Review* 51, no. 4 (July 1998): 654–679.

[23]Smith and Edmonston, *The New Americans,* 334. Somewhat similar findings are reported in Ronald Lee and Timothy Miller, "Immigration, Social Security, and Broader Fiscal Impacts," *American Economic Review* 90, no. 2 (May 2000): 350–354.

[24]Attempted illegal immigration from Mexico is estimated to be extremely sensitive to changes in Mexico's real wage rate; see Gordon Hanson and Antonio Spilimbergo, "Illegal Immigration, Border Enforcement, and Relative Wages: Evidence from Apprehensions at the U.S.–Mexico Border," *American Economic Review* 89, no. 5 (December 1999): 1337–1357.

[25]Gregory DeFreitas, *Inequality at Work: Hispanics in the U.S. Labor Force* (New York: Oxford University Press, 1991), 228. The same study showed minimal use of public services by illegal immigrants.

Thus, we cannot rule out the possibility that, despite governmental efforts to prohibit it, the "transaction" of illegal immigration is—to use the normative terminology of chapter 1—Pareto-improving. That is, the immigrants themselves clearly gain (otherwise they would go back home), while as a group, natives may well not lose! The issue is clearly an empirical one, and the net effects of illegal immigration probably deserve more study before the country decides to allocate more resources to stopping it.

EMPLOYEE TURNOVER AND JOB MATCHING

From the perspective of an individual worker, the human capital model suggests that changing jobs is a costly transaction that will be undertaken voluntarily only if the expected benefits are relatively large. Workers, then, are seen as using job mobility as a means of improving their personal well-being. From a more global perspective, however, worker mobility performs the socially useful role of matching workers with the employers who value their skills most highly. In this section we analyze the patterns of mobility that are observed.

Effects of Job Tenure and Age

Workers are unique in the sense that each one has skills and interests that are different from those of others. Employers, for their part, have differing demands for skills and other worker characteristics that are a function of consumer preferences for their products, available production technologies, and even such factors as their management styles. Given that the information workers and employers initially have about each other is incomplete and costly to obtain, the probability that both employer and employee will find they are happy with the "match" is clearly less than 100 percent. Employers will want to fire workers who are less productive within their firms than they expected, and workers will want to quit if they believe they can be treated better elsewhere. Thus, poor matches end with a separation taking place, but good matches tend to endure. The concept of matching has strong implications for job turnover by job tenure and age.

Job Tenure   The imperfect information with which employers and employees begin a job match means that the probability of a separation between them should be higher in the early months of the match and become progressively lower as the match endures. In other words, the more successful the match, the longer it will last. Indeed, among American workers in their 20s, we find that about one-third of all new full-time job matches end in the first six months and 50 percent are ended in the first year. The probability of a match's ending during the second year is 17 percent, and during the third year it has fallen to 8 percent. Cumulating these percentages, we can calculate that 75 percent of the job matches involving young workers have ended after three years.[26]

---

[26]Henry S. Farber, "Mobility and Stability: The Dynamics of Job Change in Labor Markets," in *Handbook of Labor Economics*, ed. Orley Ashenfelter and David Card (New York: Elsevier, 1999), 2439–2483.

TABLE 10.5 Number of Employers for Whom an Employee Works from Ages 20 to 60, Men, United States and United Kingdom, 1983

Age Group	Number of New Employers during Age Interval		Cumulative Number of Employers	
	U.S.	*U.K.*	*U.S.*	*U.K.*
20–29	3.1	1.9	3.1	1.9
30–39	2.1	1.2	5.2	3.1
40–49	1.4	0.9	6.6	3.9
50–59	0.9	0.6	7.5	4.5

Source: Adapted from S. W. Polachek and W. S. Siebert, *The Economics of Earnings* (Cambridge, Eng.: Cambridge University Press, 1993), 253.

Age The problems of imperfect information that put job matches at risk can be expected to fall as workers become more experienced. As they age, workers find out about their strengths and weaknesses, discover what they like best in jobs or employers, and expand their employment contacts and knowledge about the labor market. Likewise, they establish a work history that employers can use to evaluate them better in the hiring process. Thus, the quality of job matches should rise with age and labor-market experience.

Table 10.5 presents data from both the United States and United Kingdom showing the number of new employers workers have, on average, during various decades of their work lives. Although turnover at all ages is much higher in the United States than in the United Kingdom, job changing clearly declines with age in both countries. While presumably showing the effects of better job matches, this decline is also consistent with the prediction that older workers have reduced incentives to invest in job mobility.[27]

Other Patterns of Job Mobility

Our human-capital model of job changes initiated by employees suggests that decisions are made taking both benefits and costs into account. It is certainly to be expected that, because of differences in their discount rates or psychic costs of moving, individuals will differ widely in their propensities for job mobility. For example, one study found that almost half of *all* permanent separations over a

---

[27]For theoretical analyses of job matching, see Boyan Jovanovic, "Job Matching and the Theory of Turnover," *Journal of Political Economy* 87 (October 1979): 972–990, and Kenneth McLaughlin, "Rent Sharing in an Equilibrium Model of Matching and Turnover," *Journal of Labor Economics* 12, no. 4 (October 1994): 499–523. For a recent study with extensive citations to earlier work, see Alison L. Booth, Marco Francesconi, and Carlos Garcia-Serrano, "Job Tenure and Job Mobility in Britain," *Industrial and Labor Relations Review* 53, no. 1 (October 1999): 43–70.

three-year period involved the 13 percent of workers who had three or more sep-arations during the period.[28] Despite individual idiosyncrasies, however, there are clearly *systematic* factors that influence the patterns of job mobility.

Wage Effects   Human capital theory predicts that, *other things equal,* a given worker will have a greater probability of quitting a low-wage job than a higher-pay-ing one. That is, workers employed at lower wages than they could obtain elsewhere are the most likely to quit. Indeed, a very strong and consistent finding in virtu-ally all studies of worker quit behavior is that, holding worker characteristics con-stant, employees in industries with lower wages have higher quit rates. At the level of individual workers, research indicates that those who change employers have more to gain from a job change than those who stay and that, indeed, their wage growth after changing is faster than it would have been had they stayed.[29]

Effects of Employer Size   From Table 10.6, it can be seen that *quit rates tend to decline as firm size increases.* One explanation for this phenomenon is that large firms offer more possibilities for transfers and promotions. Another, however, builds on the fact that large firms generally pay higher wages.[30] This explanation asserts that large firms tend to have highly mechanized production processes, where the output of one work team is highly dependent on that of production groups preceding it in the production chain. Larger firms, it is argued, have greater needs for dependable and steady workers because employees who shirk their duties can impose great costs on a highly interdependent production process. Large firms, then, establish "internal labor markets" for the reasons suggested in chapter 5; that is, they hire workers at entry-level jobs and carefully observe such hard-to-screen attributes as reliability, moti-vation, and attention to detail. Once having invested time and effort in selecting the best workers for its operation, a large firm finds it costly for such workers to quit. Thus, large firms pay high wages to reduce the probability of quitting because they have substantial firm-specific screening investments in their workers.[31]

Gender Differences   It has been widely observed that women workers have higher quit rates, and therefore shorter job tenures, than men. To a large degree, this higher quit rate probably reflects lower levels of firm-specific human capital

[28]Patricia M. Anderson and Bruce D. Meyer, "The Extent and Consequences of Job Turnover," *Brook-ings Papers on Economic Activity: Microeconomics* (1994): 177–248.

[29]Donald O. Parsons, "Models of Labor Market Turnover: A Theoretical and Empirical Survey," in *Research in Labor Economics,* vol. 1, ed. Ronald Ehrenberg (Greenwich, Conn.: JAI Press, 1977), 185–223; Michael G. Abbott and Charles M. Beach, "Wage Changes and Job Changes of Canadian Women: Evi-dence from the 1986–87 Labour Market Activity Survey," *Journal of Human Resources* 29, no. 2 (Spring 1994): 429–460; Christopher J. Flinn, "Wages and Job Mobility of Young Workers," *Journal of Political Economy* 94, no. 3, pt. 2 (June 1986): S88–S110; and Monica Galizzi and Kevin Lang, "Relative Wages, Wage Growth, and Quit Behavior," *Journal of Labor Economics* 16, no. 2 (April 1998): 367–391.

[30]Walter Oi, "The Fixed Employment Costs of Specialized Labor," in *The Measurement of Labor Cost,* ed. Jack E. Triplett (Chicago: University of Chicago Press, 1983).

[31]This argument is developed more fully and elegantly in Walter Oi, "Low Wages and Small Firms," in *Research in Labor Economics,* vol. 12, ed. Ronald Ehrenberg (Greenwich, Conn.: JAI Press, 1991).

TABLE 10.6   **Monthly Quit Rates per 100 Workers by Firm Size, Selected Industries (1977–1981 averages)**

	Number of Employees			
Industry	*<250 Employees*	*250–499*	*500–999*	*1000 and Over*
All manufacturing	3.28	3.12	2.40	1.50
Food and kindred products	3.46	4.11	3.95	2.28
Fabricated metal products	3.33	2.64	2.12	1.20
Electrical machinery	3.81	3.12	2.47	1.60
Transportation equipment	3.90	2.78	2.21	1.41

Source: Walter Oi, "The Durability of Worker-Firm Attachments," report to the U.S. Department of Labor, Office of the Assistant Secretary for Policy, Evaluation, and Research, March 25, 1983, Table 1.

investments. We argued in chapter 9 that the interrupted careers of "traditional" women workers rendered many forms of human capital investment less beneficial than would otherwise be the case, and lower levels of firm-specific training could account for lower wages, lower job tenures, and higher quit rates.[32] In fact, once the lower wages and shorter careers of women are controlled for, there appears to be no difference between the sexes in the propensity to quit a job, especially among those with more than a high school education.[33]

Cyclical Effects   Another implication of human capital theory is that workers will have a higher probability of quitting when it is relatively easy for them to obtain a better job quickly. Thus, when labor markets are *tight* (jobs are more plentiful relative to job seekers), one would expect the quit rate to be higher than when labor markets are *loose* (few jobs are available and many workers are being laid off). This prediction is confirmed in studies of time-series data.[34] Quit rates tend to rise when the labor market is tight and fall when it is loose. One measure of tightness is the unemployment rate; the negative relationship between the quit rate and unemployment can be readily seen in Figure 10.4. Another measure of labor market conditions is the layoff rate, which tends to rise in recessions and fall when firms are expanding production. It, too, is inversely correlated with the quit rate, as Figure 10.4 shows.

---

[32]Jacob Mincer and Boyan Jovanovic, "Labor Mobility and Wages," in *Studies in Labor Markets,* ed. Sherwin Rosen (Chicago: University of Chicago Press, 1981).

[33]Anne Beeson Royalty, "Job-to-Job and Job-to-Nonemployment Turnover by Gender and Education Level," *Journal of Labor Economics* 16, no. 3 (April 1998): 392–443; Francine Blau and Lawrence Kahn, "Race and Sex Differences in Quits by Younger Workers," *Industrial and Labor Relations Review* 34 (July 1981): 563–577; and Audrey Light and Manuelita Ureta, "Panel Estimates of Male and Female Job Turnover Behavior: Can Female Non-quitters Be Identified?" *Journal of Labor Economics* 10 (April 1992): 156–181.

[34]Parsons, "Models of Labor Market Turnover," 185–223.

FIGURE 10.4
The Quit Rate and Labor Market Tightness

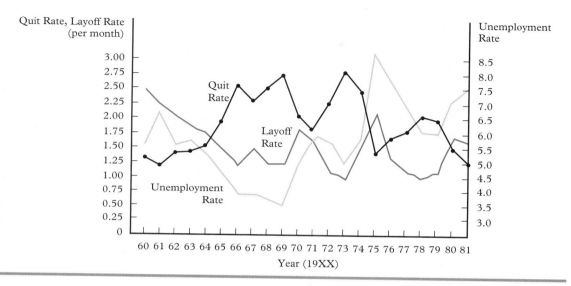

One interesting issue is whether the quality of job matches rises or falls during a recession. On the one hand, when job openings are few and job seekers are plentiful, employers have more applicants for each open position and can be more selective in making offers of employment. This reasoning suggests that match quality might increase in a recession. On the other hand, workers can expect fewer offers and may thus be more inclined during recessions to take the first offer that comes along; with workers being *less* selective, match quality might deteriorate. Recent research suggests that the latter influence dominates and that match quality during recessions is reduced.[35]

Employer Location   Economic theory predicts that when the costs of quitting a job are relatively low, mobility is more likely. Industries with high concentrations of employment in urban areas, where a worker's change of employer does not necessarily require investing in a change of residence, appear to have higher rates of turnover (holding wage rates and employee age constant) than industries concentrated in nonmetropolitan areas.[36]

---

[35]Audra J. Bowlus, "Matching Workers and Jobs: Cyclical Fluctuations in Match Quality," *Journal of Labor Economics* 13, no. 2 (April 1995): 335–350.
[36]Parsons, "Models of Labor Market Turnover," and Farrell E. Bloch, "Labor Turnover in U.S. Manufacturing Industries," *Journal of Human Resources* 14 (Spring 1979): 236–246.

Are Quits Different from Layoffs?

In studying worker mobility, we frequently make distinctions between *worker-initiated* and *employer-initiated* job separations. When an employee makes the decision to move to another job, we typically record the separation as a "quit." In contrast, if the employer decides to end the match, the separation is recorded as a "permanent layoff" or a "firing." This distinction at first seems clear, but the line between a quit and a layoff is actually blurry.

Market outcomes are the product of both employer and employee interactions. A worker with a better offer elsewhere may decide to leave, but her current employer had the option of improving her pay or working conditions if it wanted to keep her. If it chose not to take the steps to keep her, did she quit or was she forced out? Likewise, workers with whom the employer has performance issues have the option of taking steps to improve; if they choose not to take those steps, can we draw a clear distinction between their being fired and their having quit? The common distinction between a "voluntary quit" and an "involuntary layoff", however, does appear to be useful. Workers who are recorded as having quit for a nonfamily reason experience wage increases in their new jobs, while those who are laid off or fired typically are subject to wage losses.[37]

International Comparisons

It is also possible that the costs of job changing vary internationally. Data in Table 10.5, for example, suggested that workers in the United States are more likely to change employers than workers in the United Kingdom. Indeed, Table 10.7 confirms that, on average, American workers have been with their current employers fewer years than workers in most other developed economies, particularly those in Europe and Japan. We do not know for certain why Americans are more mobile, but one possibility is that they receive lower levels of company training, which could be both a cause and an effect of shorter expected job tenure. Another possibility, however, is that the costs of mobility are lower in the United States (despite the fact that Japan and Europe are more urban). What would create these lower costs?

Some argue that housing policies in Europe and Japan increase the costs of residential, and therefore *job,* mobility. Germany, the United Kingdom, and Japan, for example, have had controls on the rent *increases* that landlords can charge to existing renters, while tending to allow them freedom to negotiate any mutually agreeable rent on their *initial* lease with the renter. Thus, it is argued that renters who moved typically faced very large rent increases. Similarly, subsidized housing is much more common in these countries than in the United States, but since it is limited in supply, those British, German, or Japanese workers fortunate enough to live in subsidized units have been reluctant (it is argued)

---

[37]Keith and McWilliams, "The Returns to Mobility and Job Search by Gender."

TABLE 10.7 Average Job Tenure, Selected Countries, 1995		
	Average Tenure (in Years) with Current Employer	
Country	Men	Women
Australia	7.1	5.5
Canada	8.8	6.9
France	11.0	10.3
Germany	10.6	8.5
Japan	12.9	7.9
Netherlands	9.9	6.9
United Kingdom	8.9	6.7
United States	7.9	6.8

Source: Organisation for Economic Co-Operation and Development, *Employment Outlook: July 1997* (OECD: 1997), Table 5.6.

to give them up. The empirical evidence on the implications of housing policy for job mobility, however, is both limited and mixed.[38]

We could also hypothesize that the United States, Australia, and Canada, all of which exhibit shorter job tenures than most European countries and Japan, are countries that historically have attracted people willing to immigrate from abroad or resettle internally over long distances. In a country of movers, moving may not be seen by either worker or employer as unusual or especially costly.[39]

Is More Mobility Better?

On the one hand, mobility is socially useful, because it promotes both individual well-being and the quality of job matches. In chapter 8 we pointed out, for example, that mobility (or at least the *threat* of mobility) was essential to the creation of compensating wage differentials. Moreover, the greater the number of workers and employers in the market at any given time, the more flexibility an economy has in making job matches that best adapt to a changing environment. Indeed,

---

[38]See Patrick Minford, Paul Ashton, and Michael Peel, "The Effects of Housing Distortions on Unemployment," *Oxford Economic Papers* 40, no. 2 (June 1988): 322–345, and Axel Borsch-Supan, "Housing Market Regulations and Housing Market Performance in the United States, Germany, and Japan," in *Social Protection versus Economic Flexibility: Is There a Trade-Off?* ed. Rebecca M. Blank (Chicago: University of Chicago Press, 1994), 119–156.

[39]One study, for example, found no evidence that American employers stigmatized employees who frequently changed jobs; see Kristen Keith, "Reputation, Voluntary Mobility, and Wages," *Review of Economics and Statistics* 75, no. 3 (August 1993): 559–563.

when focusing on this aspect of job mobility, economists have long worried whether economies have *enough* mobility. A case in point is the concern whether employers have created "job lock" by adopting pension plans and health insurance policies that are not portable if the employee leaves the firm.[40]

On the other hand, however, lower mobility costs (and thus greater mobility) among workers also weaken the incentives of both employers and employees to invest in specific training or information particular to a job match. Failure to make these investments, it can be argued, reduces the productive potential of employees. Mobility costs can also introduce elements of monopsony into the labor market.

Costs of Turnover and the Monopsony Model

In chapters 3 and 4, we noted that some economists have begun to explore theoretical models that produce monopsony-like behavior by employers in situations in which they are not the sole buyers of labor in a particular market. We now briefly consider the implications for labor *demand* theory of the fact that employee turnover is costly.

Background Issues You will recall that in the standard model of labor demand, each employer is assumed to face a labor supply curve that is horizontal at the market wage rate. That is, any single firm is assumed to be a "wage taker" that can always hire additional workers at a constant (market) wage of, say, W^*. The firm has no incentive to pay *above* the market wage, because it can secure all the employees it wants at W^*, and if it paid *below* the market wage it would lose all its workers to other firms. This horizontal supply curve also means that the *marginal cost* of hiring labor is constant at W^*. With a downward-sloping marginal revenue product of labor curve, the profit-maximizing firm (which hires until marginal revenue product equals W^*) therefore has a downward-sloping labor demand curve.

From the standard model arises the *law of one price*, which states that, in equilibrium, all firms in the market for workers of the same skill will pay the same wage rate, as long as conditions of employment are the same. Two points must be made concerning the law of one price. First, a major implication of this law is that, with the exception of compensating differentials for employment conditions of one sort or another, *wages will be determined by workers' human capital characteristics*. All firms would have to pay the market wage for each skill group regardless of their level of profitability, their industry, or their size. Under this model, then, *employer characteristics*

---

[40]See Stuart Dorsey, "Pension Portability and Labor Market Efficiency: A Survey of the Literature," *Industrial and Labor Relations Review* 48, no. 2 (January 1995): 276–292; Alan C. Monheit and Philip F. Cooper, "Health Insurance and Job Mobility," and Jonathan Gruber and Brigitte C. Madrian, "Health Insurance and Job Mobility: The Effects of Public Policy on Job Lock," both in *Industrial and Labor Relations Review* 48, no. 1 (October 1994): 68–102. For a much earlier article, see Arthur Ross, "Do We Have a New Industrial Feudalism?" *American Economic Review* 48, no. 5 (December 1958): 914.

do not influence wages except when either favorable or unfavorable employment conditions give rise to compensating wage differentials.

Second, *worker mobility* is what generates the one price for labor of a given skill. If workers of equal skill were paid different wages by employers with comparable working conditions, the standard, competitive model asserts that the lower-paid ones would quit their jobs and seek employment with higher-paying firms. Wages in the lower-paying firms thereby would be driven up, while wages in the higher-paying firms would be driven down, by worker mobility. The standard model, with its horizontal labor supply curve facing each firm, implicitly assumes that mobility is costless and that the quit rate among workers is infinitely elastic with respect to wages (that is, if a firm were to cut its wages below those paid elsewhere, all its workers would quit).

Mobility Costs and the Firm's Labor Supply Curve   The human capital model of job mobility, as captured in equation (10.1), implies that a worker will *not* invest in mobility if the present value of the net benefits is negative. That is, even if the gross benefits of switching one's job are positive, making the change is not worthwhile if these benefits are small relative to the costs of searching for other offers, ending one's current employment relationship, possibly moving to a new residence, and settling into a new job.

If the costs of changing jobs make some wage (or utility) gains not worth capturing, and if these costs differ across individual workers, then we would not expect the quit rate to be infinitely responsive to wages. A small deviation from the market wage by a given firm might induce *some* workers to change employers, but a larger deviation would be required before others are induced to invest in mobility. Of course, we might reasonably expect supply to be more responsive to wages in the long run, because new entrants to the labor force are searching anyway and can choose the best opportunities (or avoid the worst) without having to incur the costs of severing ties with a current employer. However, if information is difficult to obtain and search is costly even in the long run, wage differences across workers with the same human capital characteristics and similar conditions of employment might persist more or less permanently.

Empirically, economists have estimated that workers' quit rates respond to their wages in the expected way (quits rise when wages fall), but the estimated response is considerably less than infinitely elastic.[41] Moreover, there is also evidence of persistent wage differentials across *industries* and *firm-size* groups[42] that

---

[41]See David Card and Alan B. Krueger, *Myth and Measurement: The New Economics of the Minimum Wage* (Princeton, N.J.: Princeton University Press, 1995), 375, for a summary of evidence on quit rates.

[42]Steven G. Allen, "Updated Notes on the Interindustry Wage Structure, 1890–1990," *Industrial and Labor Relations Review* 48, no. 2 (January 1995): 305–321; Richard Freeman, "Does the New Generation of Labor Economists Know More Than the Old Generation?" in *How Labor Markets Work*, ed. Bruce E. Kaufman (Lexington, Mass.: Lexington Books, 1988), 205–223; Richard Thaler, "Anomalies: Interindustry Wage Differentials," *Journal of Economic Perspectives* 3 (Spring 1989): 181–193; Jane Osborn, "Interindustry Wage Differentials: Patterns and Possible Sources," *Monthly Labor Review* 123, no. 2 (February 2000): 34–46; and Dominique Goux, "Persistence of Interindustry Wage Differentials: A Reexamination Using Matched Worker-Firm Panel Data," *Journal of Labor Economics* 17, no. 3 (July 1999): 492–533.

EXAMPLE 10.5

Monopsony in the Coal Fields? Probably Not

West Virginia coal mining at the turn of the twentieth century probably fits the archetype of a monopsony as well as any industry. Most mines were located in remote, sparsely populated areas, so miners wishing to change employers had to relocate. About 80 percent of miners lived in company housing in company towns. But despite these conditions, there is little evidence that employers enjoyed monopsony power.

Between 1897 and 1932, the West Virginia coal industry developed rapidly, but unevenly. Using annual data, William Boal investigated the size of the wage changes required to generate these employment shifts from county to county. If large wage changes were required to generate these shifts, employers would have exercised significant monopsony power, since this would imply that they faced upward-sloping labor supply curves. However, only small changes in wages were needed to attract new workers. Boal estimates that employers had the potential to exert a little monopsony power in the short run, but this power was sharply weakened by the effect of low current wages on their own future labor supply. The bottom line is that these employers faced nearly horizontal labor supply curves in the long run.

Why weren't employers able to exert monopsony power, even when there was only a single employer in town? They were handcuffed by very high turnover rates among employees, who could move to any of the hundreds of other mines in the region. Miners and their families relocated frequently, apparently using the same rail lines built to carry the coal itself from each mine to distant markets. Boal cites labor turnover rates in West Virginia ranging from 148 to 234 percent per year. (Labor turnover equals separations as a percent of average number on the payroll.) Many of the miners were single males who found moving very easy, but even married miners moved often. A U.S. Children's Bureau survey of a county in West Virginia in 1920 found that almost 60 percent of the families had lived in the same community for three years or less. In addition, the miners had plenty of information about competing job opportunities and wages. With mobile, informed workers, employers had little ability to exercise monopsony power.

Data from: William M. Boal, "Testing for Employer Monopsony in Turn-of-the-Century Coal Mining," *RAND Journal of Economics* 26, no. 3 (Autumn 1995), 519–536; and Price Fishback, *Soft Coal, Hard Choices: The Economic Welfare of Bituminous Coal Miners, 1890–1930* (New York: Oxford University Press, 1992).

researchers have not been able to explain by differences in workers' human capital or by conditions giving rise to compensating wage differentials. While there are other potential explanations for these findings, the evidence on quit rates and persistent wage differentials is certainly consistent with the presence of search and relocation costs that impede worker mobility. (As illustrated by Example 10.5, however, these costs can be surprisingly low in some cases.)

The presence of mobility costs implies that individual firms well might face upward-sloping labor supply curves over some range of wages and some finite time period. A firm could lower its wages (at least to some extent) without losing all its workers to other firms, and it could raise its wages by some amount without attracting all the workers from other firms. As was pointed out in chapter 3, the essence of the monopsonistic model of employer demand for labor is an upward-sloping labor supply curve to individual employers. It is this upward-sloping supply curve that drives the firm's marginal cost of labor above its wage rate, thus creating uncertainty about how its desired level of employment will respond to a mandated wage increase. (Recall from chapter 3 that when the marginal cost of labor is above the

FIGURE 10.5
Mobility Costs and the Extent to Which the Marginal Costs of Labor Exceed the Wage

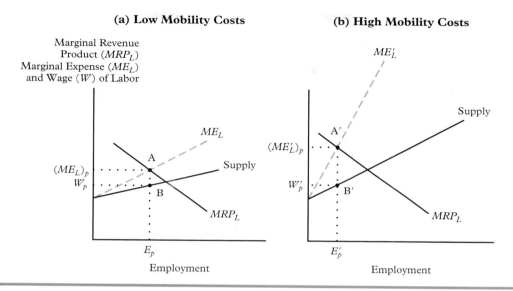

(a) Low Mobility Costs

(b) High Mobility Costs

wage, small mandated wage increases can simultaneously raise the wage level and *reduce* the marginal cost of labor.) One possible source of monopsony-like behavior by firms, then, is the presence of costs associated with job changing.[43]

The Extent of Monopsony-Like Behavior   While monopsony-like behavior by an employer is rooted in an upward-sloping labor supply curve, the *extent* to which this behavior deviates from that presumed by the standard labor demand model is a function of the *extent to which marginal costs of labor exceed the wage rate*. If marginal costs are substantially above the wage rate to begin with, for example, then even a relatively large mandated wage increase could still reduce the marginal costs of labor to the firm (and lead to theoretically ambiguous expectations about changes in the level of employment). However, if marginal costs were only slightly above the wage to begin with, the same mandated wage increase might *raise* the marginal costs of labor, which would lead us to expect the conventionally predicted fall in employment.

As illustrated in Figure 10.5, the degree to which a firm's marginal costs of labor exceed its wage rate depends on how steeply sloped its labor supply curve is.[44] When

---

[43]Card and Krueger, *Myth and Measurement*, 373–381, summarizes, and provides references to, the literature on monopsony models that are based on mobility costs.

[44]It can be mathematically proven that, with a straight-line labor supply curve to the firm, such as the ones illustrated in Figure 10.5, the accompanying marginal cost of labor curve has a slope that is *twice* that of the labor supply curve.

mobility costs are lower, the labor supply curve to an individual employer will be flatter (Figure 10.5a) and the associated marginal cost curve will rise relatively slowly. If mobility costs are higher, both the firm's labor supply curve and its marginal costs of labor rise sharply (see Figure 10.5b). Given its marginal revenue product of labor curve, if the firm were faced with a labor supply curve such as the one in panel (a), it would have a profit-maximizing employment level of E_p, would pay a wage of W_p, and the extent to which its marginal costs of labor exceeded its wage rate would be given by the distance AB. If instead the firm faced a supply curve like the one in panel (b), the gap between its marginal costs of labor and its wage rate (W'_p) at the profit-maximizing level of employment (E'_p) would be equal to the distance A'B', which is greater than AB. Thus, the *extent* to which a firm behaves like a monopsonist is a function of how steeply sloped its labor supply curve is—which is, in turn, a function of mobility costs.

REVIEW QUESTIONS

1. The licensing of such occupations as nurses and doctors in the United States requires people in those occupations to pass a test administered by the state in which they seek to work. Saying that "every time a health-care workers moves, some bureaucrat tells him he can't work," a national newspaper argued that the United States could reduce health-care costs if it removed state-to-state licensing barriers.
   a. From the perspective of positive economics, what are the labor market effects of having states, rather than the federal government, license professionals?
   b. Who would gain and who would lose from federalization of occupational licensing?
2. One way for the government to facilitate economic growth is for it to pay workers in depressed areas to move to regions where jobs are more plentiful. What would be the labor market effects of such a policy?
3. A recent television program examining the issue of Mexican immigration stated that most economists believe immigration is a benefit to the United States.

   a. State the chain of reasoning underlying this view.
   b. From a normative perspective, is the key issue wage effects on native workers or subsidies of immigrants by the host country? Why?
4. Suppose the United States increases the penalties for illegal immigration to include long jail sentences for illegal *workers*. Analyze the effects of this increased penalty on the wages and employment levels of *all* affected groups of workers.
5. Other things equal, firms usually prefer their workers to have low quit rates. However, from a social perspective, quit rates can be too low. Why do businesses prefer low quit rates, and what are the social disadvantages of having such rates "too low"?
6. The last two decades in the United States have been characterized by a very wide gap between the wages of those with more education and those with less. Suppose that workers eventually adjust to this gap by investing more in education, with the result that the wages of less-skilled workers rise faster than those of the more-skilled (so that

the wage gap between the two falls). How would a decline in the wage gap between the skilled and the unskilled affect immigration to the United States?

7. It has been said, "The fact that quit rates in Japan are lower than in the United States suggests that Japanese workers are inherently more loyal to their employers than are American workers." Evaluate this assertion that where quit rates are lower workers have stronger preferences for loyalty.

PROBLEMS

1. Rose lives in a poor country where she earns $5,000 per year. She has the opportunity to move to a rich country as a temporary worker for five years. Doing the same work, she'll earn $35,000 per year in the rich country. The cost of moving is $2,000, and it would cost her $10,000 more per year to live in the rich country. Rose's discount rate is 10 percent. Rose decides not to move because she will be separated from her friends and family. Estimate the psychic costs of Rose's move.

2. Suppose that the demand for rough laborers is $L_D = 100 - 10W$, where W = wage in dollars per hour and L = number of workers. If immigration increases the number of rough laborers hired from 50 to 60, by how much will the short-run profits of employers in this market change?

SELECTED READINGS

Abowd, John M., and Richard B. Freeman, eds. *Immigration, Trade, and the Labor Market.* Chicago: University of Chicago Press, 1991.

Borjas, George. "The Economics of Immigration." *Journal of Economic Literature* 32, no. 4 (December 1994): 1667–1717.

———. *Friends or Strangers.* New York: Basic Books, 1990.

———. *International Differences in the Labor Market Performance of Immigrants.* Kalamazoo, Mich.: W. E. Upjohn Institute for Employment Research, 1988.

Borjas, George J., and Richard B. Freeman, eds. *Immigrants and the Work Force.* Chicago: University of Chicago Press, 1992.

Borjas, George J., ed. *Issues in the Economics of Immigration.* Chicago: University of Chicago Press, 2000.

Chiswick, Barry. *Illegal Aliens: Their Employment and Employers.* Kalamazoo, Mich.: W.E. Upjohn Institute for Employment Research, 1988.

———. "Illegal Immigration and Immigration Control." *Journal of Economic Perspectives* 2, no. 3 (Summer 1988): 101–115.

Hamermesh, Daniel S., and Frank D. Bean, eds. *Help or Hindrance? The Economic Implications of Immigration for African Americans.* New York: Russell Sage Foundation, 1998.

Parsons, Donald O. "Models of Labor Market Turnover: A Theoretical and Empirical Survey." In *Research in Labor Economics,* vol. 1, ed. Ronald Ehrenberg. Greenwich, Conn.: JAI Press, 1977. Pp. 185–223.

Smith, James P., and Barry Edmonston, eds. *The New Americans: Economic, Demographic, and Fiscal Effects of Immigration.* Washington, D.C.: National Academy Press, 1997.

11

PAY AND PRODUCTIVITY:
Wage Determination within the Firm

I n the simplest model of the demand for labor (presented in chapters 3 and 4), employers had few managerial decisions to make; they simply *found* the marginal productivity schedules and market wages of various kinds of labor and hired the profit-maximizing amount of each kind. In a model like this, there was no need for employers to design a compensation policy.

Most employers, however, appear to give considerable attention to their compensation policies, and some of the reasons have already been explored. For example, employers offering specific training (see chapter 5) have a zone into which the wage can feasibly fall, and they must balance the costs of raising the wages of their specifically trained workers against the savings generated from a higher probability of retaining these workers. Likewise, when the compensation package is expanded to include such items as employee benefits or job safety (see chapter 8), employers must decide on the mix of wages and other valued items in the compensation package. We have also seen that under certain conditions employers will behave monopsonistically, in which case they *set* their wages rather than take them as given.

This chapter will explore in more detail the complex relationship between compensation and productivity. Briefly put, employers must make managerial decisions rooted in the following practical realities:

EXAMPLE 11.1

The Wide Range of Possible Productivities: The Case of the Factory That Could Not Cut Output

In 1987, a manufacturer of airguns ("BB guns") in New York State found that its sales were lagging behind production. Wanting to cut production by about 20 percent without engaging in widespread layoffs, the company decided to temporarily cut back from a five-day to a four-day workweek. To its amazement, the company found that, despite this 20 percent reduction in working hours, production levels were not reduced—its workers produced as many airguns in four days as they previously had in five!

Central to the problem of achieving its desired output reduction was that the company paid its workers on the basis of the number of items they produced. Faced with the prospect of a temporary cut in their earnings, its workers reduced time on breaks and increased their pace of work sufficiently to maintain their previous levels of output (and earnings). The company was therefore forced to institute artificial caps on employee production; when these individual output quotas had been met, the worker was not allowed to produce more.

The inability to cut output, despite cutting back on hours of work, suggests how wide the range of possible worker productivity can be in some operations. Clearly, then, careful attention by management to the motivation and morale of employees can have important consequences, both privately and socially.

1. Workers differ from each other in work habits that greatly affect productivity but are often difficult (costly) to observe before, and sometimes even after, hiring takes place;
2. The productivity of a given worker with a given level of human capital can vary considerably over time or in different environments, depending on his or her level of motivation (see Example 11.1);
3. Worker productivity over a given period of time is a function of innate ability, the level of effort, and the environment (the weather, general business conditions, or the actions of other employees);
4. Being highly productive is usually not just a matter of slavishly following orders, but rather of *taking the initiative* to help advance the employer's objectives.[1]

Employers, then, must choose management strategies and compensation policies to obtain the right (that is, profit-maximizing) kind of employees and offer them the optimum incentives for production. In doing so, they must weigh the costs of various policies against the benefits. The focus of this chapter is on the role of firms' compensation policies in optimizing worker productivity.

---

[1]For a stimulating article from which much of the ensuing discussion draws, see Herbert A. Simon, "Organizations and Markets," *Journal of Economic Perspectives* 5 (Spring 1991): 24–44. For more formal treatment of contracts and incentives, refer to James M. Malcomson, "Contracts, Hold-Up and Labor Markets," *Journal of Economic Literature* 35, no. 4 (December 1997): 1916–1957, and Canice Prendergast, "The Provision of Incentives in Firms," *Journal of Economic Literature* 37, no. 1 (March 1999): 7–63.

MOTIVATING WORKERS: AN OVERVIEW
OF THE FUNDAMENTALS

Employers and workers each have their own objectives and concerns, and the incentives imbedded in the employment relationship are critical to aligning these separate interests. We first present an overview of the key features of this relationship before moving on in later sections to analyses of various compensation schemes that employers can adopt to induce high productivity among their workers.

The Employment Contract

The employment relationship can be thought of as a contract between the employer (the "principal") and the employee (the "agent"). The employee is hired to help advance the employer's objectives in return for receiving wages and other benefits. Often there are understandings or implied promises that if employees work hard and perform well, they will be promoted to higher-paying jobs as their careers progress.

Formal Contracts   The agreement by an employee to perform tasks for an employer in return for current and future pay can be thought of as a contract. A *formal* contract, such as one signed by a bank and a homeowner for the repayment of a loan, lays out quite explicitly all that each party promises to do and what will happen if either party fails to perform as promised. Once signed, a formal contract cannot be abrogated by either party without penalty. Disputes over performance can be referred to courts of law or other third parties for resolution.

Implicit Contracts   Unlike formal contracts, most employment contracts are *incomplete* and *implicit.* They are usually incomplete in the sense that rarely are all the specific tasks that may be required of employees spelled out in advance. Doing so would limit the flexibility of employers in responding to changing conditions, and it would also require that employers and employees renegotiate their employment contract when each new situation arises—which would be costly to both parties.

Employment contracts are also implicit in the sense that they are normally a set of informal understandings that are too vague to be legally enforceable. For example, just what has an employee promised to do when she has agreed to "work hard," and how can it be proved she has failed to do so? Specifically what has a firm promised to do when it has promised to "promote deserving employees as opportunities arise"? Further, employees can almost always quit a job at will, and employers often have great latitude in firing employees; hence, the employment contract is one that usually can be abrogated by one party or the other without legal penalty.[2]

---

[2]The doctrine of *employment-at-will*, under which employers (and employees) have the right to terminate an employment relationship at any time, has historically prevailed in the United States. Those not subject to this doctrine in the United States have included unionized workers with contract provisions governing discharges, tenured teachers, and workers under some civil service systems. A number of state courts also have adopted public policy and/or implicit contract exceptions to the doctrine. For a discussion of these issues, see Ronald Ehrenberg, "Workers' Rights: Rethinking Protective Labor Legislation," in *Rethinking Employment Policy,* ed. Lee Bawden and Felicity Skidmore (Washington, D.C.: Urban Institute Press, 1989).

The severe limits on legal enforceability make it essential that implicit contracts be *self-enforcing*. We turn now to a discussion of the difficulties that must be surmounted in making employment contracts self-enforcing.

Coping with Information Asymmetries

It is often advantageous for one or both parties to cheat by reneging on their promises in one way or other. Opportunities for cheating are enhanced when information is *asymmetric*—that is, when one party knows more than the other about its own intentions or performance under the contract. For example, suppose an insurance company promises a newly hired insurance adjuster that she will receive a big raise in four years if she "does a good job." The company may later try to refuse her the raise she deserves by falsely claiming her work was not good enough. Alternatively, the adjuster, who works out of the office and away from supervisory oversight most of the time, may have incentives to "take it easy" by doing cursory or overly generous estimates of client losses. How can these forms of cheating be avoided?

Of course, sanctions against cheating are imbedded in the formal agreements made by employers and employees. Employers who break the provisions of agreements they have signed with their unions can be sued or legally subjected to a strike, for example, but this requires that cheating actually be *proved*. How can we reduce the chances of being cheated when contracts are informal and the threat of formal punishment is absent?

Discouraging Cheating: Signaling   One way to avoid being cheated is to transact with the "right kind" of person, and to do this we must find a way to induce the other party to reveal—or *signal*—the truth about its actual characteristics or intentions. Suppose, for example, that an employer wants to hire employees who are willing to defer current gratification for long-term gain (that is, it wants employees who do not highly discount the future). Simply asking applicants if they are willing to delay gratification might not evoke honest answers. There are ways, however, an employer could cause applicants to signal their preferences indirectly.

As pointed out in chapter 8, the employer could offer its applicants relatively low current wages and a large pension benefit upon retirement. Potential applicants with relatively high discount rates would find this pay package less attractive than applicants with low discount rates, and they would be discouraged from either applying for the job or accepting an offer if it were tendered.

Another way this firm could induce applicants to signal something about their true discount rate is to require a college degree or some other training investment as a hiring standard. As noted in chapter 9, people with high discount rates are less likely to make investments of any kind, so the firm's hiring standard should discourage those with high discount rates from seeking offers.

The essence of signaling, then, is the voluntary revelation of truth in *behavior,* not just statements. Many of the compensation policies discussed in the remainder of this chapter are at least partially aimed at eliciting truthful signals from job applicants or employees.[3]

Discouraging Cheating: Self-Enforcement   Even the "right kind" of people often have incentives to underperform on their promises. Economists have come to call this type of cheating *opportunistic behavior,* and it occurs not because people intend from the outset to be dishonest but because they generally try to advance their own interests by adjusting their behavior to unfolding opportunities. Thus, the challenge is to adopt compensation policies that more or less automatically induce both parties to adhere to their promises.[4]

The key to a self-enforcing agreement is that losses are imposed on the cheater that do not depend on proving a contract violation has occurred. In the labor market, the usual punishment for cheating on agreements is that the victim severs the employment relationship; consequently self-enforcement requires that *both employer and employee derive more gains from honest continuation of the existing employment relationship than from severing it.* If workers are receiving more from the existing relationship than they expect to receive elsewhere, they will automatically lose if they shirk their duties and are fired. If employers profit more from keeping their existing workers than from investing in replacements, they will suffer by reneging on promises and having workers quit.

Creating a Surplus   Incentives for both parties to live up to an implicit agreement are strongest when workers are getting paid more than they could get in alternative employment, yet less than the value of their marginal product to the firm. The gap between their marginal revenue product to the firm and their alternative wage represents a *surplus* that can be divided between employer and employee. This surplus must be *shared* if the implicit contract is to be self-enforcing, because if one party receives the entire surplus, the other party has nothing to lose by terminating the employment relationship. A graphic representation of the division of a surplus is given in Figure 11.1, where we see that attempts by one party to increase its share of the surplus will reduce the other party's losses from terminating the employment relationship.

Surpluses are usually associated with some earlier investment by the employer. In chapter 5 we saw that investments by the firm in specific training or in the hiring/evaluation process enabled workers' productivity and wages to exceed their alternatives. Firms can also create a surplus by investing in their *reputations.* For example, an employer that is well known for keeping its promises about future promotions or raises can attract workers of higher productivity at

---

[3]For a formal model that uses educational attainment as a signal for innate ability (which is difficult for an employer to observe directly), refer back to chapter 9. For a thorough review of signaling theory, see John G. Riley, "Silver Signals: Twenty-Five Years of Screening and Signaling," *Journal of Economic Literature* 39, no. 2 (June 2001): 432–478.

[4]See H. Lorne Carmichael, "Self-Enforcing Contracts, Shirking, and Life Cycle Incentives," *Journal of Economic Perspectives* 3 (Fall 1989): 65–84, for a more complete discussion of the importance of self-enforcement to implicit contracting.

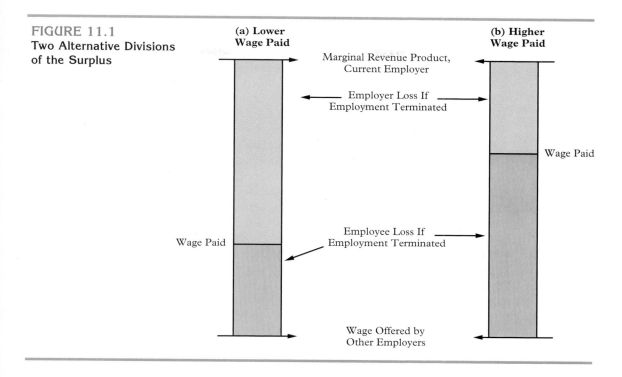

FIGURE 11.1
Two Alternative Divisions of the Surplus

(a) Lower Wage Paid

(b) Higher Wage Paid

Marginal Revenue Product, Current Employer

Employer Loss If Employment Terminated

Wage Paid

Wage Paid

Employee Loss If Employment Terminated

Wage Paid

Wage Offered by Other Employers

lower cost than can employers with poor reputations. (A firm with a poor reputation for performing on its promises must pay a compensating wage differential to attract workers of given quality away from employers with good reputations.) Because the good reputation increases productivity relative to the wage paid, a surplus is created that can be divided between the firm and its workers.

Motivating Workers

Beyond the issue of enforceability, employment contracts address the employer's need to motivate workers. Workers can be viewed as utility maximizers, and "putting forth their best efforts" may entail working hard when they are sick or distracted by personal problems, or it may involve a work pace that they find taxing. Employees can be assumed to do what they feel is in their own interests unless induced to do otherwise by the employer's system of rewards. How can we create rewards that give employees incentives to work toward goals of their employers?

Pay for Performance   The most obvious way to motivate workers is to pay them based on their individual output. Linking pay to output creates the presumption of strong incentives for productivity, but there are two general problems that incentive pay schemes must confront.[5] One problem is that using output-based pay has both benefits and costs to an employer, and both are affected by the extent to which a worker's output is influenced by forces outside his or her control. Jane, for example, may be willing to put forth 10 percent more effort if she can be sure her output (and pay) will rise by 10 percent. If machine breakdowns are so common, however, that she can only count on a 5 percent increase, she may decide that the extra 10 percent effort is not worth it. From the employer's perspective, then, output-based pay might provide only weak incentives if Jane's effort and the resulting output are not closely linked.

From Jane's perspective, a weak link between output and effort also puts her earnings at risk of variations that she cannot control—and she may be unwilling to take a job with such a pay scheme unless it pays a compensating wage differential. Thus, unless a worker's output and effort are very closely associated, output-based pay may have small benefits to the employer and yet come at added cost.[6]

The second problem facing pay-for-performance plans is the need to pick an output measure that coincides with the employer's ultimate objective. Quantitative aspects of output (such as the number of complaints handled by a clerk in the customer service department) are easier to measure than the qualitative aspects of friendliness or helpfulness—and yet the qualitative aspects are critical to building a loyal customer base. As we will see, imperfectly designed performance measures can backfire by inducing employees to allocate their effort toward what is being measured and away from other important aspects of their jobs.[7]

Time-Based Pay with Supervision   An alternative pay scheme is to compensate workers for the time they work. This reduces the risk of having Jane's pay—to continue our example—vary on a weekly basis, but guaranteeing her a wage without reference to her actual output creates a problem of *moral hazard:* why should she work hard if that effort is not rewarded? (See Example 11.2 for a comparison of actual work effort under output- and time-based pay.) The danger that workers might only "put in their time" means that employers must closely monitor their behavior.

The problem with close supervision is that it is costly. Tasks in almost any workplace are divided so that the economies afforded by specialization are possible, and workers must continually adjust to changing situations within their areas of responsibility. Extremely close supervision would require supervisors to have the same information, at the same time, on the situations facing all their subordi-

---

[5]This subsection draws heavily on David E. Sappington, "Incentives in Principal–Agent Relationships," *Journal of Economic Perspectives* 5 (Spring 1991): 45–66, and George P. Baker, "Incentive Contracts and Performance Measurement," *Journal of Political Economy* 100 (June 1992): 598–614.

[6]For a more thorough discussion of this issue, see Canice Prendergast, "What Trade-off of Risk and Incentives?" *American Economic Review* 90, no. 2 (May 2000): 421–425.

[7]A recent theoretical treatment of this issue can be found in George Baker, "The Use of Performance Measures in Incentive Contracting," *American Economic Review* 90, no. 2 (May 2000): 415–420.

EXAMPLE 11.2

Calorie Consumption and the Type of Pay

We noted in the text that time-based pay raises the question of *moral hazard*; that is, because workers are paid regardless of their output, they may not put forth their best efforts. An interesting examination of this question comes from Bukidon in the Philippines, where it is common for workers to hold several different farming jobs during a year. In some of these jobs they are paid by the hour, and in some they are paid directly for their output. Therefore, we are able to observe how hard the same individual works under the two different types of pay system.

A recent study discovered clear-cut evidence that the workers put forth much less effort in these physi-

cally demanding jobs when paid by the hour rather than for their output. Measuring effort expended by both weight change and calorie consumption, the study found that workers consumed *23 percent fewer calories* and *gained more weight per calorie consumed* when they were paid by the hour. Both facts suggest that less physical effort was put forth when workers were paid by the hour than when they were paid a piece rate.

Data from: Andrew D. Foster and Mark R. Rosenzweig, "A Test for Moral Hazard in the Labor Market: Contractual Arrangements, Effort, and Health," *Review of Economics and Statistics* 76, no. 2 (May 1994): 213–227.

---

nates, in which case they might as well make all the decisions themselves! In short, detailed supervision can destroy the advantages of specialization.

Motivating the Individual in a Group

If workers seek to maximize utility by increasing their *own* consumption of valued goods, then focusing on the link between each individual's pay and performance is sufficient in developing company policy. However, the concern for one's standing in a group is often a factor that also affects a worker's utility. The importance of the *group* in motivating *individuals* presents both problems and opportunities for the employer.

Issues of Fairness   People's concern about their treatment *relative to others* in their reference group means that *fairness* is an issue that pervades the employment relationship. A worker who obtains a 7 percent wage increase during a year in which both price and wage increases average 4 percent might be quite happy until he finds out that a colleague working in the same job for the same employer received a 10 percent increase. Workers who feel unfairly treated may quit, reduce their effort level, steal from the employer, or even sabotage output in order to "settle the score."[8]

---

[8]Interviews with managers often suggest that the perception of fairness is an important motivational tool; see, for example, Alan S. Blinder and Don H. Choi, "A Shred of Evidence on Theories of Wage Stickiness," *Quarterly Journal of Economics* 105, no. 4 (November 1990): 1003–1015. For a similar study, see David I. Levine, "Fairness, Markets, and the Ability to Pay: Evidence from Compensation Executives," *American Economic Review* 83, no. 5 (December 1993): 1241–1259.

Unfortunately for employers, however, the fairness of identical policy decisions often can be perceived differently depending on their context.

For example, a sample of people was asked to consider the case of two small companies that were not growing as planned and therefore had a need to cut costs. Each paid workers $10 per hour, but Employer A paid that in salary and Employer B paid $9 in salary and $1 in the form of a bonus. Most respondents said it would be unfair for A to cut wages by 10 percent, but they thought it fair if B were to eliminate its bonus.[9] Apparently, pay framed as "salary" connotes a greater entitlement than pay framed as "bonus."

Consider a second example from the same survey. A majority of respondents thought it would be unfair for a successful house painter to cut wages from $9 to $7 if he discovered that reliable help could be hired for less. However, they felt that if he quit painting and went into landscaping (where wages were lower), paying a $7 wage would be justified. Clearly, the employer is included among the reference groups used by workers in judging fairness, and the *context* of an employer's decision matters as much as its content!

Group Loyalty Besides concern for their own levels of consumption and their relative treatment within the group, employees are also typically concerned with the status or well-being of the entire group. While there are always temptations to "free ride" in a group by taking it easy and enjoying the benefits of others' hard work, most people are willing to make at least some sacrifices for their team, school, work group, community, or country.[10] Because the essence of "doing a good job" so frequently means taking the initiative in many small ways to advance the organization's interests, employers with highly productive workers almost universally pay attention to policies that foster organizational loyalty. While many of the steps employers can take to nurture this loyalty go beyond the boundaries of economics, some compensation schemes we will analyze relate pay to *group* performance quite directly.

Compensation Plans: Overview and Guide to the Rest of the Chapter

Along with the employer's hiring standards, supervisory policies, and general managerial philosophy, its compensation plan greatly affects the incentives of employees to put forth effort. While a detailed discussion of many managerial policies is outside

---

[9]Daniel Kahneman, Jack L. Knetsch, and Richard Thaler, "Fairness as a Constraint on Profit-Seeking: Entitlements in the Market," *American Economic Review* 76 (September 1986): 728–741.

[10]One study found that workers were over 5 percent more productive during World War II, and over 9 percent more productive in industries directly related to the war effort; see Mark Bils and Yongsung Chang, "Wages and the Allocation of Hours and Effort," National Bureau of Economic Research working paper no. 7309, August 1999. For other considerations of altruistic behavior among workers, see Simon, "Organizations and Markets," 34–38, and Julio J. Rotemberg, "Human Relations in the Workplace," *Journal of Political Economy* 102, no. 4 (August 1994): 684–717. For an analysis of peer pressure in compensation schemes, see John M. Barron and Kathy Paulson Gjerde, "Peer Pressure in an Agency Relationship," *Journal of Labor Economics* 15, no. 2 (April 1997): 234–254.

the scope of this text, the incentives created by compensation schemes fall squarely within the purview of modern labor economics. In what follows, therefore, we use economic concepts to analyze the major characteristics of compensation plans.

Three elements broadly characterize an employer's compensation scheme: the *basis* on which pay is calculated, the *level* of pay in relation to pay for comparable workers elsewhere, and—for employers with internal labor markets—the *sequencing* of pay over workers' careers. The remainder of the chapter is devoted to analyses of these elements.

PRODUCTIVITY AND THE BASIS OF YEARLY PAY

Workers can be paid for their time, their output, or some hybrid of the two. Most in the United States are paid for their time, and we must ask why output-based pay is not more widely used. Because compensation plans must satisfy both the employer and the employee, we organize our analysis around the considerations relevant to each side of the labor market.

Employee Preferences

Piece-rate pay, under which workers earn a certain amount for each item produced, is the most common form of individually based incentive pay for production workers. Another system linking earnings to individuals' output is payment by *commission,* under which workers (usually salespeople) receive a fraction of the value of the items they sell. *Gainsharing* plans, which have grown in popularity recently, are *group*-incentive plans that at least partially tie earnings to gains in group productivity, reductions in cost, increases in product quality, or other measures of group success. *Profit-sharing* and *bonus* plans attempt to relate workers' pay to the profits of their firm or subdivision; this form of pay also rewards work groups rather than individuals. Under all these systems, workers are paid at least somewhat proportionately to their output or to the degree their employer prospers.

Variability of Pay   If employees were told that their average earnings over the years under a time-based payment system would be equal to their earnings under an output-based pay plan, they would probably prefer to be paid on a *time* basis. Why? Earnings under output-based pay plans clearly vary with whatever measure of output serves as the basis for pay. As mentioned earlier, many things that affect individual or group output depend on the external environment, not just on the level of energy or commitment the individual worker brings to the job. The number of items an individual produces in a given day is affected by the age and condition of machinery, interrupted flows of supplies owing to strikes or snowstorms, and the worker's own illness or injury. Commissions earned by salespeople are clearly affected by the overall demand for the product being sold, and this demand can fluctuate for a number of reasons well beyond the control of the individual salesperson. Earnings that are dependent on some measure of *group* output will also vary with the level of effort expended by others in the group.

The possible variations in earnings under output-based pay are thought to be unappealing to workers because of their presumed *risk aversion* (that is, workers' preference for earnings certainty, even if it means somewhat lower pay). Most workers have monthly financial obligations for rent, food, insurance, utilities, and so forth. If several low-income pay periods are strung together, they might have difficulty in meeting these obligations, even if several high-income pay periods were to follow.

Because of their anxiety about periods of lower-than-usual output, employees prefer the certainty of time-based pay, other things (such as the average level of earnings) equal. To induce risk-averse employees to accept output-based pay, employers would have to pay a compensating differential.

Worker Sorting   Worker risk aversion aside, it is interesting to consider *which* workers will be attracted to piece-rate or commission pay schemes. Because time-based plans pay the same, at least in the short run, to high and low producers alike, workers who gain most from piece rates or commissions are those whose levels of motivation or ability are above average. Thus, employees who choose to work under compensation plans that reward individual productivity signal that they believe themselves to be above-average producers. For example, when an American company that installs glass in automobiles went from time-based pay to piece rates in the mid-1990s, the individual output of *incumbent employees who stayed with the firm* rose by 22 percent. However, because changing to piece rates allowed the company to attract and retain the fastest workers, the *overall* increase in worker productivity was in the neighborhood of 44 percent![11]

Pay Comparisons   There are three reasons to expect that workers paid for their output might earn more than those paid for their time: incentive pay motivates employees to work harder, it attracts the most productive workers, and it involves risk that may call forth a compensating wage differential. One study of pay in some apparel industries found that workers paid a piece rate earned about 14 percent more than workers paid by the hour. The study estimated that about one-third of this disparity was a compensating differential, with the remainder being related to the incentive and sorting effects.[12]

Employer Considerations

The willingness of employers to pay a premium to induce employees to accept piece rates depends on the costs and benefits to employers of incentive pay schemes. If workers are paid with piece rates or commissions, it is they who bear the consequences of low productivity, as noted above; thus, employers can afford

---

[11]Edward P. Lazear, "Performance Pay and Productivity," *American Economic Review* 90, no. 5 (December 2000): 1346–1361.

[12]Eric Seiler, "Piece Rate vs. Time Rate: The Effect of Incentives on Earnings," *Review of Economics and Statistics* 66 (August 1984): 363–376. For a more recent study of the topic, see Daniel Parent, "Methods of Pay and Earnings: A Longitudinal Analysis," *Industrial and Labor Relations Review* 53, no. 1 (October 1999): 71–86.

to spend less time screening and supervising workers. If workers are paid on a *time* basis, the *employer* accepts the risk of variations in their productivity; when workers are exceptionally productive, profits increase, and when they are less productive, profits decline. Employers, however, may be less anxious about these variations than employees are. They typically have more assets and can thus weather the lean periods more comfortably than individual workers can. Employers also usually have several employees, and the chances are that not all will suffer the same swings in productivity at the same time (unless there is a morale problem in the firm). Thus, employers may not be as willing to pay for income certainty as workers are.

The other major employer consideration in deciding on the basis for pay concerns the incentives for employee effort. The considerations related to three major types of incentive plans in use are discussed below.

Pay for Output: Individual Incentives   From the employer's perspective, the big advantage of individually based output pay is that it induces employees to adopt a set of work goals that are directly related to output. There are disadvantages, however.

First, the need to link output-based pay to what can be objectively determined means that workers might be induced to allocate their efforts away from aspects of their performance that are not being measured. If they get paid only for the quantity of items they individually produce or sell, they may have minimal regard for quality, safety procedures, or the performance or professional development of others on their work team.[13] These problems can create a need for costly quality-control supervision unless workers can be induced to monitor quality themselves. Self-monitoring of quality is only easily induced when a particular item or service can be traced to the worker responsible. For example, the auto glass installer mentioned earlier requires workers who have installed a windshield improperly (which usually results in its breaking) to pay for the replacement glass and then to re-install it on their own time.

A second problem is that workers may be induced to work so quickly that machines and tools are damaged through lack of proper maintenance or use. While this problem is mitigated to the extent that production downtime can cause the worker's earnings to drop, it is of enough concern to employers that they frequently require piece-rate workers to provide their *own* machines or tools.

How can firms create pay schemes with the proper incentives when the overall value of individual output is difficult to measure? In the remainder of this section, we explore two options. One is payment based on some measure of *group* output, and the other bases pay at least partly on the *subjective* judgments of supervisors.

Pay for Output: Group Incentives   When individual output is difficult to monitor, when individual incentive plans are detrimental to output quality, or when

---

[13]Robert Gibbons, "Incentives in Organizations," *Journal of Economic Perspectives* 12, no. 4 (Fall 1998): 115–132, provides a summary of this issue, with extensive citations to the literature.

output is generated by teams of interdependent workers, firms sometimes adopt group incentive pay schemes to more closely align the interests of employer and employee. These plans may tie at least a portion of pay to some component of profits (group productivity, product quality, cost reductions), or they may directly link pay with the firm's overall profit level. In still other cases workers might *own* the firm and split the profits among themselves.[14]

One drawback to group incentives is that groups are composed of individuals, and it is at the individual level that decisions about shirking are ultimately made. A person who works very hard to increase group output or the firm's profits winds up splitting the fruits of his or her labor with all the others, who may not have put out extra effort. Thus, *free-rider* opportunities give workers incentives to cheat on their fellow employees by shirking.[15] (Another downside of group incentives occurs when they attract the wrong sort of workers, and the good workers leave. One extreme case is discussed in Example 11.3.)

In very small groups, cheating may be easy to detect, and peer pressure can be effectively used to eliminate it. When the group of workers receiving incentive pay is large, however, employers may have to devote managerial resources to building organizational loyalties if shirking is to be discouraged. Interestingly, despite free-rider problems, studies have found that there is a positive correlation between profit sharing and organizational output.[16]

Group Incentives and Executive Pay   Compensation for top executives provides an interesting example of the potential and the problems of basing pay on group results. Executives run a company but do not own it, and like other employees, they want to advance their own interests.[17] How can companies align the interests of these key players with those of the owners (shareholders)?

Because firms are trying to maximize profits, we might consider basing executive pay on the firm's profits. But over what time period should profits be mea-

---

[14]For a review of the literature on productivity in worker-owned or worker-managed firms, see James B. Rebitzer, "Radical Political Economy and the Economics of Labor Markets," *Journal of Economic Literature* 31, no. 3 (September 1993): 1405–1409, and Michael A. Conte and Jan Svejnar, "The Performance Effects of Employee Ownership Plans," in *Paying for Productivity,* ed. Alan S. Blinder (Washington, D.C.: Brookings Institution, 1990), 142–181.

[15]For a more in-depth analysis of this problem, see Haig R. Nalbantian, "Incentive Contracts in Perspective," in *Incentives, Cooperation, and Risk Sharing,* ed. Haig R. Nalbantian (Totowa, N.J.: Rowman & Littlefield, 1987), and Eugene Kandel and Edward Lazear, "Peer Pressure and Partnerships," *Journal of Political Economy* 100, no. 4 (August 1992): 801–817.

[16]Martin Weitzman and Douglas Kruse, "Profit Sharing and Productivity," in *Paying for Productivity,* ed. Alan S. Blinder (Washington, D.C.: Brookings Institution, 1990); for reference to the extent and effect of profit sharing in several countries, see OECD, *Employment Outlook, July 1995* (Paris: Organisation for Economic Co-operation and Development, July 1995), ch. 4, and Sandeep Bhargava, "Profit Sharing and the Financial Performance of Companies: Evidence from U.K. Panel Data," *Economic Journal* 104, no. 426 (September 1994): 1044–1056.

[17]As noted in chapter 3's discussion of the demand for labor under monopoly, executives can buy some peace and quiet on the job by forgoing profit maximization, when possible. For an example, see Marianne Bertrand and Sendhil Mullainathan, "Is There Discretion in Wage Setting? A Test Using Takeover Legislation," *RAND Journal of Economics* 30, no. 3 (Autumn 1999): 535–554.

EXAMPLE 11.3

Poor Group Incentives Doom the Shakers

The Shakers were an unusual religious sect. They required strict celibacy and practiced communal ownership of property, with all members sharing the group's income equally—receiving the average product. They arrived in the United States in 1774 and numbered around 4,000 by 1850, but their membership dwindled thereafter. Their decline is generally attributed to their failure to reproduce and to their declining religious fervor, but economic historian John Murray argues that their group compensation plan was another important reason for their demise.

Those members with a higher-than-average marginal productivity would receive less than the value of their output—and usually less than they could make elsewhere. Thus, high-productivity members had an incentive to quit. Conversely, outsiders with a low marginal productivity had an incentive to join, receiving more than the value of their output and more than they could elsewhere.

Murray proxies marginal productivity by literacy. When the Shaker communes were established in Ohio and Kentucky, their members were full of religious zeal, which may have initially overcome the incentive problems. These members had a literacy rate of almost 100 percent, far above that of the surrounding population. By the time of the Civil War, however, illiterates were joining the group in significant numbers, and the sect's literacy rates fell below the rates in the surrounding areas. Likewise, Murray finds that literate members were 30 to 40 percent more likely to quit the community (becoming "apostates") than were illiterate members.

Contemporaries began to question the sincerity of the new entrants: they were "bread and butter Shakers," intent on free-riding on their more productive brothers and sisters. Many had been unable or unwilling to provide for themselves in the world outside the commune. Eventually, the changing composition of the Shaker communities caused a crisis in the communes; the average product of the group fell; and the group was wracked by diminishing enthusiasm, internal stress, and declining membership.

Data from: John E. Murray, "Human Capital in Religious Communes: Literacy and Selection of Nineteenth Century Shakers," *Explorations in Economic History* 32 (April 1995), 217–235.

sured? Basing this year's pay on current-year profits might create the same adverse incentives discussed earlier with piece rates. A focus on current-year profits could induce executives to pursue only short-run strategies (or accounting tricks), which run counter to the firm's long-run interests, in the hopes they can "take the money and run" to another corporation before the long-run consequences of their decisions are fully observed.

The strongest way to align the interests of corporate executives and company owners may be to pay them with company stock or the options to buy it. This seemingly rewards top executives for efforts that increase company wealth and punishes them for actions that reduce it. However, because stock prices are also influenced by overall investor "bullishness," executives paid with stock are rewarded for luck as well as effort—and they may elect to reduce effort and take a free ride when stock prices are rising in general. Beyond reducing incentives, economy-wide fluctuations in stock prices also cause executives' pay to vary because of things beyond their control, which may force firms to pay them a compensating differential for the added riskiness of their pay.

In practice, the compensation of chief executive officers (CEOs) in the United States has become increasingly responsive to shareholder value. In 1984, 17 percent of CEO pay was in the form of stock or stock options, while in 1996 the comparable figure was 23 percent.[18] (The remainder of CEO pay was in the form of salary, benefits, and bonuses based on current-year profits.) One study found that, in 1994, if the value of a firm's stock rose by 10 percent, the typical CEO's wealth rose by $1.25 million.[19] Companies in industries with higher volatility in sales—and thus for whom pay based on profits or share values exposes CEO incomes to greater variations beyond their control—rely more on salary payments, and less on company performance, to attract top executives.

It appears that paying CEOs with stock or stock options does work. Generally speaking, those firms with executive compensation plans more heavily weighted toward stock or stock options have tended to enjoy greater increases in corporate wealth. There is some evidence, however, that tying pay to stock-market values might make CEOs excessively worried about fluctuations in their own income, causing them to shy away from risky projects even when the projects appear profitable.[20]

Pay for Time, with Merit Increases Given employee risk aversion and the problem of devising appropriate measurable outcomes for individual- and group-incentive plans, most employers opt for some form of time-based pay. While satisfying employees' desires for pay stability, time pay creates an incentive problem because compensation and output are not directly linked. Employers often try to cope with this problem through the use of *merit-pay* plans, which award larger pay increases to workers whose supervisors rate them as the better performers.

On the one hand, basing pay on supervisory ratings has the potential to create superior incentives for workers, because these ratings can take account of the more subjective aspects of performance (friendliness, being a team player) that may be critical to the welfare of the employer. On the other hand, merit-based pay still faces two incentive problems similar to those with output-based pay.

If supervisors are told to base their ratings on worker contributions toward *actual* output, merit pay runs up against the (by now familiar) problem that individual effort and output may not correlate well owing to forces beyond the control of workers. For this reason, supervisors are often asked to rate their subordinates *relative* to each other, on the theory that all face the same external forces of snowstorms, machine breakdowns, and so forth.

The problem of relative rankings for merit-pay purposes is that the *effort* induced among employees may not be consistent with the employer's interests. For example, one way to enhance one's *relative* status is to sabotage the work of others.

---

[18]For a review of executive-pay issues, see John M. Abowd and David S. Kaplan, "Executive Compensation: Six Questions That Need Answering," *Journal of Economic Perspectives* 13, no. 4 (Fall 1999): 145–168.

[19]Brian J. Hall and Jeffrey B. Liebman, "Are CEOs Really Paid Like Bureaucrats?" *Quarterly Journal of Economics* 113, no. 3 (August 1998): 653–691.

[20]Abowd and Kaplan, "Executive Compensation," 158–159.

Finding pages torn out of library books on reserve shortly before major examinations is not unknown at colleges or universities, where grading is often based on relative performance. Somewhat less sinister than sabotage, but equally inconsistent with employer interests, is noncooperation; a recent study has shown that the stronger the rewards based on relative performance, the less likely employees are to share their equipment and tools with fellow workers.[21]

Because relative performance ratings usually have a subjective component, another kind of counterproductive effort may take place: *politicking*. Workers may spend valuable work time "marketing" their services or otherwise ingratiating themselves with their supervisors.[22] Thus, efforts are directed away from productivity itself to generate what is, at best, the *appearance* of productivity.[23]

PRODUCTIVITY AND THE LEVEL OF PAY

Given the difficulties created for both employer and employee by pay-for-performance plans (including merit pay), employers are often driven to search for other monetary incentives that can be used to motivate their workers. In this section we discuss motivational issues related to the *level* of pay.

Why Higher Pay Might Increase Worker Productivity

Paying higher wages is thought to increase worker productivity for several reasons. One involves the *type* of worker the firm can attract; the others are related to the productivity that can be elicited from *given* workers.

Attracting Better Workers   Higher wages can attract better employees by enlarging the firm's applicant pool. A larger pool means that the firm can be more selective, skimming the cream off the top to employ only the most experienced, dependable, or highly motivated applicants.

Building Employee Commitment   The reasons higher wages are thought to generate greater productivity from given workers all relate to the commitment to

---

[21]Robert Drago and Gerald T. Garvey, "Incentives for Helping on the Job: Theory and Evidence," *Journal of Labor Economics* 16, no. 1 (January 1998): 1–25.

[22]Paul Milgrom, "Employment Contracts, Influence Activities, and Efficient Organization Design," *Journal of Political Economy* 96 (February 1988): 42–60; and Canice Prendergast, "A Theory of 'Yes Men'," *American Economic Review* 83, no. 4 (September 1993): 757–770. For a theoretical analysis incorporating the important element of trust between workers and supervisors, see George Baker, Robert Gibbons, and Kevin J. Murphy, "Subjective Performance Measures in Optimal Incentive Contracts," *Quarterly Journal of Economics* 109, no. 4 (November 1994): 1125–1156.

[23]While we discuss individually the tools that can be used to motivate workers—incentive pay, supervision, stock ownership, or profit sharing, for example—they should all be seen as part of a firm's *system* for motivating its workers. For an article making this point, see Casey Ichniowski, Kathryn Shaw, and Giovanna Prennushi, "The Effects of Human Resource Management Practices on Productivity: A Study of Steel Finishing Lines," *American Economic Review* 87, no. 3 (June 1997): 291–313.

the firm they build. The higher the wages are relative to what workers could receive elsewhere, the less likely it is that the workers will quit; knowing this, employers are more likely to offer training and more likely to demand longer hours and a faster pace of work from their workers. Employees, on their part, realize that even though supervision may not be detailed enough to detect shirking with certainty, if they are caught cheating on their promises to work hard and are fired as a result, the loss of a job paying above-market wages is costly both now and over their remaining work life.

Perceptions of Equity   A related reason higher wages might generate more productivity from given employees arises from their concern about being treated fairly. Workers who believe they are being treated fairly are likely to put forth effort, while those who think their treatment is unfair may "get even" by withholding effort or even engaging in sabotage.[24]

One comparison workers make in judging their treatment is the extent to which they see the employer as profiting from their services. It is often considered unfair if a highly profitable employer is ungenerous in sharing its good fortune with its workers, even if the wages it pays already are relatively high. Likewise, workers who are asked to sacrifice leisure and put forth extraordinary effort on the job are likely to expect the firm to make an extraordinary financial sacrifice (that is, the offer of high pay) to them in return.[25]

Employees also judge the fairness of their pay by comparing it to what they could obtain elsewhere. Raising compensation above the level that workers can earn elsewhere, of course, has both benefits and costs to the employer, as we discuss in the following section.

Efficiency Wages

While initial increases in pay may well serve to increase productivity and therefore the profits of the firm, after a point the costs to the employer of further increases will exceed the benefits. The above-market pay level at which the marginal revenues to the employer from a further pay increase equal the marginal costs is the level that will maximize profits; this has become known as the *efficiency wage* (see Example 11.4).[26]

---

[24]This assertion is based on what psychologists call equity theory. For works by economists that employ this theory, see George A. Akerlof and Janet Yellen, "The Fair Wage–Effort Hypothesis and Unemployment," *Quarterly Journal of Economics* 105 (May 1990): 255–283, and Robert M. Solow, *The Labor Market as a Social Institution* (Cambridge, Mass.: Basil Blackwell, 1990).

[25]For a study indicating a link between profits and wages, see Andrew K. G. Hildreth and Andrew J. Oswald, "Rent-Sharing and Wages: Evidence from Company and Establishment Panels," *Journal of Labor Economics* 15, no. 2 (April 1997): 318–337.

[26]It should be clear that the efficiency wage refers to all forms of compensation, not just cash wages. Lawrence Katz, "Efficiency Wage Theories: A Partial Evaluation," in *NBER Macroeconomics Annual, 1986*, ed. Stanley Fischer (Cambridge, Mass.: MIT Press, 1986); Joseph E. Stiglitz, "The Causes and Consequences of the Dependence of Quality on Price," *Journal of Economic Literature* 25, no. 1 (March 1987): 1–48; and Kevin M. Murphy and Robert H. Topel, "Efficiency Wages Reconsidered: Theory and Evidence," in *Advances in Theory and Measurement of Unemployment*, ed. Yoram Weiss and Gideon Fishelson (London: Macmillan, 1990), offer detailed analyses of efficiency-wage theories.

EXAMPLE 11.4

Did Henry Ford Pay Efficiency Wages?

The 1908–1914 period saw the introduction of "scientific management" and assembly-line production processes at the Ford Motor Company. The change in production methods led to a change in the occupational composition of Ford's workforce, and by 1914 most of its workers were relatively unskilled and foreign born. Although these changes proved extremely profitable, worker dissatisfaction was high. In 1913, turnover rates reached 370 percent (370 workers had to be hired each year to keep every 100 positions filled), which was high even by the standards of the Detroit automobile industry at the time. Similarly, absenteeism typically averaged 10 percent a day. However, while Henry Ford was obviously having difficulty retaining and eliciting effort from workers, he had little difficulty finding replacements: there were always long lines of applicants at the factory gates. Hence, Ford's daily wage in 1913 of about $2.50 was at least at the competitive level.

In January 1914, Ford instituted a $5.00-a-day wage; this doubling of pay was granted only to workers who had been employed at the company for at least six months. At roughly the same time, residency in the Detroit area for at least six months was made a hiring standard for new job applicants. Since the company was limiting the potential applicant flow and was apparently not screening job applicants any more carefully after the pay increase, it appears the motivation for this extraordinary increase in wages was not to increase the quality of new hires.

It is clear, however, that the increase *did* affect the behavior of existing employees. Between March 1913 and March 1914, the quit rate of Ford employees fell by 87 percent and discharges fell by 90 percent. Similarly, the absentee rate was reduced by a factor of 75 percent during the October 1913 to October 1914 period. Morale and productivity increased and the company continued to be profitable.

There is some evidence that at least initially, however, Ford's productivity gains were less than the wage increase. Historians have pointed to the noneconomic factors that influenced Ford's decision, including his paternalistic desire to teach his workers good living habits. (For workers to receive these increases, investigators from Ford first had to certify that they did not pursue lifestyles that included behavior like excessive gambling or drinking.) While the wage increase thus probably did not lead to a wage level that maximized the company's profits (a smaller increase probably would have done that), the policy did have a substantial positive effect on worker turnover, effort, morale, and productivity.

Data from: Daniel Raff and Lawrence Summers, "Did Henry Ford Pay Efficiency Wages?" *Journal of Labor Economics* 5 (October 1987): S57–S86.

The payment of efficiency wages has a wide set of implications that, in recent years, have begun to be explored by economists. For example, the persistence of unemployment is thought by some to result from the widespread payment of above-market wages (see chapter 15).[27] Further, persistently different wage rates paid to qualitatively similar workers in different industries are the hypothesized result of efficiency-wage considerations.[28]

---

[27]Janet Yellen, "Efficiency Wage Models of Unemployment," *American Economic Review* 74 (May 1984): 200–208; and Andrew Weiss, *Efficiency Wages: Models of Unemployment, Layoffs, and Wage Dispersion* (Princeton: Princeton University Press, 1990).

[28]Richard Thaler, "Anomalies: Interindustry Wage Differentials," *Journal of Economic Perspectives* 3 (Spring 1989): 181–193; and Surendra Gera and Gilles Grenier, "Interindustry Wage Differentials and Efficiency Wages: Some Canadian Evidence," *Canadian Journal of Economics* 27, no. 1 (February 1994): 81–100.

For our purposes here, however, the most important implications of efficiency wages relate to their effects on productivity, and two types of empirical studies are of interest. One set of studies *infers* the effects of efficiency wages on productivity from the types of firms that pay these wages. That is, if some firms raise wages above the market level for profit-maximizing purposes, we ought to observe that those who do are the ones that (a) stand to gain the most from enhancing worker reliability (perhaps because they have a lot invested in expensive equipment), or (b) find it most difficult to properly motivate their workers through output-based pay or supervision.[29] The other kind of study directly relates the effects of efficiency wages to measures of productivity, rates of disciplinary dismissals, or changes in the employer's product market share.[30] The studies so far are limited in number, but they are generally supportive of efficiency-wage theory.

Note that the payment of wages above what workers could earn elsewhere makes sense only because workers expect to have long-term employment relationships with firms. If workers switched jobs every period, they would face no incentive to reduce shirking when a firm paid above-market wages, because firing someone who is going to quit anyway is not an effective penalty; as a result, firms would have no incentive to pursue an efficiency-wage policy. Thus, efficiency wages are likely to arise only in situations where structured internal labor markets exist. The existence of internal labor markets, however, raises *other* possibilities for using pay to motivate workers, and it is to these possibilities that we now turn.

PRODUCTIVITY AND THE SEQUENCING OF PAY

Employers with internal labor markets have options for motivating workers that grow out of their employees' expected *careers* with the organization. Applicants to, and employees of, employers with internal labor markets are concerned with the present value of *career* compensation. This "lifetime" perspective increases employers' options for developing compensation policies, because both the pay levels at each step in one's career and the swiftness of promotion to given steps can be varied by the firm while still living within the constraint of having to offer an attractive present value of career compensation. In this section we analyze several possibilities for sequencing pay over workers' careers that are thought to provide incentives for greater productivity.

---

[29]Alan B. Krueger, "Ownership, Agency and Wages: An Examination of Franchising in the Fast Food Industry," *Quarterly Journal of Economics* 106 (February 1991): 75–101; Erica L. Groshen and Alan B. Krueger, "The Structure of Supervision and Pay in Hospitals," *Industrial and Labor Relations Review* 43 (February 1990): 134S–146S; Carl M. Campbell III, "Do Firms Pay Efficiency Wages? Evidence with Data at the Firm Level," *Journal of Labor Economics* 11, no. 3 (July 1993): 442–470; and Bradley T. Ewing and James E. Payne, "The Trade-Off Between Supervision and Wages: Evidence of Efficiency Wages from the NLSY," *Southern Economic Journal* 66, no. 2 (October 1999): 424–432.

[30]Peter Cappelli and Keith Chauvin, "An Interplant Test of the Efficiency Wage Hypothesis," *Quarterly Journal of Economics* 106 (August 1991): 769–787; Jozef Konings and Patrick P. Walsh, "Evidence of Efficiency Wage Payments in U.K. Firm Level Panel Data," *Economic Journal* 104, no. 424 (May 1994): 542–555.

Underpayment Followed by Overpayment

It may be beneficial to both employer and employee to arrange workers' pay over time so that employees are "underpaid" early in their careers and "overpaid" later on.[31] This sequencing of pay, it can be argued, will increase worker productivity and enable firms to pay *higher* present values of compensation than otherwise, for reasons related both to worker sorting and to work incentives. An understanding of these reasons takes us back to the problem of avoiding cheating on an implicit contract in the presence of asymmetric information.

Worker Sorting   Pay plans that delay at least a part of employees' compensation to a time later in their careers have an important signaling component. They will appeal most (and perhaps only) to those workers who intend to stay with the employer a long time and work hard enough to avoid being fired before collecting their delayed pay. In the absence of being able to predict which workers intend to stick around and work diligently, an employer might find an underpay-now, overpay-later compensation plan attractive because of the type of workers likely to sort themselves into their applicant pool.[32]

Work Incentives   A company that pays poorly to begin with but well later on increases the incentives of its employees to work industriously. Once in the job, an employee has incentives to work diligently in order to qualify for the later overpayment. The employer need not devote as many resources to supervision each year as would otherwise be the case, because the firm has several years in which to identify shirkers and withhold from them the delayed reward. Because all employees work harder than they otherwise would, compensation within the firm tends to be higher also.

Constraints   One feasible compensation-sequencing scheme would pay workers *less* than their marginal product early in their careers and *more* than their marginal product later on. This scheme, however, must satisfy two constraints. First, the present value of the earnings streams offered to employees must be at least equal to alternative streams offered to workers in the labor market; if not, the firm cannot attract the workers it wants.

Second, the scheme must also satisfy the equilibrium conditions that the firm maximizes profits and does not earn supernormal profits. If profits are not maximized, the firm's existence is threatened; if firms make supernormal profits, new firms will be induced to enter the market. Thus, in neither case would equilibrium exist.

---

[31]Our discussion here draws on Edward Lazear, "Why Is There Mandatory Retirement?" *Journal of Political Economy* 87, no. 6 (December 1979): 1261–1284. For a review of issues raised in this and succeeding sections, see H. Lorne Carmichael, "Self-Enforcing Contracts, Shirking, and Life Cycle Incentives."

[32]The lower turnover rate among workers who have been promised larger pensions upon retirement is apparently mostly the result of self-selection, not the threat of lost pension wealth; see Steven G. Allen, Robert L. Clark, and Ann A. McDermed, "Pensions, Bonding, and Lifetime Jobs," *Journal of Human Resources* 28, no. 3 (Summer 1993): 463–481.

These two conditions will be met if hiring is done until the present value of one's career-long marginal product equals the present value of one's career earnings stream. (This career-long condition is the multiyear analogue of the single-year profit-mazimization conditions discussed in chapter 3 and the two-year profit-maximization criteria discussed in chapter 5.) Thus, for firms choosing the "underpayment now, overpayment later" compensation scheme to be competitive in both the labor and the product markets, the present value of the yearly amounts by which marginal revenue product (MRP) *exceeds* compensation early on must equal the present value of the later amounts by which MRP *falls short* of pay.

Graphical Analysis   The above compensation plan is diagrammed in Figure 11.2. We assume that MRP rises over a worker's career, but that in the first t^* years of employment compensation remains below MRP. At some point in the worker's career with the firm—year t^* in the diagram—compensation begins to exceed MRP. From t^* until retirement in year r is the period during which diligent employees are rewarded by receiving compensation in excess of what they could receive elsewhere (namely, their MRP). For the firm to be competitive in both the labor and the product markets, the *present value* of area A in the diagram must equal the *present value* of area B. (Area B is larger than area A in Figure 11.2 because sums received further in the future are subjected to heavier discounting when present values are calculated.)

Risks   To be sure, there are risks to both parties in making this kind of agreement. On the one hand, employees agreeing to this compensation scheme take a chance that they may be fired without cause or that their employer may go bankrupt before they have collected their reward in the years beyond t^*. It is easy to see that employers will have some incentives to renege, since older workers are being paid a wage that exceeds their immediate value (at the margin) to the firm.

On the other hand, employers who do not wish to fire older people face the risk that these "overpaid" employees will stay on the job longer than is necessary to collect their reward—that is, stay on longer than time r in Figure 11.2. Knowing that their current wage is greater than the wage they can get elsewhere, since it reflects payment for more than current output, older employees will have incentives to keep working longer than is profitable for the firm.

Employee Safeguards   Some safeguards for employees can be built into the employment contract when this type of pay sequencing is utilized. Employers can guarantee seniority rights for older workers, under which workers with the shortest durations of employment with the firm are laid off first if the firm cuts back its workforce. Without these seniority rights, firms might be tempted to lay off older workers, whose wages are greater than MRP, and keep the younger ones, who are paid less than MRP at this point in their careers.

Employees can also be protected later in their careers by obtaining part of their overpayment in the form of vested pension rights. Once vested (within five years of service, under federal law), employees covered by pension plans have rights to a benefit upon retirement even if they are separated from their employer before retirement age.

FIGURE 11.2

A Compensation Sequencing Scheme to Increase Worker Motivation

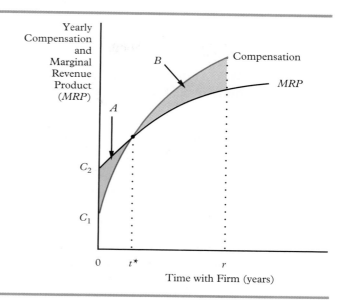

Ultimately, however, the best protection older workers have may be the employer's need to recruit *younger* workers. If a certain employer gains a reputation for firing older workers despite an implicit agreement not to do so, that employer will have trouble recruiting new employees. However, if the company is in permanent decline, if it faces an unusually adverse market, or if information on its employment policies is not easily available, incentives to renege on its promises could be very strong.

Employer Safeguards   Before 1978, many employers had mandatory retirement ages for their employees, so that they could enforce retirement at point r, for example. However, amendments to the Age Discrimination in Employment Act in 1978 and 1986 precluded mandatory retirement for most workers.[33] Age-discrimination legislation also makes it very difficult for employers to reduce the wages of workers who stay past point r. Thus, employers with underpay-over-pay plans are now faced with greater difficulties in getting employees to retire.

One action employers with these plans have taken is to offer large inducements for workers to retire at a certain age. For example, a study of pension plans in 190 of the largest companies in the United States (employing about one-quarter of all workers) found that it is common for the present value of pension benefits, summed over the expected lifetime of the retirees, to decline as retirement is

---

[33]For a study of the drop in retirements among university faculty when mandatory retirement was ended, see Orley Ashenfelter and David Card, "Did the Elimination of Mandatory Retirement Affect Faculty Retirement Flows?" National Bureau of Economic Research working paper no. 8378, July 2001.

postponed. This study discovered that for workers with typical earnings and years of service, the present value of pension benefits was over 25 percent greater if retirement occurred five years before, rather than at, normal retirement age.[34]

Who Adopts Delayed Compensation? One implication of the underpayment-overpayment compensation scheme is that it is more likely to exist for jobs in which close supervision of workers is not feasible. Indeed, a study that separated jobs into those that were conducive to close supervision and those that were not found that jobs in the latter category were more likely to have relatively high wages for older workers, and (in the past, at least) mandatory retirement rules.[35]

Promotion Tournaments

Another form of worker motivation within the context of internal labor markets might best be called a *promotion tournament.* Tournaments have three central features: who will win is uncertain, the winner is selected based on *relative* performance (that is, performance compared to that of the other "contestants"), and the rewards are concentrated in the hands of the winner, so that there is a big difference between winning and losing. Not all promotions within firms satisfy this definition of a tournament, largely because the rewards are relatively small and the winners are easy to predict. For example, one study found that promotions were typically associated with increased wage growth of 2 to 3 percent, and those who received their first promotion most quickly tended to be promoted most quickly later on as well.[36]

Promotions to very senior leadership positions, however, often take place through a process that fits the description of a tournament.[37] The fortunate vice presidents who are promoted above their rivals to CEO in America's largest corporations, for example, can expect to receive an addition to lifetime income that is in excess of $5 million.[38] The magnitude of this payoff suggests it is a prize offered

[34]Edward Lazear, "Pensions as Severance Pay," in *Financial Aspects of the United States Pension System,* ed. Zvi Bodie and John Shoven (Chicago: University of Chicago Press, 1983).

[35]Robert Hutchens, "A Test of Lazear's Theory of Delayed Payment Contracts," *Journal of Labor Economics* 5, no. 4, pt. 2 (October 1987): S153–S170. For a consideration of how age-discrimination laws affect delayed-payment pay plans, see David Neumark and Wendy A. Stock, "Age Discrimination Laws and Labor Market Efficiency," *Journal of Political Economy* 107, no. 5 (October 1999): 1081–1125.

[36]George Baker and Bengt Holmstrom, "Internal Labor Markets: Too Many Theories, Too Few Facts," *American Economic Review* 85, no. 2 (May 1995): 255–259.

[37]Edward Lazear and Sherwin Rosen, "Rank-Order Tournaments as Optimum Labor Contracts," *Journal of Political Economy* 89 (October 1981): 841–864; Sherwin Rosen, "Prizes and Incentives in Elimination Tournaments," *American Economic Review* 76 (September 1986): 701–715; and Michael L. Bognanno, "Corporate Tournaments," *Journal of Labor Economics* 19, no. 2 (April 2001): 290–315. The growth of tournaments in a variety of economic sectors, and the social disadvantages of huge gains tied to what may be small relative differences in productivity, are accessibly analyzed in Robert H. Frank and Philip J. Cook, *The Winner-Take-All Society* (New York: Free Press, 1995).

[38]Brian G. M. Main, Charles A. O'Reilly III, and James Wade, "Top Executive Pay: Tournament or Teamwork?" *Journal of Labor Economics* 11, no. 4 (October 1993): 606–628.

at the end of a tournament; after all, if one vice president were actually that much more productive than all the others, he or she would have been promoted (or the others fired) long ago! What determines a tournament's strength of incentives, and what are the problems that promotion tournaments must address?

Incentives for Effort   In any tournament, athletic or otherwise, the contestants must decide how much effort to devote to winning. In tennis, for example, a player must decide how much to risk injury by diving or straining for a ball that is difficult to reach. In the corporate world, parents need to consider whether working another week of nights at the office (on a project, say) is worth sacrificing the time with their children. We can hypothesize that contestants will decide to expend the extra effort if the marginal benefits they expect to gain exceed the added risk, inconvenience, or disutility.

The marginal benefit that the extra effort produces is a function of two things: the *increased probability of winning* and the value (including prestige) of the *winner's prize*. The extent to which one's chances of winning are improved depends on the now-familiar issue of how closely effort is linked to output. If winning is largely a matter of luck, for example, spending extra effort may have little effect on the outcome.

The value of the winner's prize, of course, depends on the *disparity* between what the winner and losers receive. Tournaments designed to elicit effort that entails great personal sacrifice, or that have so many contestants that extra effort improves one's chances only to a small degree, require a large prize to create incentives.

Tournaments also enhance output because of their sorting value. People who have confidence in their own abilities and a willingness to sacrifice now for a shot at the prize are much more likely to enter a tournament than others. Thus, employees self-select into (or out of) promotion tournaments, and by so doing they signal things about themselves that employers might otherwise find difficult to judge.

Problems   One problem with tournaments is that, as with merit pay based on relative performance, contestants may allocate effort away from increasing their own output and toward reducing the output of their rivals. Sabotage benefits them but not their employer. Another incentive problem is that, once the tournaments are over and the winners and losers have been identified, the winners may rest on their laurels and the losers may no longer have incentives to work hard—which means that the employer will have to use other means to maintain their effort (see Example 11.5).

Organizations running promotion tournaments also have to be concerned about how to treat the losers. A large disparity in earnings produces large incentives during tournament play, but it also means that the losers do relatively badly. If a firm is perceived as treating losers callously, it will have problems attracting contestants in the first place (after all, most contestants lose). Thus, the firm has to specify a disparity that is large enough to provide incentives but small enough to provide contestants!

Promotion-related incentive plans face additional problems, however, when employees find it feasible to seek careers outside their current organization and

EXAMPLE 11.5

Demanding Employers, Overworked Employees, and Neglected Families

Salaried workers often put in very long hours at work, frequently on short notice, or are expected to travel or even relocate their families at the wishes of their employers. Many feel they are required to enthusiastically respond to the unanticipated needs of their employers without the employers feeling a reciprocal obligation to support them when needs arise at home. Is this imbalance the result of powerful employers exploiting helpless workers? Maybe, but the considerations of this chapter suggest an alternative explanation: perhaps these workers are receiving efficiency wages or have chosen to compete in promotion tournaments.

There are two reasons employees who receive efficiency wages or are in tournaments work so hard. One reason is that their employers have the *ability* to make heavy demands, and the other is that their employers have an *incentive* to be demanding.

Their employers have the *ability* to demand long hours on short notice, say, because the employees receive a reward for remaining with the firm. Workers who quit a firm that offers efficiency wages face the prospect of another job at a lower wage, and those who quit a tournament obviously forfeit their chances of winning.

Incentives for the employers to be demanding stem from their need to distinguish applicants who are inherently work oriented from those who are not. Firms offering *tournaments* need to attract those who are inherently work oriented, because they do not want either the winners or the losers to slack off after the competition is over and the winner is announced. Firms paying *efficiency wages* must be careful to employ only those who will become worth their above-market wages with relatively little supervisory effort. The problem is how to identify those who are truly work oriented, either at the time of application or shortly thereafter.

All applicants will claim to be hard workers, of course, and even those who have strong preferences for leisure can pretend to be work oriented for a time after hire. Employers therefore need to elicit a signal from their applicants or employees about their true work orientation, and one way to do this is to announce to all applicants that long hours and uncompromising loyalty are expected. The expectations obviously must be reasonable enough that the firms can generate applicants, but in terms of our signaling discussion in chapter 9, the announced work requirements must be demanding enough to discourage pretenders from applying for, or accepting, employment with these firms.

Unfortunately, however, while employers offering efficiency wages and promotion tournaments will strive to make themselves unattractive to those with relatively strong preferences for leisure, they will also make themselves unattractive to anyone with significant *household* responsibilities!

Data from: James B. Rebitzer and Lowell J. Taylor, "Do Labor Markets Provide Enough Short-Hour Jobs? An Analysis of Work Hours and Work Incentives," *Economic Inquiry* 33, no. 2 (April 1995): 257–273; and Melvin W. Reder, "On Labor's Bargaining Disadvantage," in *Labor Economics and Industrial Relations: Markets and Institutions*, ed. Clark Kerr and Paul D. Staudohar (Cambridge, Mass.: Harvard University Press, 1994), 237–256.

are able to send at least some signals of their productivity to other potential employers. We turn now to an analysis of situations in which the career concerns of employees might orient their efforts toward seeking employment elsewhere.

Career Concerns and Productivity

Employees often define themselves more as members of a profession or field than as members of a particular employer. As such, they may be as motivated to impress *other* employers (in the hopes of receiving future offers) as they are their own. What are the implications of these "career concerns"?

The Distortion of Effort

Other employers can observe objective measures of performance more easily than subjective measures ("quality," for example). As a result, employees with career concerns have an incentive to allocate their efforts toward measurable areas of performance and deemphasize areas that other employers cannot observe. As discussed earlier, executives looking for opportunities elsewhere have incentives to pursue strategies that yield short-run profits (which are highly visible) even if doing so harms the long-term interests of their current employer.[39]

Piece Rates and Effort

While job possibilities with other employers can distort workers' allocations of their effort, they can also solve yet another problem with piece-rate pay. In a world in which products and technologies are constantly changing, piece rates must be continually reset. In establishing a piece rate, the employer makes a guess about how long it takes to complete the task and calibrates the piece rate so that the average hourly earnings of its workers are attractive enough to recruit and retain a workforce.

Management, however, can never know for sure just how long it takes to complete a task, given a reasonably high level of effort by production workers. Moreover, as noted earlier, workers have incentives to "go slow" in trial runs so that management will overestimate the time it takes to complete the task and set a relatively high piece rate. If workers know that the estimated time for task completion is too high, they may deliberately work slowly out of fear that the firm will later reduce the piece rate if it finds out the truth.

Employees who are mobile across firms, however, will be less concerned about their *current* employer's future actions. They are more likely to decide to work at top speed, so that other employers are sufficiently impressed to hire them in the future. Where workers' pay is at least partially based on a piece rate, then, career concerns can be helpful in eliciting maximum effort from one's employees.

The Sequencing of Effort

For employees who are concerned about future promotions, whether with their current employer or elsewhere, there are usually two general incentives for high productivity: one's current pay and the chances of future promotion. When career (that is, promotion) concerns are strong, employers may not need much in the way of current pay-for-performance incentives to motivate their employees. As career concerns weaken, firms may need to adopt more current incentives to maintain worker effort.[40]

---

[39]When workers' current employers can observe their true productive characteristics better than outsiders can, outsiders (that is, other employers) wanting to make "talent raids" may reasonably infer who are the most valuable employees from observing who is promoted. Thus, promotion itself sends information to other employers, which may help the employee who is promoted but harm his or her current employer. Several papers have addressed this issue, among which are Dan Bernhardt, "Strategic Promotion and Compensation," *Review of Economic Studies* 62, no. 2 (April 1995): 315–339, and Derek Laing, "Involuntary Layoffs in a Model with Asymmetric Information Concerning Worker Ability," *Review of Economic Studies* 61, no. 2 (April 1994): 375–392.

[40]Robert Gibbons and Kevin J. Murphy, "Optimal Incentive Contracts in the Presence of Career Concerns: Theory and Evidence," *Journal of Political Economy* 100 (June 1992): 468–505.

Workers are more likely to be motivated by career concerns, and less by pay for current performance, when they are inexperienced. Paying them for current performance runs into the problem that output is a function of ability, effort, and luck—and when workers are relatively young their abilities are unknown to themselves as well as their employers. Relating pay to the performance of inexperienced workers may not increase their incentives much because, with ability unknown, the connection between effort and output is unclear. The incentive to work hard is strong for those with career concerns, however, because they realize that employers are observing them to estimate their abilities and their willingness to put forth effort.

Moreover, the inability of employers—especially outside employers—to closely monitor workers' efforts can, in the presence of career concerns, lead to *more* effort. Employees realize that future promotions depend in large part on employers' beliefs about their *ability*. Because some of their efforts can be hidden, particularly from outside employers, inexperienced workers have incentives to put in extra, hidden effort in an attempt to mislead employers about their ability. For example, an employee expected to work 50 hours a week may put in an extra 20 hours at home to boost performance in an attempt to raise employers' perceptions of his or her ability.

As one's career progresses, however, ability becomes known with more certainty and the career-based incentives for extraordinary effort decline. Fortunately, as noted above, the case for performance-based current pay also becomes stronger. Indeed, one study found that older CEOs were paid more on the basis of current performance than younger CEOs.[41]

APPLICATIONS OF THE THEORY: EXPLAINING THREE PUZZLES

The conceptual issues outlined in this chapter can help to shed light on three questions that puzzle labor economists: why pay increases with seniority, why larger employers pay higher wages, and why employment reductions in the face of mandated wage increases are not observed as readily as simple theory would suggest. In all three cases, multiple theoretical or data-related reasons can be called upon to explain the empirical phenomenon; some of these were presented in this chapter and some were introduced earlier. This section briefly summarizes these reasons and, where relevant, reviews the results of empirical studies to evaluate which ones seem most relevant. As we will see, definitive solutions to all three puzzles await further work.

Why Do Earnings Increase with Job Tenure?

Earnings tend to rise with age, as we saw in chapter 9, but in addition, they also rise as *tenure* with one's employer increases. There are three sets of explanations for why wage increases should be associated with job tenure, all of which have different implications.[42] The simplest explanation is that workers are paid wages equal to their mar-

---

[41]Gibbons and Murphy, "Optimal Incentive Contracts in the Presence of Career Concerns."

[42]A review of this puzzle and the early empirical work on it can be found in Robert Hutchens, "Seniority, Wages, and Productivity: A Turbulent Decade," *Journal of Economic Perspectives* 3, no. 4 (Fall 1989): 49–64.

FIGURE 11.3
Alternative Explanations for the Effect of Job Tenure on Wages

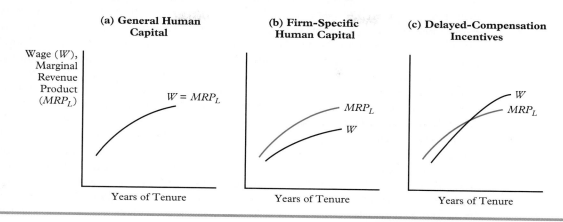

ginal revenue product, and their wages therefore rise because their productivity increases. Increasing productivity might result from workers' investments in on-the-job *general* training, which depresses their earnings initially but increases productivity later on (see chapter 9). If this simplest explanation is the correct one, then wages and productivity rise together at the same rate, as shown in panel (a) of Figure 11.3.

The second explanation for rising wages asserts that *firm-specific* investments are jointly undertaken by workers and their employers. As will be recalled from chapter 5, the joint investment creates a surplus that is *shared* by the worker and the firm; therefore, workers generally receive wage increases that are *less* than the increase in their productivity. As illustrated in panel (b) of Figure 11.3, with firm-specific human capital investments, wages are below—and rise more slowly than—marginal revenue productivity.

Finally, this chapter has offered yet a third explanation for rising wage profiles: they may be part of a delayed-compensation incentive system designed to attract and motivate workers who have long-term attachments to their employers. Under this third explanation, which is depicted in panel (c), wages rise *faster* than marginal revenue productivity and ultimately rise above it.[43]

Economists have been interested in devising empirical analyses that distinguish among these competing theories, but directly measuring *productivity* is not generally feasible. Therefore, most studies have identified workers for whom theory

[43]A variant of this third explanation is that employers offer rising wage profiles because employees *prefer* them. It is argued in Robert H. Frank and Robert M. Hutchens, "Wages, Seniority, and the Demand for Rising Consumption Profiles," *Journal of Economic Behavior and Organization* 21, no. 3 (August 1993): 251–276, that employees' utility is in part a function of their wage *increases* (not only their wage level). Therefore, to be competitive in the labor market, employers are induced to offer them wage profiles that start lower and rise faster than they otherwise would.

suggests that one or another of the above explanations is very likely (or unlikely), and then compares their wage profiles with those of other workers. Support for an explanation can be inferred if the relative wage profiles display their predicted patterns. For example, delayed-compensation plans are unnecessary if the output of a worker is easily monitored or if the worker is self-employed or paid a piece rate. If we can find evidence that wages for these workers rise *more slowly than average*, it would lend support for the existence of delayed-payment schemes.[44] Both human capital explanations are supported if workers most likely to invest in training are found to have steeper payoffs to tenure with an employer,[45] and if tenure with the employer matters less than tenure in the industry, the general-training explanation is supported.[46]

Direct attempts to compare wage and productivity profiles have generated mixed results, with one study finding support for the delayed-compensation model and another finding support for the general human capital model.[47] The authors of both studies, however, acknowledged that their estimates of productivity were sufficiently imprecise that they could not rule out either of the other two explanations. Thus, it is fair to say that the best of the explanations for rising tenure profiles has by no means been discovered—and, of course, it may well be that each correctly provides a *partial* explanation for the increase of earnings with job tenure.

Why Do Large Firms Pay More?

Roughly one-fourth of all American private sector employees work in firms with fewer than 20 workers, while another one-fifth work in firms with more than 500. Workers in the latter group, however, are much better paid; it has been estimated that they earn 12 percent more than those with the same measured human capital characteristics who work in the smallest firms. It also is the case that wages rise faster with experience in the largest firms.[48]

---

[44]Edward P. Lazear and Robert L. Moore, "Incentives, Productivity, and Labor Contracts," *Quarterly Journal of Economics* 99, no. 2 (May 1984): 275–296; and Robert Hutchens, "A Test of Lazear's Theory of Delayed Payment Contracts."

[45]James N. Brown, "Why Do Wages Increase with Tenure?" *American Economic Review* 79, no. 5 (December 1989): 971–991. For somewhat similar studies, see Sheldon E. Haber and Robert S. Goldfarb, "Does Salaried Status Affect Human Capital Accumulation?" *Industrial and Labor Relations Review* 48, no. 2 (January 1995): 322–337, and David Neumark and Paul Taubman, "Why Do Wage Profiles Slope Upward? Tests of the General Human Capital Model," *Journal of Labor Economics* 13, no. 4 (October 1995): 736–761.

[46]Daniel Parent, "Industry-Specific Capital and the Wage Profile: Evidence from the National Longitudinal Survey of Youth and the Panel Study of Income Dynamics," *Journal of Labor Economics* 18, no. 2 (April 2000): 306–323.

[47]Erling Barth, "Firm-Specific Seniority and Wages," *Journal of Labor Economics* 15, no. 3, pt. 1 (July 1997): 495–506; and Judith K. Hellerstein and David Neumark, "Are Earnings Profiles Steeper Than Productivity Profiles? Evidence from Israeli Firm-Level Data," *Journal of Human Resources* 30, no. 1 (Winter 1995): 89–112.

[48]Two papers that summarize the literature on this topic are Walter Y. Oi, "Employment Relations in Dual Labor Markets ('It's Nice Work If You Can Get It')," *Journal of Labor Economics* 8 (January 1990): S124–S149, and James E. Pearce, "Tenure, Unions, and the Relationship between Employer Size and Wages," *Journal of Labor Economics* 8 (April 1990): 251–269.

The explanations that have been offered for why larger firms pay higher wages are rooted in claims they *need better workers* and/or that they have better *opportunities* to make their workers more productive.[49] One potential explanation, for example, is that there are economies of scale in job training; larger firms are therefore more likely to offer it and, of course, have greater need to attract workers willing to undertake it.[50]

A second possible explanation is that large firms more often use highly interdependent production processes, which require that workers be exceptionally dependable and disciplined (one shirking worker can reduce the output of an entire team). Workers in a highly interdependent production environment are more regimented and have less ability to act independently, and their higher wages can be seen as a compensating wage differential for the unattractiveness of a job requiring rigid discipline.

A third hypothesis is that large firms make available to workers many steps in a career ladder, so that long-term attachments between worker and employer are more attractive than in smaller firms. As has been noted in this chapter, employers whose workers are seeking long-term attachments have more options for using pay to motivate productivity. Efficiency wages are a more effective motivator when there is an expected long-term attachment, because workers' losses from being terminated rise with both their wage level *and* the length of their future expected tenure. Deferred-compensation schemes and promotion tournaments obviously can be used *only* in the context of long-term attachment.

While large firms have more opportunities for adopting efficiency wages, deferred-compensation plans, or promotion tournaments, they may also have a greater need to adopt one or more of these schemes. Owing to sheer size, it is argued, they find it more difficult to monitor their employees and thus must turn to other methods to motivate high levels of effort. One study concluded that the firm-size effect is more related to the presence of efficiency wages than to compensating wage differentials for a demanding work environment.[51]

Finally, it has been argued that larger firms find job vacancies more costly. They tend to be more capital-intensive and, as noted above, have more interdependent production processes. Therefore, an unfilled job or an unexpected quit could more severely disrupt production in larger firms and, by idling much of its

---

[49]For studies that try to distinguish between the two factors, see Rudolf Winter-Ebmer and Josef Zweimuller, "Firm-Size Differentials in Switzerland: Evidence from Job Changers," *American Economic Review* 89, no. 2 (May 1999): 89–93, and John M. Abowd and Francis Kramarz, "Inter-Industry and Firm-Size Wage Differentials: New Evidence from Linked Employer-Employee Data," Cornell University, School of Industrial and Labor Relations Institute for Labor Market Policies, July 2000.

[50]Kevin T. Reilly, "Human Capital and Information: The Employer Size-Wage Effect," *Journal of Human Resources* 30, no. 1 (Winter 1995): 1–18; and Dan A. Black, Brett J. Noel, and Zheng Wang, "On-the-Job Training, Establishment Size, and Firm Size: Evidence for Economies of Scale in the Production of Human Capital," *Southern Economic Journal* 66, no. 1 (July 1999): 82–100.

[51]David Fairris and Lee J. Alston, "Wages and the Intensity of Labor Effort: Efficiency Wages Versus Compensating Payments," *Southern Economic Journal* 61, no. 1 (July 1994): 149–160. An extensive review of papers on both the "monitoring" and the "compensating differentials" explanations can be found in Rebitzer, "Radical Political Economy and the Economics of Labor Markets," 1417–1419.

labor and capital, impose huge costs on the firm. In an effort to reduce quits and ensure that vacancies can be filled quickly, larger firms thus decide to pay higher wages—even when the work environment is not unattractive and efficiency wages are otherwise unnecessary (because other work incentives exist).[52]

Monopsonistic Behavior by Employers

In chapter 10 we discussed how the presence of search costs can create circumstances in which firms behave monopsonistically even when they are not the sole buyers of labor services in a market. The considerations of this chapter suggest another reason the labor supply curve to a firm might slope upward. As firms grow in size, they find it more costly to monitor worker effort or to measure an individual worker's contribution to profits. To cope with the increased difficulties of ensuring employee effort, the larger a firm becomes the more it must pay in efficiency-wage premiums to elicit this effort. The need for an increased wage as a firm hires more workers means, of course, that firms face an upward-sloping labor supply curve. Because the essence of labor market monopsony is the presence of an upward-sloping labor supply curve to individual firms, monopsonistic behavior can be produced by these rising monitoring costs.[53]

---

[52]For some evidence along the lines of this argument, see James B. Rebitzer and Lowell J. Taylor, "Efficiency Wages and Employment Rents: The Employer Size–Wage Effect in the Job Market for Lawyers," *Journal of Labor Economics* 13, no. 4 (October 1995): 678–708.

[53]A more formal presentation of this "supervisory" model of monopsonistic behavior can be found in James B. Rebitzer and Lowell J. Taylor, "The Consequences of Minimum Wage Laws: Some New Theoretical Ideas," *Journal of Public Economics* 56 (1995): 245–255.

REVIEW QUESTIONS

1. Explain the underlying principle and the necessary conditions for implicit contracts in the labor market to be self-enforcing.

2. The earnings of piece-rate workers usually exceed those of hourly paid workers performing the same tasks. Theory suggests three reasons why. What are they?

3. Suppose that as employment shifts out of manufacturing to the service sector, a higher proportion of workers are employed in small firms. What effect would this growth of employment in small firms have on the types of compensation schemes used to stimulate productivity?

4. Suppose two soft-drink bottling companies employ drivers whose job it is to deliver cases of drinks to stores, restaurants, and businesses. One company pays its drivers an hourly wage, and the other pays them by the number of cases delivered each day (which can be affected by efforts of drivers to visit and sell to new customers). Which company is more likely to experience higher rates of traffic accidents among its drivers? Why?

5. "The way to get power over workers is to underpay them." Comment.

6. Some real estate brokers split the commission revenues generated by each sale with

the responsible agent. Others, however, require their agents to pay *them* (the brokers) money up front, and then allow the agents to keep the *entire* commission from each sale they make. Which agents would you predict to have the larger volume of sales, those who split all commissions with their employer or those who pay an upfront fee to their employer and then keep the entire commission? Explain.

7. In recent years, many plants have closed, forcing thousands of workers out of their jobs and into new ones. Studies of wage loss suffered by these displaced workers find that, *among groups of workers with exactly the same skills and types of training,* workers who had been with the firm for many years and were in the 55–64 age range had greater wage losses than those in the 25–34 age range. How might a com-

pensation scheme designed to enhance worker motivation lead to this result?

8. An amusement park open only in the summer hires teenagers to operate its rides, paying them $4.00 per hour and putting aside $1.50 per hour into a fund that they will receive as a lump-sum payment if they work through Labor Day (typically, its biggest day of the year).
   a. What problem is the amusement park apparently trying to solve with its compensation plan, and in what two ways does this plan help to solve the problem?
   b. Suppose the government rules that the compensation plan violates minimum wage laws because workers who quit before Labor Day receive only $4.00 per hour. How can the park now address the problem mentioned in your answer to (a)?

PROBLEMS

1. Suppose that the market wage is $5 per hour, but Charlie will work harder if his employer pays him a higher wage. The relationship between Charlie's wage and MRP_L is given in the table below. What is the efficient wage for Charlie?

Wage ($/hour)	MRP_L ($/hour)
$4	$6.00
$5	$8.00
$6	$9.50
$7	$10.25
$8	$11.00
$9	$11.50
$10	$12.00
$11	$12.25
$12	$12.50
$13	$12.75

2. A firm is considering adopting a plan in which the company pays employees less than their MRP_L early in their careers and more than their MRP_L late in their careers. For a typical worker at the firm, $MRP_L = 10 + 0.1T$, where T = the number of years which the worker has been employed at the firm and MRP_L is measured in dollars per hour. The worker's wage per hour is $W = 8 + 0.2T$. Assume that this wage is high enough to attract workers from alternative jobs, that the discount rate for the firm is zero, and that the expected tenure of a typical worker is 35 years. If workers retire after 35 years, will this plan be profitable for the firm? Explain. For how many years will the firm underpay its workers?

SELECTED READINGS

Akerlof, George A., and Janet L. Yellen, eds. *Efficiency Wage Models of the Labor Market.* New York: Cambridge University Press, 1986.

Carmichael, H. Lorne. "Self-Enforcing Contracts, Shirking, and Life Cycle Incentives." *Journal of Economic Perspectives* 3 (Fall 1989): 65–84.

Frank, Robert H., and Philip J. Cook. *The Winner-Take-All Society.* New York: Free Press, 1995.

Gibbons, Robert. "Incentives in Organizations." *Journal of Economic Perspectives* 12 (Fall 1998): 115–132.

Lazear, Edward P. "Compensation, Productivity, and the New Economics of Personnel." In *Research Frontiers in Industrial Relations,* ed. David Lewin, Olivia S. Mitchell, and Peter D. Sherer. Madison, Wis.: Industrial Relations Research Association, 1992.

Sappington, David E. "Incentives in Principal–Agent Relationships." *Journal of Economic Perspectives* 5 (Spring 1991): 45–66.

Simon, Herbert A. "Organizations and Markets." *Journal of Economic Perspectives* 5 (Spring 1991): 24–44.

12

GENDER, RACE, AND ETHNICITY IN THE LABOR MARKET

The American labor force has gone through a period of remarkable demographic change in recent decades. Some forces for change have been rooted in the different expectations of women regarding the balance between household and market work. Other forces for change have arisen from immigration, both legal and illegal, and from different birth rates among racial/ethnic groups. The result has been a pronounced and continuing change in the mix of groups in the labor force.

Table 12.1 contains both changes occurring from 1980 to 2000 and projections that are foreseeable by the year 2010. White males, who were 39 percent of the civilian labor force in 1980, constituted 35 percent by 2000, and their share is projected to fall to 34 percent by the year 2010. The share of women in the labor force has been holding steady, the share of blacks is rising, and growth rates among Asians and Hispanics are so great that their shares are expected to more than double between 1980 and 2010.

With the exception of Asians, the groups in the labor force that are growing most rapidly are those whose members earn substantially less, on average, than white males for full-time work. A glance at Figure 12.1 suggests that, as of 1999, none of the non-Asian groups with rapid growth rates averaged more than 71 percent of white male earnings for full-time work; the full-time earnings of black

TABLE 12.1   Shares of the Civilian Labor Force for Major Demographic Groups: 1980, 2000, 2010

	Year		
	1980	2000	2010 (projected)
White males (non-Hispanic)	39%	35%	34%
Women (all races)	53	52	52
Blacks (both genders)	11	12	13
Asians and Native Americans (both genders)*	2	5	6
Hispanics (all races, both genders)	6	11	13

*Includes Alaskan Natives and Pacific Islanders.
Source: Howard N. Fullerton Jr. and Mitra Toossi, "Labor Force Projections to 2010: Steady Growth and Changing Composition," Monthly Labor Review 124 (November 2001): 21–38, Table 2.

and Hispanic women averaged less than 60 percent of white male earnings. (Because Asians comprise a relatively small proportion of the population, published data on their earnings are not available on a yearly basis. Comparing full-time workers' annual earnings in 1990, however, reveals that men of Chinese and Japanese ancestry had pay that was at or above the average for all men in the United States.)[1]

The growing numerical significance of demographic groups whose members are relatively poorly paid has heightened interest in understanding the sources of earnings differences across groups. The purpose of this chapter is to analyze such differences, with special attention to the topic of discrimination.

FIGURE 12.1
Mean Earnings as a Percentage of White Male Earnings, Various Demographic Groups, Full-Time Workers over 24 Years Old, 1999

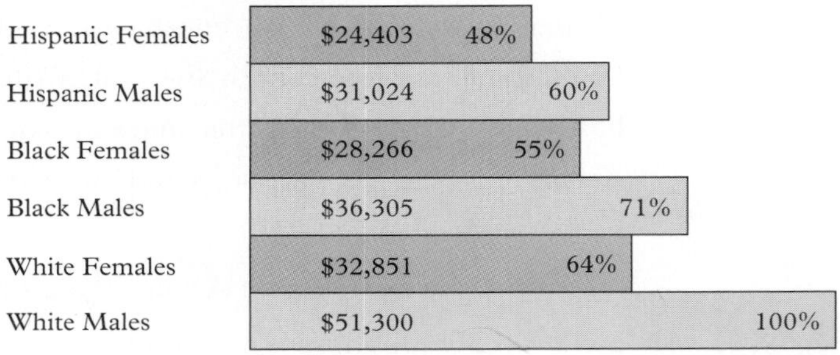

Hispanic Females	$24,403	48%
Hispanic Males	$31,024	60%
Black Females	$28,266	55%
Black Males	$36,305	71%
White Females	$32,851	64%
White Males	$51,300	100%

Source: U.S. Bureau of the Census, Money Income in the United States, 1999, Series P-60, no. 209 (Washington, D.C.: U.S. Government Printing Office, 2000), Table 10.

---

[1]See Table 12.6 later in this chapter.

MEASURED AND UNMEASURED SOURCES OF EARNINGS DIFFERENCES

This section focuses on explaining the earnings differentials for three of the larger (and partially overlapping) groups whose members have been targeted by government policy as potential victims of employment discrimination: women, blacks, and Hispanics. The focus is on these groups because data and studies are more readily available for them than for groups defined by such characteristics as physical limitation or sexual preference.[2] We analyze *earnings* rather than *total compensation* (which would be preferable) for the practical reason that data on the value of employee benefits are not generally available by demographic group.

Earnings Differences by Gender

Combining all races, women over the age of 18 who worked full-time earned an average of just 65 percent of what males earned in 1999. This percentage represents an increase from 1970 (50 percent) and 1980 (59 percent), but it suggests a huge difference in average pay that has not improved since 1990.[3] Understanding the sources of this difference is critical to a determination of what policies, if any, might be needed to address the gap in pay.

Age and Education   The first step in analyzing earnings differentials is to think of potential *sources* of difference, many of which can be measured. We know from chapter 9 that two important and measurable factors that influence earnings are education and age. While the most recent cohorts of women have levels of schooling at least equal to those of men, the same cannot be said of older cohorts. Moreover, we also know that the age/earnings profiles for women are flatter than the ones for men. Therefore, we would expect that controlling for age and education would account for at least some of the female/male differences in earnings.

The data in Table 12.2, which categorizes women and men by age and education, suggest that, as expected, female/male earnings ratios tend to fall with age. Even for the youngest cohort of women in the table, however, these ratios are so low (0.74 is the highest) that we must look elsewhere for explanations of the female/male earnings difference.

Occupation   A measurable factor that could help explain female/male earnings ratios is occupation. As can be seen in Table 12.3, women tend to be overrepresented

---

[2]For papers on these two topics, see Thomas DeLeire, "Changes in Wage Discrimination Against People with Disabilities: 1984–93," *Journal of Human Resources* 36, no. 1 (Winter 2001): 144–158, and Sylvia A. Allegretto and Michelle M. Arthur, "An Empirical Analysis of Homosexual/Heterosexual Male Earnings Differentials: Unmarried or Unequal?" *Industrial and Labor Relations Review* 54, no. 3 (April 2001): 631–646.
[3]As noted, the pay differences presented and analyzed in this chapter relate to wages and earnings, not to measures of total compensation (which would include employee benefits). There is some indication that women are less likely than comparable men to have pension, health insurance, or disability benefits; see Janet Currie, "Gender Gaps in Benefits Coverage," in *The Human Resource Management Handbook*, ed. David Lewin, Daniel Mitchell, and Mahmood Zaidi (Greenwich, Conn.: JAI Press, 1997), ch. 23.

TABLE 12.2 Female Earnings as a Percentage of Male Earnings, by Age and Education, Full-Time Workers, 1999

Age	High School Graduate	Bachelor's Degree	Master's Degree
25–34	68%	74%	74%
35–44	65	66	71
45–54	65	59	62
55–64	65	63	62

Source: U.S. Bureau of the Census, *Money Income in the United States: 1999,* Series P-60, no. 209 (Washington, D.C.: U.S. Government Printing Office, 2000), Table 9.

in low-paying occupations and underrepresented in high-paying ones; thus, at least some of the difference between the average pay of women and men is the result of different occupational distributions. Moreover, Table 12.3 also suggests that even in the *same* occupations, women earn substantially less than men. Since the higher-paying occupations selected for inclusion in Table 12.3 generally require specialized college or postgraduate education, it can be reasonably assumed that women and men entering them share a "career" orientation—yet even for these occupations in 2000, the female/male earnings ratios lay in the range of 0.73 to 0.88.

Hours and Experience   Within occupations, earnings are affected by one's hours of work and years of experience. We saw in chapter 9 that women average fewer hours of market work per week than do men in the same occupation. Putting aside the effects of part-time employment by focusing on those working full-time, Table 9.2 indicated that women in given occupations average 5 to 10 percent fewer hours per week than do men. Because salaried workers presumably receive a compensating wage differential for longer hours of work, some of the earnings differentials in Table 12.3 could be associated with lower hours of work among women.

Analyses suggest that, within occupations, women typically have less (and sometimes, interrupted) work experience and are less likely to be promoted.[4] One study of lawyers who graduated from the same law school at the same time, for example, found that women earned about 7 percent less than men initially, but after 15 years they earned 40 percent less.[5] Some of this difference at 15 years

---

[4]Edward P. Lazear and Sherwin Rosen, "Male-Female Wage Differentials in Job Ladders," *Journal of Labor Economics* 8 (January 1990 supplement): S106–S123; Erica L. Groshen, "The Structure of the Female/Male Wage Differential: Is It Who You Are, What You Do, or Where You Work?" *Journal of Human Resources* 26 (Summer 1991): 457–472; and Stephen J. Spurr and Glenn J. Sueyoshi, "Turnover and Promotion of Lawyers: An Inquiry into Gender Differences," *Journal of Human Resources* 29, no. 3 (Summer 1994): 813–842.

[5]Robert G. Wood, Mary E. Corcoran, and Paul N. Courant, "Pay Differences among the Highly Paid: The Male-Female Earnings Gap in Lawyers' Salaries," *Journal of Labor Economics* 11, no. 3 (July 1993): 417–441.

TABLE 12.3 Female/Male Earnings Ratios and Percentages of Female Jobholders, Full-Time Wage and Salary Workers, by Selected High- and Low-Paying Occupations, 2000

	Percentage Female in Occupation	Female-to-Male Earnings Ratio
High-Paying[a]		
Computer systems analysts	29	0.87
Engineers	11	0.84
Lawyers	29	0.73
Pharmacists	47	0.88
Low-Paying[a]		
Cashiers	76	0.88
Cooks, except short-order	41	0.90
Food preparation	55	0.98
Hand packers, packagers	67	0.93
Textile sewing machine operators	79	0.94

[a]"High-paying" occupations are those in which women earned more than $900 per week in 2000; "low-paying" ones are those in which men earned less than $325 per week. Occupations in which so few of either gender were employed that earnings data were not published are omitted.

Source: U.S. Bureau of Labor Statistics, *Employment and Earnings* 48 (January 2001), Table 39.

was associated with fewer current hours of work, and some was associated with less accumulated experience (women in the sample had fewer total months of experience, and more months of *part-time* work, than did their male counterparts). Given the primary role women have typically played in child-rearing, the authors attributed much of this "experience gap" to child care. Indeed, another study reports that in 1991, among all women working at age 30, those who were mothers earned 23 percent less than 30-year-old men, while those who were not mothers earned 10 percent less.[6]

Unexplained Differences Clearly, controlling for occupation, education, age, experience, and hours of work probably goes a long way toward explaining earnings differentials by gender, and other measurable variables added to this list could explain some of the rest. It is possible, however, that some differences would remain unexplained even if all measurable factors were included in our analysis. If so, there are two possible interpretations. One is that these remaining differences are the result of characteristics affecting productivity that might differ by gender but *cannot be observed* by the researcher (for example, the relative priorities individual men

[6]Jane Waldfogel, "Understanding the 'Family Gap' in Pay for Women with Children," *Journal of Economic Perspectives* 12, no. 1 (Winter 1998): 137–156.

EXAMPLE 12.1

Bias in the Selection of Musicians by Symphony Orchestras

Symphony orchestras contain about 100 musicians who must audition in front of a selection committee consisting of the conductor and some orchestra members. Prior to 1970, nearly all orchestras had auditions in which the identity of each candidate was known by the committee. This process favored males—particularly those who were students of a select group of teachers—with the result that only 10 percent of newly hired orchestra members were women. By the 1990s, some 35 percent of new hires were women. What can account for this change?

While it is likely true that the relative pool of female musicians rose during this period, another significant change occurred. Throughout the 1970s and 1980s most orchestras adopted a selection process that used a screen to conceal those auditioning from the selection committee, so that the identity and sex of the candidates could not be discovered. The fact that orchestras adopted these "blind" procedures at different times allows us to estimate the separate effects of these procedures, and one careful study found that about one-third of the 25 percentage-point increase in the hiring of women could be traced to blind auditioning. Put differently, the findings suggest that if the sex of a candidate were known to selection committees, the percentage of women hired would have fallen by about 8 percentage points (from 35 percent to 27 percent).

Data from: Claudia Goldin and Cecilia Rouse, "Orchestrating Impartiality: The Impact of 'Blind' Auditions on Female Musicians," *American Economic Review* 90, no. 4 (September 2000): 715–741.

and women assign to market and household activities, if the two conflict). Alternatively, the unexplained differential could be interpreted as resulting from *discriminatory treatment* in the labor market. (See Example 12.1 for an illustration of discriminatory behavior against women in symphony orchestras.)

Defining Discrimination   Labor market discrimination is said to exist if individual workers who have identical productive characteristics are treated differently because of the demographic groups to which they belong. Gender discrimination is alleged to take two prominent forms. First, employers are sometimes suspected of paying women less than men with the same experience and working under the same conditions in the same occupations; this is labeled *wage discrimination*. Second, women with the same education and productive potential are seen as shunted into lower-paying occupations or levels of responsibility by employers, who reserve the higher-paying jobs for men. This latter form of discrimination has been called *occupational discrimination*.

Wage Discrimination   Basic to the concept of labor market discrimination is that workers' wages are a function of both their *productive characteristics* (their human capital, the size of the firm for which they work, and so on) and the *price* each characteristic commands in the labor market. Thus, economic theory suggests that the wages of women and men might differ because of differences in their levels of job experience, for example, or they might differ because men and women are compensated differently for each added year of experience. *Wage discrimination is said to be present when the prices paid by employers for given productive characteristics are systematically different for different demographic groups.* Put differently, if men and women (or minorities and nonminorities) with equal productive characteristics are paid unequally, even in the same occupations, then wage discrimination exists.

Occupational Discrimination   Critical to a worker's human capital are the occupational preparation and skills acquired through schooling, job training, or experience. Women and men have very different occupational distributions, but proving occupational *segregation* is a lot easier than proving occupational *discrimination*.

Occupational segregation can be said to exist when the distribution of occupations within one demographic group is very different from the distribution in another. With respect to gender, occupational segregation is reflected in there being female-dominated occupations and male-dominated ones.

If occupational choices are directly limited, or if they are influenced by lower payoffs to given human capital characteristics, then occupational segregation certainly reflects labor market discrimination. If these choices reflect different preferences, however, or different household responsibilities (particularly related to child care), then two arguments can be made. One is that there is no particular problem, that occupational preferences—including those toward household work—form naturally from one's life experiences and should be respected in a market economy. The other view is that these preferences are the result of *premarket* discrimination—differential treatment by parents, schools, and society at large that points girls toward lower-paying (including household) pursuits long before they reach adulthood and enter the labor market.

We now turn to issues of measuring occupational segregation and wage discrimination. In both cases, we discuss the available measures and then briefly discuss the extent to which they can be said to accurately reflect discriminatory treatment.

Measurement: Occupational Segregation   As was seen in Table 12.3, women and men are not equally represented in the various occupations. While dramatic changes have occurred in recent decades, women are still underrepresented in higher-paying jobs and overrepresented in the lower-paying ones. Various measures are used to summarize the inequality of gender representation across detailed occupational categories, all of which are based on comparing the existing distribution of men and women in occupations to the distribution that would exist if assignment to occupations were random with respect to gender.[7]

One measure is the *index of dissimilarity*. Assuming workers of one gender remain in their jobs, this index indicates the percentage of the other gender that would have to change occupations for the two genders to have equal occupational

---

[7]Dale Boisso, Kathy Hayes, Joseph Hirschberg, and Jacques Silber, "Occupational Segregation in the Multidimensional Case: Decomposition and Tests of Significance," *Journal of Econometrics* 61, no. 1 (March 1994): 161–171; and Martin Watts, "Divergent Trends in Gender Segregation by Occupation in the United States: 1970–92," *Journal of Post-Keynesian Economics* 17, no. 3 (Spring 1995): 357–379.

distributions. If all occupations were completely segregated, the index would equal 100, while if men and women were equally distributed across occupations it would equal zero. Analyses of gender-related employment patterns in 470 narrowly defined occupations suggest that the index of dissimiliarity has declined from 68 in 1970, to 59 in 1980, to 53 in 1990.[8] A study using somewhat different occupational groupings indicated that the decline in occupational segregation continued throughout the 1990s, but that the pace slowed and the index fell by only a percentage point or two.[9]

Despite a decline in occupational segregation, studies generally find that its effects on women's wages are substantial. It is typically estimated that if American women with given educational attainment and experience levels were in the same occupations and industries as their male counterparts, their wages would rise by as much as 8–10 percent.[10] These effects of occupational segregation on the earnings of women are more pronounced than in many European countries. The reason, pointed out in Example 12.2, is that the wage differentials (for both men and women) between high- and low-paying occupations are relatively larger in the United States, so the penalty for being in a low-wage job is generally greater than in Europe.

As noted previously, however, not all gender segregation is the result of labor market discrimination; at least some may be the result of either preferences formed before labor market entry or choices made later, in the context of family decision making, for example. As yet, no measure has been devised to estimate that portion of occupational segregation that can be attributed to unequal treatment by employers.

The decline in observable occupational segregation, and our inability to measure the role of preferences in that segregation, should not imply that discrimination is no longer an issue. Even within narrowly defined occupations, men and women are often segregated across employers;[11] for example, it is common for restaurants to employ only waiters or only waitresses, but not both. Further, waitresses earn only 87 percent of what waiters earn, and a hiring audit of Philadelphia restaurants suggests that discrimination might play a role. In 1994, two matched pairs of men and women (with equivalent resumes) applied for jobs in 65 restau-

---

[8]Francine D. Blau, "Trends in the Well-Being of American Women, 1970–1995," *Journal of Economic Literature* 36, no. 1 (March 1998): 132.

[9]Francine D. Blau, Marianne A. Ferber, and Anne E. Winkler, *The Economics of Women, Men, and Work*, 4th ed. (Upper Saddle River, N.J.: Prentice-Hall, 2001), 141.

[10]Blau, Ferber, and Winkler, *The Economics of Women, Men, and Work*, 206; and Marjorie L. Baldwin, Richard J. Butler, and William G. Johnson, "A Hierarchical Theory of Occupational Segregation and Wage Discrimination," *Economic Inquiry* 39, no. 1 (January 2001): 94–110. Slightly larger effects of segregation are found in Groshen, "The Structure of the Female/Male Wage Differential," and smaller ones are reported in David Macpherson and Barry T. Hirsch, "Wages and Gender Composition: Why Do Women's Jobs Pay Less?" *Journal of Labor Economics* 13, no. 3 (July 1995): 426–471.

[11]For a study of sex segregation across manufacturing plants, including interplant segregation within occupations, see William J. Carrington and Kenneth R. Troske, "Sex Segregation in U.S. Manufacturing," *Industrial and Labor Relations Review* 51, no. 3 (April 1998): 445–464.

EXAMPLE 12.2

The Gender Earnings Gap across Countries

How do gender wage differentials in the United States compare to those in other developed countries? The ratios, listed below, of women's average weekly earnings to those of men indicate that women in the United States did relatively poorly as of the mid–1990s:

France	0.90
Australia	0.87
Sweden	0.84
Italy	0.83
Germany	0.76
United States	0.76
Switzerland	0.75
United Kingdom	0.75
Canada	0.70

The irony of the relatively low wage ratio in the United States is that women's productive characteristics are closer to those of men in the United States than in any other of the countries. Further, American women are less occupationally segregated, and American legislation concerning equal employment opportunity generally predated laws elsewhere.

The cause of this relatively large gender gap seems to be the wider pay differentials between high- and low-paid workers in the United States. It appears that wage differentials within and across occupations in the United States are larger than in other countries, so that *all* groups of workers with less experience or in lower-paid occupations are relatively worse off here than in other countries.

Data from: Francine D. Blau and Lawrence M. Kahn, "Gender Differences in Pay," *Journal of Economic Perspectives* 14, no. 4 (Fall 2000): 75–99.

rants, and it was found that the high-priced restaurants, where earnings are higher, were much less likely to interview and extend an offer to the female applicant.[12]

Measurement: Wage Discrimination We pointed out earlier that average earnings can differ between women and men either because of differences in average levels of productive characteristics or because of differences in what women and men are paid for possessing each characteristic. Ideally, wage discrimination could be identified and measured in the following four-step process:[13]

1. We would collect data, for men and women separately, on *all* human capital and other characteristics that are theoretically relevant to the determination of earnings. Based on discussions in earlier chapters, the

---

[12]David Neumark, "Sex Discrimination in Restaurant Hiring: An Audit Study," *Quarterly Journal of Economics* 111, no. 3 (August 1996): 915–941.

[13]This procedure was first described in Ronald Oaxaca, "Male-Female Wage Differentials in Urban Labor Markets," *International Economic Review* 14 (October 1973): 693–709. For refinements, see Ronald L. Oaxaca and Michael R. Ransom, "On Discrimination and the Decomposition of Wage Differentials," *Journal of Econometrics* 61, no. 1 (March 1994): 5–21, and Moon-Kak Kim and Solomon W. Polachek, "Panel Estimates of Male-Female Earnings Functions," *Journal of Human Resources* 29, no. 2 (Spring 1994): 406–428.

characteristics of age, education and training, experience, tenure with current employer, hours of work, firm size, region, intensity of work effort, industry, and the job's duties, location, and working conditions come readily to mind.

2. We would then estimate (statistically) how each of these characteristics contributes to the earnings of women. That is, we would use statistical techniques to estimate the payoffs to women associated with each characteristic. (The basic statistical technique used is called *regression analysis,* and it allows us to estimate how changes in a productive characteristic affect earnings, holding other productive characteristics constant. A computer must be used to make these estimates when, as in the case at hand, there are *several* relevant productive characteristics to be jointly analyzed. However, the general idea behind this technique is graphically illustrated in Appendix 12A, using the simple example of estimating how wages are affected by changes in a single composite measure of job "difficulty.")

3. Having measured levels of the productive characteristics typically possessed by men and women (step 1), and having estimated how changes in each productive characteristic affect the earnings of women (step 2), we would next estimate how much women *would* earn *if* their productive characteristics were exactly the same as those of men. This would be done by applying the payoffs *women* receive for each productive characteristic to the average level of those characteristics possessed by *men.*

4. Finally, we would compare the *hypothetical* average earnings level calculated for women (in step 3) with the *actual* average earnings of men. This latter comparison would yield an estimate of wage discrimination, because it reflects the effects of the different prices for productive characteristics paid to men and women. (In the absence of discrimination, women and men who have identical productive characteristics should have identical earnings.)

Can We Infer Wage Discrimination?   There are two problems with this "ideal" measure of wage discrimination: not all potentially measurable productive characteristics are included in available data sets, and some important characteristics are inherently unmeasurable. Such characteristics as native intelligence or the presence of emotional disorders are randomly distributed across the population, so that their effects on women's average earnings are expected to be about the same as they are on men's. Other unobserved characteristics may be differently distributed between women and men. Because of greater household responsibilities, for example, women may be more likely to seek work closer to home, may be less available for work outside normal business hours, or may more often be the parent on call if a child becomes ill at school. These factors reduce the earnings of women, but because they are unmeasured they tend to show up statistically as reduced payoffs to the observed characteristics.

Thus, not all of the wage differences that would remain if observed productive characteristics were equalized between women and men can be unambiguously identified as the result of discrimination in the labor market. As with occupational segregation, some of the differences may reflect choices on the supply side of the market.

Analyzing Wage Differences   These measurement problems notwithstanding, it is interesting to follow the four-step procedure outlined above and see what the earnings gap between women and men would be if observed productive characteristics were equalized. A study using 1988 data estimated that, while women in the sample earned about 72 percent as much as men, if their productive characteristics (including occupation) had been equalized, they would have earned about 88 percent as much.[14] Other studies try to account for the effects of some *unobserved* characteristics (preferences, for example) by using data on *changes* in wages and productive characteristics over time for the *same*—presumably unchanging—individuals. Studies taking this latter approach find that the level of possible wage discrimination is cut roughly in half, but this implies, of course, that some wage discrimination may remain.[15]

The observed productive characteristic that contributes most to the wage gap between women and men in the same occupation is labor market *experience.* Women typically have *less* work experience than men of comparable age, education, and occupation; further, an extra year of total experience also appears to have a *lower payoff* to women. One study, however, suggests that we need to go beyond measuring total years of experience to analyze the effects on wages of the *frequency* and *timing* of periods when women (and men) are out of the labor force, and another suggests that it is experience as a *full-time* worker that is crucial for both men and women.[16] Thus, in the absence of data on the frequency and timing of nonwork spells (data not normally available to the researcher), at least some of the lower payoff to work experience for women may be the result of an unmeasured productive characteristic.

Overall, the *combined* effects of occupational segregation and wage discrimination could possibly reduce women's wages by up to 10 or 20 percent.

---

[14]Blau, Ferber, and Winkler, *The Economics of Women, Men, and Work,* 207.

[15]Kim and Polachek, "Panel Estimates of Male-Female Earnings Functions"; and Sharmila Choudhury, "Reassessing the Male-Female Wage Differential: A Fixed Effects Approach," *Southern Economic Journal* 60, no. 2 (October 1993): 327–340.

[16]Audrey Light and Manuelita Ureta, "Early-Career Work Experience and Gender Wage Differentials," *Journal of Labor Economics* 13, no. 1 (January 1995): 121–154. A study by Francine D. Blau and Lawrence M. Kahn, "Swimming Upstream: Trends in the Gender Wage Differential in the 1980s," *Journal of Labor Economics* 15, no. 1, pt. 1 (January 1997): 1–42, finds that women's returns to *full-time* experience were lower than men's in 1979 but similar by 1988. For a study with similiar implications, see Audra J. Bowlus, "A Search Interpretation of Male-Female Wage Differentials," *Journal of Labor Economics* 15, no. 4 (October 1997): 625–657. T. D. Stanley and Stephen B. Jarrell, "Gender Wage Discrimination Bias? A Meta-Regression Analysis," *Journal of Human Resources* 32, no. 4 (Fall 1998): 947–973, summarizes and references several studies of gender wage discrimination.

TABLE 12.4 **Earnings Ratios of Full-Time, Full-Year Workers, by Race and Gender, 1970–1999**

	Earnings Ratios		
Year	*Black Men/ White Men*	*Black Women/ White Men*	*Black Women/ White Women*
1970	.65	.47	.84
1980	.70	.53	.92
1990	.70	.58	.90
1999	.71	.55	.86

Source: U.S. Bureau of the Census, *Money Income of Households, Families and Persons*, Series P-60. no. 80 (1971), Table 52; no. 132 (1982), Table 58; no. 174 (1991). For 1999, see Figure 12.1.

These estimates are interesting, but they are hardly a precise measure of the effects of discrimination. On the one hand, current labor market discrimination of this magnitude could discourage women from making certain human capital investments that men might find attractive, thus affecting the level of the productive characteristics women bring with them to the labor market.[17] On the other hand, there is as yet no completely satisfactory way to distinguish the effects of discrimination from those caused by unmeasured differences that are associated with gender. Therefore, we do not know whether the 10 to 20 percent differential that apparently would remain if measured productive characteristics were equalized over- or understates the magnitude of discrimination against women.

Earnings Differences between Black and White Americans

We saw in Figure 12.1 that black males who worked full-time in 1999 earned just 71 percent as much as white males; black females earned just 55 percent as much. These percentages represent increases from their levels in 1970, but as the data in Table 12.4 indicate, the gains took place primarily in the 1970s and there has been little improvement since then.

The earnings of full-time workers, however, do not tell the whole story of the economic disparities between black and white Americans. There is no major difference in the fraction of adult male employees in the two groups who work part-time, and there is a *lower* percentage of employed black women (16 percent) than

---

[17]One attempt to measure the effects of current labor market discrimination on subsequent human capital accumulation is reported in David Neumark and Michele McLennan, "Sex Discrimination and Women's Labor Market Outcomes," *Journal of Human Resources* 30, no. 4 (Fall 1995): 713–740.

TABLE 12.5   Employment Ratios, Labor Force Participation Rates, and
Unemployment Rates, by Race and Gender,[a] 1970–2000

	Employment Ratio		Labor Force Participation Rate		Unemployment Rate	
			Men			
Year	Blacks	Whites	Blacks	Whites	Blacks	Whites
1970	71.9%	77.8%	77.6%	81.0%	7.3%	4.0%
1980	62.5	74.0	72.1	78.8	13.3	6.1
1990	61.8	73.2	70.1	76.9	11.8	4.8
2000	63.4	72.9	69.0	75.4	8.1	3.4
			Women			
1970	44.9	40.3	49.5	42.6	9.3	5.4
1980	46.6	48.1	53.6	51.4	13.1	6.5
1990	51.5	54.8	57.8	57.5	10.8	4.6
2000	58.7	57.7	63.2	59.8	7.2	3.6

[a]For 1970 and 1980, data on blacks include other racial minorities. Data in all years are for persons age 16 or older.

Sources: U.S. Bureau of Labor Statistics, *Employment and Earnings* 17 (January 1971), Table A–1; 28 (January 1981), Table A-3; 38 (January 1991), Table 3; 48 (January 2001), Table 3.

white women (26 percent) who work part-time. There are significant disparities, however, in the *employment-to-population ratios* (the ratios of employed adults to the entire population of adults in a particular demographic group). It can be seen in the first two columns of Table 12.5 that, as compared to the white population, a much lower percentage of the black population is employed. The differences are particularly striking for males. We begin our analysis of black/white disparities by first considering these differences in the employment ratios..

Differences in Employment Ratios   The employment ratio for a given demographic group is completely determined by the percentage of the group seeking employment (the labor force participation rate) and the percentage of those seeking employment who find it. Because the latter is equal to 100 percent minus the group's unemployment rate, the employment ratio can be expressed as a function of two widely published rates: the group's labor force participation rate and its unemployment rate.

Table 12.5 contains data on labor force participation rates and unemployment rates by race and gender. Looking first at labor force participation, we see that black women have had *higher* labor force participation rates than white women over the 1970 to 2000 period. Among men, however, the picture is much different. Black men have had consistently lower participation rates than white men, and while both groups of men experienced reductions in labor force participation rates from 1970 to 2000, the reductions were greater for blacks.

The declining labor force participation rates of men are not just the result of earlier labor force withdrawal among older men or more postsecondary schooling by the young (although as we saw in chapter 6, both phenomena have played a role).[18] The participation rates even of men age 35 to 44 have dropped for both blacks and whites, with these reductions being more or less confined to those with a high school education or less. The wages of poorly educated workers—especially men—have fallen in recent years, and many of these men apparently have become "discouraged workers" and have dropped out of the labor force. It appears that at least some of the larger declines in labor force participation among black males are a consequence of their lower average levels of education.[19]

Table 12.5 also suggests that the higher unemployment rates of blacks are a cause of their lower employment-to-population ratios. In 1970, the unemployment rates of black men and women were about 1.8 times higher than those of whites, but since 1980, unemployment rates among blacks have been over *twice* as high. These patterns are *not* just a function of differences in education, age, experience, or region of residence; the black unemployment rate has been roughly double the rate for whites in *every* group.[20]

The relative constancy of the black/white *ratio* of unemployment rates suggests that this ratio is not affected much by the business cycle. It would be erroneous to conclude from this constancy, however, that recessions have equal proportionate effects on black and white employment; in fact, the constant ratio means that black workers suffer *disproportionately* in a recession.

Suppose, for example, that the white unemployment rate were 5 percent and the black unemployment rate were 10 percent; these rates imply, of course, that 95 percent of the white labor force, and 90 percent of the black labor force, is employed. Suppose now that a recession occurs, and that the white and black unemployment rates rise to 8 and 16 percent, respectively. Among whites, the employment rate falls from 95 to 92 percent, which implies that a bit over 3 percent of whites who had jobs lost them (3/95 = 0.032). Among blacks, however, the employment rate falls from 90 to 84 percent, indicating that almost 7 percent of employed blacks lost their jobs (6/90 = 0.067). The greater sensitivity of black employment to aggregate economic activity has led many observers to conclude that blacks are the last hired and first fired.

---

[18]Among men in their 50s, the poorer health of blacks seems to account for much of the difference in labor force participation; see John Bound, Michael Schoenbaum, and Timothy Waidman, "Race Differences in Labor Force Attachment and Disability Status," *The Gerontologist* 36, no. 3 (1996): 311–321.

[19]See Amitabh Chandra, "Labor-Market Dropouts and the Racial Wage Gap: 1940–1990," *American Economic Review* 90, no. 2 (May 2000): 333–338; and John Bound and Richard B. Freeman, "What Went Wrong? The Erosion of Relative Earnings and Employment of Young Black Men in the 1980s," *Quarterly Journal of Economics* 107, no. 1 (February 1992): 202–232.

[20]For a recent analysis of the growth in the unemployment ratio, see Robert W. Fairlie and William A. Sundstrom, "The Emergence, Persistence, and Recent Widening of the Racial Unemployment Gap," *Industrial and Labor Relations Review* 52, no. 2 (January 1999): 252–270.

Occupational Segregation and Wage Discrimination   Among black workers who are employed, analyses similar to those for women can be made to measure the extent of occupational segregation and the degree to which measurable productive characteristics explain the black/white gap in earnings. Occupational segregation appears to be less prevalent by race than by gender. Recent studies that calculated indices of occupational dissimilarity by both race and gender found that the indices comparing black and white occupational distributions had values roughly *half* the size of indices comparing male/female occupational distributions. While racial occupational dissimilarities are smaller and have fallen faster over time than gender-related ones, economists continue to study what role, if any, discrimination plays in generating occupational differences by race.[21]

Turning to the issue of *wage discrimination,* researchers have attempted to determine what factors are most responsible for the large gap that exists between blacks and whites. Analyses that use conventional data on education, experience, age, hours of work, region, occupation, industry, and firm size conclude that these easily measured factors account for much, but clearly not all, of the observed earnings gap between black and white men. One study, for example, estimated that if black men had the same conventionally measured productive characteristics (including occupation) as white men, they would receive earnings 89 percent of those received by whites.[22] As in the case of gender earnings differentials, however, one is left with the question of whether the remaining 11 percent differential reflects current wage discrimination or unmeasured productive characteristics.

One normally unmeasured productive characteristic that plays a key role in explaining black/white wage differentials is cognitive achievement, as measured by scores on the Armed Forces Qualification Test (AFQT). Black Americans have lower AFQT scores, on average, which is associated with poorer-quality schooling and the influences of poverty on home and neighborhood characteristics. Studies that are able to include AFQT scores among their measures of productive characteristics have been limited to young people, but they generally estimate that differences in cognitive achievement alone explain most of the overall black/white earnings gap.[23] Typically,

---

[21]Andrew M. Gill, "Incorporating the Cause of Occupational Differences in Studies of Racial Wage Differentials," *Journal of Human Resources* 29, no. 1 (Winter 1994): 20–41. For a study of racial segregation across firms, see William J. Carrington and Kenneth R. Troske, "Interfirm Segregation and the Black/White Wage Gap," *Journal of Labor Economics* 16, no. 2 (April 1998): 231–260.

[22]Francine D. Blau and Lawrence M. Kahn, "Race and Gender Pay Differentials," in *Research Frontiers in Industrial Relations and Human Resources,* ed. David Lewin, Olivia S. Mitchell, and Peter D. Sherer (Madison, Wis.: Industrial Relations Research Association, 1992), 381–416. Similar estimates have been found in other, including more recent, studies; see Joseph G. Altonji and Rebecca M. Blank, "Race and Gender in the Labor Market," in *Handbook of Labor Economics,* ed. Orley Ashenfelter and David Card (New York: Elsevier, 1999): 3143–3259.

[23]Derek A. Neal and William R. Johnson, "The Role of Premarket Factors in Black-White Wage Differences," *Journal of Political Economy* 104, no. 5 (October 1996): 869–895. For a lively discussion of what the estimated AFQT effects mean, see two articles in the *Journal of Economic Perspectives* 12, no. 2 (Spring 1998): William A. Darity Jr. and Patrick L. Mason, "Evidence on Discrimination in Employment: Codes of Color, Codes of Gender," 63–90, and James J. Heckman, "Detecting Discrimination," 101–116.

these analyses conclude that if AFQT scores and other productive characteristics were equalized, the wages of young black Americans would fall somewhere in the range of 8 percent less to 8 percent more than those of comparable whites.

The effects of differences in cognitive achievement levels are clearly serious. Gaps between black and white Americans in schooling attainment and measured school quality (expenditures per pupil, for example) have narrowed considerably in recent decades, although the effects of these gains have been masked by increased relative wages of workers with the highest levels of educational attainment. Differences in AFQT scores remain substantial, however, and the uncertain ability of additional schooling resources to influence cognitive achievement (see chapter 9) raises questions about how public policies can now help to equalize achievement scores.

While there is evidence of important premarket differences between blacks and whites, on average, most studies do not find that these differences explain the *entire* wage gap that exists. Further, there is ample direct evidence (from hiring audits and government complaints) that labor market discrimination exists.[24] Moreover, as long as black unemployment rates are twice those of whites, blacks will continue to fall short of whites, on average, in terms of job experience and the tenure-related benefits of on-the-job training.[25]

Earnings Differences by Ethnicity

Increased immigration has sparked a renewed interest in the relative earnings of various ancestral groups in the United States, most especially because the earnings differences are so pronounced. Table 12.6 contains earnings data on men from the 1990 *Census of Population.* The first column displays full-time earnings of men from selected ancestral groups relative to the U.S. average, and from it we can note the relatively high earnings of men whose ancestry was Russian, Italian, or Japanese. Conversely, men whose ancestry is Native American, Mexican, or Puerto Rican had especially low earnings.

Drawing upon our discussion of earnings differences across gender and race, we must ask to what extent these differences resulted from different levels of productive characteristics. Educational attainment, for example, across ethnic groups is widely divergent. Men of Japanese, Chinese, and Russian ancestry had average levels of college attainment roughly twice the national average of 1.6 years in 1990, while men from Puerto Rican and Mexican backgrounds had average levels that were under half the national average. The second column in Table 12.6 presents estimates of what earnings in each group would have been if observed productive characteristics, including education and fluency in English, were equalized across all

---

[24]Darity and Mason, "Evidence on Discrimination in Employment" (but also see Heckman, "Detecting Discrimination"), and U.S. President, *Economic Report of the President,* 1998 (Washington, D.C.: U.S. Government Printing Office, February 1998), ch. 4.

[25]Edwin A. Sexton and Reed Neil Olsen, "The Returns to On-the-Job Training: Are They the Same for Blacks and Whites?" *Southern Economic Journal* 61, no. 2 (October 1994): 328–342.

TABLE 12.6 **Male Earnings Differences, by Ancestry, 1990**

Ancestral Group	Earnings as a Percent of U.S. Average	Estimated Earnings as a Percent of U.S. Average if Productive Characteristics of Group Were Average
U.S. total	100	100
Mexican	71	95
Puerto Rican	87	98
Cuban	90	102
Chinese	99	95
Japanese	133	115
Native American	85	95
English	113	102
Italian	121	109
Russian	157	118

Source: William Darity Jr., David Guilkey, and William Winfrey, "Ethnicity, Race and Earnings," *Economics Letters* 47 (1995): 401–408.

groups. The results suggest that if observed productive characteristics were equalized, men of Japanese or Russian ancestry would have earned 15–18 percent more than average, while those of Mexican, Chinese, or Native American ancestry would have earned roughly 5 percent less.[26]

Because of social concern about labor market discrimination, it is natural to focus on groups whose earnings appear to be low, given their productive characteristics. In recent years, however, there has also been interest in the diversity of earnings across white ethnic groups, for which discrimination is of less concern. Of particular interest is whether there are unmeasured qualitative differences in education or background across ethnic groups. Indeed, recent studies have found evidence that there are important intergenerational transfers of "ethnic human capital," some of which is manifest in divergent rates of return to education.[27]

Research interest in ancestral groups that are suspected victims of labor market discrimination have centered on "Hispanics," a categorization including people

---

[26]An analysis of wage differences in rural America estimates that equalizing the productive characteristics of Native Americans would result in their earning 3 to 7 percent less than rural whites. See Jean Kimmel, "Rural Wages and Returns to Education: Differences between Whites, Blacks, and American Indians," *Economics of Education Review* 16, no. 1 (February 1997): 81–96. Similar findings come from a study of native groups in Canada; see Peter George and Peter Kuhn, "The Size and Structure of Native–White Wage Differentials in Canada," *Canadian Journal of Economics* 27, no. 1 (February 1994): 20–42.

[27]George J. Borjas, "Ethnic Capital and Intergenerational Mobility," *Quarterly Journal of Economics* 107 (February 1992): 123–150; and Barry R. Chiswick, "The Skills and Economic Status of American Jewry: Trends over the Last Half-Century," *Journal of Labor Economics* 11, no. 1, pt. 1 (January 1993): 229–242.

from such diverse backgrounds as Mexican, Puerto Rican, Cuban, and Central and South American. While these groups share a common linguistic heritage, one can infer from Table 12.6 that they have somewhat different earnings and human capital levels.

The influx of Spanish-speaking immigrants into the United States has resulted in the growth of a group of workers characterized by its youth, low levels of education, inexperience in the American labor market, and relatively low levels of proficiency in English. Motivated in part by concerns about discrimination, recent research on earnings differences between Hispanics and non-Hispanic whites has focused on the effects of English-language proficiency on earnings. Language proficiency is not measured in the data sets normally used to analyze earnings, yet it clearly affects productivity in just about any job; hence, if measures of it are omitted from the analysis, we cannot conclude anything about the presence or absence of discrimination against immigrant groups.

The handful of studies (including the one underlying the data in Table 12.6) that have had access to data on language proficiency estimate that equalizing all productive characteristics, including language proficiency, would bring the earnings of Hispanics up to within 3 to 6 percent of those received by non-Hispanic whites. One study, however, found that the effects on earnings of either unmeasured productive characteristics or labor market discrimination are far larger for black than for non-black Hispanics.[28]

THEORIES OF MARKET DISCRIMINATION

We cannot rule out the presence of discrimination against women and minorities in the labor market. Before designing policies to end discrimination, however, we must understand the *sources* and *mechanisms* causing it. The goal of this section is to lay out and evaluate the different theories of discrimination proposed by economists.

Three general sources of labor market discrimination have been hypothesized, and each source suggests an associated model of how discrimination is implemented and what its consequences are. The first source of discrimination is *personal prejudice,* wherein employers, fellow employees, or customers dislike associating with workers of a given race or sex.[29] The second general source is *statistical prejudgment,* whereby employers project onto individuals certain perceived

---

[28]William Darity Jr., David Guilkey, and William Winfrey, "Ethnicity, Race, and Earnings," *Economics Letters* 47 (1995): 401–498. For other studies that include language proficiency, see David E. Bloom and Gilles Grenier, "The Earnings of Linguistic Minorities: French in Canada and Spanish in the United States," *Quarterly Journal of Economics* 106 (May 1991): 557–586; Francisco L. Rivera-Batiz, "English Language Proficiency and the Economic Progress of Immigrants," *Economic Letters* 34 (1990): 295–300; Barry R. Chiswick and Paul W. Miller, "The Endogeneity between Language and Earnings: International Analyses," *Journal of Labor Economics* 13, no. 2 (April 1995): 246–288; and Anthony P. Carnevale, Richard A. Fry, and B. Linsay Lowell, "Understanding, Speaking, Reading, Writing, and Earnings in the Immigrant Labor Market," *American Economic Review* 91, no. 2 (May 2001): 159–163.

[29]The models of personal prejudice are based on Gary S. Becker, *The Economics of Discrimination*, 2d ed. (Chicago: University of Chicago Press, 1971).

group characteristics. Finally, there are models based on the presence of *noncompetitive* forces in the labor market. While all the models generate useful, suggestive insights, we will see that none has been convincingly established as superior.

Personal-Prejudice Models: Employer Discrimination

The models based on personal prejudice assume that either employers, customers, or employees have prejudicial tastes; that is, they have preferences for not associating with members of certain demographic groups. Suppose first that white male *employers* are prejudiced against women and minorities but (for simplicity's sake) that customers and fellow employees are not. Further, assume for the purposes of this model that the women and minorities in question have the same productive characteristics as white males. (This assumption directs our focus to labor market discrimination by putting aside premarket factors.)

If employers have a decided preference for hiring white males in high-paying jobs despite the availability of equally qualified women and minorities, they will act *as if* the latter were less productive than the former. By virtue of our assumption that the women and minorities involved are equally productive in every way, the devaluing of their productivity by employers is purely subjective and is a manifestation of personal prejudice. The more prejudiced an employer is, the more actual productivity will be discounted.

Suppose that *MRP* stands for the actual marginal revenue productivity of all workers in a particular labor market and *d* represents the extent to which this productivity is subjectively devalued for minorities and women. In this case, market equilibrium for white males is reached when their wage (W_M) equals *MRP*:

$$MRP = W_M \tag{12.1}$$

For the women and minorities, however, equilibrium is achieved only when their wage (W_F) equals their *subjective* value to firms:

$$MRP - d = W_F \tag{12.2}$$

or

$$MRP = W_F + d \tag{12.2a}$$

Since the actual marginal revenue productivities are equal by assumption, equations (12.1) and (12.2a) are equal to each other, and we can easily see that W_F must be less than W_M:

$$W_M = W_F + d \tag{12.3}$$

or

$$W_F = W_M - d \tag{12.3a}$$

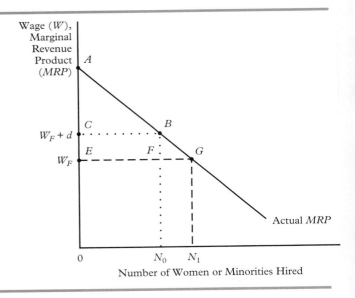

FIGURE 12.2

Equilibrium Employment of Women or Minorities in Firms That Discriminate

What this says algebraically has a very simple economic logic: if the actual productivity of women and minorities is devalued by employers, workers in these groups must offer their services at lower wages than white males to compete for jobs.

Profits under Employer Discrimination   This model of employer discrimination has two major implications, as illustrated by Figure 12.2, which is a graphic representation of equation (12.2a). The first concerns profits. A discriminatory employer faced with a market wage rate of W_F for women and minorities will hire N_0, for at that point $MRP = W_F + d$. *Profit-maximizing* employers, however, will hire N_1; that is, they will hire until $MRP = W_F$. The effects on profits can be readily seen in Figure 12.2 if we remember that the area under the MRP curve represents total revenues of the firm. Subtracting the area representing the wage bill of the discriminatory employer ($0EFN_0$) yields profits for these employers equal to the area $AEFB$. Profits for a profit-maximizing (nondiscriminatory) employer, however, are AEG. These latter employers hire women and minorities to the point where their marginal product equals their wage, while the discriminators end their hiring short of that point. Given the wages of women and minorities (W_F), discriminators give up profits in order to indulge their prejudices.

Pay Gaps under Employer Discrimination   The second implication of our employer discrimination model concerns the size of the gap between W_M and W_F. The determinants of this gap can best be understood by moving to an analysis of the *market* demand curve for women or minorities. In Figure 12.3, the market's demand for women or minorities is expressed in terms of their wage rate *relative* to

FIGURE 12.3

Market Demand for Women or Minorities as a Function of Relative Wages

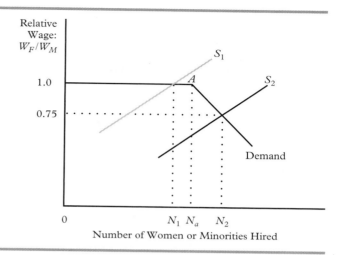

the wage for white males. The figure assumes that there are a number of nondiscriminatory employers, who will hire up to N_a women or minorities at a relative wage of unity (that is, at $W_F = W_M$). For those employers with discriminatory preferences, W_F must fall below W_M to induce them to hire women or minorities. These employers are assumed to differ in their preferences, with some willing to hire women or minorities at small wage differentials and others requiring larger ones. Thus, the market's relative demand curve is assumed to bend downward at point A, reflecting the fact that to employ an increased number of women or minorities would require a fall in W_F relative to W_M.

If the supply of women or minorities is relatively small (supply curve S_1 in Figure 12.3), then such workers will all be hired by nondiscriminatory employers and there will be no wage differential. If the number of women or minorities seeking jobs is relatively large (see supply curve S_2), then some discriminatory employers will have to be induced to hire women or minorities, driving W_F down below W_M. In Figure 12.3, combining supply curve S_2 with the demand curve drives the relative wage down to 0.75.

Besides changes in the labor supply curves of women or minorities, there are two other factors that can cause the market differential between W_F and W_M to change. First, given the supply curve, if the number of nondiscriminators were to increase, as shown in Figure 12.4, the wage differential would decrease. The increase in the nondiscriminators shows up graphically in the figure as an extension of the horizontal segment of the demand curve to A', and the relative wage is driven up (to 0.85 in the figure). Behaviorally, the influx of nondiscriminators absorbs more of the supply than before, leaving fewer workers who must find employment with discriminatory employers. Moreover, the few who must still find

FIGURE 12.4

Effects on Relative Wages of an Increased Number of Nondiscriminatory Employers

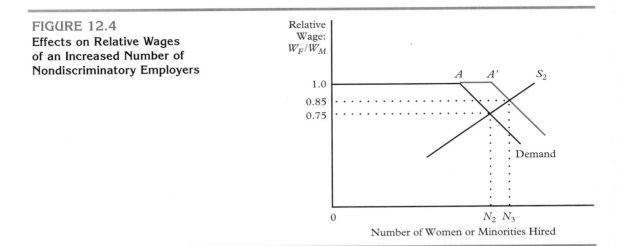

work with discriminatory employers are able to bypass the worst discriminators and can go to work for those with smaller preferences for discrimination.

Second, the same rise in W_F relative to W_M could occur if the number of prejudiced employers stayed the same but their discriminatory preferences were reduced. Such reduction would show up graphically as a flattening of the downward-sloping part of the market's relative demand curve, shown in Figure 12.5. The changes hypothesized in this figure cause W_F to rise relative to W_M, because the inducement required by each discriminatory employer to hire women or minorities is now smaller.

Which Employers Can Afford to Discriminate?   The employer discrimination model implies that discriminators maximize *utility* (satisfying their prejudicial preferences) instead of *profits*. This practice should immediately raise the question of how they survive. Since profit-maximizing (nondiscriminatory) firms would normally make more money from a given set of assets than would discriminators, we should observe nondiscriminatory firms buying out others and gradually taking over the market. In short, if competitive forces were at work in the product market, firms that discriminate would be punished and discrimination could not persist unless their owners were willing to accept below-market rates of return.

Theory suggests, then, that employer discrimination is most likely to persist when owners or managers do not have to maximize profits in order to stay in business. The opportunity to indulge in discriminatory preferences is especially strong among monopolies that face government regulation, because the costs of this wasteful practice make profits look smaller to regulatory bodies.

Studies of both the banking and trucking industries provide evidence consistent with the greater presence of race and gender discrimination among regulated

FIGURE 12.5

Effects on Relative Wages of a Decline in the Discriminatory Preferences of Employers

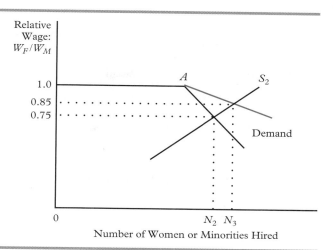

monopolies. Both industries were regulated in ways that limited competition, both were deregulated in recent decades, and in both cases race and gender wage differentials were considerably narrowed by greater product-market competition.[30]

Personal Prejudice Models: Customer Discrimination

A second personal-prejudice model stresses *customer* prejudice as a source of discrimination. Customers may prefer to be served by white males in some situations and by minorities or women in others. If their preferences for white males extend to jobs requiring major responsibility, such as physician or airline pilot, then occupational segregation that works to the disadvantage of women and minorities will occur. If women or minorities are to find employment in these jobs, they must either accept *lower wages* or be *more qualified* than the average white male, because their value to the firm is lower than that of *equally qualified* white males owing to customers' prejudices.

One of the implications of customer discrimination is that it will lead to segregation in the occupations with high customer contact. Firms that cater to discriminatory customers will hire only the preferred group of workers, pay higher wages, and charge higher prices than firms that employ workers from disfavored groups and that serve nondiscriminatory customers. To continue their discriminatory ways, then, customers must be willing to pay the added costs.

[30]Sandra E. Black and Philip E. Strahan, "The Division of Spoils: Rent-Sharing and Discrimination in a Regulated Industry," *American Economic Review* 91, no. 4 (September 2001): 814–831; and James Peoples Jr. and Wayne K. Talley, "Black-White Earnings Differentials: Privatization versus Deregulation," *American Economic Review* 91, no. 2 (May 2001): 164–168.

Empirical studies have found evidence consistent with customer discrimination. For example, the racial composition of a firm's customers is reflected in the racial composition of its employees, especially in jobs with high customer contact.[31] Similarly, a recent study of television viewership for professional basketball games in the United States found that ratings rose, other things equal, when there was greater participation by white players. Because a team's revenues are affected by its television viewership, the latter finding implies that customer discrimination causes white players to have higher marginal revenue product—and higher pay—than black players with comparable skills.[32]

Personal Prejudice Models: Employee Discrimination

A third source of discrimination based on personal prejudice might be found on the supply side of the market, where white male workers may avoid situations in which they will have to interact with minorities or women in ways they consider distasteful. For example, they may resist taking orders from a woman or sharing responsibility with a minority member.

If white male workers, for example, have discriminatory preferences, they will tend to quit or avoid employers who hire and promote on a nondiscriminatory basis. Employers who wish to employ workers in a nondiscriminatory fashion, therefore, would have to pay white males a wage premium (a compensating wage differential) to keep them.

If employers were nondiscriminatory, however, why would they pay a premium to keep white males when they could hire equally qualified and less expensive women or minorities? One answer is that white males constitute a large fraction of the labor force, so it is difficult to imagine producing without them. Moreover, the pressure for women and minorities to be employed outside of "traditional" occupations is relatively recent, so white males hired under one set of implicit promises relating to future promotion possibilities now must adjust to a new set of competitors for positions within the firm. Firms realize that changing their practices involves reneging on past promises, so they may seek to accommodate the preferences for discrimination among their workers. Put differently, employee discrimination may be costly to employers, but so is getting rid of it.

One way to accommodate employee discrimination is to hire on a segregated basis. While it is usually not economically feasible to completely segregate a plant, it *is* possible to segregate workers by job title. Thus, both the employee and the customer models of discrimination can help to explain the finding of one study that

---

[31]Harry J. Holzer and Keith R. Ihlanfeldt, "Customer Discrimination and Employment Outcomes for Minority Workers," *Quarterly Journal of Economics* 113, no. 3 (August 1998): 835–867. The evidence in Neumark, "Sex Discrimination in Restaurant Hiring," also suggests the existence of customer discrimination.

[32]Mark T. Kanazawa and Jonas P. Funk, "Racial Discrimination in Professional Basketball: Evidence from Nielsen Ratings," *Economic Inquiry* 39, no. 4 (October 2001): 599–608.

EXAMPLE 12.3

Fear and Lathing in the Michigan Furniture Industry

In the late nineteenth century, America attracted several hundreds of thousands of immigrants every year. Ethnicity was very important, as people divided along ethnic lines into separate neighborhoods, churches, trade unions, and social clubs. This flood of immigrants encouraged a growing tide of nativism during the late 1800s. The most recognizable face of this nativism was hostility by the American-born toward Catholics and the new immigrant groups from southern and eastern Europe. In addition, many of the newcomers distrusted and disliked one another, carrying over animosities from the old country.

How did these ethnic sensibilities play out in the labor market? Data from the Michigan furniture industry in 1889 allow us a remarkable view, as they include the wages of workers and measures of their human capital, plus information on the ethnicity of co-workers and supervisors.

During this period, the supervisors or foremen had tremendous latitude in hiring and setting the wages of those who worked under them. If *employers* were the source of discrimination, then we would expect a worker to earn more when supervisors were from the same ethnic group and less when they were not. If fellow *employees* were the source of discrimination, we would expect a compensating wage differential to arise, with workers receiving higher pay to offset the disamenity of working with members of other ethnic groups, and lower pay when working only with members of their own ethnic group.

Both of these indications of discrimination occurred in the Michigan furniture industry, but employee-based discrimination appears to have been much more important. Working with foremen from one's own ethnic group was associated with earning wages about 2 percent higher.

However, the ethnicity of co-workers had a fairly large effect: workers who were the only member of their ethnic group in the workplace earned about 11 percent *more* than those whose ethnic group made up about one-quarter of the labor force. Those working in a factory where over 90 percent of co-workers were from their own ethnic group earned about 9 percent *less*. Thus, a worker could pay a big price for avoiding—and could reap big rewards from working with—workers from the other ethnic groups.

Data from: David Buffum and Robert Whaples, "Fear and Lathing in the Michigan Furniture Industry: Employee-Based Discrimination a Century Ago," *Economic Inquiry* 33, no. 2 (April 1995), 234–252.

employers usually hire only women or only men into any single job title—even if *other* employers hire members of the opposite sex into that job title.[33]

The most direct test for the presence of employee discrimination comes from a study that found young white males earned more in *racially integrated* workplaces than if they worked in segregated environments. Further, recent work suggests that the lack of women in top executive jobs may be related to distaste among men for working under female bosses.[34] (Example 12.3 provides an interesting historical example of employee discrimination.)

---

[33]Erica Groshen, "The Structure of the Male/Female Wage Differential."

[34]James F. Ragan Jr. and Carol Horton Tremblay, "Testing for Employee Discrimination by Race and Sex," *Journal of Human Resources* 23, no. 1 (Winter 1988): 123–137; Baldwin, Butler, and Johnson, "A Hierarchical Theory of Occupational Segregation and Wage Discrimination"; and Marianne Bertrand and Kevin F. Hallock, "The Gender Gap in Top Corporate Jobs," *Industrial and Labor Relations Review* 55, no. 1 (October 2001): 3–21.

Statistical Discrimination

We discussed in chapter 5 the need for employers to acquire information on their job applicants in one way or another, all of which entail some cost. Obviously, the firm will evaluate the *personal* characteristics of its applicants, but in seeking to guess their potential productivity it may also utilize information on the average characteristics of the groups to which they belong. If group characteristics are factored into the hiring decision, *statistical discrimination* can result (at least in the short run) even in the absence of personal prejudice.[35]

Statistical discrimination can be viewed as a part of the *screening problem* which arises when observable personal characteristics that are correlated with productivity are not perfect predictors. By way of example, suppose two grades of workers apply for a secretarial job: those who can type 70 words per minute (wpm) over the long haul and those who can type 40 wpm. These actual productivities are unknown to the employer, however. What the employer can observe are the results of a five-minute keyboarding test whose results reflect skill but also are affected by test-taking abilities and luck.

Figure 12.6 shows the test-score distributions for both groups of workers. Those who can actually type 70 wpm score 70 on average, but half score less. Likewise, half of the other group score better than 40 on the test. If an applicant scores 55, say, the employer does not know if the applicant is a good (70 wpm) or a bad (40 wpm) keyboarder. If those scoring 55 are automatically rejected, the firm will be rejecting some good workers, and if it accepts those scoring 55, some bad workers will be hired.

Suppose the employer, in an effort to avoid the above dilemma, does some research and finds out that applicants from a particular training school are specifically coached to perform well on five-minute keyboarding tests. Thus, applicants who can actually type X words per minute over a normal day will tend to score *higher* than X wpm on a five-minute test. Recognizing that students from this school will have average test scores above their long-run productivity, the firm might decide to reject all applicants from this school who score 55 or below (on the grounds that, for most, the test score overestimates their ability), even though some who score less than 55 really can do better.

The general lesson of this example is that firms can legitimately use both *individual* data (test scores, educational attainment, experience) and *group* data in making hiring decisions when the former are not perfect predictors of productivity. However, this use of group data can give rise to market discrimination because people with the same *measured productive characteristics* (test scores, education, etc.) will be treated differently depending on *group* affiliation. The use by employers of race and sex in evaluating job applicants could lead them to prefer white

---

[35]For references to the literature on this topic, see Joseph G. Altonji and Charles R. Pierret, "Employer Learning and Statistical Discrimination," *Quarterly Journal of Economics* 116, no. 1 (February 2001): 313–350.

FIGURE 12.6
The Screening Problem

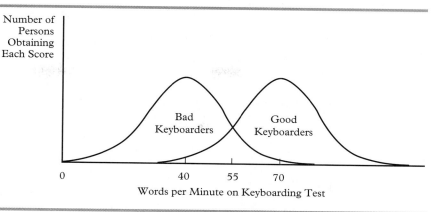

males over other groups. While it is obvious that this preference could be rooted in prejudice, it is also possible that it is based on nonmalicious grounds (for example, the fact that women work fewer hours on average than men). However, if statistical discrimination does not derive from prejudice, then employers will show evidence of "learning" (relying less on group affiliation) as more accurate information on individuals becomes available.[36]

Noncompetitive Models of Discrimination

The discriminatory models discussed so far have traced out the wage and employment implications of personal prejudices or informational problems for labor markets in which firms were assumed to be wage takers. The rather diverse models to which we now turn are all based on the assumption that individual firms have some degree of influence over the wages they pay, either through *collusion* or through some source of *monopsonistic* power.

Crowding The existence and extent of occupational segregation, especially by gender, have caused some to argue that it is the result of a deliberate *crowding* policy intended to lower wages in certain occupations. Graphically, the "crowding hypothesis" is very simple and can be easily seen in Figure 12.7. Panel (a) illustrates a market in which supply is small relative to demand and the wage (W_H) is thus relatively high. Panel (b) depicts a market in which crowding causes supply to be large relative to demand, resulting in a wage (W_L) that is comparatively low.

While the effects of crowding are easily seen, the phenomenon of crowding itself is less easily explained. If men and women were equally productive in a given

---

[36]Altonji and Pierret, "Employer Learning and Statistical Discrimination," finds evidence of this learning—and little evidence of statistical wage discrimination based on race.

FIGURE 12.7
Labor Market
Crowding

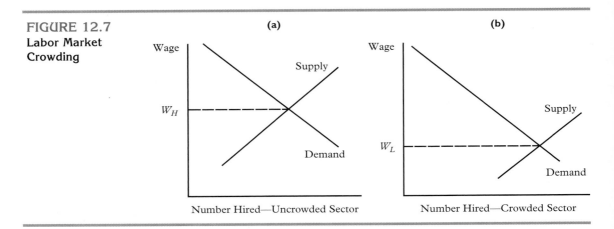

job or set of jobs, for example, one would think that the lower wages of women caused by their being artificially crowded into certain jobs would make it attractive for firms now employing only men to replace them with less-expensive women workers; this profit-maximizing behavior should eventually eliminate any wage differential. The failure of crowding, or occupational segregation, to disappear suggests the presence of noncompeting groups (and therefore barriers to employee mobility), but we are still left with trying to explain why such groups exist in the first place. Over the past seventy years, various possible explanations have been put forth: the establishment of some jobs as "male" and others as "female" through social custom, differences in aptitude that are either innate or acquired, and different supply curves of men and women to monopsonistic employers (discussed later). None of these explanations is complete in the sense of getting at the ultimate source of discrimination, but it is undeniable that the more female-dominated an occupation is, the lower its wages are, even after controlling for the human capital of the workers in it.[37]

Dual Labor Markets   A variant of the crowding hypothesis with more recent origins is the view that the labor market is divided into two noncompeting sectors: a *primary* and a *secondary* sector. Jobs in the primary sector offer relatively high wages, stable employment, good working conditions, and opportunities for advancement. Secondary-sector jobs, however, tend to be low-wage, unstable, dead-end jobs with poor working conditions; the returns to education and experience are thought to

---

[37]See Elaine Sorenson, "The Crowding Hypothesis and Comparable Worth," *Journal of Human Resources* 25, no. 1 (Winter 1990): 55–89. An excellent history of crowding theories is provided in Janice F. Madden, *The Economics of Sex Discrimination* (Lexington, Mass.: Lexington Books, 1973), 30–36. Also see Barry T. Hirsch and Edward J. Schumacher, "Labor Earnings, Discrimination, and the Racial Composition of Jobs," *Journal of Human Resources* 27, no. 4 (Fall 1992): 602–628.

be close to zero in this sector. Workers (primarily minorities and women) relegated to the secondary sector are tagged as unstable, undesirable workers and are thought to have little hope of acquiring primary-sector jobs.

The dual labor market description of discrimination does not really explain why noncompeting sectors arose or why women and minorities were confined to the secondary sector. Some view the dual labor market as arising out of employer collusion (see the section below on collusive behavior), and others see it as rooted in the factors that lead to internal labor markets and efficiency wages.[38] Whatever the cause, there is evidence that two distinct sectors of the labor market exist—one in which education and experience are associated with higher wages and one in which they are not.[39]

Such evidence in favor of the dual labor market hypothesis offers an explanation of why discrimination can persist. It calls into question the levels of competition and mobility that exist and suggests that the initial existence of noncompeting race/sex groups will be self-perpetuating. In short, the dual labor market hypothesis is consistent with any of the models of discrimination analyzed above; what it does suggest is that if any of these theories *are* applicable, we cannot count on natural market forces to eliminate the discrimination that results.

Search-Related Monopsony   The crowding and dual labor market explanations for discrimination are grounded in the assumption that workers are "assigned" to occupational groups from which mobility to other groups is severely restricted; how or why assignments are made is not entirely clear. A third model of restricted mobility is built around the presence of job search costs for employees.[40] This model combines a monopsonistic model of firm behavior, such as the one discussed in the final section of chapter 10, with the phenomenon of prejudice discussed earlier.

Suppose that some, but not all, employers refuse to hire minorities or women owing to their own prejudices, those of their customers, or those of their employees. Suppose further that, in contrast, no employers rule out the hiring of white males. Minorities and women looking for jobs do not readily know who will refuse them out of hand, so they have to search longer and harder than do white men to generate the same number of job offers. As we saw at the end of chapter 10, employee job search costs cause firms' labor supply curves to slope upward, and the monopsonistic outcomes that follow become more pronounced when these search costs are greater.

---

[38]See, for example, Jeremy Bulow and Lawrence Summers, "A Theory of Dual Labor Markets with Application to Industrial Policy, Discrimination, and Keynesian Unemployment," *Journal of Labor Economics* 4 (July 1986): 376–414; Claudia Goldin, "Monitoring Costs and Occupational Segregation by Sex: A Historical Analysis," *Journal of Labor Economics* 4 (January 1986): 1–27; and James Rebitzer, "Radical Political Economy and the Economics of Labor Markets," *Journal of Economic Literature* 31, no. 3 (September 1993): 1417.

[39]William Dickens and Kevin Lang, "A Test of Dual Labor Market Theory," *American Economic Review* 75 (September 1985): 792–805.

[40]For a more rigorous discussion of this model, see Dan H. Black, "Discrimination in an Equilibrium Search Model," *Journal of Labor Economics* 13, no. 2 (April 1995): 309–334.

FIGURE 12.8
Search-Related Monopsony and Wage Discrimination

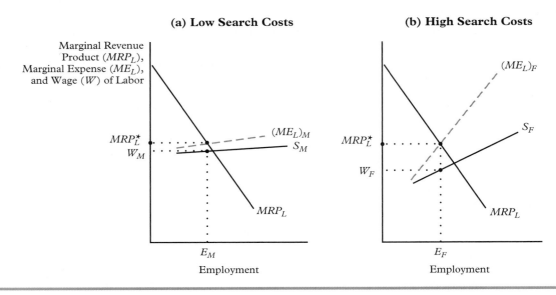

Figure 12.8 graphically illustrates the implications of a situation in which two groups of workers have the same productivity (that is, they both have a marginal revenue product of labor equal to MRP_L^*), but one group has higher search costs than the other. Panel (a) depicts the supply and the marginal revenue product of labor curves for the group (white males, presumably) with relatively low search costs. The labor supply curve of this group to their employers (S_M) is relatively flat, which also means that the associated *marginal* expense of labor curve (ME_L)$_M$ is relatively flat. Profit-maximizing employers will hire E_M workers from this group and pay them a wage of W_M, which is only slightly below MRP_L^*.

Panel (b) illustrates the relevant curves for a group (minorities or women) with higher search costs created by the existence of prejudice. These workers are assumed to have exactly the same marginal revenue product of labor, but their higher search costs imply a more steeply sloped labor-supply curve (S_F), a more steeply sloped marginal expense of labor curve (ME_L)$_F$, and a greater divergence between marginal revenue product and the wage rate. E_F workers in this group are hired, and they are paid a wage of W_F. Comparing panels (a) and (b), it is readily seen that despite having the same marginal productivity, workers with higher search costs are paid lower wages (that is, $W_F < W_M$). At a practical level, if members of both groups are hired by a given firm, those with higher search costs may be placed into lower job titles.

Our discussion of search-related monopsony invites two comments. First, in chapters 3 and 4 we introduced the monopsony model as a potential explanation for the small and uncertain responses of employment to *mandated* wage increases under minimum wage laws. The monopsony model has also been invoked to explain the lack of employment declines associated with mandated wage increases for women under the United Kingdom's Equal Pay Act of 1970.[41]

Second, if prejudice increases the job search costs for women and minorities, so that members of these groups are less likely to search for alternative offers of employment, their job matches will be of lower quality than the job matches for white men. Individual women and minority-group members, then, would be less likely to find the employers who can best utilize their talents. Thus, even within narrowly defined occupational groups, minorities and women would tend to be less productive and receive less pay than white men, owing to poorer-quality matches.

Collusive Behavior   Some theories are grounded in an assumption that employers collude with each other to subjugate minorities or women, thus creating a situation in which monopsonistic wages can be forced on the subjugated group. One of the more explicit collusive theories of discrimination argues that prejudice and the conflicts it creates are inherent in a capitalist society because they serve the interests of owners.[42] Workers divided by race or gender are harder to organize and, if they *are* unionized, are less cohesive in their demands. Hence, it is argued that owners of capital gain, while *all* workers—but particularly minorities and women—lose from discrimination.

If discrimination is created or at least perpetuated by capitalists, however, how do we account for its existence in precapitalist or socialist societies? Further, it may be true that if all white employers conspire to keep women and minorities in low-wage, low-status jobs, they can all reap monopoly profits. However, if employers A through Y adhere to the agreement, employer Z will always have incentives to *break* the agreement. Z can hire women or minorities cheaply because of the agreement among *other* employers not to hire them, and Z can enhance profits by hiring these otherwise equally productive workers to fill jobs that A through Y are staffing with high-priced white males. Since every other employer has the same incentives as Z, the conspiracy will tend to break down unless cheaters can be disciplined in some way. The collusive-behavior model does not tell us how the conspiracy is maintained and coordinated among the millions of U.S. employers.

A Final Word on the Theories of Discrimination

It would appear that all models of discrimination agree on one thing: any persistence of labor market discrimination is the result of forces that are either noncompetitive

---

[41]Alan Manning, "The Equal Pay Act as an Experiment to Test Theories of the Labour Market," *Economica* 63, no. 250 (May 1996): 191–212.

[42]Michael Reich, "The Economics of Racism," in *Problems in Political Economy: An Urban Perspective,* ed. David M. Gordon (Lexington, Mass.: D. C. Heath, 1971), 107–113.

or very slow to adjust to competitive forces. While no one model yet can be demonstrated to be superior to the others in explaining the facts, the various theories and the facts they seek to explain suggest that government intervention might be useful in eliminating the noncompetitive (or sluggish) influences. In analyzing these governmental programs, it will be helpful to keep in mind that discriminatory pressures can come from a variety of sources and that discrimination is not necessarily profitable for those who engage in it.

FEDERAL PROGRAMS TO END DISCRIMINATION

Broadly speaking, the government has taken two somewhat conflicting approaches to combat the causes or effects of discrimination. One approach is to mandate *nondiscrimination*, which implies that race, ethnicity or sex should play no role in hiring, promoting, or compensating workers. The other approach can be characterized as *affirmative action,* in which employers are required to be conscious of race, ethnicity, and gender in their personnel decisions and take steps to ensure that "protected" groups are not under-represented.

Equal Pay Act of 1963

Before the 1960s, sex discrimination was officially sanctioned by laws that limited women's total weekly hours of work and prohibited them from working at night, lifting heavy objects, and working during pregnancy. Not all states placed all these restrictions on women, but the effect of these laws was to limit the access of women to many jobs. These laws were overturned by the Equal Pay Act of 1963, which also outlawed separate pay scales for men and women using similar skills and performing work under the same conditions.

The act was seriously deficient as an antidiscrimination tool, however, because it said nothing about equal opportunity in hiring and promotions. This flaw can be easily understood by a quick review of our theories of discrimination. If there is prejudice against women from whatever source, employers will treat female employees as less productive or more costly to hire than equally productive males. The market response is for female wages to fall below male wages, because otherwise women cannot hope to be able to successfully compete with men in obtaining jobs. The Equal Pay Act took a step toward the elimination of wage differentials, but in so doing it tended to suppress a market mechanism that helped women obtain greater access to jobs.[43] The act failed to acknowledge that if labor market discrimination is to be eliminated, legislation must require *both* equal pay *and* equal opportunities in hiring and promotions for people of comparable productivity.

---

[43]Some critics of the Equal Pay Act of 1963 argued that its motivation was to help men compete with lower-paid women. See Nancy Barrett, "Women in the Job Market: Occupations, Earnings, and Career Opportunities," in *The Subtle Revolution,* ed. Ralph E. Smith (Washington, D.C.: Urban Institute, 1979), 55.

Title VII of the Civil Rights Act

Some defects in the Equal Pay Act of 1963 were corrected the next year. Title VII of the Civil Rights Act of 1964 made it unlawful for any employer "to refuse to hire or to discharge any individual, or otherwise to discriminate against any individual with respect to his compensation, terms, condition, or privileges of employment, because of such individual's race, color, religion, sex or national origin." Title VII applies to all employers in interstate commerce with at least 15 employees and is enforced by the Equal Employment Opportunity Commission (EEOC), which has the authority to mediate complaints, encourage lawsuits by private parties or the U.S. attorney general, or bring suits itself against employers. To enhance the force of the law, the courts permitted individual plaintiffs to expand their suits into *class actions* in which the potential discriminatory impact of an organization's employment practices on an entire group of workers is assessed.

Over the years, the federal courts have fashioned two standards of discrimination that may be applied when discriminatory employment practices are alleged—*disparate treatment* and *disparate impact.* Disparate treatment occurs under Title VII if individuals are treated differently because of their race, sex, color, religion, or national origin, and if it can be shown that there was an intent to discriminate. The difficulty raised by this standard is that policies that appear to be neutral in the sense that they ignore race, gender, etc., may nevertheless perpetuate the effects of past discrimination. For example, word-of-mouth recruiting (a seemingly neutral policy) in a plant with a largely white workforce would be suspect under Title VII even if the selection of new employees from among the applicants was done on a nondiscriminatory basis.

The concern with addressing the present effects of past discrimination led to the *disparate impact standard.* Under this approach it is the result, not the motivation, that matters. Policies that appear to be neutral but lead to different effects by race, gender, etc., are prohibited under Title VII unless they can be related to job performance.[44] As a result, plaintiffs, employers, and the courts have become interested in how closely the race or gender composition of those selected for employment, promotion, training, or termination accords with the race or gender composition of the pool of workers available for selection.

Enforcing Title VII using the disparate impact standard has raised several issues regarding hiring, promotion, and pay decisions. One is defining who should be considered in a firm's potential hiring pool; for example, should prospective applicants residing quite far from the workplace be given the same weight as those who live in nearby neighborhoods? Another is statistical: what constitutes convincing (significant) evidence of under-representation? Two other issues relate to how employers award seniority to workers and how to judge "equal pay" when occupations are segregated.

---

[44]*Griggs* v. *Duke Power Company* 401 U.S. 424 (1971).

Seniority   Many firms use seniority as a consideration in allocating promotion opportunities. Moreover, employees are frequently laid off in order of reverse seniority, the least-senior first, in a recession. Seniority can be calculated either as tenure within the *plant* or as time served within a *department* of the plant; in both cases such systems have worked against minorities and women who have been hired or promoted to nontraditional jobs as a result of Title VII or some other antidiscrimination program. The most egregious cases occurred under departmental seniority systems when, during a business downturn, women or minorities who recently had been promoted to new departments were laid off ahead of those who had less plant seniority! The argument that the effects of seniority systems lock in past discrimination led to much litigation, but departmental seniority systems are still permitted[45] and laying off more-senior white employees instead of recently-hired minorities to preserve racial balance has been ruled unconstitutional.[46]

Comparable Worth: In Theory   Many contend that achieving "equal pay for equal work" would be a rather hollow victory, since occupations are so segregated by gender that men and women rarely do "equal work." As a result, some have come to support the goal of equal pay for jobs of "comparable worth." Proponents of comparable worth can point to the fact that the "male" occupation of maintaining *machines* (general maintenance mechanic) pays $11 per hour, for example, while the "female" job of maintaining *children* (child-care worker) pays $7. Why, they might ask, should those who take care of human beings be paid less than those who take care of machines?

When asked why mechanics are paid more than child-care workers, economists answer in terms of market forces: for some reason, the supply of mechanics must be smaller relative to the demand for them than the supply of child-care workers. Perhaps this reason has to do with working conditions, or perhaps it is more difficult to learn and keep abreast of the skills required of a mechanic, or perhaps occupational crowding increases the supply of child-care workers. Whatever the reason, it is argued, wages are the price of labor—and prices play such a critical *practical* role in the allocation of resources that they are best left unregulated.

Thus, in fighting discrimination, most economists would advise modifying the demand or supply behaviors that *cause* unequal outcomes rather than treating the *symptoms* by regulating wages. If the wages of child-care workers were to be raised above their market-clearing level, to take the case at hand, a surplus would be created in that labor market. Above-market wages would mean fewer jobs and more unemployed applicants—hardly the outcome envisioned by those wanting to end discrimination. (A lengthy analysis of these unintended side effects is given in Example 12.4, in the context of equalizing the pay of university professors across the various disciplines.)

---

[45]*International Brotherhood of Teamsters* v. *United States* 431 U.S. 324, 14 FEP 1514 (1977).
[46]*Franks* v. *Bowman Transportation* 424 U.S. 747, 12 FEP Cases 549 (1976); *Fire Fighters Local 1784* v. *Stotts*, U.S. S. Ct. no. 82–206, June 12, 1984; and *Wygant* v. *Jackson Board of Education*, U.S. S. Ct. no. 84–1340, May 19, 1986.

Comparable Worth: In Practice   Comparable worth policies have generally relied on job-rating schemes often used by employers with internal labor markets to determine or justify pay differentials associated with various job titles or promotion steps. The process involves assigning points to each job according to the knowledge and problem-solving abilities required, its level of accountability, the physical conditions of work, and perhaps other characteristics. Jobs with equal point values would receive equal pay and, of course, jobs assigned higher point values would receive higher pay (Appendix 12A provides an example). The process by which points are awarded to each job is obviously critical, and both sides of the comparable-worth issue see it as a problem. Opponents claim that job ratings can be used to unjustifiably raise the pay in targeted jobs above market levels, while proponents argue that the job ratings now used within firms unfairly lower the value of women's jobs.[47]

The relatively few cases in which comparable-worth policies have been used to address unequal pay in the United Kingdom and the United States have required equalization only *within the boundaries of a single employer.* In contrast to the United Kingdom, however, where cases involving both public and private employers have come before the tribunals specially created to hear comparable-worth complaints,[48] the major push for comparable worth in the United States has come in the state and local government sector.

To date, the estimated effects of implementing comparable worth in the United States and the United Kingdom have been neither as positive as its proponents had hoped nor as dire as its critics had portended. The effects on male/female wage differentials appear small,[49] as do any negative effects on female employment.[50]

The Federal Contract Compliance Program

In 1965 the U.S. Office of Federal Contract Compliance Programs (OFCCP) was established to monitor the hiring and promotion practices of federal contractors (firms supplying goods or services to the federal government). OFCCP requires contractors above a certain size to analyze the extent of their underutilization of women

---

[47]See Donald J. Treiman and Heidi L. Hartmann, eds., *Women, Work and Wages: Equal Pay for Jobs of Equal Value* (Washington, D.C.: National Academy Press, 1981), and Steven E. Rhoads, *Incomparable Worth* (Cambridge, Eng.: Cambridge University Press, 1993), 160–165.

[48]Rhoads, *Incomparable Worth,* 148–160.

[49]See, for example, Peter E. Orazem, J. Peter Mattila, and Sherry K. Welkum, "Comparable Worth and Factor Point Pay Analysis in State Government," *Industrial Relations* 31 (Winter 1992): 195–215; Mark R. Killingsworth, *The Economics of Comparable Worth* (Kalamazoo, Mich.: W. E. Upjohn Institute for Employment Research, 1990); and Rhoads, *Incomparable Worth,* 166.

[50]See, for example, Killingsworth, *The Economics of Comparable Worth;* Shulamit Kahn, "Economic Implications of Public Sector Comparable Worth: The Case of San Jose, California," *Industrial Relations* 31 (Spring 1992): 270–291; Ronald G. Ehrenberg and Robert S. Smith, "Comparable Worth Wage Adjustments and Female Employment in the State and Local Sector," *Journal of Labor Economics* 5 (January 1987): 43–62; and Manning, "The Equal Pay Act as an Experiment to Test Theories of the Labor Market."

EXAMPLE 12.4

Comparable Worth and the University

Some of the difficulties involved with the concept of *comparable worth* can be illustrated by an example in which gender does not even enter. Consider the labor market for university professors in the fields of computer science and English, and suppose that initially the demand and supply curves for both are given by D_{0C} and S_{0C}, and D_{0E} and S_{0E}, respectively. As the figure indicates, in this circumstance the same wage (W_0) will prevail in both markets, and N_{0C} computer science professors and N_{0E} English professors will be hired. Suppose also that in some objective sense the quality of the two groups of professors is equal.

Presumably this is a situation that advocates of comparable worth would applaud. Both types of professors require the same amount of training, represented by a Ph.D., and both are required to engage in the same activities, teaching and research. Unless we are willing to assign different values to the teaching and research produced in different academic fields, we must conclude that the jobs are truly comparable. Hence, if the two groups are equal in quality, equal wages would be justified according to the concept of comparable worth.

Suppose now, however, that the demand for computer science professors rises to D_{1C} as a result of the increasing numbers of students who want to take computer science courses. Suppose at the same time the demand for English professors falls to D_{1E} because fewer students want to take elective courses in English. At the old equilibrium wage rate there is now an excess demand for computer science professors of $N_{1C} - N_{0C}$ and an excess supply of English professors of $N_{0E} - N_{1E}$.

How can universities respond? One possibility is to let the market work; the wage of computer science professors will rise to W_{1C} and that of English professors will fall to W_{1E}. Employment of the former will rise to N_{2C} while employment of the latter will become N_{2E}.

Another possibility is to keep the wages of the two groups of professors equal at the old wage rate of W_0. Universities could respond to the excess demand for computer scientists and the excess supply of English professors by lowering hiring standards for the former and raising them for the latter. Since the average quality of English professors would then exceed the average quality of computer scientists, the wage paid per "quality-unit" would now be higher for the computer scientists. Hence, true comparable worth—equal pay for *equal-quality* workers performing comparable jobs—would not be achieved. Moreover, employment and course offerings in this situation would not change to meet changing student demands.

Alternatively, some advocates of comparable worth might argue that universities should respond by raising the wages of *all* professors to W_{1C}. While this would eliminate the shortage of computer science professors, it would exacerbate the excess supply of English professors, raising it to $N_{4E} - N_{3E}$. Universities would respond by reducing the employment of

and minorities and to propose a plan to remedy any such underutilization. Such a plan is called an *affirmative action plan*. Contractors submitting unacceptable plans or failing to meet their goals are threatened with cancellation of their contracts and their eligibility for future contracts, although these drastic steps are rarely taken.

Affirmative action planning is intended to commit firms to a schedule for rapidly overcoming unequal career opportunities afforded women and minorities. Such planning affects both *hiring* and *promotion* practices, and like requirements under the disparate impact standard, the contract compliance program requires covered employers to take race, ethnicity, and gender into account when developing personnel policies.

EXAMPLE 12.4

Comparable Worth and the University *(continued)*

English professors to N_{3E} (and reducing course offerings). Moreover, the excess supply again would permit universities to raise hiring standards for English professors, so again average quality would rise. As a result, once more the wage per quality-unit of English professors would be less than that of computer science professors, and again true comparable worth would not be achieved.

The message we can take away from this example is that it is difficult to "trick the market." In the face of changing relative demand conditions, either wage differentials for the two types of professors must be allowed to arise or quality differentials will arise. In neither case, however, can comparable worth be achieved. Put another way, the value of a job cannot be determined independently of market conditions.

The Market for Computer Science and English Professors

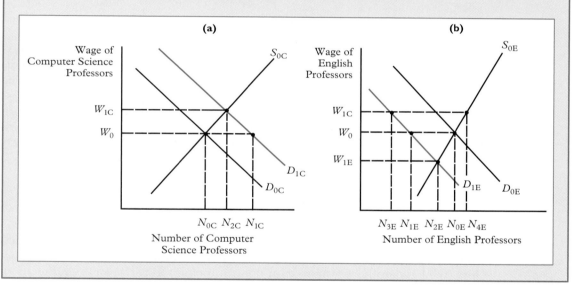

Those who favor affirmative action point out that even if nondiscrimination in personnel actions were to be scrupulously followed, it still would not be an expeditious way to overcome the adverse effects of past discrimination. For example, consider the data in Table 12.7 for a hypothetical firm that has just agreed to follow a policy of nondiscrimination in hiring. Black workers represent 12 percent of the firm's hiring pool, but right now they are only 6.25 percent of the firm's 1600-person workforce. The firm is not growing, so the only hiring opportunities come when workers quit, which they do at a rate of 20 percent each year. Because of these limited hiring opportunities, and because 20 percent of black workers hired subsequently leave each year, nondiscriminatory hiring in this case would

TABLE 12.7   Change in the Racial Composition of a 1,600-Person Job Group with Nondiscriminatory Hiring from a Pool That Is 12% Black (20% yearly turnover rate)

	Year						
	0	1	2	3	4	5	10
Number of blacks							
Loss		20	24	26	29	31	36
New hires		38	38	38	38	38	38
Net gain		18	14	12	11	7	2
Cumulative level	100	118	132	144	155	162	181
Percent black	6.25	7.37	8.25	9.00	9.69	10.12	11.31

not achieve proportionate representation even in ten years (progress would be even slower with a lower quit rate).

Besides the argument that affirmative action represents *reverse* discrimination (against white males), the potential effects of the contract compliance program have been questioned on two other grounds. First, if under-represented groups are to be given preference in hiring, will firms be required to hire less-qualified workers? Second, because the program covers only federal contractors, will qualified minorities and women just be shifted from the noncovered to the covered sector, with no overall gain in employment? These questions lead us to a review of the effects that antidiscrimination programs have had in the United States.

Effectiveness of Federal Antidiscrimination Programs

A recent, comprehensive review of federal affirmative action programs concluded that they have redistributed employment opportunities among federal contractors (who generally pay more than noncontractors) toward blacks and women, although the extent of this redistribution does not seem to have been very large. It also appears that, with respect to women, there is no evidence that affirmative action was associated with lower hiring standards or job performance. Weaker labor-market credentials were found among minorities hired, but there is scant evidence that job performance levels were lower.[51] Can we conclude that the improvements for minorities and women in this one sector have trans-

---

[51]Harry Holzer and David Neumark, "Assessing Affirmative Action," *Journal of Economic Literature* 38, no. 3 (September 2000): 483–568. For a study of an apparently successful program aimed at improving opportunities for black workers among defense contractors during World War II, see William J. Collins, "Race, Roosevelt, and Wartime Production: Fair Employment in World War II Labor Markets," *American Economic Review* 91, no. 1 (March 2001): 272–286.

lated to improvements overall? This question has been most extensively addressed with respect to African Americans.

The ratio of black to white incomes has risen since 1960, and it is natural to ask if this rise was a result of government efforts, or were other forces working to accomplish this result? Three other forces are commonly cited. First, an improvement in the *educational attainment* of black workers relative to that of whites during this period is thought to have played an important role in raising the ratio of black to white earnings; in fact, one study estimated that increased educational attainment accounts for 20–25 percent of the post-1960 gain in the earnings ratio.[52] Second, there is evidence that the *quality* of schooling improved more after 1960 for blacks than for whites, and one study has estimated that from 15 to 20 percent of the increased earnings ratio can be attributed to enhanced school quality.[53] Finally, it has been argued that because the relatively large reduction in labor-force participation rates among blacks was centered in the least-educated group of workers, the average earnings of those who remained employed were thereby increased, giving the *appearance* of overall improvement. Roughly 10 to 20 percent of the improved earnings ratio has been attributed to this last factor.[54]

Taking the upper estimates of the three sources of earnings increases cited above, at least a third of the improvement in the black/white earnings ratio for men remains to be explained. Is it possible that federal efforts to reduce discrimination in the labor market were responsible? One review of the literature and the evidence on this issue concluded that, overall, federal efforts were successful in raising earnings levels of African Americans.[55]

One important fact about black economic progress is that there was a discontinuous jump in the black/white earnings ratio between 1960 and 1975. This sudden improvement coincided with the onset of federal antidiscrimination programs, and it cannot be explained by the rather continuous increases taking place in such other factors as schooling quality or attainment. A second important fact is that the greatest gains in the black/white earnings ratio during the 1960–1975 period were in the South, where segregation was most blatant and where federal antidiscrimination efforts were greatest.

---

[52]James P. Smith and Finis R. Welch, "Black Economic Progress after Myrdal," *Journal of Economic Literature* 27, no. 2 (June 1989): 519–564.

[53]David Card and Alan B. Krueger, "School Quality and Black-White Relative Earnings: A Direct Assessment," *Quarterly Journal of Economics* 107, no. 1 (February 1992): 151–200.

[54]John J. Donohue III and James Heckman, "Continuous versus Episodic Change: The Impact of Civil Rights Policy on the Economic Status of Blacks," *Journal of Economic Literature* 29 (December 1991): 1603–1643.

[55]Donohue and Heckman, "Continuous versus Episodic Change." For a thumbnail sketch of this comprehensive review, see James Heckman, "Accounting for the Economic Progress of Black Americans," in *New Approaches to Economic and Social Analyses of Discrimination*, ed. Richard R. Cornwall and Phanindra V. Wunnava (New York: Praeger, 1991), 331–337. A paper by Kenneth Y. Chay, "The Impact of Federal Civil Rights Policy on Black Economic Progress: Evidence from the Equal Employment Opportunity Act of 1972," *Industrial and Labor Relations Review* 51, no. 4 (July 1998): 608–632, supports the view that federal efforts helped to reduce the black/white pay gap.

The conclusion that federal antidiscrimination efforts may have been at least partially responsible for raising the relative earnings of blacks must be acknowledged as somewhat surprising, because studies of individual programs (such as the federal contract compliance program) have estimated rather meager results. The paradox of overall improvement resulting from programs that appear to have been individually weak may be resolved by noting that each program was part of a comprehensive set of programs—largely aimed at the South—to dismantle all forms of racial segregation, register blacks to vote, and provide legal remedies for victims of discrimination. In the words of one analyst:

> There is evidence that southern employers were eager to employ blacks if they were given the proper excuse. This produced a strong leverage effect for the new laws.... An entire pattern of racial exclusion was challenged. This helps to explain how an apparent straw (the Equal Employment Opportunity Commission and the Office of Federal Contract Compliance) could have broken the back of southern employment discrimination. They were only the tip of a federal iceberg launched against the South.[56]

While optimism about the effects of federal antidiscrimination programs in the 1960s and 1970s is warranted, it is not clear that such programs were successful after 1980, when the market for less-educated workers turned poor. It might be possible to argue that the earnings of blacks after 1980 would have been even *lower* were it not for federal efforts, but the evidence so far is that once the most blatant forms of discrimination were attacked, the effects of federal efforts have weakened.[57]

---

[56]Heckman, "Accounting for the Economic Progress of Black Americans," 336.
[57]Donohue and Heckman, "Continuous versus Episodic Change," 1640. Harry J. Holzer, "Why Do Small Establishments Hire Fewer Blacks Than Large Ones?" *Journal of Human Resources* 32, no. 4 (Fall 1998): 896–914, documents that small firms lag behind larger ones in the hiring of blacks. While the source of this lag is unknown, the lag does indicate a sector in which further gains might be possible.

REVIEW QUESTIONS

1. Chinese and Japanese Americans have average earnings that are equal to, or above, those of white Americans. Does this fact imply that they are not victims of labor market discrimination?

2. "In recent years, the wage gap between skilled and unskilled workers in the United States has grown. This growth means that measured labor market discrimination against unskilled Mexican immigrants is also growing." Comment on whether the second part of this statement is implied by the first part.

3. A recent Associated Press article quoted a report saying that male high school teachers were paid more than female high school teachers. Assuming this is true, what information would you require before judging this to be evidence of wage discrimination?

4. Assume there is a predominantly black, central-city school district surrounded by white, suburban districts that recruit teachers from the same pool. Black teachers are equally willing to teach in both places, but white teachers are reluctant to take jobs in the central city (assume their prejudice extends only

to students, not to black teachers). Assume further that there are not enough black teachers to fully staff the central-city schools. If the law requires teachers in the same district to be paid equally, but allows salaries across districts to vary, will black teachers earn more, the same, or less than white teachers? Why?

5. Suppose that the United States were to adopt, on a permanent basis, a wage subsidy to be paid to employers who hire black, disadvantaged workers (those with relatively little education and few marketable skills). Analyze the potential effectiveness of this subsidy in overcoming (a) labor market discrimination against blacks, and (b) premarket differences between blacks and whites in the long run.

6. You are involved in an investigation of charges that a large university in a small town is discriminating against female employees. You find that the salaries for professors in the nearly all-female School of Social Work are 20 percent below average salaries paid to those of comparable rank elsewhere in the university. Is this university exhibiting behavior associated with *employer* discrimination? Explain.

7. Suppose a city pays its building inspectors (all male) $16 an hour and its public health nurses (all female) $10 an hour. Suppose that the city council passes a comparable-

worth law that in effect requires the wages of public health nurses to be equal to the wages of building inspectors. Evaluate the assertion that this comparable-worth policy would primarily benefit high-quality nurses and low-quality building inspectors.

8. In the 1920s, South Africa passed laws that effectively prohibited black Africans from working in jobs that required high degrees of skill; skilled jobs were reserved for whites. Analyze the consequences of this law for black and white South African workers.

9. Assume that women live longer than men, on the average. Suppose an employer hires men and women, pays them the same wage for the same job, and contributes an equal amount per person toward a pension. However, the promised monthly pension after retirement is smaller for women than for men because the pension funds for them have to last longer. According to a decision by the Supreme Court, the above employer would be guilty of discrimination because of the unequal monthly pension benefits after retirement.

   a. Comment on the Court's implicit definition of discrimination. Is it consistent with the definition normally used by economists? Why or why not?

   b. Analyze the economic effects of this decision on men and women.

PROBLEMS

1. Calculate the Index of Dissimilarity for males and females given the information below.

Occupation	Males	Females
A	40	20
B	40	25
C	20	25
Total	100	70

2. Suppose that $MRP_L = 20 - 0.5L$ for left-handed workers, where L = the number of left-handed workers and MRP_L is measured in dollars per hour. The going wage for left-handed workers is $10 per hour, but employer A discriminates against these workers and has a discrimination coefficient, D, of $2 per hour. Graph the MRP_L curve and show how many left-handed workers

employer A hires. How much profit has employer A lost by discriminating?

3. Suppose that (similar to Figure 12.3 in the text) the market demand for female workers depends on the relative wage of females to males, W_F/W_M, in the following manner. $W_F/W_M = 1.1 - 0.0001N_F$ if the number of female workers is less than 1,000, where N_F is the number of female workers hired in the market; $W_F/W_M = 1$, if the number of female workers is between 1,001 and 5,000; $W_F/W_M = 1.5 - 0.0001N_F$ if the number of female workers is above 5,000. Graph this demand curve and calculate the relative wage of female workers when the number hired is 200, 2,000, and 7,000. When does discrimination harm female workers in this market?

4. (Appendix). In the market for delivery truck drivers, $L_S = -45 + 5W$ and $L_D = 180 - 10W$, where $L =$ number of workers and $W =$ wage in dollars per hour. In the market for librarians, $L_S = -15 + 5W$ and $L_D = 190 - 10W$. Find the equilibrium wage and employment level in each occupation, and explain what will happen if a comparable worth law mandates that the librarians' wage be increased to equal the delivery truck drivers' wage. Use a graph.

SELECTED READINGS

Aigner, Dennis J., and Glen G. Cain. "Statistical Theories of Discrimination in Labor Markets." *Industrial and Labor Relations Review* 30 (January 1977): 175–187.

Altonji, Joseph G., and Rebecca M. Blank. "Race and Gender in the Labor Market." In *Handbook of Labor Economics,* ed. Orley Ashenfelter and David Card. New York: Elsevier, 1999.

Becker, Gary. *The Economics of Discrimination.* 2d ed. Chicago: University of Chicago Press, 1971.

Blau, Francine D., and Lawrence M. Kahn. "Gender Differences in Pay." *Journal of Economic Perspectives* 14, no. 4 (Fall 2000): 75–99.

Blau, Francine D., Marianne A. Ferber, and Anne E. Winkler. *The Economics of Women, Men, and Work.* 4th ed. Upper Saddle River, N.J.: Prentice-Hall, 2001.

Cain, Glen G. "The Challenge of Segmented Labor Market Theories to Orthodox Theory: A Survey." *Journal of Economic Literature* 14 (December 1976): 1215–1257.

Cornwall, Richard R., and Phanindra V. Wunnava, eds. *New Approaches to Economic and Social Analyses of Discrimination.* New York: Praeger, 1991.

Donohue, John H. III, and James Heckman. "Continuous versus Episodic Change: The Impact of Civil Rights Policy on the Economic Status of Blacks." *Journal of Economic Literature* 24 (December 1991): 1603–1643.

Goldin, Claudia. *Understanding the Gender Gap: An Economic History of American Women* (New York: Oxford University Press, 1990).

Holzer, Harry, and David Neumark. "Assessing Affirmative Action." *Journal of Economic Literature* 38, no. 3 (September 2000): 483–568.

Killingsworth, Mark R. *The Economics of Comparable Worth.* Kalamazoo, Mich.: W. E. Upjohn Institute for Employment Research, 1990.

Smith, James P., and Finis R. Welch. "Black Economic Progress after Myrdal." *Journal of Economic Literature* 27 (June 1989): 519–564.

12A

Estimating "Comparable-Worth" Earnings Gaps: An Application of Regression Analysis

Although many economists have difficulty with the notion that the worth of a job can be established independently of market factors, formal job evaluation methods have existed for a long time. The state of Minnesota is one of the few states that began to implement comparable-worth pay adjustments for their employees based on such an evaluation method. How might we use data from job evaluations to estimate whether discriminatory wage differentials exist?[1]

Minnesota, in conjunction with Hay Associates, a prominent national compensation consulting company, began an evaluation of state government jobs in 1979. Initially evaluated were 188 positions in which at least ten workers were employed and which could be classified as either *male* (at least 70 percent male incumbents) or *female* (at least 70 percent female incumbents) positions. Each position was evaluated by trained job evaluators and awarded a specified number of *Hay Points* for each of four job characteristics or factors: required know-how, problem solving, accountability, and working conditions. The scores for each factor were then added to obtain a total Hay Point, or job evaluation, score for each job. These scores varied across the 188 job titles from below 100 to over 800 points.

Given these job evaluation scores, the next step is to ask what the relationship is between the salary (S_i) each male job pays and its total Hay Point (HP_i) score. Each dot in Figure 12A.1 represents a male job, and this figure plots the monthly salary for each job against its total Hay Point score. On average, it is clear that jobs with higher scores receive higher pay.

---

[1]For a more complete discussion of the Minnesota job evaluation and comparable-worth study, see *Pay Equity and Public Employment* (St. Paul, Minn.: Council on the Economic Status of Women, March 1982).

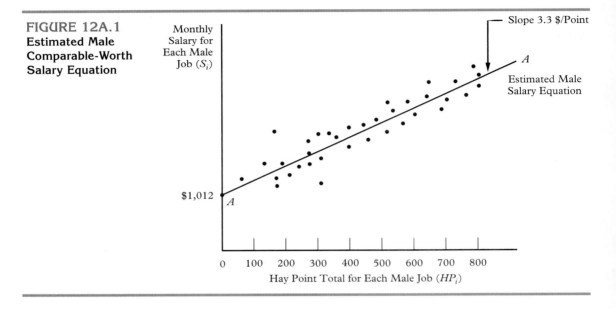

FIGURE 12A.1
Estimated Male Comparable-Worth Salary Equation

Although these points obviously do not all lie on a single straight line, it is natural to ask what straight line fits the data best. An infinite number of lines can be drawn through these points, and some precise criterion must be used to decide which line fits best. As discussed in Appendix 1A, the procedure typically used by statisticians and economists is to choose that line for which the sum (across data points) of the squared vertical distances between the line and the individual data points is minimized. The line estimated from the data using this method—the *method of least squares*—has a number of desirable statistical properties.[2]

Application of this method to data for the *male* occupations contained in the Minnesota data yielded the estimated line:[3]

$$S_i = 1012 + 3.3 \, HP_i \qquad (12A.1)$$

So, for example, if male job i were rated at 200 Hay Points, we would predict that the monthly salary associated with job i would be $1,012 + (3.3)(200)$, or $1,672. This estimated male salary equation is drawn in Figure 12A.1 as line AA.

Now, if the value of a job could be determined solely by reference to its job evaluation score, one would expect that, in the absence of wage discrimi-

---

[2]See Appendix 1A.
[3]These estimates are obtained in Ronald Ehrenberg and Robert Smith, "Comparable Worth in the Public Sector," in *Public Sector Payrolls,* ed. David Wise (Chicago: University of Chicago Press, 1987).

FIGURE 12A.2

Using the Estimated Male Comparable-Worth Salary Equation to Estimate the Extent of Underpayment in Female Jobs

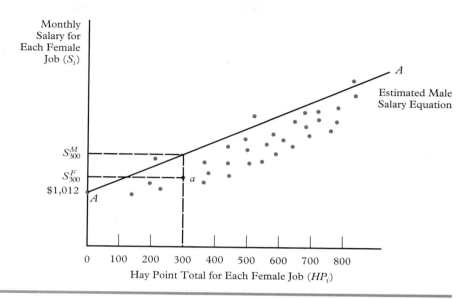

nation against women, male and female jobs rated equal in terms of total Hay Point scores would pay equal salaries (at least on average). Put another way, the same salary equation used to predict salaries of male jobs could be used to provide predictions of salaries for female jobs, and any inaccuracies in the prediction would be completely random. Hence, a test of whether female jobs are discriminated against is to see if the salaries they pay are systematically less than the salaries one would predict they would pay, given their Hay Point scores and the salary equation for male jobs.

Figure 12A.2 illustrates how this is done. Here each dot represents a salary/Hay Point combination for a female job. Superimposed on this scatter of points is the estimated male job salary equation, AA, from Figure 12A.1. The fact that the vast majority of the data points in Figure 12A.2 lie below the male salary line suggests that female jobs tend to be underpaid relative to male jobs with the same number of Hay Points. For example, the female job that is rated at 300 Hay Points (point a) is paid a salary of S_{300}^F. However, according to the estimated male salary line, if that job were a male job it would be paid S_{300}^M. The difference in percentage terms between S_{300}^M and S_{300}^F is an estimate of the comparable-worth earnings gap—the extent of underpayment—for the female job. Indeed, calculations suggest that the average (across all the female occupations) comparable-worth earnings gap in the Minnesota data was over 16 percent.[4]

This brief presentation has glossed over a number of complications that must be addressed before such estimates can be considered estimates of wage discrimination against female jobs.[5] These include issues relating to the reliability and/or potential sex bias in the evaluation methods, whether salaries and Hay Point scores may be related in a nonlinear fashion, whether the *composition* of any given total Hay Point score (across the four sets of job characteristics) affects salaries, and whether variables other than the job evaluation scores can legitimately affect salaries. Nonetheless, it should give the reader a sense of how "comparable-worth wage gap" estimates are computed.

---

[4]See Ehrenberg and Smith, "Comparable Worth in the Public Sector." Analogous estimates for four other states are presented there and in Elaine Sorensen, "Implementing Comparable Worth: A Survey of Recent Job Evaluation Studies," *American Economic Review* 76 (May 1986): 364–367.

[5]For a more complete discussion of these issues and empirical studies relating to comparable worth, see Ehrenberg and Smith, "Comparable Worth in the Public Sector"; M. Anne Hill and Mark R. Killingsworth, eds., *Comparable Worth: Analyses and Evidence* (Ithaca, N.Y.: ILR Press, 1989); Robert T. Michael, Heidi L. Hartmann, Brigid O'Farrell, eds., *Pay Equity: Empirical Inquiries* (Washington, D.C.: National Academy Press, 1989); and Killingsworth, *The Economics of Comparable Worth.*

13

UNIONS AND THE LABOR MARKET

Our analysis of the workings of labor markets has, for the most part, omitted any mention of the role of labor unions and collective bargaining. Because many people have strong and conflicting opinions about the role of unions in our society, it is often difficult to remain objective when discussing them. Some people view labor unions as forms of monopolies that, while benefiting their own members, impose substantial costs on other members of society. In contrast, others view unions as *the* major means by which working persons have improved their economic status and as important forces behind much social legislation.

The purpose of this chapter is to analyze the goals, major activities, and overall effects of unions in the context of economic theory. We begin with some general descriptive material on unions internationally, with a more comprehensive description of unions in the United States, and then move to a fundamental theoretical question: What are the economic forces on the demand side of the market that constrain unions in their desire to improve the welfare of their members? With these constraints in mind, we devote the last half of the chapter to analyzing the primary activities of the collective bargaining process and to discussing empirical evidence on how unions affect wages, employment, labor productivity, and profits.

UNION STRUCTURE AND MEMBERSHIP

Labor unions are organizations of workers whose primary objectives are to improve the pecuniary and nonpecuniary conditions of employment among their members. Unions can be classified into two types: an *industrial* union represents most or all of the workers in an industry or firm regardless of their occupations, and a *craft* union represents workers in a single occupational group. Examples of industrial unions are the unions representing automobile workers, bituminous-coal miners, and rubber workers; craft unions include those representing the various building trades, printers, and dockworkers.

Unions bargain with employers over various aspects of the employment contract, including pay and employee benefits; conditions of work; policies regarding hiring, overtime, job assignment, promotion, and layoff; and the means by which grievances between workers and management are to be resolved. Bargaining can occur at different levels.

At one end of the spectrum, bargaining can be highly *centralized,* with representatives of entire industries sitting at the bargaining table to decide on contracts that bind multiple employers. At the *decentralized* end of the spectrum, bargaining can take place between a union and a single company—or even between the workers and management at a single plant within a company. In the middle are multiemployer agreements reached at the local level between a union and several employers; an example of such agreements would be the ones typically signed between construction craft unions (plumbers, say) and the construction contractors that operate in a given metropolitan area.

As large collective organizations, unions also represent a *political* force in democratic countries. Often, unions will use the political process in the attempt to gain benefits they could not as easily win through collective bargaining. In some countries (Great Britain, for example), unions have their own political party. In others, such as the United States, unions are not affiliated with any single political party; rather, they act as lobbyists for various bills and policies at the federal, state, and local levels of government.

International Comparisons of Unionism

Table 13.1 displays two measures of unionization in several countries. One measure is the percentage of workers who are members of unions, and the other is the percentage of workers in each country whose conditions of employment are covered by a collective bargaining agreement. Two characteristics of this table stand out. First, the United States and Japan are notable in the relatively small percentages of their workers who are covered by collectively bargained agreements. Collective bargaining in these countries and Canada takes place at the level of firms and plants, and provisions of the resulting agreements rarely extend beyond the membership of the unions that signed them. Second, in Australia and most European countries collective bargaining coverage is extended to a very high fraction of workers who are not members of unions. In Austria, for example, collective bargaining is highly centralized, in that agreements are national in their scope, and

TABLE 13.1 **Union Membership and Bargaining Coverage, Selected Countries, 1994**

Country	Union Membership as a Percentage of Workers	Percentage of Workers Covered by a Collective Bargaining Agreement
Austria	42	98
France	9	95
Germany	29	92
Italy	39	82
Netherlands	26	81
Sweden	91	89
Switzerland	27	50
Australia	35	80
United Kingdom	34	47
Canada	38	36
Japan	24	21
United States	16	18

Source: Organisation for Economic Co-operation and Development, *Employment Outlook, July 1997* (Paris: OECD, 1997), p. 71.

in most of continental Europe the parties at the bargaining table represent entire sectors of the economy. The correlation between the coverage and the centralization of bargaining is far from perfect, however; Australia has less-centralized bargaining than Switzerland, for example, yet a higher fraction of its workers are covered by collective bargaining agreements.[1] Clearly, the historical and legal contexts within which unions operate in each country are critical to an understanding of the differing levels of membership.

These different legal contexts across countries also mean that union membership levels and union power are not easily correlated. In Sweden, for example, where almost everyone is in a union, some unions are much weaker in bargaining power than others. In Germany, to take another example, both union and nonunion workers are represented on workplace councils, which decide at the plant level on various personnel issues that in other countries are addressed by local collective bargaining agreements. Finally, government tribunals have played an important role in the Australian system of wage determination, with collective bargaining used to negotiate supplements to the governmental wage awards.[2]

---

[1]Organisation for Economic Co-operation and Development, *Employment Outlook, July 1997* (Paris: OECD, 1997), 71.

[2]Harry Katz, "The Decentralization of Collective Bargaining: A Literature Review and Comparative Analysis," *Industrial and Labor Relations Review* 47, no. 1 (October 1993): 3–22; and Richard B. Freeman, "American Exceptionalism in the Labor Market: Union–Nonunion Differentials in the United States and Other Countries," in *Labor Economics and Industrial Relations: Market and Institutions,* ed. Clark Kerr and Paul D. Staudohar (Cambridge, Mass.: Harvard University Press, 1994), 272–299.

Much of the empirical work on unions has been done on the United States, where bargaining is decentralized and, as we have seen, the majority of workers are nonunion. While the study of unions in one country does not easily generalize to others, given the different legal and historical environments, this empirical work may be of growing interest elsewhere owing to what may be a trend toward a greater decentralization of bargaining in most developed economies during the last decade.[3] No matter how well (or poorly) studies of U.S. unions generalize, however, their results must still be understood within the context of American institutions. We therefore turn to a brief history of the legal structure within which American unions have operated.

The Legal Structure of Unions in the United States

Public attitudes and federal legislation have not always been favorably disposed toward labor unions and the collective bargaining process in the United States. For example, during the early part of the twentieth century, employers were often able to claim that unions acted like monopolies in the labor market and hence were illegal under existing antitrust laws. Such employers were often able to get court orders or injunctions that prohibited union activity and aided them in stopping union organization drives. Given this environment, it is not surprising that the fraction of the labor force who were union members stood at less than 7 percent in 1930. Since that date, however, legislation has changed the environment in which American unions operate.

National Labor Relations Act   The National Labor Relations Act (NLRA) of 1935 required employers to bargain with unions that represented the majority of their employees and made it illegal for employers to interfere with their employees' right to organize collectively. The National Labor Relations Board (NLRB) was established by the NLRA and given power both to conduct *certification elections* to see which union, if any, employees wanted to represent them, and to investigate claims that employers were either violating election rules or refusing to bargain with elected unions.[4] In the event violations were found, the NLRB was given further power to order violators to "cease and desist."

Taft-Hartley Act   After World War II the pendulum shifted decidedly in an antiunion direction. The Labor-Management Relations Act of 1947 (better known as the Taft-Hartley Act) restricted some aspects of union activity and permitted workers

---

[3]Katz, "The Decentralization of Collective Bargaining." Michael Wallerstein, Miriam Golden, and Peter Lange, "Unions, Employers' Associations, and Wage-Setting Institutions in Northern and Central Europe, 1950–1992," *Industrial and Labor Relations Review* 50, no. 3 (April 1997): 379–401, presents evidence for Austria, Germany, Belgium, the Netherlands, and Scandinavia suggesting that a general process of decentralization has not occurred in those countries.

[4]Actually, the NLRA was much less pro-labor than our brief discussion indicates; the NLRA also gave the NLRB power to investigate employers' claims that their employees, or unions, were violating provisions of the act.

to vote in elections that could decertify a union from representing them in collective bargaining. Perhaps its most famous provision is Section 14B, which permits individual states to pass *right-to-work laws*. These laws prohibit the requirement that a person become a union member as a condition of employment. Twenty-two states, located primarily in the South, Southwest, and Plains areas, have passed such laws.

Landrum-Griffin Act   In 1959, Congress passed the Labor-Management Reporting and Disclosure Act (the Landrum-Griffin Act). This law, which was designed to protect the rights of union members in relation to their leaders, contained provisions that increased union democracy. As argued below, such provisions may well have had the side effect of increasing the level of strike activity in the economy.

Government Unions   The laws that have been discussed to this point relate only to the private sector, where unionism in the United States first flourished. Indeed, prior to the 1960s, public sector workers were prohibited from organizing. In 1962, however, President Kennedy signed Executive Order 10988, which gave federal workers the right to organize and bargain over working conditions, but not wages.[5] The influence of federal unions on wages, then, operates primarily through the political pressure they can exert on the president to recommend, or on Congress to approve, pay increases.

Beginning with Wisconsin in 1959, a number of states have extended to employees of state and local governments (including teachers) the rights to organize and collectively bargain. Generally speaking, public sector unions are barred from going on strike, so that laws permitting their right to bargain were accompanied by provisions for some form of binding arbitration (through which neutral parties would ultimately decide on disputes that could not be voluntarily resolved).[6]

Union Membership   Union membership as a fraction of all American workers peaked in the years following World War II at about one-third. Since then, the percentage of all workers who are union members has dropped continuously, except among government workers. Figure 13.1 graphs the trends in union membership starting in 1973, when the membership percentages in the private and public sectors (and hence, overall) were about 24 percent. Since then, membership among private sector workers has fallen to 9 percent, membership among government workers has risen to over 37 percent, and the overall rate of membership now stands at 13.5 percent.

Unionized workers in the United States are members of "local" unions, organized at the level of the plant, the employer, or (especially for construction unions)

---

[5]There were some major exceptions—namely, postal workers and employees of federal government authorities, such as the Tennessee Valley Authority (TVA). In each of these cases the prices of the products or services produced (mail delivery, hydroelectric power) can be raised to cover the cost of the contract settlement. In other federal agencies, salaries are paid out of general revenues.

[6]See Richard B. Freeman, "Unionism Comes to the Public Sector," *Journal of Economic Literature* 24 (March 1986): 41–86, for a more complete discussion of the evolution of legislation governing bargaining in the public sector.

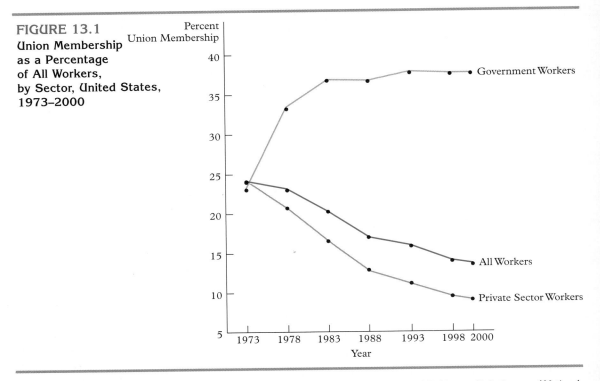

FIGURE 13.1

Union Membership as a Percentage of All Workers, by Sector, United States, 1973–2000

Source: Barry T. Hirsch and David A. Macpherson, *Union Membership and Earnings Data Book 2001* (Washington, D.C.: Bureau of National Affairs, 2001), Table 1.

the metropolitan area. We have noted that in the United States bargaining is relatively decentralized, so it is local unions that bear the brunt of negotiations. These locals, however, are usually members of larger "national" or "international" (usually meaning they include Canadian workers) unions, which provide help and advice to the locals with their organization drives and, later, their negotiations. If bargaining is being done at the industry level, or with one firm at the national level, it is representatives of the national or international union who sit at the bargaining table.

In turn, most of the nationals and internationals (and therefore some three-quarters of all union members) are affiliated with the AFL-CIO, which stands for the American Federation of Labor and Congress of Industrial Organizations. The AFL-CIO is not a union, but rather an association of unions organized both nationally and at the state level. Its main functions are to provide a unified political voice for its diverse member unions, to recommend and coordinate membership initiatives among its affiliates, and to provide research and information to its members. It does not directly negotiate with employers.

Table 13.2 provides another way of looking at union membership in the United States. From this table we can see that men are more likely to be union-

TABLE 13.2 Percentage of U.S. Wage and Salary Workers Who Are Union Members, by Selected Characteristics, 2000	
Men	15.2
Women	11.5
Black	17.1
Hispanic	11.4
White	13.0
By Age	
16–24	5.0
25–34	11.9
35–44	14.9
45–54	18.8
55–64	17.8
65 and over	8.4
By Industry	
Mining	10.9
Construction	18.3
Manufacturing	14.8
Transportation, Public Utilities	24.0
Wholesale, Retail Trade	4.7
Finance, Insurance	1.6
Services	5.6

Source: U.S. Bureau of Labor Statistics, *Employment and Earnings* 48, no. 1 (January 2001), Tables 40, 42.

ized than women, and that minorities and middle-aged workers have higher rates of unionization. The highest rates of unionization are found in the transportation and public utility, construction, and manufacturing industries.

CONSTRAINTS ON THE ACHIEVEMENT OF UNION OBJECTIVES

The founder of the American Federation of Labor, Samuel Gompers, was once asked what unions wanted. His answer was quite simple: "More." Hardly anyone who has studied union behavior believes unions' objectives are quite that simple, but it is self-evident that unions want to advance the welfare of their members in one way or another. Some of their objectives are *procedural*; they want to give workers some voice in the way employers manage the workplace, especially in the handling of various personnel issues such as job assignment, the allocation of overtime, the handling of worker discipline and grievances, and the establishment of joint labor–management safety committees and work teams. Procedural objectives are not always costly to the employer, who (especially with modern management techniques) may want a mechanism through which employee participation in management decisions can be achieved.[7] Other procedural objectives, however, put constraints on managerial prerogatives that, while difficult to quantify, are often seen by employers as costly.

Wanting "more" is usually associated with the union goal of increasing the *compensation* levels of its members. The most visible element of compensation is the wage rate, but bargaining in the United States also occurs over such employee benefits as pensions, health insurance, and vacations. (In many other developed countries, these benefits are mandated by the government and therefore are not subject to collective bargaining.) The attempts to achieve "more," of course, take place in the context of *constraints*. Employers are on the other side of the bargaining table, and they must make agreements that permit them to operate successfully both with their workers *and* within their product markets. Increased compensation for their workers will give them incentives to *substitute* capital for labor, and to the extent that their costs of production rise, there also will be pressures to reduce the *scale* of operations. In short, unions must ultimately reckon with the downward-sloping demand curve for labor. As a result, both the position and the elasticity of this curve become fundamental market constraints on the ability of unions to accomplish their objectives.

To see this, ignore employee benefits and working conditions for the moment and consider Figure 13.2, which shows two demand curves, D_e^0 and D_i^0, that intersect at an initial wage W_0 and employment level E_0. Suppose a union seeks to raise the wage rate of its members to W_1. To do so would cause employment to fall to E_e^1 if the union faced the relatively elastic demand curve D_e^0, or to E_i^1 if it faced the relatively inelastic demand curve D_i^0. Other things equal, the more elastic the demand curve for labor is, the greater will be the reduction in employment associated with any given increase in wages.

Suppose now that the demand curve D_i^0 shifts out to D_i^1 while the negotiations are under way, owing perhaps to growing demand for the final product. If the union succeeds in raising its members' wages to W_1, there will be no absolute decrease in employment in this case. Rather, the union will have only slowed the rate of growth of employment to E_i^2 instead of E_i^3. More generally, other things equal, the more rapidly the labor demand curve is shifting out (in), the smaller (larger) will be the reduction *in employment* or the reduction *in the rate of growth of employment* associated with any given increase in wages. Hence, unions' ability to raise their members' wages will be strongest in rapidly growing industries with inelastic labor demand curves. Conversely, unions will be weakest in industries

---

[7]See William N. Cooke, "Employee Participation Programs, Group-Based Incentives, and Company Performance: A Union–Nonunion Comparison," *Industrial and Labor Relations Review* 47, no. 4 (July 1994): 594–609.

FIGURE 13.2
Effects of Demand Growth and the Wage Elasticity of Demand on the Market Constraints Faced by Unions

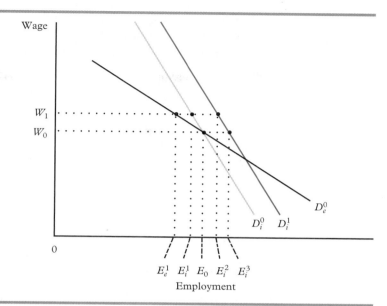

in which the wage elasticity of demand is highly elastic and in which the demand curve for labor is shifting in.

We now turn to two alternative models of how unions and employers behave in their agreements about wages and benefits, given the market constraints they face. Each of the models analyzes the interaction of—and trade-offs between—wages and employment.

The Monopoly-Union Model

The simplest model of the union–employer relationship has been called one of *monopoly unionism*, whereby the union sets the price of labor and the employer responds by adjusting employment to maximize profits, given the new wage rate with which it is confronted. This model is formally illustrated by Figure 13.3, which shows the labor demand curve, D, facing workers as a simple function of the wage rate (for simplicity, we abstract from other elements in the compensation package).

In Figure 13.3, we assume that the union values both the wages and the employment levels of its members and that it can aggregate its members' preferences so that we can meaningfully speak of a union utility function that depends on these two variables. This utility function is summarized by the family of indifference curves U_0, U_1, U_2, U_3. Each curve represents a locus of employment/wage combinations about which the union is indifferent. The indifference curves are negatively sloped, because to maintain a given utility level the union

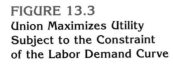

FIGURE 13.3
Union Maximizes Utility Subject to the Constraint of the Labor Demand Curve

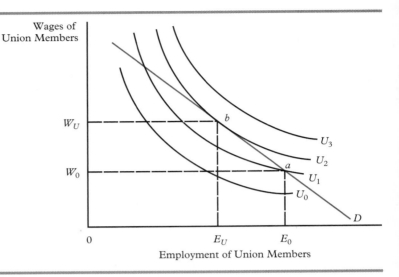

must be compensated for a decline in one variable (employment or wages) by an increase in the other. They exhibit the property of diminishing marginal rates of substitution (they are convex to the origin) because we assume the loss of employment that unions are willing to tolerate in return for a given wage increase grows smaller as employment falls. Finally, higher indifference curves represent higher levels of union utility.

Suppose that, in the absence of a union, market forces would cause the wage to be W_0 and employment to be E_0 (point a in Figure 13.3). How does collective bargaining affect this solution? One possibility is that the union and the employer will agree on a higher wage rate and then, given the wage rate, the employer will determine the number of union members to employ. Given a bargained wage rate, the employer will maximize profits and determine employment from its labor demand curve. Since the union presumably knows this, its goal is to choose the wage that maximizes its utility subject to the constraint that the resultant wage/employment combination will lie on the labor demand curve.

In terms of Figure 13.3, the union will seek to move to point b, where indifference curve U_2 is just tangent to the labor demand curve. At this point wages would be W_U and employment E_U. Given the constraint posed by the labor demand curve, point b represents the highest level of utility the union can attain.

The Efficient-Contracts Model

An interesting feature of the simple monopoly-union model is that it is not "efficient." Instead of having unions set the wage and then having employers determine employment, both parties could be better off if they agreed to jointly determine wages and employment. Put succinctly in terms of Figure 13.3, there is a whole set of wage/employment combinations that at least one of the parties would prefer and that would leave the other no worse off; these combinations have been called *efficient contracts*. (While the term "efficient" recalls our discussion of *Pareto efficiency* in chapter 1, it is being used more narrowly here. Pareto efficiency refers to *social* welfare, and a transaction is said to be Pareto-improving if *society* is made better off—that is, some gain and no one else loses. "Efficiency" in the current context denotes only that the welfare of the two parties can be improved; it does not imply that society, as a whole, gains. Indeed, we will see in the next subsection that, in general, these efficient contracts lead to a socially wasteful use of labor.)

The Formal Model   To begin our analysis, we must recall from chapter 3 that the labor demand curve is defined by the employer's choosing an employment level that maximizes profits at each wage rate. In Figure 13.3, for example, if we start at point a on the demand curve with the wage at W_0 and employment at E_0, profits would fall if the employer were to either expand or contract employment. Thus, if employment were to be changed from E_0, a lower wage rate would have to be paid to keep profits from falling. The larger the deviation of employment from E_0, the lower wages would have to be to keep profits constant.

We can formalize this by reintroducing the concept of *isoprofit curves*, first discussed in chapter 8. Here an isoprofit curve is a locus of wage/employment combinations along which an employer's profits are unchanged. Figure 13.4 shows three isoprofit curves for the employer whose labor demand curve is D. As discussed above, each curve reaches a maximum at its intersection with the demand curve; as we move along a given isoprofit curve in either direction away from the demand curve, wages must fall to keep profits constant. A higher isoprofit curve represents a lower level of employer profits because the wage associated with each level of employment is greater along the higher curve. So, for example, the employer would prefer any point on I_0, which includes the original wage/employment combination (point a), to any point on I_2, which includes the monopoly-union wage/employment solution (point b).

Figure 13.5 superimposes the family of employer isoprofit curves from Figure 13.4 onto the family of union indifference curves from Figure 13.3 and illustrates why the monopoly-union solution, point b, is not an *efficient contract*. Suppose, rather than locating at point b, the parties negotiated a contract that called for them to locate at point d, where the wage rate (W_d) would be lower but employment of union members (E_d) higher. At point d the union would be better off, since it would now be on a higher indifference curve, U_3, while the firm would be no worse off, since it still would be on isoprofit curve I_2.

Similarly, suppose that rather than negotiating a contract to wind up at b, the parties agreed to a contract that called for them to locate at point e, with a wage rate of W_e and an employment level of E_e. Compared to the monopoly-union solution (point b) the union is equally well off, since it remains on indifference curve U_2, but now the firm is better off because it has been able to reach isoprofit curve I_1. Because I_1 lies below I_2, it represents a higher level of profits.

In fact, there is a whole set of contracts that both parties will find at least as good as point *b*; these are represented by the shaded area in Figure 13.5. Among this set, the ones that are efficient contracts—contracts in which no party can be made better off without hurting the other—are the ones in which employer isoprofit curves are just tangent to union indifference curves, such as at points *d* and *e*. Indeed, there is a whole locus of such points, and they are represented in the figure by the curve *ed*. Each point on *ed* represents a tangency of a union indifference curve and an employer isoprofit curve; these are points at which the employer and the union are equally willing to substitute wages for employment at the margin (so that no more mutually beneficial trades of wages for employment are possible).

All of the points on *ed*, which is often called the *contract curve* (or locus of efficient contracts), will leave both parties at least as well off as at point *b*, and at least one party better off. However, the parties are not indifferent to where along *ed* the settlement is reached. Obviously the union would prefer to be close to *d* and the employer close to *e*. Where on the contract curve a settlement actually occurs in this model depends upon the bargaining power of the parties.[8]

The Contract Curve   Two points need to be made about the contract curve. First, as shown in Figure 13.5, it lies off and to the right of the firm's labor demand curve. This implies that the firm is using more labor at any given wage rate than it would if it had unilateral control over employment, and it implies that the collective bargaining agreement will contain clauses that create (more precisely, ratify the use of) excess labor in the plant. For example, there may be clauses pertaining to minimum crew sizes or to rigid rules governing which workers must do specific tasks; some agreements may even have no-layoff clauses for certain workers. While the employer may be better off with these clauses, because it can induce the union to agree to a lower wage, its failure to minimize costs is socially wasteful (society could increase its aggregate output if labor were reallocated and used more productively).

Second, it is not necessary that the slope of the contract curve be up and to the right, as shown in Figure 13.5. Depending on the shapes of the union's indifference curves and the firm's isoprofit curves, the contract curve could slope up and to the left or even be vertical.

An interesting special case involving a vertical contract curve is created when the curve is *vertical at the original (preunion) level of employment.* In this case, the firm agrees to maintain employment at the level that *maximizes profits,* given the *market* wage rate. The union and firm in effect bargain over how these profits are split; every dollar gained by the union is a dollar lost by the employer and there are no changes in output or employment. If the union succeeds in raising wages above their original (market) level, however, it is reasonable to ask how the firm could afford to pay higher wages, maintain its original employment

---

[8]For an attempt to model how bargaining power affects the nature of contract settlements, see Jan Svejnar, "Bargaining Power, Fear of Disagreement, and Wage Settlements: Theory and Empirical Evidence from U.S. Industry," *Econometrica* 54 (September 1986): 1055–1078.

FIGURE 13.4
Employer Isoprofit Curves

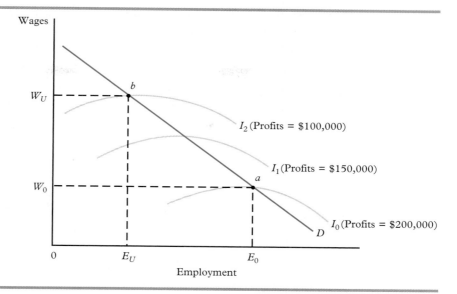

FIGURE 13.5
The Contract Curve—The Locus of Efficient Contracts

level, and still operate successfully in the product market. The answer must be that it is in a *noncompetitive* product market and is therefore receiving profits in excess of those required for it to remain in business; a reduction in these excess profits might make management unhappy, but it does not cause the employer

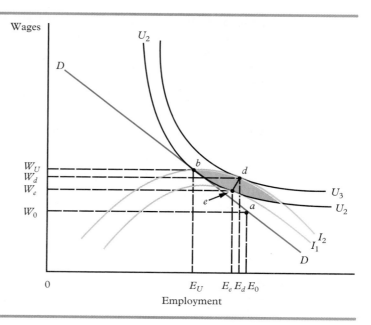

to change its behavior.[9] Further implications of a vertical contract curve are discussed in the final section of this chapter, in which the social gains or losses of unionization are considered.

Are Contracts Really "Efficient?"   How realistic is the efficient-contracts model as a description of the wage-determination process in unionized workplaces in the United States? The most obvious way to answer this question would be to look at the language of collective bargaining agreements to see if there is evidence of joint agreement on employment levels. Many contracts covering public school teachers specify maximum class sizes or minimum teacher/student ratios, and a few private sector contracts include no-layoff provisions for certain core workers, but the world is too uncertain for an employer to explicitly guarantee a certain *level* of employment.

Contracts, however, often contain language that perpetuates the use of excess labor. Many require that duties cannot be performed "out of job title," so that a custodian, for example, could not paint a scuffed wall (a painter would be required), or an off-stage actress could not perform any of the duties of a lighting technician. These rigidities in job assignment clearly are designed to protect jobs even though the level of employment is not explicitly determined in the contract.

There are also *indirect* tests of the efficient-contracts model. This model and the monopoly-union model yield different implications about how wages and employment will vary in response to changes in variables that affect either the demand for labor or union preferences. A number of studies have analyzed these implications, and it is fair to say that at the moment there is evidence that both supports and goes against the efficient-contracts model.[10]

THE ACTIVITIES AND TOOLS OF COLLECTIVE BARGAINING

Having analyzed the general constraints facing unions as they seek to accomplish their goals, we turn now to an economic analysis of several activities that affect their power. We begin with a simple model of union *membership* and use it to help understand the decline in membership faced by U.S. unions in recent decades. Next, we briefly discuss the ways in which unions use the *political* process in an attempt to alter the market constraints they face. Finally, we analyze the ultimate threats—of calling a *strike* or having an unresolved dispute decided by third-party *arbitration*—that unions can carefully use in the collective bargaining process.

---

[9]Brian E. Becker, "Union Rents as a Source of Takeover Gains among Target Shareholders," *Industrial and Labor Relations Review* 49, no. 1 (October 1995): 3–19. An empirical test for a vertical contract curve can be found in John M. Abowd, "The Effect of Wage Bargains on the Stock Market Value of the Firm," *American Economic Review* 79, no. 4 (September 1989): 774–800.

[10]Walter J. Wessels, "Do Unions Contract for Added Employment?" *Industrial and Labor Relations Review* 45 (October 1991): 181–193, cites previous literature. John Pencavel, *Labor Markets under Trade Unionism* (Cambridge, Mass.: Basil Blackwell, 1991), ch. 4, presents an analysis of the results on this topic, most especially of the evidence for a vertical contract curve.

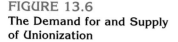

FIGURE 13.6
The Demand for and Supply of Unionization

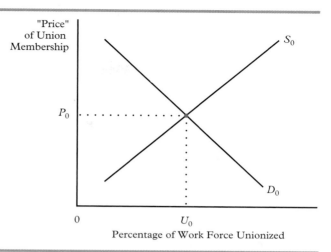

Union Membership: An Analysis of Demand and Supply

A simple model of the demand for and supply of union activity can be used to explain the forces that influence union membership.[11] On the demand side, employees' desire to be union members will be a function of the "price" of union membership; this price includes initiation fees, monthly dues, the value of the time an individual is expected to spend on union activities, etc. Other things equal, the higher the price, the lower the fraction of employees that will want to be union members, as represented by the demand curve D_0 in Figure 13.6.

It is costly to represent workers in collective bargaining negotiations and to supervise the administration of union contracts. Therefore, it is reasonable to conclude that, other things equal, the willingness of unions to supply their services is an upward-sloping function of the price of union membership, as represented by the supply curve S_0 in Figure 13.6. The intersection of these demand and supply curves yields an equilibrium percentage of the workforce that is unionized (U_0) and an equilibrium price of union services (P_0).

What are the forces that determine the *positions* of the demand and supply curves? Anything that causes either the demand curve *or* the supply curve to shift to the right will increase the level of unionization in the economy, other things equal.

---

[11]This model is based upon the approach found in Orley Ashenfelter and John Pencavel, "American Trade Union Growth, 1900–1960," *Quarterly Journal of Economics* 83 (August 1969): 434–448, and John Pencavel, "The Demand for Union Services: An Exercise," *Industrial and Labor Relations Review* 24 (January 1971): 180–191.

Conversely, if either of these curves shifts to the left, other things equal, the level of unionization will fall. Identifying the factors that shift these curves would enable us to explain *changes* in the level of unionization in the economy over time.

On the demand side, it is likely that individuals' demand for union membership is positively related to their perceptions of the *net benefits* from being union members. For example, the larger the wage gain they think unions will win for them, the further to the right the demand curve will be. Another factor is *tastes*; if individuals' tastes for union membership increase, perhaps because of changes in social attitudes, the demand curve will also shift to the right.

On the supply side, anything that changes the *costs* of union organizing activities will affect the supply curve. Introduction of labor legislation that makes it easier for unions to win representation elections will shift the supply curve to the right. Changes in the composition of employment that make it more difficult to organize the workforce will shift the curve to the left and reduce the level of unionization.[12]

The decline in unionization rates that has taken place in the United States since the mid-1950s is hypothesized to be at least partially explained by five factors related to the demand for, or supply of, union services: demographic changes in the labor force, a shifting industrial mix, a heavier mix of employment in states in which the environment is not particularly favorable for unions, increased competitive pressures, and increased employer resistance to union organizing efforts.[13]

Demographic Changes   The fraction of the labor force that is female has increased substantially (see chapter 6), and women historically have tended not to join unions. The benefits from union membership are a function of individuals' expected tenure with firms; seniority provisions, job security provisions, and retirement benefits are not worth much to individuals who expect to be employed at a firm for only a short while. *In the past*, women tended to have shorter expected job tenure than men and to have more intermittent labor force participation. Given the *growing* labor force attachment of women, however, demographic changes are an unlikely explanation for the decline in union membership.[14]

---

[12]Rebecca S. Demsetz, "Voting Behavior in Union Representation Elections: The Influence of Skill Homogeneity and Skill Group Size," *Industrial and Labor Relations Review* 47, no. 1 (October 1993): 99–113, finds that plants with more homogeneously skilled workers are more supportive of unions, other things equal.

[13]For a discussion of the factors underlying the rise and fall of unionization rates in the United States, see the essays by Edward P. Lazear, Richard B. Freeman, and Melvin W. Reder in *Journal of Economic Perspectives* 2, no. 2 (Spring 1988): 59–110. For quantitative estimates of the extent to which the factors discussed in this section are responsible for the decline in unionization, see Henry Farber, "The Decline of Unionization in the United States: What Can Be Learned from Recent Experience?" *Journal of Labor Economics* 8, no. 1, p. 2 (January 1990): S75–S105, and Henry Farber and Alan Krueger, "Union Membership in the United States: The Decline Continues," in *Employee Representation: Alternatives and Future Decisions*, ed. Bruce Kaufman and Morris Kleiner (Madison, Wis.: Industrial Relations Research Association, 1993).

[14]Farber and Krueger, "Union Membership in the United States: The Decline Continues," argue that demographic changes have played almost no role in the decline.

Changing Industrial Mix   A second possible factor in the decline of union membership is the shift in the industrial composition of employment, first discussed in chapter 2. The fraction of workers in government, the most heavily unionized sector in the United States, has held more or less constant since the mid-1970s, while there has been a substantial decline in the employment shares of the most heavily unionized industries in the *private* sector (see Table 13.2): manufacturing, mining, construction, transportation, and public utilities. Employment has increased most notably in wholesale and retail trade, in finance, insurance and real estate, and in the service industries—all of which are the least-unionized sectors of the economy.

Why do the latter industries tend not to be unionized? These industries tend to be highly competitive, with high price elasticities of product demand and therefore high wage elasticities of labor demand, which limit unions' abilities to increase wages without suffering substantial employment declines. For this reason, the net benefits individuals perceive from union membership may be lower in these industries, and an increase in their importance in the economy would shift the demand for union services to the left in Figure 13.6, thereby reducing the percentage of the workforce that is unionized.

These industries also tend to be populated by small establishments. The demand for unionization is thought to be lower for employees who work in small firms, because they often feel less alienated from their supervisors. Similarly, since it is more costly to try to organize 1,000 workers spread over 100 firms than it is to organize 1,000 workers at one plant, it is often thought that the supply of union services would shift left as the share of employment going to small firms increased. Both of these factors tend to suggest (in terms of Figure 13.6) that unionization will decline as the share of employment in small establishments increases, providing another reason the shift in industrial distribution of employment may have affected the extent of unionization.

Regional Shifts in Employment   A third factor that may have contributed to the decline in union strength is the movement in population and employment that has occurred since 1955 from the industrial Northeast and Midwest to the South and West. As noted earlier, the South and Southwest are heavily represented among the twenty-two states that have right-to-work laws. Such laws raise the costs of expanding union membership, because individuals who accept employment with a firm cannot be compelled to become union members as a condition of employment. In terms of Figure 13.6, these laws shift the supply curve of union services to the left, thereby reducing the level of unionization. Between 1955 and 2000 the proportion of employees working in right-to-work states increased from 24 to over 38 percent. This shifting geographic distribution of the workforce, coupled with the existence of these laws, undoubtedly tended to depress union membership.

It is not at all obvious, however, that the decline in unionization occasioned by the move to the South and West can be attributed to right-to-work laws per se. The extent of unionization in right-to-work states tended to be lower than that

EXAMPLE 13.1
The Effects of Deregulation on Trucking and Airlines

Before the late 1970s, the heavily unionized trucking and airline industries were regulated by the United States government, which restricted the entry of potential competitors and granted existing carriers a degree of monopoly power. From 1978 to 1980, however, these restrictions were largely removed. The resulting increase in product market competition increased the price elasticity of product demand and, of course, the wage elasticity of labor demand in those industries—thus reducing the power of unions to raise wages.

These changes reduced the desirability of being unionized, and indeed, both industries experienced sharp declines in unionized employment. In the airline industry, for example, the employment of union mechanics had fallen 15–20 percent by 1983. In trucking, the rate of unionization throughout the industry fell from 88 percent before deregulation to 65 percent by 1990.

Data from: David Card, "The Impact of Deregulation on the Employment and Wages of Airline Mechanics," *Industrial and Labor Relations Review* 39, no. 4 (July 1986): 527–538; and Michael H. Belzer, *Sweatshops on Wheels: Winners and Losers in Trucking Deregulation* (New York: Oxford University Press, 2000).

in other states even before the passage of the laws. These laws may only reflect attitudes toward unions that already exist in these communities.[15]

Competitive Pressures   A fourth factor is increased foreign competition in manufacturing and the deregulation of the airline, trucking, and telephone industries (see Example 13.1). In these industries, which tended to be highly unionized, increased product market competition has served to increase the price elasticities of product demand, and hence the wage elasticities of labor demand. To the extent that union members' wages did not fall substantially in the face of increased product market competition, unionized employment within these industries could have been expected to fall. Indeed, the share of unionized employment in these previously heavily unionized industries has fallen substantially in the past two decades as competition from both foreign firms and new, nonunion employers in the deregulated industries has increased.[16]

By making labor demand curves more elastic, increased competitive pressures reduce the benefits to workers of collective action, hence shifting the demand curve for union membership to the left. Moreover, increased product market competition may well call forth *employer* responses that affect workers' demand for unions. For example, if firms find that foreign competition has intensified, they may seek to relocate in areas where workers are less likely to unionize; similarly, they may

---

[15]For a recent study that cites earlier literature on the effects of right-to-work laws, see Steven E. Abraham and Paula B. Voos, "Right-to-Work Laws: New Evidence from the Stock Market," *Southern Economic Journal* 67, no. 2 (October 2000): 345–362.

[16]Evidence that the effects of foreign competition are felt primarily in union members' employment levels, not in their wages, is found in John Abowd and Thomas Lemieux, "The Effects of International Trade on Union Wages and Employment: Evidence from the U.S. and Canada," in *Immigration, Trade, and the Labor Market*, ed. John Abowd and Richard Freeman (Chicago: University of Chicago Press, 1991).

seek to employ workers in demographic groups whose demands for union membership are relatively low. Increased competition may also cause employers to resist union organizing efforts more vigorously, which could well increase the costs of such efforts and shift the supply curve of union services to the left.

Employer Resistance   U.S. employers can, and often do, play an active role in opposing union organizing campaigns, using both legal and illegal means. For example, under the National Labor Relations Act it is legal for employers to present arguments to employees detailing why they think it is in the workers' best interests to vote against a union and for employers to hire consultants to advise them how to best conduct a campaign to prevent a union from winning an election. However, it is illegal for an employer to threaten to withhold planned wage increases if the union wins the election or for a firm to discriminate against employees involved in the organizing effort. If a union believes an employer is involved in illegal activities during a campaign, it can file an unfair labor practices charge with the National Labor Relations Board which, if sustained, can lead the NLRB to issue a formal complaint.

Table 13.3 chronicles, from 1970 to 1999, the number of union representation elections, the percent won by the union, and the number of unfair labor practice complaints filed by the NLRB against employers. While not all unfair practices occur during representation elections, the ratio of such complaints to the number of elections held gives us at least some idea of the intensity of employer resistance. This ratio rose steeply in the 1970s and 1980s, peaked in 1993 (at a ratio over five times greater than it had been two decades earlier), and then fell during the 1990s. This measure of resistance appears more closely associated with the *number* of elections (which fell steadily through the period before bottoming-out in the mid-1990s) than in the *percentage* won by the union.

TABLE 13.3   Union Representation Elections and Unfair Labor Practice Complaints Issued by NLRB, 1970–1999

	Representation Elections		*NLRB Complaints against Employers*	
Year	*Number*	*Percent Won by Union*	*Number*	*Ratio: Complaints to Elections*
1970	8,074	55.2	1,474	0.183
1975	8,577	48.2	2,335	0.272
1980	8,198	45.7	5,164	0.630
1985	4,614	42.4	2,840	0.616
1990	4,210	46.7	3,182	0.756
1993	3,586	47.6	3,576	0.997
1996	3,277	44.8	2,919	0.891
1999	3,585	50.5	2,036	0.568

Source: Annual Report of the National Labor Relations Board, Appendix Tables 3A, 13 (various years).

Why did employers offer increased resistance to unions in the early 1990s? Some argue that employers were more disposed, on ideological grounds, to maintain union-free workplaces. Others suggest, however, that the change in employer behavior was the result of an increase in the costs that employers expected to face if the unions won. During the 1970s and early 1980s, wages of unionized workers grew more rapidly than the wages of nonunion workers just as competition from foreign producers increased sharply. Thus, the perceived economic benefits to nonunion employers of keeping their workplaces nonunion increased. This factor, it is argued, encouraged them to increasingly and aggressively combat union election campaigns, through both legal and illegal means.[17] A recent study, however, suggests the reduction in union organizing activity, as measured by the number of successful elections, has contributed little to the overall decline in unionization in the United States.[18]

Union Actions to Alter the Labor Demand Curve

Many actions that unions take are direct attempts to relax the market constraints they face: either to increase the demand for union labor or to reduce the wage elasticity of demand for their members' services. Many of these attempts have *not* occurred through the collective bargaining process per se. Rather, they have occurred through union support of legislation that at least indirectly achieved union goals and through direct public relations campaigns to increase the demand for products produced by union members.

Shifting Product Demand   To shift the demand for the final product, unions have lobbied for import quotas, which restrict the quantities of foreign-made goods that can be imported into the United States, and for *domestic content* legislation, which requires goods from abroad to have a certain percentage of American-made components. Unions have also lobbied strongly against legislation, such as the North American Free Trade Act (NAFTA), that reduces tariffs on imported goods. Some unions have sought to directly influence people's tastes for the products they produce, urging consumers to "Buy American" or "Look for the union label."

Restricting Substitution: Legislation   Unions have also sought, by means of legislation, to pursue strategies that increase the costs of other inputs that are potential substitutes for union members. For example, labor unions have been among the primary supporters of higher minimum wages.[19] While such support

---

[17]William T. Dickens, "The Effect of Company Campaigns on Certification Elections: Law and Reality Once Again," *Industrial and Labor Relations Review* 36 (July 1983): 560–575; Robert Flanagan, *Labor Relations and the Litigation Explosion* (Washington, D.C.: Brookings Institution, 1987); and Henry Farber, "The Decline in Unionization in the United States."

[18]Henry S. Farber and Bruce Western, "Round Up the Usual Suspects: The Decline of Unions in the Private Sector, 1973–1998," *Journal of Labor Research* 22, no. 3 (Summer 2001): 459–485.

[19]For evidence that union support for minimum wage legislation is often transformed into pro-minimum wage votes by members of Congress, see James Cox and Ronald Oaxaca, "The Determinants of Minimum Wage Levels and Coverage in State Minimum Wage Laws," in *The Economics of Legal Minimum Wages,* ed. Simon Rottenberg (Washington, D.C.: American Enterprise Institute for Public Policy Research, 1981).

may be motivated by a concern for the welfare of low-wage workers, increases in the minimum wage also raise the relative costs to employers of less-skilled nonunion workers, thereby both increasing the costs of the products they produce and reducing employers' incentives to substitute nonunion workers for higher-paid union workers.

Another example of how unions can influence the demand for union labor is their position on immigration policy. The AFL-CIO has been quite explicit, both historically and in recent years, about its concern that immigrants depress wages as they are substituted for unionized American workers. With respect to the problem of illegal immigration in the early 1980s, the AFL-CIO asserted that

> while the nation should continue its compassionate and humane immigration policy, it is apparent that large numbers of illegal immigrants are being exploited by employers, thus threatening hard-won wages and working conditions. U.S. immigration policy should foster reunification of families and provide haven for refugees from persecution, while taking a realistic view of the job opportunities and the needs of U.S. workers.[20]

It is not surprising, then, that unions have historically supported legislation restricting immigration.

Restricting Substitution: Bargaining   Union attempts to restrict the substitution of other inputs for union labor typically occur by means of the collective bargaining process. In the past, some unions, notably those in the airline, railroad, and printing industries, sought and won guarantees of minimum crew sizes (for example, at least three pilots were required to fly certain jet aircrafts). Such *staffing requirements* prevented employers from substituting capital for labor.[21] Other unions have won contract provisions that prohibit employers from *subcontracting* for some or all of the services they provide. For example, a union representing a company's janitorial employees may win a contract provision preventing the firm from hiring external firms to provide it with janitorial services. Such provisions may limit the substitution of nonunion for union workers.

Craft unions often negotiate specific contract provisions that restrict the functions that members of each individual craft can perform, thereby limiting the substitution of one type of union labor for another. They also limit the substitution of unskilled union labor for skilled union labor by establishing rules about the maximum number of *apprentice* workers that can be employed relative to the experienced *journeymen* workers. Apprenticeship rules also limit the supply of skilled workers to a craft, which is another way to limit substitution for current union members.

---

[20]*The AFL-CIO Platform Proposals: Presented to the Democratic and Republican National Conventions 1980* (Washington, D.C.: AFL-CIO, 1980), 14.

[21]In cases in which these requirements call for the employment of workers whose functions are redundant—for example, fire stokers in diesel-operated railroad engines—*featherbedding* is said to take place. For an economic analysis of this phenomenon, see George Johnson, "Work Rules, Featherbedding and Pareto Optimal Union Management Bargaining," *Journal of Labor Economics* 8, no. 1, pt. 2 (January 1990): S237–S259.

Bargaining and the Threat of Strikes

How do unions persuade employers to agree to changes that reduce the wage elasticity of demand or shift the demand curve for union labor to the right? Given the elasticity and position of demand curves, how are unions able to bargain for, and win, real wage increases when in most cases an increase in the price of an input reduces a firm's profits?

In some cases a union and an employer may agree to a settlement in which real wages are increased in return for the union's agreeing to certain work-rule changes that will result in increased productivity. If such an agreement is explicit and is tied to the resulting change in productivity, the process is often referred to as *productivity bargaining*. More typically, however, unions are able to win management concessions at the bargaining table because of the unions' ability to impose costs on management. These costs typically take the form of work slowdowns and strikes. A *strike* is an attempt to deny the firm the labor services of all union members.

Strikes, for all the publicity generated when they occur, are relatively rare—and becoming ever rarer—in the United States. In 1970, for example, there were 381 work stoppages in the United States involving 1,000 or more workers, and these strikes caused a loss of about one-fourth of one percent of all work hours in the economy. By way of contrast, in 1997 (a year of comparable economic activity, as measured by the unemployment rate) there were 29 strikes involving 1,000 or more workers, and these caused a one-hundreth of one percent loss of overall work hours.[22] Despite their infrequency, the *threat* of a strike hangs over virtually every bargaining situation in the private sector, and therefore models of the bargaining process and its outcomes must address this threat.

A Simple Model of Strikes and Bargaining   The first, and also simplest, model of strikes in the bargaining process was developed by Sir John Hicks.[23] Suppose that management and labor are bargaining over only one issue: the size of the wage increase to be granted. How would the percentage increase that the union demands and the increase that the employer is willing to grant vary with the expected duration of a strike? Hicks analyzed this question with a diagram like the one shown in Figure 13.7, in which $\dot{W}$ is the percentage wage increase over which labor and management are bargaining.

On the employer side, the firm's highest pre-strike wage offer is assumed to be $\dot{W}_f$. If that offer is rejected and a strike ensues, the employer may be able to service its customers for a relatively short period of time through accumulated inventories or the use of nonstriking employees (including managers) in production jobs. As a strike progresses, however, the costs of lost business or dissatisfied customers mount, and the employer can be expected to increase its wage offer in an effort to end the strike. The expected willingness of employers to increase their

---

[22]*World Almanac and Book of Facts, 1999* (Mahwah, N.J.: World Almanac Books, 1999), 145, 152.
[23]John R. Hicks, *The Theory of Wages*, 2d ed. (New York: St. Martin's Press, 1966), 136–157.

FIGURE 13.7
**Hicks's Bargaining Model
and Expected Strike Length**

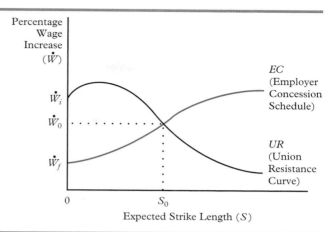

wage offers as a strike lengthens is depicted by the upward-sloping *employer concession schedule, EC,* in Figure 13.7.

The union is assumed initially willing to accept some wage increase ($\dot{W}_i$) without a strike, but after a strike begins worker attitudes may harden, and the union may actually increase its wage demands early on. After some point in the strike, however, the loss of income workers are suffering begins to color their attitudes, and the union will begin to reduce its wage demands. This reduction is indicated by the *union resistance curve, UR,* in Figure 13.7, which eventually becomes downward-sloping.

As the strike proceeds, we expect the union's demands to decrease and the employer's offer to increase, until at strike duration S_0 the two offers will coincide. At this point a settlement is reached on a wage increase of $\dot{W}_0$ and the strike is expected to end. This simple model has several implications.

Implications of the Model   First, holding the *EC* schedule constant, anything that shifts the *UR* schedule upward (that is, increases union resistance to management) will both lengthen the expected strike duration and raise the wage increase that can be expected. This heightened resistance may be manifest in either a higher "no-strike" wage demand (an increase in $\dot{W}_i$) or a flatter slope to the *UR* curve, which would indicate that the union is less willing to modify its wage demands as the strike proceeds.[24] Union resistance can be expected to increase, for example, if the unemployment rate is so low that strikers can easily obtain temporary jobs or if strikers are able to collect some form of unemployment benefits

---

[24]For evidence on the hypothesized downward slope to the *UR* curve, see Sheena McConnell, "Strikes, Wages, and Private Information," *American Economic Review* 79 (September 1989): 801–815, and David Card, "Strikes and Wages: A Test of an Asymmetric Information Model," *Quarterly Journal of Economics* 105 (August 1990): 625–659.

(either from the government or from the union). Indeed, we do find that strikes are both more likely and of longer duration in periods of relative prosperity; the availability to strikers of unemployment benefits similarly affects strike activity.[25]

A second implication of the simple Hicks model is that anything strengthening the resistance of employers will lower the *EC* curve, thereby lengthening expected strike duration and reducing the expected wage settlement. Thus, firms will be more likely to resist—and less likely to raise their wage offers very much as the strike progresses—if they are less profitable, face an elastic product demand curve, can stockpile product inventories in advance of a strike, or can easily hire replacement workers (see Example 13.2).[26]

A final implication is that strikes appear to be unnecessarily wasteful. Had the expected settlement of $\dot{W}_0$ been reached *without* a strike, or with a *shorter* strike, both sides would have been spared some losses. When strikes are likely to be very costly to both parties, the two might agree in advance to certain *bargaining protocols* that will help avert future strikes. For example, the parties might agree to start bargaining well in advance of a contract's expiration date, to limit the number of contract items they will discuss, or to submit the dispute to binding arbitration if they fail to reach agreement on their own. Indeed, there is some evidence that strikes are less frequent, and shorter, when the *joint costs* of any strike are likely to be greater.[27]

If strikes are costly, and if they can be averted in advance, why do they occur at all? Some argue that, to enhance their bargaining positions and retain the credibility of the *threat* of a strike, unions have to periodically use the strike weapon; that is, a strike may be designed to influence *future* negotiations. Strikes also may be useful devices by which the internal solidarity of a union can be enhanced against the common adversary—the employer. More fundamentally, however,

[25]Orley Ashenfelter and George Johnson, "Bargaining Theory, Trade Unions, and Industrial Strike Activity," *American Economic Review* 59 (March 1969): 35–49; Susan B. Vroman, "A Longitudinal Analysis of Strike Activity in U.S. Manufacturing: 1957–1984," *American Economic Review* 79 (September 1989): 816–826; Peter C. Cramton and Joseph S. Tracy, "The Determinants of U.S. Labor Disputes," *Journal of Labor Economics* 12, no. 2 (April 1994): 180–209; and Robert Hutchens, David Lipsky, and Robert Stern, "Unemployment Insurance and Strikes," *Journal of Labor Research* 13 (Fall 1992): 337–354. For similar evidence on strikes and the business cycle in Canada and Great Britian, see Alan Harrison and Mark Stewart, "Is Strike Behavior Cyclical?" *Journal of Labor Economics* 12, no. 4 (October 1994): 524–553, and A. P. Dickerson, "The Cyclicality of British Strike Frequency," *Oxford Bulletin of Economics and Statistics* 56, no. 3 (August 1994): 285–303.

[26]Melvin W. Reder and George R. Neumann, "Conflict and Contract: The Case of Strikes," *Journal of Political Economy* 88, no. 5 (October 1980): 867–886; John F. Schnell and Cynthia L. Gramm, "The Empirical Relations between Employers' Striker Replacement Strategies and Strike Duration," *Industrial and Labor Relations Review* 47, no. 2 (January 1994): 189–206; and Peter Cramton, Morley Gunderson, and Joseph Tracy, "The Effect of Collective Bargaining Legislation on Strikes and Wages," *Review of Economics and Statistics* 81, no. 3 (August 1999): 475–487.

[27]Barry Sopher, "Bargaining and the Joint-Cost Theory of Strikes: An Experimental Study," *Journal of Labor Economics* 8, no. 1, pt. 1 (January 1990): 48–74.

EXAMPLE 13.2

Permanent Replacement of Strikers

The collective bargaining laws of most nations permit a company whose workforce is on strike to hire *temporary* replacement workers to keep the business operating. The United States is one of the few nations that permit firms to hire *permanent* replacement workers. That is, workers on strike in the United States are at risk of permanently losing their jobs.

Although the right of companies to hire permanent replacements dates back to a 1938 Supreme Court decision, only since the early 1980s are large companies doing so, or seriously threatening to do so. In 1981, for example, the Reagan administration "broke" the air traffic controllers' union by permanently replacing striking controllers. Subsequently a number of large companies, including Eastern Airlines and Greyhound, permanently replaced striking workers. One study estimated that the increased threat of using permanent replacements reduced strikes in the 1980s by about 8 percent.

Why did large companies begin using permanent replacement workers in the 1980s when they had typically failed to do so during the previous four decades? Some attributed it to increasingly antiunion attitudes on the part of the federal government, a declining number of high-wage union jobs, and high unemployment—which led many workers to apply for permanent replacement positions, even at the risk of being called "scabs." Still others attributed it to the pressures of international competition, which increased employers' needs to cut costs.

Does the increased use of permanent replacements, which reduced union bargaining power, portend the end of unions in the United States? The answer is probably no. While employers may derive benefits from the use of permanent replacements, they also face costs. The costs are particularly high when new employees must be carefully screened and training needs to be extensive. There is also likely to be friction between replacements and any union workers brought back after the strike, and the commitment of workers to the employer may suffer in the long run.

Reference: Peter Cramton and Joseph Tracy, "The Use of Replacement Workers in Union Contract Negotiations: The U.S. Experience, 1980–1989," *Journal of Labor Economics* 16, no. 4 (October 1998): 667–701.

strikes are thought to occur because the information that both sides have about each other's goals and intentions to resist may be imperfect.

Strikes and Asymmetric Information   Most recent economic analyses of strike activity in the United States are based on some kind of information asymmetry. Workers may want to share in the firm's profits, for example, but they will doubt management's willingness to be completely truthful about current and expected profit levels. The reason is not difficult to understand: management knows more about the firm's profitability than does labor, and if it can convince workers that the enterprise is not very profitable, the union can be expected to moderate its wage demands.

Knowing management's informational advantages and its incentives to understate profitability, the union may try to elicit a signal from management about the true level of profits. A strike would be one such signal. If the firm is lying, and profits are greater than stated, the firm may be unwilling to put up a fight (management may figure that, since giving in is financially feasible, it is better off avoiding the costs of a strike). If, however, the firm is telling the truth about its low level of profits, giving in may not be feasible; taking a strike, then, sends a signal that the firm believes labor's demands are far enough above what it can feasibly pay that they must be strongly resisted.

An implication of the asymmetric-information model of strike activity is that greater uncertainty about an employer's willingness and ability to pay for wage increases should raise both the probability that a strike will occur and the duration of the strike. It does appear that the more variable a firm's profitability is over time, other things equal, the greater this uncertainty will be and the greater will be the expected incidence and duration of strike activity.[28] If the parties realize this, however, they may avert a strike by establishing a reputation for revealing their true positions rather quickly.

Union Leaders and the Union Members   One barrier to elimination of the misunderstandings caused by asymmetric information is that there are really *three* major parties to a negotiation, not just two. On the employee side of the negotiations are two groups: union *leaders* and the *rank-and-file* union members, who rely on their leaders for information.[29] The rank and file may understandably suspect their leaders of withholding information from them so that their negotiations are less stressful; put differently, the rank and file may suspect their leaders will sell them out. Conversely, the leadership may be unsure just how strongly their members feel about certain demands being made of management. Thus, there are also information asymmetries (and hence possibilities for misunderstandings) within the *employee* side of the negotiating table.

Union leaders have much better information than rank-and-file union members about the employer's true financial position. If the offered settlement is smaller than the membership wants, union leaders face two options.

On the one hand, they can return to their members, try to convince them of the employer's true financial picture, and recommend that management's offer be accepted. The danger is that the members may vote down the recommendation, accuse the leaders of selling out to management, and ultimately vote them out of office.

On the other hand, union leaders can return to their members and recommend that the members go out on strike. This recommendation will allow them to appear to be strong, militant leaders, even though the leaders themselves know that the strike probably will not lead to a larger settlement. After a strike of some duration, however, in accordance with the notion of the union resistance curve in Figure 13.7, union members will begin to moderate their wage demands, and ultimately a settlement for which the union leaders will receive credit will be reached.

---

[28]Joseph Tracy, "An Empirical Test of an Asymmetric Information Model of Strikes," *Journal of Labor Economics* 5 (April 1987): 149–173, and "An Investigation into the Determinants of U.S. Strike Activity," *American Economic Review* 76 (June 1986): 423–436. For other evidence supporting the asymmetric information model, see Peter Kuhn and Wulong Gu, "Learning in Sequential Wage Negotiations: Theory and Evidence," *Journal of Labor Economics* 17, no. 1 (January 1999): 109–140.

[29]The model described here was put forth by Ashenfelter and Johnson, "Bargaining Theory, Trade Unions, and Industrial Strike Activity."

Because the latter strategy is the one that is more likely to maintain the union's strength *and* keep the leaders in office, it is the strategy leaders may opt for even though it is clearly not in their members' best interests in the short run (the members have to bear the costs of the strike). Interestingly, strike activity rose markedly right after passage of the Landrum-Griffin Act in 1959, possibly because this act increased union democracy—thereby giving the wishes of the rank and file greater weight in the bargaining process.[30]

Bargaining in the Public Sector: The Threat of Arbitration

Although some states have granted to selected public sector employees the right to strike in one form or another, most have continued historic prohibitions against strikes by state and local government workers. When strikes are forbidden, however, laws often provide for third parties to enter the dispute-resolution process if bargaining between the parties comes to an impasse. The first step in this process is typically some form of *mediation,* in which a neutral third party attempts to facilitate a settlement by listening to each party separately, making suggestions on how each might modify its position to have more appeal to the other, and doing anything else possible to bring the parties to a voluntary settlement.

If a mediator is unable to bring the parties to a settlement, the dispute-resolution process sometimes calls for the next step to be *fact-finding,* in which a neutral party, after listening to both sides and gathering information, writes a report that proposes a settlement. The report is not binding on either party, but it may be considered by each to be a forecast of the settlement that binding arbitration would impose if the impasse were to continue.

If noncoercive methods fail to bring a voluntary settlement, *arbitration* becomes the final step of the dispute-resolution process. A single arbitrator may hear the case, or the case may be heard by a panel, usually consisting of one representative from labor, one from management, and one "neutral." Whether the parties *choose* to go to arbitration to settle their dispute, or whether by law they *must* go to arbitration, once the arbitration report is issued the parties are bound by its contents. Arbitration associated with the bargaining process is called *interest arbitration* (to distinguish it from the *grievance*-arbitration process so widely used in resolving contract-administration disputes during the life of a contract).

Forms of Arbitration   Interest arbitration can take two forms. With *conventional arbitration,* the arbitrators are free to decide on any wage settlement of their choosing. They listen to both sides make their case and then render their own decision. Some have suspected that under this conventional procedure, arbitrators tend to split the difference between the two parties, thereby encouraging the parties to take extreme positions (in the hope of dragging the arbitrator toward their true goal).

---

[30]Ashenfelter and Johnson, "Bargaining Theory, Trade Unions, and Industrial Strike Activity."

Some jurisdictions have chosen to adopt *final-offer arbitration,* in which the arbitrator is constrained to choose the final, prearbitration offer either of the union or of management; no other option is possible for the arbitrator. Final-offer arbitration, it was theorized, would induce the parties to make more reasonable final offers to each other, because by so doing they would increase the chances of their offer being the one accepted by the arbitrator.

The Contract Zone   No matter what form arbitration may take, going to arbitration is a risk for both parties because neither knows how the arbitrator will decide. A party wins the gamble only if the arbitrator's decision grants a higher wage increase than it could get through voluntary agreement. Thus, in deciding whether to continue bargaining—or, instead, take a rigid position and let the dispute go to arbitration—a party needs to develop expectations of various possible arbitrator decisions. By calculating the likelihood of each possible outcome *and* the utility associated with it, the party can develop a set of voluntary agreements it would prefer over taking its chances with arbitration. If the preferred sets of the two parties happen to overlap, there is a *contract zone* of possible voluntary agreements that *both* parties will prefer to the gamble of arbitration. If there is no overlap, the parties cannot agree voluntarily and the dispute will definitely go to arbitration.

A party's preferences for negotiation over gambling on arbitration are increased by greater aversion to risk and greater uncertainty about how the arbitrator might decide. If the parties become increasingly averse to losing, or if they become increasingly unable to predict what arguments or facts an arbitrator will find persuasive, then the set of negotiated outcomes they prefer to the arbitration gamble will widen. (Appendix 13A presents a more formal model underlying this conclusion.)

While logic dictates that a bargaining situation with *no* contract zone will produce no voluntary agreement, it is not obvious that a wider contract zone will make reaching a voluntary agreement more likely.[31] A wider contract zone opens up more feasible outcomes to the two parties, so one might think that the chances of voluntary agreement are enhanced, but it also gives the parties more to argue about. To take an extreme example, if there were only one wage increase that both parties preferred to arbitration, then perhaps agreement would be reached more quickly and with more certainty than if there were several possible outcomes to be thoroughly debated.

Persuading the Arbitrator   Although going to arbitration is clearly risky, the parties are not helpless in their abilities to influence the arbitrator's decision. If they are going to final-offer arbitration, they can improve their chances of winning by developing a final, prearbitration offer that the arbitrator is likely to regard as reasonable. The influence they exert in final-offer arbitration, then, amounts to guessing what the arbitrator thinks the outcome should be and then crafting an offer that

---

[31]Vincent Crawford, "Arbitration and Conflict Resolution in Labor–Management Bargaining," *American Economic Review* 71 (May 1981): 205–210.

approaches it. (Obviously, the union will approach it from *above* and management will approach it from *below*, as each tries to drag the arbitrator in its direction.)

If the parties are going to conventional arbitration, it is less certain how their offers can influence the arbitrator's decision. Some people might reason that the arbitrator will decide on a wage increase that lies between those of the two parties, or in the extreme, simply split the difference. If so, the parties might then be tempted to make final offers that are far from where they eventually expect to end up.

It might be more reasonable to believe, however, that arbitrators initially have their own views of a proper settlement, which can then be modified by listening to the arguments and positions of each party. Their own beliefs of what constitutes a reasonable outcome are not easily changed, and if a party's position (offer) is far from the outcome they consider appropriate, little weight will be given to it.[32] This latter view of how arbitrators behave implies that the parties can gain influence only by making offers that are close to what they think the arbitrator will decide. If both parties make the same (correct) guess about the arbitrator's preferred outcome, their final offers will bracket the arbitrator's decision. To outsiders it will look as though the arbitrator followed a simple, split-the-difference rule, but what really happened was that the parties strategically placed their offers around the arbitrator's expected position.[33]

Effects of Arbitration   If arbitrators have their own, strongly held views on the appropriate outcome in a particular case, and if the parties position their offers around what they expect to be the arbitrator's preferred outcome, then whatever form of arbitration is used, the behavior of the parties and the arbitrator should be more or less the same. Indeed, one study of police officers' contracts in a state where either form could be used found the wage outcomes chosen by the arbitrators were very similar in both conventional and final-offer arbitration.[34] But how do arbitrated settlements compare to negotiated ones?

It is not surprising that negotiated wage settlements are comparable to arbitrated settlements in states requiring that disputed settlements go to arbitration, because all negotiations in those states take place under the threat of arbitration. What is somewhat surprising, however, is that another study of police contracts found wages in states requiring arbitration of disputed settlements are more or less the same as those in states *without* that requirement.[35] Thus, it may well be that the effect of arbitration on wage levels is actually quite small.

---

[32]For experimental evidence in support of this view of arbitrator behavior, see Henry S. Farber and Max H. Bazerman, "The General Basis of Arbitrator Behavior: An Empirical Analysis of Conventional and Final-Offer Arbitration," *Econometrica* 54, no. 4 (July 1986): 819–844.

[33]Henry S. Farber, "Splitting-the-Difference in Interest Arbitration," *Industrial and Labor Relations Review* 35 (October 1981): 70–77.

[34]Orley Ashenfelter and David Bloom, "Models of Arbitrator Behavior: Theory and Evidence," *American Economic Review* 74 (March 1984): 111–124.

[35]Orley Ashenfelter and Dean Hyslop, "Measuring the Effect of Arbitration on Wage Levels: The Case of Police Officers," *Industrial and Labor Relations Review* 54, no. 2 (January 2001): 316–328.

THE EFFECTS OF UNIONS

Economists have long been interested in the effects of unions on wages, and recently attention has also been given to their effects on total compensation (including employee benefits), employment levels, hours of work, productivity, and profits. In this section we review the theory and the evidence on these effects.

The Theory of Union Wage Effects

Suppose we had data on the wage rates paid to two groups of workers identical in every respect except that one group was unionized and the other was not. Let W_u denote the wage paid to union members and W_n the wage paid to nonunion workers. If the difference between the two could be attributed solely to the presence of unions, then the *relative wage advantage (R)* that unions would have achieved for their members would be given, in percentage terms, by

$$R = (W_u - W_n)/W_n \tag{13.1}$$

This relative wage advantage does *not* represent the absolute amount, in percentage terms, by which unions would have increased the wages of their members, because unions both directly and indirectly affect *nonunion* wage rates also. Moreover, we cannot say for sure whether estimates of R will overstate or understate the absolute effect of unions on their members' real wage levels. To illustrate the difficulties in interpreting union–nonunion wage differentials, we begin with the simple model of the labor market depicted in Figure 13.8.

Figure 13.8 represents two sectors of the labor market, both of which hire similar workers. Panel (a) is the union sector and panel (b) is the nonunion sector. Suppose *initially* that both sectors are nonunion and that mobility between them is costless. Workers will therefore move between the two sectors until wages are equal in both. With demand curves D_u and D_n, workers will move between sectors until the supply curves are S_u^0 and S_n^0, respectively. The common equilibrium wage will be W_0, and employment will be E_u^0 and E_n^0, respectively, in the two sectors.

Once one sector becomes unionized, and its wage rises to W_u^1, what happens to wages in the other sector depends on the responses of employees who are not employed in the union sector. In the subsections below, we discuss four possible reactions.[36]

---

[36]Much of the discussion in this section is based upon the pioneering work of H. G. Lewis, *Unionism and Relative Wages in the United States* (Chicago: University of Chicago Press, 1963). In Figure 13.8, our analysis employs a two-sector model with labor supply curves to each sector. Remember that a labor supply curve to one sector is drawn holding the wages in other sectors ("alternative wages") constant; whenever the wage in one sector changes, the labor supply curve to the other sector may shift. We *sometimes* ignore this complexity below to keep our exposition as simple as possible and to highlight the various behaviors that might occur in either sector in response to unionization.

FIGURE 13.8
Spillover Effects of Unions on Wages and Employment

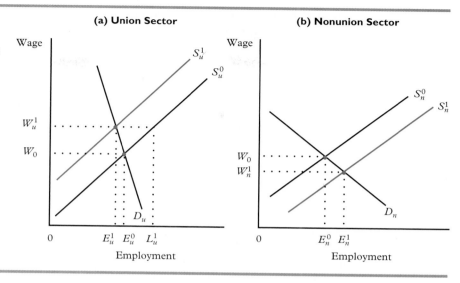

Spillover Effects   If the union succeeds in raising wages in the union sector to W_u^1, this increase will cause employment to decline to E_u^1 workers, resulting in $L_u^1 - E_u^1$ unemployed workers in that sector. If all the unemployed workers *spill over* into the nonunion sector, the supply curves in the two sectors will shift to S_u^1 and S_n^1, respectively. Unemployment will be eliminated in the union sector; in the nonunion sector, however, an excess supply of labor will exist at the old market-clearing wage, W_0. As a result, downward pressure will be exerted on the wage rate in the nonunion sector until the labor market in that sector clears at a *lower* wage (W_n^1) and a higher employment level (E_n^1).

In the context of this model, the union has succeeded in raising the wages of its members who kept their jobs. However, it has done so by shifting some of its members to lower-wage jobs in the nonunion sector and, because of this spillover effect, by actually lowering the wage rate paid to individuals initially employed in the nonunion sector. As a result, the observed union *relative wage advantage* (R_1), computed as

$$R_1 = (W_u^1 - W_n^1)/W_n^1 \tag{13.2}$$

will tend to be greater than the true *absolute* effect of the union on its members' real wage. This true absolute effect (A), stated in percentage terms, is defined as

$$A = (W_u^1 - W_0)/W_0 \tag{13.3}$$

Because W_n^1 is lower than W_0, R_1 is greater than A.

Threat Effects   Another possible response by nonunion employees is to want a union to represent them as well. Nonunion employers, fearing that a union would increase labor costs and place limits on managerial prerogatives, might seek to buy off their employees by offering them above-market wages.[37] Because there are costs to workers (as noted earlier) of union membership, some wage less than W_u^1 but higher than W_0 would presumably be sufficient to assure employers that the majority of their employees would not vote for a union (assuming that the employees are happy with their nonwage conditions of employment).

The implications of such *threat effects*—nonunion wage increases resulting from the threat of union entry—are traced in Figure 13.9. The increase in wage in the union sector, and resulting decline in employment there, is again assumed to cause the supply of workers to the nonunion sector to shift to S_n^1. In response to the threat of union entry, however, nonunion employers are assumed to *increase* their employees' wages to W_n^*, which lies between W_0 and W_u^1. This wage increase causes nonunion employment to decline to E_n^*; at the higher wage nonunion employers demand fewer workers. Moreover, since the nonunion wage is now not free to be bid down, an excess supply of labor, $L_n^* - E_n^*$, exists, resulting in unemployment. Finally, because the nonunion wage is now higher than the original wage, the observed union relative wage advantage

$$R_2 = (W_u^1 - W_n^*)/W_n^* \tag{13.4}$$

is smaller than the absolute effect of unions on their members' real wages.

Wait Unemployment   Do workers who lose (or do not have) a union job necessarily leave the union sector and take jobs in the nonunion sector? Even with reduced employment in the union sector, job vacancies occur as a result of retirements, deaths, and voluntary turnover. Some of those who do not have union jobs will find it attractive to search for work in the union sector, and their search might be more effective if they are not simultaneously employed elsewhere. Workers who reject lower-paying nonunion jobs so that they can search for higher-paying union ones create the phenomenon of *wait unemployment* (they are waiting for union jobs to open up).[38]

The main behavior behind the wait-unemployment response is that workers will move from one sector to another if the latter offers higher *expected* wages. Expected wages in a sector are equal to the sector's wage rate multiplied by the probability of obtaining a job in that sector. Thus, even if one were always able to find a job in the nonunion sector, rejecting employment there might be beneficial if there were a reasonable chance (even if it were less than 100 percent) of obtaining a higher-paying union job. The importance of the resultant wait unemployment for our current discussion is that not everyone who loses a job in the union sector will spill over

---

[37]For a more formal discussion of this possibility, see Sherwin Rosen, "Trade Union Power, Threat Effects, and the Extent of Organization," *Review of Economic Studies* 36 (April 1969): 185–196.

[38]See Jacob Mincer, "Unemployment Effects of Minimum Wages," *Journal of Political Economy* 84, no. 4, pt. 2 (August 1976): S87–S104. Although Mincer discusses minimum wage effects, union-imposed "minimum wages" can be analyzed analogously.

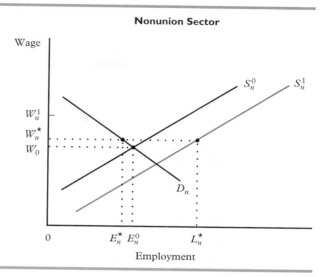

FIGURE 13.9
Threat Effects of Unions on Wages and Employment in Nonunion Sector

into the nonunion sector; in fact, it is even theoretically possible that some workers originally in the nonunion sector would quit their jobs to take a chance on finding work in the union sector.

The presence of wait unemployment in the union sector will reduce the spillover of workers to the nonunion sector, thus moderating downward pressure on nonunion wages. Moreover, if enough nonunion workers decide to search for union jobs, the labor supply curve to the nonunion sector could even shift to the left. In this case, unionization in one sector could cause wages in the nonunion sector to rise, just as with the threat effect (in fact, a "threat" here is being carried out: workers are leaving the nonunion employers to search for union jobs).

Shifts in Labor Demand   Finally, recall that we discussed earlier the activities unions undertake to alter the demand for their members' labor services. In some cases these activities involve attempts to shift the product demand curve facing unionized firms (and hence their labor demand curve) to the right. If unions were successful in their efforts to increase product demand in the unionized sector, perhaps at the expense of the nonunion sector, the rightward shift in the union-sector labor demand curve—and the associated leftward shift in the labor demand curve in the nonunion sector—would again serve to lower wages in the nonunion sector below what they were originally.[39]

---

[39]Our discussion of these four responses has assumed a partial equilibrium model. Once one considers a general equilibrium framework and allows capital to move between sectors, even more possibilities may exist. On this point, see Harry Johnson and Peter Mieszkowski, "The Effects of Unionization on the Distribution of Income: A General Equilibrium Approach," *Quarterly Journal of Economics* 84 (November 1969): 539–561.

Evidence of Union Wage Effects

Because the presence of unions can influence both the union and the nonunion wage rate, it is not possible to observe the wage that would have existed in the absence of unions (W_0). Hence, estimates of a union's absolute effects on the level of its members' real wages (A)—see equation (13.3)—cannot be obtained. Care must be taken not to mistake the relative wage effects we can observe (equations 13.2 and 13.4) for the absolute effects.

Economists have expended considerable effort to estimate the extent to which unions have raised the wages of their members relative to the wages of comparable nonunion workers in the private sector. These studies have tended to use data on large samples of individuals and sought to estimate how much more union members get paid than nonunion workers, after controlling for any differences between the two groups in other factors that might be expected to influence wages. Most of the work has been done on the United States, where levels of unionization are so modest that it is relatively easy to find comparable nonunion workers.

Because the studies of union-nonunion wage differences have used various data sets and statistical methodologies, there is no single estimate of the gap upon which all researchers agree. Enough work has been done on the topic, however, for certain patterns to emerge.

1. The union relative wage advantage in the United States appears to fall into the range of *10 to 20 percent.* That is, our best estimate is that American union workers receive wages that are some 10 to 20 percent higher than those of comparable nonunion workers.[40]

2. The *private sector* union wage advantage in the United States is larger than that in the *public* sector. For example, one study that used the same data and the same statistical methodology for both sectors estimated that the private sector wage gap was 15 to 19 percent in the 1990s, while in the public sector over the same period it was in the 10 to 13 percent range.[41]

3. The union relative wage advantage in the United States is larger than it is in other countries for which comparable estimates are available. One study that used the same data set and the same methodology for the United States and three other countries estimated the following wages gaps for 1985–1987: United States, 18 percent; United Kingdom,

---

[40]For surveys of these estimates, see Richard Freeman and James Medoff, *What Do Unions Do?* (New York: Basic Books, 1984); H. Gregg Lewis, *Union Relative Wage Effects: A Survey* (Chicago: University of Chicago Press, 1986); Barry T. Hirsch and John T. Addison, *The Economic Analysis of Unions: New Approaches and Evidence* (Boston: Allen and Unwin, 1986); Pencavel, *Labor Markets under Trade Unionism.* For a recent article with citations to the latest studies, see Stephen Raphael, "Estimating the Union Earnings Effect Using a Sample of Displaced Workers," *Industrial and Labor Relations Review* 53, no. 3 (April 2000): 503–521.

[41]Barry T. Hirsch and David A. Macpherson, *Union Membership and Earnings Data Book: Compilations from the Current Population Survey* (Washington, D.C.: Bureau of National Affairs, 2002), 19–20.

10 percent; West Germany, 6 percent; Austria, 5 percent.[42] A study of Australia for the same time period also indicated smaller union wage effects there than in the United States.[43]

4. Unions everywhere tend to reduce the dispersion of earnings among workers. They raise the wages of less-skilled workers relative to higher-skilled workers within the union sector, thereby reducing the payoff to human-capital investments. They standardize wages within and across firms in the same industry, and they reduce the earnings gaps between production and office workers.[44] They also reduce the wage gap between white and black workers in the United States.[45]

5. The union relative wage advantage in the United States has historically tended to be larger during recessionary periods.[46] Studies suggest, for example, that the union–nonunion wage gap increased significantly during the early 1980s, when unemployment rates were relatively high. Firms find it easier to substitute capital for labor when new capital investments are being made. Therefore, during periods when output and investments are not expanding, substitutions of capital for labor are more difficult and the union confronts a less elastic demand curve for labor.

6. Although the findings do not yet fit a pattern, researchers have attempted to discover whether greater levels of unionization tend to increase or decrease wages in the *nonunion* sector. These studies have tried to see whether the spillover or the threat effect dominates among nonunion employers. The evidence so far is ambiguous. A recent study found, for example, that threat effects dominated within *cities* (that is, in more highly

---

[42]David G. Blanchflower and Richard B. Freeman, "Unionism in the United States and Other Advanced OECD Countries," *Industrial Relations* 31, no. 1 (Winter 1992): 56–79. For Canada, see Peter Kuhn and Arthur Sweetman, "Wage Loss Following Displacement: The Role of Union Coverage," *Industrial and Labor Relations Review* 51, no. 3 (April 1998): 384–400. For union effects in South Africa, see Kristin F. Butcher and Cecilia Elena Rouse, "Wage Effects of Unions and Industrial Councils in South Africa," *Industrial and Labor Relations Review* 54, no. 2 (January 2001): 349–374.

[43]Robert Kornfeld, "The Effects of Union Membership on Wages and Employee Benefits: The Case of Australia," *Industrial and Labor Relations Review* 47, no. 1 (October 1993): 114–128.

[44]Lawrence M. Kahn, "Wage Inequality, Collective Bargaining and Relative Employment 1985–94: Evidence from 15 OECD Countries," *Review of Economics and Statistics* 82, no. 4 (November 2000): 564–579; David Card, "The Effect of Unions on Wage Inequality in the U.S. Labor Market," *Industrial and Labor Relations Review* 54, no. 2 (January 2001): 296–315; Barry T. Hirsch and Edward J. Schumacher, "Unions, Wages, and Skills," *Journal of Human Resources* 33, no. 1 (Winter 1998): 201–219.

[45]James Peoples Jr., "Monopolistic Market Structure, Unionization, and Racial Wage Differentials," *Review of Economics and Statistics* 76, no. 1 (February 1994): 207–211; Richard Freeman and James Medoff, *What Do Unions Do?* ch. 5.

[46]Lewis, *Unionism and Relative Wages;* Peter Linneman and Michael Wachter, "Rising Union Premiums and Declining Boundaries among Noncompeting Groups," *American Economic Review* 76 (May 1986): 103–108; and William Moore and John Raisian, "Union–Nonunion Wage Differentials in the Public Administration, Educational and Private Sectors," *Review of Economics and Statistics* 69 (November 1987): 608–615.

unionized cities, the wages of nonunion workers were higher). It also found, however, that the spillover effect dominated within *industries* (in more highly unionized industries, nonunion wages tended to be lower). These contradictory results mirror those of earlier studies.[47]

Evidence of Union Total Compensation Effects

Estimates of the extent to which the wages of union workers exceed the wages of otherwise comparable nonunion workers may prove misleading for two reasons. First, such estimates ignore the fact that wages are only part of the compensation package. It has often been argued that *employee benefits,* such as paid holidays, vacation pay, sick leave, and retirement benefits, will be higher in firms that are unionized than in nonunion firms. The argument states that, because tastes for the various benefits differ across individuals and because there is no easy way to communicate the preferences of the average employee to the employer in a nonunion firm, nonunion firms tend to pay a higher fraction of total compensation in the form of money wages. Empirical evidence tends to support this contention; employee benefits and the share of compensation that goes to benefits do appear to be higher in union than in nonunion firms. Further, studies also suggest that unionization increases the probability that workers apply for government benefits for which they are eligible.[48] Ignoring benefits may therefore *understate* the true union/nonunion total-compensation differential.

Second, ignoring *conditions of employment* may cause one to *overstate* the effect of unions on their members' overall welfare levels compared to those of nonunion workers. For example, studies have shown that for blue-collar workers, unionized firms tend to have more-structured work settings, more-hazardous jobs, less-flexible hours of work, faster work paces, lower worker job satisfaction, and less employee control over the assignment of overtime hours than do nonunion firms.[49] This situation may arise because production settings that call for more interdependence among workers and the need for rigid work requirements by employers also give rise to unions. While unions often strive to affect these working

---

[47]See David Neumark and Michael L. Wachter, "Union Effects on Nonunion Wages: Evidence from Panel Data on Industries and Cities," *Industrial and Labor Relations Review* 49, no. 1 (October 1995): 20–38.

[48]Richard Freeman, "The Effect of Trade Unions on Fringe Benefits," *Industrial and Labor Relations Review* 34 (July 1981): 489–509; Kornfeld, "The Effects of Union Membership on Wages and Employee Benefits"; Barry T. Hirsch, David A. Macpherson, and J. Michael Dumond, "Workers' Compensation Recipiency in Union and Nonunion Workplaces," *Industrial and Labor Relations Review* 50, no. 2 (January 1997): 213–236; John W. Budd and Brian P. McCall, "The Effects of Unions on the Receipt of Unemployment Insurance Benefits," *Industrial and Labor Relations Review* 51, no. 3 (April 1997): 478–492; and Thomas C. Buchmuller, John DiNardo, and Robert G. Valletta, "Union Effects on Health Insurance Provision and Coverage in the United States," working paper no. 30, Center for Labor Economics, University of California, Berkeley, March 2001.

[49]Greg Duncan and Frank Stafford, "Do Union Members Receive Compensating Wage Differentials?" *American Economic Review* 70 (June 1980): 355–371; and Keith A. Bender and Peter J. Sloane, "Job Satisfaction, Trade Unions, and Exit-Voice Revisited," *Industrial and Labor Relations Review* 51, no. 2 (January 1998): 222–240.

conditions, they do not always succeed. Part of the estimated union/nonunion earnings differential thus may be a premium paid to union workers to compensate them for these unfavorable working conditions. One study estimates that two-fifths of the estimated union/nonunion earnings differential reflects such compensation, suggesting that the observed earnings differential may overstate the true differential in overall levels of worker well-being.[50]

The Effects of Unions on Employment

If unions raise the wages and employee benefits of their members, and if they impose constraints on managerial prerogatives, economic theory suggests their presence will have a negative effect on employment. In recent years, several studies have investigated this theoretical prediction, and the results suggest that unions do reduce employment growth. A study of plants in California during the late 1970s, for example, estimated that employment grew some 2 to 4 percentage points more slowly per year in union than in nonunion firms; in fact, the growth rates were so different that about 60 percent of the decline in California's unionization rate was attributed to slower employment growth in union jobs.[51] Other studies have found similar employment effects for the United States as a whole, as well as for Canada and the United Kingdom.[52] Finally, even when employment is not much changed in the face of unionization, the total yearly hours of work might still fall.[53]

The Effects of Unions on Productivity and Profits

There are two views on how unions affect labor productivity (output per worker). One is that unions *increase* worker productivity, given the firm's level of capital, by providing a "voice" mechanism through which workers' suggestions and preferences can be communicated to management.[54] With a direct means for expressing their

---

[50]Duncan and Stafford, "Do Union Members Receive Compensating Wage Differentials?"

[51]Jonathan S. Leonard, "Unions and Employment Growth," *Industrial Relations* 31, no. 1 (Winter 1992): 80–94.

[52]Timothy Dunne and David A. Macpherson, "Unionism and Gross Employment Flows," *Southern Economic Journal* 60, no. 3 (January 1994): 727–738; Stephen G. Bronars, Donald R. Deere, and Joseph Tracy, "The Effects of Unions on Firm Behavior: An Empirical Analysis Using Firm-Level Data," *Industrial Relations* 33, no. 4 (October 1994): 426–451; Robert G. Valletta, "Union Effects on Municipal Employment and Wages: A Longitudinal Approach," *Journal of Labor Economics* 11, no. 3 (July 1993): 545–574; Richard J. Long, "The Impact of Unionization on Employment Growth of Canadian Companies," *Industrial and Labor Relations Review* 46, no. 4 (July 1993): 691–703; David G. Blanchflower, Neil Millward, and Andrew J. Oswald, "Unions and Employment Behaviour," *Economic Journal* 101, no. 407 (July 1991): 815–834; and Kahn, "Wage Inequality, Collective Bargaining and Relative Employment 1985–94."

[53]William M. Boal and John Pencavel, "The Effects of Labor Unions on Employment, Wages, and Days of Operation: Coal Mining in West Virginia," *Quarterly Journal of Economics* 109, no. 1 (February 1994): 267–298.

[54]For a more complete statement of this argument, see Freeman and Medoff, *What Do Unions Do?* Note that there is another, more mechanical way in which unions can raise worker productivity. We have seen that unions raise wages, and theory suggests that the response by profit-maximizing employers will be to reduce employment and substitute capital for labor. Thus, as firms move up and to the left along their marginal product of labor curves, the marginal product of labor rises in response to the wage increase.

ideas or concerns, workers may have enhanced motivation levels and be less likely to quit. With lower quit rates, firms have more incentives to invest in firm-specific training, which should also raise worker productivity.

The other view on how unions affect worker productivity stresses the limits they place on managerial prerogatives, especially with respect to using cost-minimizing levels of the labor input. We argued earlier that if unions care about the employment, as well as the wages, of their members, they will put pressure on management to agree to staffing requirements, restrictions on work out of job title, cumbersome methods through which the disciplining of nonproductive workers must take place, and other policies that increase labor costs per unit of output.

Empirical analyses of union productivity effects have yielded conflicting results. The effects of unions on workers' output apparently depend very much on the quality of the relationship between labor and management in each particular collective bargaining setting.[55]

If unions raise wages, but do not clearly raise worker productivity, then we might expect them to reduce firms' profits. Some studies directly analyze unionization and profit levels, holding other things constant; these rather consistently estimate that profits in unionized firms are lower, both in the United States and in the United Kingdom.[56] Another way of studying unions' effects on profits, however, is to make use of evidence that the stock market quickly and accurately reflects changes in a firm's profitability. The stock-price studies that have been done to date also find evidence consistent with the hypothesis that unionization reduces the profitability of employers.[57] Example 13.3 considers the effects of right-to-work legislation on expected profits, as reflected in stock prices.

Normative Analyses of Unions

We have seen throughout this text that economic theory can be used in both its *positive* and its *normative* modes. The analyses of union effects in this section so far have been of a positive nature, in that we have summarized both theory and evidence on how unions affect various labor market outcomes. We turn now to a normative question that often underlies discussions of unions and the government

---

[55]Blanchflower and Freeman, "Unionism in the United States and Other Advanced OECD Countries"; and Sandra Black and Lisa Lynch, "How to Compete: The Impact of Workplace Practices and Information Technology on Productivity," *Review of Economics and Statistics* 83, no. 3 (August 2001): 434–445.
[56]Bronars, Deere, and Tracy, "The Effects of Unions on Firm Behavior"; Blanchflower and Freeman, "Unionism in the United States and Other Advanced OECD Countries"; Barry T. Hirsch, "Unionization and Economic Performance: Evidence on Productivity, Profits, Investment, and Growth," in *Unions and Right-to-Work Laws*, ed. Fazil Mihlar (Vancouver: Fraser Institute, 1997), 35–70; and Richard B. Freeman and Morris M. Kleiner, "Do Unions Make Enterprises Insolvent?" *Industrial and Labor Relations Review* 52, no. 4 (July 1999): 510–527.
[57]Richard S. Ruback and Martin B. Zimmerman, "Unionization and Profitability: Evidence from the Capital Market," *Journal of Political Economy* 92 (December 1984): 1134–1157; Becker, "Union Rents as a Source of Takeover Gains among Target Shareholders"; and Abraham and Voos, "Right-to-Work Laws: New Evidence from the Stock Market."

EXAMPLE 13.3

Do Right-to-Work Laws Matter?

Many observers argue that state right-to-work laws are mostly symbolic. These observers contend that such laws are passed in states where workers are less attracted to unions anyway, and thus that they merely *reflect*—rather than cause—union weakness in those states. Others believe that the laws do affect union power, reducing the probability of organizing, shrinking membership in previously organized units, and tipping the bargaining scales in favor of employers.

A recent study distinguished between these two interpretations by examining how investors responded when right-to-work laws were passed in Louisiana (1976) and Idaho (1985–1986). The study matched firms in both states to similar firms operating elsewhere and compared movements in their stock prices. An investor's valuation of a company's stock depends on expectations about the company's future profits. Thus if the passage of a right-to-work law is expected to increase profits of a firm operating in the state,

investors will bid up the price for which a share of the firm sells in the stock market. If the law is purely symbolic, investors won't expect any change in profits and stock prices won't change.

The study found that as news favorable to the passage of these right-to-work bills came out of the states' legislatures, courts and governors' offices, stock prices of in-state companies rose. The cumulative effect of passing these laws was to increase the stock market value of Louisiana firms by 2.2 to 4.5 percent and Idaho firms by 2.4 to 9.5 percent. While right-to-work laws may have some symbolic value, investors—who must put their money on the line—have concluded that right-to-work laws are good for firms and boost their expected profits.

Data from: Steven E. Abraham and Paula B. Voos, "Right-to-Work Laws: New Evidence from the Stock Market," *Southern Economic Journal,* 67, no. 2 (October 2000), 345–362.

---

policies that affect them: Do unions enhance or reduce social welfare? As one might expect, opinions differ.

Potential Reductions in Social Welfare   We saw in chapter 1 that the role of any market, including the labor market, is to facilitate mutually beneficial transactions by providing a mechanism for voluntary exchange. The ultimate goal of this exchange is to arrive at an allocation of goods and services that generates as much utility as is possible, given a society's resources, for the individuals in that society. If a market has facilitated *all* such transactions, then it can be said to have arrived at a point of Pareto efficiency. A requirement for the existence of Pareto efficiency is that all productive resources, including labor, be used in a way that generates maximum utility for society (this includes the utility of the workers as well as that of the consumers who purchase the goods or services they produce).

Arguments that unions reduce social welfare stem generally from the proposition that they represent the interests of only their members, not of others.[58] One argument points to the production lost (the labor resources wasted) when workers

---

[58]Assar Lindbeck and Dennis J. Snower, "Insiders versus Outsiders," *Journal of Economic Perspectives* 15, no. 1 (Winter 2001): 165–188.

go on strike. A second argument is similar: When labor and management agree to restrictive work rules (as noted in our discussion of the efficient-contracts model), the use of excess workers in the production process creates wastage—and therefore social loss—in the use of labor. A third argument is more subtle, however.

Simple reasoning suggests that for Pareto efficiency to be achieved, resources that have the same *potential* productivity must have the same *actual* productivity. Consider, for example, a group of workers who are equally skilled, experienced, and motivated. If some of these workers are in jobs that produce $15 worth of goods or services per hour, while others in the group are in jobs that produce only $10, the value of society's output could be enhanced by the voluntary movement of members from the latter subset into the higher-productivity jobs. Reducing the number of workers in the $10 jobs would serve to raise the marginal productivity of those who remain in those jobs, while increasing the number of workers in the $15 jobs would put downward pressure on the wage (and marginal productivity) in that sector. As long as the marginal productivities of workers in the skill group continue to differ, however, the value of society's output could be increased still further by having members of the lower-paid subset move into the higher-paying jobs. Only when the marginal productivities are equal, and all Pareto-improving moves by workers have been completed, can it be said that Pareto efficiency is achieved.

The third argument that unions reduce social welfare, then, rests on two propositions. The first is that unions create wage (and therefore productivity) differentials among equivalent workers by raising wages in the union sector above those in the nonunion sector. The second proposition is that the higher and inflexible union wage prevents workers in lower-paying jobs from moving into the higher-productivity sector, with the result that society's output is lower than it would be otherwise. Some economists have attempted to estimate these losses, and their estimates have generally been small—in the range of 0.2 to 0.4 percent of national output.[59]

Potential Increases in Social Welfare   Arguments that unions reduce social welfare lose some of their force if, in the absence of unions, labor or product markets are not as competitive as assumed by standard economic theory. Suppose, for example, that the cost of mobility is so great that workers do not freely move to preferable jobs. Compensating wage differentials may fail to correctly guide the allocation of workers across jobs that have varying levels of unpleasant (or pleasant) characteristics. If so, too many workers may end up in dangerous or otherwise unpleasant jobs, which they would gladly leave (even for a lower-paying one) if they had the chance.

With respect to working conditions, there are two general means by which employer behavior can be influenced. The mechanism relied upon by the market, with its individual transactions, is one of *exit and entry*. If a worker is unhappy with certain conditions of employment, he or she is free to leave; if enough workers do so, the employer will be forced to alter the offending condition or else increase wages enough to induce the workers it has to remain. An alternative to the exit

---

[59]Freeman and Medoff, *What Do Unions Do?* 57.

mechanism is the mechanism of *voice:* workers can vocalize their concerns and hope that the employer will respond.

The voicing of requests by *individuals* is potentially very costly. First, many workplace conditions (such as lighting, scheduling, safety precautions) are examples of "public goods" within the plant. All workers are benefited by any improvements, whether or not they contributed to the campaign to secure them. Therefore, the possibility of free riders inhibits individuals (acting alone) from bearing the costs of a campaign to change workplace conditions. Second, because the employer may respond to complaints by firing "troublemakers," an individual worker who uses the voice mechanism without some form of job protection must be prepared to suffer the costs of exit.

Those who hold the view that unions improve social welfare argue that, in the face of high mobility costs, unions offer workers the mechanism of *collective* voice in the establishment of their working conditions. They solve the free-rider problem and relieve their members of the risks and burdens associated with individual voice. Further, collective bargaining agreements almost always establish a grievance procedure through which certain employee complaints can be formally addressed by a neutral third party. In short, unions provide mechanisms of collective voice that substitute for an expensive-to-use exit mechanism in the determination of the workplace conditions that affect workers' utility. They therefore promote Pareto-improving transactions that otherwise would not have been induced because of the high costs of employee mobility.

Other arguments that unions enhance (or at least do not reduce) social welfare also rest on market conditions that call into question key assumptions underlying the standard economic model of employer behavior. For example, one possibility (mentioned earlier in this chapter) is that unionized employers have substantial monopoly power in their product markets, which yields them excess profits. If the efficient-contracts model of bargaining holds, and if the associated contract curve is vertical, then employment remains equal to its preunionization level, and the union and the employer end up simply splitting the employer's excess profits. Income is transferred from owners to workers, but because total output is unaffected, there would be no social losses associated with higher union wages.

Another argument is that employers are not as knowledgeable about how to maximize profits as standard economic theory assumes. Because management finds it costly to search for better (or less costly) ways to produce, so the argument goes, we cannot be sure that it will always use labor in the most productive ways possible. (Clearly, this argument rests on the implicit assumption that entry into the product market is difficult enough that inefficient producers are not necessarily punished by competitive forces.) When unions organize and raise the wages of their members, firms may be shocked into the search for better ways to produce. Moreover, by establishing formal channels of communication between workers and management, unionization at least *potentially* provides a mechanism through which employers and employees can more effectively communicate about workplace processes.[60]

---

[60]For a fuller development of this argument, see Freeman and Medoff, *What Do Unions Do?* 15.

REVIEW QUESTIONS

1. Suppose that a proposal for tax reductions associated with the purchase of capital equipment is up for debate. Suppose, too, that union leaders are called upon to comment on the proposal from the perspective of how it will affect the welfare of their members as workers (not consumers). Will they all agree on the effects of the proposal? Explain your answer.

2. Some collective bargaining agreements contain "union standards" clauses that prohibit the employer from farming out work normally done in the plant to other firms that pay less than the union wage.
   a. What is the union's rationale for seeking a union standards clause?
   b. Under what conditions will a union standards clause most likely be sought by a labor union?

3. The Jones Act mandates that at least 50 percent of all U.S. government-financed cargo must be transported in U.S.-owned ships and that any U.S. ship leaving a U.S. port must have at least 90 percent of its crew composed of U.S. citizens. What would you expect the impact of this act to be on the demand for labor in the shipping industry and the ability of unions to push up the wages of U.S. seafarers?

4. It has been observed that unions in the capital-intensive steel industry were able to negotiate higher-than-average wage increases during the very period in which steel output in the United States was declining. Using economic theory, how can this pattern be explained?

5. In Germany temporary layoffs and dismissals on short notice are often illegal. A dismissal is illegal if it is "socially unjustified," and it is considered "socially unjustified" if the worker could be employed in a different position or establishment of the firm, even one requiring retraining. Workers illegally dismissed may sue their employers. What are the likely consequences of this German law for the ability of German unions to raise wages?

6. In the mid–1980s, the teachers' union of a large American city was given a choice: it could accept a 10 percent cut in the salaries paid to teachers and suffer no employment losses, or it could keep salaries constant and accept a 10 percent cut in employment levels (and a corresponding 10 percent increase in class sizes). Given that union leaders are elected by the membership, answer the following:
   a. Predict and explain the union's decision, assuming that its collective bargaining agreement with the city specifies that any layoffs will occur among those teachers most recently hired.
   b. Explain whether the decision in (a) would have been different if the collective bargaining agreement had specified that all layoffs would occur on a random basis, independent of seniority, teaching field, or any other teacher characteristics.

7. A publication of the AFL-CIO stated, "There is accumulating evidence that unionized workers are more productive than nonunion workers and that unionization raises productivity in an establishment. This suggests that employers and American society generally should take a much more positive approach to unionism and collective bargaining." Comment on this quotation.

8. Is the following statement true, false, or uncertain? "The empirical studies indicating that unions raise the wages of their members by 10 to 20 percent relative to the wages of comparable nonunion workers imply that unions have a negative effect on national output." Explain your answer.

PROBLEMS

1. Suppose that the employer concession schedule is $W = 1 + .02S$ and the union resistance curve is $W = 5 + .02S - .01S^2$, where W = percentage wage increase and S = expected strike length in days. Using Hicks's simplest model, determine the length of the strike and the percentage wage increase.

2. The Brain Surgeons' Brotherhood faces an own-wage elasticity of demand for their labor that equals -0.1. The Dog Catchers' International faces an own-wage elasticity of demand for their labor which equals -3.0. Suppose that leaders in both unions push for a 20 percent wage increase but have no power to set employment levels directly. Why might members of the Dog Catchers' International be more wary of the targeted wage increase?

3. Suppose that unionized workers in the retail sales industry earn $10 per hour and that nonunionized workers in the industry earn $8 per hour. What can be said about the relative wage advantage of unionized workers and the absolute effect of the union on its members' real wage?

SELECTED READINGS

Atherton, Wallace. *Theory of Union Bargaining Goals.* Princeton, N.J.: Princeton University Press, 1973.

Freeman, Richard B., and James L. Medoff. *What Do Unions Do?* New York: Basic Books, 1984.

Hirsch, Barry T., and John T. Addison. *The Economic Analysis of Unions: New Approaches and Evidence.* Boston: Allen and Unwin, 1986.

Kerr, Clark, and Paul D. Staudohar, eds. *Labor Economics and Industrial Relations: Markets and Institutions.* Cambridge, Mass.: Harvard University Press, 1994.

Lewis, H. G. *Union Relative Wage Effects: A Survey.* Chicago: University of Chicago Press, 1986.

Pencavel, John. *Labor Markets under Trade Unionism.* Cambridge, Mass.: Basil Blackwell, 1991.

13A

Arbitration and the Bargaining Contract Zone

W hat incentive do the parties to collective bargaining negotiations have to settle their negotiations on their own rather than go to arbitration and have an outside party impose a settlement? The answer may well be that the uncertainty about an arbitrator's likely decision imposes costs on both parties that give them an incentive to come to an agreement on their own. This appendix provides a simple model that illustrates this proposition; it highlights the roles of both *uncertainty* about an arbitrator's likely decision and the parties' *attitudes toward risk* in determining whether a negotiation will wind up in arbitration.[1]

Consider a simple two-party bargaining problem in which the parties, A and B, are negotiating over how to split a "pie" of fixed size. Each party's utility function depends only on the share of the pie that it receives. Figure 13A.1 plots the utility function for party A. When A's share of the pie is zero, A's utility (U_A) is assumed to be zero, and as A's share (S_A) increases, A's utility increases. Crucially, this utility function is also assumed to exhibit the property of *diminishing marginal utility*; equal increments in S_A lead to progressively smaller increments in U_A. As we shall show below, this is equivalent to assuming that the party is *risk averse*, which means that the party would prefer the certainty of having a given share of the pie to an uncertain outcome that, on average, would yield the same share.[2]

Now suppose party A believes that, on average, the arbitrator would award it one-half of the pie if the negotiations went to arbitration. If it knew with certainty that the arbitrator would do this, party A's utility from going to arbitration would be $U_A(1/2)$, at point a in Figure 13A.1. Suppose, however, that party A is uncer-

---

[1]The discussion here is a simplified version of some of the material found in Henry S. Farber and Harry C. Katz, "Interest Arbitration, Outcomes, and the Incentive to Bargain," *Industrial and Labor Relations Review* 33 (October 1979): 55–63.
[2]Refer to Appendix 8A, especially note 4, for an introduction to this use of cardinal utility functions.

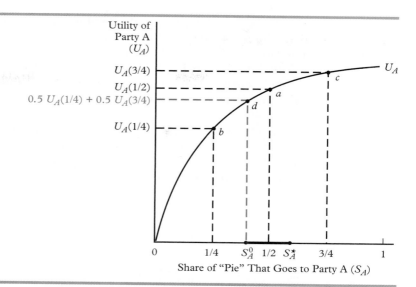

FIGURE 13A.1

Utility Function for a Risk-Averse Party: Uncertainty about Arbitrator's Decision Leads to a Contract Zone

tain about the arbitrator's decision and instead believes the arbitrator will assign it one-quarter of the pie with probability one-half, or three-quarters of the pie also with probability one-half. Utility in these two states is given by $U_A(1/4)$, point b, and $U_A(3/4)$, point c, respectively. Although, on average, party A expects to be awarded one-half of the pie, its average or *expected* utility in this case is $0.5U_A(1/4) + 0.5U_A(3/4)$, which, as Figure 13A.1 indicates (see point d), is less than $U_A(1/2)$. This reflects the fact that party A is risk averse, preferring a certain outcome (point a) to an uncertain outcome (point d) that yields the same expected share.

Note that if party A were awarded the share S_A^0 with certainty, it would receive the same utility level it receives under the uncertain situation, where it expects, with equal probability, the arbitrator to award it either one-quarter or three-quarters of the pie. Indeed, it would prefer any *certain* share above S_A^0 to bearing the cost of the uncertainty associated with having to face the arbitrator's decision. The set of contracts it potentially would voluntarily agree to, then, is the set S_A such that

$$S_A^0 \leq S_A \leq 1; S_A^0 < 1/2 \tag{13A.1}$$

Suppose party B is similarly risk averse and has identical expectations about what the arbitrator's decision will look like. It should be obvious, using the same logic as above, that the set of contracts, S_B, that party B potentially would voluntarily agree to is given by a similar expression:

$$S_B^0 \leq S_B \leq 1; S_B^0 < 1/2 \tag{13A.2}$$

Now, any share that party B voluntarily agrees to receive implies that what B is willing to give party A is 1 minus that share. Since the *minimum* share B would agree to receive, S_B^0, is less than one-half, it follows that the *maximum* share B would voluntarily agree to give A in negotiations, S_A^* (which equals $1 - S_B^0$), is greater than one-half. Party B potentially would be willing to voluntarily agree to any settlement that gives party A a share of less than S_A^*.

Referring to Figure 13A.1, observe that party A would be willing to voluntarily agree to contracts that offer it at least S_A^0, while party B would be willing to agree to contracts that give party A S_A^* or less. Hence, the set of contracts that *both* parties would find preferable to going to arbitration (and thus *potentially* would voluntarily agree to) is given by all the shares for A (S_A) that lie between these two extremes:

$$S_A^0 \leq S_A \leq S_A^* \tag{13A.3}$$

This set of potential voluntary solutions to the bargaining problem is indicated by the bold-line segment on the horizontal axis of Figure 13A.1 and is called the *contract zone*. As long as both parties are risk averse and are uncertain what the arbitrator will do, a contract zone will exist.

FIGURE 13A.2
Increased Uncertainty about Arbitrator's Decision Increases Size of the Contract Zone

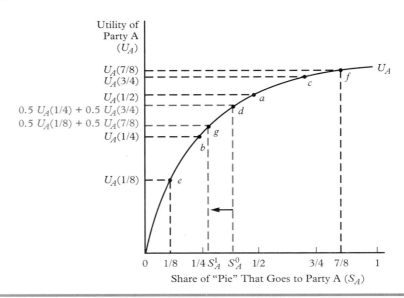

Share of "Pie" That Goes to Party A (S_A)

FIGURE 13A.3
**Utility Function for a Risk-Neutral Party: Contract Zone Is Reduced
to a Single Point**

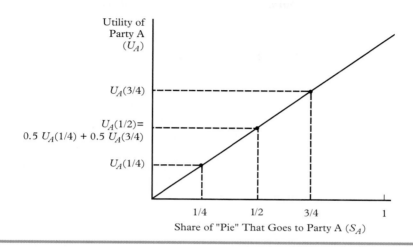

The extent of the parties' *uncertainty* about the arbitrator's decision and the extent of their *risk aversion* are important determinants of the size of the contract zone. To see this, first suppose that party A continues to expect that, on average, the arbitrator will assign it one-half of the pie, but now believes that this will occur by receiving shares of one-eighth and seven-eighths with equal probability. Figure 13A.2 indicates its utility in each of these states (points *e* and *f*) and shows that, while its expected share is still one-half, the greater uncertainty—or "spread" of possible outcomes—has led to a reduction in its expected utility (compare points *d* and *g*). Indeed, now party A would be as happy to receive the share S_A^1 with certainty as it would to face the risks associated with going to arbitration. Since S_A^1 is less than S_A^0, the size of the contract zone has increased. Hence, increased uncertainty about the arbitrator's decision leads to a larger contract zone.

Next consider Figure 13A.3, where we have drawn a utility function for a *risk-neutral* party. A risk-neutral party has a linear utility function because its utility depends only on its expected share, not the uncertainty associated with the outcome. So, for example, in Figure 13A.3, party A gets the same utility from having a share of one-half with certainty as it does from facing an arbitrated outcome in which there is equal probability that the arbitrator will award it either a share of one-quarter or a share of three-quarters. As a result, faced with the possibility of going to arbitration, there is no share less than one-half that party A would voluntarily agree to settle for prior to arbitration. If party B had similar expectations about the arbitrator's behavior and was similarly risk neutral, it also would refuse to settle for any share of less than one-half, which on average is what it expects to win from the arbitrator. Hence, the contract zone would reduce to one point, the point where both parties receive a share of one-half. The only voluntary agreement the parties will reach is what they expect to receive on average if they go to arbitration. (This illustrates how the arbitration process per se may influence the nature of negotiated settlements.)

More generally, one can show that as a party's risk aversion increases (the utility function becomes more curved), the size of the contract zone will increase. Hence, increases in either the parties' risk aversion or their uncertainty about the arbitrator's decision will increase the size of the contract zone.

Larger contract zones mean that there are more potential settlements that *both* parties would prefer to an arbitrated settlement, and some people have argued that this increased menu of choices increases the probability that the parties would settle on their own prior to going to arbitration.[3] An immediate implication of this argument is that, if one believes it is preferable for the parties to settle on their own, the arbitration system should be structured so that the arbitrator's behavior does not become completely predictable. As we discussed in the text, however, others argue that a *smaller* contract zone implies the parties have less to argue about, and that therefore smaller zones lead to more rapid voluntary settlements.

---

[3]Farber and Katz, "Interest Arbitration, Outcomes, and the Incentive to Bargain."

14

INEQUALITY IN EARNINGS

Workers as individuals, and society as a whole, are concerned with both the *level* and the *dispersion* of income in the economy. The level of income obviously determines the consumption of goods and services that individuals find it possible to enjoy. Concerns about the distribution of income stem from the importance that we, as individuals, place on our relative standing in society, and the importance that our society as a collective places on equity.

For purposes of assessing issues of poverty and relative consumption opportunities, the distribution of *family incomes* is of interest. An examination of family incomes, however, involves an analysis of unearned as well as earned income; thus, it must incorporate discussions of inheritance, investment returns, welfare transfers, and tax policies. It must also deal with family size and how families are defined, formed, and dissolved. Many of these topics are beyond the scope of a labor economics text.

Consistent with our examination of the labor market, the focus of this chapter is on the distribution of *earnings*. While clearly only part of overall income, earnings are a reflection of marginal productivity, the investment in (and returns to) education, training and migration activities, and the access to opportunities. This chapter begins with a discussion of how to conceptualize and measure the equality or inequality of earnings.

MEASURING INEQUALITY

To understand certain basic concepts related to the distribution of earnings,[1] it is helpful to think in graphic terms. Consider a simple plotting of the number of people receiving each given level of earnings. If everyone had the same earnings, say $20,000 per year, there would be no dispersion. The graph of the earnings distribution would look like Figure 14.1.

If there were disparities in the earnings people received, these disparities could be relatively large or relatively small. If the average level of earnings were $20,000 and virtually all people received earnings very close to the average, the *dispersion* of earnings would be small. If the average were $20,000, but some made much more and some much less, the dispersion of earnings would be large. Figure 14.2 illustrates two hypothetical earnings distributions. While both distributions are centered on the same average level ($20,000), distribution A exhibits smaller dispersion than distribution B. Earnings in B are more widely dispersed and thus exhibit *a greater degree of inequality.*[2]

Graphs can help illustrate the concepts of dispersion, but they are a clumsy tool for *measuring* inequality. Various quantitative indicators of earnings inequality can be devised, and they all vary in ease of computation, ease of comprehension, and how accurately they represent the socially relevant dimensions of inequality.

The most obvious measure of inequality is the *variance* of the distribution. Variance is a common measure of dispersion, calculated as follows:

$$\text{Variance} \ = \ \frac{\sum\limits_{i}(E_i - \overline{E})^2}{n} \tag{14.1}$$

---

[1]Ideally, the focus would be on total compensation, so that the analyses would include employee benefits. As a practical matter, however, data on the *value* of employee benefits are not widely available in a form that permits an examination of their *distribution* either over time or across individuals. Including private pensions with earnings apparently affects measures of inequality only slightly in the United States, except in the union sector (where pensions are more unequally distributed than earnings). See Mary Ellen Benedict and Kathryn Shaw, "The Impact of Pension Benefits on the Distribution of Earned Income," *Industrial and Labor Relations Review* 48, no. 4 (July 1995): 740–757.

[2]A summary of various inequality measures can be found in Frank Levy and Richard J. Murnane, "U.S. Earnings Levels and Earnings Inequality: A Review of Recent Trends and Proposed Explanations," *Journal of Economic Literature* 30 (September 1991): 1333–1381. It is also interesting to inquire whether the distribution of earnings is *symmetric* or not. If a distribution is symmetric, as in Figure 14.2, then as many people earn $X less than average as earn $X more than average. If not, we say it is *skewed*, meaning that one part of the distribution is bunched together and the other part is relatively dispersed. For example, many less-developed countries do not have a sizable middle class. Such countries have a huge number of very poor families and a tiny minority of very wealthy families (the distribution of income is highly skewed to the right).

FIGURE 14.1
Earnings Distribution with Perfect Equality

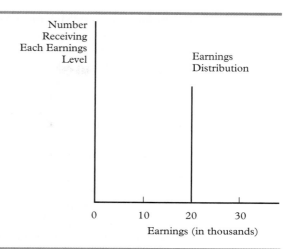

where E_i represents the earnings of person i in the population, n represents the number of people in the population, $\bar{E}$ is the mean level of earnings in the population, and the symbol Σ indicates that we are summing over all persons in the population. One problem with using the variance, however, is that it tends to rise as earnings grow larger. For example, if all earnings in the population were to double, so that the ratio of each person's earnings to the mean (or to the earnings of anyone else, for that matter) remained constant, the variance would still quadruple. Variance is thus a better measure of the absolute than of the *relative* dispersion of earnings.

    An alternative to the variance is the *coefficient of variation:* the square root of the variance (called the *standard deviation*) divided by the mean. If all earnings were

FIGURE 14.2
**Distributions of Earnings
with Different Degrees
of Dispersion**

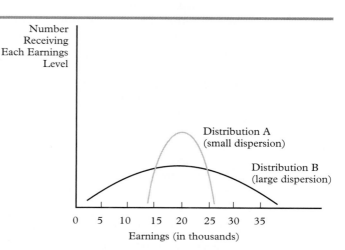

to double, the coefficient of variation, unlike the variance, would remain unchanged. Because we must have access to the underlying data on each individual's earnings to calculate the coefficient of variation, however, it is impractical to construct it from published data. Unless the coefficient of variation is itself *published,* or unless the researcher has access to the *entire* data set, other more readily constructed measures must be found.

The most widely used measures of earnings inequality start with ranking the population by earnings level and establishing into which percentile a given level of earnings falls. For example, in 1999, men over the age of 25 with earnings of $34,850 were at the *median* (50th percentile), meaning that half of all men earned less and half earned more. Men with earnings of $17,153 were at the 20th percentile (20 percent earned less, 80 percent earned more), while those with earnings of $60,585 were at the 80th percentile.

Having determined the earnings levels associated with each percentile, we can either compare the earnings *levels* associated with given percentiles or compare the *share* of total earnings received by each. Comparing shares of total *income* received by the top and bottom fifth (or "quintiles") of families in the population is a widely used measure of *income* inequality. Using this measure we find, for example, that in 1999 households in the top fifth of the income distribution received 49.3 percent of all income, while those in the bottom fifth received 3.7 percent.[3]

Unfortunately, information on *shares* received by each segment of the distribution is not as readily available for individual *earnings* as it is for family income. Comparing the earnings *level* associated with each percentile is readily feasible, however. A commonly used measure of this sort is the ratio of earnings at, say, the 80th percentile to earnings at the 20th. Ratios such as this are intended to indicate how far apart the two ends of the earnings distribution are, and as a measure of dispersion they are easily understood and readily computed.

How useful is it to know that in 1999, for example, men at the 80th percentile of the earnings distribution earned 3.53 times more than men at the 20th? In truth, the ratio in a given year is not very enlightening unless it is *compared* to something. One natural comparison is with ratios for prior years. An increase in these ratios over time, for example, would indicate that the earnings distribution was becoming stretched, so that the distance between the two ends was growing and earnings were becoming more unequally distributed.

As a rough measure of increasing distance between the two ends of the earnings distribution, the ratio of earnings at the 80th and 20th percentiles is satisfactory; however, this simple ratio is by no means a complete description of inequality. Its focus on earnings at two arbitrarily chosen points in the distribution ignores what is happening on either side of the chosen percentiles. For example, if earnings at the 5th percentile fell and those at the 20th percentile rose, while all other earnings remained constant, the above ratio would decline even though the very low-

---

[3]U.S. Bureau of the Census, *Money Income in the United States: 1999,* Series P–60, no. 209 (September 2000). A more sophisticated measure would take into account the shares of income received by each of the five quintiles, and a way to quantify the deviation from strict equality (when the income share of each quintile is 20 percent) is discussed in the appendix to this chapter.

est end of the distribution had moved down. Likewise, if earnings at the 20th and 80th percentiles were to remain the same, but earnings in between were to become much more similar, this step toward greater overall earnings equality would not be captured by the simple 80:20 ratio.

These drawbacks notwithstanding, we present in the next section descriptive data on changes in earnings inequality based on comparisons of earnings *levels* at the 80th and 20th percentiles of the distribution. While crude, these measures indicate that during the decade of the 1980s there was a growing inequality of earnings among both men and women in the United States. The trend slowed for men, and was reversed for women, in the 1990s.

EARNINGS INEQUALITY SINCE 1980: SOME DESCRIPTIVE DATA

Table 14.1 displays, for men and women separately, the recent trends in the ratio of earnings at the 80th percentile to those at the 20th. Among men, earnings inequality grew from 1975 to 1999, with the 80:20 ratio increasing by 37 percent. Interestingly, this growth in inequality took place in the context of generally

TABLE 14.1   The Dispersion of Earnings by Gender, Ages 25 and Over, 1975–1999 (expressed in 1999 dollars)

	Earnings at		
	80th Percentile (a)	20th Percentile (b)	Ratio: (a) ÷ (b)
Men			
1975	$58,655	$22,701	2.58
1980	58,456	20,844	2.80
1985	58,645	18,227	3.22
1990	55,682	16,383	3.40
1999	60,585	17,153	3.53
Women			
1975	30,058	6,819	4.41
1980	30,528	7,518	4.06
1985	34,657	8,175	4.24
1990	34,826	7,578	4.60
1999	38,856	9,194	4.23

Sources: U.S. Bureau of the Census, *Money Incomes of Households, Families, and Persons in the United States,* Series P–60: no. 105 (1975), Table 49; no. 132 (1980), Table 54; no. 156 (1985), Table 38; no. 174 (1990), Table 29; no. 209 (1999), Table 10.

stagnant real earnings at the 80th percentile and significantly falling real earnings at the 20th percentile.[4]

For women, the picture is very different in three ways. First, real earnings generally *rose* at both points in the female earnings distribution throughout the 1980s and 1990s. Second, the 80:20 ratio for women fluctuated modestly from 1975 to 1999. Third, earnings at the 20th percentile are so low that they are unlikely to be received by women who are working full-time (in 1999, 36 percent of women worked less than full time); therefore the 80:20 ratio for women is not a reliable indicator for what has happened to their *wages* at these two points in the earnings distribution. Indeed, once we turn to an analysis of earnings among full-time workers, we will see that similar trends in inequality prevail for both men and women.

Mathematically, earnings inequality could grow in two ways from one year to another. First, inequality could grow by moving people originally in the middle of the distribution to either end. For example, if middle-class jobs were disappearing and being replaced by highly technical jobs at one end of the distribution and by totally unskilled jobs at the other, then the earnings distribution would become more stretched. Second, the earnings of individuals originally at the upper end of the distribution might grow faster (or fall more slowly!) than the earnings of individuals originally in the lower tail. This rise in relative earnings could be caused by increases in relative wages or by relative changes in the hours of work. The different possible dimensions of change from 1975 to 1999 are explored below.

The Occupational Distribution

One possible cause of growing earnings inequality is the destruction of middle-income jobs and their replacement by both higher- and lower-paying occupations. Table 14.2 presents data, for men and women separately, on the occupational distribution in 1983 and again in 1990 and 2000 (unfortunately, changes in occupational definitions occurred in 1983, so earlier data are noncomparable). More specifically, Table 14.2 charts changes in the percentages of all workers who were in the highest-paying and lowest-paying occupational groups over those years. From the table we can see some shrinkage of jobs in the middle of the distribution, but only because of growth at the upper end of the distribution. The share of jobs in the lowest-paying occupations declined slightly during this period.

---

[4]Recall from the discussion of Table 2.2 in chapter 2 that the Consumer Price Index, which we use in Table 14.1 to adjust all earnings figures to 1999 dollars, may overstate inflation by about one percentage point per year. If that is the case, then the real earnings of men at the 80th percentile *grew* (by some 30 percent) over the 24 years from 1975 to 1999, while those for men at the 20th percentile stayed constant. The major point made in Table 14.1, however, is that the 80:20 ratio has grown for men over this period, and it is important to realize that the *ratios* in any given year are not affected by assumptions about inflation (because the same inflationary adjustments are made to both the numerator and the denominator of the ratio).

TABLE 14.2   Changes in the Occupational Distributions of Men and Women, 1983–2000

	Median Weekly Earnings, 1983	Percent of Workforce in Occupation		
		1983	1990	2000
Men				
Highest-Paying Occupations		**24.5**	**25.8**	**29.5**
Executive, managerial, administrative	$530	12.8	13.8	15.6
Professional specialty	$506	11.7	12.0	13.9
Lowest-Paying Occupations		**21.1**	**20.8**	**20.6**
Machine operators, assemblers, inspectors	$319	7.9	7.5	6.7
Handlers, cleaners, helpers, laborers	$251	6.1	6.2	6.3
Service, except private household and protective workers	$217	7.1	7.1	7.6
All Other Occupations		**54.4**	**53.4**	**49.9**
Total		100.0	100.0	100.0
Women				
Highest-Paying Occupations		**21.9**	**26.2**	**32.3**
Executive, managerial, administrative	$339	7.9	11.1	14.6
Professional specialty	$367	14.0	15.1	17.7
Lowest-Paying Occupations		**36.5**	**34.9**	**33.3**
Sales occupations	$204	12.8	13.1	13.1
Machine operators, assemblers, inspectors	$202	7.4	6.0	4.4
Service, except private household and protective workers	$176	16.3	15.8	15.8
All Other Occupations		**41.6**	**38.9**	**34.4**
Total		100.0	100.0	100.0

Sources: U.S. Bureau of Labor Statistics, *Employment and Earnings* 31 (January 1984), Table 21; 38 (January 1991), Table 21; 48 (January 2001) Table 23. Earnings data from U.S. Bureau of the Census, *Statistical Abstract of the United States 1991* (Washington, D.C.: U.S. Government Printing Office, 1991), Table 678.

Among men, executive and professional jobs increased as a percentage of the total, from 24.5 percent in 1983 to 29.5 percent in 2000. The share of jobs in the lowest-paying occupational groups, however, has remained more or less constant at about 21 percent. For women, though, there was a small decline in the share of the lowest-paying occupational groups and a relatively large increase in the share of employment in the highest-paying groups. Among both women and men, then, the growth of higher-paying jobs took place at the expense of jobs in the middle and, to a lesser extent, the lower end of the occupational earnings distribution. Thus, changes in the occupational distribution contributed to growing inequality in the 1980s and 1990s, but these changes do not tell the whole story.

Changes in Relative Wages

A second possible dimension of growing inequality is the increased disparity of earnings among those who remained in high- and low-paying jobs. This disparity could result from either an increase in the disparity of wage rates or an increased disparity in hours worked. We first analyze changes in earnings among *full-time, full-year* workers, because eliminating part-time workers from the data represents a simple way to at least crudely control for hours of work, and it serves the purpose of moving the analysis from earnings to *wage rates*. In the subsection that follows, we look separately at changes in hours worked among full-time workers and at changes in part-time employment.

We know from chapter 9 that, within age groups, those with four or more years of college tend to have the highest wages or salaries. Within educational groups, pay tends to be highest among older workers. Thus, patterns that could be associated with growing inequality are a rising payoff to a college education or a rising payoff to age or experience.

Table 14.3 summarizes some aspects of change in the returns to education and experience from 1975 to 1999. The top panel focuses on the returns to a four-year college education for full-time, year-round workers in mid-career (ages 35–44). The data clearly show, as did slightly different data in chapter 9, that the salaries of college graduates rose relative to those of high school graduates after 1980. Among men, this increase was the product of slowly growing real earnings after 1980 for college graduates and *falling* real earnings for high school graduates. Among women, the real, full-time earnings of four-year college graduates grew substantially from 1980 to 1999, while the earnings of high school graduates remained more or less constant.

The bottom panel of Table 14.3 summarizes changes in the returns to experience among full-time workers. In this panel we display the mean earnings of 45- to 54-year-olds relative to those of 25- to 34-year-olds. While there was some small growth in the returns to experience among women with a high school education, the ratios shown in panel B of Table 14.3 have not risen for men, and for women they have not changed nearly as much as the returns to schooling shown in panel A.

Relative Changes in Hours of Work

Do the changes in relative earnings noted in Table 14.3 really reflect changes in relative *wages* of full-time workers, or might they reflect changes in their *hours* of work? Table 14.4 charts changes from 1983 to 2000 in the hours of work for full-time workers in high-paying occupational groups, usually requiring a college education, and

TABLE 14.3 Returns to Education and Experience among Full-Time, Year-Round Workers, Selected Ages, 1975–1999 (expressed in 1999 dollars)

A. Returns to Education

	Mean Earnings Men, Ages 35–44			Mean Earnings Women, Ages 35–44		
	College Grads (a)	High School Grads (b)	Ratio: (a) ÷ (b) (c)	College Grads (d)	High School Grads (e)	Ratio: (a) ÷ (b) (f)
1975	65,492	43,348	1.51	32,696	24,070	1.36
1980	58,371	41,423	1.41	32,347	23,744	1.36
1985	58,896	40,143	1.47	34,629	24,769	1.40
1990	60,422	36,873	1.64	40,319	25,349	1.59
1999	65,469	37,155	1.76	43,471	24,258	1.79

B. Returns to Experience
(Mean Earnings, Ages 45–54) ÷ (Mean Earnings, Ages 25–34)

	Men		Women	
	College Grads	High School Grads	College Grads	High School Grads
1975	1.54	1.24	1.15	1.06
1980	1.59	1.22	1.10	1.03
1985	1.54	1.30	1.06	1.06
1990	1.43	1.28	1.07	1.17
1999	1.44	1.24	1.15	1.19

Sources: U.S. Bureau of the Census, *Money Income of Households, Families, and Persons in the United States,* Series P–60: no. 105 (1975), Table 48; no. 132 (1980), Table 52; no. 156 (1985), Table 36; no. 174 (1990), Table 30; no. 209 (1999), Table 9.

for those in low-paying, less skilled groups. Hours of work generally rose slightly for all groups shown, with no indication that they rose more markedly for higher-paid than lower-paid workers.[5] Hence, changing work hours among those working full-time do not appear to have been a cause of rising earnings inequality.

While it seems clear that a major cause of growing earnings inequality after 1980 was an increased gap between the wages or salaries of more-educated and

[5]For a recent study of the hours worked by those in high- and low-paid occupations, see Dora Costa, "The Wage and the Length of the Work Day: From the 1890s to 1991," *Journal of Labor Economics* 18, no. 1 (January 2000): 156–181.

TABLE 14.4   Average Weekly Hours of Work by Occupation, for Full-Time, Year-Round Workers, 1983–2000

	1983	1985	1990	2000
Men				
Highest-Paying Occupations				
Executive, managerial, administrative	46.4	47.1	47.5	47.7
Professional specialty	45.2	45.6	46.2	45.8
Lowest-Paying Occupations				
Machine operators, assemblers, inspectors	42.0	42.7	43.0	43.1
Handlers, cleaners, helpers, laborers	41.1	41.5	41.9	41.3
Service, except private household and protective workers	42.1	42.5	42.6	42.3
Women				
Highest-Paying Occupations				
Executive, managerial, administrative	42.4	43.0	43.2	43.3
Professional specialty	41.3	41.6	41.8	42.1
Lowest-Paying Occupations				
Sales occupations	41.5	42.0	42.2	41.8
Machine operators, assemblers, inspectors	40.0	40.3	40.7	40.7
Service, except private household and protective workers	40.6	40.8	41.2	40.7

Source: U.S. Bureau of Labor Statistics, *Employment and Earnings* 31 (January 1984), Table 34; 33 (January 1986), Table 34; 38 (January 1991), Table 34; 48 (January 2001), Table 23.

less-educated workers, another possibility is that lower-paid workers saw their full-time jobs converted to part-time, or that they experienced more spells of unemployment during a given year. In 1983, 60 percent of men with a high school education or less worked full-time, year-round; by 1999, 72 percent did so. Among women with a high school education or less, the percentage working full-time year-round rose from 47 to 56. Thus, the conversion of full-time jobs to part-time or part-year jobs among lower-paid workers was *not* a phenomenon during this period.

Growth of Earnings Dispersion within Human Capital Groups

While one factor in the growing diversity of earnings is the enlarged gap between the average pay of more-educated and less-educated workers, another possibility is that earnings *within* narrowly defined human capital groups became more diverse. If, for example, the distribution of earnings within groups of workers with the same age and education had become more stretched, the overall diversity of

TABLE 14.5   Ratio of Earnings at the 80th to 20th Percentiles for Males, by Age and Education; 1980–1997

	1980	1990	1997
Male College Graduates			
Ages 25–34	2.27	2.49	2.54
35–44	2.47	2.52	2.68
45–54	2.62	2.93	2.75
Male High School Graduates			
Ages 25–34	2.47	2.78	2.73
35–44	2.48	2.85	2.61
45–54	2.45	2.75	2.75

Source: U.S. Bureau of the Census, *Money Incomes of Households, Families, and Persons in the United States*, Series P–60: no. 132 (1980), Table 51; no. 174 (1990), Table 29; tables at http://ferrett.bls.census.gov/macro/031998/perinc/toc.htm.

earnings would have grown. A greater diversity of earnings among 45- to 54-year-old college graduates, for example, could have raised earnings at the 80th percentile, while more diversity among younger workers with a high school degree or less would be likely to have reduced earnings at the 20th percentile.

Perhaps the best way to judge, using published data, whether wages *within* age/education categories grew more unequally through the 1980s and 1990s is to calculate the earnings ratios of those at the 80th to those at the 20th percentiles for each category. Table 14.5 reports on the 80:20 earnings ratios only for homogenously grouped men, because those for women are heavily influenced by the dominance of part-time earnings at the lower end of the earnings distribution. The evidence for men clearly indicates that earnings within age/education groups became more unequal over this period, especially during the 1980s. Thus, as argued above, the growing disparities among older, college-educated workers could have pulled up earnings at the 80th percentile of the *overall* earnings distribution, while wider disparities among younger, less-educated men could have dragged down earnings at the 20th percentile.[6]

Summarizing the Dimensions of Growing Inequality

It can be concluded from our analyses in this section that the most important dimension of the growth in inequality after 1980 was the increased returns to a college education. These increases were observed among both women and men, and they were especially rapid after 1985. For men in midcareer, the increased returns to college

---

[6]One author concludes that growing within-group inequality has played a rather significant role in the rising disparity of earnings overall, and that it has been fueled to a significant degree by rising instability of individuals' earnings over time. See Peter Gottschalk, "Inequality, Income Growth, and Mobility: The Basic Facts," *Journal of Economic Perspectives* 11, no. 2 (Spring 1997): 21–40.

EXAMPLE 14.1

Labor's Share of Total Income: "Raw" Labor vs. Human Capital

The labor force includes everyone from brain surgeons (who must invest highly in training and experience) to tomato pickers, who have little need for any skills beyond the ability to use their eyes, arms and legs. We saw in Chapter 1 that about 70 percent of national income goes to employees, and it is interesting to ask how much of this income is paid to workers because of their raw (untrained) abilities, and how much is paid to them for the human capital that they accumulate through education and experience.

A recent study attempted to answer this question by estimating the amount by which wages rose with each year of schooling and experience. It then used this relationship to predict the wages of a hypothetical worker with no work experience and no formal education. It concluded that from 1959 to 1979, roughly 15 to 17 percent of employee earnings were associated with raw labor—implying, of course, that 83 to 85 percent of employee pay was a return on human capital investments. From 1979 to 1989, however, the payments for raw skill dropped to about 9 percent of total pay, and it had dropped to a bit over 6 percent by 1996. This study, therefore, supports the argument that the returns to human capital rose dramatically in the 1980s and 1990s, with an associated fall in the payments going to completely unskilled labor.

Data from: Alan Krueger, "Measuring Labor's Share," *American Economic Review, Papers and Proceedings* 89 (2), May 1999, pp. 45–51.

were created by the sharply falling real earnings of high school graduates in an environment in which the real earnings of college graduates grew only slowly. For women, however, the returns rose because the real earnings of college graduates grew quickly while those of high school graduates remained more or less constant. Although using a different approach, the study underlying Example 14.1 supports the finding that the relative imporance of human capital grew substantially after 1980.

Two other dimensions of the growth in inequality were identified by our analyses, but their quantitative significance appears to be smaller. First, the disparity of earnings *within* narrowly defined human capital groups generally rose. Second, changes in the occupational distribution among both men and women tended to increase the share of high-paying jobs, and this increase was at the expense of jobs mostly in the middle of the earnings distribution.

THE UNDERLYING CAUSES OF GROWING INEQUALITY

The major phenomenon we must explain is the widening gap between the wages of highly educated and less-educated workers, and our basic economic model suggests three possible causes. First, the *supply* of less-educated workers might have risen faster than the supply of college graduates, driving down the relative wages of less-skilled workers. Second, changes in *institutional* forces, such as the decline

FIGURE 14.3
Changes in Supply as the Dominant Cause of Wage Changes

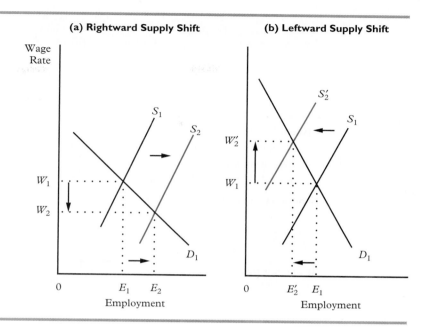

of unionism, might have reduced the wages of less-educated, production workers relative to the more highly educated. Third, the *demand* for more-educated workers might have increased relative to the demand for less-educated workers. We discuss these possibilities below.

Changes in Supply

In reality, shifts in supply and demand curves, and even changes in the influence of institutions, occur both simultaneously and continually. Sophisticated statistical studies can often sort through the possible influences underlying a change and estimate the separate contributions of each. For the most part, however, the details of these studies are beyond the scope of this text; instead, our focus will be on identifying the *dominant* forces behind the growth of wage inequality in recent years.

For the market-clearing wage rate of a particular group of workers to be reduced primarily by a shift in *supply*, that shift must be rightward and therefore accompanied by an increase in employment (see panel a of Figure 14.3 for a graphic illustration). Conversely, if a leftward shift in the supply curve is the dominant cause of a wage increase, this wage increase will be accompanied by a decrease in the market-clearing level of employment (see panel b of Figure 14.3). Other things equal, the larger these shifts are, the larger will be the effects on the equilibrium wage.

TABLE 14.6   Employment Shares (within Gender) of Groups Classified by Their Relative Change in Earnings, 1980 to 1999

	Share of Gender's Total Employment (%)		
	1980	*1990*	*1999*
Groups Whose Relative Earnings Rose			
A. Women with four years of college, all ages	10.2	13.9	20.0
B. Men with four years of college, all ages	11.4	14.0	19.9
C. Female high school graduates, ages 45–54	7.5	7.5	8.2
Groups Whose Relative Earnings Fell			
D. Female high school graduates, all ages	46.4	42.1	33.4
E. Male high school graduates, all ages	38.2	38.1	32.2
F. Female high school graduates, ages 25–34	12.3	11.1	6.7

Source: U.S. Bureau of the Census, *Money Income of Households, Families, and Individuals in the United States,* Series P–60: no. 132 (1980), Table 52; no. 174 (1990), Table 30; no. 209 (1999), Table 9.

The major phenomenon we are trying to explain is the increasing gap between the wages of highly educated and less-educated workers. If *supply* shifts are primarily responsible, we should observe that the employment of less-educated workers *increased* relative to the employment of the college-educated workforce. Table 14.6 contains data indicating that supply shifts could *not* have been the primary cause. It is clear from comparing rows A and B, respectively, with rows D and E of the table, that the groups with the larger wage increases also had larger *increases* in employment over the period! The shares of aggregate employment going to female and male college graduates both rose, while the corresponding shares of employment going to high school graduates both fell. Thus, shifts in supply cannot be the dominant explanation for the growing returns to education.[7]

To say that shifts in supply were not the *dominant* influence underlying the increased returns to education is not to say, of course, that they had no effect at all. We saw in chapter 10 that immigration to the United States rose during the period, and that it was especially heavy among unskilled, less-educated workers—

---

[7]The generally small role played by *supply* shifts in generating recent wage inequality is also found in more sophisticated studies: Lawrence F. Katz and Kevin M. Murphy, "Changes in Relative Wages, 1963–1987: Supply and Demand Factors," *Quarterly Journal of Economics* 107 (February 1992): 35–78; John Bound and George Johnson, "Changes in the Structure of Wages in the 1980s: An Evaluation of Alternative Explanations," *American Economic Review* 82 (June 1992): 371–392; and John Bound and George Johnson, "What Are the Causes of Rising Wage Inequality in the United States?" *Federal Reserve Bank of New York Economic Policy Review* 1, no. 1 (January 1995): 9–17.

the very groups whose relative earnings fell most during that period. One study has estimated that one-third of the decreased relative wages of high school *dropouts* (a group that has done particularly poorly since 1980) was caused by immigration.[8] Because of immigration, then, the percentage of less-skilled workers in the labor force fell less than it would otherwise have fallen, and therefore the supply-related upward pressures on unskilled wages were probably smaller.

The analysis to this point has concentrated on *quantitative* shifts in labor supply. It is also possible that the *quality* of labor supplied changed in such a way that the gap between the wages of college and high school graduates grew in the 1980s and 1990s. We mentioned in chapter 9, for example, that there is a positive relationship between wage levels and performance on tests of cognitive achievement. Did changes in cognitive achievement scores play a major role in the growing wage dispersion after 1980?

For changes in labor quality to have widened the gap between the wages of college and high school graduates after 1980, the scores of high school graduates would have had to *fall* relative to those of college graduates during that period. Studies of this question are few in number, but they suggest that relative changes in labor quality, insofar as we can measure it, did not play a role in the growing disparity of wages, at least through 1990.[9]

Changes in Institutional Forces

We know from chapter 13 that the percentage of the labor force that is unionized fell during the 1980s. This decline was especially pronounced among less-educated workers in the private sector, the very group that had the highest union wage premiums. Thus fewer less-educated workers received the wage premiums union members have historically enjoyed, and correspondingly greater numbers earned lower, nonunion wages. Further, declining union influence also could have led to reduced wage premiums among those workers who remained unionized.

It can be argued, then, that the reduced role of unions in wage determination strengthened the importance of market forces. In the past, when unions took wage determination out of the market to a greater extent than they do now, the returns to education were relatively low in the union sector (it will be recalled from chapter 13 that unions have tended to compress wage differentials across

---

[8]See George J. Borjas, Richard B. Freeman, and Lawrence F. Katz, "On the Labor Market Effects of Immigration and Trade," in *Immigration and the Work Force*, ed. George J. Borjas and Richard B. Freeman (Chicago: University of Chicago Press, 1992), 213–244. For a recent article that does not find that immigration of the unskilled has influenced inequality much, see James J. Heckman, Lance Lochner, and Christopher Taber, "Explaining Rising Wage Inequality: Explorations with a Dynamic General Equilibrium Model of Labor Earnings and Heterogeneous Agents," *Review of Economic Dynamics* 1, no. 1 (January 1998): 1–58.

[9]See John Bishop, "Is the Test Score Decline Responsible for the Productivity Growth Decline?" *American Economic Review* 79 (March 1989): 190.

skill groups). Now that market forces have greater influence in the determination of wages, it is natural to expect that the returns to education should have risen.

There are three a priori reasons to doubt that the decline of labor unions has been a significant causal factor of the increased returns to education after 1980. First, as noted in chapter 13, the declining share of unionized workers in the United States is a phenomenon that started in the 1950s and has continued unabated throughout each decade—even in the 1970s, when the returns to education *fell* (see chapter 9). Second, women are less highly unionized than men (see chapter 13), and yet increases in the returns to education were as large among women as among men, or larger, after 1980. Third, as also noted in chapter 13, the wage premiums obtained by unions for their members actually rose in the early and mid–1980s, suggesting that *within* the union sector, at least, forces toward greater dispersion could not have started much before 1985.

Studies that have empirically investigated the contribution of declining unionization to overall wage inequality have concluded that, for men, perhaps 15 to 20 percent of the rise in inequality since the mid–1970s can be attributed to changes in unionization. The role of unionization in the growing earnings inequality among women, however, appears to have been negligible.[10]

Another institutional factor that has been considered as a possible explanation for the rising returns to education is the declining real level of the minimum wage throughout much of the period, especially the 1980s. The nominal minimum wage rate was held constant at $3.35 from 1981 to 1990, a period during which the average nominal wage in manufacturing, for example, grew. Consequently, the minimum wage fell from 44 percent of the average hourly wage in manufacturing in 1981 to just 33 percent by 1996. While this decline could have reduced the relative wages of very poorly paid workers, it cannot have played a dominant role in the increased earnings gap between college and high school graduates, because few of the latter have earnings near the minimum. The declining value of the real minimum wage, however, has been estimated to have played some role in rising inequality.[11]

Changes in Demand

Because changes in labor supply and institutional forces did not play dominant roles in the growing wage dispersion after 1980, shifts in labor *demand* must have been at the root of growing wage inequality. Recalling our introductory discus-

---

[10]David Card, "The Effect of Unions on Wage Inequality in the U.S. Labor Market," *Industrial and Labor Relations Review* 54, no. 2 (January 2001): 296–315; Nicole M. Fortin and Thomas Lemieux, "Institutional Changes and Rising Wage Inequality: Is There a Linkage?" *Journal of Economic Perspectives* 11, no. 2 (Spring 1997): 75–96; Bound and Johnson, "Changes in the Structure of Wages."

[11]David S. Lee, "Wage Inequality in the United States During the 1980s: Rising Dispersion or Falling Minimum Wage?" *Quarterly Journal of Economics* 114, no. 3 (August 1999): 977–1023.

sions of labor demand in chapters 3 and 4, the demand for labor is a function of both *product* demand (which affects the *scale* of production) and decisions about the cost-minimizing *mix of capital and various kinds of labor* used to produce the profit-maximizing level of output.

Product Demand   Over time, the demand for products produced in the United States shifts as incomes or preferences change, and as relative product prices increase or decrease. Moreover, developments in the international economy, from reductions in trade barriers to products newly produced abroad, also affect domestic demand. If the increased demand for college-trained workers relative to high school graduates were the result mainly of shifts in product demand, we would expect to observe a faster expansion of employment in industries that are heavily dependent on a highly educated workforce. The result would be an increased share of total employment among those industries that use the largest number of highly educated workers.

As shown in Table 14.7 (panel A), there were notable shifts in the distribution of employment across industries in the 1980s and 1990s. The largest gains came in the private service sector, especially in such business services as advertising, computer and data processing, accounting, management consulting, and temporary-help agencies. The largest relative declines were in manufacturing, where

---

TABLE 14.7   **The Distribution of Employment across Industries, 1983–2000**

A. Percentages of Employment in Major Industries

	1983	1990	2000
Manufacturing	19.8%	18.0%	14.7%
Trade (wholesale, retail)	21.0	20.6	20.6
Private services (business, health, personal, recreational, and social services)	21.6	25.3	27.8
Government	15.4	15.0	14.1
Others	22.2	21.1	22.8

B. Percentages of Employment by Selected Occupation, Major Industries

	Managerial, Professional			Operators, Laborers, Service Workers		
	1983	1990	2000	1983	1990	2000
Manufacturing	17.7%	20.5%	24.8%	43.5%	42.1%	39.4%
Trade	9.8	10.5	11.6	31.7	31.3	32.1
Private services (except household) and government	41.0	42.5	48.3	26.9	25.8	23.4

Source: U.S. Bureau of Labor Statistics, *Employment and Earnings* 38 (January 1991), Tables, 23, 28; 31 (January 1984), Tables 25, 28; 48 (January 2001), Tables 12, 17, 18.

the rising gap between imports and exports during the 1980s was most felt. The share of employment in both government and retail and wholesale trade fell slightly. Were these shifts a dominant force in changing the relative demand for highly educated workers?

Panel B of Table 14.7 suggests that the biggest loser of employment, manufacturing, uses relatively few highly educated workers (managers and professionals) and relatively more workers in jobs requiring less education. In contrast, the service sector, which grew the most, uses more highly educated workers and fewer less-educated ones. We might think, then, that shifts in employment *across* industries played a dominant role in causing the earnings gap between more-educated and less-educated workers to grow after 1980.

Most studies of product demand shifts and wage inequality have concentrated on the effects of international trade. As restrictions on such trade were liberalized, imports as a fraction of all purchases in the United States rose from 7 percent in 1980 to 15 percent in 1999.[12] The most rapid growth of imports was in durable manufactured goods, which are produced in the United States with the very workers whose relative earnings dropped most dramatically: less-educated men. The findings among economists who have analyzed the effects of trade on inequality are not unanimous, but the predominant conclusion is that the contributions of international trade to the changes in wage inequality after 1980 were rather small.[13]

Changing the Mix of Productive Factors   A change in the mix of productive factors, perhaps by substituting highly educated labor for less-educated labor, will be manifest primarily in *intra*-industry changes in the distribution of employment across occupations. Table 14.7, panel B, contains some data pertinent to these intra-industry changes. Comparing the distribution of high- and low-education jobs within each industry in 1983 and 2000 indicates that, *within* each major industry displayed, the number of managers and professionals grew relative to those in jobs requiring less education. These intra-industry percentage-point gains for highly educated workers, and the losses among those with less education, translate to large changes in the *numbers* demanded because they are applied to a base that equals *total* employment in each industry. (In contrast, the percentage changes in the cross-industry mix of employment highlighted in panel A imply smaller numerical changes in demand for skilled and

---

[12]U.S. President, *Economic Report of the President* (Washington, D.C.: U.S. Government Printing Office, 2001), Table B–2.

[13]A comprehensive review of various studies, by both labor economists and international trade specialists, is found in Gary Burtless, "International Trade and the Rise in Earnings Inequality," *Journal of Economic Literature* 33, no. 2 (June 1995): 800–816. Similiar findings are contained in David H. Autor, Lawrence F. Katz, and Alan B. Krueger, "Computing Inequality: Have Computers Changed the Labor Market?" *Quarterly Journal of Economics* 113, no. 4 (November 1998): 1169–1213; Eli Berman, John Bound, and Stephen Machin, "Implications of Skill-Biased Technological Change: International Evidence," *Quarterly Journal of Economics* 113, no. 4 (November 1998): 1245–1279; and George E. Johnson, "Changes in Earnings Inequality: The Role of Demand Shifts," *Journal of Economic Perspectives* 11, no. 2 (Spring 1997): 41–54.

unskilled workers because they are applied to a base that equals only the *change* in each industry's employment.[14])

The most plausible explanation for demand-side increases in the returns to education after 1980 is technological change. It has been widely observed that the introduction of new technology increased dramatically in the 1980s, as firms sought to become more competitive by adopting the use of advanced computers, robots, more-flexible manufacturing systems, and new office technologies. Conventional technological improvements, such as larger or faster machines, were adopted at a slower pace, with the result that in manufacturing, for example, the new, high-tech capital rose from 9.5 percent of the total capital stock in 1976 to 25.7 percent in 1986.[15] The percentage of all workers who used computers in their jobs, to take another example, rose from 25 to 37 percent from 1984 to 1989, and to 47 percent by 1993.[16]

As noted in chapter 4, technological change is equivalent to a decrease in the price of capital, and the effects on the demand for labor depend on the relative size of scale and substitution effects. If a category of labor is a complement in production with the capital whose price has been reduced, or if it is a substitute in production but a *gross* complement, then technological change will increase the demand for labor. If the category of labor is a gross substitute with capital, however, then technological change will reduce the demand for labor.

There are several reasons to suspect that the spread of high-tech capital, especially computers, played a key role in the changing demand for more-educated and less-educated workers in the 1980s and 1990s. First, it can be hypothesized that the relative demand for highly educated workers increases during periods of rapid technological innovation, because (as we argued in chapter 9) those who invest

---

[14]To take a simple example, assume C = managerial/professional employment and that we want to explain the changes in this variable from 1983 to 1990; that is, we want to calculate $C_{90} - C_{83}$ in a certain industry. If E = total employment in the industry and k = the percentage of the total constituted by managers and professionals, then

$$C_{90} - C_{83} = E_{90}(k_{90}) - E_{83}(k_{83})$$

If $E_{90}(k_{83})$ is subtracted from the first term on the right-hand side and added to the second, the equation becomes

$$C_{90} - C_{83} = E_{90}(k_{90} - k_{83}) + k_{83}(E_{90} - E_{83})$$

Note that in the first expression on the right-hand side of the equation, the *intra*-industry changes in k are applied to total employment. Changes in C caused by growth or decline in the industry (the second expression) are based only on *changes* in employment; these latter changes form the basis for *inter*-industry effects. See Autor, Katz, and Krueger, "Computing Inequality: Have Computers Changed the Labor Market?" and Berman, Bound, and Machin, "Implications of Skill-Biased Technological Change: International Evidence," for articles concluding that the relative demand for skilled workers has shifted more *within* industries than *between* them. For a somewhat different view of growing wage inequality within industries, see the entire issue of *Industrial and Labor Relations Review* 54, no. 2A (March 2001).

[15]Ernst R. Berndt and Catherine J. Morrison, "High-Tech Capital Formation and Economic Performance in U.S. Manufacturing Industries: An Exploratory Analysis," *Journal of Econometrics* 65, no. 1 (January 1995): 9–43.

[16]Autor, Katz, and Kreuger, "Computing Inequality: Have Computers Changed the Labor Market?" Table 4.

in education tend to be those who have the greatest comparative advantage at learning. Rapid change requires rapid learning, and it can be argued that the better-educated are more adaptable.

Second, we know from chapter 4 that, in general, capital and skilled labor tend to be gross complements, while capital and less-skilled labor are more likely to be gross substitutes. If these general patterns apply specifically to high-tech capital, then the falling price of such capital, and its consequent spread, would have shifted the demand curve for skilled labor to the right and the demand curve for less-skilled labor to the left.

Third, it has been estimated that those industries with the largest increases in high-tech capital were those with both the highest proportions of college-educated workers and the largest shifts away from the use of less-educated production workers. Indeed, computer usage in 1993 was greater for the college-educated (70 percent) than for high school graduates (35 percent), and it was greater for women (53 percent) than men (41 percent).[17] One study, in fact, concludes that the greatest declines in the wages of less-educated men took place in regions that experienced the largest increases in the labor force participation rates of highly skilled women.[18]

Finally, it has been estimated that workers who used computers on their jobs in 1993 received some 20 percent more in wages than they otherwise would have received, a larger differential than in 1984.[19] Thus, it appears that the widespread adoption of high-tech capital, especially the personal computer, increased the demand for highly educated workers relative to those with less education.

Growth in Supply of Educated Workers While a rightward shift in the demand for highly educated workers, which was associated with technological change, appears to have been a powerful force underlying growing inequality, this rightward shift could only have raised relative wages if shifts in supply failed to keep pace. As will be recalled from chapter 9, during the 1970s, when rates of return to college educations were low, there was a decline in the proportion of male high school graduates going to college. This decline slowed the growth of college graduates in the overall labor force during the 1980s, and even as the rate of return later rose rapidly, the supply response was relatively modest (the proportion of males enrolling in college actually fell a bit from 1985 to 1990 before rising in the 1990s). Had the *supply* response to the increased demand for highly educated workers been larger, their wage growth would have been slower.[20]

---

[17]Autor, Katz, and Krueger, "Computing Inequality: Have Computers Changed the Labor Market?"
[18]Robert H. Topel, "Regional Trends in Wage Inequality," *American Economic Review* 84, no. 2 (May 1994): 17–22. For a study finding that computer usage accounts for much of the increased substitution of high-skilled women for low-skilled men, see Bruce A. Weinberg, "Computer Use and the Demand for Female Workers," *Industrial and Labor Relations Review* 53, no. 2 (January 2000): 290–308.
[19]Autor, Katz, and Krueger, "Computing Inequality: Have Computers Changed the Labor Market?"
[20]For a discussion of the supply response to increases in the returns to human capital investments, see David Card, "Can Falling Supply Explain the Rising Return to College for Younger Men? A Cohort-Based Analysis," *Quarterly Journal of Eocnomics* 116, no. 2 (May 2001): 705–746; Chinhui Juhn, "Wage Inequality and Demand for Skill: Evidence from Five Decades," *Industrial and Labor Relations Review* 52, no. 3 (April 1999): 424–443; and Robert H. Topel, "Factor Proportions and Relative Wages: The Supply-Side Determinants of Wage Inequality," *Journal of Economic Perspectives* 11, no. 2 (Spring 1997): 55–74.

EXAMPLE 14.2

Changes in the Premium to Education at the Beginning of the Twentieth Century

While the premium to education has recently risen and is currently relatively high, the premium appears to have been even higher at the beginning of the twentieth century. However, the premium did not stay high for too long because, despite increasing demand for educated workers, the *supply* increased at an even more rapid clip. In 1914, office workers, whose positions generally required a high school diploma, earned considerably more than less-educated manual workers. Female office workers earned 107 percent more than female production workers, while male office workers earned 70 percent more than male production workers. This premium fell rapidly during World War I and the early 1920s, so that by 1923, the high school premium was only 41 percent for females and merely 10 percent for males. These rates drifted just a little higher during the remainder of the 1920s and 1930s.

What makes these dramatically falling premiums for a high school degree so surprising is that changes in the economy were increasing the relative demand for these workers. New office machines (such as improved typewriters, adding machines, address machines, dictaphones, and mimeo machines) lowered the cost of information technology and increased the demand for a complementary factor of production: high school–educated office workers. In the two decades after 1910, office employment's share of total employment in the United States rose by 47 percent.

Counteracting this demand shift, however, was an even more substantial shift in the supply of high school graduates, as high schools opened up to the masses throughout much of the country. Between 1910 and 1920, for example, high school enrollment rates climbed from 25 to 43 percent in New England and from 29 to 60 percent in the Pacific region. The internal combustion engine, paved roads, and consolidated school districts brought secondary education to rural areas for the first time during the 1920s. Within cities, schools moved away from offering only college preparatory courses and attracted more students. From 1910 to 1930, the share of the labor force made up of high school graduates increased by almost 130 percent.

Thus, relative growth in the demand for more-educated workers was similar in the early and late decades of the twentieth century, but changes in the premiums for education diverged. As emphasized throughout this text, demand *and* supply are important in understanding wages!

Data from: Claudia Goldin and Lawrence F. Katz, "The Decline of Non-Competing Groups: Changes in the Premium to Education, 1890–1940," NBER working paper, no. 5202, August 1995.

We do not fully understand why the growth in the supply of college-educated workers was so slow in the United States, but it is an important part of the explanation of why inequality grew so much in the face of technological change. Indeed, in the early 1900s, important changes in office technology also increased the relative demand for better-educated workers, but during that period wage premiums for those with more education actually *fell* (see Example 14.2).

Technological Change and Within-Group Dispersion   The increased disparity of earnings *within* narrowly defined age/education groups possibly could be attributed to the adoption of new technology as well. It could be argued, for example, that rapid technological change, when combined with product demand shifts, has created a greater than normal number of new job opportunities, on the one hand, and job loss on the other. Those in each human capital group lucky enough to obtain jobs in expanding sectors did well, while those unfortunate enough to have lost jobs did poorly, with the result that disparities between the "lucky" and the "unlucky" grew.

An alternative explanation that could tie growing within-group disparities to the new technology focuses on the willingness of workers to adapt to change. It might be argued that, within human capital groups, some workers are more adaptable and ready for new challenges than others. The adaptable ones profit most during periods of change, while the less adaptable fall behind.

INTERNATIONAL COMPARISONS OF CHANGING INEQUALITY

In the previous section, we analyzed the changes over *time* in the extent of wage inequality within the United States. It is also instructive to analyze these changes using a different point of reference: the experience of *other developed countries* during the same time period. After briefly describing trends in wage inequality elsewhere, we will analyze the contributions of demand, supply, and institutional forces toward explaining the different trends across countries.

We begin our international comparisons with Table 14.8, which compares the wages of full-time workers at the 90th and 10th percentiles across several countries for which comparable data are available (unlike those in Table 14.1, the data contained in Table 14.8 are only for full-time workers). As can be seen from the table, Canada and the United States have relatively high *levels* of wage inequality compared to the other advanced economies. Regardless of the level of such inequality, however, all but one of the countries shown exhibited *increases* in inequality during the 1980s.

The greatest increases in wage inequality throughout the 1980s were in the United Kingdom and the United States; the British 90:10 ratio grew slightly over 30 percent for both men and women, while the American ratios for men and women grew by 19 and 36 percent, respectively. Taking into account increases in the 90:10 ratios for both men and women, increases in the other countries were less than half as large. Thus, one question that arises is why inequality grew so much faster in Great Britain and the United States than elsewhere during the decade.

Another development is that, as we have seen, growing earnings disparities in the United States took place in the context of *stagnant* or *falling real wages* for male workers. For American men, growing inequality arose from the fact that earnings near the bottom of the distribution fell sharply (the same was true for Canadian men, although the rates of decline were somewhat smaller).[21] For American women, and more generally for workers in the comparison countries outside of North America, increased inequality was accompanied by at least modest real wage

---

[21]David Card and Richard B. Freeman, *Small Differences That Matter: Labor Markets and Income Maintenance in Canada and the United States* (Chicago: University of Chicago Press, 1993), 49.

TABLE 14.8   International Comparisons of Wage Inequality, Full-Time Workers, 1979 and 1990

| | Ratio of Wages at 90th Percentile to Those at 10th | | | | | |
| | Men | | | Women | | |
Country	1979	1990	Percentage Increase in 90:10 Ratio	1979	1990	Percentage Increase in 90:10 Ratio
United Kingdom	2.41	3.19	32	2.32	3.03	31
United States	3.42	4.06	19	2.61	3.56	36
Canada	3.49	3.97	14	3.74	3.97	6
Australia	1.99	2.22	12	1.75	1.95	12
Japan	2.59	2.83	9	2.20	2.34	6
Austria	2.64	2.75	4	3.35	3.53	5
France	3.29	3.42	4	2.61	2.77	6
Netherlands	2.75	2.75	0	na	na	na
Sweden	2.16	2.16	0	1.70	1.82	7

Source: Richard B. Freeman and Lawrence F. Katz, "Introduction and Summary," *Differences and Changes in Wage Structures,* ed. Richard Freeman and Lawrence Katz (Chicago: University of Chicago Press, 1995), 13.

growth at the bottom of the earnings distribution. This latter pattern was especially evident in Great Britain, where men at the 10th percentile saw their real wages increase by some 12 percent from 1979 to 1989 (as compared to a 12 percent decrease for American men).[22] Thus, a second question that needs to be addressed concerns the causes and the consequences of falling real wages for less-educated American men as compared to generally rising real wages elsewhere.

Why Did Inequality Grow Most in Great Britain and the United States?

We have seen that most economists who have studied the growth of inequality in the United States attribute it to what might be called *skill-biased technological change*—that is, technological change that increased the demand for skilled workers relative to that for less-skilled ones. The shifts in labor demand curves that resulted from this technological change were not accompanied by supply-curve

[22]Lawrence F. Katz, Gary W. Loveman, and David G. Blanchflower, "A Comparison of Changes in the Structure of Wages in Four OECD Countries," in *Differences and Changes in Wage Structures,* ed. Richard B. Freeman and Lawrence F. Katz (Chicago: University of Chicago Press, 1995), 30–31.

shifts of equal magnitude in the United States; therefore, in an environment in which institutions did little to inhibit wage changes, the wages of skilled workers rose relative to those for unskilled workers.

Because the comparison countries have similar standards of living, and access to labor and capital of similar quality, it is quite likely that skill-biased technological change occurred in all these countries.[23] It is also quite likely that these countries were also affected in roughly similar ways by international trade and the growing production of manufacturing durables elsewhere. Hence, unless the pace of change was slower in continental Europe for some reason, it is unlikely that differences on the *demand* side of the labor market account for the different growth rates of earnings disparities across these countries.

In the presense of skill-biased technological change, the countries with smaller (or zero) increases in the returns to human capital investments must have experienced either (or both) of two phenomena. They must have had either relatively *large increases in the supply of highly skilled workers,* or very *strong institutional forces* that served to prop up the wages of the unskilled in the face of reduced demand.

Increases in the Supply of Skills   For reasons that have not yet been thoroughly analyzed, increases in the supply of college-educated workers were smaller in the United States during the 1980s than elsewhere. Further, growth rates of the highly educated were smaller in the countries (such as Great Britain and Japan) that experienced rising returns to education than in the countries (such as France) that did not.[24] Thus, it appears that the rates at which the supply of college-educated workers increased in the various countries affected the returns to educational investments observed in each.

Institutional Forces   We noted in chapter 13 that unions tend to raise the wages of less-skilled workers relative to those of skilled workers, and that the United States is far less unionized than other developed countries. It is not surprising, then, that the *level* of American wage inequality is higher than elsewhere.[25] We are seeking to understand *changes* in wage inequality, however, so we must therefore look for changes (or the lack of them) in the power of unions to affect the structure of wages within other countries.

---

[23]Berman, Bound, and Machin, "Implications of Skill-Biased Technological Change: International Evidence."
[24]Peter Gottschalk and Timothy M. Smeeding, "Cross National Comparisons of Earnings and Income Inequality," *Journal of Economic Literature* 35, no. 2 (June 1997): 633–687; and Katz, Loveman, and Blanchflower, "A Comparison of Changes in the Structure of Wages in Four OECD Countries." Katz, Loveman, and Blanchflower also point out that less-educated workers in the United States are less trained (and perhaps less trainable) than in many other developed countries; thus, when the demand for their services fell, they were less likely than workers elsewhere to move up into higher-skilled jobs.
[25]For an analysis of inequality and unionization in Canada and the United States, see Thomas Lemieux, "Unions and Wage Inequality in Canada and the United States," in *Small Differences That Matter,* ed. Card and Freeman. In addition, see Francine D. Blau and Lawrence M. Kahn, "International Differences in Male Wage Inequality: Institutions versus Market Forces," *Journal of Political Economy* 104, no. 4 (August 1996): 791–837.

In some countries, such as Canada, unionization rates were not much changed throughout the 1980s.[26] In others, such as France, union membership fell sharply during the decade, but in France collective bargaining takes place at the industry level and the provisions bargained by unions are often extended to nonunion workers by the government (which also maintained a rather high minimum wage during this period).[27] Thus, declining unionization in France was not associated with real wage declines for low-skilled workers.

In Great Britain and the United States, union membership *declined* in the context of bargaining structures that were relatively *decentralized* to begin with. That is, collective bargaining in these two countries was most significant at the firm and plant levels, where market forces are apt to be felt most keenly (product and labor demand curves are likely to be most elastic at the level of the firm). Further, in both countries, bargaining tended to become *more* decentralized throughout the decade.[28] Some analysts conclude that the twin phenomena of declining union membership and growing decentralization of collective bargaining contributed to the larger growth of inequality in Great Britain and the United States than elsewhere.[29] As the rates of unionization declined, and as collective bargaining agreements became increasingly responsive to market forces, unions in the United States and Britain lost some of their power to narrow the wage gap between skilled and less-skilled workers.

Causes and Effects of Different Real Wage Changes among the Unskilled

We should reiterate from the discussion immediately above that the effects of unions in a given country are a function of both the level of their membership and the centralization of the country's wage-determination process. Bargaining is tending to decentralize in many countries, a move that is probably a response to the dramatic technological changes taking place. It can be argued that in environments of rapid change, local conditions are likely to vary widely, so centralized bargainers are especially ill informed about appropriate wage settlements (or the consequences of inappropriate ones). Thus, when the very rapid advances of high-technology capital were evident in the 1980s, many countries moved to decentralize their bargaining, at least to some degree.[30]

---

[26]W. Craig Riddell, "Unionization in Canada and the United States: A Tale of Two Countries," in *Small Differences That Matter*, ed. Card and Freeman, 110.

[27]Katz, Loveman, and Blanchflower, "A Comparison of Changes in the Structure of Wages in Four OECD Countries," 54.

[28]Harry C. Katz, "The Decentralization of Collective Bargaining: A Literature Review and Comparative Analysis," *Industrial and Labor Relations Review* 47, no. 1 (October 1993): 3–22.

[29]Freeman and Katz, "Introduction and Summary" in *Differences and Changes in Wage Structures*, 18–19; and Gottschalk and Smeeding, "Cross-National Comparisons of Earnings and Income Inequality."

[30]Richard B. Freeman and Robert S. Gibbons, "Getting Together and Breaking Apart: The Decline of Centralized Collective Bargaining," in *Differences and Changes in Wage Structures*, 345–370; and Katz, "The Decentralization of Collective Bargaining."

Despite this market response of collective bargaining in most advanced economies, the power of *institutions* to affect the wage structure is much stronger in European countries than in North America. European levels of unionization are relatively high, and beyond that, many European governments tend to be quite active in the wage-setting process. The result is that, when faced with similar technological changes and product market forces (for example, the decline of manufacturing), European institutions tended to ensure that the real wages of relatively unskilled workers did not fall. In Great Britain, for example, where wage inequality grew rapidly, "wage councils" set industry-wide minimum wages up through the early 1990s. While the councils were weakened in the 1980s, which contributed to growing inequality, the real wages of unskilled workers were not allowed to fall as they did in the United States and Canada.[31]

Using the experience of the United States (which has the most market-dominated wage-determination process) as a point of reference, changes on the demand side of the labor market were apparently putting strong downward pressures on the market equilibrium wages of the unskilled. Unless the unskilled could be quickly trained for more-skilled jobs, the failure of their real wages to fall in Europe suggests that we will observe sharp increases in their unemployment rates. This is precisely what we do observe. In Great Britain, for example, the unemployment rate among college graduates rose by 3.1 percentage points from 1979–1987, while among the least-educated workers it rose by 14 percentage points. The least-skilled were also increasingly over-represented among those unemployed for more than one year.[32]

In France and Germany, the decade of the 1980s also witnessed huge increases in unemployment among the least-skilled members of the workforce. As we noted at the end of chapter 2, the unemployment rate among the lowest-paid workers in France jumped by some 6 percentage points in the decade, while in Germany it increased by over 9 percentage points. These increases were large relative to the 1.3 and 3 percentage-point increases (respectively) in American and Canadian unskilled unemployment rates; they were also large compared to the *overall* increases in France and Germany. In Australia, where the overall ratio of employment to the population was somewhat higher in 1990 than in 1980, the ratio among the least-skilled males fell by 14 percent.[33]

It is apparently the case, then, that in countries in which the real wages of unskilled workers did not fall after 1980, unemployment among the unskilled

---

[31]John Schmitt, "The Changing Structure of Male Earnings in Britain, 1974–1988," in *Differences and Changes in Wage Structures,* 203; and Stephen Machin and Alan Manning, "The Effects of Minimum Wages on Wage Dispersion and Employment: Evidence from the U.K. Wage Councils," *Industrial and Labor Relations Review* 47, no. 2 (January 1994): 319–329. In 1992, when the wage councils were abolished, the United Kingdom became the only European Community country without a minimum wage system.

[32]Schmitt, "The Changing Structure of Male Earnings in Britain," 188–190.

[33]Robert G. Gregory and Francis Vella, "Real Wages, Employment, and Wage Dispersion in U.S. and Australian Labor Markets," in *Differences and Changes in Wage Structures*, 210, 218.

rose most precipitously. In other words, where the wages of unskilled workers did not fall, substitution and scale effects worked in the direction of reducing their employment rather sharply.[34]

_____

[34]See Blau and Kahn, "International Differences in Male Wage Inequality: Institutions versus Market Forces."

REVIEW QUESTIONS

1. Analyze how increasing the investment tax credit given to firms that make expenditures on new capital affects the dispersion of earnings. (For a review of relevant concepts, see chapter 4.)

2. Assume that the "comparable worth" remedy for wage discrimination against women will require governmental and large private employers to increase the wages they pay to women in female-dominated jobs. The remedy will not apply to small firms. Given what you learned earlier about wages by firm size and in female-dominated jobs, analyze the effects of comparable worth on earnings inequality among women. (For a review of relevant concepts, see chapter 12.)

3. One of organized labor's primary objectives is legislation forbidding employers to replace workers who are on strike. If such legislation passes, what will be its effects on earnings inequality? (For a review of relevant concepts, see chapter 13.)

4. Proposals to tax health and other employee benefits, which are not now subject to the income tax, have been made in recent years. Assuming that more highly paid workers have higher employee benefits, analyze the effects on earnings inequality if these tax proposals are adopted. (For a review of relevant concepts, see chapter 8.)

5. "The labor supply responses to programs designed to help equalize _incomes_ can either narrow or widen the dispersion of _earnings_." Comment on this statement in the context of an increase in the subsidy paid under a "negative income tax" program to those who do not work. Assume that this program creates an effective wage that is greater than zero but less than the market wage, and assume that this effective wage is unchanged by the increased subsidy to those who do not work. (For a review of relevant concepts, see chapter 6.)

6. Discuss the role of geographic mobility in decreasing or increasing the dispersion of earnings. (For a review of the relevant concepts, see chapter 10.)

7. Suppose a country's government is concerned about growing inequality of incomes and wants to undertake a program that will increase the total earnings of the unskilled. It is considering two alternative changes to its current payroll tax, which is levied on employers as a percentage of the first $50,000 of employee earnings:

   a. Extending employer payroll taxes to all earnings over $50,000 per year, and increasing the cost of capital by eliminating certain tax deductions related to plant and equipment;

   b. Reducing to zero employer payroll taxes on the first $20,000 of earnings but taxing employers on all employee earnings between $20,000 and $50,000 (there would be no taxes on earnings above $50,000).

   Analyze proposal a and proposal b separately (one, but not both, will be adopted). Which is more likely to accomplish the aim of increasing the earnings of the unskilled? Why?

PROBLEMS

1. (Appendix). Ten college seniors have accepted job offers for the year after they graduate. Their starting salaries are given below. Organize the data into quintiles and then, using these data, draw the Lorenz curve for this group. Finally, calculate the relevant Gini coefficient.

Becky	$42,000
Billy Bob	$20,000
Charlie	$31,000
Kasia	$24,000
Nina	$34,000
Raul	$37,000
Rose	$29,000
Thomas	$35,000
Willis	$60,000
Yukiko	$32,000

2. Suppose that the wage distribution for a small town is given below.

Sector	Number of Workers	Wage
A	50	$10 per hour
B	25	$5 per hour
C	25	$5 per hour

Assume a minimum wage law is passed that doesn't affect the market in high-wage sector A but boosts wages to $7 per hour in sector B, the covered sector, while reducing employment to 20. Displaced workers in sector B move into the uncovered sector, C, where wages fall to $4.50 per hour as employment grows to 30. Has wage inequality risen or fallen? Explain.

SELECTED READINGS

Bound, John, and George Johnson. "Changes in the Structure of Wages in the 1980s: An Evaluation of Alternative Explanations." *American Economic Review* 82 (June 1992): 371–392.

Burtless, Gary, ed. *A Future of Lousy Jobs? The Changing Structure of U.S. Wages.* Washington, D.C.: Brookings Institution, 1990.

Freeman, Richard B., and Lawrence F. Katz, eds. *Differences and Changes in Wage Structures.* Chicago: University of Chicago Press, 1995.

Katz, Lawrence F., and Kevin M. Murphy. "Changes in Relative Wages, 1963–1987: Supply and Demand Factors." *Quarterly Journal of Economics* 107 (February 1992): 35–78.

Levy, Frank, and Richard J. Murnane. "U.S. Earnings Levels and Earnings Inequality: A Review of Recent Trends and Proposed Explanations." *Journal of Economic Literature* 30 (September 1992): 1333–1381.

Lorenz Curves and Gini Coefficients

The most commonly used measures of distributional inequality involve grouping the distribution into deciles or quintiles and comparing the earnings (or income) received by each. As we did in the main body of this chapter, we can compare the earnings levels at points high in the distribution (the 80th percentile, say) with points at the low end (the 20th percentile, for example). A richer and more fully descriptive measure, however, employs data on the *share* of total earnings or income received by those in each group.

Suppose that each household in the population has the same income. In this case of perfect equality, each fifth of the population receives a fifth of the total income. In graphic terms, this equality can be shown by the straight line *AB* in Figure 14A.1, which plots the cumulative share of income (vertical axis) received by each quintile and the ones below it (horizontal axis). Thus, the first quintile (with a 0.2 share, or 20 percent of all households) would receive a 0.2 share (20 percent) of total income, the first and second quintiles (four-tenths of the population) would receive four-tenths of total income, and so forth.

If the distribution of income is not perfectly equal, then the curve connecting the cumulative percentages of income received by the cumulated quintiles—the *Lorenz curve*—is convex and lies below the line of perfect equality. For example, in 1992 the lowest fifth of U.S. households received 3.8 percent of total income, the second fifth received 9.4 percent, the third fifth 15.8 percent, the next fifth 24.2 percent, and the highest fifth 46.9 percent. Plotting the cumulative data in Figure 14A.1 yields Lorenz curve *ACDEFB*. This curve displays the convexity we would expect from the clearly unequal distribution of household income in the United States.

Comparing the equality of two different income distributions results in unambiguous conclusions if one Lorenz curve lies completely inside the other (closer to the line of perfect equality). If, for example, we were interested in comparing the American income distributions of 1980 and 1992, we could observe that plotting the 1980 data results in a Lorenz curve, *AcdefB* in Figure 14A.1, that lies everywhere closer to the line of perfect equality than the one for 1992.

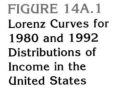

FIGURE 14A.1

Lorenz Curves for 1980 and 1992 Distributions of Income in the United States

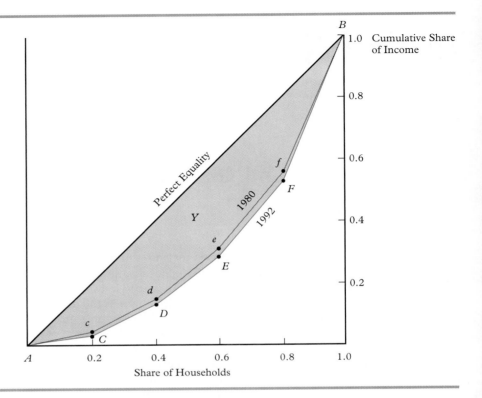

If two Lorenz curves cross, however, conclusions about which one represents greater equality are not possible. Comparing curves *A* and *B* in Figure 14A.2, for example, we can see that the distribution represented by *A* has a lower proportion of total income received by the poorest quintile than does the distribution represented by curve *B*; however, the cumulative share of income received by the lowest two quintiles (taken together) is equal for *A* and *B*, and the cumulative proportions received by the bottom three and bottom four quintiles are higher for *A* than for *B*.

Another measure of inequality, which seems at first glance to yield unambiguous answers when various distributions are compared, is the *Gini coefficient*: the ratio of the area between the Lorenz curve and the line of perfect equality (for 1992, the area labeled *Y* in Figure 14A.1) to the total area under the line of perfect equality. Obviously, with perfect equality the Gini coefficient would equal zero.

One way to calculate the Gini coefficient is to split the area under the Lorenz curve into a series of triangles and rectangles, as shown in Figure 14A.3 (which repeats the Lorenz curve for 1992 shown in Figure 14A.1). Each triangle has a base equal to 0.2—the horizontal distance for each of the five quintiles—and a height equal to the percentage of income received by that quintile (the cumulative percentage less the percentages received by lower quintiles).

FIGURE 14A.2
Lorenz Curves
That Cross

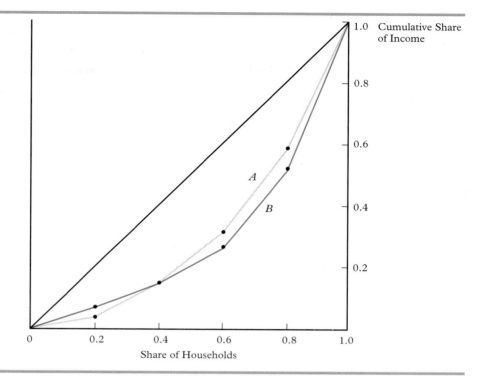

Because the base of each triangle is the same and their heights sum to unity, the *sum* of the areas of each triangle is always equal to $0.5 \times 0.2 \times 1.0 = 0.1$ (one-half base times height).

The rectangles in Figure 14A.3 all have one side equal to 0.2 and another equal to the cumulated percentages of total income received by the previous quintiles. Rectangle $Q_1CC'Q_2$, for example, has an area of $0.2 \times 0.038 = 0.0076$, while $Q_2DD'Q_3$ has an area of $0.2 \times 0.132 = 0.0264$. Analogously, $Q_3EE'Q_4$ has an area of 0.0580 and $Q_4FF'Q_5$ an area of 0.1064; together, all four rectangles in Figure 14A.3 have an area that sums to 0.1984.

The area under the Lorenz curve in Figure 14A.3 is thus $0.1984 + 0.1 = 0.2984$. Given that the total area under the line of perfect equality is $0.5 \times 1 \times 1 = 0.5$, the Gini coefficient for 1992 is calculated as follows:

$$\text{Gini coefficient (1992)} = \frac{0.5 - 0.2984}{0.5} = 0.4032 \qquad (14A.1)$$

For comparison purposes, the Gini coefficient for the income distribution in 1980 can be calculated as 0.3768—which, because it lies closer to zero than the Gini coefficient for 1992, is evidence of greater equality in 1980.

FIGURE 14A.3
Calculating the Gini
Coefficient for the
1992 Distribution of
Household Income

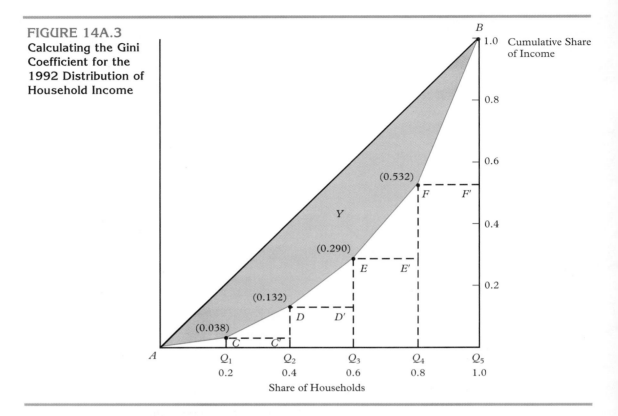

Unfortunately, the Gini coefficient will become smaller when the rich give up some of their income to the middle class as well as when they give up income in favor of the poor. Thus, the Gini coefficient may yield a "definitive" answer about comparative equality when none is warranted. As we saw in the case of Figure 14A.2, in which the Lorenz curves being compared cross, judging the relative equality of two distributions is not always susceptible of an unambiguous answer.

To this point in the appendix, we have analyzed the Lorenz curve and Gini coefficient in terms of *household income,* for the simple reason that published data permit these calculations. The underlying data on the *shares* of individual *earnings* are not published, but the Gini coefficients associated with earnings distributions were published on a comparable basis from 1967 to 1992. The Gini coefficients for the *earnings* distributions of both men and women who worked full-time year-round were relatively stagnant in the 1970s, but rose roughly 15 percent in the 1980s.[1]

_____

[1]U.S. Bureau of the Census, *The Changing Shape of the Nation's Income Distribution, 1947–1998,* P–60, no. 204 (June 2000), pp. 2–3.

15

UNEMPLOYMENT

A s noted in chapter 2, the population can be divided into those people who are in the labor force (L) and those who are not (N). The labor force consists of those people who are employed (E) and those who are unemployed but would like to be employed (U). The concept of unemployment is somewhat ambiguous, since in theory virtually anyone would be willing to be employed in return for a generous enough compensation package. Economists tend to resolve this dilemma by defining unemployment in terms of an individual's willingness to be employed at some prevailing market wage. Government statistics take a more pragmatic approach, defining the unemployed as those who are on temporary layoff waiting to be recalled by their previous employer or those without a job who have actively searched for work in the previous month (of course, "actively" is not precisely defined).

Given these definitions, the unemployment rate (u) is measured as the ratio of the number of the unemployed to the number in the labor force:

$$\mathbf{u} = \frac{U}{L} \tag{15.1}$$

Much attention is focused on how the national unemployment rate varies over time and how unemployment rates vary across geographic areas and age/race/gender/ethnic groups.

It is important, however, to understand the limitations of unemployment rate data. They *do* reflect the proportion of a group that, at a point in time, actively want to work but are not employed. For a number of reasons, however, they *do not* necessarily provide an accurate reflection of the economic hardship that members of a group are suffering. First, individuals who are not actively searching for work, including those who searched unsuccessfully and then gave up, are not counted among the unemployed (see chapter 7). Second, unemployment statistics tell us nothing about the earnings levels of those who are employed, including whether these exceed the poverty level. Third, a substantial fraction of the unemployed come from families in which other earners are present—for example, many unemployed are teenagers—and the unemployed often are not the primary source of their family's support. Fourth, a substantial fraction of the unemployed receive some income support while they are unemployed, in the form of either government unemployment compensation payments or private supplementary unemployment benefits.

Finally, while unemployment rate data give us information on the fraction of the *labor force* that are not working, they tell us little about the fraction of the *population* that are *employed*. Table 15.1 contains U.S. data on the aggregate unemployment rate, the labor force participation rate, and the *employment rate*—the last being defined as employment divided by the adult population—for 2000 and for two pairs of earlier years over which roughly equal changes in the unemployment rate were experienced. From 1948 to 1958, for example, the unemployment rate rose from 3.8 to 6.8 percent, and the employment rate fell from 56.6 to 55.4 percent. In contrast, from 1968 to 1991, the unemployment rate rose by a similar magnitude, but the employment rate *rose* substantially! The reason for the opposite correlations between the unemployment

TABLE 15.1   Civilian Labor Force Participation, Employment, and Unemployment Rates in the United States (in percentages)

Year	Unemployment Rate (U/L)	Labor Force Participation Rate (L/POP)	Employment Rate (E/POP)
1948	3.8	58.8	56.6
1958	6.8	59.5	55.4
1968	3.6	59.6	57.5
1991	6.7	66.0	61.6
2000	4.0	67.2	64.5

U = number of people unemployed.
L = number of people in the labor force.
E = number of people employed.
POP = total population over age 16.

Source: U.S. Department of Labor, *Employment and Earnings* 48, no. 1 (January 2001), Table 1.

and the employment rates for these two periods is that in the earlier period labor force participation grew only slowly, while in the latter period it was growing very rapidly.

Nonetheless, the unemployment rate remains a useful indicator of labor market conditions. This chapter will be concerned with the causes of unemployment and with how various government policies affect, in an either intended or unintended manner, the level of unemployment.

A STOCK-FLOW MODEL OF THE LABOR MARKET

We begin with a simple conceptual model of a labor market that emphasizes the importance of considering the *flows* between labor market states (for example, the *movement* of people from employed to unemployed status) as well as the *number* of people in each labor market state (for example, the *number* of the unemployed). Knowledge of the determinants of these flows is crucial to any understanding of the causes of unemployment.

Data on the number of people who are employed, unemployed, and not in the labor force are provided each month from the national Current Population Survey (CPS). As Figure 15.1 indicates, in May 1993 (when the overall unemployment rate averaged 6.9 percent) there were 119.2 million employed, 8.9 million unemployed, and 65.2 million adults age 16 and over not in the labor force. The impression we get when tracing these data over short periods of time is that of relative stability; for example, it is highly unusual for the unemployment rate to change by more than a few tenths of a percentage point from one month to the next.

Taking month-to-month snapshots of the number of people who are employed, unemployed, or out of the labor market misses a considerable amount of movement into and out of these categories *during* the month. Figure 15.1 contains data on the

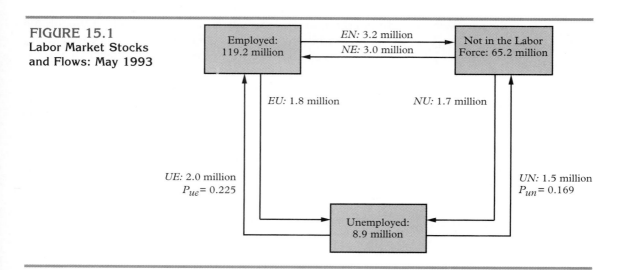

FIGURE 15.1
Labor Market Stocks and Flows: May 1993

flows of workers between the various categories during the one-month period April to May 1993, when the total number of workers unemployed was the same at the end as it was at the beginning. During this month, approximately 2.0 million unemployed individuals found employment (the flow denoted by UE in Figure 15.1), and 1.5 million of the unemployed dropped out of the labor force (the flow denoted by UN). These numbers represent the proportions 0.225 (P_{ue}) and 0.169 (P_{un}) of the stock of the unemployed, respectively; thus, we can conclude that approximately 40 percent of the individuals who were unemployed at the beginning of that month left unemployment by the next month. These individuals were replaced in the pool of unemployed by equivalent flows of individuals into unemployment from the stocks of employed individuals (the flow EU) and those not in the labor force (the flow NU).[1] The flow EU consists of individuals who voluntarily left or involuntarily lost their last job, while the flow NU consists of people entering the labor force. The fact that the flows *into* unemployment equaled the flows *out of* unemployment meant that the number of unemployed workers remained constant from April to May.

Sources of Unemployment

When we think of the unemployed, the image of an individual laid off from his or her previous job often springs to mind. However, the view that such individuals constitute all, or even most, of the unemployed is incorrect. Table 15.2 provides some data that bear on this point for years between 1970 and 2000, during which the unemployment rate varied between 4.0 and 9.7 percent. Only in the relatively high unemployment years, such as 1982, were more than half of the unemployed job losers. In each year, more than one-third of the unemployed came from out-of-labor-force status—that is, they were individuals who were either entering the labor force for the first time (*new entrants*) or individuals who had some previous employment experience and were reentering the labor force after a period of time out of the labor force (*reentrants*). Some of these reentrants, of course, will be job losers who dropped out of the labor force for a time. Finally, although the vast majority of individuals who quit their jobs obtain new jobs prior to quitting and never pass through unemployment status, in most years at least 10 percent of the unemployed were voluntary job leavers.

Among those who lose their jobs, the duration and the consequences of unemployment depend on whether the layoff is temporary or permanent. Of the 0.6 per-

---

[1]Joseph A. Ritter, "Measuring Labor Market Dynamics: Gross Flows of Workers and Jobs," *Review, Federal Reserve Bank of St. Louis* 75 (November/December 1993): 39–57. From the perspective of actual measurement, those who are classified as "unemployed" are distinguished from those considered "out of the labor force" only by self-reported information on job search. Thus, the empirical distinction between the two categories, as well as errors in recording movements between them, have attracted the attention of researchers. For an analysis of the former issue, see Füsun Gönsül, "New Evidence on Whether Unemployment and Out of the Labor Force Are Distinct States," *Journal of Human Resources* 27, no. 2 (Spring 1992): 329–361. On the latter topic, see Paul Flaim and Carma Hogue, "Measuring Labor Force Flows: A Special Conference Examines the Problems," *Monthly Labor Review* (July 1985): 7–15.

TABLE 15.2   **Sources of Unemployment, United States, Various Years**

Year	Unemployment Rate	Percent of Unemployed Who Were:			
		Job Losers	Job Leavers	Reentrants	New Entrants
1970	4.9	44.3	13.4	30.0	12.3
1974	5.6	43.5	14.9	28.4	13.2
1978	6.1	41.6	14.1	30.0	14.3
1982	9.7	58.7	7.9	22.3	11.1
1986	6.9	48.9	12.3	26.2	12.5
1990	5.5	48.3	14.8	27.4	9.5
1994	6.1	47.7	9.4	34.8	7.6
2000	4.0	44.1	13.7	34.6	7.6

Source: U.S. Department of Labor, *1982 Employment and Training Report of the President* (Washington, D.C.: U.S. Government Printing Office, 1982), Table A–36; U.S. Department of Labor, *Monthly Labor Review,* various issues.

cent of American workers who were laid off in the average month during the 1990s, a bit less than half were laid off temporarily and returned relatively quickly to their jobs (usually within three to six weeks). Those who were permanently discharged—whether for cause or because of plant closure or "downsizing"—were unemployed for over twice as long. Further, when they returned to work it was typically at a much lower pay level.[2] Unfortunately, layoffs in the 1990s were less likely to be temporary than in earlier decades, reflecting the permanent adjustments required by a business environment that was becoming increasingly competitive.

Rates of Flow Affect Unemployment Levels

Although ultimately public concern focuses on the level of unemployment, to understand the determinants of this level we must analyze the flows of individuals between the various labor market states. A group's unemployment rate might be high because its members have difficulty finding jobs once unemployed, because they have difficulty (for voluntary or involuntary reasons) remaining employed once a job is found, or because they frequently enter and leave the labor force.

---

[2]See Hoyt Bleakley, Ann E. Ferris, and Jeffrey C. Fuhrer, "New Data on Worker Flows During Business Cycles," *New England Economic Review* (July-August 1999): 49–76. For more on the subject of permanent displacement, see Bruce C. Fallick, "A Review of the Recent Empirical Literature on Displaced Workers," *Industrial and Labor Relations Review* 50, no. 1 (October 1996): 5–16; Kenneth A. Couch, "Earnings Losses and Unemployment of Displaced Workers in Germany," *Industrial and Labor Relations Review* 54, no. 3 (April 2001): 550–572; and Lori G. Kletzer, "Job Displacement," *Journal of Economic Perspectives* 12, no. 1 (Winter 1998): 115–136.

The appropriate policy prescription to reduce the unemployment rate will depend upon which one of these labor market flows is responsible for the high rate.

Somewhat more formally, we can show that if labor markets are roughly in balance, with the flows into and out of unemployment equal, the unemployment rate (**u**) for a group depends upon the various labor market flows in the following manner:

$$\mathbf{u} = F(\overset{+}{P}_{en}, \overset{-}{P}_{ne}, \overset{-}{P}_{un}, \overset{+}{P}_{nu}, \overset{+}{P}_{eu}, \overset{-}{P}_{ue}) \tag{15.2}$$

In this equation,

F means "a function of"
P_{en} = fraction of employed who leave the labor force
P_{ne} = fraction of those not in the labor force who enter the labor force and find employment
P_{un} = fraction of unemployed who leave the labor force
P_{nu} = fraction of those not in the labor force who enter the labor force and become unemployed
P_{eu} = fraction of employed who become unemployed
P_{ue} = fraction of unemployed who become employed

So, for example, if there were initially 100 employed individuals in a group and 15 of them became unemployed during a period, P_{eu} would equal 0.15.

A plus sign over a variable in equation (15.2) means that an increase in that variable will increase the unemployment rate, while a minus sign means that an increase in the variable will decrease the unemployment rate. The equation thus asserts that, other things equal, increases in the proportions of individuals who voluntarily or involuntarily leave their jobs and become unemployed (P_{eu}) or leave the labor force (P_{en}) will increase a group's unemployment rate, as will an increase in the proportion of the group that enters the labor force without first having a job lined up (P_{nu}). Similarly, the greater the proportion of individuals who leave unemployment status, either to become employed (P_{ue}) or to leave the labor force (P_{un}), the lower a group's unemployment rate will be. Finally, the greater the proportion of individuals who enter the labor force and immediately find jobs (P_{ne}), the lower a group's unemployment rate will be.[3]

Equation (15.2) and Figure 15.1 make clear that social concern over any given level of unemployment should focus on both the incidence of unemployment (on the fraction of people in a group who become unemployed) and the duration of

---

[3]The specific functional form for equation (15.2) is found in Stephen T. Marston, "Employment Instability and High Unemployment Rates," *Brookings Papers on Economic Activity* 1976–1, 169–203. An intuitive understanding of why each of the results summarized in equation (15.2) holds can be obtained from the definition of the unemployment rate in equation (15.1). A movement from one labor market state to another may affect the numerator or the denominator, or both. For example, an increase in P_{en} does not affect the number of unemployed individuals directly, but it does reduce the size of the labor force. According to equation (15.1), this reduction leads to an increase in the unemployment rate.

spells of unemployment. Society is probably more concerned if small groups of individuals are unemployed for long periods of time than if many individuals rapidly pass through unemployment status. Until recently, it was widely believed that the bulk of measured unemployment could be attributed to the fact that many people were experiencing short spells of unemployment. However, evidence suggests that, while many people do flow quickly through the unemployed state, prolonged spells of unemployment for a relatively small number of individuals characterize those found in the *stock* of the unemployed at any given time.

The various theories of unemployment discussed in the following sections all essentially relate to the determination of one or more of the flows represented in equation (15.2). That is, they provide explanations of why the proportions of individuals who move between the various labor market states vary over time or across geographic areas, including countries. The types of unemployment we examine are frictional, structural, demand-deficient (cyclical), and seasonal.

FRICTIONAL UNEMPLOYMENT

Suppose a competitive labor market is in equilibrium in the sense that, at the prevailing market wage, the quantity of labor demanded just equals the quantity of labor supplied. Figure 15.2 shows such a labor market, in which the demand curve is D_0, the supply curve is S_0, employment is E_0, and the wage rate is W_0. Thus far the text has treated this equilibrium situation as one of full employment and has implied that there is no unemployment associated with it. However, this implication is not completely correct. Even in a market-equilibrium or full-employment situation there will still be some *frictional unemployment,* because some people will be between jobs.

FIGURE 15.2
A Market with Full Employment Initially

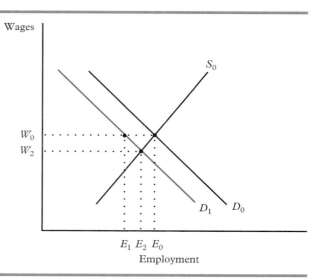

Frictional unemployment arises because labor markets are inherently dynamic, because information flows are imperfect, and because it takes time for unemployed workers and employers with job vacancies to find each other. Even if the size of the labor force is constant, in each period there will be new entrants to the labor market searching for employment while other employed or unemployed individuals are leaving the labor force. Some people will quit their jobs to search for other employment (see chapter 10).[4] Moreover, random fluctuations in demand across firms will cause some firms to close or lay off workers at the same time that other firms are opening or expanding employment. Because information about the characteristics of those searching for work and the nature of the jobs opening up cannot instantly be known or evaluated, it takes time for job matches to be made between unemployed workers and potential employers. Hence, even when, in the aggregate, the demand for labor equals the supply, frictional unemployment will still exist.

The Theory of Job Search

The level of frictional unemployment in an economy is determined by the flows of individuals into and out of the labor market and the speed with which unemployed individuals find (and accept) jobs. The factors that determine this speed are captured in an analysis of the job search process, to which we now turn.

A Model of Job Search   Workers who want employment must search for job offers, and because information about job opportunities and workers' characteristics is imperfect, it will take time and effort for matches to be made between unemployed workers and potential employers. Other things equal, the lower the probability that unemployed workers will become employed in a period (that is, the lower P_{ue} is), the higher will be their expected duration of unemployment and the higher will be the unemployment rate. To understand what can affect P_{ue}, we develop a formal model of job search, based on the key assumption that wages are associated with the characteristics of jobs, not with the characteristics of the specific individuals who fill them.[5]

Suppose that employers differ in the set of minimum hiring standards they use. Hiring standards may include educational requirements, job training, work experience, performance on hiring tests, etc. A very simple model of the hiring process assumes that this set of attributes can be summarized in a single variable, K, which denotes the minimum skill level a job requires. Associated with each job

---

[4]For an analysis of the relative advantages of searching for work while employed and while unemployed, see Christian Belzil, "Relative Efficiencies and Comparative Advantages of Job Search," *Journal of Labor Economics* 14, no. 1 (January 1996): 154–173.

[5]Our discussion here draws heavily on Dale T. Mortensen, "Job Search, the Duration of Unemployment, and the Phillips Curve," *American Economic Review* 60 (December 1970): 846–862. Also see Theresa Devine and Nicholas Kiefer, *Empirical Labor Economics: The Search Approach* (New York: Oxford University Press, 1990).

is a wage, $W(K)$—a wage that is assumed to be a function of the required skill level and not of the particular characteristics of the people hired. We also assume that the wage rate is an increasing function of the minimum required skill level and that two employers using the same standard will offer the same wage.

Because different employers have different hiring standards, our simple model implies that there will be a distribution of wage offers associated with job vacancies in the labor market. This distribution of wage offers is denoted by $f(W)$ in Figure 15.3. As we move to the right in the figure, the minimum skill level and offered wage on a job increase. Since $f(W)$ represents a probability distribution of wage offers, the area under the curve sums to 1 (that is, the distribution contains 100 percent of all wage offers in the market). Each wage offer (on the horizontal axis) is shown in relation to that offer's share in the distribution (on the vertical axis).

Now suppose a given unemployed individual has skill level K^*. Since no firm will hire a worker who does not meet its hiring standards, the maximum wage this individual could hope to receive is $W^*(K^*)$. An individual who knew which firms had a hiring standard of K^* would apply to those firms and, since the individual meets their hiring standards, would be hired at a wage of W^*.

Suppose, instead, that job market information is imperfect in the sense that, while an applicant knows the shape of the distribution of wage offers, $f(W)$, he or she does *not* know what each particular firm's wage offer or hiring standard will be. We can then conceptualize job search as a process in which the person randomly visits firms' employment offices. If the firm's hiring standard exceeds K^*, the person is rejected for the job, but if the hiring standard is K^* or less, the person is offered the job. While the individual might find it advantageous to accumulate a number of job offers and then accept the best, job seekers—especially those at the lower end of the skill ladder—are not always allowed such a luxury. Rather, they must instantly decide whether to accept a job offer, because otherwise the offer will be extended to a different applicant.

FIGURE 15.3
Choice of Reservation Wage in a Model of Job Search

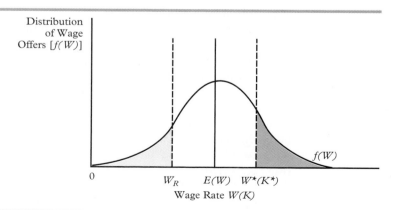

The Reservation Wage   How does an unemployed worker know whether to accept a particular job offer? One strategy is to decide on a *reservation wage* and then to accept only those offers above this level. The critical question then is, "How is this reservation wage determined?"

To answer this question, suppose W_R is the reservation wage chosen (in Figure 15.3) by a person who has skill level K^*. Now observe that this individual's job application will be rejected by any firm that offers a wage higher than $W^*(K^*)$; the person will not meet its minimum hiring standards. Similarly, the person will reject any job offers that call for a wage less than W_R. Hence, the probability that he or she will find an acceptable job in any period is simply the unshaded area under the curve between W_R and W^*. The higher this probability, the lower the expected duration of unemployment. Given that the person finds a job, his or her *expected* wage is simply the weighted average of the job offers in the W_R to W^* range. This average (or expected) wage is denoted by $E(W)$ in Figure 15.3.

If the individual were to choose a slightly higher reservation wage, his or her choice would have two effects. On the one hand, since the person would now reject more low-wage jobs, his or her expected wage (once employed) would increase. On the other hand, rejecting more job offers also decreases the probability of finding an acceptable job in any given period, thus increasing the expected duration of unemployment. Each unemployed individual will choose his or her reservation wage so that, at the margin, the expected costs of longer spells of unemployment just equal the expected benefits of higher post-unemployment wages.

Implications of the Model   This simple model and associated decision rule lead to a number of implications. First, as long as the reservation wage is not set equal to the lowest wage offered in the market, the probability of finding a job will be less than 1, and hence some *search unemployment* can be expected to result. *Search unemployment* occurs when an individual does not necessarily accept the first job that is offered—a rational strategy in a world of imperfect information.

Second, since the reservation wage will always be chosen to be less than the wage commensurate with the individual's skill level, $W^*(K^*)$, virtually all individuals will be *underemployed* once they find a job (in the sense that their expected earnings will be less than W^*). This underemployment is a cost of imperfect information; better labor market information would improve the job-matching process.

Third, otherwise identical individuals will wind up receiving different wages. Two unemployed individuals with the same skill level could choose the same reservation wage and have the same *expected* post-unemployment wage. However, the wages they actually wind up with will depend upon pure luck—the wage offer between W_R and W^* they happen to find. In a world of imperfect information, then, no economic model can explain all the variation in wages across individuals.

Fourth, anything that causes unemployed workers to intensify their job search (to knock on more doors per day) will reduce the duration of unemployment, other things equal. More efficient collection/dissemination of information on both jobs and applicants can increase the speed of the search process for all parties in the market; enhanced computerization among employment agencies is one example of an innovation that could reduce unemployment. You will recall from chapter 7, however, that even unemployed workers have alternative uses for their time (they can spend it in "household production"). Thus, the intensity of job search is also influenced by the value of their time in household production and the payoffs to job search that they expect; if the value of the former is high and the expected payoffs to the latter are low, unemployed workers may become discouraged and quit searching altogether—in which case they are counted as being "out of the labor force."

Finally, if the cost to an individual of being unemployed were to fall, the person should be led to increase his or her reservation wage (that is, the person would become more choosy about the offers deemed to be acceptable). A higher reservation wage, of course, would increase both the expected duration of unemployment and the expected post-unemployment wage rate. One important influence on the cost of being unemployed, and hence on the reservation wages of unemployed workers, is the presence and generosity of governmental unemployment insurance (UI) programs.

Effects of Unemployment Insurance Benefits

Virtually every advanced economy offers its workers who have lost jobs some form of unemployment compensation, although these systems vary widely in their structure and generosity.[6] In the United States, the unemployment insurance system is actually composed of individual state systems. Although the details of the individual systems differ, we can easily sketch the broad outlines of how they operate.

When U.S. workers become unemployed, their eligibility for unemployment insurance benefits is based on their previous labor market experience and reason for unemployment. With respect to their experience, each state requires unemployed individuals to demonstrate "permanent" attachment to the labor force, by meeting minimum earnings or weeks-worked tests during some base period, before they can be eligible for UI benefits. In all states, covered workers who are *laid off* and meet these labor market experience tests are eligible for UI benefits. In some states, workers who voluntarily quit their jobs are eligible for benefits in certain circumstances. Finally, new entrants or reentrants to the labor force and workers fired for cause are, in general, ineligible for benefits.

After a waiting period, which is one week in most states, an eligible worker can begin to collect UI benefits. The structure of benefits is illustrated in Figure 15.4, where it can be seen that benefits are related to an individual's previous earnings level. As shown in panel (a), all eligible unemployed workers are

---

[6]Organisation for Economic Co-operation and Development, *Employment Outlook, July 1996* (Paris: OECD, 1996), 28–43, contains a description and comparison of unemployment insurance programs in various countries. A description of the characteristics of the American UI system is found in *Highlights of State Unemployment Compensation Laws* (Washington, D.C.: National Foundation for Unemployment Compensation and Workers' Compensation, 2001).

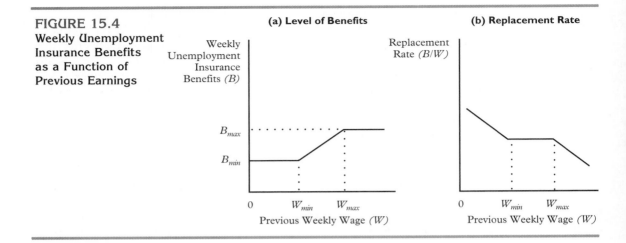

FIGURE 15.4
Weekly Unemployment Insurance Benefits as a Function of Previous Earnings

entitled to at least a minimum benefit level, B_{min}. After previous earnings rise above a critical level (W_{min}), benefits increase proportionately with earnings up to a maximum earnings level (W_{max}), past which benefits remain constant at B_{max}. A few states also have dependents' allowances for unemployed workers, although in some of these states the dependents' allowance cannot increase an individual's weekly UI benefits above B_{max}.

An implication of such a benefit structure is that the ratio of an individual's UI benefits to previous earnings varies according to his or her past earnings (see panel b). This ratio is often called the *replacement rate*, the fraction of previous earnings that the UI benefits replace. Over the range between W_{min} and W_{max}, where the replacement rate is constant, most states aim to replace around 50 percent of an unemployed worker's previous earnings.

Once UI benefits begin, an unemployed individual's eligibility for continued benefits depends on his or her making continual "suitable efforts" to find employment; the definition of suitable efforts varies widely across states. In addition, there is a maximum duration of receipt of benefits that is of fixed length in some states (usually 26 weeks) and varies in other states with a worker's prior labor market experience (workers with "more permanent attachment" being eligible for more weeks of benefits). Congress has also passed legislation that allows states where the unemployment rate is high to extend the length of time unemployed workers can receive benefits; the typical extension is 13 weeks.

Do Generous Benefits Increase Unemployment?   Our theory of job search outlined above leads to the expectation that, by reducing the costs associated with being unemployed, more generous UI benefits should cause an increase in the reservation wages of unemployed workers. Increased reservation wages will tend to reduce P_{ue} and P_{un}, which will lengthen the duration of unemployment. Longer durations, in turn, will increase the unemployment rate if other things remain

EXAMPLE 15.1

The Unemployment Insurance Bonus Experiment

Between mid–1984 and mid–1985 the state of Illinois conducted a *claimant bonus* experiment to test whether providing cash bonuses to unemployment insurance (UI) recipients who found a new job "quickly" would be an effective way to reduce their durations of unemployment without adversely affecting their post-unemployment wages. The idea was that the promise of a cash bonus for rapid reemployment would cause UI recipients to increase the fraction of time they spent searching for new employment and that they would thus find acceptable jobs more quickly.

UI recipients in the experiment were randomly assigned to two groups. The first served as a control group and received regular UI benefits. Members of the second group were promised an additional cash bonus of $500 if they found a full-time job within eleven weeks and held that job for at least four months. Given that individuals were randomly assigned to the two groups, one would expect the two groups to exhibit, on average, roughly equivalent durations of unemployment and post-unemployment wages in the absence of any "bonus effect."

It turned out that people eligible for the bonus experienced one less week of unemployment, on average, than did members of the control group. Further, their post-unemployment wages were about the same as those among the control group. Thus, it appeared that offering the cash bonus to UI recipients achieved its goal.

Data from: Bruce D. Meyer, "Lessons from the U.S. Unemployment Insurance Experiments," *Journal of Economic Literature* 33, no. 1 (March 1995): 91–131

---

equal. (One way to shorten durations is to offer workers a bonus if they accept offers more quickly; see Example 15.1.)

Because the generosity of UI benefits varies widely across states, numerous studies have sought to empirically test the hypothesis that more-generous benefits serve to raise the unemployment rate beyond what it would otherwise be. Evidence from these studies suggests that higher UI replacement rates are indeed associated with longer durations of unemployment for recipients. Estimates differ, of course, on how responsive durations actually are to changes in the replacement rate, but one study estimated that if the United States had ended its UI program in 1976, the average duration of unemployment that year would have fallen from 4.3 to 2.8 months.[7] It is more realistic, of course, to consider how responsive durations are to more-modest changes in UI benefits, and most estimates imply that a 10 percentage-point increase in the replacement rate would increase the length of unemployment spells by about one week.[8] Studies of the

---

[7]James M. Poterba and Lawrence H. Summers, "Unemployment Benefits and Labor Market Transitions: A Multinomial Logit Model with Errors in Classification," *Review of Economics and Statistics* 77, no. 2 (May 1995): 207–216.

[8]Anthony B. Atkinson and John Micklewright, "Unemployment Compensation and Labor Market Transitions: A Critical Review," *Journal of Economic Literature* 29 (December 1991): 1679–1727, and Gary Burtless, "Unemployment Insurance and Labor Supply: A Survey," in *Unemployment Insurance: The Second Half-Century*, ed. W. Lee Hansen and James Byers (Madison: University of Wisconsin Press, 1990), provide surveys of these studies.

effects of unemployment compensation in other countries also support the hypothesis that more-generous UI benefits tend to increase the unemployment rate.[9]

Effects of Benefit Eligibility   Aside from benefit levels, the mere *eligibility* of workers for unemployment compensation benefits has also been found to influence workers' job-search behavior. In the United States, for example, there is a huge jump in the probability of a worker taking a job during the week his or her eligibility for UI benefits ends.[10] Further evidence concerning the eligibility for UI benefits is seen in an analysis of the differences between the unemployment rate in Canada and the United States. In 1981, an unemployed Canadian worker was 3 times more likely to qualify for UI benefits than was an unemployed worker in the United States, and by the end of the 1980s unemployed Canadians were 3.5 times more likely to be receiving benefits. Accompanying that change was a rise in the Canadian unemployment rate relative to that in the United States; in fact, one study concluded that the majority of the widening gap in unemployment between Canada and the United States was probably caused by differential eligibility for UI benefits.[11]

Do More Generous Benefits Improve Job Matches?   Referring back to our theory of job search, the increased reservation wage accompanying more-generous UI benefits will tend to increase the duration of unemployment spells, but it should also raise the expected post-unemployment wage. Indeed, one purpose of unemployment compensation is precisely to permit workers to search for a suitable match. Unfortunately, there is only weak evidence that more generous UI benefits do raise the quality of the subsequent job match.[12]

STRUCTURAL UNEMPLOYMENT

Structural unemployment arises when there is a mismatch between the skills demanded and supplied in a given area or an imbalance between the supplies of and demands for workers across areas. *If* wages were completely flexible *and* if costs

---

[9]Jennifer Hunt, "The Effects of Unemployment Compensation on Unemployment Duration in Germany," *Journal of Labor Economics* 13, no. 1 (January 1995): 88–120; and Kenneth Carling, Bertil Holmlund, and Altin Vejsiu, "Do Benefit Cuts Boost Job Finding? Swedish Evidence from the 1990s," *Economic Journal* 111, no. 474 (October 2001): 766–790.

[10]Lawrence Katz and Bruce Meyer, "Unemployment Insurance, Recall Expectations and Unemployment Outcomes," *Quarterly Journal of Economics* 105, no. 4 (November 1990): 993–1002. Orley Ashenfelter, David Ashmore, and Olivier Deschenes, "Do Unemployment Insurance Recipients Actively Seek Work? Randomized Trials in Four U.S. States," working paper no. 412, Industrial Relations Section, Princeton University, Dec. 1998, reports findings that unemployment insurance recipients *do* search for work while receiving benefits; thus, taking a job just as benefits are about to end may be mostly a function of reducing one's reservation wage at that time.

[11]David Card and W. Craig Riddell, "Unemployment in Canada and the United States: A Further Analysis," in *Trade, Technology and Economics: Essays in Honour of Richard G. Lipsey,* ed. B. Curtis Eaton and Richard G. Harris (Cheltenham, U.K.: Edward Elgar Publishers, 1997).

[12]Christian Belzil, "Unemployment Insurance and Subsequent Job Duration: Job Matching versus Unobserved Heterogeneity," *Journal of Applied Econometrics* 16, no. 5 (September–October 2001): 619–636.

of occupational or geographic mobility were low, market adjustments would quickly eliminate this type of unemployment. In practice, however, these conditions may fail to hold, and structural unemployment may result.

Occupational and Regional Unemployment Rate Differences

A two-sector labor market model, represented by Figure 15.5, can be used to illustrate how structural unemployment can arise. For the moment, we shall assume the sectors refer to markets for occupational classes of workers; later we shall assume that they are two geographically separate labor markets.

Occupational Imbalances   Suppose that market A is the market for production workers in the automobile industry and market B is the market for skilled computer specialists, and suppose that initially both markets are in equilibrium. Given the demand and supply curves in both markets, (D_{0A}, S_{0A}) and (D_{0B}, S_{0B}), the equilibrium wage/employment combinations in the two sectors will be (W_{0A}, E_{0A}) and (W_{0B}, E_{0B}), respectively. Because of differences in training costs and nonpecuniary conditions of employment, the wages need not be equal in the two sectors.

Now suppose that the demand for automobile workers falls to D_{1A} as a result of foreign import competition, while the demand for computer specialists rises to D_{1B} as a result of the increased use of computers. If real wages are inflexible downward in market A because of union contract provisions, social norms, or government legislation, employment of automobile workers will fall to E_{1A}. Employment and wages of computer specialists will rise to E_{1B} and W_{1B}, respectively. Unemployment of $E_{0A} - E_{1A}$ workers would be created in the short run.

FIGURE 15.5
Structural Unemployment Due to Inflexible Wages and Costs of Adjustment

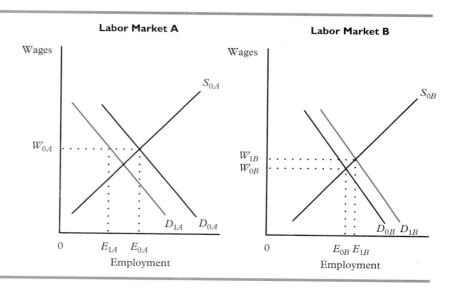

If automobile employees could costlessly become computer specialists, these unemployed workers would quickly move to market B, where we assume wages are flexible, and eventually unemployment would be eliminated.[13] Structural unemployment arises, however, when costs of adjustment are sufficiently high to retard or even prevent such movements. The cost to displaced individuals, many in their fifties and sixties, may prove to be prohibitively expensive, given the limited time horizons they face until retirement. Moreover, it may be difficult for them to borrow funds to finance the necessary job training.

Geographic Imbalances   Geographic imbalances can be analyzed in the same framework. Suppose we now assume that market A refers to a Snowbelt city and market B to a Sunbelt city, both employing the same type of labor. When demand falls in the Snowbelt and unemployment increases because wages are not completely flexible, these unemployed workers may continue to wait for jobs in their home city for at least three reasons. First, information flows are imperfect, so workers may be unaware of the availability of jobs hundreds of miles away. Second, the direct money costs of such a move, including moving costs and the transaction costs involved in buying and selling a home, are high. Third, the psychological costs of moving long distances are substantial because friends and neighbors and community support systems must be given up. As noted in chapter 10, such factors inhibit geographic migration, and migration tends to decline with age. These costs are sufficiently high that many workers who become unemployed as a result of plant shutdowns or permanent layoffs express no interest in searching for jobs outside their immediate geographic area.[14]

Structural factors can cause substantial differences in unemployment rates across states in a given year, but these differences usually do not persist indefinitely.[15] If a state's unemployment rate is higher than the national average, many unemployed workers will eventually leave the state and new entrants will tend to avoid moving there; both sets of decisions serve to reduce the unemployment rate. Conversely, states with unemployment rates lower than average will attract workers looking for jobs.

For example, in 1981 Indiana had an unemployment rate of 10.1 percent, while the national average was 7.6 percent. During the next decade, Indiana's labor force increased more slowly than average, and by 1991 its unemployment rate, at 5.9 percent, was almost one percentage point below the national average. Similarly, New Hampshire had an unemployment rate of 5 percent in 1981, but over the

---

[13]Actually, this statement is not quite correct. As noted in chapter 13, when analyzing the effects of unions using a similar model, *wait unemployment* may arise. That is, as long as the wage rate in market A exceeds the wage rate in market B, and unemployed workers in market A expect that normal job turnover will eventually create job vacancies in A, it may be profitable for them to remain attached to market A and wait for a job in that sector.

[14]For a recent study of inter-industry mobility among those likely to be permanently displaced, with references to other mobility studies related to this group, see Elisabetta Magnani, "Risk of Labor Displacement and Cross-Industry Labor Mobility," *Industrial and Labor Relations Review* 54, no. 3 (April 2001): 593–610.

[15]See Olivier Jean Blanchard and Lawrence F. Katz, "Regional Evolutions," *Brookings Papers on Economic Activity*, 1992–1, 1–75.

next decade it experienced a labor-force growth rate that was about three times the national average; by 1991 its unemployment rate was above average at 7.2 percent.

International Differences in Long-Term Unemployment

In terms of equation (15.2), structural unemployment exists when the unemployed have a small probability of finding work (P_{ue} is low) and their duration of unemployment is consequently long. We saw in chapter 2 that the percentage of the labor force unemployed for more than one year is much higher in most of Europe than in the United States, and it is natural to wonder what differences might be causal.

The flow of workers out of unemployment is accelerated when worker retraining is encouraged and when workers find it less costly to make geographical moves. It will also be accelerated when employers find it less costly to create new jobs—and thus create them at a faster pace. While the United States spends much less on government training programs than most of Europe,[16] it may compensate for this by having a relatively high rate of geographical mobility. The biggest difference, however, seems to be in the rates at which new jobs are created.

European countries typically have job-protection policies that are intended to reduce layoffs. Such policies, however, are thought to reduce the rate at which new jobs are created and thus increase the duration of unemployment. In France, for example, dismissals involving ten workers or more require notification to the government, consultations with worker representatives, a relatively long waiting period, and severance pay. In contrast, the United States requires some employers to notify their workers in advance of large-scale layoffs, but these requirements are much less burdensome than in most of Europe.[17] These job-protection policies are of special interest when analyzing structural unemployment because they also make it more costly for an employer to *hire* workers (who may have to be laid off in the future). Indeed, a recent comparative study found that as the stringency of job-protection laws rose so did the average duration of unemployment.[18]

Do Efficiency Wages Cause Structural Unemployment?

Suppose that employers are unable to completely monitor the performance of their employees and decide to pay above-market (*efficiency*) wages to reduce the incentives

---

[16]France, Germany, and Sweden, for example, spend roughly 0.30 to 0.45 percent of national income on government training programs for the unemployed, while the United States spends about a tenth of that (0.04 percent). See Organisation for Economic Co-operation and Development, *Employment Outlook: June 1999* (Paris: OECD, 1999), Table H.

[17]Katherine G. Abraham and Susan N. Houseman, "Does Employment Protection Inhibit Labor Market Flexibility? Lessons from Germany, France, and Belgium," in *Social Protection Versus Economic Flexibility: Is There a Trade-Off?* ed. Rebecca Blank (Chicago: University of Chicago Press, 1994), 59–93.

[18]Olivier Blanchard and Pedro Portugal, "What Hides Behind an Unemployment Rate: Comparing Portuguese and U.S. Labor Markets," *American Economic Review* 91, no. 1 (March 2001): 187–207.

for workers to shirk their duties. As you will recall from chapter 11, efficiency wages are thought to increase worker productivity for two reasons.[19] First, by giving workers the gift of a generous wage, employers might expect that employees would reciprocate by giving them the gift of diligent work. Second, if an employee's effort is not diligent, the employee can be fired and faced with earning a lower wage or, as we argue below, with unemployment.

Efficiency Wages Affect Unemployment   If all employers were to follow the above strategy and offer wages higher than the market equilibrium wage, then clearly supply would exceed demand and unemployment would result. If only *some* firms paid efficiency wages, then there would be a high- and a low-wage sector. Workers employed at lower-paying firms could not obtain employment at a high-wage firm by offering to work at some wage between the low (market-clearing) and the high (efficiency) wage levels, because the high-wage employers would want to maintain their wage advantage to discourage shirking. However, because jobs in the high-wage sector are preferable, and because such jobs will occasionally become available, some workers in the low-wage sector may quit their jobs, attach themselves to the high-wage sector, and wait for jobs to open up. That is, using reasoning similar to that used in chapter 13, where a high-wage sector was created by unions, *wait unemployment* will tend to arise in the presence of an efficiency-wage sector.[20]

Unemployment Affects Efficiency Wages   The wage premium that efficiency-wage employers must pay to discourage shirking depends upon the alternatives open to their employees. Other things equal, the higher the unemployment rate in an area, the poorer are the alternative employment opportunities for their workers and thus the less likely the workers are to risk losing their jobs by shirking. The employers, then, need not pay wage premiums that are as high. This leads

---

[19]Our argument here draws on, and abstracts from many of the complications discussed in, the articles in George Akerlof and Janet Yellen, eds., *Efficiency Wage Models of the Labor Market* (Cambridge, Eng.: Cambridge University Press, 1986), and Andrew Weiss, *Efficiency Wages: Models of Unemployment, Layoffs and Wage Dispersion* (Princeton, N.J.: Princeton University Press, 1990).

[20]Suppose that employees are *risk neutral* (that is, they do not lose utility if their earnings *fluctuate* over time around some mean value). In equilibrium, they would move from the low-wage to the high-wage sector and remain as unemployed job seekers as long as the expected wage from choosing to wait exceeds the expected wage of searching for work while employed in the low-wage sector. Put algebraically, a worker who is unemployed will wait for a high-wage job if

$$P_e W_e > P_0 W_e + (1 - P_0) W_0$$

where W_e and W_0 are the wages in the high- and low-wage sectors (respectively), P_e is the probability of finding a job paying W_e if one is unemployed, and P_0 is the probability of finding a high-wage job if one takes employment in the low-wage sector. Presumably P_e is greater than P_0 because individuals can search for work more intensively if they are not employed. The above inequality can be rewritten as

$$(P_e - P_0) W_e > W_0 (1 - P_0)$$

and, as we can see from this latter expression, whether one chooses wait unemployment depends on the increased probability of finding a high-wage job if unemployed ($P_e - P_0$) as well as on the difference between W_e and W_0.

FIGURE 15.6
The Wage Curve

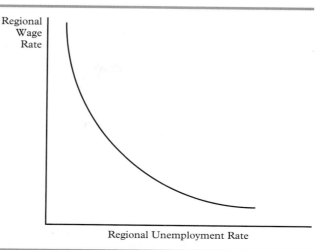

to the prediction that, other factors held constant, there should be a negative association between average wage rates and unemployment rates across areas.

Efficiency Wages and the Wage Curve   The efficiency-wage explanation of structural unemployment receives indirect support from a remarkable empirical finding. An exhaustive study of data on wages and regional unemployment rates within 12 countries found that, after controlling for human-capital characteristics of individual workers (some 3.5 million of them), there was a strong negative relationship between regional unemployment rates and real wages in all countries. That is, in regions within these countries with *higher* rates of unemployment, wage levels for otherwise comparable workers were *lower*. This negative relationship between the region's unemployment rate and its real wage level, seen in Figure 15.6, has been called the *wage curve*.

The wage curve is remarkable on three accounts. First, it seems to exist in every country for which enough data are available to estimate it. Second, the curves for each country are surprisingly similar; a 10 percent increase in a region's unemployment rate is associated with wage levels that are lower by 0.4 to 1.9 percent in eleven of the twelve countries studied.[21]

Finally, the wage curve is remarkable because it is a finding in search of an explanation. Using a standard demand-and-supply-curve analysis, one would think that higher unemployment and *higher* wages would be associated with each

---

[21]See David G. Blanchflower and Andrew J. Oswald, "An Introduction to the Wage Curve," *Journal of Economic Perspectives* 9, no. 3 (Summer 1995): 153–167; David Card, "The Wage Curve: A Review," *Journal of Economic Literature* 33, no. 2 (June 1995): 785–799; and Lutz Bellmann and Uwe Blien, "Wage Curve Analyses of Establishment Data from Western Germany," *Industrial and Labor Relations Review* 54, no. 4 (July 2001): 851–863.

other (in other words, there would be a positively sloped wage curve). Using this analysis, if wages were above market-clearing levels, supply would exceed demand, and the result would be workers who want jobs and cannot find them (unemployment); the higher that wages were above equilibrium, the more unemployment there would be. Thus, a downward-sloping relationship, such as depicted in Figure 15.6, is not what simple economic theory suggests.

Simple theory does suggest, of course, that when unemployment is relatively high, real wages will *fall*. The problem with this explanation for the wage curve is that the curve plots the relationship between unemployment and the wage *level*, not wage *changes*; thus, this implication of standard theory also fails to explain what we observe. If simple theory is not providing explanations for the wage curve, is there a more complex theory that does?

One reason we might observe a negatively sloped wage curve can be found in the efficiency-wage explanation of structural unemployment reviewed above. Suppose, for example, that one cause of long-term unemployment is the widespread payment of above-market wages by employers in an effort to reduce shirking among their employees. In regions where this and other causes happen to create higher levels of unemployment, the efficiency-wage premiums needed to reduce shirking would be lower—which would cause the negative association we observe between regional unemployment rates and wage levels.

DEMAND-DEFICIENT (CYCLICAL) UNEMPLOYMENT

Frictional unemployment arises because labor markets are dynamic and information flows are imperfect; structural unemployment arises because of long-lasting imbalances in demand and supply. *Demand-deficient unemployment* is associated with fluctuations in business activity (the "business cycle"), and it occurs when a decline in aggregate demand in the output market causes the *aggregate* demand for labor to decline in the face of downward inflexibility in real wages.

Returning to our simple demand and supply model of Figure 15.2, suppose that a temporary decline in aggregate demand leads to a shift in the labor demand curve to D_1. If real wages are inflexible downward, employment will fall to E_1, and $E_0 - E_1$ additional workers will become unemployed. This employment decline occurs when firms temporarily lay off workers (increasing P_{eu}) and reduce the rate at which they replace those who quit or retire (decreasing P_{ne} and P_{ue}). That is, flows into unemployment increase while flows into employment decline.

Unemployment, however, is not the inevitable outcome of reduced aggregate demand. Employers, for example, could reduce the wages they pay to their workers. If the latter response occurred, employment would move to E_2 and real wages to W_2 in Figure 15.2. Although employment would be lower than its initial level, E_0, there would be no measured demand-deficient unemployment, because $E_0 - E_2$ workers would have dropped out of the labor force in response to this lower wage. We will analyze two features of the U.S. labor market thought to contribute to demand-deficient unemployment: (1) institutional and profit-maximizing reasons for rigid money wages, and (2) the way in which the U.S. unemployment compensation program is financed.

Downward Wage Rigidity

Stock and commodity prices fluctuate with demand and supply, and product market retailers have sales or offer discounts when demand is down, but do the wage rates paid to individual workers fall when the demand for labor shifts to the left? If such decreases are not very likely, what might be the reasons?

Wages, of course, can be measured in both nominal and real terms. Nominal wages (the money wages quoted to workers) may be rigid, yet the real wage (the nominal wage divided by an index of prices) can fall if prices are rising. It will come as no great surprise that the real wages received by individual workers quite commonly fall; all that needs to happen for real wages to fall is for the increase in nominal wages to be less than the increase in prices. One study that followed individuals in the United States from 1970 to 1991 found that when the unemployment rate went up by 1 percentage point, the average real hourly earnings among workers who did not change employers went down by about 0.5 percent. Hourly earnings reductions were greatest among those paid by piece rates or commissions, while those paid by salary were least likely to experience such reductions.[22]

Despite evidence of at least modest downward flexibility of *real* wages, it is also important to see how common cuts in workers' *nominal* wages are. If real wages fall only when prices rise, they may not be able to fall fast enough to prevent an increase in unemployment during business downturns. One study of workers who did not change employers found that nominal wages fell from one year to the next in 18 percent of the cases between the years 1976 and 1988; similiar estimates come from a study using different employee-provided data, although this latter study extended into the early 1990s, when some 18 to 20 percent of hourly paid workers experienced nominal-wage cuts.[23] These studies, and another that used data obtained from employers,[24] suggest that nominal wages are not completely rigid in a downward direction. However, the studies also conclude that nominal wages are resistant to cuts, and as a result, employment adjustments during periods of downturn are larger and more common than they would be with complete nominal-wage flexibility.

Explanations for why employment levels are more likely to be reduced than nominal wages during business downturns must confront two questions: why do

---

[22]Paul J. Devereux, "The Cyclicality of Real Wages within Employer-Employee Matches," *Industrial and Labor Relations Review* 54, no. 4 (July 2001): 835–850.

[23]Shulamit Kahn, "Evidence of Nominal Wage Stickiness from Microdata," *American Economic Review* 87, no. 5 (December 1997): 993–1008; and David Card and Dean Hyslop, "Does Inflation Grease the Wheels of the Labor Market?" in *Reducing Inflation: Motivation and Strategy,* ed. Christina D. Romer and David H. Romer (Cambridge, MA: National Bureau of Economic Research, 1997): 71–121.

[24]Harry J. Holzer and Edward B. Montgomery, "Asymmetries and Rigidities in Wage Adjustments by Firms," *Review of Economics and Statistics* 75, no. 3 (August 1993): 397–408.

firms find it more profitable to reduce employment than wages, and why are workers who face unemployment not more willing to take wage cuts to save their jobs? The hypotheses concerning wage rigidity that have come to the forefront recently address both questions.

Wage Rigidity and Unions According to one explanation for rigid money wages, employers are not free to unilaterally cut nominal wages because of the presence of unions. This cannot be a complete explanation for the United States, because less than 15 percent of American workers are represented by unions (see chapter 13), and unions could, in any case, agree to temporary wage cuts to save jobs instead of subjecting their members to layoffs. Why they fail to make such arrangements is instructive.

A temporary wage reduction would reduce the earnings of all workers, while layoffs would affect, in most cases, only those workers most recently hired. Because these workers represent a minority of the union's membership in most instances, because union leaders are elected by majority rule, and because these leaders are most likely drawn from the ranks of the more experienced workers (who are often immune from layoff), unions tend to favor a policy of layoffs rather than one that reduces wages for all members.[25] A variant of this explanation is the *insider-outsider hypothesis,* which sees union members as *insiders* who have little or no concern for nonmembers or former members now on layoff (*outsiders*); these insiders gain from keeping their numbers small and may choose to negotiate wages that effectively prevent the recall or employment of outsiders.[26]

Wage Rigidity and Specific Human Capital Layoffs do occur in *nonunion* firms, although perhaps less frequently than in unionized ones, so wage rigidity cannot be completely attributed to unionization. One possible explanation lies with employer investments in workers. In the presence of firm-specific human capital investments, for example, employers have incentives both to minimize voluntary turnover and to maximize their employees' work effort and productivity. Across-the-board temporary wage reductions would increase all employees' propensities to quit and could lead to reduced work effort on their part. In contrast, layoffs affect only the least-experienced workers, the workers in whom the firm has invested the smallest amount of resources. It is likely, then, that the firm will find the layoff strategy a more profitable alternative.[27]

---

[25]See James Medoff, "Layoffs and Alternatives under Trade Unions in United States Manufacturing," *American Economic Review* 69 (June 1979): 380–395, for evidence. This hypothesis suggests that unions are much more likely to bargain for wage reductions when projected layoffs exceed 50 percent of the union's membership. For evidence that this occurred in the early 1980s, see Robert J. Flanagan, "Wage Concessions and Long-Term Union Flexibility," *Brookings Papers on Economic Activity,* 1984–1, 183–216.
[26]Assar Lindbeck and Dennis J. Snower, "Insiders versus Outsiders," *Journal of Economic Perspectives* 15, no. 1 (Winter 2001): 165–188.
[27]See Truman F. Bewley, *Why Wages Don't Fall during a Recession* (Cambridge, MA: Harvard University Press, 1999), and Weiss, *Efficiency Wages: Models of Unemployment, Layoffs and Wage Dispersion.* Wendy L. Rayack, "Fixed and Flexible Wages: Evidence from Panel Data," *Industrial and Labor Relations Review* 44 (January 1991): 288–298, presents empirical evidence that the sensitivity of wages to unemployment is confined largely to workers with short job tenure.

Wage Rigidity and Asymmetric Information   Employers with internal labor markets frequently promise, at least implicitly, a certain path of earnings to employees over their careers. As we saw in chapter 11, firms may pay relatively low salaries to new employees with the promise (expectation) that if they work diligently these employees will be paid relatively high wages toward the end of their careers. The firm's promises are, of necessity, conditional on how well it is performing, but the firm has more accurate information on the true state of its demand than do its workers. If a firm asks its employees to take a wage cut in periods of low demand, the employees may believe that the employer is falsely stating that demand is low and, noting that the employer loses nothing by the wage cut, resist the request. If, instead, a firm temporarily lays off some of its workers, it loses the output these workers would have produced, and workers may therefore accept such an action as a signal that the firm is indeed in trouble (that wages exceed marginal productivity). Put another way, the *asymmetry of information* between employers and employees may make layoffs the preferred policy.[28]

Wage Rigidity and Risk Aversion   Firms with internal labor markets, and therefore long employer–employee job attachments, may be encouraged by the risk aversion of older employees to engage in seniority-based layoffs (last hired, first laid off) rather than wage cuts for all its workers. That is, the desire to have a constant income stream, rather than a fluctuating one with the same average value over time, is something for which older, more-experienced workers may be willing to pay.[29] Thus, if the risks of income fluctuation are confined to one's initial years of employment, the firm may be able to pay its experienced workers wages lower than otherwise would be required. Of course, during the initial period, workers will be subject to potential earnings variability and may demand higher wages then to compensate them for these risks. However, if the fraction of the workforce subject to layoffs is small, on average employers' costs could be reduced by seniority-based layoffs.

Wage Rigidity: Worker Status and Social Norms   The explanations above pertain mainly to firms with internal labor markets, which can be roughly thought of as large employers. If these firms have rigid wages and lay off workers during a business downturn, why don't workers who are laid off take jobs with smaller employers? These smaller firms pay lower wages and have few of the reasons cited above to avoid reducing them further when aggregate demand falls; hence, increased employment in these jobs would lower the average nominal wage paid in the economy and help reduce unemployment. Some theorists believe that the

---

[28]See, for example, Sanford Grossman, Oliver Hart, and Eric Maskin, "Unemployment with Observable Aggregate Shocks," *Journal of Political Economy* 91 (December 1983): 907–928; Sanford Grossman and Oliver Hart, "Implicit Contracts, Moral Hazard and Unemployment," *American Economic Review* 71 (May 1981): 301–307; and Costas Azariadis, "Employment with Asymmetric Information," *Quarterly Journal of Economics* 98 (Supplement, 1983): 157–172.

[29]This line of reasoning follows that in Costas Azariadis, "Implicit Contracts and Underemployment Equilibria," *Journal of Political Economy* 83 (December 1975): 1183–1202, and Martin Baily, "Wages and Employment under Uncertain Demand," *Review of Economic Studies* 41 (January 1974): 37–50.

failure of unemployed workers to flock to low-wage jobs derives from their sense of status (their relative standing in society). These economists postulate that individuals may prefer unemployment in a good job to employment in an inferior one, at least for a period longer than the typical recession.[30] It is this sense of *status* that prevents the expansion of jobs and the further reduction of wages in the low-wage sectors during recessionary periods.

Some analysts have stressed, however, that prevailing market wages, even those paid by small, competitive firms, may be accepted as *social norms* that inhibit the unemployed from trying to undercut the wages of employed workers to find employment.[31] As explained below, that unemployed workers are apparently more willing to face unemployment than a reduced wage may have more to do with future considerations than with status.

Suppose there are many identical unemployed workers, each with the same *reservation wage*, the minimum wage they will accept (which is influenced by the implicit monetary value each individual places on leisure time plus the unemployment benefits or other monetary payments each receives while unemployed). If each planned to remain in the labor force only for a single period, it would be rational to bid down wages in an effort to secure employment. As long as the wage ultimately received was greater than the workers' common reservation wage, unemployed workers would be better off working.

Suppose, however, that each unemployed worker planned to remain in the labor force for a number of periods. In this case, if workers offer to work for below the prevailing wage in the current period, they will reveal to employers that their common reservation wage is lower than originally thought, and employers might decide to permanently cut wages in future periods as well. In this case individuals may be better off remaining unemployed until a job is ultimately found at the current wage. In fact, the individual's incentive not to undercut the current market wage is larger the greater the number of periods he or she plans to remain in the labor force and the greater the chance of finding work if the market wage is not undercut. Hence, this theory suggests that market wages are more likely to be inflexible in a downward direction when workers have more permanent attachment to the labor force and when increases in the unemployment rate are relatively small.

Financing U.S. Unemployment Compensation

The incentives for employers to prefer temporary layoffs to fluctuations in real wages are affected by a key characteristic of the U.S. unemployment insurance (UI) system: *its methods of financing benefits.* As we will see, the way in which

---

[30]See Alan S. Blinder, "The Challenge of High Unemployment," *American Economic Review* 78 (May 1988): 1–15.

[31]See Robert M. Solow, *The Labor Market as an Institution* (Cambridge, Mass.: Basil Blackwell, 1990), ch. 2.

the government raises the funds to pay for UI benefits has a rather large effect on cyclical layoffs.

The UI Payroll Tax   The benefits paid out by the UI system are financed by a payroll tax. Unlike the Social Security payroll tax, in almost all states the UI tax is paid solely by employers.[32] The UI tax payment (T) that an employer must make for each employee is given by

$$T = tW \quad \text{if } W \leq W_B \tag{15.3a}$$

and

$$T = tW_B \quad \text{if } W > W_B \tag{15.3b}$$

where t is the employer's UI tax rate, W is an employee's earnings during the calendar year, and W_B is the *taxable wage base* (the level of earnings after which no UI tax payments are required). In 2001, the taxable wage base ranged from \$7,000 to \$12,000 in about two-thirds of the states; thus, depending on the state, employers had to pay UI taxes on just the first \$7,000 to \$12,000 of each employee's earnings. The other one-third of the states had taxable wage bases that were higher.

The employer's UI tax rate is determined by general economic conditions in the state, the industry the employer is operating in, and the employer's *layoff experience*. The last term is defined differently in different states; the underlying notion is that since the UI system is an insurance system, employers who lay off workers frequently and make heavy demands on the system's resources should be assigned a higher UI tax rate. This practice is referred to as *experience rating*.

Imperfect Experience Rating   Experience rating is typically *imperfect* in the sense that the marginal cost to an employer of laying off an additional worker (in terms of a higher UI tax rate) is often less than the added UI benefits the system must pay out to that worker. Imperfect experience rating is illustrated in Figure 15.7, which plots the relationship between an employer's UI tax rate and that firm's layoff experience. (We shall interpret *layoff experience* to mean the probability that employees in the firm will be on layoff. Clearly, this probability depends both on the frequency with which the firm lays off workers and the average duration of time until they are recalled to their positions.)

Each state has a minimum UI tax rate, and below this rate (t_{min} in Figure 15.7) the firm's UI tax rate cannot fall. After a firm's layoff experience reaches some critical value (l_{min}) the firm's UI tax rate rises with increased layoff experience over some range.[33] In each state there is also a ceiling on the UI tax rate (t_{max}); after this

---

[32]Recall from our discussion in chapter 3 that this fact tells us nothing about who really bears the burden of the tax.

[33]In actuality the UI tax rate changes discretely (as a step function) over the range l_{min} to l_{max}, not continuously as drawn in Figure 15.7. For expository convenience, we ignore this complication.

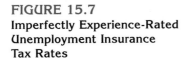

FIGURE 15.7

Imperfectly Experience-Rated Unemployment Insurance Tax Rates

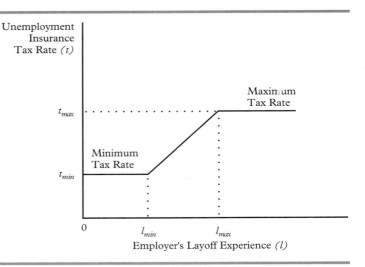

tax rate is reached, additional layoffs will not alter the firm's tax rate. The system is *imperfectly* experience-rated because for firms below l_{min} or above l_{max}, variations in their layoff rate have no effect on their UI tax rate.[34] Further, over the range in which the tax rate is increasing with layoff experience, the increase is not large enough in most states to make the employer's marginal cost of a layoff (in terms of the increased UI taxes the firm must pay) equal to the marginal UI benefits the laid-off employees receive.

Does the UI Tax Encourage Layoffs?   The key characteristic of the UI system that influences the desirability of temporary layoffs is the *imperfect experience rating* of the UI payroll tax. To understand the influence of this characteristic, suppose first that the UI system were constructed in such a way that its tax rates were perfectly experience rated. A firm laying off a worker would have to pay added UI taxes equal to the full UI benefit (50 percent of normal earnings) received by the worker, so it saves just half of the worker's wages by the layoff. Now suppose instead that the UI tax rate employers must pay is totally independent of their layoff experience (no experience rating). In this case, a firm saves a laid-off worker's *entire* wages because its UI taxes do not rise as a result of the layoff. Thus, compared to a UI system with perfect experience rating, it is easy to see that a system with incomplete experience rating will tend to enhance the attractiveness of layoffs to employers.

Empirical analyses of the effect of imperfect experience rating on employer behavior suggest that it is substantial. These studies have estimated that

---

[34]Such a system of UI financing leads to inter-industry subsidies, in which industries (such as banking) with virtually no layoffs still must pay the minimum tax, and these industries subsidize industries (such as construction) that have very high layoffs but pay only the maximum rate.

unemployment would fall by 10–33 percent if UI taxes in the United States were perfectly experience rated (so that employers laying off workers would have to pay the full cost of the added UI benefits).[35]

SEASONAL UNEMPLOYMENT

Seasonal unemployment is similar to demand-deficient unemployment in that it is induced by fluctuations in the demand for labor. Here, however, the fluctuations can be regularly anticipated and follow a systematic pattern over the course of a year. For example, the demand for agricultural employees declines after the planting season and remains low until the harvest season. Similarly, the demand for production workers falls in certain industries during the season of the year when plants are retooling to handle annual model changes.

The issue remains, why do employers respond to seasonal patterns of demand by laying off workers rather than reducing wage rates or hours of work? All the reasons cited for the existence of cyclical unemployment and temporary layoffs for cyclical reasons also pertain here. Indeed, one study has shown that the expansion (in the early 1970s) of the unemployment insurance system that led to the coverage of most agricultural employees was associated with a substantial increase in seasonal unemployment in agriculture. Studies of seasonal layoffs in nonagricultural industries also suggest that imperfect experience rating of the unemployment insurance taxes significantly increases seasonal unemployment.[36] (See Example 15.2 for a longer-term perspective on unemployment insurance and seasonal unemployment.)

We may question why workers would accept jobs in industries in which they knew in advance they would be unemployed for a portion of the year. For some workers, the existence of UI benefits along with the knowledge that they will be rehired as a matter of course at the end of the slack-demand season may allow them to treat such periods as paid vacations. However, since UI benefits typically replace less than half of an unemployed worker's previous gross earnings and even smaller fractions for high-wage workers (see Figure 15.4), most workers will not find such a situation desirable. To attract workers to seasonal industries, firms will have to pay workers higher wages to compensate them

---

[35]Patricia M. Anderson and Bruce D. Meyer, "The Effects of the Unemployment Insurance Payroll Tax on Wages, Employment, Claims, and Denials," *Journal of Public Economics* 78, no. 1–2 (October 2000): 81–106; and Robert H. Topel, "Financing Unemployment Insurance: History, Incentives, and Reform," in *Unemployment Insurance: The Second Half-Century*, ed. W. Lee Hansen and James F. Byers (Madison: University of Wisconsin Press, 1990), 108–135.

[36]Barry Chiswick, "The Effect of Unemployment Compensation on a Seasonal Industry: Agriculture," *Journal of Political Economy* 84 (June 1976): 591–602; Patricia M. Anderson, "Linear Adjustment Costs and Seasonal Labor Demand: Evidence from Retail Trade Firms," *Quarterly Journal of Economics* 108, no. 4 (November 1993): 1015–1042; and David Card and Phillip B. Levine, "Unemployment Insurance Taxes and the Cyclical and Seasonal Properties of Unemployment," *Journal of Public Economics* 53 (January 1994): 1–29.

EXAMPLE 15.2

Unemployment Insurance and Seasonal Unemployment: A Historical Perspective

The current American unemployment insurance system was established during the Great Depression of the 1930s. At that time labor economist John Commons urged that legislation include a penalty on firms with higher unemployment rates. He believed that employers had enough leeway to reduce seasonal and other layoffs substantially, and he thus championed a system that included incentives to avoid higher layoffs. Others were unconvinced that employers had much discretion over unemployment. But ultimately, the Commons plan was adopted in most states. It was rarely adopted outside the United States, however.

Evidence on seasonal unemployment seems to support Commons's contentions: over time, as the economy has diversified, seasonal unemployment has fallen, but it has fallen much more rapidly where employers are penalized for layoffs. A recent study shows that within the United States, seasonal differences in employment growth rates have fallen the most in states where experience rating is highest. Even more striking is the comparison between the United States and Canada, which established an unemployment insurance system without *any* experience rating. Seasonality in the Canadian construction industry (an industry notorious for its seasonality) fell by half between 1929 and the 1947–1963 period, as construction practices improved and changed. However, in states along the Canadian border, seasonality dropped by an even greater two-thirds!

Data from: Katherine Baicker, Claudia Goldin, and Lawrence F. Katz, "A Distinctive System: Origins and Impact of U.S. Unemployment Compensation," in Michael D. Bordo, Claudia Goldin, and Eugene N. White, eds., *The Defining Moment: The Great Depression and the American Economy in the Twentieth Century* (Chicago: University of Chicago Press, 1998), 259.

for being periodically unemployed. One recent study, for example, found that agricultural workers in seasonal jobs earned about 10 percent more per hour than they would have earned in permanent farm jobs.[37]

The existence of wage differentials that compensate workers in high-unemployment industries for the risk of unemployment makes it difficult to evaluate whether this type of unemployment is voluntary or involuntary in nature. On the one hand, workers have voluntarily agreed to be employed in industries that offer higher wages *and* higher probabilities of unemployment. On the other hand, once on the job, employees usually prefer to remain employed rather than becoming unemployed. Such unemployment may be considered either voluntary or involuntary, then, depending upon your perspective.

WHEN DO WE HAVE FULL EMPLOYMENT?

Governments constantly worry about the unemployment rate, because it is seen as a handy barometer of an economy's health. An unemployment rate that is

---

[37]Enrico Moretti, "Do Wages Compensate for Risk of Unemployment? Parametric and Semiparametric Evidence from Seasonal Jobs," *Journal of Risk and Uncertainty* 20, no. 1 (January 2000): 45–66.

deemed to be too high is seen as a national concern, because it implies that many people are unable to support themselves and that many of the country's workers are not contributing to national output. Often, governments will take steps to stimulate the demand for labor in one way or another when they believe unemployment to be excessive.

Governments also worry about unemployment being too low. An unusually low rate of unemployment is thought by many to reflect a situation in which there is excess demand in the labor market. If labor demand exceeds supply, wages will tend to rise, it is argued, and wage increases will lead to price inflation. In addition, excessively low unemployment rates may increase shirking among workers and reduce the pool of available talent upon which new or expanding employers can draw.

Defining the Natural Rate of Unemployment

If both too much and too little unemployment are undesirable, how much is just right? Put differently, what unemployment rate represents full employment? The *full-employment* (or *natural*) rate of unemployment is difficult to define precisely, and there are several alternative concepts from which to choose. One defines the natural rate of unemployment as that rate at which wage and price inflation are either stable or at acceptable levels. Another defines full employment as the rate of unemployment at which job vacancies equal the number of unemployed workers, and yet another defines it as the level of unemployment at which any increases in aggregate demand will cause no further reductions in unemployment. A variant of the latter defines the natural rate as the unemployment rate at which all unemployment is voluntary (frictional and perhaps seasonal). Finally, a recent definition of the natural rate is that rate at which the level of unemployment is unchanging and both the flows into unemployment and the duration of unemployment are normal.[38]

All the various definitions above try to define in a specific way a more general concept of full employment as the rate that prevails in "normal" times. If we assume that frictional and seasonal unemployment exist even in labor markets characterized by equilibrium (i.e., markets having neither excess demand nor excess supply), it is clear that the natural rate of unemployment is affected by such factors as voluntary turnover rates among employed workers, movements in and out of the labor force, and the length of time it takes for the unemployed to find acceptable jobs. These factors vary widely across demographic groups, so the natural rate during any period is strongly influenced by the demographic composition of the labor force.

Unemployment and Demographic Characteristics

Table 15.3 presents data on actual unemployment rates for various age/race/gender/ethnic groups in 2000. The patterns indicated in Table 15.3 for 2000 are similar

---

[38]James Tobin, "Inflation and Unemployment," *American Economic Review* 62 (March 1972): 1–18; and John Haltiwanger, "The Natural Rate of Unemployment," in *The New Palgrave*, ed. J. Eatwell, M. Milgate, and P. Newman (New York: Stockton Press, 1987), 610–612.

TABLE 15.3   Unemployment Rates in 2000 by Demographic Groups

Age	White Male	White Female	Black Male	Black Female	Hispanic Male	Hispanic Female	All
16–17	15.2	12.5	28.6	25.7	22.5	22.9	
18–19	10.4	9.0	25.0	21.5	12.8	15.7	
20–24	5.9	5.8	16.7	13.5	6.5	8.9	
25–54	2.5	2.9	5.9	5.4	3.6	5.4	
55–64	2.4	2.4	2.7	3.3	4.1	5.1	
Total	3.4	3.6	8.1	7.2	4.9	6.7	4.0

Source: U.S. Department of Labor, *Employment and Earnings* 48 (January 2001), Tables 3, 4. "Hispanic" refers to those of Hispanic origin; depending upon their races these individuals are also included in both the white and black population group totals.

to the patterns for other recent years: high unemployment rates for teens and young adults of each race/gender group relative to older adults in these groups; black unemployment rates roughly double white unemployment rates for most age/gender groups, with Hispanic American unemployment rates tending to lie in between; and female unemployment rates roughly equal to, or lower than, male unemployment rates for each group except Hispanics and those of prime age. The high unemployment rates of black teenagers, which ranged between 21 and 29 percent in 2000, have been of particular concern to policymakers.

Over recent decades, the demographic composition of the labor force has changed dramatically with the growth in labor force participation rates of females and substantial changes in the relative size of the teenage, black, and Hispanic populations. Between 1960 and 2000, the proportion of the labor force that was female grew from 33 to 47 percent. Similarly, between 1973 (when statistics were first collected) and 2000, the Hispanic American labor force grew almost three times faster than average, going from 4.1 to 10.9 percent of the overall labor force. In contrast, while between 1960 and 1978 the proportion of teenagers in the labor force grew from 7.0 to 9.5 percent, by 2000 it had fallen to 5.9 percent.[39]

Demographic Change and the Natural Rate

Until quite recently, women tended to have higher unemployment rates than men. As a result, the increases in the relative labor force shares of women, Hispanics, and teenagers through 1978 were increases in the shares of groups that had relatively high unemployment rates; this led to an increase in the overall unemployment rate

[39]See U.S. Department of Labor, *Employment and Earnings* 48 (January 2001), Tables 1–5, and earlier years' issues. For an analysis of the racial gap in unemployment rates, see Robert W. Fairlie and William A. Sundstrom, "The Emergence, Persistence, and Recent Widening of the Racial Unemployment Gap," *Industrial and Labor Relations Review* 52, no. 2 (January 1999): 252–270.

associated with any given level of labor market tightness. Indeed, one investigator concluded that demographic shifts in the composition of the labor force from the 1960s to the late 1970s probably raised the overall unemployment rate at least 1 percentage point for any given level of overall labor market tightness.[40]

Over the last two decades, however, demographic forces have probably worked to reduce the natural rate.[41] The share of teenagers in the labor force has declined. In addition, while the share of women in the labor force has continued to expand, female unemployment rates have fallen relative to male rates because much of U.S. employment growth has occurred in sectors, such as the service sector, that employ proportionately more females.

What Is the Natural Rate?

Economists' estimates of the natural rate have varied over time, going from something like 5.4 percent in the 1960s, to about 7 percent in the 1970s, to 6 or 6.5 percent in the 1980s. Recent work suggests that at the low rates of inflation experienced by the United States in the last decade, the natural rate might fall below 5 percent.[42] We must wonder, though, how useful estimates of the natural rate are for policy purposes if they keep changing; indeed, Milton Friedman, a Nobel-prizewinner in economics and a leader in the development of the natural-rate concept, disavows any attempts at forecasting it. He says, "I don't know what the natural rate is…and neither does anyone else."[43]

Is unemployment a serious problem? Certainly some level of frictional unemployment is unavoidable in a dynamic world fraught with imperfect information. Moreover, as we have seen, the parameters of the UI system encourage unemployment associated with both search, cyclical or seasonal layoff. Nonetheless, when unemployment rises above its full-employment or natural level, resources are being wasted. Some thirty years ago, Arthur Okun pointed out that every 1-percentage-point decline in the aggregate unemployment rate was associated with a 3-percentage-point increase in the output the United States produces. More recent estimates suggest that the relationship is now more in the range of a 2-percentage-point increase in output.[44] Even this last number, however, suggests the great costs a society pays for excessively high rates of unemployment.

---

[40]James Tobin, "Stabilization Policy Ten Years After," *Brookings Papers on Economic Activity,* 1980–1, 19–72.

[41]Richard Krashevski, "What Is So Natural about High Unemployment?" *American Economic Review* 78 (May 1988): 289–293.

[42]George A. Akerlof, William T. Dickens, and George L. Perry, "Near-Rational Wage and Price Setting and the Long-Run Phillips Curve," *Brookings Papers on Economic Activity,* 2000–1, 1–44.

[43]Amanda Bennett, "Business and Academia Clash over a Concept: 'Natural' Jobless Rate," *Wall Street Journal,* January 24, 1995, A8.

[44]Arthur Okun, "Potential GNP: Its Measurement and Significance," reprinted in *The Political Economy of Prosperity,* ed. Arthur Okun (Washington, D.C.: Brookings Institution, 1970); and Clifford L. F. Attfield and Brian Silverstone, "Okun's Coefficient: A Comment," *Review of Economics and Statistics* 79, no. 2 (May 1997): 326–329.

REVIEW QUESTIONS

1. A presidential hopeful is campaigning to raise unemployment compensation benefits and lower the unemployment rate. Comment on the compatibility of these goals.

2. Government officials find it useful to measure the nation's "economic health." The unemployment rate is currently used as a major indicator of the relative strength of labor supply and demand. Do you think the unemployment rate is a useful indicator of labor market tightness? Why?

3. Recent empirical evidence suggests that unemployed workers' reservation wages decline as their spells of unemployment lengthen. That is, the longer they have been unemployed, the lower their reservation wages become. Explain why this might be true.

4. Is the following assertion true, false, or uncertain? "Increasing the level of unemployment insurance benefits will prolong the average length of spells of unemployment. Hence, a policy of raising UI benefit levels is not socially desirable." Explain your answer.

5. In recent years the federal government has introduced and then expanded a requirement that unemployment insurance beneficiaries pay income tax on their unemployment benefits. Explain what effect you would expect this taxation of UI benefits to have on the unemployment rate.

6. In the 1970s, Sweden adopted several new labor market policies affecting layoffs. Three were notable: (1) Plants that provided in-plant training instead of laying off workers in a recession received government subsidies. (2) All workers had to be given at least one month's notice before being laid off, and the required time in the average plant was two to three months. (3) Laid-off workers had to be given first option on new jobs with the former employer. What probable effects would these policies, taken as a whole, have on wages, employment, and unemployment in the long run?

7. The "employment-at-will" doctrine is one that allows employers to discharge workers for any reason whatsoever. This doctrine has generally prevailed in the United States except where modified by union agreements or by laws preventing discrimination. Recent policies have begun to erode the employment-at-will doctrine by moving closer to the notion that one's job becomes a property right that the worker cannot be deprived of unless there is a compelling reason. If employers lose the right to discharge workers without "cause," what effects will this have on the unemployment rate?

8. The present value of benefits in many pension plans is greater if a person retires before the normal retirement age. In short, there is a large inducement for many private sector workers to retire early. What effect will increasing the inducements to retire early have on the unemployment rate of older men? Fully explain your answer, making use of the assumption that retired workers withdraw from the labor force and do not seek or obtain other jobs.

PROBLEMS

1. Suppose that at the beginning of the month, the number employed, *E*, equals 120,000,000; the number not in the labor force, *N*, equals 70,000,000; and the number unemployed, *U*, equals 10,000,000. During the course of the month, the following

flows have occurred (see table below). Assuming that the population has not grown, calculate the unemployment and labor force participation rates at the beginning and end of the month.

EU	1.8 million
EN	3.0 million
UE	2.2 million
UN	1.7 million
NE	4.5 million
NU	1.3 million

2. Suppose that initially the Pennsylvania economy is in equilibrium with no unemployment: $L_S = -1,000,000 + 200W$ and $L_D = 19,000,000 - 300W$, where W = annual wages and L = number of workers. Then structural unemployment arises because the demand for labor falls in Pennsylvania but wages there are inflexible downward and no one moves out of state. If labor demand falls to $L_D = 18,000,000 - 300W$, how many workers will be unemployed in Pennsylvania? What will be its unemployment rate?

3. Suppose that the unemployment insurance system is structured so that B_{min} = \$200, B_{max} = \$500, and $B = .5W + 100$ in between, where W = previous weekly wage and B = weekly unemployment insurance benefits. Graph this benefit formula and calculate the benefits and replacement rate for workers whose previous weekly wages are \$100, \$500, and \$2,000.

SELECTED READINGS

Atkinson, Anthony, and John Micklewright. "Unemployment Compensation and Labor Market Transitions: A Critical Review." *Journal of Economic Literature* 29 (December 1991): 1679–1727.

Blanchflower, David G., and Andrew J. Oswald. *The Wage Curve.* Cambridge, Mass.: MIT Press, 1994.

Blank, Rebecca M., ed. *Social Protection versus Economic Flexibility: Is There a Trade-off?* Chicago: University of Chicago Press, 1994.

Freeman, Richard, and Harry Holzer, eds. *The Black Youth Unemployment Crisis.* Chicago: University of Chicago Press, 1986.

Lang, Kevin, and Jonathan Leonard, eds. *Unemployment and the Structure of Labor Markets.* New York: Basil Blackwell, 1987.

Meyer, Bruce D. "Lessons from the U.S. Unemployment Insurance Experiments." *Journal of Economic Literature* 33 (March 1995): 91–131.

Reducing Unemployment: Current Issues and Policy Options. Kansas City, Mo.: Federal Reserve Bank of Kansas City, 1994.

Rees, Albert. "An Essay on Youth Joblessness." *Journal of Economic Literature* 24 (June 1986): 613–628.

Answers to Odd-Numbered Review Questions and Problems

CHAPTER 1

Review Questions

1. The basic value premise underlying normative analysis is that if a given transaction is beneficial to the parties agreeing to it and hurts no one else, then accomplishing that transaction is said to be "good." This criterion implies, of course, that anyone harmed by a transaction must be compensated for that harm (a condition tantamount to saying that all parties to a transaction must voluntarily agree to it). The labor market will reach a point of optimality when all mutually beneficial transactions have been accomplished. If there are mutually beneficial transactions remaining unconsummated, the labor market will not be at a point of optimality.

   One condition preventing the accomplishment of a mutually beneficial transaction would be ignorance. A party to a transaction may voluntarily agree to it because he or she is uninformed about some adverse effect of that transaction. Likewise, a party to a potential transaction may fail to enter into the transaction because he or she is uninformed about a benefit of the transaction. Informed individuals may fail to consummate a transaction, however, because of underlying transaction barriers. These may arise because of government prohibitions against certain kinds of transactions, imperfections in the market's ability to bring buyers and sellers together, or the nonexistence of a market where one could potentially exist.

3. Although a draft and a voluntary system of labor recruitment could conceivably result in the same number of employees working on the levee, the system of voluntary acceptance has one major normative advantage: It assures society that all employees working on the levee view the job as improving their welfare. When workers are drafted, at least some are being compelled to accept a transaction that they view as detrimental to their interests; allowing these workers to change employment would improve social welfare through simply reallocating (not increasing) resources. A system of

537

voluntary recruitment, then, increases the welfare of society as compared to a system that relies on conscription.

5.   a. This behavior is entirely consistent with the model of job quitting described in the text. Workers are assumed by economic theory to be attempting to maximize utility (happiness). If all other aspects of two jobs are similar, this theory predicts that workers will prefer a higher-paying to a lower-paying job. However, two jobs frequently differ in many important respects, including the work environment, personalities of managers, and the stresses placed on employees. Thus, one way to interpret this woman's behavior is that she was willing to give up 50 cents an hour to be able to work in an environment freer of stress.

   b. There is no way to prove that her behavior was grounded in "rationality." Economists define rationality as the ability to make considered decisions that are expected (at the time the decision is made) to advance one's self-interest. We cannot tell from any one individual act whether the person involved is being rational or not. Certainly, as described above, this woman's decision to quit could be interpreted as a move calculated to increase her utility (or level of happiness). However, it could also be that she became uncontrollably angry and made her decision without any thought of the consequences.

   c. Economic theory does not predict that everyone will act alike. Since economic agents are assumed to maximize utility, and since each person can be assumed to have a unique set of preferences, it is entirely consistent with economic theory that some workers would respond to a given set of incentives and that others would not. Thus, it could not be correctly concluded from the situation described that economic theory applied to one group of workers but not to another. It might well be that the other workers were less bothered by stress and that they were not willing to give up 50 cents an hour to avoid this stress.

7. The prohibitions of child labor laws would seem to violate the principle of mutual benefit by outlawing certain transactions that might be voluntarily entered into. However, there are at least two conditions under which such prohibitions would be consistent with the principles of normative economics. First, the children entering into an employment transaction may be uninformed of the dangers or the consequences of their decision to work in a particular environment. By their very nature children are inexperienced, and society frequently adopts legislation to protect them from their own ignorance.

Second, society may adopt child labor legislation to protect children from their parents. A child forced by a parent to work in a dangerous or unhealthy environment has not voluntarily agreed to the employment transaction. Thus, a law prohibiting such a child from engaging in certain employment would not be violating the principle of mutual benefit when parental compulsion was present.

Problems

1. (Appendix) Plotting the data shows that age and wage rise together. The appropriate linear model would be $W_i = a_0 + a_1 A_i + e_i$, where W_i is the wage of the ith person, A_i is the age of the ith person, a_0 and a_1 are the parameters of the line, and e_i is the random error term for the ith person. Notice that wage must be the dependent variable and age the explanatory variable, not the other way around.

3. (Appendix) Yes, the t-statistic (the coefficient divided by the standard error) equals .3/.1, or 3. When the t-statistic exceeds 2, one can be fairly confident that the true value of the coefficient is not 0.

CHAPTER 2

Review Questions

1. As shown in the figure, the outflow of construction workers shifted the labor supply curve relevant to Egypt's construction sector to the *left* (from S_1 to S_2), while the demand curve for the services of construction workers shifted to the *right* (D_1 to D_2). Because both shifts, by themselves, tended to increase the equilibrium wage rate from W_1 to W_2, we would clearly expect wages in the Egyptian construction sector to have risen faster than average. However, the two shifts by themselves had opposite effects on employment, so the expected net change in employment is theoretically ambiguous.

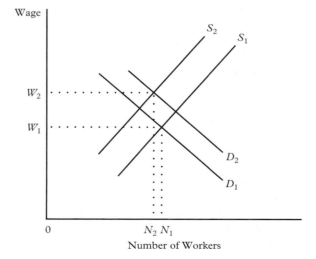

3. Many engineers are employed in research and development tasks. Therefore, if a major demander of research and development were to reduce its demand, the demand curve for engineers would shift left, causing their wages and employment to fall.

5. If the wages for arc welders are above the equilibrium wage, the company is paying more for its arc welders than it needs to and as a result is hiring fewer than it could. Thus, the definition of overpayment that makes the most sense in this case is one in which the wage rate is above the equilibrium wage.

   A ready indicator of an above-equilibrium wage rate is a long queue of applicants whenever a position in a company becomes available. Another indicator is an abnormally low quit rate as workers (in this case arc welders) who are lucky enough to obtain the above-equilibrium wage cling tenaciously to their jobs.

7.

7(a)

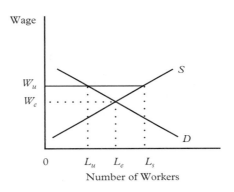

7(b)

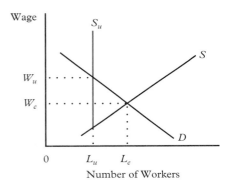

9. This regulation essentially increases the cost of capital and will have an ambiguous effect on the demand curve for labor. On the one hand, the increased cost of capital will increase the cost of production and cause a scale effect that tends to depress employment. On the other hand, this regulation will increase the cost of capital relative to labor and could stimulate the substitution of labor for capital. Thus, the substitution effect will work to increase employment while the scale effect will work to decrease it. Which effect is stronger cannot be known a priori.

Problems

1. Unemployment rate = 100 × (number unemployed)/(number unemployed + number employed) = 100 × (5 million)/(135 million) = 3.7 percent. Labor force participation rate = 100 × (number employed + number unemployed)/adult population = 100 × (135 million)/(210 million) = 64.3 percent.

3. The quickest place to find the relevant data is probably at http://www.bls.gov, "Average Hourly Earnings" (Table B-3), and "CPI" (Table 1). If average hourly earnings are rising faster than the CPI, then real wages have been rising. In

addition, we should consider the impact of mismeasurement in the CPI. If the CPI overstates inflation (as discussed in the text), then real wages have risen more rapidly than the official statistics suggest. The Bureau of Labor Statistics Web site contains links to recent changes in the construction of the CPI that are intended to remove some of the historical bias.

CHAPTER 3

Review Questions

1. Profit maximization requires that firms hire labor until marginal revenue productivity equals the market wage. If wages are low, a profit maximizer will hire labor in abundant quantity, driving the marginal revenue productivity down to the low level of the wage. This statement, then, seems to imply that firms are not maximizing profits.

3. The potential employment effects of OSHA standards differ with the type of approach taken. If the standards apply to capital (machinery), they will increase the cost of capital equipment. This increase in cost has a scale effect, which will reduce the quantity demanded of all inputs (including labor). On the other hand, it also provides employers with an incentive to substitute labor (which is now relatively cheaper) for capital in producing any given desired level of output. This substitution will moderate the decline in employment.

   In contrast, requiring employers to furnish personal protective devices to employees increases the cost of labor. In this case, employers have an incentive to substitute now relatively cheaper capital for labor when producing any given level of output (as above, the increased cost of production causes a scale effect that also tends to reduce employment).

   Other things equal, then, the employment reduction induced by safety standards will be greater if the personal protective device method is used. However, to fully answer the question requires information on the costs of meeting the standards using the two methods. For example, if the "capital" approach increases capital costs by 50 percent while the "personal protective" approach increases labor costs by only 1 percent, the scale effect in the first method will probably be large enough that greater employment loss will be associated with the first method.

5. The wage and employment effects in both service industries and manufacturing industries must be considered. In the service sector the wage tax on employers can be analyzed in much the same way as payroll taxes are analyzed in the text. That is, a tax on wages, collected from the employer, will cause the demand curve to shift leftward if the curve is drawn with respect to the wage that employees take home. At any given hourly wage that employees take home, the cost to the employer has risen by the amount of the tax. An increase in cost associated with any employee wage dampens the employer's appetite for labor and causes the demand curve to shift down and to the left.

The effects on employment and wages depend on the shape of the labor supply curve. If the labor supply curve is upward-sloping, both employment and the wage employees take home will fall. If the supply curve is vertical, employment will not fall but wages will fall by the full amount of the tax. If the supply curve is horizontal, the wage rate will not fall but employment will.

The reduced employment and/or wages in the service sector should cause the supply of labor to the manufacturing sector to shift to the right (as people formerly employed in the service sector seek employment elsewhere). This shift in the supply curve should cause employment in manufacturing to increase even if the demand curve there remains stationary. If the demand curve does remain stationary, the employment increase would be accompanied by a decrease in manufacturing wages. However, the demand for labor in manufacturing may also shift to the right as consumers substitute away from the now more expensive services and buy the now relatively cheaper manufactured goods. If this demand shift occurs, the increase in employment would be accompanied by either a wage increase or a smaller wage reduction than would occur if the demand curve for labor in manufacturing were to remain stationary.

7. The imposition of financial penalties on employers who are discovered to have hired illegal immigrants essentially raises the cost of hiring them. The employers now must pay whatever the prevailing wage of the immigrants is, and they also face the possibility of a fine if they are discovered to have illegally employed workers. This penalty can be viewed as increasing the cost of hiring illegal workers so that this cost now exceeds the wage. This effect can be seen as a leftward shift of the demand curve for illegal immigrants, thus reducing their employment and wages.

The effects on the demand for skilled "natives" depend on whether skilled and unskilled labor are gross substitutes or gross complements. Raising the cost of unskilled labor produces a scale effect that tends to increase the cost of production and reduce skilled employment. If skilled and unskilled labor are complements in production, the demand for skilled labor will clearly shift to the left as a result of the government's policy. However, if they are substitutes in production, the increased costs of unskilled labor would stimulate the substitution of skilled for unskilled labor. In this case, the demand for skilled labor could shift either right (if the substitution effect dominated the scale effect) or left (if the scale effect dominated).

Problems

1. The marginal product (as measured by these test scores) is 0.
3. See the figure below. Since the supply curve is vertical, the workers will bear the entire tax. The wage will fall by $1 per hour, from $4 to $3.

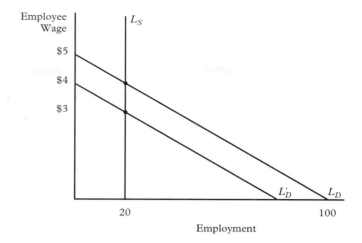

5. (Appendix) As the chapter explains, to minimize cost, the firm picks K and L so that $W/MP_L = R/MP_K$. Rearrange this to $W/R = MP_L/MP_K$ and substitute in the information from the problem:

$$12/4 = 30K^{0.25}L^{-0.25}/10K^{-0.75}L^{0.75}$$
$$3 = 3K/L$$
$$K = L$$

CHAPTER 4

Review Questions

1. The overall conditions making for a smaller employment loss among teenagers are (a) a small substitution effect, and (b) a small scale effect. The substitution effect is relatively small when it is difficult to substitute capital or adult workers for teenagers, or when those substitutes rise in price when the demand for them grows. A small scale effect is associated with having the labor cost of teenagers be a small part of overall cost, and with the industry's product demand curve being relatively inelastic.

3. The tax credit for capital purchases effectively lowers the cost of capital, so the question thus becomes under what conditions will a reduced price of capital increase employment the most? Employment will be most beneficially affected if a particular industry has a large scale effect, and a small substitution effect, associated with the tax credit. The scale effect will be largest when the share of capital is relatively large (so that the reduced price of capital results in a relatively large reduction in product price) and when the product demand

elasticity facing the industry is relatively large (the product price decline caus-es a large increase in product demand). The substitution effect will be non-exis-tent if labor and capital are complements in production; it will be relatively small when they are substitutes in production but capital is not easily substi-tuted for labor, or when the supply of labor is inelastic (so that if the demand for labor goes down as capital is substituted for it, its price will also go down—which will blunt the substitution effect).

5. Both options increase the costs of firms not already providing employees with acceptable health coverage. Since noncoverage is a characteristic mostly of small firms, all options would increase costs of small firms relative to costs in large firms. This would create a scale effect, tending to reduce employment in small firms relative to that in large ones. The magnitude of this scale effect will be greater the more elastic product demand is and (usually) the greater labor's share is in total cost.

Option A has, in addition to the scale effect, a substitution effect that tends to decrease the number of workers a firm hires. This substitution effect will be larger the more easily capital can be substituted for labor and the more elastic the supply of capital is.

Option B is a tax on a firm's revenues, so it would have just a scale effect on the demand for labor, not a substitution effect. It would increase total costs and cause downward pressures on employment and wages, but it does not raise the ratio of labor costs to capital costs. Thus, its effects on wages and employment would be smaller than under option A.

7. a. An increased tariff on steel imports will tend to make domestic product demand, and therefore the demand for domestic labor, more inelastic.

b. A law forbidding workers from being laid off for economic reasons will dis-courage the substitution of capital for labor and therefore tend to make the own-wage elasticity of demand for labor more inelastic.

c. A boom in the machinery industry will shift the product demand curve in the steel industry to the right, thereby shifting the labor demand curve to the right. The effects of this shift on the own-wage elasticity of demand for labor cannot be predicted (except that a parallel shift to the right of a straight-line demand curve will reduce the elasticity at each wage rate).

d. Because capital and labor are most substitutable in the long run, when new production processes can be installed, a decision to delay the adoption of new technologies reduces the substitutability of capital for labor and makes the labor demand curve more inelastic.

e. An increase in wages will move the firm along its labor demand curve and does not change the shape of that curve. However, if the demand curve happens to be a straight line, movement up and to the left along the demand curve will tend to increase elasticity in the range in which firms are operating.

f. A tax placed on each ton of steel output will tend to shift the labor demand curve to the left, but will not necessarily change its elasticity. However, if the demand curve happened to be a straight line, this leftward shift would tend to increase the elasticity of demand for labor at each wage rate.

Problems

1. Elasticity of demand = $\%\Delta$(quantity demanded)/$\%\Delta$(wage) = $(\Delta L_D/L_D)/(\Delta W/W)$ = $(\Delta L_D/\Delta W) \times (W/L_D)$. At $W = 100$, $L_D = 3000$, so that $W/L_D = 100/3000$. You will note that $(\Delta L_D/\Delta W)$ is the slope of the labor demand function (the change in employment demanded brought about by a one-unit change in the wage). This slope equals -20. Therefore, own-wage elasticity of demand = $-20 \times (100/3000) = -2/3$. The demand curve is inelastic at this point.

   Use the same approach to calculate the elasticity at $W = 200$. In this case, the own-wage elasticity of demand = $-20 \times (200/1000) = -4$. The demand curve is elastic at this point.

3. a. See the figure below. The higher wage will cause a movement along the demand curve, and L_D will fall from 220 ($300 - 20 \times 4$) to 200 ($300 - 20 \times 5$).

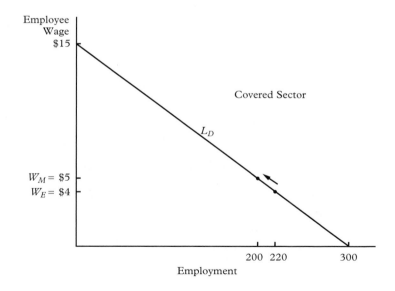

b. The initial equilibrium wage in the uncovered sector is $4 per hour and $L = 220$. Then the labor supply curve shifts over by 20 to $L_{S'} = -80 + 80W$. The new equilibrium is $W = \$3.80$ per hour and $L = 224$ (see figure below).

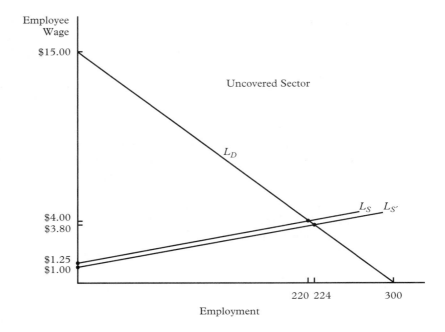

CHAPTER 5

Review Questions

1. What low-skilled workers and high-paid college professors have in common is that neither group receives much firm-specific training. The former group can be thought of as having received no training and the latter group as having received highly general training. In either case, we know that the workers' marginal productivity in their current firm is the same as their marginal productivity with other firms. In competitive labor markets, the latter will represent the wage other firms will be willing to pay them. As a result, if the wage at their current firm falls below their marginal productivity, both types of workers have an incentive to quit their jobs.

   One might contrast the behavior of these groups with the behavior of individuals who have received a good deal of firm-specific training. We know from the text that (a) by the definition of specific training, the marginal productivity of these individuals at their current firm exceeds their marginal productivity elsewhere, and (b) their wage at the current firm is less than their marginal productivity there. As long as this wage is greater than their potential marginal productivity elsewhere, these workers have reduced incentives to quit their jobs.

3. This change would convert a quasi-fixed labor cost to a variable one, inducing employers to substitute added workers for weekly hours (especially overtime hours) of work. Because this new financing scheme increases the cost of higher-paid workers relative to lower-paid ones, it also induces firms to substitute unskilled for skilled workers. (Both these effects emphasize labor–labor substitution; scale effects are minimal if total premiums are held constant.)

5. If the new employers of these displaced workers needed to provide specific training to anyone they hired, then they would find that the shorter expected tenures of older workers would make training them less attractive, other things equal. The decreased attractiveness of older workers (as objects of human capital investments) would drive down their wage offers relative to those of otherwise comparable younger workers.

7. Employee benefits such as insurance impose per-worker costs on the employer, while wages impose hourly costs. If hourly costs of labor rise and per-worker costs remain the same or fall, employers will tend to substitute added workers for added hours per worker if they must increase labor input.

Problems

1. The present value of the three-period contract must be greater than the present value of the alternative wage stream, which is $200 + $200/(1 + .10) + $200/(1 + .10)^2 = $200 + $181.82 + $165.29 = $547.11. The present value of the three-period contract is $180 + $200/(1 + .10) + X/(1 + .10)^2. Set this equal to $547.11 and solve for X: $180 + $181.82 + X/1.21 = $547.11. X = $185.29 × 1.21 = $224.20. The firm must pay more than $224.20 in the third period.

3. The firm cannot recoup its costs of providing general human capital, so the worker must pay for the training: $W = MP_L -$ cost of training = $3000 − $1000 = $2000.

CHAPTER 6

Review Questions

1. False. An inferior good is defined as one that people consume less of as their incomes rise (if the price of the good remains constant). A labor supply curve is drawn with respect to a person's wage rate. Thus, for an individual's labor supply curve to be backward-bending, the supply curve must be positively sloped in some range and then become negatively sloped in another. A typical way of illustrating a backward-bending supply curve is shown below.

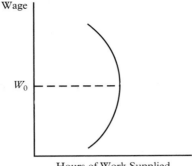

Hours of Work Supplied

  Along the positively sloped section of this backward-bending supply curve, the substitution effect of a wage increase dominates the income effect, and as wages rise the person increases his or her labor supply. However, after the wage reaches W_0 in the figure, further increases in the wage are accompanied by a reduction in labor supply. In this negatively sloped portion of the supply curve, the income effect dominates the substitution effect.

  We have assumed that the income effect is negative and that, therefore, leisure is a normal good. Had we assumed leisure to be an inferior good, the increases in wealth brought about by increased wages would have worked *with* the underlying substitution effect and caused the labor supply curve to be unambiguously positively sloped.

3. The graphs for each option are shown below, with the new constraints shown as dashed lines. By mandating that 5 percent of each hour be worked for free, option A reduces lawyers' wages, creating income and substitution effects that work in opposite directions on their desired labor supply.

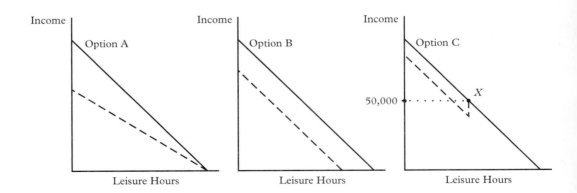

  Option B essentially reduces the time lawyers have available for leisure and paid work, which shifts the budget constraint to the left in a parallel manner (keeping the wage rate constant). This creates an income effect that increases their incentives to work for pay.

Option C leaves unchanged the budget constraint of lawyers who work relatively few hours, but for those who work enough to earn over $50,000 there is an income effect that tends to increase work incentives. For some whose incomes were only slightly above $50,000, however, the $5,000 tax may drive them to reduce hours of work, thereby reducing their earnings to $50,000 and avoiding the tax. These lawyers find their utilities are maximized at point X in the graph of option C's budget constraint.

5. Absenteeism is one dimension of labor supply, so the proposals must be analyzed using labor supply theory. Both proposals increase worker income, because employees now have paid sick days; this increase in income will tend to increase absenteeism through the income effect. The first proposal also raises the *hourly wage,* however, because any unused sick leave can be converted to cash in direct proportion to the unused days. Thus, this first proposal will tend to have a substitution effect accompanying the income effect, so that the overall expected change in absenteeism is ambiguous.

The second proposal raises the cost of the *first* sick day because, if absent, the worker loses the entire promised insurance policy. Thus, there is a huge substitution effect offsetting the income effect for the first day of absence. However, once sick leave is used at all, *further* days of absence cause no further loss of pay; thus, after the first day there is no substitution effect to offset the income effect, and this will tend to increase the incentives for absenteeism.

7. In the figure below, the straight line *AB* represents the person's market constraint (that is, the constraint in a world with no subsidies). *ACDEB* is the constraint that would apply if the housing subsidy proposal became effective.

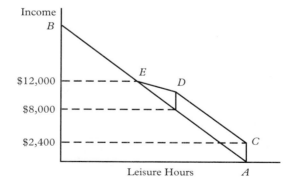

The effects on labor supply depend on which segment of *ACDEB* the person finds relevant. There are four possible cases. First, if the indifference curves are very steeply pitched (reflecting a strong desire to consume leisure), the housing subsidy proposal will not affect work incentives. The person strongly desiring leisure would continue to not work (would be at point C), but would receive the housing subsidy of $2,400. The second case occurs when the person has a tangency along segment CD. Along this segment the person's effective wage rate is the same as the market wage, so there is a pure income effect tending to reduce work incentives.

If the person has a tangency point along segment DE, there are likewise reduced incentives to work because the income effect caused by the northeast shifting out of the budget constraint is accompanied by a reduction in the effective wage rate. Finally, those with tangency points along EB will not qualify for the housing subsidy program and therefore will not alter their labor supply behavior. (An exception to this case occurs when a person with a tangency point near point E before the initiation of the housing subsidy program now has a tangency point along segment DE and, of course, works less than before.)

Problems

1. a. See the figure below, where the initial budget constraint is given by ACE. After the new law is passed, the budget constraint bends upward after 8 hours of work. Thus, the new wage rate and overtime constraint is given by ABCD, which intersects the old constraint at point C—the original combination of income and working hours (10 hours of work in this example).

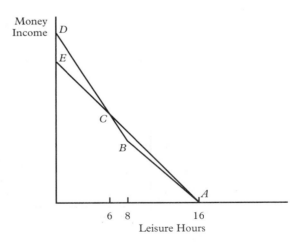

b. Initially, earnings were $11 \times 10 = \$110$. The new earnings formula is $8W + 2 \times 1.5W$, where W = the hourly wage. Pick W so that this total equals $110. Since $11W = \$110$, we calculate that $W = \$10$ per hour.

c. See the figure above. If the workers were initially at a point of utility maximization, their initial indifference curve was tangent to the initial budget constraint (line *ACE*) at point *C*. Since the new budget constraint (along segment *BD*) has a steeper slope ($15 per hour rather than $11 per hour), the workers' initial indifference curve cannot be tangent to the new constraint at point *C*. Instead, there will be a new point of tangency along segment *CD*, and hours of work must increase—tangency points along *CD* lie to the left of point *C*. This decision is similar to the labor force participation decision in Figure 6.11. (Income in the vicinity of point *C* is effectively being held constant, and the substitution effect always pulls in the direction of less leisure whenever the wage rate has risen.)

CHAPTER 7

Review Questions

1. a. 6,000 − 5,600, or 400.
   b. The labor force participation rate drops from 60 percent to 56 percent, a reduction of 4 percentage points.
   c. One implication of hidden unemployment is that the unemployment rate may not fully reflect the degree of joblessness. That is, some people who want to work but do not have work are not counted as unemployed because they place such a low probability on obtaining employment that they stop looking for work. While this observation may suggest that hidden unemployment should be included in the published unemployment figures, to do so would call into question the theoretical underpinnings of our measure of unemployment. Economic theory suggests that unemployment exists if there are more people willing to work at the going wage than there are people employed at that wage. If economic conditions are such that at the going wage some decide that time is better spent in household production than in seeking market work, our theory suggests that they have in fact dropped out of the labor force.

3. Jimmy Carter's statement reflects the "additional-worker hypothesis." Stated briefly, this hypothesis suggests that, as the economy moves into a recession and some members of the labor force are thrown out of work, other family members currently engaged in household production or leisure will enter the labor force to try to maintain family income. While Carter's statement of the additional-worker hypothesis is an apt description of that hypothesis, his statement fails to reflect the fact that studies show the "discouraged-worker" effect dominates the added-worker effect (that is, as the economy moves into a recession and workers are laid off, the labor force shrinks, on balance).

5. To parents who must care for small children, this subsidy of day care is tantamount to an increase in the wage rate. For those parents who are currently out

of the labor force, the increased wage will be accompanied by a dominant substitution effect that induces more of them to work outside the home (the substitution effect dominates in *participation* decisions). For those who are currently working outside the home, this increase in the take-home wage will cause both an income and a substitution effect, the net result of which is not theoretically predictable. If the substitution effect is dominant, then the change in policy would increase the hours of work. If the income effect is dominant, then this increase in the take-home wage rate might cause a reduction in work hours.

7. For workers close to retirement age, this change in government policy creates a significant decrease in postretirement income. The basic postretirement pension has been cut in half, so these workers experience a substantial income effect that would drive them in the direction of more work (delayed retirement).

   For very young workers, the reduction in pension benefits facing them in their retirement years is offset by a reduction in payroll taxes (which, of course, acts as an increase in their take-home wage rate). Thus, if we assume that these workers will pay for their retirement benefits through the payroll taxes they pay over their careers, this change in Social Security might leave their lifetime wealth unaffected. If so, the cut in payroll taxes would increase their wages without causing an increase in lifetime wealth, which would create a "pure" substitution effect inducing more labor supply (and possibly later retirement).

9. a. The budget constraint facing this teenager is shown below, with line *ABC* representing the constraint associated with her job with the caterer, and *AD* the constraint as a babysitter (assuming she needs 8 hours per day for sleep and personal care).

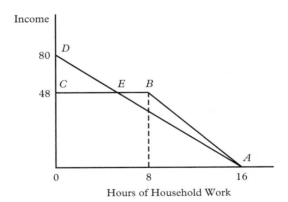

   b. The value to her of studying and practicing would be shown by indifference curves, with more steeply sloped curves indicating a greater value. If she places a high value on her household activities, she will either not work (corner solution at point *A*) or choose to work as a caterer along constraint *AB*. In this case the state law has no effect. With a flatter indifference curve, however, she may maximize utility at point *B* (catering job) or along *ED*. In these cases, the state law reduces her earnings and her utility, but the effects on her hours at home are unclear. If she ends up at point *B*, she spends more time at home than she would if unconstrained, but along *ED* the income and substitution effects of the law work in opposite directions and the effects of the law on hours at home are ambiguous.

CHAPTER 8

Review Questions

1. The demand curve shows how the marginal revenue product of labor (MRP_L) is affected by the number employed; if few workers are employed, they are placed in jobs in which their MRP_L is relatively high. The supply curve indicates the number of workers willing to offer their services at each wage rate. Because fewer construction workers are willing to offer their services at any given wage if working conditions are harsh (as in Alaska), construction wages will be higher than in the continental United States. Further, the higher wage that must be paid restricts employment in harsh conditions to the performance of projects that have a very high MRP_L.

3. A society unwilling to use force or trickery to fill jobs that are dangerous, say, must essentially bribe workers into voluntarily choosing these jobs. To induce workers to choose a dangerous job over a safer one requires that the former be made more attractive than the latter in other dimensions, and one way is to have elevated compensation levels. These increased levels of compensation are what in this chapter we have called compensating wage differentials.

   These compensating wage differentials will arise if workers are well informed and can select from an adequate number of job choices. If workers are without *choice*, then society essentially forces them to take what is offered through the threat of being jailed or of not being able to obtain a means of livelihood.

   If, instead of lacking choice, workers lack information about working conditions in the jobs from which they have to choose, then society is in effect using trickery to allocate labor. That is, if workers are ignorant of true working conditions and remain ignorant of these conditions for a long period after they have taken a job, they have not made their choice with full information. They have been tricked into making the choice they have made.

5. False. Whether government policy is required in a particular labor market depends on how well that market is functioning. If the outcomes of the market take into account worker preferences (with full information and choice), then

the labor market decisions will lead to utility maximization among workers. In this case, efforts by government to impose a level of safety greater than the market outcome could lead to a reduction in worker welfare (as argued in the text).

If the market fails to take full account of worker preferences, owing to either lack of information or lack of choice, then the private decision makers do not weigh all the costs and benefits of greater safety. There is a very good chance that the market outcome will not be socially optimal, and an appropriate setting of governmental standards could improve the utility of workers.

Of course, if society does not trust workers' preferences or seeks to change those preferences, it would not want to rely on the market even if it were functioning perfectly, because the market would reflect worker preferences.

7. Men and women who work in their homes do not have to bear the expenses of commuting and child care that factory workers do. Moreover, many prefer the flexibility of working at home to the regimen of a factory, because they can perform farming chores or do other household tasks that would be impossible to do during a factory shift. These intrinsically desirable or cost-saving aspects of working at home suggest that the same level of utility could be reached by homeworkers at a lower wage rate than factory workers receive. Thus, at least part of the higher wage paid to factory workers is a compensating wage differential for the cost and inconvenience of factory employment.

9. From the perspective of positive economics, banning Sunday work drives down the profits of employers, which will have a scale effect on employment, and drives up the cost of labor relative to capital (machines are not banned from running on Sunday). Overall, firms will tend to hire less labor.

Further, in the absence of government prohibitions, most workers presumably preferred to celebrate a Sabbath, and in Germany Sunday was most likely the typical choice. With most workers preferring Sunday off, employers who wanted to remain open had to hire from a small pool of workers who did not celebrate Sunday as a Sabbath. If this pool was small relative to the demand for Sunday workers, employers had to pay a compensating wage differential to lure workers into offering their services on Sundays. The workers most easily lured were those who cared least about having Sunday off. These workers will lose their premium pay (unless exempt from the law).

Normatively, this law prevents some voluntary transactions. It makes society worse off by preventing workers who are willing to work on Sundays (for a price) from transacting with employers who want Sunday workers, and it thus discourages some mutually beneficial transactions.

Problems

1. See the figure below. A's wage at 3 meters is $10 + .5 \times 3 = \$11.50$ per hour. At 5 meters, B's wage is $10 + .5 \times 5 = \$12.50$ per hour. A's indifference curve must

be tangent to the offer curve at 3 meters—B's must be tangent at 5 meters. Because both indifference curves are tangent to a straight line, both must have the same slope at their points of tangency; therefore, both workers are willing to pay (or receive) 50 cents per hour for reduced (added) depth of one meter. Worker A, who chooses to work at 3 meters, has a steeper indifference curve (a greater willingness to pay for reduced depth) at each level of depth; that is why worker A chooses to work at a shallower depth.

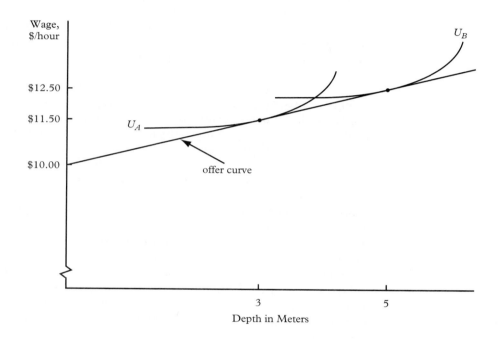

3. (Appendix) He will be fully compensated when his expected utility is the same on the two jobs.

Utility from the first job is $\sqrt{Y} = \sqrt{40{,}000} = 200$.

Utility from the second job is $U = .5 \times \sqrt{Y_{bad}} + .5 \times \sqrt{Y_{good}} = .5 \times \sqrt{22{,}500} + .5 \times \sqrt{Y_{good}}$. This equals the utility of the first job when $Y_{good} = 62{,}500$. ($.5 \times 150 + .5 \times \sqrt{Y_{good}} = 200$.) If he earns $22,500 half the time, and $62,500 half the time, his expected earnings are $42,500. Thus, his expected extra pay for the layoff risk is $2,500 per year.

CHAPTER 9

Review Questions

1. Understanding why women receive lower wages than men of comparable age requires an analysis of many possible causes, including discrimination. This answer will explore the insights provided by human capital theory.

   Women have traditionally exhibited interrupted labor market careers, which shortens the time over which human capital investments can be recouped. Even recently, when educational attainment levels between relatively young men and women have equalized, women graduates are still bunched in occupations for which an interrupted working life is least damaging. Lower human capital investments and occupational bunching are undoubtedly associated with lower wages.

   The fact that female age/earnings profiles are relatively flat, while men have age/earnings profiles that are upward-sloping and concave, can also be explained by human capital analysis. If men acquire more on-the-job training in their early years than women do, their wages will be relatively depressed by these investments (this will cause wages of men and women at younger ages to be more equal than they would otherwise be). In their later years, those who have made human capital investments will be recouping them, and this will cause the wages of men and women to become less equal.

3. Delaying reduces tuition costs, but it also delays the benefits of a medical education (generally measured as the difference between what doctors earn and what can be earned without a medical degree). This difference in benefits will be greatest for those with the smallest alternative (pre-medical-school) earnings. Further, it reduces by one the number of years that the investment's payoff can be recouped. Thus, those expecting the greatest payoff to an investment in medical education, and those who are older and therefore have fewer years over which to recoup its returns, will be least likely to take this offer.

5. One cost of educational investment is related to the time students need to devote to studying in order to ensure success. People who can learn quickly are going to have lower costs of obtaining an education. If one assumes that learning ability and ability in general (including productive capacity in a job) are correlated, then the implication of human capital theory is that the most-able people, other things being equal, will obtain the most education.

7. Government subsidies will, of course, lower the costs to individuals of obtaining an education (of making a human capital investment). Reduced university costs will, from an individual perspective, raise the individual rate of return to making an investment in education. This will induce more people to attend college than would have attended otherwise. Students who would, in the absence of a college subsidy, have required a postcollege earnings differential (as compared to that of a high school graduate) of $2,000 per year may now be induced

to attend college if the earnings differential is only $1,000 per year. From a social perspective, however, the increase in productivity of $1,000 per year may be insufficient to pay back society for its investments in college students.

Problems

1. She needs to compare the present value of the costs and benefits from getting the MBA. Costs equal forgone income at ages 48 and 49, plus tuition. The cost of an apartment is not included, because she will need to live somewhere whether she's working or in school. Benefits equal the $15,000 in extra wages that she'll get at ages 50 through 59. The present value of costs = $50,000 + $50,000/(1.06) = $97,170. Present value of benefits = $15,000/(1.06)^2 + $15,000/(1.06)^3 + ... + $15,000/(1.06)^{10} + $15,000/(1.06)^{11} = $104,152.

   Thus Becky enrolls in the MBA program, because the present value of the net benefits of doing so is $6,982.

CHAPTER 10

Review Questions

1. a. State licensing increases the costs of interstate mobility among licensed professionals, thus tending to reduce the overall supply to these occupations and to drive up their wages. In addition, the flows from low- to high-earnings areas are inhibited, which slows the geographic equalization of wages among these professionals.

   b. The gainers from federalization would be licensed professionals who are in low-earnings areas, because their labor market mobility is enhanced. (One could also argue that clients in high-earnings areas similarly gain from the enhanced mobility of the professionals from whom they purchase services.) The losers are already licensed professionals in high-earnings areas, who face increased competition now because of enhanced mobility.

3. a. Immigrant workers create goods or perform services that have value to the rest of society. Thus, whether their presence enriches native-born Americans (in the aggregate) depends on the total value of these services, net of what they are paid. If immigrants receive no more than their marginal revenue product, the native-born cannot lose and in fact will reap inframarginal gains. If immigrants are subsidized by the native-born, so they are net consumers of goods and services, then the native-born could be worse off in the aggregate.

   b. There are two critical issues from a normative perspective. The first is whether immigrants are subsidized, on balance, by the native-born (as noted above). If they are not, then there is a second issue: Are there mechanisms whereby the native-born gainers from immigration can compensate the losers? Many economists argue that compensation of losers must take place for a potentially Pareto-improving policy to be socially defensible, so identifying whose wages are reduced and by how much is a critical social issue.

5. One factor inducing quit rates to be low is that the cost of job changing may be high (pension losses, seniority losses, and difficulties finding information about other jobs are examples of factors that can increase the cost of quitting). If there are cost barriers to mobility, then employees are more likely to tolerate adverse conditions within the firm without resorting to leaving.

   Firms also are more likely to provide their employees with firm-specific training if quit rates are low. Thus, if firms need to train their employees in firm-specific skills, they clearly prefer a low quit rate.

   Finally, firms prefer low quit rates because hiring costs are kept to a minimum. Every time a worker quits, a replacement must be hired, and to the extent that finding and hiring a replacement is costly, firms want to avoid incurring these costs.

   From a social perspective, the disadvantage of having a low quit rate is related to the failure of the market to adjust quickly to shortages and surpluses. Changing relative demands for labor require constant flux in the employment distribution, and factors that inhibit change will also inhibit adaptation to new conditions.

   Further, high costs of quitting will be associated not only with lower quit rates but also with larger wage differentials across firms or regions for the same grade of labor. Since firms hire labor until marginal productivity equals the wage they must pay, these large wage differentials will also be accompanied by large differentials in marginal productivities within the same skill group. As implied by our discussion of job matching, if marginal productivities differ widely among workers with the same skills, national output could be increased by reallocating labor so that marginal productivities of the low-paid workers are enhanced.

7. It is possible that Japanese workers, say, do have stronger preferences for loyalty (meaning that they are more willing to pass up monetary gains from mobility for the sake of "consuming" loyalty to their current employers). It is also true that quit rates are affected by incentives as well as preferences, and incentives for lower quit races can be altered by employer policies. Thus, quit rates do not by themselves allow us to measure differentials in inherent employee loyalties.

   Lower quit rates in Japan could result from poorer information flows about jobs in other areas, greater costs of changing jobs (employee benefits may be strongly linked to seniority within the firm so that when workers quit they lose benefits that are not immediately replaced by their new employer), smaller wage differentials among employers, or other employer policies adopted because of a greater reliance on firm-specific human capital investments by Japanese employers.

Problems

1. The present value of net benefits from the move is given by equation 10.1 in the text. Assuming that the benefits of the two identical jobs are summarized by the real wage, the present value of the gains from moving are $20,000 + $20,000/1.1 + $20,000/1.1^2 + $20,000/1.1^3 + $20,000/1.1^4 = $83,397.

   Because she doesn't move, we know that the costs of moving outweigh the benefits. The direct cost of the move is only $2,000, so the psychic costs must be greater than $81,397.

CHAPTER 11

Review Questions

1. With an implicit labor-market contract, which is not legally enforceable, the punishment for cheating is that the other party terminates the employment relationship. Therefore, the principle underlying self-enforcement is that both parties must lose if the relationship is terminated. For both parties to lose, workers must be paid above what they could get elsewhere, but below what they are worth to the employer. The latter conditions imply the existence of a surplus (a gap between marginal revenue product and alternative wages) that is divided between employer and employee.

3. Compensation schemes such as efficiency wages, deferred payments, and tournaments are made feasible by an expected long-term attachment between worker and firm. If small firms do not offer long enough job ladders to provide for career-long employment, long-term attachments will become less prevalent and the above three schemes less feasible. The growth of small firms, then, may mean more reliance on individual or group output-based pay schemes (or on closer supervision).

5. If management already has power over workers because workers' ability to go to other jobs is severely limited by unemployment or monopsony, then low wages may result. However, paying low wages is definitely not the way to *acquire* power if management currently lacks it. Underpaid workers have no incentives to tolerate demanding requirements from management, because their current job is not better (and may be worse) than one they could find elsewhere. However, if workers are paid more by one firm than they could get elsewhere, they will tolerate heavy demands from their supervisors before deciding to quit. One way to acquire power over workers, therefore, is to overpay, not underpay, them.

7. The compensation scheme that pays workers less than they are worth initially, and more than they are worth later on, could result in this outcome. Older workers end up getting pay that is high relative to their productivity, and when they

have to find another employer their pay drops substantially. Younger workers, who are lower paid under this scheme to begin with, do not experience such a drop in wages.

Problems

1. Charlie's employer will pay him $6 per hour. Increasing his wage from $5 to $6 per hour induces enough extra output to cause revenue to climb from $8 to $9.50—i.e., a raise of $1 per hour yields $1.50 per hour in extra output, so the employer benefits from increasing his wage from $5 to $6. Increasing his wage beyond $6 per hour won't benefit his employer. An increase from $6 to $7 induces an increase in output from $9.50 to $10.25—only 75 cents per hour, not enough to pay for a $1 per hour increase in his wage.

CHAPTER 12

Review Questions

1. Labor market discrimination is said to exist when workers who are productively equivalent are systematically paid different wages based on their race or ethnicity (or some other demographic characteristic unrelated to productivity). Because simple averages of earnings do not control for these characteristics, we cannot tell from them if labor market discrimination exists (Chinese and Japanese Americans, for example, may have average productive characteristics that greatly exceed those of white Americans).

3. Wage discrimination in the labor market is present when workers with the same productive characteristics are systematically paid differently because of the demographic group to which they belong. The critical issue in judging discrimination in this case is whether male and female high school teachers have the same productive characteristics.

    One area of information we would want to obtain concerns the human capital characteristics: do male and female teachers have the same levels of education and experience, and do they teach in comparable fields? A second area of information concerns working conditions. Are male teachers working longer hours (coaching sports or sponsoring clubs) or working in geographical areas that are associated with compensating wage differentials?

5. a. A wage subsidy paid to employers who hire disadvantaged black workers will shift the demand curve for such workers (stated in terms of the employee wage) to the right. This shift can cause employment to increase, the wage rate paid to black disadvantaged workers to increase, or both. The mix of wage and employment changes will depend on the shape of the supply curve of these workers. The changes in wages and employment induced by

the subsidy will tend to overcome the adverse effect on unskilled blacks of labor market discrimination.

   b. Increasing the wages and employment opportunities of unskilled black workers will reduce incentives of these workers to invest in the training required to become skilled. Thus, one consequence of a wage subsidy just for unskilled black workers is that the subsidy may induce more to remain unskilled than would otherwise have been the case.

7. When nursing wages are raised above market-clearing levels, a surplus of nursing applicants will arise. The high wages, of course, will attract not only a large number of applicants but also a large number of very high-quality applicants; the fact that applicants are so plentiful allows the city to select only the best. Therefore, comparable worth may reduce the number of nursing jobs available, but it will also tend to increase the employment of high-quality nurses.

   Since the wages of nurses are tied to those of building inspectors, the city will be very reluctant to raise the wages of building inspectors even if there are shortages. Rather than raising wages as a recruiting device for building inspectors, the city may be tempted to lower its hiring standards and to employ building inspectors it would previously have rejected. Thus, employment opportunities for low-quality building inspectors may be enhanced by the comparable worth law.

9.   a. Wage discrimination exists when compensation levels paid to one demographic group are lower than those paid to another demographic group that is exactly comparable in terms of productive characteristics. Using this definition, there would be no discrimination because both men and women would receive equal yearly compensation while working. This equal yearly compensation would, in fact, result in a pension fund for each man and woman that would have exactly the same present value at retirement age. However, because women live longer than men, this retirement fund would be paid out over a longer period of time and thus would be paid out to retired women in smaller yearly amounts. The Supreme Court decision would require employers to put aside more pension funds for women, and it thus requires that working women have greater yearly compensation (while working) than comparable men.

   b. The decision essentially mandates greater labor costs for women than for men of comparable productive characteristics, and by raising the firm's costs of hiring women, it could give firms incentives to substitute male for female workers (or capital for female workers).

Problems

1. Assuming that workers of one gender remain in their jobs, the index of dissimilarity indicates the percentage of the other group that would have to change occupations for the two genders to have equal occupational distributions. Assume that the males stay in the same jobs and then find the number of females in each job that would give them the same percentage distribution as males.

Occupation	Actual Female Distribution	If Female % = Male %	No. Needing to Change
A	20	40% = 28	28 – 20 = 8
B	25	40% = 28	28 – 25 = 3
C	25	20% = 14	14 – 25 = –11

As this table shows, 11 females need to change jobs—these 11 leave occupation C and move into occupations A and B. Eleven females equals 15.7 percent of the total, which is the index of dissimilarity.

3. See the figure below.

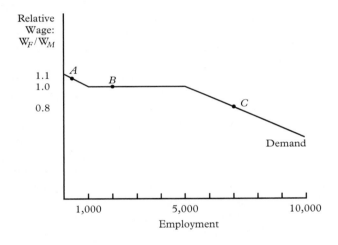

$W_F/W_M = 1.08$ when 200 women are hired at point A.
$W_F/W_M = 1$ when 2,000 women are hired at point B.
$W_F/W_M = 0.8$ when 7,000 women are hired at point C.

Discrimination only hinders female workers in this market if there are more than 5,000 hired. In fact, discrimination goes in favor of female workers when there are fewer than 1,000 hired.

CHAPTER 13

Review Questions

1. Since a reduction in the price of capital equipment will stimulate the purchase of capital equipment, a union should be concerned whether its members are

gross complements or gross substitutes with capital. In the former case, the proposed policy (reducing the price of capital) would cause the demand for union members to rise, while in the latter their demand would fall. Other things equal, the more rapidly the demand for labor is shifting out, the smaller will be the reduction in employment associated with any union-induced wage gain (assuming the collective bargaining agreement lies on the labor demand curve). Hence, unions representing groups that are gross complements (substitutes) with capital would benefit (lose) from the policy change.

Evidence cited in the text suggests that capital and skilled labor may be gross complements, but capital and unskilled labor are gross substitutes. This suggests that union leaders representing the latter type of workers will be opposed to the legislation, while union leaders representing the former may favor it.

3. The provisions of the Jones Act affect the demand for labor in the U.S. shipping industry in at least two ways. First, the provision that 50 percent of all U.S. government cargo must be transported in U.S.-owned ships makes the price elasticity of demand for U.S. shipping in the output market less elastic. Second, the restriction that at least 90 percent of the crews of U.S. ships must be U.S. citizens reduces the ability of ship owners to substitute foreign seamen for U.S. citizens. Both changes cause the wage elasticity of demand for U.S. seamen to be less elastic than it would otherwise be.

To the extent that the U.S. shipping industry is heavily unionized and there is little competition between union seamen and nonunion seamen (a reasonable assumption), the wage elasticity of demand for union seamen would become less elastic under the Jones Act. As stressed in the text, inelastic labor demand curves permit unions to push for increases in their members' wages without large employment losses, at least in the short run.

5. This law makes it more difficult and more costly to substitute capital for labor. Any worker replaced by capital (or another substitute factor of production) must be retrained and employed elsewhere in the firm, which clearly raises the cost of this substitution. Thus, this law tends to reduce the elasticity of demand for union labor, and it increases the ability of unions to raise wages without reducing their members' employment very much.

7. Unions may raise worker productivity for several reasons. One of the more obvious is that, as wages are increased, firms cut back employment and substitute capital for labor. Both actions tend to raise the marginal productivity of labor. To survive in a competitive market, profit-maximizing firms must raise the marginal productivity of labor whenever wages increase.

Another reason unions raise productivity is that the high wages unionized employers offer attract a large pool of applicants, and employers are able to select the best applicants. Moreover, the reduction in turnover that we observe in unionized plants increases firms' incentives to provide specific training to their workers, and the seniority system that unions typically implement encourages older workers to help train younger workers (they can do so without fear that the younger workers will compete for their jobs when fully trained).

Because many of these sources of increased productivity are responses by firms to higher wages, they tend to mitigate the effects of unionization on costs. Some nonunion firms deliberately pay high wages to attract and retain able employees, and they often pursue this strategy even without the implicit threat of becoming unionized. However, the fact that firms generally pay the union wage only after their employees become organized suggests that they believe unions raise labor costs to a greater extent than they raise worker productivity.

What the quotation in question 7 overlooks is that increases in productivity must be measured against increases in costs. If unions enhance productivity to a greater extent than they increase costs of production, then clearly employers should take a much less antagonistic approach to unions. If, however, enhancements in labor productivity are smaller than increases in labor costs, employer profitability will decline under unionization.

Problems

1. Set the employer concession schedule equal to the union resistance curve and solve for W:

$1 + .02S = 5 + .02S - .01S^2$ simplifies to $.01S^2 = 4$, or $S^2 = 400$, or $S = 20$ days. Plugging S into the equations yields $W = 1.4\%$.

3. The relative wage advantage is $R = (W_{union} - W_{nonunion})/W_{nonunion} = (\$10 - \$8)/\$8 = .25$. Union workers earn 25 percent more than nonunion workers. The absolute effect of the union cannot be determined because we don't know what the wage of the unionized workers would be in the absence of the union. We don't know the extent of spillover effects, threat effects, and wait unemployment, for example.

CHAPTER 14

Review Questions

1. Increasing the investment tax credit reduces the price of capital, and therefore has two possible effects on the demand for labor. If labor and capital are complements in production or are gross complements, then the tax credit will shift the labor demand curve to the right and tend to increase wages and employment. If, however, capital and labor are gross substitutes, then this tax credit could result in a decreased demand for labor.

We learned from chapter 4 that capital and unskilled labor are more likely to be substitutes in production than are skilled labor and capital; therefore, this investment tax credit is more likely to negatively affect the demand for unskilled labor than for skilled labor. If so, there will be more downward pressure on the wages of unskilled workers, and the resulting decline in the relative wages of the lowest-paid workers tends to widen the dispersion of earnings.

3. Forbidding employers to replace striking workers will have ambiguous effects on the dispersion of earnings. On the one hand, we know that forbidding striker replacement should increase the power of unions to raise the wages of their members, and we know that unions have historically raised the wages of less-skilled members relative to the wages of those who are more skilled. Thus, if union power is enhanced, the primary beneficiaries will be lower-skilled union workers, and this effect should tend to equalize the distribution of earnings.

   On the other hand, we need to consider the effects on those who would have worked as replacements. We know that unions are more prevalent in large firms, which pay higher wages anyway, and we can suppose that workers who wish to work as replacements are attracted to these jobs because they can improve their earnings. By encouraging higher wages in large, unionized firms, forbidding striker replacement could cause a spillover effect that reduces wages in the nonunionized sector. Thus, prohibiting striker replacement may actually drive down wages paid to those now in the small-firm, nonunion sector and create a greater dispersion in earnings.

5. Increasing the subsidy guaranteed to those who do not work, but holding constant a nonzero effective wage rate, will clearly cause a reduction in labor supply. This reduction will take two forms: Some who worked before may decide to withdraw from the labor force, and some who worked before may reduce their hours of work. These two forms of labor supply reduction have quite different effects on the distribution of *earnings*.

   It is reasonable to suppose that the expected labor supply reductions will come mainly from workers with the lowest level of earnings. Thus, when labor force *withdrawal* takes place, those with the lowest earnings are leaving the labor force, and this withdrawal will tend to equalize the distribution of earnings (those at the lower end exit from the distribution).

   Reduced hours of work among those who continue in the labor force, however, will have the opposite effect on the distribution of earnings if this labor supply response is also focused among those with the lowest level of earnings. Reductions in working hours will lower the earnings of these low-wage workers further, which will tend to widen the dispersion of earnings. Therefore, while this increased generosity of the negative income tax program serves to equalize the distribution of *income* (which includes the subsidies), the labor supply responses can tend to either narrow or widen the dispersion of earnings.

7. Proposal "a" increases the cost of employing high-wage (skilled) labor and capital. This will have ambiguous effects on the demand curve for unskilled workers. On the one hand, it will tend to cause unskilled workers to be substituted for skilled workers and/or capital (assuming they are substitutes in production). On the other hand, the costs of production rise and the scale effect will tend to reduce both output and the demand for all workers (including the unskilled).

   If the substitution effect dominates, the demand curve for the unskilled shifts to the right, tending to increase their employment and wage rate. If the scale effect dominates (or if the unskilled are complements in production with skilled labor and capital), then the demand curve for them shifts left, and their wage rate and employment level would decrease.

Proposal "b" cuts the cost of employing all labor, but the percentage decrease is greatest for the low-paid (unskilled). Thus, the proposal cuts the cost of unskilled labor relative to that of both capital and skilled labor. This will unambiguously shift the demand for unskilled labor to the right (keeping the employee wage on the vertical axis), because both the scale and the substitution effects work in the same direction. This will tend to increase both unskilled employment and the wages received by employees.

Proposal "b" is better for accomplishing the government's goal of improving the earnings of the unskilled, because the scale effect tends to increase, not reduce, the demand for their services.

Problems

1. (Appendix) First order the students by income to find the poorest 20%, next poorest 20%, middle 20%, next richest 20%, and richest 20% (see the table below). Then find the total income—in this case, $344,000. Divide the income in each 20% group by the total income to find its share of income. Finally calculate the cumulative share of income.

   Now graph this information, making sure that cumulative share of income goes on the vertical axis and cumulative share of households goes on the horizontal axis (see the figure below). (An even more precise Lorenz curve can be graphed by breaking the data into tenths rather than fifths.)

Name	Income	Share of Income	Cumulative Share of Income
Bottom 20%			
Billy Bob	$20,000	$44,000/$344,000 = .128	.128
Kasia	$24,000		
2nd 20%			
Rose	$29,000	$60,000/$344,000 = .174	.128 + .174 = .302
Charlie	$31,000		
Middle 20%			
Yukiko	$32,000	$66,000/$344,000 = .192	.302 + .192 = .494
Nina	$34,000		
4th 20%			
Thomas	$35,000	$72,000/$344,000 = .209	.494 + .209 = .703
Raul	$37,000		
Top 20%			
Becky	$42,000	$102,000/$344,000 = .297	.703 + .297 = 1.000
Willis	$60,000		

To find the Gini coefficient, use the method outlined in the Appendix to find the area below the Lorenz curve. This area equals .1 plus the area of the four rectangles whose bases are .2 and whose heights are the cumulative shares of income for the first four income groups. Area = .1 + (.2 × .128) + (.2 × .302) + (.2 × .494) + (.2 × .703) = .1 + .3254 = .4254. The Gini Coefficient equals (0.5 − area under the Lorenz curve)/0.5 = (0.5 − .4254)/0.5 = .1492.

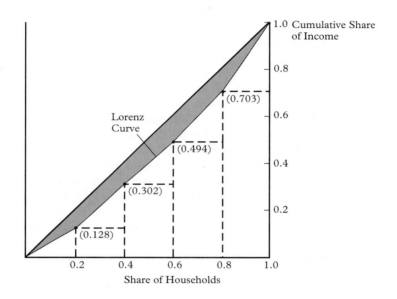

CHAPTER 15

Review Questions

1. The two policy goals are not compatible in the short run. An increase in unemployment compensation benefits reduces the costs to unemployed workers of additional job search; this will lead them to extend their duration of unemployment and search for better-paying jobs. In the short run, increasing unemployment compensation benefits will increase the unemployment rate.

   In the long run, however, the two policy goals may be compatible. If the prolonged durations of job search lead to better matches of workers and jobs, the chances that workers will become unemployed in the future will diminish. That is, the better matches will reduce both the probability that workers will quit their jobs and the probability that they will be fired. This reduced probability of entering unemployment will reduce the unemployment rate in the long run. Whether the reduction in the unemployment rate due to the smaller incidence of unemployment outweighs the increase due to the longer spells of unemployment is an open question.

3. When a worker first becomes unemployed, he or she may be optimistic about employment opportunities and set a high reservation wage. However, if over time only very low wage offers are received, the individual may realize that the distribution of wage offers is lower than initially assumed. This revision of expectations would also cause a downward revision of the reservation wage.

   In fact, even if workers' initial perceptions about the distribution of wage offers were correct, this distribution might systematically shift down over time. For example, employers might use the length of time an individual had been unemployed as a signal of the individual's relatively low productivity and might moderate wage offers accordingly. A systematically declining wage-offer distribution that arises for this reason would similarly cause reservation wages to decline as durations of unemployment lengthened.

5. This policy should have two effects on the unemployment rate. First, by reducing the value of benefits to unemployed workers, it should reduce the duration of their spells of unemployment. In other words, by taxing unemployment insurance benefits, the government is in effect reducing those benefits, and the reduction in benefits increases the marginal costs of remaining unemployed for an additional period of time. Thus, workers will tend to be less choosy about job offers they accept and should be induced to reduce the amount of time they spend searching for additional job offers. However, by reducing job search, the taxation of UI benefits may lead to poorer matches between worker and employer, thus creating higher turnover (and more unemployment) in the long run.

   Second, because unemployed workers are now receiving less compensation from the government, those in jobs in which layoffs frequently occur will find them less attractive than they previously did. Employers who offer these jobs will have more difficulty attracting employees unless they raise wages (assuming workers have other job options). This compensating wage differential will act as a penalty for high layoff rates, and this penalty should induce firms to reduce layoffs to some extent. A reduced propensity to lay off workers, of course, should reduce the unemployment rate (other things being equal).

7. The level of unemployment is affected by flows into and out of the pool of unemployed workers. Restricting employers' ability to fire workers will reduce the flow of workers *into* the pool, thus tending to reduce unemployment. However, because these restrictions increase the costs of hiring workers (the costs of firing them are a quasi-fixed cost of employment), firms will tend to reduce their *hiring* of labor. This reduction will slow the flows out of the unemployed pool, so that one cannot predict the overall effect of the restrictions on the unemployment rate.

Problems

1. To make the calculations easier, we can drop the millions terms. The initial unemployment rate is $100 \times U/(U + E) = 100 \times 10/(10 + 120) = 8.33\%$

   The initial labor force participation rate is $100 \times (U + E)/(U + E + N) = 100 \times (10 + 120)/(10 + 120 + 70) = 65.0\%$.

The new levels of the three measures (in millions) are:

$U_1 = U_0 + EU + NU - UE - UN = 10 + 1.8 + 1.3 - 2.2 - 1.7 = 9.2$
$E_1 = E_0 + UE + NE - EU - EN = 120 + 2.2 + 4.5 - 1.8 - 3.0 = 121.9$
$N_1 = N_0 + EN + UN - NE - NU = 70 + 3.0 + 1.7 - 4.5 - 1.3 = 68.9$

The new rates are:

Unemployment rate $= 100 \times 9.2/131.1 = 7.02\%$

Labor force participation $= 100 \times 131.1/200 = 65.55\%$

3. See the figure below.

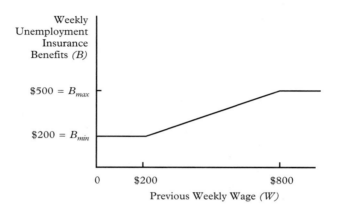

Case 1: If wage = $100, then the worker receives the minimum, $B = \$200$, and the replacement rate, $B/W = \$200/\$100 = 2$.

Case 2: If wage = $500, then the worker receives $B = .5 \times 500 + 100 = \$350$, and the replacement rate is $\$350/\$500 = .7$.

Case 3: If wage = $2,000, then the worker receives the maximum, $B = \$500$, and the replacement rate is $\$500/\$2,000 = .25$.

NAME INDEX

Subject Index

TABLE 6.1 Labor Force Participation Rates of Females in the United States over 16 Years of Age, by Marital Status, 1900–1999 (percent)

Year	All Females	Single	Widowed, Divorced	Married
1900	20.6	45.9	32.5	5.6
1910	25.5	54.0	34.1	10.7
1920	24.0			9.0
1930	25.3	55.2	34.4	11.7
1940	26.7	53.1	33.7	13.8
1950	29.7	53.6	35.5	21.6
1960	37.7	58.6	41.6	31.9
1970	43.3	56.8	40.3	40.5
1980	51.5	64.4	43.6	49.8
1990	57.5	66.7	47.2	58.4
1999	60.0	68.7	49.1	61.2

Sources: 1900–1950: Clarence D. Long, *The Labor Force under Changing Income and Employment* (Princeton, N.J.: Princeton University Press, 1958), Table A–6.

1960–1995: U.S. Department of Labor, Bureau of Labor Statistics, *Handbook of Labor Statistics*, Bulletin 2340 (Washington, D.C.: U.S. Government Printing Office, 1989), Table 6; and Eva E. Jacobs, ed., *Handbook of U.S. Labor Statistics* (Lanham, Md.: Bernan Press, 2001), 11, 18.

TABLE 6.2 Labor Force Participation Rates for Males in the United States, by Age, 1900–1999 (percent)

Year	Age Groups					
	14–19	16–19	20–24	25–44	45–64	Over 65
1900	61.1		91.7	96.3	93.3	68.3
1910	56.2		91.1	96.6	93.6	58.1
1920	52.6		90.9	97.1	93.8	60.1
1930	41.1		89.9	97.5	94.1	58.3
1940	34.4		88.0	95.0	88.7	41.5
1950	39.9	63.2	82.8	92.8	87.9	41.6
1960	38.1	56.1	86.1	95.2	89.0	30.6
1970	35.8	56.1	80.9	94.4	87.3	25.0
1980		60.5	85.9	95.4	82.2	19.0
1990		55.7	84.4	94.8	80.5	16.3
1999		52.9	81.9	93.0	80.7	16.9

Sources: 1900–1950: Clarence D. Long, *The Labor Force under Changing Income and Employment* (Princeton, N.J.: Princeton University Press, 1958), Table A–2.

1960: U.S. Department of Commerce, Bureau of the Census, *Census of Population, 1960: Employment Status,* Subject Reports PC(2)–6A, Table 1.

1970: U.S. Department of Commerce, Bureau of the Census, *Census of Population, 1970: Employment Status and Work Experience,* Subject Reports PC(2)–6A, Table 1.

1980–1999: Eva E. Jacobs, ed., *Handbook of U.S. Labor Statistics* (Lanham, Md.: Bernan Press, 2001), 24, 33.